ISBN 978-1-333-62858-1
PIBN 10528384

1 MONTH OF
FREE
READING

at
www.ForgottenBooks.com

By purchasing this book you are eligible for one month membership to ForgottenBooks.com, giving you unlimited access to our entire collection of over 1,000,000 titles via our web site and mobile apps.

To claim your free month visit:

www.forgottenbooks.com/free528384

English
Français
Deutsche
Italiano
Español
Português

www.forgottenbooks.com

Mythology Photography **Fiction**
Fishing Christianity **Art** Cooking
Essays Buddhism Freemasonry
Medicine **Biology** Music **Ancient**
Egypt Evolution Carpentry Physics
Dance Geology **Mathematics** Fitness
Shakespeare **Folklore** Yoga Marketing
Confidence Immortality Biographies
Poetry **Psychology** Witchcraft
Electronics Chemistry History **Law**
Accounting **Philosophy** Anthropology
Alchemy Drama Quantum Mechanics
Atheism Sexual Health **Ancient History**
Entrepreneurship Languages Sport
Paleontology Needlework Islam
Metaphysics Investment Archaeology
Parenting Statistics Criminology
Motivational

MARKLAND

OR

NOVA SCOTIA

Its History, Natural Resources and
Native Beauties

BY

ROBERT R. McLEOD

PUBLISHED BY THE
MARKLAND PUBLISHING COMPANY
1903

MARKLAND

OR

NOVA SCOTIA

Its History, Natural Resources and Native Beauties

BY

ROBERT R. McLEOD

PUBLISHED BY THE

MARKLAND PUBLISHING COMPANY

1903

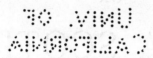

MANUFACTURED BY
THE J. L. NICHOLS COMPANY LIMITED
TORONTO, CANADA.

PREFACE.

The idea of producing this book originated with W. V. Brown, Esq., of Berwick, N. S. My acquaintance with him began in the winter of 1901 when he laid before me the general plan of the work, and desired that I would aid him with suggestions touching the contents, and their arrangement, and write the book in the main, but making such compilation from other sources as best satisfied myself. Not finding very much printed matter in the shape that suited my purpose, I have been obliged to write nearly all from beginning to end. It devolved upon Mr. Brown to secure the means to carry out the project, and this he has accomplished by the exercise of much energy, diligence, and intelligence. We have done our portions of the work, and now submit the book to the public for whom it was prepared. We are no longer young men, and the labor involved has severely taxed our strength. Mr. Brown has done all the business connected with raising the money, securing a publisher, and obtaining the photographs for illustrations. As President of the Company that issues this work Prof. E. M. Keirstead, M. A., D. D., of Acadia University, has lent his valuable name and official assistance, and Mr. S. C. Parker of Berwick, Secretary of the Nova Scotia Fruit-Growers' Association, as Secretary Treasurer of the Markland Company has aided the business in many ways.

There seemed to be a demand for something like what we have produced.' It is true that there are in existence Histories of Nova Scotia, and no small amount of literature relating to the economic interests of the Province. The latter portion is not readily accessible, as much of it is scattered here and there in rare books, or hidden away in publications of societies, and newspaper files. There has not existed up to this date a book wherein could be found the information desired by men of business, by tourists, and sportsmen, and students of natural science. Hitherto our fine scenery away from railway routes, had not been brought before the public by means of the camera and otherwise, in a way that extends to all parts of the Province.

This book will show that Nova Scotia has been mightily enriched by nature. We have scarcely done more than make a beginning in the work of drawing upon these sources of wealth. To make more

3

M15375

widely known our interesting history, our resources of land and sea, and the native charms of this choice bit of the globe, is the object in producing this work. We who are responsible for it, have no schemes to boom, no properties for sale, and no small ends to answer in this way. No man's money has been taken for advertisements of his business or of himself. To insure a more lasting character the book is largely devoted to subjects and topics that do not readily become obsolete. A word about the title "Markland." It is my own suggestion. About a thousand years ago the Norwegians who had settled in Iceland, and discovered Greenland, were not satisfied with such tame enterprises, and therefore without chart, or compass, or quadrant ran their intrepid prows southward into our waters. Written accounts of these voyages exist in the Icelandic language. There has been a good deal of controversy about the locality of the lands they made. Until within a dozen years or thereabouts it has been quite generally believed that when Captain Leif Erikson touched a land "covered with wood, white sands were far around where they went, and the shore was low, and he said this land shall be named after its qualities, and called it Markland," that Nova Scotia was thus designated. That this view is not now so generally accepted is due to the researches of Professor Storm, a Danish scholar, who has convinced himself, and some others that Nova Scotia is the Vinland of the Norse explorers. However, the name is a pleasing word, and for all that any one surely knows to the contrary may be the very one that Leif bestowed upon these wooded shores and sandy beaches. At any rate it will be a restful variation from Acadia, which is another word of doubtful meaning if we are to listen to some respectable critics. This is the "Woodland" where the forests primeval still shelter the moose, and caribou, and bear and other wild things, and for the purposes of this book "Markland" may stand with propriety.

For my own part I would have been pleased had the choice of a writer fallen upon one who could have excelled my performance. It is beyond my expectation to please all my readers, but to that end I have spared no pains, and shirked no duty in the matter, and in the words of Apocryphal Scripture, "If I have done well, and as is fitting the story, it is that which I desired; but if slenderly and meanly, it is that which I could attain to."

ROBERT RANDALL McLEOD.

Brookfield, Queens County, Nova Scotia, July, 1902.

ANTIC OCEAN

WARD IS

C.Breagu

East C.   Margarie R.
          Seal Ig
          Broadcove

and R.

Peter Boy
le Madame
C Canso

Mary

Milip

C. mackan
Ship Harr
in B.

g.t Mouton
Herbert

ANNAPOL

Annapolis
Port Royal

Bay Gut

Plymouth

B Y

N

CONTENTS.

LIST OF CHAPTERS AND SUBJECTS.

8   CONTENTS.

W. V. BROWN.

CHAPTER I.

9

W. V. BROWN.

In the order of Nature warfare is an ordained factor of prime importance in the animal world. In human affairs it has often seemed that nothing short of the arbitrament of the sword could settle questions of great interest to mankind.

Any country where such epoch-making struggles have been thus decided, is thereby invested with unusual interest.

Geography destined Nova Scotia to become the arena where issues of the gravest national importance to future generations were to be decided by the ordeal of war. Less than one hundred and fifty years ago it was not determined whether French, or English rule should dominate North America. No human foresight could see what decision the "Tablets of Destiny" contained on their hidden faces. A question so pregnant with mighty issues for unborn generations of people must have been decided by the inscrutable will of Providence. If France could have kept what she had claimed in America, and thus held the whole of it except the fringe of English Colonies along the Atlantic Coast, from Massachusetts southward, then we may be confident that there would have been no Revolutionary War to gain independence of England, only to be swallowed up by a people foreign to them in blood, in laws, in religion, and in the common usages of social and public life. Indeed it is quite certain that in the event of French occupancy of all other portions wherein she had fastened her hold, that these British Colonies would have been added by conquest to that vast domain, and their populations scattered and lost in the general masses. In other words, less than a century and a half ago it was, so far as human power could discern, an unsettled question, whether or not there was to be a United States, and a British Canada. "Great doors turn on small hinges." Apparently the decision oscillated in the balance, and might have been easily decided against English interests.

Nova Scotia stands out like a great wharf into the restless Atlantic. Its coastline is a succession of harbors inviting the early explorers to shelter and new supplies of food, wood, and water.

We shall never know whose were the human voices that first broke the solitudes of this region; whose was the hand that opened hostilities upon the innocent wild things that ranged the unbroken forest without dread of such armed, and tireless, enemies as mankind. He may have been a "rugged type of primal man," whose kinsmen left their stone implements where they were buried in the glacial gravels of Trenton, New Jersey, while they retreated before this invasion of ice, at a time so distant that the Niagara gorge was not begun. If these were the original explorers of Nova Scotia, then the time came nearly one hundred thousand years ago, when the slowly increasing cold and accumulated snow, drove them from this peninsula that became a world of arctic desolation for thousands of years. Whether the primeval men of pre-glacial America, who retreated southward before the ice-sheet till beyond its reach, survived in their decendants and camped again on their old lines of retreat in after ages as they returned northward, is a matter of speculation for the present. Out of that stock may have sprung the rude sons of the forest who greeted the first white men, and were so long in the land that their fathers had named the natural aspects of the country in a musical tongue that was a mimicry of the murmuring streams and the whispering winds in the restless pines. These Red Men were in the Stone Age of their history; further progress was barred until iron ore could be melted and forged into implements. Here they dwelt, not without some virtues, but not greatly in advance of the bears and the moose, save in point of intelligence. They called the peninsula Acadie, meaning a land of plenty.

Surely it was no Canaan flowing with milk and honey; but there were fresh fish, and game, and berries, and nuts, and roots. They hailed with delight the Frenchmen who brought hatchets and guns, and knives, and bartered them for skins of beavers, bears, and moose. They did not perceive that the superiority of the men who furnished these weapons would inevitably make them the rulers of the land. Here on these Acadian shores was begun the New France that once bid fair to rival the glories of the Motherland. Here was poured out the treasures of a nation to build a Fortress Town to scare the British ships from adjacent seas, and make hopeless all attempts to overthrow her power. The utter ruin and pathetic desolation that marks the site of that city is a stern rebuke to human pride and national ambitions of conquests. Such a challenge as Louisburg constituted did not pass unheeded by her only rival on these shores. Before Englishmen had settled at Jamestown or Plymouth the French had begun colonization at least at two points, and when the Mayflower with her pilgrim passengers in 1620 sailed into Plymouth there had been for fifteen years a post and plantation at Port Royal or Annapolis. Nature at this point had furnished a most admirable site and noble surroundings for a city. No wonder the locality was pitched upon for such a purpose. Its great land-locked basin fringed with ample meadows, and fenced by lofty hills that rise almost to mountain magnitude and clothed with noble forests to their summits, are but leading lineaments of a scene calculated to charm the eye and win the approbation of the remarkable men who named it Port Royal and began its permanent settlement before Henry Hudson had discovered the noble river that bears his name, or Jamestown was founded, or any colony planted north of Spanish dominions at St. Augustine, Florida. Hereabouts was shed the first blood in the long conflict that was to decide whether France or England should hold this Continental Domain from the Gulf of Mexico to Hudson's Bay. No less than three armaments commanded and manned by New Englanders have sailed into this peaceful haven to lay in ruins the forts and settlements, and a Virginian half-freebooter, sailing under orders, struck the infant colony within ten years of its founding.

For a long time the history of Annapolis is the history of Nova Scotia, for the most part, and there is no proper understanding to be had of the founding of Anglo-Saxon rule in America without careful study of the annals of this province.

Beyond question the Norsemen touched these shores a thousand years ago. It is almost a certainty that Sebastian Cabot in 1498 made a landing on this peninsula. Very probable that Jacques Cartier in 1534 saw the coast of Cape Breton. French fishermen and fur-traders frequented the Atlantic seaboard from then till the beginning of the next century, but made no real attempt to form a permanent settlement. Thus matters stood until 1604 when Henry Fourth of France appointed a Governor-General of this country in the person of Pierre du Guast Sieur de Monts, a native of Saintonge, a man who had distinguished himself in the service of the King and gained his confidence. This enterprising gentleman had already made a pleasure trip across the ocean four years previously with the Sieur Chavin on a trading voyage to Tadousac on the St. Lawrence. His commission extended from the 40th to the 46th degree north latitude, and he was "to people and cultivate said lands, search for gold and silver, build forts and towns, and grant lands," etc. He and his associates, certain merchants, had the exclusive right to trade in furs and other merchandise in all this wide region. This looked like what in modern parlance we call a gilt-edged business proposition, and there were not wanting men of large means and uncommon ability to furnish the financial sinews, for the concern had no government backing in money. They fitted out ships and got together a large company of men from various walks of life from a baron to a blacksmith. The Baron Jean de Poutrincourt was to become a notable figure in this enterprise, but a man of historic fame was in that group—no other than Samuel de Champlain of Brouage on the Bay of Biscay, the founder of Quebec, who gave his name to the great lake, surveyed and made maps of the Canadian coast, wrote invaluable history of his voyages, and died in his bed after all his perilous adventures on land and sea. The four vessels sailed from Havre de Grace on the 7th day of April, and on the 16th day of May three of the ships had put into Liverpool Harbor and there de Monts found an opportunity to exercise his authority. An adventurous and thrifty countryman of his was there with his vessel carrying on a trade in fur with the natives, which he had a right to do so far as he was aware, or it was possible for him to learn. The news had not reached him that de Monts and his associates had the exclusive right under a royal permit to all this trading themselves. De Monts showed a callous disregard of proprieties and failed in showing a decent respect for the wholesome opinions of mankind. He confiscated the vessel of this fellow-citizen in a lone land; took her supplies to help out his failing stock, and sailed away to the westward in search of some goodly territory yet to be discovered within the limits of his ample patent. Rossignol was the name of the man he had distressed. It was for a time retained by the harbor and now lingers as a designation of the largest lake in the province, on the waters of the Liverpool River.

The vessels rounded Cape Sable and dallying in St. Mary's Bay pushed out into the Bay of Fundy. They named it the La Baye Francois, and found their way into the spacious Annapolis Basin, that they called Port Royal. Poutrincourt, the baron who was looking for some place to make a home in the new world, was so much pleased with this locality that he requested and obtained a grant of it from de Monts, and the King confirmed his title two years later.

The expedition did not tarry long at beautiful Port Royal, and the River Dauphin, but sailed out and up the bay into the Basin of

Minas. That was the name they bestowed upon a locality in which they had discovered copper. Wherever they had landed a search was made for mines as they were bound to do by the terms of their charter. The imagination had enriched these unknown strands with precious things. At St. Mary's Bay they had lost and left in the woods Father Aubry, a priest with an enthusiasm for the new things of this unexplored world. By good luck the poor man was discovered weeks afterwards and restored to his companions.

One of their pilots turned chief prospector and picked out of a rock a smooth blue stone, an amethyst, and generously broke it in two and presented the halves to de Monts and the Baron, who were so pleased with these pretty specimens of quartz that they presented them to the King and Queen after a goldsmith had adorned them in settings of gold. They would be of great interest now in our Provincial Museum, and they have doubtless survived among royal trinkets.

Failing to discover a mine did not prevent them from fixing the name on the Basin, and they stood across the Bay of Fundy and discovered a great river on the 24th day of June, the festival of St. John the Baptist, and named the noble stream after this ancient worthy. They made some explorations and were greatly pleased with the scenery, the fish, and the game, but were so hard to suit that they set sail again and stood up the western coast not many leagues to the River St. Croix. Selecting an island in the river they began to make preparations to spend the winter there. Certainly they had left behind them situations far better adapted to their purposes and their needs, as they learned to their sorrow when wood and water failed. Baron Poutrincourt took passage for home in one of the vessels, but de Monts and most of his party spent a tedious winter on that undesirable spot where thirty-five men perished of scurvy and other ills. In the spring they sailed westward to Cape Cod and returned to St. Croix, where they were happily joined by the vessel that sailed in the autumn for France, under Pontgrave, who brought out forty men and new supplies.

They concluded to abandon St. Croix and return to Port Royal for a settlement. Placing Pontgrave in charge of this work, de Monts, seeing it well forward, sailed for France, leaving the afterwards famous Champlain to pass another rather uncomfortable winter there, and charged them to explore the country as best they could. Not till the next 27th of July, 1606, did de Monts return, and by that time many misfortunes had befallen them, but when they met again there was a great jubilation. The Baron had come, and with him Lawyer Marc Lescarbot, a handy learned man to whom we are indebted for a history for what befell them in all these times. He says the Baron opened a hogshead of wine and set up the drink in a fashion so lavish that "Some were so drunk that their caps turned round." A very practical man was this Parisian advocate, for he found them grinding their grain in hand-mills, and grumbling over the wretched toil. He devised a mill, the first in the province to be turned by water power, and aided in many other ways the material needs of the settlement.

Baron Poutrincourt had a taste for agriculture and a desire to get this place into a condition inviting to his family, so he had cleared ground and sown wheat in the fall. Meantime de Monts with M. de Champdore for master set sail for home again.

The winter was passed in comfort; they built two small vessels in the spring for their convenience and anxiously awaited the return of de Monts. He did not come, but a vessel brought letters informing them that the King had been induced to remove the terms of the patent by which he had exclusive rights of trading with the Indians, and thus the bottom dropped out of the enterprise before it had got on its feet. The King acted upon the advice of the Ministry to whom fishermen and traders made bitter complaints of the failure of their business, owing to de Monts forbidding their barter with the natives. One is at liberty to believe that the treatment of poor Rossignol in Liverpool Harbor was largely resented and the penalty, though long delayed, was not escaped.

Thus ended the attempt to make great fortunes in a short time. De Monts and his associates could do nothing but withdraw from such a venture and make the best of a bad bargain. Port Royal was abandoned and de Monts engaged Champlain to make a settlement in Quebec. Thus we see that at the close of 1607 this settlement was a deserted locality. Baron Poutrincourt had a grant of that place and was determined not to give up without an effort what had been so well begun. He was back again in the early summer of 1610 and with him came a priest, Messire Jossé Flesche, who baptized several Indians shortly after the arrival. This event was deemed of so much importance, from a business point of view, that the Baron dispatched the vessel with his son Biencourt to France with the welcome news to the King, and on the resulting flood-tide of good feeling expected to obtain some aid for the colony that he was founding out of his own none-too-deep pocket.

After many trials this young man returned the next June, 1611, and with him two Jesuit Fathers, Pierre Biard and Raimond Masse. There were in all thirty-six people on board this small craft of sixty tons that had been the plaything of the Atlantic since the 26th of January. They saw great icebergs, and singularly enough fell in with Champlain as he was making his way to Quebec and was detained by the ice, but arrived at Tadoussoc on the St. Lawrence May 11th. The Baron was not overjoyed with the results of the trip. Thirty-six were added to his family of twenty-three, besides the old Mic-mac Chief, Membertou, and his relatives, who had not become Christians out of religious considerations alone. This venerable man, who considered himself more than one hundred years of age, was obliging enough to die that summer, and then there were a few mouths less to fill.

The very next month the Baron sailed away for home to secure further aid, and there he carried out a transaction by which a woman secured a grant of the whole Province of Nova Scotia, Port Royal excepted. She was Madame la Marquise de Gucherville, lady of honor to the Queen, the wife of the Sieur de Liancourt, first esquire of his Majesty and Governor of Paris. This grand lady, once renowned for grace and beauty, was deeply interested in missions, and was instrumental in sending out the Jesuit Fathers with young M. Biencourt. To this woman the Baron went directly for assistance. She had already invested some money there as a missionary venture, and she was now persuaded to drop a thousand crowns more into this pious enterprise that the enthusiastic Poudrincourt represented in glowing colors. The noble madame concluded to look a little closer into this proposition, and the result was that she found de Monts yet held the Province except Port Royal, and although he was not very active still he had vessels there at that very date. She obtained from de Monts a release of his rights, and the King gave her a grant of the whole region from the St. Lawrence to Florida, excepting Port Royal. The Baron remained at home and naturally fell out with the madame. He dispatched a vessel to Port Royal that made the voyage in twenty-three days, arriving on the 23d of January, 1612. Matters at Port Royal were far from prosperous or harmonious, and meantime the Marchioness fitted out a ship and dispatched it to form a new settlement in her ample domain, that extended westward to Cape Cod. There were forty-eight in all. They landed at Cape Le Héve on the 16th of May, 1613. A fishing station was existing at that point, and there unexpectedly were found Biard and Masse, the two missionaries, with three others from Port Royal, where it was no longer desirable to remain on account of short rations and dissensions. Taking with them these two Fathers, they sailed westward to the entrance of the Bay of Fundy, and thence further west along the coast to near Mount Desert, in the vicinity of the Penobscot River, where they began to make a settlement, not without considerable contentions.

Now we come to an event of some real historical interest. At this point was fired the first gun in the contest between England and France for the possession of this western world, that was to have its final decision on the Plains of Abraham nearly a century and a half later.

The Englishmen who had been making a settlement during the last seven years in Virginia claimed to northward all the coast and lands, including Acadia. This claim was not new, but dated from the voyages of the Cabots in 1497 and 1498.

These Virginian pioneers were an enterprising community, and they were soon harvesting the seas for fish on the coasts of Maine. It chanced in that very summer of 1613 there sailed into these northern waters Captain Samuel Argall with an armed vessel convoying a fishing fleet. This was the very man who captured Pocahontas and brought her to Jamestown, where she married Mr. Rolfe. Innocently an Indian told him of the white men and their doings not far away. The Captain was a man of action, troubled with no fine scruples about making an attack upon Frenchmen at a time when the parent states were at peace. He rather liked the prospect of an encounter with these invaders of British territory, as he wished to believe. He lost no time and soon had them at his mercy. The valiant Frenchmen, taken unawares by a ship of fourteen guns and sixty men, .made some resistance, but surrendered after a loss in dead and wounded. This is a long story, of which we have the details, but the upshot of the affair was this—about one-half of the people were permitted to sail away in their own shallops and get home again if they could, and they succeeded. The other half were taken to Jamestown and treated badly by the colonists. Among these were Captain Flury, who was master of the French ship, and three Jesuit Fathers.

The Governor of Virginia, Sir Thomas Dale, was so well pleased with the success of this expedition that he at once dispatched Argall on another, with three vessels, to destroy the settlement of Port Royal and everything of French occupancy he could discover. Argall took with him Captain Flury and the Jesuits, and cleared for Acadie with this roving commission to carry fire and sword into the disputed territory. The first landfall he made was at St. Sauveur, the scene of his late victory, where he had not made as clean a sweep of all improvements as suited his taste in such matters. There he pulled down a cross, to gratify his religious feelings, and burned the buildings, and doubtless would have sowed the clearing in salt, after the Oriental custom, if that article had been on hand. In the old Norman fashion he made a lavish use of the firebrand and left nothing that would burn.

He stood across the bay to Port Royal and there all was deserted. The few who lingered took to the woods at sight of the enemy in such force. However, they ventured back and Biencourt, son of the Baron, failed to make terms of peaceable trade, and Argall destroyed the fort and houses that had cost a hundred thousand crowns, and even picked out of the stone the names of de Monts and his official associates, and sailed away in triumph. To the Baron this was the last straw that was to break the back of the enterprise that he had abandoned, and he then entered the service of the King and managed to get honorably killed in a besiegement where a fellow "wickedly moved a catapult and struck him on the breast, and the subsequent proceedings interested him no more," 1615, in the fifty-eighth year of his age. He was a notable and interesting figure in the earliest annals of our Province. Captain Argall was getting on in the world. He was realizing that nothing succeeds like success. The Earl of Warwick for mercenary reasons took him under his influential patronage, and he was made Deputy Governor of Virginia, where he enforced the Sabbath laws with edifying rigor. Had there been another French settlement in all Acadie when he had wiped out Port Royal we may be sure it would not have been spared. There were no longer any homes of white men in all this region. While a serious check had been placed upon French colonization by this act of Argall's, still the fishermen and fur traders continued their vocations in no very small way. More than five hundred vessels sailed annually from France to these western waters to engage in fishing and trading with the "*sauvages*," as they were always

2

called, even after they had become Christians, but the word did
not refer to their dispositions but to their life in the forests. Biencourt, in a measure, rebuilt his ruined post, and in 1618 wrote to
the authorities of the city of Paris urging upon them the advantages
of establishing fortified posts in Acadie to defend it from the incur-
sions of the English, who continued hostile. It was very evident
that French occupancy of this continent was not to be had without
a stern contest with English claimants, who fell back upon Cabot's
discoveries as the moral ground of their contention. In 1621
James I was King, and Sir William Alexander, a favorite courtier,
could get most anything he dared ask for. He was a younger son
of a large landed proprietor in Scotland, and having some talent
for writing dramas and verses was able to flatter the pedantic monarch by praising the royal performances in that line. In 1621 Sir
William applied to the King for a grant of Acadie, for the purpose
of colonizing it on a large scale. He had no difficulty in securing
what no one but himself and his associates wanted; and in his
patent the region was called Nova Scotia for the first time, in a
formal fashion.   It was then a large unlimited domain, of which
neither the King nor anyone else in the British Isles knew very
much; but they had stores of misinformation. Before this scheme
got into practical shape James paid the debt of nature, and Charles
reigned in his stead. He confirmed the grant of his father and
founded the order of the Knights of Nova Scotia, that resulted in
neither good nor harm. This was in 1624. It is currently reported
that at this date an expedition had been sent out and made no
landing, but returned with the report that the French were everywhere strongly in possession. If that was the case, matters were
later in better shape, and a new start was made by certain London
merchants under the patronage of Alexander. Among them was
Gervase Kirke, an Englishman of Derbyshire who had long resided
in Dieppe, and there married a French woman, who bore him at least
three sons of more than ordinary spirit and enterprise. Three small
armed ships were fitted out and commanded respectively by the
three brothers, David, Lewis, and Thomas Kirke. Letters of marque
were obtained and the adventurers were authorized to drive out the
French from Acadia and Canada. Many Huguenot refugees were
among the crews. Having been expelled from New France as
settlers, the persecuted sect embraced this opportunity to return

as enemies. Ties of blood and patriotism combined were not so powerful as the sentiment of religion, and thus it is always.

The plucky little outfit got away in the year 1627 and had a good run of luck, capturing several vessels but doing nothing at colonizing, unless it was to clear the adjacent seas of the enemy. Annapolis was taken as a matter of course, and in all Nova Scotia there was no other settlement worthy of attention. The next summer David Kirke was before the little Fort of Quebec summoning the great Champlain to surrender. But that he did not do—such conduct was not in his line. Doubtless there would have been no other course, had it not been to the interest of Kirke to be elsewhere to intercept the enemy's unarmed vessels of which he had gained some tidings. The next summer the three captains sailed up the St. Lawrence. David, who was in command of the armament, tarried at Tadoussac, a busy fishing station, and sent forward his brothers to Quebec to demand its surrender. Sickness and hunger had made resistance useless, and Champlain offered no resistance. It was a bitter reward for the dangers and indescribable hardships of nearly a quarter of a century. His country had shown but little appreciation of his heroic and patriotic services. This surrender was one hundred and thirty years before it was taken by Wolfe. The French had been dislodged everywhere by the Kirke captains, and when all was done King Charles, by the Treaty of Saint Germain, 1632, returns it to France. It will be of interest to know how much had been accomplished toward the settling up of Acadie and Canada in the twenty-eight years since de Monts had made the beginning. Charlevoix, writing a little more than a hundred years later, says: "Cape Breton at that date, 1632, was of but little importance—the fort at Quebec, surrounded by some inferior buildings, and some sheds, two or three cabins in the Island of Montreal, perhaps as many more at Tadoussac and other places on the River St. Lawrence, the beginning of a settlement at Three Rivers, and the ruins of Port Royal—in these consist New France, and all the fruits of the discoveries of Verazoni, Jacques Cartier, Roberval and Champlain, of the great expense of the Marquis de la Roche and M. de Monts, and of the industry of a great number of Frenchmen, which might have made there a great establishment, if they had been well conducted." This was a poor showing indeed. It had not been due to anything so much as bad management. Commercial greed and religious strife had been active factors from the day of de Mont's arrival. At any rate, the country was worth the conquest and a good deal more, but the men who furnished the money and the pluck never were repaid. David was knighted and Sir William Alexander was created an Earl, and these decorations did not cost King nor country a farthing. The King did not value this western domain very highly, for we are now aware that he traded it away for the balance of his Queen's dowry, about two hundred thousand dollars. Had the British crown kept these possessions it would have prevented incalculable bloodshed, and suffering, and waste of property during more than a century, to end at last on the Plains of Abraham, so recently that our old people have conversed with those who witnessed the death of General Wolfe. It is depressing to consider how often the course of human history has been turned hither and thither by the whim of a vain woman, the obstinacy of a stupid monarch, the vice of a royal tyrant, the barking of a dog, and the cackling of geese! There seems to be more order and proper direction in an ant-hill than there is in the history of the human race. I do not say there *is*, but it looks that way. For twenty years after this treaty the French were undisturbed in the western world and wrought as they would. A dozen years before the treaty was signed, the historic Mayflower landed her passengers on Plymouth Rock: this was the beginning of the end of French rule on this continent. The Puritan stock took firm root in that New England region and grew apace. They had no liking for their French neighbors, since they were separated from them by religion, race, and language. The Puritans of England and their co-religionists in America had never looked with favor upon the surrender of all the northern country by the Treaty of Saint Germain, so it turned out that when Cromwell, who was of their own gloomy faith, came to rule, he did not wait for a declaration of war with France, but having a little business in that line with the Dutch in New York in 1654 he sent out ships to Boston, to be there reinforced, and after their main business was over they were to proceed to the French settlements and reduce them to British authority. The Dutch encounter did not come off, as the matter was meanwhile settled by treaty; but under Major Sedgewick, of Charlestown, and Captain Leverett, of Boston, they were soon away on their errand of war. The result is all we can notice. Everything went as they desired, and soon all Acadie was in English hands again. France protested against this Cromwellian policy, but all in vain, for Oliver stoutly asserted that the cession of that country by Charles was a piece of unbearable folly, that he took upon himself to set right again. Sir Thomas Temple, Charles la Tour and others obtained patents from the Protector, and set to work to develop the resources of the Province in a way that would eventually replenish their own pockets, if all went as they hoped. They had been two years making ready for permanent business, when the stout heart of the Protector stood still forever. He died on the anniversary of his great victories of Dunbar and Worcester. In less than two years after this notable event in English history Charles II became King in title, but there was nothing kingly in him, and but a poor substitute for the man whose genius had raised England from a low estate to unparalleled power and influence in the world. Temple and his partners were actively at work repairing the forts and regulating the fish business and other affairs, and all the time spending large sums of money, and as yet getting no full return for their outlay. Charles had neither knowledge nor interest in this wild, bleak land beyond the ocean. He had more interest in decorating his mistresses with fine titles than he did with the affairs of state. In the seventh year of his reign he concluded a treaty with the French, at Breda, by which he restored to that nation "all the country called Acadia, situated in North America, which the most Christian King had formerly enjoyed." The result was that Temple was commanded to hand over all the forts and improvements to the representative of France, Chevalier de Grand Fontain, an act that he performed with bad grace, after a delay of more than two years that brings us to 1670. ·At this time there was but·a very thin population scattered along the rivers that empty into the Bay of Fundy. The outlook for much increase in this direction was not encouraging. The eager expectation of discovering rich mines had long ago been given up. Considering how fairly common in many parts of this Province gold-bearing quartz was scattered on top of the ground, and the precious metal plainly to be seen with naked eyes, it is unaccountable that the Indians had not noticed it, and that white men were equally blind to its existence till within the last forty years. The farming lands were not extensive; the marshes could only be dyked at considerable expense and special skill. Add to these circumstances the hostility of spirit between the New Englanders and the French, and the prospect was very dark for the settlement of Nova Scotia. During the twenty years succeeding the treaty of Breda, there was but little done in the way of improvement. Small groups of peasants occasionally arrived from France; yet the population did not reach one thousand, and in all New France there were less than six thousand souls.

No events of importance transpired till we reach the date of 1689, when war was declared between France and England. James II had played the hypocrite, the coward, and the tyrant with such admirable talent that he was deprived of his crown, and Mary, his daughter, and William, her cousin and husband, reigned jointly in his stead. War with the old-time enemy soon followed, for the fugitive King had found an aid and safety in the French court. At that date New England had reasons enough for making haste to settle up accounts that had accumulated during a score of years, during which her border settlements had suffered unspeakable horrors from the attacks of Indians, who were instigated and rewarded by the French in Quebec. In less than one year there sailed out of Boston a frigate of forty guns, a ship of sixteen guns, and another of eight guns, together with transports for 700 men, and this fleet cleared for Port Royal under the command of Sir William Phipps. This man was a remarkable character. He was born in the State of Maine, 1650, son of a gunsmith and a mother who had twenty-six children, and William was one of the youngest. While yet a child his father died, and the boy was hired to herd sheep, and continued in this most peaceful of all employments till he was eighteen years of age, when he was apprenticed to a shipbuilder, with whom he learned the trade and built some vessels on his own account. He was a restless spirit, and sailed away in his ship and kept at it until he was captain himself. When he was thirty-seven years of age he found a sunken Spanish treasure-ship off the Bahamas, from which was taken nearly one million dollars, and of this sum about sixty thousand fell to the discoverer, and he was knighted by James as a further reward for his intelligent energy. He was appointed Governor of Massachusetts in 1692. His fiery temper soon got him in collision with the collector of customs, for which he was demanded in England to answer for his conduct. He died there in 1695. This was the man who cleared his ships from Boston on the 28th day of May, 1690, or May 9th as we now reckon it. M. de Menneval was the Governor of Acadie and resided at Port Royal, where he had a garrison of only eighty-six men, and there were only eighteen unmounted cannon, while the forts were insignificant affairs. We may well believe there was no small degree of consternation when this formidable armament sailed into the peaceful Basin. M. de Menneval surrendered without attempting a defence. It was a case of where he might as well come down at once. In common parlance, Sir William had the drop on him, and there was nothing left to do but secure the best possible terms, and this was accomplished very adroitly. No one was hurt, the Governor was comfortably carried away, and some of his people shared his captivity. A few inhabitants nearest the fort were sworn allegiance to William and Mary. A sergeant was left in charge, and after ten days the ships departed with considerable plunder that must have seemed trifling to the man who had seen a million fished out of a Spanish wreck, buried in water, sand, and seaweed. The New Englanders were well pleased with the bloodless expedition, although the result was not very important; in reality the French occupancy was only interrupted for a little while at one or two points. Fighting went on for a half dozen years with a good deal of savagery on both sides. The battle-field extended from the frontiers of New York, through the forests and settlements, to central Maine. Frenchmen of noble blood did not hesitate to accompany the Indians on these expeditions against the English settlements and become parties to, and participants in, the attacks where women and children were murdered, and scalped, or dragged away to torture, or imprisonments. That such orgies of cruelty could have been witnessed and instigated by men who considered themselves Christian gentlemen seems almost incredible. The redskins wore crucifixes about their swarthy necks, that were often dabbled in the blood of babies whose mothers' scalps, gouted in gore, were stuck in the girdles of the murderers. The naked savage might plead in defence his ignorance and bad breeding, but the well-tailored savage at his side, who had been daintily cradled in the lap of European civilization, could not avail himself of such a defence. An hundred years later this thin veneer of savagery was thrown aside, and the world witnessed with uplifted hands of horror the deeds of the French Revolution, that showed an unparalleled aptitude for wholesale cruelty. The only defence ever urged for it is, that it was the reaction of even greater atrocities. Is it true that one need not scratch deeper than the skin in any nationality to start the savage blood?

Retaliation took what shape it could, and one of the forms was to equip Col. Ben Church, of Plymouth, to harry the coast where-ever the enemy could be found. This leader was a seasoned veteran of the terrible Indian war of Phillip that had sorely crippled New England in men and money. His services had been repeatedly solicited in the later French-and-Indian war, where he had proved his courage, energy, and intelligence. Our school history for Nova Scotia contemptuously remarks that "a fitting instrument of revenge was found in old Ben Church, who had many years before gained renown in Indian war." In fact he was but fifty-five years of age— ten years younger than General Roberts—when he won his best reputation. Church was so far from being considered a back number that his services were sought eight years later in another raid on the ancient enemy in Acadia, and he did not fail to remind them of a former visit. Church was no carpet knight, but a man of action, who did not turn pale at sight of blood. He had looked upon fearful sights in his day, the results of Indian atrocities. In his life, written by his own hand, they are related in graphic detail, too shocking for these pages. He felt justified in fighting fire with fire, and about· concluded "that there are no good Indians but dead ones," as the western pioneer came to believe long afterwards. In the summer of 1696 Church sailed eastward in a fleet of whaleboats and shallops, and made it a memorable occasion at St. John, and Beau Basin, in Cumberland county. Not so many were killed, but great was the number scared by even the name of this intrepid soldier. He was most intent on killing Indians, but his anger was greatly kindled by the French tactics that employed these merciless natives in their warfare. To show them how fine a thing it was, he brought along two or three score of these red men who had gone over to him in Phillip's war long ago. These he called "our savages," and he caused his French prisoners at Beau Basin no small degree of terror by reminding them how easy it would be to give them more than a taste of the tender mercies that these fellows would be pleased to exhibit on a word from him. Colonel Church evidently believed that he had shown mercy wherever it could be prudently extended: that he had conducted himself like a Christian and a patriot. We should not tread on dead lions!

On the 25th of September, 1697, was ratified the treaty of Ryswick by William III, and by its terms Nova Scotia was again admitted to be French territory and its boundaries were to be fixed by a commission. The treaty had no sooner gone into effect than Governor Villibon put forth a manifesto claiming everything east of the Kennebec River, together with the fisheries. But little attention wàs paid to his large pretensions, because he was not able to enforce them at the cannon's mouth. Fighting continued on sea and land and the English frontier suffered never more severely from French and Indians combined. War was again declared in 1702, but whether it was declared or not, armed hostilities went on the same. It was an irrepressible conflict. These nations, with all their ancient feuds, and radical racial differences, could not peaceably divide this land between them. The question of ultimate possession must be settled by the sword, but not necessarily with the horrid adjuncts of fiendish tortures, the tomahawk, and scalping knife. The burden of maintaining and extending English settlements fell almost wholly on New England.

They had the true Anglo-Saxon turn of temperament that rooted them to the soil through all their known history. They stood stubbornly above their furrows like their forefathers of old, and fought for *home,* a word that cannot be fully translated into the French language; *le foyer* is not the equivalent of HOME, that may embrace a whole kingdom, a city, a village, or a cottage. It has a moral quality that does more than suggest a cookery or a huddling place for shivering bodies. The Saxon home-instinct strongly inclines him to indoor comforts of floors and furniture and general tidiness, in strong contrast to the Celtic usages. An Englishman will take more pains to make himself comfortable in a place where he expects to stay but a year than a Highland crofter or an Irishman will in a house where he intends to remain for a natural lifetime. An Isle of Skye fisherman will spend all his indoor days weeping in a reek of smoke that has no escape but a hole in the roof that it finds after every corner is full. An Irish peasant will not be inconvenienced by the presence of a pig in the living room at his discretion, when a Saxon in the same station of life would not tolerate the beast on any terms. Among the French peasantry, if we are to believe good authority, there is the same lack of tidiness and comfort. Since ever these Saxon men of the soil touched England, some fifteen centuries ago, they have exhibited this important disposition and determination to attach themselves to the soil, wherever they made what was taken to be a permanent halting place, and there make them homes to be kept inviolate from conquest if possible, and if not possible, then to get the best terms within reach, but still cling to the plow and the hoe and the sickle. That was no alien stock that within four months from the date of their landing from the

Mayflower, in December, 1620, had invaded the stingy soil with their hoes and mattocks; and Governor Bradford, who was a participant, writes: "Afterward they, as many as were able, began to plant their corne, in which service Squanto stood them in great stead, showing them both ye maner how to set it and after how to dress and tend it." This early example in tilling the soil was characteristic of the people, and the beginning of their ultimate conquest of all that was in dispute. It showed that, in their estimation, to hold the soil by means of agriculture was of first importance. The axes of vigorous pioneers rung out on the frosty air of the wood-crowned heights that overlooked the distant coasts, and ever further, and further receded the sounds of peaceful conquest that dared the dangers of skulking savages, and faced the toil and poverty of the situation to make homes for themselves and their children's children. With all this thriftiness went the unfailing Saxon love of independence, that got itself expressed in the common law of England and again in Magna Charta. The town meetings among the bleak hills of Massachusetts and New Hampshire were but the lineal descendants of the ancestral Folkmote, or folk-meet, wherein every person had a right to be heard. These New Englanders were farmers, sailors, fishers, mechanics, and tradesmen, but everywhere and always a citizen, a somebody to be reckoned with in public affairs. They knew that every kingdom or state must be founded in agriculture if it was to be a permanent institution. Meanwhile New France was invaded by keen and greedy traders in furs, who had even opened the graves and stripped the dead of their ample robes of peltry. When every Indian encampment from Penobscot to Quebec was not without a French trader, adventurer, or loafer, there was not an Englishman voluntarily among these redskins in all New England. They never said, "I will wed a savage woman; she shall rear my dusky race," but the bluest blood of old France was mingled in the veins of these children of the forest. Such differences are unbridgeable chasms. They are constitutional, and the results of their activities will work out on lines of precision as rigid as Fate, which is only another name for natural laws. French dominacy was foredoomed in the very nature of the problem to be worked out on these western shores. These embattled Anglo-Saxon farmers were determined not to be conquered by garrison troops, by trappers, and traders and Indians combined. They struck their blows, now here and now there, and then returned to their furrows and their several vocations, and hung up their muskets and their powder-horns, till the next demand for their services. Among their French adversaries there was no lack of courage, and devotion to King and country. Of the pioneers, Champlain stands easily at the head, and yet so lightly were his great services appreciated that his now honored dust lies in an unknown grave. Not only for great services on field and flood and in the lonely forests, but for wise counsel that went unheeded, did this fine hero deserve great things from his country. He saw the vast importance of agricultural pursuits in this new world, and set the example in that line.

We have paused a moment here in the recounting of raids and counter raids, and treaties and declarations of war, to point out what seems to be the most important features in the enactment of the great historical drama in this western world. The marvelous spread of the English language and British power till 130,000,000 people express their thoughts in the language of Shakespeare and Milton, and more than one-quarter of the population of the world live under the tricolor of Britain, demand some adequate explanation, and I believe it will be largely found in the virtues of the Saxon stock that have been scarcely more than mentioned in this connection.

That I may not seem to be viewing the situation through national prejudice, it may be well to remark that within three or four years a notable book appeared in Paris written by an eminent author, M. Edmond Demolins, entitled, in English, "Anglo-Saxon Superiority; to What It Is Due." This book ran through a dozen editions, and got itself translated into other languages. The author could be quoted at great length, to show that he attributes Anglo-Saxon superiority, that has manifested itself by overspreading one-quarter of the populations of the world, and carrying with it the best features of the civilization of today, to the qualities I have here pointed out. Great was the comment of the French journals on this bold and startling production. It will be well to notice here and there an expression from these sources. The famous critic and writer, Jules Lemaitre, in "Le Figaro" said: "An infinitely painful book is that of M. Demolins; but we must swallow the bitter cup to the dregs. The book ought to be read." From "La Depeche Coloniale" the editor says: "M. Demolins has just worked out on a large scale a study which every one who has lived in our colonies has dreamt to accomplish locally: Why is England successful with her colonies, whilst we get nothing out of ours?" It would be easy matter to

fill a goodly volume with extracts of this quality, all bearing witness
to the inefficiency of French methods and means of colonization.
The closer we look into the matter, the clearer become revealed · ·
the causes of their ultimate defeat in America. The history of this
little peninsula of Nova Scotia takes us upon the arena where great
questions of national destiny were settled forever.· History as a
mere relation of royal successions, court intrigues, military marching,
and battles by sea and land, is scarcely worth reading; but it
is the philosophy of history that sets us to thinking, the moving
why they did thus and so, why empires rise and fall, why a handful
becomes a great nation, why national ambitions are humbled in
the dust, and "right doing exalteth a nation."

To resume the thread of the narrative: The hostilities grew even
more intense and disastrous as the means for carrying them out
increased with property and population. In 1704 Colonel Church
was again sent to Nova Scotia to inflict what injury he could upon
the enemy. He visited Minas, or Horton, and destroyed their
dykes and some other property; called in at Beau Basin to renew his
previous acquaintance, and left them the poorer for his visit. ·

Three years later a rather formidable armament was despatched
to capture Port Royal. It was under the command of Colonel
March, who was aided by two of her Majesty's ships of war, but
the expedition proved a failure. The fort was commanded by the
brave Subercase, who was well equipped to receive the enemy. The
attack was conducted in a way that reflected no credit on March or
his advisers, and there was nothing to do but return and face the
ridicule and contempt of those who despatched them on such
weighty business. Their reception, as it proved, was not one to be
envied. Meantime the enemy was extremely active and successful
on sea and land. Their privateers had captured no less than thirty
Boston vessels, with valuable cargoes and many prisoners. New
England was thoroughly aroused, and agents were sent to England
to represent their condition and procure some substantial aid. The
result was that on the 29th of September, 1710, a fleet of British
and New England warships and transports, having on board regiments
of soldiers, and altogether in such strength that it was sure to
prove irresistible if once it got safely into the Basin of Port Royal.
Colonel Nicholson was in command, and with him were Samuel
Vetch and Paul Mascarene, both of them to become well-known
figures in the history of this Province. Governor Subercase knew

that he had no adequate opposition to offer this array of war, that was now in competent hands; but he made an heroic defence during a whole week, and thus called into action the best resources of the enemy. When he had exhausted all means, then honorable terms were secured, and the Union Jack again floated over the walls of this historic outpost where it was destined to remain to this day. The garrison was sent home to France. Samuel Vetch had in his pocket a royal commission, made in anticipation of this conquest, by which he became Governor of Annapolis Royal. He was a Scotchman, the son of a Presbyterian clergyman. He had seen service in the continental war, he had taken part in a scheme to found a city on the Isthmus of Darien, that turned out a failure, when he took passage to New York, where his excellent family connections enabled him to make a prosperous match with a daughter of Livingston, the Secretary for Indian Affairs. He was a trader in Boston and got on in the world, not without being accused of making profit by trading with the Acadian French. This was the new Governor, who was left to represent her Majesty in Nova Scotia, an able, worthy man, who remained in office six or seven years, and after many efforts to secure pay for his services died a prisoner for debt in the King's Bench, London, 1732.

Beyond an unsuccessful attempt on the part of French and Indians to capture the fort, there is nothing of much importance to recount for the next three years, and at the end of that time, 1713, Acadia was ceded to the Queen of Great Britain by the treaty of Utrecht and ever since it has remained a dependency of the British Crown.

When by the treaty of Utrecht, 1713, Nova Scotia and Newfoundland were ceded to England, then was the beginning of the end of the contest that left France in less than a century without a foot of territory on the North American continent.

She had remaining Cape Breton and Prince Edward Island, to guard her fisheries and the entrance of the St. Lawrence, as a kind of bulwark of Canada, where at this late date there were but two towns of any importance, Quebec and Montreal, and their total population did not equal that of Boston. In fact the entire population of Canada did not exceed thirty-five thousand souls—only about one-half that of Massachusetts—and their commerce was insignificant compared to that of the English colonies. Their only trade was in furs, and while there was no lack of adventurous spirits

like Joliet, Marquette and La Salle, to explore the vast West and
the Mississippi Valley and River, there was lacking the true colonizing spirit that their English neighbors were everywhere exhibiting
on land and sea. It was very evident that Cape Breton and Prince
Edward Island, or L'Isle St. Jean, as they called it, would not long
remain a French possession, unless extraordinary means were taken
to resist an enemy in force. The first intimation of war between the
parent states would be the signal for the hostile New Englanders
to seize those coveted islands. Now that Nova Scotia and Newfoundland were most convenient accessories, offering shelter and
supplies of one kind and another, the danger was apparent to even the
authorities, to whom had been pointed out years before, by competent men, the desirability of erecting a great stronghold at Louisburg, if all was not to be lost of this great New France, that had ·
in no wise justified its grand name.

Seven years after the treaty, in 1720, was begun the "Dunkirk
of America," the namesake of the King of France; and Cape Breton
was renamed in the same spirit Isle Royal, and St. Peters became
Port Dauphin. In all this there was a good deal of the grand flourish that can never be the equivalent of lowly and useful qualities
that keep close to the ground and well at work along lines of
economic laws and material principles.

It is most interesting and instructive to note that nation-building
goes on with a distinct understanding on the part of the Power that
operates as Nature, that prosperity and endurance shall not be the
results of outraged principles. It is surely an indispensable qualification of statesmanship to recognize and respect the soundness
and integrity of natural laws applied to the local and political life of
mankind, and never attempt to accommodate principles to the demand of the hour, as if it were a light thing to have a demand that
cannot be accommodated to the trend of principles.

History of mankind is only worth relating on account of the
moral significance of its various phases; otherwise one might as well
chronicle cock-fights and ant battles. The French Revolution was
not a suddenly generated cyclone, but the awful culmination of a
long series of events, and ever since that country has been in a
state of unstable equilibrium, and her birth rate falling behind her
death tally is Nature's response to the tyrant who robbed the land
of the best men and sacrificed them to aggrandize himself and satisfy the national vanity. Pity that a state so great in science, and

art, and literature should have lacked the proper strength of moral fiber to carry her forward to some high destiny. Greece, Rome and Egypt are the tragical examples that assure us of the truth that no excellence of art, no flights in literature, and delving of philosophy are adequate equivalents of right conduct. neither in the individual nor the nation.

Here was a continental dominion to be awarded to one, or the other of two contestants. It had long been evident that there could be no peaceful division of the territory, vast as it was. France, although crippled by disastrous wars, and dissolute courts, was not in the least minded to give up the Isle Royal without a struggle. The government had come to realize its importance to the Canadian domain, and Louisburg was the visible sign of this realization. The locality was selected with good judgment, and the best military engineering skill of the nation was employed, and six millions of dollars were expended on the fortifications, and defences of one kind and another, together with public buildings.

This great naval and military station became both a menace and a challenge to the English colonies, although all the plans of the engineers had not been carried out in twenty-five years from the beginning; still it had long been a walled town that well merited a comparison with the great fortress that threatened the English in their own waters.

From 1713 to 1744 there were no stirring events in the Peninsula of Nova Scotia. It was a time of peace, and beyond the military post of Annapolis, where a lieutenant-governor resided, and a few soldiers and petty officials and some French families retained their homes, there was but little other evidence of English possession. The Acadian peasants, numbering 2,500 souls in all the Province, were for the most part settled about the marsh lands of Annapolis, Cornwallis, Horton, Windsor and Amherst. A few in Port La Tour, Shelburne County, and others in Pubnico, and Barrington, and Bedford and Pictou. They were a simple minded people entirely under the guidance of their priests, who, if they had taught them as wisely touching their duties and obligations to the British sovereign as they did in the affairs of social and religious life, there never would have been enacted the tragedy of nearly a half century later, to be defended, denounced and deplored: the subject of moving verse and heated disputes without end. When the ownership of the Province changed hands for the last time in 1713, these people were doubtless

placed in a sore strait, for all their sentiments were wounded and
traversed by this new arrangement, that did not take into consideration the feelings of a few settlers in remote districts of a far-
away province. Hearts are breaking all the time; a few, more or
less, are not to be considered in the deliberations of international
affairs. They took the oath of allegiance with mental reservations
and unexpressed wishes and resolves. Very naturally they preferred
the rule of their own country to that of the English, and they just
as naturally hoped for a release from this undesirable condition.
That people thus situated would improve every safe opportunity to
bring about what they most ardently desired is but a rational supposition. No man can serve two masters; the result of their attempt in
that line is a sorrowful instance in proof of the saying.

When Annapolis was taken in 1710 Samuel Vetch became Governor, and held that office till October, 1712, when he was displaced by the connivance and influence of his old companion in
arms, Col. Francis Nicholson, who was a false friend, and a most
undesirable person to place in charge of affairs at Annapolis. He
never made but one brief visit, and that to ruin Vetch if he could,
and his term of office expired January 20, 1715, and not 1717, school
historians and all others to the contrary notwithstanding. But
Vetch was again commissioned Governor, and held the office without returning to Nova Scotia, till Col. Richard Phillips, son of Sir
John Phillips, of Picton Castle, in North Wales, was appointed
Governor of Nova Scotia and Placentia. He remained five years in
this Province and returned to England, where he continued to draw
his salary for twenty-seven years, and meantime the affairs of the
Province were administered by a lieutenant governor and his
council. The first of these officials was Captain Laurence. Armstrong, who had been connected with military affairs of the
Province. His term of office began in 1725 and he ended it in 1739
with his own sword in a fit of melancholy. His successor was Paul
Mascarene, a picturesque figure of those days. He was a French
Protestant of the Huguenot sect, whose parents had been driven out
of France by the events which followed the revocation of the Edict
of Nantes. His life had been spent in the English military service.
He filled the new post in a very acceptable way during ten years, till
the coming of Lord Cornwallis to found Halifax in 1749, and the
end of all came to him in 1760.

During the years of peace between France and England, from

VIEWS OF DIGBY AND ANNAPOLIS BASIN.

BRIDGETOWN, ANNAPOLIS COUNTY.

1713 to 1744, the Indians of Nova Scotia, New Brunswick and Maine were hostile and caused a great deal of suffering and difficulties by their raids here, and there. They declared that they were not a party to the treaty, and the whole land was theirs. The French authorities of Quebec and the peasant Acadians supported them in this contention, and through all their conduct we may see the preparations for the scenes of 1755, when the long account was settled with a heavy hand, that left naked chimneys and yawning cellars, where had been the homes of a prosperous but misguided people. In 1744 the peace was broken. War was declared by the French against the English on March 20th of that year, and the news did not reach Boston till June 2d, but it had been sent by a special fast sailing craft to Louisburg, where it thus became known much earlier, and while I am writing these lines Marconi towers are being erected with Louisburg almost in sight from their summits, and there the first message will be received as it leaps the span of the Atlantic. Let us hope this wireless mystery will never be degraded by the transmission of declarations of war. In fact, had the finer sentiments kept pace in their development with the achievement of the intellect, we would now be as far advanced from war as this new telegraphy exceeds the old ocean greyhound that brought the war news to Louisburg.

To be thus informed of the hostile attitude of the parent states so long in advance of the English colonies was taken to be of some advantage by a few hot-headed parties. Accordingly several small vessels carrying seventy soldiers and three hundred militia, under the command of M. Duvivier, aide-major of Louisburg, were dispatched to Canseau, where they were joined by three hundred Indians. At that point there was not much to be captured beyond a fisherman-built blockhouse, a small garrison, and a village, and that business was soon accomplished. The next move was to capture Annapolis, but that ended in failure. A naval force had also been sent to take Placentia in Newfoundland, but that met with no better fate. Although these efforts to regain their old domain had in two instances failed, still it was evident that better fortune might well crown a determined effort that would not hesitate to attack the colonies to the southwestward.

Although these New Englanders had actively traded with the French as they built their fortress town, yet they had looked with

3

deep concern upon the massive walls of Louisburg, whose towers
rose like giants above the northern seas.

This summer of 1744 was a season of great unrest and depression
of business among the people of New England. They had been
driven from the fisheries of Newfoundland, and Canseau was wiped
out. Privateers fitted out from Louisburg captured their vessels
almost in sight of home, and Boston might be called upon any day
to meet an irresistible force. "Courage mounts with occasion;"
the people were made of stern stuff. They knew what it meant to
leave their plows in the furrows and fight for their homes. They
acted at once. Sent aid to Annapolis; declared war against the
Indians east of Passamaquoddy, who had taken part in the hostilities against Canseau and Annapolis, and put their coast defences in
order. At this juncture a most heroic measure was proposed. It
was nothing less than the audacious project of capturing Louisburg
itself.

There are several claimants for the honor of having first suggested the expedition against the city. The fact is, the project was
almost in the air. It was well known that the great fortress was in
no condition to withstand a determined and well conceived attack;
the soldiers were mutinous, and the officers incompetent. Very
likely that William Vaughn of Damoriscouta was the original sug-
gester of a movement of this kind; but Governor Shirley of Massachusetts it was who gave it official recognition as a feasible project,
and brought it before the Massachusetts Legislature in secret session, where it was rejected as foolish and chimerical in the extreme.
But Shirley was not the man to be discouraged by a rebuff of that
kind, and he set about at once and got a numerously signed petition
of New England merchants and traders, wherein were recited the
injuries received by them from the privateers of Louisburg. Armed
with this the Governor called the Legislature, or General Court, to
reconsider their previous determination, and then by *one vote* his
project was carried. He then sent circular letters to all the colonies
as far south as Pennsylvania, asking their support. But everywhere outside of New England it was regarded as a wild, imprac-
ticable scheme. Passing over much of detail, the expedition was
formed under the command of William Pepperell, and was ready to
sail on the 23d of March. It consisted of 4,070 men, of whom
Massachusetts contributed 3,250, New Hampshire 340, Connecticut
516. Maine was not then separated from Massachusetts, and con-

tributed nearly one-third of the whole force. The Colonial fleet was composed as follows: Massachusetts frigate, 24 guns; Shirley galley, 24 guns; Cæsar, 20 guns; beside there were one galley, three ships 16 guns each, one sloop 12 guns, one of 14 carriage guns and 12 swivels, one of 14 guns, two of 8 guns each, a private of 20 guns, and a large number of transports.

Before the expedition sailed a day of fast and prayer was held throughout Massachusetts, to invoke the blessing of Heaven on the enterprise. Whether this proceeding moved Heaven or not, it moved the men who went up against the stronghold of the enemy and made them a formidable host. It is worth something to feel assured that the stars in their courses do not fight against you, that your efforts are in line with all the destiny-controlling powers. It seemed like going up against the walls of Jericho with ram's horns, or attacking Leviathan with darts, to challenge the might of this northern stronghold. It is not a part of my purpose to relate the affairs of this memorable siege, but, in short, they accomplished their purpose. Fortune favored them at every turn; good luck was with them throughout. The siege lasted forty-seven days, and deservedly ranks as one of the greatest exploits ever achieved by a body of undisciplined volunteers.

Great was the rejoicing in England and New England when the news of the capture of the famous stronghold reached them. France heard the tidings with startled concern. It seemed incredible that a body of farmers, fishermen, mechanics and sailors, with slight aid from the royal navy, had dealt such a blow to the interests of New France. The nation was thoroughly aroused, and a plan speedily matured by which not only Cape Breton, but Newfoundland and Nova Scotia, were to be recaptured, while Boston and other English seaports were to feel the sharp retribution of war on a formidable scale. To this end a vast fleet sailed away the next summer under the command of the Duke d'Anville, an illustrious nobleman, but an incompetent sailor.

Almost from the start began the disasters and fatalities that are quite phenomenal. If the New Englanders in their attack on Louisburg were given the advantage of every imaginable turn of good luck, to a degree that rationally supported their belief that Heaven was with them from beginning to end, then on the other hand with the French it seemed that nothing had been lacking to show the disapproval of Providence. Eleven ships of the line mounting from fifty to sixty guns each, twenty frigates and about thirty-four transports, together with 3,000 soldiers, and abundant arms and ammunition, sailed out of Rochelle late in June, after being detained by head winds. Before it got out of the Bay of Biscay great gales had made havoc of much sails and rigging, and several ships were struck by lightning, and a number of men killed and injured. Sickness broke out in the overcrowded quarters and hundreds perished on the way.

The fleet did not reach our coast till early in September. When in the vicinity of Sable Island a storm broke upon them, and several vessels were lost; and when, a little later, he arrived at Chebucto (Halifax), the chosen rendezvous of the fleet, only one vessel was there, and in all only four battered ships, and of the rest no account could be given. Under the strain of such adversity the Admiral broke down, and died in his own cabin very suddenly. The same day arrived the vice-admiral with some of the missing vessels. More than a thousand men had been buried at sea, and they were yet dying fast every day. The vice-admiral, d'Estournel, then in charge, was so perplexed and disheartened that he ran his sword through his body. The command, by his dying order, fell upon the Marquis Tonguiere, governor-elect of Canada. More than one thousand men died in their rude encampments on the shore. The crippled fleet sailed away on the 13th of October, casting dead bodies overboard as it went out of the harbor. Its destination was Annapolis, and on board there were fifty volunteer Acadians from that region, who had come across by way of Windsor, and were ready to pilot the fleet into the basin. This is the spirit that resulted in the deportation of the Acadians less than ten years later.

The season was tempestuous; gale succeeded gale, and sickness raged, and the battered remnant never reached Annapolis, but got away to Port Louis, and thence to France. Had the fleet met with anticipated success, the subsequent history of North America would have been different, so far as human vision can penetrate. Before the fall of Louisburg it was evident that France intended to confine the English to the narrow region embraced between the coast and the great bend of the Alleghanies, no doubt with the expectation of making conquest of that domain at a later date. While this plan had been rudely shattered by the fortunes of war, it was by no means abandoned. In two years from the October that witnessed the clearance from our coast of d'Anville's fleet, the unexpected happened. The Treaty of Aix-la-Chapelle brought the war to a close and actually restored Louisburg to the French,, in exchange for comparatively worthless considerations. It reveals even at that late date the utter ignorance among English statesmen of the great value of Cape Breton from many points of view.

No wonder that the New Englanders were irritated, and even enraged at the paltry spirit shown at home, where their great conquest had never been, and has never been, appreciated and duly acknowledged. And there was begun the "little rift within the lute": the misunderstanding that widened into the breach of the Revolution thirty years later, when these "embattled farmers" turned their muskets on the red-coats and never desisted till the British sovereign was thrown across the sea. And oh the pity of it, that blundering kings and pig-headed advisers should separate so long what in the nature of things must be one people. This treaty really settled nothing; in pugilistic phrase, it was only "sparring for wind" on both sides.

The next step of interest to Nova Scotia was the decision of the Home Authorities to establish a naval and military station at Halifax, and this matter was so speedily arranged that within nine months of signing the treaty Lord Cornwallis sailed into Chebucto harbor with men and means to make a vigorous beginning of this new departure. This step announced the resolution of Britain to hold Nova Scotia. It was quite time for some sign of awakening interest, for she had nothing more to show for the thirty-nine years' occupancy of the peninsula than the military post at Annapolis, and the ruins of a fishing station at Canso. Meantime the Acadians had greatly multiplied, and were far from being friendly British subjects. Whoever wishes to get a further glimpse of the founding of Halifax can find it in this work, where the history of Halifax County is retold.

We see that the Indians proved a sore trouble in this enterprise, and were beyond question on terms of good understanding with the Acadians, as indeed they had ever been. Not only at Halifax and Dartmouth, but at Lunenburg, where a body of German immigrants were making a settlement, these savages were a constant source of suffering. None doubted but they were welcome visitors at the homes of the Acadians when they returned with the scalps of English victims in their belts. When the day of reckoning came there were those who had good reason for closing their ears to the cry for mercy.

The next year after the founding of Halifax the French began to build a formidable fort on the western banks of the Misseguash River, that now forms the line separating Nova Scotia and New Brunswick. This was one of the chain of forts that reached from the Gulf of St. Lawrence to the St. John River. Meantime the English were at work on the opposite side of the river, building a stronghold to check any future inroads. There were settled many French families in this fertile and beautiful locality that they well named Beaubassin, and where they would not have been disturbed, but their evil genius in the person of the priest La Loutre, prevailed upon these thousand people to quit their homes and then sent his Indian converts to set them on fire. Here were two forts, Beausejour and Lawrence frowning across the low fertile acres; both of them were garrisoned. Meantime Governor Lawrence, who had succeeded Cornwallis, was very desirous of settling the country with people of British stock. He could not prevail on the Acadians, who now numbered 10,000 people, to take the oath of allegiance, unless it was qualified by the condition that they should not be obliged to bear arms. It was very well understood that peace could be of short duration, and in no case would there be occasion to meet other than a French foe. This point the Acadians had in view, and they did not intend to be found in arms against their countrymen. Lawrence was quite well aware that they would not remain neutral when a contest was urged. Of their incapacity for that attitude they had given ample evidence already in their conduct with the Indians. Beyond all doubt it was a perplexing problem. Had a plague swept them swiftly out of existence it would have been a happy solution of the difficulty.

Lawrence and Governor Shirley were both Englishmen who did not stick at trifles, nor faint at the sight of blood, and they laid their heads together with the result that the fiat went forth that these Acadians should no longer endanger British interests. They were to come up by the roots this time, when a real radical policy took hold of them. They did not wait for declarations of war in a formal fashion in those days in America, so in this instance there was not much delay. New England was the main reliance for carrying out a measure of this kind. They had long been the sufferers from these Acadians, who in more ways than one provoked their indignation. Massachusetts especially considered that her fate was bound up with the Acadian region. These two men, Lawrence and Shirley, are responsible for the expulsion of the Acadians. They acted like men who foresaw an impending blow, and meant to make the first move in the struggle. Colonel Monckton was dispatched by Lawrence to Boston to confer with Shirley, and, if possible, raise an expedition to join forces with the garrison at Fort Lawrence and capture Fort Beausejour, and then pass up the bay to the Basin of Minas, and so on to Grand Pre and other adjacent points, and collect the people as best they could; place them aboard of transports that would carry them away to the English colonies where they might in some way manage to live.

Colonel Monckton was in command, and by the 3d of May, 1755, the expedition sailed from Boston with two thousand men. They were reinforced at Annapolis by three hundred regulars from that garrison, and then proceeded up the Bay to Chignecto, and landed at Fort Lawrence on the 3d of June, and on the 16th the fortress surrendered. Captain Rouse was at once dispatched with an armed vessel to drive the French from the mouth of the St. John River.

The New England volunteers were under the command of Colonel Winslow, of old Puritan stock. His journal has come down to us. We know the details of his movements. Colonel Monckton assigned to Winslow the unenviable job of deporting the Acadians, and destroying their homes. There are many proofs in his journal that his heart was touched by the scenes that were inseparably connected with such a task. He looked upon it as a piece of surgery that must be carried out if the English were to be left standing room in North America. He did his work orderly and thoroughly; there was no needless cruelty, unless it was in the separation of families. This very likely arose from lack of careful attention at every point, more than it did from any desire to inflict needless suffering. We must not be over captious in these matters concerning the hardships of three or four thousand people, when at this very date far more distressing scenes are being enacted in South Africa and the Philippine Islands by this same world-dominating Anglo-Saxon stock. Such dreadful experiences are incidental to the progress of the world; they are the growing pains of the race: Jeremiah of old cried his eyes out in imperishable lamentations over the sack of Jerusalem and the captivity of the people by Nebuchadnezzar, and yet this Gentile monarch is declared by the same prophet to be "the servant of the Lord."

The expulsion of the Acadians has been made the most of in song and story. It was a mere fly-bite compared to thousands of experiences incidental to such work, or arising out of perverted ideas of religion. And while all right feeling persons will regret the cruel scenes, perhaps not one of us placed in the circumstances of Shirley and Lawrence would know what better course to take. In a short time the Acadians were quite content to return and comply with the conditions required of them, and very largely they found their way back, and began anew to make homes in Digby, Cumberland, Halifax, Yarmouth Counties, and in parts of the Island of Cape Breton, and their descendants are numerous among us.

It was clearly perceived by Lawrence that settlers must be induced to make homes in this Province. With the exception of a body of Germans who had come over under the administration of Cornwallis and settled in Lunenburg County, there had been no attempts to form villages and towns. The year 1755 closed on a gloomy prospect. All the Acadian settlements had been laid waste, and hundreds of the younger men had fled to the woods, where they joined the Indians, to become a terror to every family exposed to them. Hand in hand they went with the red man, both had grievances and both were quite willing to square accounts in a barbarous fashion. Lawrence issued a proclamation, inviting British settlers to take the confiscated lands of the Acadians, or select any desirable point, and come along. There was a response from New England, but it was tardy. For six years the fields and furrows of the expelled settlers lay unclaimed, and then people came from the State of Connecticut and took possession of the region of Grand Pre, Canard and Habitant, and they were joined into the Township of Cornwallis.

In 1760 Liverpool was founded by settlers from Plymouth, Chatham, and adjacent towns. About this time Colchester County secured many families from Londonderry, New Hampshire, and also from the North of Ireland. Amherst and that region was settled by New England families, and Pictou County had some pioneers from Philadelphia and Scotland. Shelburne and Yarmouth Counties, and a few other localities had thus made beginnings of settlements in 1760 and a little later.

We must now retrace our steps for a moment and get upon the

main trend of historical development, in which this Province played a conspicuous part. The "Seven Years War" between France and England began in 1756. It was the result of a vast European muddle, wherein blockhead statesmen, unscrupulous kings, and corrupt courts had come to blows all around. It is a consolation to find two real men of steel and brain, stride out of the distressing mediocrity of the day: Frederick the Great, and William Pitt. One with a drop of King Alfred's blood in his veins, and the other blending in his line, the wide commonalty of England, for whom he became "The Great Commoner." But for his master spirit it is difficult to see what would have prevented the complete domination of North America by the French. Their plans in that direction were laid with consummate skill and were fast maturing. · Virginia and Pennsylvania were determined that the Ohio Valley should not become closed to them, and with equal resolution the French declared that it was theirs by every proper right, and they were prepared to hold it against all comers. There was no waiting for declaration of war at home, and the struggle began in 1754, two years before that event. With at least dramatic interest we see the figure of George Washington emerge from the smoke of the first volley for which he had given his little company the word to fire.

One year later, in June, he was at the side of Braddock when he fell amid a hail of bullets, wherein there was not one for him—a man of destiny, whose hour had not yet come. We must bear in mind the fact that Braddock was dead and his army wiped out but four months previous to the expulsion of the Acadians, and English reverses at other points had been quite sufficient to cause much alarm throughout the colonies. Disasters followed close on one another. The military genius of Montcalm was nowhere matched by the English officers. Great preparations for the destruction of Louisburg were made by Earl Loudon, who actually had in the harbor of Halifax fifteen ships of the line and three frigates and twelve thousand troops. Yet all this outlay was wasted through official incapacity.

The forts at Oswego had been destroyed, Fort William Henry had fallen, and, in short, at the close of the year 1757 the English had been worsted everywhere, and her prestige humbled by the incapacity of Braddock and Shirley and the cowardice of Webb at Fort Edward and Loudon and Holbourne the admiral.

At this critical juncture the genius of William Pitt came into play.   He was equal to the occasion, his plans directed, and his spirit animated the achievements of the British arms in all directions where they were engaged.   It was either a deep design of Providence, or a great piece of good fortune for England, that such a man was in a position to control her destiny at such a momentous period of her history.   With marvelous foresight he discerned the quality of men. Clive and Wolfe, Amherst and Boscawen, and others, stood the test of his rigid demands.   The result was soon felt, for Louisburg with its garrison of 5,000 men surrendered after a siege of seven weeks under Amherst, Wolfe and Boscawen, in 1758.

The next year in northern New York General Amherst captured Forts Crown Point and Ticonderoga.   Fort du Quesne, on the site of Pittsburg, was taken by Farlies and Washington, and Armstrong, and this great gateway of the West bears the name of the most prominent statesman of the day.

In the next summer there were 50,000 British and Colonial forces under arms, and Parliament voted twelve million pounds to carry on the war.   There was to be a complete conquest of all Canada if the ambition and desire of Pitt could be carried out; not a smoldering ember was to be left according to the program. Quebec and Montreal were marked out for the next actions, and on the 25th of September Quebec surrendered, but Wolfe and Montcalm were no more; a little within one year after Montreal had been captured.   Practically this completed the conquest of Canada, but the war lingered on in naval actions during three years more.   Then the Treaty of Paris, February 10, 1763, was concluded, and by its terms the French King. lost his possessions in the western world. The cherished dream of a "New France" had passed away in a rude awakening, and so far as human vision can penetrate the world has been the better for the decision that gave this vast domain to the Anglo-Saxon people, the best stock to be entrusted with a responsibility so vast and vital to human interests.   Throughout the enactment of this historic drama, extending across the centuries, we have shown that Acadia and Cape Breton have been localities where often centered tragic interests, and the scenes wherein figured great characters, and momentous events.

A convenient point to close a chapter was the date of the Treaty of Paris, 1763.   By its terms were ceded to England "Canada with all its dependencies, as well as the Island of Cape Breton and all other islands and coasts on the Gulf and River St. Lawrence, and in generai everything that depends on the said countries, islands, and coasts; with the sovereignty, property, and possession, and all rights acquired by treaty or otherwise which the most Christian King and the Crown of France have had till now over the said countries."

From that date till the present these possessions have remained continuously under the British flag. The island of Cape Breton was annexed to the government of Nova Scotia by proclamation of King George the Third, October 3, 1763; but it was little more than an empty performance, as there were no legal voters on the island to elect a member to the Legislature. At that time there were not more than one thousand people in Cape Breton, and they were a mixed lot, in which there was but very little material well calculated to found a colony. The peninsula of Nova Scotia was in no very promising condition. Halifax had then been in existence fourteen years, and was a small garrison town of five hundred families, where the principal business was rumselling among commercial people, and wrangling and squabbling over political matters among the officials. The total number of white families for the whole Province was 797, and divided as follows:

Halifax 500
Lawrence Town 3
Chester 30
Lunenburg 300
New Dublin 50
Liverpool 100
Barrington 50
Yarmouth 50
Annapolis 60
Granville 50
Cornwallis 128
Horton 154
Falmouth 80
Newport 65

The total population of the Province was estimated to be about 13,900 whites, and one-fifth of these were French Acadians. This was no great showing after more than one hundred and fifty years of occnpancy by French and English. There were no carriage roads; the settlements were isolated and poor, where the pioneers were struggling with great privations and difficulties. The Indians were not trusted and the Acadians were held in but little better estimation. The Governors of the Province had been desirous of securing loyal British stock for this region, but there were no great inducements to offer such people. They must come from Great Britain or the American colonies where they were already settled in reasonable comfort. Here was no paradise of plenty, no golden strand, no delightful clime; but quite otherwise. However, there are always adventurous spirits, and thus it was that slowly came the families that dared be pioneers in districts where now their descendants scarcely know of the struggles of their ancestors but three or four generations removed.

There is very little to set down in a general history of Nova Scotia after the Treaty of Paris during a dozen years. The population had increased by a couple of thousands, but there was a hard struggle in the backwoods to keep the wolf from the door while the settlers got a footing on the soil that would make some proper return for their labors.

In these days there were perilous trials in the home land. The old British ship of state had no longer at the helm the peerless pilot of 1758 who declared: "I am sure that I can save this country, and that nobody else can do it," and save it he did. There came a time in the history of the Jews when King Saul resorted to a witch in his extremity, declaring that the "Lord answered him not, neither by dreams nor by Urim, nor by prophets." So it was in England in those days. There was neither oracle nor prophet. Statesmanship was at a low ebb. Political corruption was rampant among all parties. The genius of Pitt was not quenched in death, but was under a deep eclipse of ill health, and declining powers, from which it never again emerged. By a series of unwise enactments, discontent had been bred in New England. Commercial restrictions had already been a heavy burden, not borne without resistance; but the attempt to tax these colonies in a more direct fashion was the last straw to break the camel's back.

With nothing but commonplace material from which to make a selection, a dull, obstinate King pitched upon Lord North as a proper person to place at the head of the Government at this critical period. He was quite ready to humor the temper and whims of his royal master. The end of it all was the entire independence of the American colonies that had for years been in armed rebellion against the mother country. Sooner or later this was sure to come, but it is much to be regretted that the animosities then engendered have continued to actively exist more or less on both sides up to the present moment.

During this struggle from 1775 to 1783 Nova Scotia was outside of the storm center that tore wildly through the neighboring colonies. It is true that American privateers caused some loss of property, and there were signs here and there that the revolutionists were not without sympathizers among their countrymen in this Province. Indeed it is quite certain that no great effort would have been required to draw Nova Scotia into the struggle for independence. There is abundant evidence that a majority of the American settlers favored the cause of the revolutionists, and there was no military force of any importance at Halifax or Annapolis. Early in the struggle the attention of Washington was directed to this Province by those who were informed of the temper of the people, and the defenceless conditions where any opposition might be expected.

In reply to a formal proposition to make conquest of this region, Washington reported as follows, with his usual good sense:

"Camp at Cambridge, Aug. 11th, 1775.

"Gentlemen :—

"I have considered the papers you left with me yesterday. As to the expedition proposed against Nova Scotia by the inhabitants of Machias, I cannot but applaud their spirit and zeal, but after considering the reasons offered for it, several objections occur which seem to me unanswerable. I apprehend such an enterprise to be inconsistent with the general principle upon which the colonies have proceeded. That Province has not acceded it is true, to the measures of Congress, but it has not commenced hostilities against them, nor are any to be apprehended. To attack it, therefore, is a measure of conquest rather than defence, and may be apprehended with very dangerous consequences. It might perhaps be easy, with the force proposed, to make an incursion into the Province, and overcome those of the inhabitants who are inimical to our cause, and for a short time prevent them from supplying the enemy with provisions; but to produce any lasting effect the same force must continue. As to furnishing vessels of force: you, gentlemen, will anticipate me in pointing out our weakness, and the enemy's strength at sea. There would be a great danger that with the best preparations we could make, they would fall an easy prey either to the men-of-war on that station, or to some that would be detached from Boston. I have been thus particular to satisfy any Gentleman of the Court who should incline to adopt the measure. I could offer many other suggestions against it, some of which I doubt not will suggest themselves to the honourable Board. But it is unnecessary to enumerate them, when our situation as to ammunition, absolutely forbids our sending a single ounce of it out of the camp at present.

"I am Gentlemen, &c.,

"Go Washington."

As the war dragged on from year to year stragglers from the scene of conflict were making their way into this Province, where they would be at least safe from the incidents of war. Some of them were Britishers who had no taste for dangers, others there were too old for active service, or otherwise inclined. To the general reader there is not much of interest to relate in the history of Nova Scotia after the capture of Louisburg. Her affairs no longer have vital connections with great historic movements. The growth of population has been slow, and the development of natural resources until very recently has been on a very restricted scale.

When the American war closed in 1783 there were but 14,000 white inhabitants. A large proportion of these were Americans who had come a score of years before. At this date the population was suddenly increased twice over by the arrival of a multitude from the United States, where the able-bodied men had fought in the royal regiments and lost not only their cause, but their homes. Over there they were called "Tories" and "traitors;" over here they were dubbed "Loyalists." For the most part they must have followed their consciences. When the war was over they were strenuously urged to find a shelter beneath the flag they fought for, instead of remaining as a dangerous element while the new ship of state was trying to "find itself" amid the perils of national convulsions—a task that required all the tact and skill the occasion could command.

This was not magnanimous treatment, but there was no great show of this fine virtue among the nations in those times. Magnanimity signifies at bottom, greatness of mind, and it depends on rare and complex conditions. It is not like common honesty or hospitality, whose existence is fairly to be presumed; but rather is it a virtue that however often it exists as bud, or promise, but rarely comes to fruit. Among savages it has no place; it requires a strong imagination and lively sympathy, and a large measure of unselfishness. Smallness of mind is the common order of things, and the more pinched, and poor, and ignorant the people, the less are the chances for magnanimity. Half starved men on floating

wrecks snap and snarl like dogs, and finally kill and eat each other
. as a matter of course. "Skin for skin; all that a man hath will he
give for his life." We must judge people by their times and circumstances. King David sawed asunder his prisoners of war; he
dragged them under harrows; he cast them into hot brick kilns,
and this on a large scale; but he did not invent these atrocities, he
merely practiced them in common with his neighbors, and was
neither better nor worse than those about him. When the British
colonies gained their independence they were in no mood for magnanimous treatment of men who had suffered from the same hardships that had goaded them into open hostilities, and yet took sides
with the King who had been the author of all their woes and indig-
nities.

No unprejudiced person with the facts before him can fail to see
that the grievances imposed upon these colonies by Great Britain
were more than men of spirit could well endure. But a few years
before they were a patriotic people, shedding their blood freely in
the interest of King and country. Even Washington was at the
right hand of Braddock when he fell in the forest massacre, and
Franklin was employing his fertile genius and risking his fortune to
help on the ill-starred campaign. It must have been a grave
affront to manly sensibilities that estranged these American Englishmen and turned their powder-seasoned muskets against the Royal
regiments. Some of our historians would have us believe that Sam
Adams, after failing in shopkeeping in a Boston suburb, raised a
ruction in his own interest and drew into it a few scamps like
Warren, Otis, and Hancock, as if a large percentage of the population
was not smarting under injustice, and ripe for insurrection.

The Continental Congress that met in Philadelphia to consider
what course to take in this dire extremity was composed of men
of extraordinary talent. It was no hole-in-the corner meeting of an
intriguing cabal, but it was a collection of men such as the English
speaking world alone could furnish. Said the illustrious Lord
Chatham: "I must avow and declare that in all my reading of
history—and it has been my favorite study—I have read Thucydides
and admired the master states of the world—that for solidity of
reasoning, force of sagacity, and wisdom of conclusions under such
a complication of circumstances, no nation, or body of men, can
stand in preference to the General Congress assembled in Philadelphia." This was the representative body that directed the

American Revolution. They had not come together to hatch
treason, nor to inflame popular prejudices, but to devise some way.
by which they might honorably escape from unbearable burdens that
a stupid King and a corrupt ministry had imposed upon a free people. They sought in vain to conciliate their English brethren. In
one of the most remarkable state papers ever written they rehearsed
the history of their wrongs, and demanded nothing but to be
restored to the condition in which they were in 1763. Appealing
at last to the justice of the British nation for a Parliament which
should overthrow the "power of a wicked and corrupt ministry,"
they used this admirable language: "Permit us to be as free as
yourselves, and we shall ever esteem a union with you to be our
greatest glory and our greatest happiness; we shall ever be ready to
contribute all in our power to the welfare of the Empire; we shall
consider your enemies as our enemies, your interests as our own.
But if you are determined that your Ministers shall sport wantonly
with the rights of mankind, if neither the voice of justice, the dic-
tates of the law, the principles of the constitution, nor the suggestions of humanity can restrain your hands from shedding blood in
such an impious cause, we must tell you that we will never submit
to be hewers of wood or drawers of water for any Ministry or
nation in the world."

It took more than a thousand years of English experience to
breed the spirit that glows in that language. I set this much down,
because we have had over-much praise of the Tories who found
refuge and rations within our borders, and took care to transmit
to their posterity an ill-mannered detraction of their own brothers
and fathers, and other kin, who had struck the blow for freedom,
that they from mixed motives would never sanction. That they
had a keen remembrance of the discomforts that went with a losing
cause is no matter of wonder, for, as Dr. Johnson remarked: "One
will have no difficulty to remember the man who kicked him out
of doors!" These Loyalists more than doubled the scanty population of the Province, and on the whole were good material for
settlers; but there were many soft handed gentlemen among them
who were hankering for a chance to hold down an office chair rather
than looking for an opportunity to tackle some bit of forest
primeval. They are responsible for a narrow prejudice long existing among our people that held in small esteem the "Yankee" over
the line. Until the coming of this Loyalist migration there was

no such sentiment in this Province, for by far the greater portion were either New Englanders by birth, or but a generation removed. They had been foremost in every step that advanced the interests of Nova Scotia. For many reasons they might well look upon this country as a mere extension of their own' borders, as it had been for years the battleground where contending interests had called them forth to bloody conflicts.

When it became necessary in 1754 to organize a court of law, Governor Lawrence called upon the son of a Massachusetts Governor in the person of Jonathan Belcher to become the Chief Justice, and this man of varied accomplishments,. who had been graduated at Harvard College, and trained at the English bar, has never been excelled by any of his successors. He it was who directed the attention of the lords of trade to the important constitutional question, whether the Governor and Council of Nova Scotia had the power to pass laws without an Assembly.

Lawrence withstood this encroachment on his prerogative, but in vain. The question was decided against him by the home authorities, and he was obliged to call upon his Council to take action in the matter. This they did in January, 1757, and their names are: Belcher, Green, Morris, Collier, and Grant. Benjamin Green was a native of Massachusetts, a scholarly men of affairs, son of a Salem minister, secretary of the expedition against Louisburg in 1745, where he remained as manager of finances. Charles Morris was a native of New England, and was also at the siege of Louisburg, under Pepperell, and was one of two engineers to lay out the town of Halifax. These three New Englanders in the Council became well-known in the after history of the Province for valuable and honorable services; and they were the men who insisted upon the rights of the people to a representative assembly.

With Cornwallis, when he came to found Halifax, were certain gentlemen looking for remunerative offices, but the new Governor appointed his Council, and here are the names: Col. Paul Mascarene, long time lieutenant governor of Nova Scotia, a Huguenot, who spent his life in the service of England, and died in Boston, even though he was not born there; Col. John Gorham, a native of Massachusetts, who had seen service at Louisburg; Benjamin Green, (just noticed); Captain Edward Howe, from the same region, an accomplished and valuable man, who soon lost his life through the treachery of La Loutre; John Salisbury, an Englishman, worthless

in the extreme, who soon returned to England to live on the bounty
of his relatives, who must have been delighted at an opportunity to
attend his funeral—a slight interest attaches to him as the father of
Mrs. Thrale, the friend of Dr. Sam Johnson; and, last of all, Hugh
Davidson, who came with Cornwallis, was the first Provincial Secretary, and returned to England after one year under charges of
trading in the supplies and stores of the settlers.   Who can doubt
but these New England men were the only serviceable persons in the
Council, and year after year they left their mark for good in the
history of the Province.

During many years from the establishment of an House of Assembly to 1848, there had been popular government only in name. There
was an upper branch of the Legislature, consisting of a council of
twelve, in which were the Chief Justice, the Bishop of the English
Church, the Attorney General, the Provincial Secretary, and some
other high officials.   This Council exercised both executive and
legislative functions.   They sat with closed doors, and every act
passed by the House of Assembly must receive their sanction.   This
was not a government by the people, but in reality a government
by a clique, responsible to no one, and the greatest difficulty they
encountered was, not to be found out.   Macaulay observes that certain politicians could be tracked after the fashion employed with
moles, which are sure to cast up a heap of dirt at intervals along
their burrows.   The home authorities were very reluctant to grant
popular rights after they had their experience with the thirteen run-
away colonies in a bunch, in which such privileges existed.

In Halifax the big-bugs were quite content with the old order of
things remain; they were well taken care of, and reforms were not
in their line or their interest: "Doth the wild ass bray while there is
yet grass."

In 1828 a young printer, twenty-four years of age, became owner
and editor of a weekly paper called the Nova Scotian. He was the
son of a British Tory, born in Boston; a Loyalist refugee. This
young man was Joseph Howe, and he gave his time and splendid
talents during nearly a score of years to securing a form of responsible government, which we have enjoyed during more than half a
century. While he was engaged in the leadership of that reform
his father, brothers, and all others of English proclivities voted
against him or his measures.   Let us remember that this man was
a New Englander by an ancestry of several generations, and the

mere matter of Halifax birth in no way raises a claim for the liberal spirit that belonged to the land from which his father came. Without entering into details in this direction, we may briefly recall other names of notable Nova Scotians of New England derivation: Thomas Chandler Haliburton, the judge, historian and humorist; Sir Samuel Cunard, who won fame and fortune by his intelligent enterprise; Governor Sir John Wentworth; Bishop Inglis; and General Inglis; Bishop Binney; Sir Charles Tupper, whose eminent services have been recognized in many ways; Herbert Huntington, the sturdy aid of Howe in his contest for responsible government; Hon. W. S. Fielding, the clever minister of finance; Hon. J. W. Longley, these many years Attorney General of Nova Scotia, orator, and writer of repute; Dr. Borden, Minister of Militia; Dr. Silas Rand, eminent scholar, who deserved more honors than he received; Governor Alfred Jones, long distinguished for valuable services in Parliament; Dr. Gesner, geologist and writer on our natural resources. This list might readily be greatly lengthened, but here are enough names to show that the history of Nova Scotia cannot be written without giving a large place to the so-called Yankee element. It is far from my thought to claim for this New England stock superiority over that derived from Great Britain; but simple justice demands a recognition of our debt, and good manners requires that we who are altogether or in part of the same blood as our neighbors shall not disparage their virtues nor magnify their faults.

Our people have been drawn from several sources, but let it be remembered that this New England blood far exceeds in quantity all the others combined, and to its virile qualities we owe the largest share of blessings we enjoy as a free people. In spite of political rancor and false representations, our sons and daughters have left us by tens of thousand during many years, and made their homes in the United States. They are to be found over all the wide country engaged in many industries and many professions; and as a rule giving a good report of themselves. Perhaps we are now to see a development of our great resources that will tempt our young people to stay at home. We have lacked enterprise in that direction; but there are now unmistakable signs that Nova Scotia is entering upon an era of industrial prosperity, and the future historian will be able to write the chapter in which will be related the founding of great works, the development of mines and quarries, the planting of vast orchards, the harnessing electrically of myriad water-powers that will enrich and adorn a long-neglected but highly-favored portion of the world.

From the close of the Revolutionary War, in 1783, to the War of 1812 between Great Britain and the United States, there was a slow but steady development of the Province. Villages grew into towns; the population increased everywhere; public roads were built and new districts opened up.

The war caused some stir and flutter of excitement here and there. Old blockhouses were repaired, cannon were mounted at the entrance of some of the harbors, privateers were sent against the enemy, and Halifax fairly awoke from a long slumber to find the port thronged with warships and prizes. After a couple of years the strife was all over, and both parties, like two tipsy combatants, could hardly tell what it was all about; if they could, they did not mention it when it came time to put up their guns and stop their foolishness.

"Peace hath her victories no less renowned than war," says Milton, and the one to be chronicled for Nova Scotia was the opening up of a few miles of railway between Halifax and Windsor, in February, 1855. It was the beginning of railway construction. Great had been the contention over the project and the work, for the scheme, that seems to have originated with Mr. Howe, got into politics, where there was next to no end of disputes. Since then a good deal of railroad has been constructed in the Province, where there is still a demand for considerable extension on the Atlantic slope of the peninsula. Before July 1, 1867, there was no Dominion of Canada known to the world of politics. Before that date Nova Scotia stood alone; since then she is a member of a confederation of Provinces that stretches across the continent. In many ways it was a bad bargain for her, but the step was inevitable sooner or later. In this union there is strength. A forecast of the future can hardly fail to see this great Dominion become an independent nation, a powerful factor in the great Anglo-Saxon confederacy that seems destined to long direct the affairs of the human race.

CHAPTER II.

The material for many volumes has been assorted to make a choice of the matter for this chapter. Not much beyond broad outlines and prominent features have been discussed. A century ago there was no geology; the infant Science was cradled amid fierce disputes over the nature and age of fossils and strata. Religious dogmatists became alarmed. We smile at their idle fears while we read their irrational and obsolete tirades. All this has passed away; the lamb and the lion have lain down together, and the lamb is not *inside* the lion, either.

Geology has its honored teachers in all seats of learning, and every civilized nation has organized and supported geological surveys that have proved to be of great economical value. These surveys have employed men of exceptional ability, and their reports and maps have widened the horizon of knowledge and generously contributed to the available wealth of the world. This chapter will have a meaning to those who are acquainted with the elements of this Science. Here they may learn something of a history that must have begun more than fifty million years ago, and has been actively continued to the present moment. We will find it convenient now to leave the Island of Cape Breton out of our considerations. The oldest rocks of this peninsula are the Slates and Quartzites of the Atlantic slope covering about 5,000 square miles. By common consent they are placed at the very remote time of Lower Cambrian, and this is provisional. Later they are not, earlier they may be. In this formation are the gold fields where considerable work has been carried on sometimes to a depth of several hundred feet, and not a certain trace of living thing has been found.

This formation is naturally divided into two groups. The Lower, where Quartzites are interbedded with slates to a thickness of about three miles; and the Upper or Slate group, about two miles in thickness. These rocks were deposited as sediment in the ocean, and were, of course, originally horizontal. Ages ago this formation was subjected to a force that pushed it and folded it into a succession of waves till it came to occupy about half the area that at first was covered. The movement was exceedingly slow and thus the crests of the rock waves were attacked by erosive agencies and scoured away to several miles in depth. The result is that the denuded surface now presents a series of anticlinal ridges and synclinal valleys with a general east and west direction that approximately corresponds with the coast. The gold mines are all located in these anticlinals that extend from end to end of the Province, Cape Breton excepted. These mines are interesting features to the geologist, who will find a further account of them in a succeeding chapter. This Cambrian Formation extends under the Atlantic, but to what distance is not known. It is surely made from the wreck of a land that very probably lay eastward, where now the sea has possession. If we go inland from the Atlantic shore, the land gradually rises between there and the Bay of Fundy to an elevation, varying from four to six hundred feet in a distance of forty and fifty miles. The surface is covered with forests, meadows, bogs, barrens, hills of gravel, and mud and sand. Granite boulders rounded and smoothed on the unexposed sides are scattered over this Atlantic slope. The outcrops of bed-rock are numerous and sometimes extensive, and the ledges are often planed and grooved and scratched by glacial action.

How far inland this Cambrian formation once extended we cannot know, because long after it was crowded and buckled into waves, and quartz veins were formed, there was a great theatre of profound disturbance along the axial crest of the peninsula and reached the eastern coast in the counties of Halifax, Lunenburg, Shelburne and Yarmouth. The fact is that the slates and quartzites, as a rule, at distances from five to forty miles came into contact with granite. The line of junction is very uneven in its course and ragged and broken in detail. The sedimentary rocks have been apparently invaded by an extensive outbreak of granite that occupies by far the greater portions of Annapolis and Kings Counties, extends in a large area into Digby, Lunenburg and Halifax, and appears as isolated outbreaks in Shelburne, and Southern Queens and Guysborough. The contact of the Cambrian slates and quartzites with this granite is marked with many features due to heat, suffering great alterations and in some instances graduating into mica schists and gneiss. The granite often extends into the older rocks on the southern border in long tongues and veins, but does not overflow them as a lava would have done had it broken forth on such a scale, for the granite covers about 4,000 square miles. Some discussion has arisen as to the origin of this granite. Both theory and facts strongly support the view that it is a highly altered condition of the Cambrian formation. It is evident that the granite invasion did not take place till after the other rocks through their miles of thickness had been crowded and crumpled and thrust into anticlinals and synclinals. What can we imagine to have previously occupied the present granite area but the northward extension of the Cambrian slates and quartzites that were invaded by great heat that accomplished the changes in the rock structure that is now a striking feature in the Geology of Nova Scotia?

On the northern boundary of the granite in the Counties of Digby, and Annapolis, there are at least two exposed areas where Silurian and Devonian rocks form the line of contact. These formations are determined by their abundant fossils. The positions of these slates, and their metamorphic equivalents, like the Cambrian of the Atlantic side, were sharply inclined and complexly folded before the appearance of the granite, as the numerous tongues and veins and altered rocks completely testify. Dawson says of this locality: "This junction is of great interest as showing the gradual alteration of slaty beds holding fossils into gneissose rock with garnets, within the distance in some places of a few hundred feet." Again he says: "It would appear that the general direction of the dip is toward the granitic mass, as if the Devonian and Upper Silurian beds had sunk into a cauldron· of molten granite," and continuing his remarks he adds: "The intrusion of this great mass of granite without material disturbance of the strike of the slates conveys. the impréssion that it has melted quietly through the stratified deposits, or that these have been . locally crystallized into granite in Situ." With this evidence before him, yet Dawson was not entirely persuaded that the granite was but the highly altered stratified rocks.

In the County of Yarmouth the granite is wholly in contact with the Cambrian formation and nearly all the County of Digby presents a similar line of junction. Elsewhere on the northerly side, with the exception of a small isolated area at Nictaux, the contact of the granite is with the New Red Sandstone of the Triassic Period, a formation that extends from the Basin of Minas to the Annapolis Basin and beyond to St. Mary's Bay. In the Nictaux River, that has made a fine' exposure of the strata of the South Mountain, the Devonian rocks with their characteristic fossils are seen to emerge from beneath the New Red Sandstone. Although the Coal measures are only from fifty to seventy-five miles distant in Cumberland County, where they give extraordinary proof of great duration in forming so many seams, still the Annapolis Valley has no recognized Carboniferous formation. It is very certain that during that age there was no South Mountain, and no North Mountain, and the sea extended over this region. The later Devonian fossils cannot be held to a hard and fast line that they are not also early Carboniferous.

To the northward, the New Red Sandstone forms a contact with the great Trap ridge called the North Mountain over 100 miles in length, that did not exist in the Carboniferous Age, that was followed, or perhaps more properly described as closed, by great disturbances. The New Red Sandstone, while belonging to the Secondary or Mesozoic Age, was evidently at this point well within the theatre of great changes that had been at their maximum elsewhere long before. The Bay of Fundy in those days rolled unobstructed to the South Mountain, and the Sandstones derived from that shore were distributed by the tides over what is now the Annapolis Valley and far northward into the bay beyond where now is the North Mountain. The bottom of the bay was a subsiding trough, and the crust broke along the major axis of this depression, and lavas issued from them under the water and built a frowning wall of black basalt from Blomidon to Briar Island, that through the millions of years from then till now has been a sheltering rampart to that bit of territory that has become famous in song and story, and also gained the title of the "Garden of Nova Scotia."

The Granite occupies about one-half of Kings County on the south; almost reaches the Avon River on the east, where it makes a contact with the Cambrian gold-bearing series, and turns abruptly southward in a broad belt about fifteen miles wide, its eastern contact running westward of Halifax a few miles, and extends to the coast and forms the shore-line from Sambro to the vicinity of Chester, in Lunenburg County. Thus about one-third the area of Hants is granite, about one-third Cambrian, and the other third Carboniferous and Devonian. The adjoining County of Colchester to the eastward and northward is outside the granite outcrop, and Silurian, Devonian and Carboniferous formations are the "Country rocks" of the region. Cumberland County is an extension of Colchester on the north. The pre-Cambrian, Silurian, Devonian, Upper and Lower Carboniferous formations are exposed at various points. The Cobequid range of mountains offered problems in classifications not readily solved, but the Geological Survey assigns the region to the undelimited field of pre-Cambrian.

Pictou County, joining Colchester on the northeast, has the following strata as tabulated by the Geological Survey: Triassic, Permian, Carboniferous, Devonian, Silurian, Cambro-Silurian; these, it will be observed, are in an unbroken descending order. On the southern boundary the Cambro-Silurian rocks most abound and evidently underlie all the other formations.

Antigonish County is a continuation to the northeast of Carboniferous and Devonian formations that appear on the Cape Breton shore of the Strait of Canso. The southern portion of the County has the outcrop of the old Cambrian rocks that continue into Guysborough County, where they are more or less overlain by Devonian and Carboniferous formations on its northern border, while the southern region bounded by the ocean is entirely Cambrian of the gold-bearing series, with intrusions of granite areas at various points. Continuing westward along the shore in Halifax County we have the Cambrian formation with extensive tracts of granite, in one instance thirty-five miles in length and from five to fifteen in width, extending from near Sheet Harbor to Waverley, running nearly parallel with the coast.

We now cross the Strait of Canso to Cape Breton with a land area of 4,376 square miles. This is divided into four counties. The Island is very largely occupied with the Carboniferous and Cambrian formations. The Carboniferous extends on the western side from Canso to Cape North on the other extremity of the Island and includes the Coal Mines at Broad Cove. The high lands of the northern portion are Cambrian, or perhaps older, and make up the greater part of Victoria County. The Devonian of Guysborough underlies the Strait of Canso and covers large areas of Richmond County where the Carboniferous and Cambrian rocks disappear. Cape Breton County contains the famous coal mines of Sydney, and there also the other formations common to the Island are outcropping over large tracts.

The writer of this sketch is well aware how mere an outline it is, but the design of this book does not permit a more extensive notice, in this chapter at least, and the County Histories of this volume contain additional information.

CHAPTER III.

It has been thought advisable to write a brief history of each county. In this way information is arranged in desirable and convenient groups, and the pictorial illustrations fall into their natural places. The Nova Scotians who live abroad, and own this book, will readily find in compact form a good deal of information about the portion of this Province that was once their home.

Tourists who are contemplating a visit to our shores will be aided by consulting these brief histories.

After due consideration, I have concluded to give an outline of the geological formation of each county. A keen sense of the value of this feature has induced me to supply it, although its omission would have brought me no reproach.

Says Sir William Dawson: "It is scarcely too much to say that absolute ignorance of the structure and history of the earth, and more especially of the geology of the district in which we reside, is scarcely compatible with the mental health of any educated man, as it is quite inconsistent with any intelligible comprehension of the geography and resources of our country. Every traveler who wishes to understand the topography, scenery, productions, history, and modes of life of the countries which he may visit, should know something of geology."

This earth is a solid globe of metals and minerals. Three-quarters of its surface is covered by oceans and lakes. All the land would be naked rocks if it were not that they are more or less slowly disintegrated by air and water, heat and cold, by which agencies are made the sands, and gravels, and clay in which vegetation finds a rootage. This surface is never very deep, and the bed-rocks in ledges and mountain flanks protrude like bones through the gaunt hide of some living thing. These rocks are of various ages and origins. They may belong to the most ancient of all known formations, or they may have come into existence but a million years ago. Even in Nova Scotia, a comparatively small area, there is no little diversity in the rocks, and each county has important and distinctive features that are due to the underlying bed-rock. The soil, the forests, the bogs, barrens and lakes, the industries, the scenery, the birds and beasts, all these and more, are largely affected and determined by the geology of the district. A feature so important deserves to be noticed, but it is so generally neglected that I am constrained to make this word of explanation for taking another course.

The Geology of each County will. go no further than outlines, and technical names will be avoided as far as possible.

The oldest known rocks are called Laurentian; the next age is Cambrian, the next Silurian, the next Devonian, the next Carboniferous, the next Mesozoic, the next Tertiary, the next Quarternary.

To reach our times many million. years must be allowed for each Age. The more distant the Age, the more extended the time within its limits. ˙ For some Counties it has been a matter of considerable difficulty to obtain knowledge of their early settlement, but in all cases these histories contain valuable information that has not all been gained by resort to books. In other instances I have been greatly aided by County Histories and other sources of written information.

CHAPTER IV.

This county takes the first place in the alphabetical order, but it has a natural priority by reason of its historical importance. The town of Annapolis is the most ancient permanent settlement north of Florida on this continent. At Canso and other points there were fishing stations, for temporary accommodations, but no attempt was made to make preparations for homes till Seur de Monts cleared ground on the Annapolis Basin in 1605. He had been the first to sail into those waters a year before, but concluded to look further to see if there was not a locality more inviting for his purpose. He was not "on pleasure bent," but there was speculation in his eyes, and he hoped to make a great fortune out of a Royal Patent that enabled him alone to barter glass beads, iron tomahawks, and other trinkets, for the fine furs that the natives desired to exchange for these articles. He was also quite confident that valuable mines could be discovered in this region where their imaginations had located exhaustless treasures of precious metals.

In view of the fact that a large portion of this peninsula is gold-bearing, and also that the gold in considerable nuggets may often be seen in quartz boulders and outcrop of veins, it is rather remarkable that the Indians had no specimens to show these eager adventurers, or their successors. A few specimens would have kindled a great flame of excitement then and there. However, De Monts did not tarry long in the beautiful Basin; his pilot was Samuel Champlain, the greatest mariner of his age. He had sailed the southern seas, and visited the City of Mexico; he had been up the St. Lawrence, and everywhere he had made extensive notes of his voyages, and constructed charts of the new coasts. With such a restless spirit on board, De Monts was not likely to settle down on the first bit of fine scenery he came upon.

· Champlain was in his element. Here were unexplored coasts and unsailed seas. They stood up the bold North Mountain shore and entered the Basin over whose entrance Blomidon stands guard, and there they found, as we may today, pretty specimens of amethyst and bits of native copper. We may well believe that Sieur De Monts, Champlain, Baron Poudrincourt, Champdor, and Portgrave, the leading persons in this enterprise, were all in fine spirits on these June

MIDDLETON, ANNAPOLIS COUNTY.

MIDDLETON, ANNAPOLIS COUNTY.

days, as they saw the new coastlines enclosing the ample Bay that invited to new discoveries. How eagerly must they have entered the great river that they piously named the St. John because they found it on the 24th of June, the day set apart in honor of St. John the Baptist. It is a noble stream, and these explorers did not leave it without considerable examination. They sailed southwestward along the coast until they reached the Passamaquoddy Bay, where a bad selection was made for a fort and winter quarters. After a dismal, and to many of them, a fatal experience, they returned to Port Royal in the Spring, and there began in earnest to get a permanent footing by constructing a fort and erecting suitable buildings.

The experiences of this town are related in some detail in the portion of this volume devoted to the history of Nova Scotia, and will not be repeated here. English and French monarchs were granting charters of the same territory, vesting large rights and privileges to royal favorites with itching palms, and adventurous spirits. In such a state of affairs there were clashing interests among unscrupulous people by no means reluctant to fight. The town of Annapolis was founded at this time, when the greater its prosperity the more certain its destruction by the English. During nine years to 1614 considerable progress had been made, and word to that effect readily reached the ears of the Governor of Virginia in his one settlement of James-town, and he despatched Captain Argall with orders to destroy all the French settlements in Acadia. And this thinly disguised bucca-neer, who was not new to this kind of business, laid Port Royal in ruins, although there was no war at the time between England and France. From this event till the treaty of Utrecht, a full century, there had been many claims and counter claims of Acadia; and Port Royal, as the French called it, became famous as the spot where the fierce disputes concentrated in besiegements, assaults and surrenders, till the town had no rival in that kind of business on the whole Continent. It has been taken by force five times by the English—by Argall 1614, by Kirk 1621, by Sedgewick 1654, by Phipps in 1690, and by Nicholson in 1710. It was by them abandoned or restored to the French four times—by Argall, by the treaty of St. Germain 1632, by treaty of Breda 1667, and by treaty of Ryswick 1697. It was unsuccessfully attacked by the English three times—by Ben Church 1694, by March 1707, and by Wainwright in 1707. It was unsuccessfully attacked by the French and Indians twice—in July,

1744, by Abbie De Loutre, and in September, 1744, by Duvivier. It was taken, sacked and abandoned twice—once by pirates in 1690, and once by United States Revolutionary forces in 1781.

Considering that it is less than three hundred years old, this is an extraordinary record. And now that it is side-tracked by the railroad, its cup of grievances is full; but nothing can stale the variety of its charms, or detract from the interest of its historic memories. While the world endures, the investing waters, and mountains, and islands, and meadows, and groves will continue to please the eye with their varied combinations that put on new aspects of beauty with the passage of the seasons and the hours of the day. The imagination, enriched by a knowledge of its early history, restores the ancient activities and environments, sees the leading characters that acted their part in the stirring dramas of the day; sees French nobles, famous navigators, and grave Jesuits; sees military captains, naval commanders, and strenuous adventurers whose names are indelibly intermingled with the history of Anglo-Saxon America; sees Champlain, the chivalrous gentleman, the bold mariner, and brave soldier, as he paced the outworks that commanded the ample bay, and longed for the return of De Monts, that he might lead some great enterprise of discovery and colonization, and thus lay the foundation of future Commonwealths. Space forbids me to call the roll of noted men whose presence on this scene bespoke the importance of the locality as a storm center of clashing interests of international importance and continental dimensions.

If nature did not intend this place for a brisk commercial center, she nevertheless dowered the spot with riches that no art can furnish, and no money can buy. It remains for human enterprise to utilize these advantages and make the old town so comfortable, so inviting, that it can never be neglected while there are tired mortals in search of refreshing scenes that appeal to the eye, and the intellect, and the imagination of intelligent people.

It was on that ground was grown the first wheat ever raised in America, and in the rocky suburbs was constructed the first waterwheel to turn a millstone on this Continent, and the builder, Le Escarbot, a Parisian lawyer, proved more useful in the New World in his mechanical employment than he would have been in the Old World in a more genteel vocation. In spite of many discouragements from 1605 to 1755, the French population, and there was no other European, had vigorously multiplied in this goodly land, and made for themselves comfortable homes in the choicest localities. By the treaty of Utrecht they had become subjects of England. This was repugnant to their most sacred sentiments of religion and patriotism. At any rate, right or wrong, the French were to go. The "mailed fist" of unrelenting authority made short work of these "vermin," as General Amherst termed them three years later in an order to General Wolfe. Their deserted lands and the ashes of their homes were the unwritten records of a tragedy for which there are some excuses.

About sixteen hundred people in this County were either deported, or settled among the Indians in the forest. Their settlements extended east to the Township line. The next Summer of 1756 the whole scene from end to end of the valley, from Basin to Basin, was one of desolation, and vividly suggestive of suffering on a great scale.

New England troops had carried out the work of destruction, and they were best calculated for the task, if we are to believe Captain Alexander Murray, in charge of a garrison at Windsor, who wrote to Colonel Winslow at Grand Pre, a month before the deportation began there:

"FORT EDWARD, 8th. Sept. 1755.

"Dear Sir:

"I received your favor and am extremely pleased that things are so clever at Grand Pre, and that the poor devils are so resigned. When I think of Annapolis I applaud our thoughts of summoning them in. I am afraid there will be some lives lost before they are got together. You know our soldiers hate them, and if they can find a pretence to kill them they will."

Having cleared the land of these undesirable owners, the next step was an effort to find other occupants who would give the Government no trouble in the matter of allegiance. With the departure of the Acadians from all their settlements in the peninsula south of Canseau, the white population was reduced to less than 1,000 in Halifax and about 1,500 Germans in Lunenburg. The French were in possession of Cape Breton. Only a half dozen years since Cornwallis had made a beginning at Halifax, and but two years since ground was broke at Lunenburg. Both settlements had suffered severely from Indians, who were quite willing to indulge their cruel propensities and receive rewards from their French friends.

Both Shirley and Lawrence were not only desirous of ridding the Province of the troublesome Acadians, but to replace them by settlers whose presence was a guarantee of security to English interests. The French were not expelled in order that their property might be divided among greedy adventurers who longed to possess their fertile lands and fruitful orchards, as we are sometimes informed. So there are certain wiseacres who tell us that the present war in the Transvaal is but a scramble on the part of Great Britain to secure the gold and diamond fields of that region. Had it been designed to deport the Acadians in order to bestow their inheritance upon covetous friends, then there would have been a reasonable effort made to protect their holdings and occupy them the next season. The firebrand was liberally used, and every house and barn belonging to them laid in ashes, and the land was largely injured in the interval before other hands were there to plow and sow and fence once more. These people never would have been expelled in order to despoil them of their property, but, having designed to get clear of them for other reasons, it was clearly the intention to bestow them upon more desirable settlers.

Writing while the deportation was going forward, Lawrence says:

"Though every means was used to point out to the deputies [of the Acadians] their true interest, and sufficient time given them to deliberate, nothing could induce them to acquiesce in any measure consistent with H. M. honor and the security of the province. * * * As soon as the French are gone, I shall use my best endeavours to encourage people to come from the Continent to settle their lands, and if I succeed in this point we shall soon be in a condition of supplying ourselves with provisions, and I hope in time be able to strike off the great expense of victualling the troops. This was one of the happy effects I proposed to myself from driving them off the Isthmus; and the additional circumstance of the inhabitants evacuating the County will, I flatter myself, greatly hasten this event, as it furnishes us with a large quantity of good land ready for immediate cultivation."

During four years, from 1755 to 1760, these fields lay waste and rapidly decreasing in value. The orchards were unpruned, weeds ran riot in the gardens, unclaimed cattle, dazed with their new conditions, wandered over unfenced farms in Summer, and secured a living in the shelter of the forests in the Winter, after the manner of moose and caribou. The old Town, so long the capital, had been outgrown in importance by Halifax, and, deprived of that distinction, fell into a second place.

Several families of British origin continued to reside there, and

GRANVILLE FERRY, ANNAPOLIS.

ANNAPOLIS, FROM GRANVILLE.

OLD POWDER MAGAZINE IN OLD FRENCH FORT, ANNAPOLIS.

OLD FRENCH FORT, ANNAPOLIS.

it remained with a garrison and all its concomitants of commissary and chaplain, etc.

It became evident that the new settlers for these lands must be tempted from the rural districts of New England. The whole story of the expulsion of the Acadians was familiar to them. With the exception of Annapolis, this work had been carried out either entirely as at Grand Pre, or very largely elsewhere, by men from Massachusetts 'and nearby States. The wretched business had not been "done in a corner." ·

So far as New England was concerned, there is no evidence that the farmers of that region were eager to possess those lands that Lawrence, in a proclamation issued on the 12th day of October, 1758, inviting settlers from the old Colonies, describes as "one hundred thousand acres, of which the country had produced wheat, rye, barley, oats, hemp, flax, etc., without failure for the last century; and an·other hundred thousand acres had been cleared and stocked with English grass, planted with orchards, and embellished with gardens, the whole so intermixed that every individual farmer might have a proportionate quantity of plowed land, grass land, and woodland."

This tempting bait, officially dangled before the eyes of men who were wresting a livelihood from the stingy soil of New England hills, got something more than a tentative nibble. Agents came to Halifax from these localities to know what more was to be thrown into this offer. There must be guarantee of civil and religious liberties, and explicit statement of terms of occupancy, before these desirable settlers would quit their homes. Governor Lawrence, in response to this demand, issued another proclamation on the 11th of January, 1759, that satisfied the interested parties, and active preparations went forward to bring the new pioneers. In the next May, 1760, came forty-five of these people, with some live stock and utensils for the farms. They came on a vessel called the "Charming Molly," and their names are of sufficient importance to be given here: Jonathan Thayer, Gideon Albe, Isaac Kent, Stephen Rice, Daniel Summer, Joseph Marshall, Thomas Hooper, wife and sons and three daughters, William Williams, John Hill, Abner Morse, Nathaniel Rawson, Samuel Perkins, Ebenezer Felch, Thomas Damon, John Damon, Edmund Damon, William Curtis and wife, Daniel Moore, Samuel Bent, Uriah Clarke, Samuel Morse, Jonathan Church, Benjamin Mason, Michael Spurr and wife, three sons and three daughters, John Winslow, John Whit-

5

man, Michael Law, John Bacon, Daniel Felch, Benjamin Rice, Beriah Rice.

Later in the season arrived the following persons: Captain Phineas Lovitt, Obadiah Wheelock, Aaron Hardy, Moses Thayer, Joseph Daniels, Benjamin Eaton, Thomas Smith, Job Cushing, Ebenezer Perry, John Baker, William Jennison, Paul Hazeltine. William Bowles. The work of settlement went steadily forward. Other houses were built and other homes were made on the goodly acres of the expatriated Acadians, who were dying by hundreds of homesickness, want and fear in the midst of inhospitable strangers. The more hardy of these deported people were venturing back to their beloved Acadia. After eight years, in 1768, a census was taken, and the returns show a population of 513; among them are four French families. The present population of this county is largely composed of the descendants of these families from New England. The population was strongly increased between 1775 and 1783 by the arrival from the Colonies, that afterwards became the United States, of many people who are known as "Loyalists." The greater portion of these came at the latter date when they were expelled by the victorious party. The newborn nation was not minded to have in their midst an obstructive element, that had almost proved fatal to their cause in the long struggle for independence. So with genuine Anglo-Saxon bluntness they were made to distinctly understand that their room was better than their company, such a policy resulting in great hardships. Much of the best brains and culture was turned out of doors, and Nova Scotia was greatly enriched by the portion of these refugees that fell to her share. Their descendants are numerous in Annapolis County, where their thrift and intelligence have left a distinctive mark upon that portion of the Province. The thrifty villages and fine farms of this region bespeak a superior population. To describe these localities in much detail is not possible within the limits of this brief history, but the most notable must claim a word of description.

Annapolis Town is the county capital. It is situated at the head of Annapolis Basin, and has a population of about 6,000. It is a trading center for the adjacent district and by rail and shipping it is in touch with general outside business; a delightful locality for summer visitors, who can enjoy the tempered sea air, the pleasant drives and walks, and find opportunities for sailing, fishing and other diversions. About 28 acres are covered with the old fortifications, now fallen into desuetude, but still replete with memories of distant days, when there were stirring times among the pioneers who were so often obliged to defend by force of arms their slender holdings that they had wrested from Nature. Here are churches, good schools, a newspaper, and comfortable hotels.

Bridgetown is fourteen miles from Annapolis up the valley, and at the head of navigation on the river. It is in the midst of a favored farming district, and has a population of about 1,000. It lacks the water outlook of Annapolis, and the interesting history of that town, but we cannot live on scenery, however much it contributes to our enjoyment. Bridgetown has its own charms, and is central to fine fishing in the streams to the southward. The town is on the D. A. R. line of railroad, and has a newspaper, several churches, good hotels, and other evidences of prosperity and promises of comfort to those who seek her hospitalities.

Paradise, Lawrencetown, and Middleton, in the above order, extend eastward up the valley on the line of railroad. They are all prosperous towns situated amid fine farms and extensive orchards. From Paradise a road crosses the North Mountain to Port Williams, distance about seven miles, on the Bay of Fundy, where some three hundred people are principally engaged in fishing.

From Middleton the Central Railroad crosses the South Mountain, and extends to Lunenburg Town on the Atlantic Coast. Southward from Middleton, fout miles on this line, is Nictaux, a farming village largely on the hills, where there are immense deposits of valuable iron ore. The present outlook is favorable for extensive operations in this mining district. The Nictaux River, a considerable stream, descends into the valley over a precipitous course from the upper regions of the watershed, and thus makes available a large store of power to be utilized in the mining industry. To the southward of Nictaux are the rural villages of Springfield, New Albany, and Dalhousie. The small villages and hamlets are too numerous to describe, but they all have merits and charms of their own in this sheltered and fertile region of the valley. Returning to the Annapolis Basin, we come to Granville, on the north shore, where the first settlement was made by Sieur De Monts. This is a considerable township, delightfully situated. Communication with the town of Annapolis is maintained with a ferry-boat, but a bridge should be built for that purpose. On the south shore of the basin is Clementsport, a beautiful village, and Deep Brook is a most inviting locality. Bear River is on the county line, and the thriving town among the hills is famous for cherries, steep roads and religious gatherings. A large portion of the county on the southern side is a forest, valuable for lumber and pulp. This soil is not suitable for farming purposes. On this extreme border, adjoining Queens, are the small villages of Maitland, Milford, and Northfield, while Milford and Greywood are intermediate hamlets on the highway between Annapolis and Liverpool. We come now to consider the general geological features of this county. About three-quarters of the county is granite; the remainder is Triassic red sandstone, Devonian and Silurian quartzites and shales, and Cambrian quartzites. In more detail, we may say, from the southern edge of the valley to the Queens County line all is granite except a small area of Devonian strata wherein are the Nictaux and Torbrook iron mines, and about fifty square miles of the same formation in the southwestern extremity of the county, through which run Deep Brook and Bear River in a portion of their courses. From Clementsport to the Digby County line, and from the shore of the basin southward five or six miles, the older or underlying Cambrian quartzites occur. The Annapolis Valley is very near the western extremity of the granite axis of the Peninsula of Nova Scotia. It is discussed somewhat in the chapter on the Geology of Nova Scotia. The valley itself is also remarkable for the few exposures of the bed rock, which proves to be red sandstone of the Triassic Age, that are certainly not so old as the North Mountain, where portions of this formation may be seen at the "Devil's Kitchen," some three hundred feet or more above the general level of the valley. The remaining area is covered by the North Mountain, which is an extrusion of lava that once issued from a fracture in the trough of the Bay of Fundy. These varied geological features result in a corresponding variety of scenery and economic products.

CHAPTER V.

The gold-bearing rocks extend from the Strait of Canso to the western extremity of the Province, with a breadth varying from ten to thirty-five miles, and with an area of 6,000 square miles. This formation of slates and quartzites is bounded on the south by the ocean, on the north by a granite contact. Thus much for a mere outline, but it will be worth while to dwell a moment on the origin of these rocks. A diagram representing the succession of geological Ages, one over another, will have the Cambrian, or Lower Silurian, at the very bottom of the undisputed fossiliferous rocks, and to this formation the gold measures of Nova Scotia have been provisionally assigned. They have not yielded for certain a single trace of life, although manifestly of sedimentary origin, not altered by heat to a degree destructive to fossils, and of a nature fairly well calculated to preserve even delicate organisms. Further investigation may well classify them as Pre-Cambrian. At any rate they are made from the ruins of an older land whose site they largely occupy. . The ceaseless assault of the wallowing waves, the myriad-handed agencies of sun, air, and water, reduced the frowning naked rocks to sand and mud; and the under-tow of the broken billows, and the tireless tides, distributed these sediments along the coast in the same way that they are now, after so vast a time, being redistributed before our eyes.

Nothing need be clearer than the sedimentary origin of these gold-bearing rocks. Beyond all intelligent question they were once before in form of solid formations, and then reduced to sediments. From reliable data, this series of rocks is estimated to be about three miles in thickness.

There is not now, nor ever has been, a coast where the surroundings at once fell into such abysmal depths as that: The explanation is that the plastic crust of a newer world yielded to the weight of sediment and slowly subsided as the strata accumulated, and the adjacent land may well have been elevated in a corresponding degree. To-day these old sands, mud, and clay are quartzites and slates, but they are no longer in horizontal beds. They are standing on edge at all angles, showing everywhere that they have been operated upon by a force that pushed them into an area of about one-half they once occupied. In other words, the very foundations on which as sediments they were deposited shrank into vastly smaller dimensions, and this shrinkage, as a matter of course, must result in folds, and waves, and many complications of structure. Very likely these movements were due to cooling of the crust of the globe. A marked feature of these rocks is a succession of east and west waves running roughly parallel to the Atlantic coast, and with a marked general regularity. These rock waves were so slow in their elevation that perhaps they were never to be seen as actual undulations, for the erosive agencies of air, and heat, and wind, and water leveled them as they rose, and we have now before us the scored away crests, and the once profound depth, open to investigation. The ordinary structure of this formation is plainly shown in Fig. 1, copied from a map of the Geological Survey of the County of Halifax, and originally made from actual observations. It is a vertical section of about one-half mile in depth and nine miles in length, with a north and south course across the dips or inclinations of the denuded waves of the strata. No observations have been made to this depth, but the planes of stratification, as they appear at the various and extensive outcrops above the surface drift, are abundant evidence of the nature of the deep structure. The dotted lines above and below the diagram are intended to show about where the crumpled rocks would have reached, some five to eight miles in altitude, had they not been largely worn away by erosive agencies as they arose above the general level. The dotted lines below indicate in a general manner

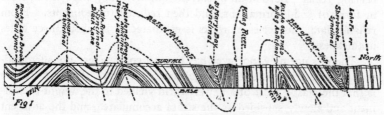

Fig 1

the characteristic features of the deeper portion of the formation. It will be noted that the truncated or cut-off crest of these waves or folds are called anticlinals. Such important localities may be quite readily found where there are occasional exposures of the bed-rock above the ground, and other loose material, and to the prospector it is a matter of prime importance to locate the anticlinal. These rocks are all formed in layers, or strata, varying in thickness from a few inches to many feet, and when we find them on opposite sides of a bit of country a mile, more or less, in width, dipped or slanted away as they go down from a line, or axis, drawn easterly and westerly through that middle ground somewhere, then we are certain that the anticlinal axis is, roughly speaking, where there is no dip. One may see this illustrated in Fig. 1 in all the three anticlinals. Between two waves, whether of rocks or of water, there must be a valley. In the rock formation we must bear in mind that it is continuous and everywhere responds, as a whole, to the forces that acted upon it, as a human hand would manipulate a lump of dough. Therefore the same strata that buckle and fold along some line of least resistance, and push their fractured crests towards the clouds, must have their corresponding areas of depression, and these are the synclinals, where the dips of the strata are towards a synclinal axis, the very reverse of the anticlinal. An examination of Fig. 1 will reveal the fact that the deepest rocks that are exposed on the surface are to be found on the axes of the anticlinals, and this also is a fact of the first importance to the prospectors and miners, as we shall see in the proper connection, for *all the gold mines are located on these anticlinals.*

Another geological feature of great practical importance to those engaged in gold mining is the fact that this immense formation is naturally divided into an upper and lower. There is no line of unconformity between them, but there is a difference in the rocks themselves. While both are of sedimentary origin, they were manifestly made up of different varieties of sediments that were deposited under different conditions, the depth of water being an important factor. The lower division is principally quartzite, with thin beds of slate between the strata of this harder rock. Quartzite is an altered or metamorphic sandstone. The thickness of this lower group is estimated to be about three miles by Mr. Faribault, C. E., of Geological Survey, and he is better qualified to express an approximate estimate than any other person.

The upper division is slate of different varieties, and estimated by Mr. Faribault to be two miles in thickness. These figures, of course, are to be applied to the original beds before they were folded into their present condition, and not taken as an estimate of the perpendicular depths of these folded and enormously eroded formations. We may with entire confidence believe that even the perpendicular measurement would extend beyond the limits of mining.

Having briefly discussed the rock formation, we come now to consider the quartz veins. Gold in small quantities is widely distributed.

It exists as a dissolved chloride in all sea-water, and is found in the rocks of all the geological divisions as a small part of their metallic contents. Gold in quantities that can be profitably mined is found either as loose particles in sand and gravel, or in veins and dikes. These alluvial or surface washings are either on the beds of living, or dead rivers, or on the present seashore or on some ancient shore, like the conglomerates of South Africa. In all these instances the gold has been derived from veins of quartz, or dikes of intrusive rocks, but the latter source is but an exception to a rule. Beyond reasonable doubt, all the gold worth getting out of the earth has once been scattered broadcast through the rocks as invisible particles, and from that condition collected into cracks and crevices with other metals and minerals, till a vein is formed. The great body of these veins consist of quartz, or silica, and that mineral is an oxide of silicon, that con-stitutes about one-third of the earth's crust. Although so hard that it scratches glass, so refractory that it is melted with difficulty, still it is dissolved in water everywhere; minute creatures in countless millions secrete it for their shells, and plants take it up through their roots from the water of soil and use it in their own way in their structures. Even in rocks there is water in circulation, and as a rule it will, under such conditions, have quartz dissolved and mingled with it. Nothing is more common than to see fragments of rocks by the wayside or the streets with veins of quartz running through them. Sometimes they are mere threads, or the thin sheet is cut across. Na-ture has used this enduring material to heal the numberless gaps, and gashes, and fissures that have resulted from the shrinking of this globe. The mineral crust has rested uneasily on the viscous and ever-changing foundations, where Titanic forces accumulate and then break forth till earthquakes record in a shudder the tremendous occurrence. As the heat is lost in the cold of space, the fact is registered deeper and deeper into the fiery heart of our planet. Slowly and ceaselessly responsive, the cool crust is crowded into smaller areas, and finds relief in wrinkles and folds, and faults, and thrusts, and fissures, till the oldest forma-tions seem almost cruelly contorted in age-long agony. Deep hidden from all eyes, vast strata bend, and arch, and break on a scale so gi-gantic that an earthquake records the disaster, and the sea responds with a wave that crosses the Pacific. As a result to this shrinking— the ocean bed has here and there risen above the waves with the accu-mulated sediments of ages, miles in depth, and tilted them into moun-tain summits above the limits of eternal snow.

When the gold-bearing rocks of Nova Scotia were thus forced from their horizontal position they would have out-distanced the highest peaks of the loftiest known ranges, reaching an altitude of eight miles, as we may determine from the downward dip or angle of strata as we find them exposed. To what altitude they actually arose we cannot decide, but it is most probable that the eroding agencies held them in check from extreme heights. The sediment resulting from this constant denuding must have been transported to the synclinal valleys, where it is reasonable to suppose that we have it in the now upper slate group, as we see it indicated in Fig. 1, in the synclinals of St. Mary's

Fig. 11

Granite
—— Anticlinal Axis
Dome of Anticline
O Gold Districts

Bay and Sherbrooke, where we can readily see by the diagram that its position is above the quartzite division where the gold-yielding veins occur.

Since the gold is confined to the vicinity of these anticlinal axes, it is of vital importance to know how often they occur. In a distance of thirty-five miles across the formation in Halifax County there are nine of these folds that appear, as I have said, as truncated waves, billows of rocks scored away to a level with the old valleys between them. They are running nearly parallel with the coast, and more or less out of line, as the result of "faults," or breaks and dislocation of the strata on a great scale. Fig. 2 is a reduced map in general features from the Geological Survey of portions of Halifax and Guysboro Counties. There the anticlinals are indicated, also the faults, the discovered mines, and granite areas. The latter are but portions of a formation that marks a contact with the auriferous Cambrian rocks throughout the Western Counties. We may note on this map that the anticlinal folds are on an average about four miles apart, and the mines thus far located upon them are distant from each other from ten to twenty-five miles. The ordinary veins of this formation are inter-bedded between the various layers or strata, and generally are found at the point where quartzite and slate once came into contact till wrenched apart by the folding movement. It is very desirable that a clear idea of these veins be conveyed to the ordinary reader—for such persons I am writing —so we will resort to an illustration: If we take a couple of dozen sheets of colored wet blotting paper and place at intervals a few sheets of writing paper separated by three or four sheets from one another, and then double all till the outer edges nearly meet, we will then have the writing paper in the position of the veins, only with more regularity than usually found in nature. Now if we remove with some sharp instrument the upper portion of this fold, the edges of the writing paper that represent the veins will be exposed in the horizontal section and they will be dipped away from the anticlinal axis. Unless all the sheets are cut away, which is not desirable, then the writing paper may be seen to be continuous over the crown of the anticlinal, forming a saddle with two legs inclined outward. In some instances, notably at Oldham, this structure is to be seen in the rocks. If the veins were continuous for miles, then we should be sure that they all crossed the anticlinal axis at one time before the crest was eroded, and that deeper mining would discover all of them still unexposed folded over the axis. In spite of much fracturing and dislocation of the strata, this is the general plan of the arrangement of these leads. I introduce here Fig. 3 to illustrate this plan; it is copied from a Geological Survey made of the Oldham District in the County

FIG. III

OLDHAM ANTICLINAL.

of Halifax. These veins could not have been formed until the strata had been folded and dislocated to a degree that resulted in openings between the tilted beds along the region that yielded to the pressure and doubled into these anticlines. That the formation of the veins began before these disturbances closed is probable in theory and borne out by appearances. The process, beyond reasonable doubt, extended over millions of years, and for the most part was carried on far beneath what is now the surface. The gold coming mostly from a great depth was brought to the higher levels in a state of solution, and the same watery solvent held the silica or quartz and the base metal sulphides. It is a very common experience to find the enclosing wall-rocks of the quartz veins containing abundance of iron sulphides, and sometimes gold is found in the slate and quartzite walls where they come in contact with the quartz, or very near to that junction. Pieces of wall-rock are found enclosed in the quartz now and then, showing that it was once plastic. These veins vary in width from a half inch to several feet, but the usual thickness of working leads is from four inches to a foot. These leads generally occurring between beds of slate and quartzite, have the advantage of the slate as a "working belt," and thereby greatly facilitating the mining operations.

The gold in paying quantities is almost entirely confined to certain portions known as "pay streaks" or "ore chutes." This valuable ground will extend along the vein from one hundred to several hundred feet; its downward boundaries are quite abrupt, and generally are not perpendicular, but dip eastward or westward with considerable regularity throughout the district. The aggregating of these values into smaller areas is one of the fortunate aspects, for had the same amount been scattered throughout the vein, mining would be out of the question. The same lead in some instances will have more than one such gold zone or "pay streak." The depth of such ore bodies has never been tested. Even within the limits of this chute there are comparatively barren areas, and others of phenomenal richness. A further study of them is desirable, to throw additional light on their origin.

The precious metals have certain affinities that are not satisfied by chemical union, and thus it turns out that they are always more or less intimately associated in the mines with sulphides of iron, and lead, and zinc, and "white iron," or mispickel, a chemical combination of arsenic, iron, and sulphur. The latter mineral is very common. Quartz veins in which one or more of these minerals are not to be found will carry no gold.

These minerals, as I shall notice further on, are all enriched with invisible gold. Often the precious metal is embedded among the crystals of these base ores, that chemistry alone can deal with. As a rule, and rather a rigid one in Nova Scotia, quartz in which no gold can be seen with the naked eye will have no value worth attention. It often turns out that these common minerals exist abundantly, but no gold can be found in the quartz. It will, however, be a great mistake in prospecting to conclude that a vein is valueless because no gold is found in one or even many trials along its outcrop or exposures, for very often gold abruptly makes its appearance within a few feet of barren ground. These interbedded veins belong, all of them, to one system, but there are others known as "angulars" or "cross-leads." In mining the "regular" interbedded leads, the common experience is that small veins emerge from the walls at all angles. As a rule they do not extend very far into the rocks, and when they carry gold the main lead will be enriched at the junction of these "angulars." They evidently had their origin in the general fracturing and dislocation that made possible the interbedded leads.

There is also another system of lodes that may properly be termed fissure veins, for they were formed in extensive cracks that traversed at various angles the "strike" of the formation. These veins are among the most productive, and they occur all over the gold districts.

Thus far we have described the great east and west folds because they are the most conspicuous and important geological feature of this gold-bearing formation.

Due to some agency, apparently pressure, there are at intervals of ten and fifteen miles along the anticlinal folds, certain areas where the surface of the rock pitches away eastward and westward at a low angle with the horizon along the axis of the anticlinal, and thus elliptical "domes" are formed in which are located the gold mines of the Province. It is only in exceptional instances that veins can be located entirely around the dome, but a clear knowledge of their relation to it is an item of importance in prospecting and mining.

Hitherto, and up to this time, the rock-structure has been neglected to the great detriment of the gold-mining industry. Says Mr. E. R. Faribault, C. E., who has for several years been in charge of a portion of the Geological Survey, mapping the gold fields of Nova Scotia: "The study of the structure of these rocks over that region has afforded an opportunity of acquiring important data and facts by means of which gold mining may be carried on with more confidence, under

NICTAUX FALLS

PROSPECTING AT MOLEGA.

more exact conditions and with greater economy. A thorough knowledge of the anticlinal folds becomes necessary to locate the gold-bearing quartz deposits on the surface and to develop them in depth."

These important statements from this source are in direct contradiction to the opinions of the average prospector of this region, who solemnly asserts that "gold is where you find it, just as the Bible says," and thus, as he supposes, brings Scripture to support his position. This old saying originated in placer "diggins," where the gold was washed from old river beds where it had been the sport of the currents, and lodged here and there in favoring localities that no science or experience could locate and the pick and shovel alone could tell. When gold is in veins there is no such field for the haphazard miner. These deposits have been formed within the lines of natural laws, and order reigns amid apparent disorder.

Although the existence of gold in Nova Scotia has been known about forty years, and the returns have compared well with gold mines in various parts of the world, still the prospecting and mining, as a rule, have not been prosecuted with much energy or good judgment. ·Provincial capital was in the hands of men afraid to invest it in this new kind of speculation, and outside companies distinguished themselves by notorious bad management in many directions, but notably in the selection of officials who were utterly inexperienced or otherwise incompetent for their positions. Failures have again and again resulted from causes that would have insured the like disastrous termination had they existed in any other line of business. Intemperance, extravagance, ignorance, this wretched triplet includes the signal sins of foreign companies, and the visible monuments of their evil activities are to be seen all over the Province in abandoned shafts and dismantled mills. Not a company or individual has had the intelligent enterprise to sink to a depth of 1,000 feet perpendicular and explore by cross-cuts the axis of an anticlinal to which science and outside experience have pointed as most inviting ground. Capital sufficient for this purpose has often been squandered in expensive plants and unsystematic search for bonanzas near the surface. Whether the gold-bearing zones along the anticlinal axes extend to a great depth is a problem on the solution of which largely depends the prosperity and perpetuation of the gold-mining industry of Nova Scotia. This fact affords ample reasons for discussing the question in these pages that are intended to afford reliable information to those who take the trouble to consult them. Without in the least yielding to the common fallacy that greater depth will be likely to yield higher values of precious metal, still we may say that natural conditions may so far alter cases that *this very thing may be true,* or at any rate the ore will not depreciate with depth.

Mr. E. K. Faribault, C. E., whom I have already introduced as of the Canadian Geological Survey, is the person best calculated to give a sound opinion on this question. He has in 1899 published a pamphlet devoted to aspects of this problem, and comes to a favorable conclusion. We will, by quotations and use of some of his diagrams, enable our reader to follow his reasoning. When veins are formed between the bedding planes of folded strata, it is evident that they may or will continue over the apex of an anticlinal fold; at that point the ore-body is called a "saddle," and the extensions downward on each side are termed "legs."

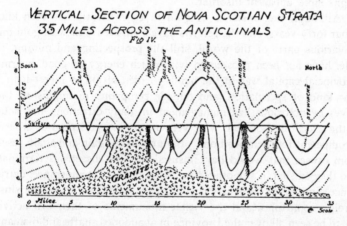

VERTICAL SECTION OF NOVA SCOTIAN STRATA
35 MILES ACROSS THE ANTICLINALS
FIG IV.

Fig. 4, constructed in the main by Faribault from actual surveys, shows us the structure of the rocks and the location of the mines on the anticlinal folds. All above the "surface" line is an ideal formation based upon the dip of the rocks as we now have them. That the summits of the great folds were over eight miles higher than now is not at all probable, but they would have been had there been no denuding agencies to attack them. Beyond question the old surface was once far higher than now, and the veins that are today outcropping were once deeply entombed in the earth.

If we can point to gold mines in other quarters of the world under general conditions very like those in Nova Scotia, that have proved profitable to a depth of more than 2,000 feet, and the end not reached, then we have a strong argument from that quarter in favor of deep mining in Nova Scotia. A notable instance of this kind is found in Bendigo, Australia.

In Fig. 5 we have a section to scale of this folded formation, showing the mines on the anticlinal folds as they are in this Province, and

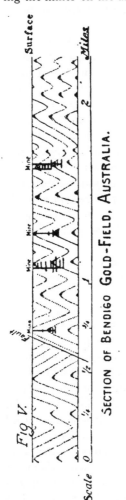

the recurring ore-bodies at different levels. In Fig. 5 we have a diagram from actual measurements to a depth of 2,000 feet, in which the ore-bodies appear as "saddles" and "legs" bestriding the anticlinal axis or fold. These saddles constitute the "saddle-reefs" of that country. "They are at Bendigo not only of great size and of remarkable persistence in length, but are also notable for recurring ·in depth one below the other. At the Lazarus Mine there are from the surface to the 2,200-foot level no less than twenty-four of these saddle reefs, thirteen of which are auriferous to a payable degree and some of great size. At Bendigo, on the 31st of December, 1897, six mines were worked over 3,000 feet in depth, and twelve over 2,700 feet, the deepest was down 3,352 feet, and these are all worked on the anticlinal folds." Continuing, says Faribault:

"No operation has yet been carried to any depth through the arch-core of the folds in Nova Scotia, but the development done along the anticlinal axis at Salmon River, the Richardson Mine, Waverly, Oldham and Mooseland should be sufficient to convince the most skeptical that quartz saddle-reefs and legs may be found underneath one another, to even a greater depth than in Bendigo.

Mr. Walter H. Prest, formerly a valued member of the Geological Survey, and of long experience in our mines, and of natural aptitude, has given special attention to this problem of deep mining in Nova Scotia, and in a published monograph reaches the following conclusions:

"1st. The probability of the hydro-thermal origin and resulting great depths of our mineral veins and pay streaks.

2nd. That the original was far above the present surface, and even the upper beds of the series show evidence of great erosion and still higher beds.

3rd. That what are now called surface deposits were then many thousands of feet deep.

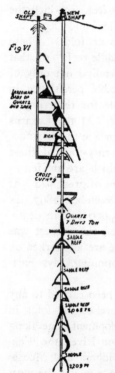

Fig VI

4th. That denudation (or geological deep mining) has already exposed our pay streaks to a depth of 25,000 feet below the original surface.

5th. And finally, modern mining has only exposed those pay streaks 500 or 600 feet lower down, thus only slightly extending the former geological work. When the question of deep mining is fully considered in all its varied geological relations, I cannot see why there should exist any doubt as to its successful prosecution. Judging future mining from past geological work, there is no evidence that our auriferous leads either decrease in size or richness with increasing depth."

The first report of Samuel Creelman, the first Chief Gold Commissioner for the Province of Nova Scotia, bears date of 1862.

By way of introduction we are therein informed that "The earliest discovery of gold in the Province, made known to the public, occurred during the summer of 1860, at a spot about twelve miles north from the head of Tangier Harbor, on the northeast branch of the Tangier River, Halifax County. The discoverer, John Pulsiver of Musquodoboit, was induced from what he had heard of the gold-bearing quartz of California to search for the same substance amongst the rocks on the upper waters of the Tangier River; and while in company with some Indians whom he had hired, Mr. Pulsiver found several pieces of gold in quartz in a brook, at a place known as Mooseland Diggings. This discovery being known, a number of persons from various parts of the Province gathered to the spot during the summer and succeeding autumn for the purpose of prospecting; but gold not being found in remunerative quantity, the place was abandoned before the close of the year.

"In the month of October of the same year, Peter Mason, a fisherman and land-owner near the head of Tangier Harbor, concluded that he had found the precious metal there.

"On the 11th of April, 1861, the Government took possession of the district."

This report of 1862 gives the returns from Tangier, Wine Harbor, Sherbrooke, Stormont, Oldham, and Renfew. The total number of tons of ore 1,294, yielding gold to the value of $49,707. During the intervening years from 1862 to 1901 about fourteen million dollars have been won from the mines. During several years the business was carried on by crude methods and subjected to many disadvantages in other ways. Many failures were not due to natural causes, but to the ill-considered attempts of men to become suddenly rich. As in other affairs, something has been learned by such failures and disasters, and real progress has been made in treatment of ores and in some instances in the management of mines.

The following table, copied from the Report of the Department of Mines for 1900, will give a general idea of the output of the mines from their discovery till now:

PRODUCTION BY DISTRICTS FROM 1862 TO 1900.

DISTRICT.	Tons Crushed.	TOTAL YIELD OF GOLD.			AVERAGE YIELD PER TON.			Value at $19.00 Per Oz.
		Oz.	Dwts.	Grs.	Oz.	Dwts.	Grs.	
Caribou and Moose River	124,500	41,814	6	18	.	6	17	$ 794,472.42
Montague	26,140	40,606	10	14	1	11	1	771,524.06
Oldham	48,243	52,382	..	12	1	1	17	995,258.48
Renfrew	48,601	38,320	4	..	.	15	18	728,083 80
Sherbrooke	226,169	138,406	16	9	.	12	5	2,629,729.56
Stormont	176,170	66,545	16	3	.	7	13	1,264,370.32
Tangier	46,938	22,831	14	15	.	9	9	433,802.90
Wniacke	54,362	38,509	15	7	.	14	4	731,685.53
Waverly	123,383	61,711	15	5	.	10	..	1,172,523.45
Salmon River	117,175	41,487	5	20	.	7	2	788,258.55
Brookfield	43,975	21,098	17	22	.	9	14	400,879.03
Whiteburne	6,394	9,554	17	18	1	9	21	181,542.87
Lake Catcha	23,023	24,340	8	15	1	1	3	462,467.80
Raudon	12,178	9,594	15	10	.	15	18	182,300.65
Wine Harbor	49,070	26,872	8	2	.	10	22	510,575.68
Fifteen Mile Stream	32,893	16,403	9	5	.	9	23	311,665.75
Malaga	20,292	18,563	2	8	.	18	7	352,699.22
Other Districts	81,800	48,837	6	5	.	11	22	9.17,908.90
Total	1,261,306	717,881	10	10	.	......	......	$13,639,748.97

6

The surface of the gold-bearing formation is quite generally covered with gravel, clay, sand, loam, rocks, and black mud. The latter is largely of vegetable origin, but all the other materials are the products of erosion. They are contributions from the slates and quartzites of the gold measures and from the granite area that makes a contact on the north. Granite boulders, rounded and smooth, and often weighing a dozen tons, are plentifully scattered over this Atlantic slope of Cambrian rocks. Ice and water have been the agencies at work upon all this material. The frequent bed-rock exposures are grooved, and scratched in parallel lines with a southeastward direction that have their evident origin in a glacial movement. The gravels, sands, etc., are about where the subsiding waters left them, arranged in hills and knolls, or distributed over level areas, where loose rocks cover a stratum of compact clay and gravel. These latter are generally grown up in small trees and shrubs, such as wire birches, poplars, whortleberry, etc. The hills and knolls are naturally covered with forests of hardwood—oak, beeches, birches, and maples being the principal trees. Extensive forests of coniferous trees—pines, hemlocks, spruces, firs— are found in areas of rather level, damp, rocky, clayey soil. Bogs occupy ancient lake beds that have been gradually filled with vegetable matter grown on the spot. Swamps are a conspicuous feature and cover such lower portions of the old rock surface as favored certain forms of vegetation that preferred a damp or even wet situation. These areas are grown up in meadow grass, black spruce, swamp maple, alders, choke cherries, ilex, and lowly shrubs and plants.

At the beginning of the Glacial Period the quartz veins had been stripped to some extent by natural erosion that left them in some instances standing a few feet above the surface; in other cases they had cracked along planes of crystallization and tumbled down in fragments on the strike or course of the vein. When the snow had accumulated to glacier dimensions of thousands of feet in depth in ice, it began to move down to the low incline of 600 feet in 35 miles to the Atlantic seaboard. Protruding quartz veins were broken off by this imperceptibly crawling ice sheet. Under such enormous pressure the friction produced heat enough to melt the ice next the bed-rock. Thus by means of ice and water the fragments of the veins were transferred, along with gravels and sands, to the southward, to distances of a quarter of a mile, or even several miles in some instances. These fragments of quartz are known as "float" or "drift;" they are the telltales of the hidden treasure somewhere, not very distant, in a vein.

The fragments or "float" furthest away from the parent vein are on the surface, and as the source is approached they are to be found embedded in the ground, deeper and deeper, till the vein is reached. A competent prospector coming upon good "drift" on the surface does not begin *there* to dig, but he searches on the surface to the northward; when he can find no more in that way, he will begin a north and south trench, but never going to bed-rock, as a rule, while he can find the quartz, which he will readily recognize, although other veins will be represented in the excavation. When this float is found on the bed-rock in the bottom of the trench, then one may expect the desired vein is quite or nearly reached. Having thus followed the float to the source, it may turn out that the vein is barren at that point, for no vein is gold-bearing to a profitable degree throughout its whole course, as I have previously explained. The "pay streak" may stop quite abruptly, and consequently the experienced prospector will test it by cuttings at short intervals of fifty feet or less.

In some instances the "float" may have had its origin in a "cross" or fissure lead, with a strike or course at a considerable angle across the strata and their regular interbedded veins. In a case of that kind a north and south trench might fail to uncover the vein that had furnished the "drift" quartz. In dealing with such an occurrence, the float will itself quite often have some peculiarity, or there will be clinging to it a portion of the wall rock, or some other clue will be noted by experienced and observant eyes that will generally put one on the right track.

In rare instances the "float" is found to the northward of its vein for a short distance of a hundred feet or thereabouts, its unusual location being due to a backset of the current or a thrust of an upturned ice-cake, but one will of course direct his operations by the rule, but with a knowledge of exceptions.

MINING.

I have already made it plain that the veins dip at various angles from almost perpendicular to 45 degrees, rarely more where worked. Generally there is a stratum of slate on one side of the veins, and forms a cheap working belt. The walls are kept secure by scaffolds of poles arranged on stout "stulls" or cross-sills that are fitted into "hitches" cut in the wall-rock. These scaffolds are loaded with the waste rock of the mine. The foot-wall affords a good opportunity for a skip-way used in hoisting the ore and rock.

The cost of mining will very largely depend upon management, upon width of vein, and hardness of the working belt.

Miners' wages from $1.25 to $1.40.

Dynamite from 22 cents to 25 cents.

Cordwood $2 to $3 per cord.

Blacksmiths and carpenters about $1.75 per day.

The numerous waterfalls in all this gold-bearing region are sources of sufficient energy to operate all the mines and mills if they were electrically harnessed to the work, but up to this date (1901) not a wheel has been turned by electrical transmission of this power. Within three and four miles of quartz mills, now expensively operated by steam, there are hundreds and even thousands of horse power in water-falls that are absolutely unused. Intelligent use of capital will put a stop to this short-sighted policy and place many mines on a paying basis that are now lying idle.

FREE GOLD IN THE SAND AND GRAVEL, OR ALLUVIAL GOLD.

Either from ancient river bed, from sea-shore or living river banks and bottoms, mankind obtained the first gold. Doubtless the pretty particles attracted the attention long before the art of milling metals was known. The gold of all these localities had its origin in quartz veins that have been broken up on the surface by natural agencies that set free the particles and nuggets of gold. These agencies were air, frost, heat, running water, and ocean waves. Gold-bearing quartz in rapidly running streams would be crushed, and the gold by its great weight would collect in natural receptacles among the rocks. The early mines of California, 1849, were all of this description. At Cape Nome, in Alaska, great quantities of gold are being recovered from the seashore, where the waves have trampled down the gold-bearing rocks, and their ancient conquest of the land has been elevated above the water by oscillations of the crust of the earth. The gold of the Klondyke is all alluvial gold and has its source in the bed-rock schists of that region.

Theoretically Nova Scotia should have rich and extensive alluvial gold mines. The highest authorities agree that denudation on an enormous scale has taken place on the gold measures since the veins were formed—miles in depth eroded and swept away into the ocean. Whatever might have become of the sand and mud, the gold did not go far, except in a very fine condition. As a rule the gold of Nova

Scotia is coarse and nuggety, in many instances to a degree not exceeded elsewhere in rock mining.

The rivers of these gold fields have an average fall of about 500 feet in 35 or 40 miles, and their courses are across the veins. But these rivers are not located where the pre-glacial drainage of this area found a way to the sea, and in them, if we knew where they are, might be the gold that belonged in the anticlinal domes that were planed down for thousands of feet millions of years before the advent of the Age of Ice. One ancient river bed carrying gold in paying quantities, and belonging to a drainage system of pre-glacial times, may be seen at the village of Coldstream, six miles from the Shubenacadie railroad station, in Colchester County. In the opinion of Sir William Dawson, Dr. Honeyman, C. F. Hartt, and the Canadian Geological Survey, this deposit belongs to the lower Carboniferous, a very far away epoch, before there was even a creature on land so lowly as a lizard, and fishes were the head of creation. This river-bed deposit is a conglomerate formed from the debris of the rocks over which it ran, and these are Cambrian slates of the gold measures. Now it is a most interesting fact that when the river ran, those slates were already folded into anticlinals, that had been scored away miles in depth, and left the upturned edges of the strata standing at sharp angles, forming steep ledges, and these were penetrated by longitudinal fissures or seams across the cleavage of the slates. The river ran at right angles to these ledges, and filled these fissures of crystalline origin, that were less than an inch in width, with mud and sand and gold. This was a rapid current, carrying along large fragments of rocks, and in once instance a quartz boulder weighing 500 pounds or more, and smooth in every part almost as a kidney, a shape it rather resembled. The writer speaks from personal experience while in charge on this ground. The veins from which the gold was derived have not been discovered, but we get a glimpse into that far-away age and see that agencies were at work then, as now, to form gold-bearing alluvia.

Dr. T. Sterry Hunt, in his Report on Gold Fields of Nova Scotia, 1868, says: "The existence in Nova Scotia of gold-bearing alluvions older than the boulder clay is a contingency not to be lost sight of; the presence of considerable quantities of gold at Gay's River in Colchester County, in conglomerate beds at the base of the Carboniferous series, which are nothing more than consolidated alluvions of that period, shows the great antiquity of alluvial gold in this region."

In the Province of Quebec the boulder-clay is generally destitute of gold, but in his report on the gold of that Province, Geological Survey, 1866, Mr. Michel has shown that beneath this sterile clay is an ancient deposit of alluvial gravel, abounding in gold, of which the rich washings of the Gilbert River, in the Chaudiere District, are an example. Analogous conditions are presented by the rich alluvial deposits of Victoria, Bolivia, and California. Mr. Michel, therefore, insists upon the importance of carefully searching in certain parts of Nova Scotia for similar ancient alluvions beneath the boulder clay or glacial drift. Such deposits, when we consider the abundance of gold in the quartz lodes of the region, may reasonably be expected to be of great richness.

Pay gravel has been discovered in the glacial drift and worked at Moose River, Isaac's Harbor, Wine Harbor, Tangier, Gold River, the Ovens, and other localities in the Province.

Carefully conducted prospecting, backed with an adequate capital, would doubtless result in other discoveries of more importance in these later accumulations.

CONCENTRATES.

The gold-bearing quartz contains Iron pyrites, Copper pyrites, Arsenical iron or Mispickel, Lead sulphide or Galena, and Zinc sulphide. These are more or less intimately associated with the gold. The precious metal is often found imbedded among the iron crystals, or mingling with the cubes of galena. They all huddle together in a sort of gregarious fashion. The proportion by weight of these base metals varies from one to thirty per cent; the average would be about five.

These minerals carry very fine gold in their structure. It must have been present in a form or condition favorable to be included as native gold in the crystal structures of these sulphides and arsenides of iron and lead. Whatever its mode of entrance into this chemical combination as an outsider in it, but not of it, we do not know, but we do know that this gold cannot be saved in a stamp mill. It is too finely divided; very little of it is set free, and that is lost in the flow of sand and water. By passing the whole amount of sands or tailings from the end of the plates over concentration machines, these metallic substances can be secured, and they are known as "concentrates." From different veins they have different values, running from $15 to several hundred per ton; an average of $25 would probably be near the mark. This gold can be won from the concentrates by chemical processes. There is but one chlorination plant in the Province for this purpose, and that is at North Brookfield, Queens County, where a large, well-equipped concern treats the concentrates from the premises and will treat the shipments from other localities that arrive on the completion of a railroad now in course of construction.

MILLING.

The ore is crushed in mills of from five to fifty stamps, weighing in the later plants about 900 pounds, and run at a speed of 70 to 100 drops a minute. The gold, as a rule, is coarse, and by far the greater part is lodged in the mortars, becoming packed in the gravel among the dies; the remainder is splashed through the wire screen by the action of the stamps as they strike the water in the mortars. This fine gold is amalgamated with quicksilver as it passes over copper plates prepared for that purpose. There is always some loss of the finest gold, that is carried away in the tailings or battery sand. These mills, no matter how well built, are clumsy contrivances doing undesirable things that result in waste, but nothing better has come to stay, out of the many devices of rollers and wheels, etc.

The Island of Cape Breton contains 4,375 square miles, and four counties of the Province of Nova Scotia are included in this area. The geological structure of the Island presents many points of difference from the main peninsula. The slate and quartzite gold measures of the Atlantic slope that we have discussed are not certainly identified there, and consequently the gold that has been discovered occurs under different conditions.

Quartz veins carrying free gold have been found at Middle River, and other localities, as Wycocomah and Chetticamp, have yielded the precious metal in placer or gravel washings, and associated with pyrites and arseno-pyrites in veins. To this time, however, no mines have been operated.

The Provincial Government owns the gold mines. They are Crown property, but the Crown does not get the gold. A mining area is 230 feet by 150 feet. The Government will give a prospecting license good for one year for fifty cents per area, and one hundred areas may be included in one such license, but the number of licenses is not limited for one person. These areas may be on lands owned in fee simple, to whom damages will be awarded if there is proper ground for such action. The Government will also lease for forty years, a hundred areas or less, for the consideration of $2 cash down and 50 cents annual rental for each area.

A royalty tax of two per cent is exacted on the gross yield of the mines in gold.

CHAPTER VI.

The history of this county begins with the founding of Halifax City, in 1749. This was carried out at Government expense under the charge of Col. The Hon. Edward Cornwallis, M. P., who was officially designated as Captain General and Governor of Nova Scotia. During 36 years since the Treaty of Utrecht, by the terms of which this Province became a portion of the British dominions, no progress had been made in its colonization. The importance of this territory had scarcely dawned upon the authorities. At this date there was a small garrison of two or three hundred troops at Annapolis Royal, where the Governor resided. All the rest of the population, numbering a few thousand, were Acadian French peasants, settled around the Basin of Minas, Annapolis Basin, and intermediate points. A few of them were in Cumberland County, and at Canso was a handful more of these people. More than a thousand Indians, hostile to English interests, were ready to act with the Acadians, to whom they were already allied more or less by ties of blood and religion.

It was high time that some active measures were taken to protect British interests in this quarter of the world. The French Governor of Canada claimed all the country from the St. Lawrence to Maine. Governor Shirley, of Massachusetts, clearly perceived the necessity of some effectual check upon this spirit of aggression. Now that Louisburg was restored to the French, there was an ample base of action. That stronghold had been a menace to New England till her yeomanry had seized it only four years previous to the treaty that returned it to the ancient enemy; a paltry concession that in less than ten years bore such evil fruit that English arms reduced it to a possession, where it, with the whole of Cape Breton Island, has ever since remained. In the midst of such a turmoil of affairs the city of Halifax had its beginning. The claim is made that Governor Shirley and other Boston men had long suggested the erection of a military and nava' station on this fine harbour so central to the whole peninsula. At any rate, the project was long in the air before it took shape in a material form. The Board of Trade and Plantations finally matured the plan that received the approbation of the Government. George Montague, Earl of Halifax, was President of the Board, and active in the support

of the scheme, hence the name of the new city. The Government very
well knew that desirable settlers would not venture into that houseless
wilderness to make their homes unless special inducements were offered. These were speedily forthcoming. Settlers would be conveyed there free of all charges, and maintained at public expense during
twelve months. They were to be supplied with arms and ammunition
and implements for clearing the land, building houses, and prosecuting
the fisheries. Officers and private men lately discharged from the
army and navy were particularly designated as desirable persons. The
speedy response was 1,176 volunteer settlers, together with their families, making a total of 2,576, and of this number 500 were man-of-war
sailors. There were three majors, six captains, and nineteen lieuten-
ants in the army, three ensigns, twenty-three midshipmen, one attorney, one clergyman, and several "gentlemen."

Cornwallis considered them a poor lot when he got them all together. He wrote to the Lords of Trade "that the number of active
men proper to carry on a new settlement is very small. Of soldiers
there are only 100; of tradesmen, sailors, and others willing to work,
not above 200."

He lumped the balance as idle and worthless, who took up with
the opportunity to get lodged and fed a twelvemonth free of all charge.

There was evident lack of foresight, or such a state of affairs would
not have occurred. Cornwallis, however, was not a man to be discouraged by ordinary difficulties. He was obliged to fight the battle
with a broken sword. His own reputation and the safety of British
possessions in America depended upon the successful founding of this
stronghold.

Within six months winter would be upon them, and shelter must
be provided without delay. Boards and hewed timber were brought
from Boston at a high price to meet the first demands. Excellent
citizens came from New England. From Louisburg, just then evacu-
ated by the English, came considerable numbers, and 116 came from
England in August. Within one month a good start had been made.
One of the settlers writing at that time (July 25th, 1749) to England,
says: "On our arrival we found the Sphinx, of twenty guns, which
had come into harbor a few days before us; as I write the transports
are entering the harbor with the two regiments of Hopson and War-
burton on board from Louisburg. We have already cleared about
twenty acres, and every one has a hut by his tent. There are already
several wharves built, and one gentleman is erecting a saw mill.

BAND STAND, PUBLIC GARDENS

PUBLIC GARDENS

A DRIVE BY THE SEA

PROVINCIAL BUILDING.

VIEWS OF HALIFAX AND VICINITY.

A SCENE ON THE N. W. ARM.

CITY HALL.

THE ARMORIES.

REGATTA, N. W. ARM.

VIEWS OF HALIFAX AND VICINITY.

Public storehouses are also building. We have received constant supplies of plank and timber for building, and fresh stock, and rum in great quantities, twenty schooners frequently coming in one day. We have also 100 cows, and some sheep brought down to us by land from Minas. In short, everything is in a very prosperous way. But I should be equally unjust and ungrateful were I to conclude without paying the tribute which is due to our Governor. He seems to have nothing in view but the interest and happiness of all."

Before the middle of October 350 houses had been completed and two of the square forts built. The Indians came and made treaties for the sake of the presents that went with them. In reality they were hostile and completely under French influence from Quebec and the Acadian settlements. Their outrages were numerous and terrifying. They lurked in the cover of the woods with deadly purpose, and fatal results to those who ventured within their power. The Governor, before the first winter was over, offered ten pounds sterling for every Indian scalp or prisoner. The bounty was not often claimed, but the scalps were forthcoming now and then, as witness when John Connor and James Grace came in with six of these gruesome trophies and were not required to make it clear who had owned them. It was a harsh measure, but one must sometimes fight fire with fire. The redskins knew where to find a market for this human peltry among their French friends. They were not out for their health; neither were they crouching hungry and cold in the forest for the mere love of killing a fellow mortal. To the shame of white men, these ignorant people were used to further ends of conquest, and one might well wish that in a later struggle the English had not resorted to the same means.

At the expiration of one year, 1749, Cornwallis had expended £76,000, and £40,000 was rated for the next year. There was no little haggling and fault-finding by the Lords of Trade over this demand for money, that far exceeded their original intentions. As matters turned out, there was never made a better national investment. In reply to their complaints the Governor writes to them:

"Not a pound shall be expended by me unnecessarily, but without money you could have no town. 'Tis very certain the public money cleared the ground, built the Town, secured it, kept soldiers and sailors from starving with cold, and has brought down over 1,000 settlers from the other Colonies."

The first winter was moderate and the spring opened early, but it had been a tedious and heart-breaking time to many of them. About a thousand persons had been carried off by an epidemic in the autumn. There had been a constant state of preparation for an attack by the French and Indians, and, last but not least, there was great disorder created by the sale of rum, in spite of stringent regulations and penalties, including the stocks and the whipping post. In fact, this cause of intemperance has ever since been the greatest enemy to the prosperity of this town.

Occasional glimpses of the early days of Halifax reveal the great extent of this evil. Here, for instance, is an extract from a letter written by Mr. Grant, a member of the Council, to Rev. Dr. Stiles of Boston, dated May, 1760, when the place had been eleven years in the making:

"We have upwards of 100 licensed houses, and perhaps as many more which retail spirituous liquors without license; so that the business of one-half of the town is to sell rum, and the other half drinks it. You may, from this single circumstance, judge of our morals, and naturally infer that we are not enthusiastic in religion."

Twenty-two years later Murdoch says of it: "The moral condition of the town had become dreadful in the extreme. Eight or ten thousand soldiers, sailors, and prisoners of war let loose in a little town of less than 10,000 inhabitants can well be imagined."

The world has improved since those days, and Halifax has rather slowly moved forward in response to the spirit of the age. It was founded as a naval and military station, and for that purpose it has been of incalculable value to British interests, but this very fact was not favorable to some other important phases of civic and commercial development.

The conservative spirit has been very pronounced, but the spirit of the age is effectually dealing with ancient evils, and the city with its abundance of elbow room, and fine surroundings, and magnificent harbor, will never be less than a city of great importance to British America. In spite of the dark side of its early existence, there was no lack of heroic and patriotic spirits who were determined that Englishmen should not be crowded out of this new world by her ancient enemy. The second summer great progress was made in laying out and building the streets, and in increasing the fortifications and providing accommodations for new arrivals. Cornwallis after two and one-half years resigned the government, and Hon. Peregrine T. Hopson was appointed in his stead. His greatest difficulties were the result of French hostilities. In a letter to the Board of Trade during the first

HALIFAX HARBOR, SHOWING H. M. S. "OPHIR" AND OTHER SHIPS OF WAR.

REGATTA, N. S. HARBOUR, HALIFAX.

year in office he says: "Your Lordships may imagine how disagreeable it is to me to see His Majesty's rights encroached upon, and those encroachments openly avowed and supported by the Governors of Canada and Louisburg, when it is not in my power to prevent it. I have barely sufficient force to protect the settlers from insult of an Indian war, under pretense of which the French take an opportunity to commit hostilities upon His Majesty's subjects. I am informed that the French have often been mixed among them in the expeditions, and am convinced past doubt that they are fed and protected from our pursuit, and are encouraged to disturb us as openly and in as great a degree as in time of war." In two or three years after the above was written, the Acadian French were removed from this Province, and one can readily see by this letter that there was a sharp demand for heroic treatment for this unbearable disorder.

The old proverb has it that no one becomes suddenly bad; neither did the Provincial Government become suddenly bad. One must know the provocations that have resulted in great severity before one can pass upon its merits or demerits. It is very evident that the Acadians were unconsciously preparing for themselves a landslide of calamities, to be told in song and story to the end of time. Their tale of woes will always excite pity in tender hearts, and their mischievous conduct will afford a large measure of excuse for Lawrence and Shirley, who saw no other way out of the difficulty but to thrust out of the country, root and branch, this constant menace to British interests that demanded just then a great effort, or there would be an end of them on this continent.

From the mass of expelled Acadians there escaped to the woods, and found sustenance among the Indians, about 500 young men of the most hardy and audacious of the villagers. They fled when the alarm 'was given. If they were hostile to the English from patriotic sentiment before the expulsion, they were now deadly enemies, eager to retaliate for the deeds done upon their homes and their families. The actual danger from these outlaws and their red allies was very great. Atrocities were reported from various directions, until Lieutenant-Governor Lawrence, with the advice of the Council, on the 14th day of May, 1756, offered a reward of thirty pounds for every male Indian prisoner above the age of sixteen years brought in alive; for scalps of such male Indian, twenty-five pounds; for every Indian woman or child brought in alive, twenty-five pounds. Said General Sherman, "War is hell,' and this was one illustration.

It was an instance of a skin for a skin. It is said that the scalps brought in were not carefully examined to decide whether they belonged on French or Indian heads.

In the year 1755 a census of Halifax reports only 1,755 inhabitants, and of this number more than half were women, and 256 masters of families. This was far from encouraging. The people very largely went to New England or some other portion of the old colonies to the southward, until not one-half of the original number remained, and they were dependent on the money put in circulation by the Government through the army and navy.

In a half dozen years this town had cost the British nation £560,000 sterling, and not a penny of it returned to the British taxpayer, but it was the thing to do if Anglo-Saxon supremacy was to be maintained on this continent.

On May 8, 1758, Halifax was aroused by the arrival of an English fleet destined for Louisburg, and 12,000 soldiers belonging to that expedition. The Dunkirk of America was doomed. Lawrence went with them, and left Colonel Monckton in charge. "It's an ill wind that blows no one any good," and the sack of the Cape Breton city enriched Halifax in men and means.

From the founding of the city, the Governor and Council were the seat of authority, and possessed both executive and legislative powers. Lawrence, who had a keen liking for his office, and all its concomitants of this kind, was strongly disposed to maintain this state of things. He was obliged to yield to superior opinion and take steps to secure a representative system. A resolution to that effect passed the Council January, 1757, and the General Assembly met on Monday, the 2nd of October, 1758, in the Court House in Halifax.

Lawrence yielded with a bad grace to this natural demand of British subjects. Only five days previous to the meeting of this Assembly he wrote to the Lords of Trade that he hoped he should not find in any of the representatives a disposition to embarrass or obstruct His Majesty's service, or to dispute the royal prerogative. And he further observes "that too many of the members chosen are such as have not been the most remarkable for promoting unity or obedience to H. M. Government here, or indeed that have the most natural attachment to the Province."

All the representatives came from Halifax and Lunenburg—16 from the former and 4 from the latter locality. There were no other places where there were fifty qualified electors.

Their names and standing are as follows:

Joseph Gerrish,	William Fay,
Robert Sanderson,	William Nesbitt,
Henery Newton,	Joseph Rundell,
	Esquires.
William Best,	William Pantree,
Alex Kedie,	Joseph Fairbanks,
Jonathan Binny,	Phillips Hammond,
Henery Ferguson,	John Fillis,
George Suckling,	Lambert Falkers,
Robert Campbell,	Phillip Knaut,
	Gentlemen.

They made Sanderson Speaker, and got down to business and found that the duties on spirituous liquors from 1751 amounted to £7,045, of which a balance remained of £2,204, and this was drawn on to build a lighthouse at Sambro and a workhouse in the town. Through the use of these liquors the latter building became necessary; thus it was very appropriate to use the money for that purpose. In 1759 the Province was divided into five counties—Annapolis, Kings, Cumberland, Lunenburg, and Halifax. The latter division comprised all the mainland and islands lying easterly of the County of Lunenburg and southerly and easterly of Kings County, and all the other lands and islands within the Province of Nova Scotia not already included— a sort of "common count" for the possible benefit of Halifax is this last clause.

At this date New Brunswick region was included in Nova Scotia and the separation was not made till 1784. These were stirring and decisive times, in which important history was rapidly enacted. In 1759 Quebec had fallen and before the end of September of the next year the conquest of all Canada was complete. Surrender of French and Indians was the order of the day, and Governor Lawrence was deeply occupied with this business when he suddenly died on October 11, 1760. He had been eleven years actively employed in the affairs of the Province, and nearly all this time as Lieutenant Governor or Governor. He was not a person of kindly graces: He did not flinch at sight of blood, but was withal a man for the place and times, vigorous, patriotic, and intelligent. A little later in the same year passed away at Boston, in a ripe old age, Col. Paul Mascarene, a Huguenot refugee, an English military officer, and Lieutenant Governor of the fort at Annapolis and Administrator of the Government of Nova Scotia from

1740 to 1749. This chivalrous gentleman had all the virtues that Lawrence lacked.

The administrations of Cornwallis and Lawrence cover the actual founding of Halifax, but it is outside my purpose here to follow in detail its further history. It did not come into existence as a natural result of economic features, like Winnipeg and Toronto, and most other towns and cities, but it was born out of the political exigencies of the times. A good harbor for the navy, a shore well adapted to fortifications, were the first considerations. Neither the soil nor its products, nor the rocks and their contents, were taken into consideration. For these reasons the town was a military and naval station dependent for years wholly on English guineas and always largely leaning on that support. There were no ample streams contributory to its harbor to afford water-power and a cheap highway for timber. The only good times were when there was war on the carpet. For years the place dozed and slept, ruled by a Council who slammed their chamber doors in the face of the public. In 1817 there were only 11,000 inhabitants. What money they did not get from England as grants for public purposes they realized out of lotteries, and taxes on rum. The conservative spirit struggled hard under the new order of things that comes with steam and electrical devices. There have been no leaps and bounds in its growth. And never were there any frisky antics that resulted in rapid improvements. But in spite of many opposing elements and features there has been for a half century or more a continuous betterment until Halifax can boast of many objects and institutions to its credit. It is distinguished for its charitable institutions, its beautiful public gardens, and charming scenery at Point Pleasant Park and other localities.

A large business is now carried on in the fisheries, and many vessels are fitted out by the city merchants. Halifax is also the commercial center of the Province; and railroad and steamboat connections of later years have given new life to mercantile business.

With this extended notice of the city, we cross over to Dartmouth, on the eastern side of the harbor, and find there a prosperous and pretty town. It was laid out the next year after Halifax was founded. A settlement was begun and a sawmill built, but the Indian soon carried death and destruction among these pioneers. Little was done to make another beginning for nearly thirty years, till Governor Parr in 1784 encouraged thirty families to remove thither from Nantucket to carry on the whaling business. In less than ten years, however,

YACHTING IN HALIFAX HARBOUR.

MINIATURE LAKE, PUBLIC GARDENS, HALIFAX.

MOUNTED RIFLES EMBARKING AT DOCKYARD, HALIFAX,
FOR SOUTH AFRICA.

A WALK IN THE PUBLIC GARDENS, HALIFAX.

these families went to England and matters were at a low ebb. Since then it has slowly grown, and now has a population of about 3,000. Among the attractive features of Dartmouth are its beautiful lakes. They are a portion of a waterway that extends to the Bay of Fundy waters, in connection with the Shubenacadie River. Three-quarters of a century ago a company was formed to open up this to canal navigation. The Legislature voted £15,000 for that purpose, and work was begun, but both money and enthusiasm were soon lacking, and the project ended in failure. There are a number of thriving manufactories in Dartmouth, and the lakes yield valuable crops of ice, which are duly harvested. Many people engaged in business in Halifax have fine residences in Dartmouth. On the west shore of Bedford Basin, a capacious and beautiful extension of Halifax harbor, is the village of Bedford, a delightful summer resort on the Intercolonial Railroad, where there are first-class hotel accommodations, fine scenery, good boating and fishing, and the enchantments of unspoiled forests at the very doors. Beginning at the seaboard and going eastward, there are more harbors and coves than there is space here to enumerate. All of these are centers of population, the homes of fishermen, farmers, miners, traders and mariners. The Musquodoboit River and its productive region were known, and in some measure settled by the French a half century or more before the founding of Halifax, but appears to have been deserted at that time. In 1692 the King confirmed a grant to Sieur De Gautiers of one league above and one below the mouth of the river, and two leagues wide going up the river and the harbor. The Indian name is Mooskudoboogett, meaning, flowing out square.

At Chezzencook, a few miles from Halifax and near Musquodoboit, are settled some Acadian French. When Halifax was founded Mr. Morris, the Government surveyor, found there and at Musquodoboit the deserted buildings of the French. From Halifax westward to St. Margaret's Bay the coast line is rugged in the extreme, and settled by fishermen wherever there is a coign of vantage for their business.

The geology of this county in general outline is very simple. In the matter of area it is about equally divided between the Cambrian slates and quartzites of the one part, and granite intrusions of the other, with the exception of a patch of Carboniferous on the upper Musquodoboit. To the westward of Halifax all is granite. Beginning at Waverly a broad belt of granite extends eastward and inland almost to Sheet Harbor, within ten miles of the county line of Halifax and Guysborough. Within the area of the Cambrian formation are the gold mines of this county. They are located on the anticlinals of the formations that may be considered as the denuded crests of rock waves running easterly and westerly, from nine to ten miles apart. The richest of these mines is at Montague, some half dozen miles from Halifax. Other mines are at Oldham, Waverly, Caribou, Fifteen Mile Stream, Tangier, Killag, Oxford, Moose River, Gold Lake, Beaver Dam, Salmon River, and Lawrence Town.

There are many other points where gold has been discovered, but these are the principal localities in which mining has been carried on, only however in such a small way that a depth of a thousand feet has not yet been reached. The Carboniferous area in the Musquodoboit region overlies these gold-bearing rocks, and they may be productive of coal, when properly explored.

CHAPTER VII.

Nova Scotia has natural game preserves that are now well stocked with wild animals. Nothing more will be required to keep up this state of things than wise laws strictly observed. When the age of glacial ice and water closed in this Province many thousand years ago, it was evident that a great portion of the peninsula would never be used for agricultural purposes. Hundreds of square miles scattered here and there in areas of that extent, were strewn with boulders and ribbed with ledges. These in the long run became barrens that supported a vegetable life of hardy shrubs, and stunted trees. These areas were diversified with hills, and hillocks, and long banks or kames composed of gravel, and sand and stones on which have grown oaks, beeches, maples, birches, and other northern species of trees. There were portions far more extensive of flat clayey wet land now covered with cone-bearing trees. The area of the Province is 20,000 square miles, about two-thirds of this surface is covered with barren-ground growth. This territory will never be brought under the plow. It is not adapted to agricultural purposes, and as matters stand, it is more valuable for its forest products.

Over this region roam moose, caribou, wild-cats, and foxes; and the swamps abound with hares. The ruffed grouse is common, spruce grouse is rare except in certain localities, but they are protected by law all the time. Nova Scotia abounds in lakes; and during the autumn, a sportsman will be able to vary his bill of fare with black-ducks and wood-ducks, and woodcock. Moose are quite common over all the Province in favorable localities, but caribou are rare, now only to be found in the back portions of Queens, Digby, Shelburne, Cumberland, and Yarmouth Counties, and the northern parts of Cape Breton. One might well expect them to be more plentiful, as they are so keen of scent, so wary and fleet of foot that they are seldom killed. They eat the trailing moss, or more properly lichens, that grow on the branches of cone-bearing trees, and on the bogs they feed upon another species of this nutritious group of vegetation.

With the invention of modern firearms, all game is more seriously threatened than ever before. The law aims to give them adequate protection, and every true sportsman is their natural guardian; but many people who carry guns into these woods find pleasure in killing almost every wild thing. Nothing short of eternal vigilance on the part of game wardens and sportsmen will save our large animals from extinction in the near future. At present not only are the woods stocked with game, but the seashore affords excellent duck, and snipe shooting.

The best localities for large game are, of course, in the districts most remote from settlement. Beginning at the western extremity of the Province, we first note a large area of wild land containing about a thousand square miles, wherein there are no houses. It abounds in lakes, and the following streams take their rise in this elevated wilderness, viz: The Liverpool, or Mersy, Broad River, Sable River, Jordan River, Roseway River, Clyde River, Tusket River, Sisiboo River, and Bear River. From Liverpool, or Shelburne, or Yarmouth, or Annapolis, sportsmen can be readily guided to this unfenced domain of rugged and unspoiled beauty. The whole southern portion of Annapolis and Kings Counties is a game country. Halifax County is the largest, containing 2,000 square miles. By far the greater part is forest abounding in large game, with good shooting on the shores. In the back settlement of Lunenburg and Hants and Cumberland Counties moose are not uncommon, especially in Cumberland.

Guysborough and Antigonish are not without large game, but these localities are not the most favorable hunting grounds. Crossing the Straits of Canseau to Cape Breton and pushing northward to Baddeck, one will be on the border of a great wilderness that stretches sixty miles to Cape North along the water divide; and all the way without a human dwelling. This region is the home of moose and caribou, and has been but little hunted.

There are more men who find amusement with rod than the gun, and here is a word for those who are casting about for some promising pools and sylvan streams where they can indulge their liking to some purpose; but for my own part I am suited in sentiment with Foss when he writes that,

> I go a-gunning, but take no gun,
>   I fish without a pole,
> And I bag good game and catch such fish
>   As suits a sportsman's soul,

For the choicest that the forest holds,
And the best fish of the brook,
Are never brought down by a rifle shot,
And are never caught with a hook.

So away for a hunt in the fern-scented woods
Till the going down of the sun;
There is plenty of game still left in the woods
For the hunter who has no gun.
So away for the fish by the moss-bordered brook
That flows through the velvety sod,
There are plenty of fish still left in the streams
For the angler who has no rod.

The woods were made for the hunters of dreams,
The brooks for the fishers of song;
To the hunters who hunt for gunless game
The streams and the woods belong.

There are thoughts that moan from the soul of the pine
And thoughts in a flower-bell curled,
And thoughts that are blown with the scent of the fern
Are as new and as old as the world.

If a reader does not like the look of this bit of verse he can skip it, but I am sure that he who finds in himself some response and sanction to the sentiment they contain will get the most out of his fishing and hunting.

It is really a fine thing to whip the waters in vain for fish and all the time enjoy the charm of beautiful surroundings. Nature is communicative on the Marconi system of telegraphing. She is perpetually dispatching in every direction all manner of marvelous communications, but one must have a receiving instrument within himself in order to intercept and record them. Isaac Walton, in his "Complete Angler," quotes the famous Sir Henry Wotton as saying that "Angling after tedious study was a rest to his mind, a cheerer of his spirits, a diverter of sadness, a calmer of unquiet thoughts, a moderator of passions, a procurer of contentedness"; and "that it begat habits of peace and patience in those that professed and practiced it." Says Walton: "Indeed, my friend, you will find angling to be like the virtue

of humility, which has a calmness of spirit and a world of other blessings attending upon it."

Unless men who come from business offices and stock boards can
leave behind them the telephones and tickers at the gates of the forest
they will make no connections with their finest opportunity, though
they return with big catches and sun-bronzing, galore.

Says Emerson: "The tempered light of the woods is like a per-
petual morning, and is stimulating and heroic. The anciently reported
spells of these places creep on us. The incommunicable trees begin
to persuade us to live with them and quit our life of solemn trifles."

Now we will proceed to tell of some localities where there are
trout and salmon in Nova Scotia. To mention them all requires more
space than we can afford. If one land in Yarmouth, the most likely
place, because the most convenient, he will find good fishing not far
away on the Tusket River waters, where trout and salmon may be
taken.

The numerous lakes on this stream and their many tributaries
afford excellent opportunities for good sport. In fact, the upper waters
of all the larger rivers are stocked with trout, but as a matter of course
some are better than others. The Liverpool, near the mouth, is fished
for salmon with good results, and on all its higher points and extensive system of lakes and tributaries there is excellent trout fishing,
notably so at the Indian Gardens, the Eelweir, and far out to Milford
on the Annapolis and Liverpool road. On the Port Medway River,
Queens County, there is probably the best salmon fishing in the Province, from the mouth upward some twelve miles to Greenfield, where
there is a pretty village at the foot of the Ponhook Lake. About
eight miles of this distance the river runs through an unbroken forest
of unusual beauty. Along the banks there is a good carriage road,
and wholesome accommodations are to be had at Mills Village and
Greenfield, the two extremes of the fishing ground.

The Lahave River at various points affords good salmon fishing.
In the days of early settlement this stream was famous for the great
abundance of this fish.

·   From the ocean to Bridgewater, about fifteen miles, the river is
a succession of fine views and navigable all the way.

·   Gold River, near Chester, in Lunenburg County, is also a large
stream, with numerous lakes and well worth a sportsman's attention.

·   In Halifax County the Musquodoboit River has the reputation of
good fishing grounds whereon trout are to be had for the effort. At

Sheet Harbor, in this county, the East and Middle Rivers and their tributaries are well stocked with trout and are but little fished. The village of Sheet Harbor is easily reached both by steamer from Halifax and stage from Shubenacadie, on the Intercolonial Railroad, every day.

Cumberland County has a large area of secluded forest and many streams where trout are plentiful.

In Guysborough County the Saint Mary's and Salmon Rivers penetrate the wilderness and are sure to repay a visit to those who are in search of opportunities to cast their lines in pleasant and promising places.

Crossing the Straits of Canso to Cape Breton one has entered a region far famed for its historic interest and economic wealth of mines, and forests, and fisheries. If its fine salmon and trout fishing are not to be reckoned among the natural riches, they certainly deserve no second place among the many attractions of the island, that has resources enough for an independent kingdom of no mean importance.

The Margaree River, in Inverness County, is easily reached by different routes, and once there good accommodations may be readily secured.

On the Northeast Margaree is an angler's ideal spot for enjoyment of his sport. Samuels, in his fine book entitled "The Rod and Gun," has this to say of that region: "Here may be found a comfortable stopping place at one of the farm-houses, and the angler may obtain such sport as he perhaps never dreamed of. The Margaree is one of the finest rivers in America. It abounds in sea trout of great size and gaminess, and salmon occur in goodly numbers. It is, moreover, so easily fished that one may almost dry-shod for many miles of its length cast the fly in many grand pools which are scattered along its length. For upwards of thirty miles the river flows through meadows, pastures, and cultivated fields, and its angling possibilities are unsurpassed. In leaving Northeast Margaree the angler will do well to return to Baddeck by way of Wycocomah, visiting Lake Ainslie on the journey. Here he will find near the head of the lake a large, deep pool at one end of the inlet, which is in the summer sometimes literally packed with sea trout and salmon. So numerous are the sea trout in this pool that before it was protected from the attacks of the poachers a single jig-hook has taken out upwards of three barrels in one day!"

Aspy Bay, in the extreme north of 'the island, has the reputation of exceptionally good fishing for sea trout. It is a most delightful locality, reached by post-road from Baddeck or by steamer from Sydney.

On the St. Lawrence side of the island northward of Margaree are several streams of good repute and but little fished. There are other localities in this famous island where anglers may indulge in their favorite sport, but these are places of local fame, and a little enquiry will discover those not so well known yet deserving a call or a visit. At any rate, Cape Breton is worth seeing even if there were no fish to be had.

LUNENBURG HARBOUR.

LUNENBURG, WESTERN SUBURBS.

CHAPTER VIII.

Lunenburg County is bounded by Queens, Annapolis, Kings, Hants, and Halifax Counties, and the ocean. It contains 1,116 square miles, and has a population of about 30,000. This county is a highly favored region. The natural scenery is unsurpassed in the Province. The soil is fertile, the forest varied and thrifty, the sea a never-failing source of wealth in its fine fisheries. Farming, ship-building, fishing, these have been the ordinary industries; of recent years gold mining has added a new item that bids fair to become a business of considerable magnitude and profit. The La Have River is a broad, beautiful stream, navigable to a distance of about 15 miles for ordinary shipping, and extending northward beyond the county line, affording ample water-power for saw-mills, and pulp-mills, and other machinery, and forming a cheap highway for the timber that grows abundantly near its source. Throughout nearly the whole distance, this river runs through a fertile region, and is bordered by fine farms and good houses. The lakes are numerous, and the drainage by the river systems admirably adapted to the convenience of the people.

The coast is greatly diversified with bays and harbors and inlets, making one hundred and fifty miles of actual seaboard, although in a straight line the county is but forty miles in width.

Islands in great number, either inhabited or clad in forests, greatly heighten the picturesque effects of this delightful scene.

Such, in brief, is the county as Nature made it.

We now turn to its occupation by white men. From 1604 to 1713 the Province had been largely in the hands of the French, but not without counter claims on the part of the English and actual treaty rights. Neither France nor England showed a proper appreciation of the country. The New England colonies looked upon the French settlements as a menace to their safety, and did not hesitate to deal sturdy and ruinous blows on more than one occasion. The French were never good colonizers, and they were not at their best in those times and in this Province. In Lunenburg County they had established a fishery at Malagash or Merliguesche, the site of the present town of Lunenburg, where some old cellars long furnished the only trace of the settlement. We have not space to follow in any detail

this period of county history. In it there is but little of the charm
of romance, nor much that is of any practical value in the life of today.

The real colonization of Nova Scotia by the English begins with
the gazetting of the Hon. Edward Cornwallis as Governor of Nova
Scotia, on May 9, 1749. He founded the city of Halifax, and the
township of Lunenburg was the next oldest settlement formed by the
English Government in Nova Scotia. The next year, 1750, steps were
taken to secure settlers from Germany. To this end notice was set   .
up in several towns and cities in that country, offering very liberal
terms to those who would come to this Province. The result was that
Germans and Swiss to the number of 1,615 landed in Halifax between
the 13th of July, 1751, and early in 1753. They had been subjected
to great hardships on the voyage, and the new country and hostile
savages filled their hearts with regrets for their venture and fears for
the future. After some casting about for a suitable locality, Governor
Hopson decided upon the present site of Lunenburg. The name was
that of the old home of many of these settlers. Lunenburg, a town of
Hanover, they left behind, and they set to work with no lightness of
heart to create a namesake on these new shores. For the most part
they were farmers, but they had not been accustomed to clear up the
primeval forests and face the dangers and difficulties that met them
on every hand. They were inadequately provided with tools and agricultural implements, and destitute of cattle and other live stock till the
next year, when the Government distributed gratis among them 74
cows, 967 sheep, 114 swine, 164 goats, and much poultry. Rations during the first year of their settlement were supplied by the Government,
and they were continued to the aged and sick. From the same source
each family received 700 feet of boards, 500 brick, and nails in proportion. Matters were bad enough with them without the crowning distress of savages lying in wait for their lives and their persons. Many of
them suffered torture, and death, and captivity. Governor Lawrence
became exasperated at these and other outrages and proposed a stern
remedy. By proclamation he offered a reward of thirty pounds for every
male Indian over sixteen years of age, and twenty-five pounds for the
scalp of such a savage, and Haliburton says there was a proportionable
reward for scalps of women and children, or captured alive. The
price was liberal and the desire to win the money was not lacking,
but the Indians had so much reluctance to parting with their lives or
their persons that not one of these settlers ever claimed the bounty.
These natives were not fighting for their homes nor their country;

they were set on by their French friends, and were not unwilling to gratify their ferocity. The day of reckoning for these misguided Frenchmen was near at hand. During seven years these Indian outrages continued, and they were so fatal that the population had only increased by seven persons in that period. From this date hostilities ceased in a large measure, and the people ventured further away from the town of Lunenburg and founded various settlements in the county. During one hundred years these people for the most part retained their German speech and national usages, and many women had command of no other language. In some households older members of the family still cling to this tongue, but it is corrupted by English words and other agencies, and will soon be heard for the last time in this region. Until the establishment of a common school system, nearly forty years ago, the people had but small opportunities of learning to even read and write, but they were a vigorous stock and managed to supply their actual needs during years of hard times. The older people still retain more than a mere suggestion of their nationality, and might be set down in their ancestral home across the ocean and found to fit exactly into their surroundings. Superstitions that were once believed by everybody, and that have been for the most part dislodged by the schoolhouses, are still found nestling in the minds of the oldest portions of this community. The "witch doctor" is not unknown. Horseshoes over the barn doors, and lucky days for many of the agricultural undertakings are still common enough. In 1891, out of a population of about 30,000, 8,854 could neither read nor write. Now schools are established in every community; all the children are taught English and ordinary branches of learning. The present generation of young married men and women have also had these advantages, and the result has been to fertilize their minds with new ideas and separate them from the older generations about to leave the stage. That they may not lack the sturdy worth of their fathers is a most desirable wish. Many of the young men and women have gone to the United States, where some have made permanent homes, and others are looking around for opportunities of profitable employment. Whoever will drive through this county, up, and down, and across, will be impressed with the general air of neatness and thrift, and in some localities of a high degree of prosperity. This is especially discernible on the lower portions of the La Have River, where the fisheries have proved veritable bonanzas for the intrepid men who follow this calling.

With this general review we will pass on to notice the towns and villages in brief mention. Writing in 1828, Haliburton said:

»   "Lunenburg Town is situated on a peninsula and is built on the side of a hill of moderate ascent, and when approached by water presents a neat and pleasing appearance. The harbor is about a quarter of mile deep and half a mile wide, of easy access and possessing good anchorage. It is sheltered by Cross Island, which is near its entrance, and is about thirty feet high, containing 253 acres. Inside of this island the water is deep, decreasing as it approaches the wharves, alongside of which it is from twelve to fourteen feet. The town is constructed on a regular plan, the streets crossing each other at right angles. It contains upwards of 230 dwelling houses, stores, and other buildings, many of which are spacious, substantially built, and neatly finished."

In the census of 1891, the latest now accessible, the population of this town is returned as 4,894. Haliburton would not now recognize Lunenburg by his description. Because of its pre-eminence in the fisheries it has been well named the Gloucester of Nova Scotia. The latent energy of the old stock has been aroused by the spirit of the age, and this quaint old German outpost, that dozed and dreamed amid vacated blockhouses and cabbage yards for a century, awoke to its opportunities, and Lunenburg is full of life, and thrift, and hope, and beautiful for situation, as it overlooks the restful view of ocean, and islands, and headlands that fade into the dim perspective of distance.

The Lunenburg fishery business has grown to such proportions that an extended notice will be acceptable to all who take an interest in our natural resources, and their intelligent and energetic use of them. To this end I insert letters written for the Halifax Herald of November, 1901, by gentlemen well entitled to attention. The first is from the pen of Col. C. E. Kaulbach, M. P., and runs as follows:

(Written for the special South Shore edition of the Halifax Herald by Lieutenant Colonel Kaulbach, M. P.)

'No description of Lunenburg is complete that does not deal with its chief industry—the fisheries. The history of this industry as now conducted—the deep-sea, or bank fishery—dates back to the early sixties. Previous to that time the fishing industry of Lunenburg was entirely confined to the Labrador and shore fishery, and trawling, and trapnetting was an unknown art to Lunenburg fishermen. In 1865 the

SOUTHERN SIDE OF LUNENBURG HARBOUR.

GRAND BAND STAND. LUNENBURG

BRIDGEWATER.

OAK ISLAND. WHERE CAPTAIN KIDD'S GOLD WAS BURIED (?).

first banker—the "precursor" of our splendid fleet of today—was fitted out by Benjamin Anderson for the western banks. The venture was a new departure and was not looked upon with favor by the fishermen of that day. So doubtful were they of its success that Mr. Anderson was compelled to guarantee the crew wages equivalent to the earnings of a Labrador trip. But the voyage being a successful one, he was followed the next year by others, thus opening up a wider and richer field which the enterprise of Lunenburg fishermen was not slow to grasp. From such small beginnings has developed her present gigantic fishing industry, exceeding in value that of any port in the Dominion, and outstripping in number of vessels engaged in deep-sea fishing the once famous fishing fleet of the New England States, until today Lunenburg is justly entitled "The Gloucester" of Canada. The vessels composing the fleet are of the finest type of marine architecture, combining speed, safety, and utility. Up to 1895 the average fishing vessel was about 70 tons burthen, costing about $3,000. Since then the tendency has been and is to build larger vessels, as is evidenced by the fact that the present average is 93 tons, valued at about $4,500.

NEW VESSELS ON THE STOCKS.

As an evidence of the growth of this industry within the thirty years since its inception we have only to show that, compared with the one solitary vessel then, we have today a fleet of 153 bankers, employing crews to the number of 2,745 men! A record surely to be proud of. To this fleet additions are being made every year. Last year there were launched from the ship yards of this county thirty-six beautifully modeled fishing crafts, and there are now on the stocks and engaged to be built (in time for the coming fishing season) as many more. As this article is supposed to deal exclusively with the fishing industry of Lunenburg, I shall make no comment with reference to the fleet of vessels registered at this port, except to say that the total number of vessels (sea-going) owned and employed is far in excess of that of any other county in Canada, and that Lunenburg has built and registered more vessels within the last three years than any other port in Canada.

CAPITAL AND EARNINGS.

The value of the fishing industry to the county of Lunenburg can scarcely be estimated in dollars and cents. The total value of vessels engaged represents $800,000, to which is to be added $250,000 for outfits, which is certainly a large showing of capital invested, the return for which is estimated this present year at $1,016,000. The catch for 1901 being upward of 254,000 quintals. In addition to the deep-sea fishery we have to reckon as a part of Lunenburg's great fishing industry the shore fisheries. According to the fishery report for 1900 (the latest available statistics) this much of the industry represents a value of $222,830 in boats and fishing gear, with a catch valued at $250,000. This estimate, however, does not include another branch of this same industry, the lobster fishery. Unfortunately there are no statistics of the value of outfits employed in this business, but the yield is valued in the fishery report for 1900 as $29,409. This would give, as a grand total, the value of the fishing industry of Lunenburg as $2,568,239. Certainly a grand showing, the indirect benefits of which cannot be estimated in dollars and cents, embracing as it does every other industry, and giving employment to farmers, lumbermen, artisans, and laborers of every class. It is also the basis of our foreign trade, and is to the people of this country the one great primal, central source of a wealth and prosperity unsurpassed by few, if any, of the counties of Nova Scotia.

FURTHER DEVELOPMENT.

In connection with the further development of this great industry of fishing, it has occurred to me that the establishment of a biological station on our coast would be a very important factor in the interest of the fisheries, and as Nova Scotia has pushed the industry of fishing with grand results, making what I have described it, I feel that a scientific laboratory should be founded in Nova Scotia to make possible the still greater prosecution of fishing and marine researches similar to those promoted with signal success in other countries, by which the more technical and complex features, now very doubtfully understood, can be the more easily grasped and carried into practical use. It is a significant fact that the artificial propagation of marine food fish is rapidly extending among all nationalities having extensive fisheries, and encouraged and supported by governments planting marine hatcheries at various intervals along the coasts of their territories.

The decrease in the supply of food fishes as population increases by reason of the improved methods of catch, is the experience of all fishing countries, and practical and scientific men and governments are everywhere giving increased attention to artificial propagation as a means in promoting and increasing the wealth of the sea.

VALUE OF HATCHERIES.

To give an idea of the commercial value that would accrue to a country were artificial cultivation of the products of the sea cared for by the use of fish hatcheries, formed by natural ponds, indentations of the coast, where the tide ebbs and flows, or by incubators in charge of good, practical men, paid by the Government for their services, who will receive all mother-fish and dispose of them as he considered best—if for the incubator, to strip them of their eggs, whether they be lobster or cods, excepting all unripe lobsters, which should be returned to the sea—incalculable benefits would be derived in the sea's reproduction of fish, for the food and wealth of the fisherman. Every twelve-inch lobster contains by actual count on an average 22,000 eggs; allow 2,000 less for stripping and bad eggs, and you have 20,000 net return from each lobster. The average of cod ova is about the same as that of the lobster, which will given an idea of the immense beneficial results that would accrue were the Government to adopt the methods I suggest, whereby the waters would be recuperated or fructified and the fishermen benefited.

THE FISHERMEN.

We have, as I stated, 2,745 men engaged as fishermen in this county—Lunenburg—a class of hardy men, inured to a life upon the sea, quick of thought, keen of intellect, robust of body, ready in resource, sturdy in purpose, perfectly fearless and, in my opinion, unsurpassed in the world today for bravery: expert boatsmen, capable of enduring hardship, competent in all things pertaining to the sea, and from this source we in Lunenburg mainly depend for competent and skillful masters and mates in our mercantile marine service, which is no small benefit when we consider that this source of supply is from the fishermen who at the present time man our Lunenburg fishing fleet, which Commisioner Prince, in a speech delivered before the School of Science the past summer, described as the finest fishing fleet in the world. Therefore, as a means of developing this class of men, encouraging shipbuilding, and developing and sustaining the fisheries, not only of Lunenburg, but the Atlantic coast, I would urge upon the Government the adoption of the principles and views which I have advanced in this article.   C. E. KAULBACH.

Lunenburg, November, 1901.

(Written for the special South Shore edition of the Halifax Herald by
Mr. W. C. Acker.)

The bank fishing in the county of Lunenburg, from a small beginning, has increased until today this county stands pre-eminently at the
head of that business on the continent.

In 1865 the Lunenburg banking fleet consisted of four small vessels, which fished on the Banks only during April and May, after
which they went to Labrador for the remainder of the fishing season.
From that insignificant attempt at Bank fishing, the industry has developed to the splendid proportions we find it at the present time. ·

Bank fishing in those early days was done from the deck, hand
lining, so called, although Yankee and Western Nova Scotia vessels at
that time did trawl fishing in a small way, by the method known as
"hauling and setting."

Mr. Benjamin Anderson, who was the master of one of the first
four vessels, can truthfully be said to be the pioneer trawler· and the
father of Bank fishing as carried on from this county at the present
time.

THE FIRST TRAWLER.

About the year 1871 he fitted the schooner "Dielytris" with dories
and trawls, and decided to spend the whole season on the banks instead
of going to Labrador, as formerly.

He saw other fishermen using the trawl "hauling and setting,"
and he conceived the idea that that method could be improved on,
and by experimenting evolved the "under-running" method of trawl
fishing as used today by the Lunenburg fleet. It might be said that
the introduction of that easy and scientific way of fishing has been the
lever which has raised Lunenburg to the prominence she now occupies.

Mr. Anderson was successful, others quickly followed, the fleet
increased year by year, and is still growing. Mr. Anderson followed
fishing up to about twelve years ago, when he retired, and is today
enjoying the fruits of his labors. He earned for himself more than
a local reputation as the pioneer trawler and a most successful fisherman.

REMARKABLE GROWTH.

From that small beginning thirty years ago has grown the splendid
fishing industry of Lunenburg County, which this year consisted of a
fleet of 158 vessels, employing 2,745 men.

Gloucester and other New England towns, about fifteen years ago,

LUNENBURG.

LINCOLN STREET, LUNENBURG, LOOKING WEST.

had some 200 vessels, employing 3,800 men, engaged in salt cod fishing. Last year that fleet consisted of about 60 vessels and 1,000 men, and it is said these are fishing with no profit, which will tend to lessen that fleet, while ours continues to grow steadily. We have no great manufacturing, mining, or farming interests, but the heritage of the sea is ours, and "what we have we hold." No other section of the continent can compete with us. So long as the succulent codfish frequent the Banks our men and vessels will be there to catch them. Judging from experience, the fish are there for all time. Our fishermen found the fish as plentiful the past season as in any previous year (a report from Yankee fishermen to the contrary notwithstanding). It would take a generation for any other section to develop the class of men suitable for Bank fishing. Our men are born, bred, and reared to the calling, usually making their debut as "throaters" or "headers" when mere boys.

A "HOME" PEOPLE.

They are a "home" people, and few, if any, of our fishermen go from the county to fish in foreign vessels. From these original German farmers who settled in Lunenburg County some one hundred and forty-eight years ago, have come these hardy men of the sea, who are equal, if not superior, to any other class of working men in the world.

A more intelligent, industrious, courageous, temperate, and moral people as a whole cannot be found. The splendid churches in every town and village in the county emphasize the latter fact. In the spring, when some fifteen hundred men at one time are about our streets, where the ardent is easily procurable, drunkenness and quarrelling are rare.

The toilers of the sea are everywhere a people renowned for industry and courage, daily risking their lives with no great pecuniary reward. Our fishermen are no exception. The splendid cottages owned and occupied by our fishermen throughout the county testify to their frugality and industry.

They are as a class intelligent readers, generally well informed, and ready to adopt any improved method to their work. Men from amongst them occupy positions in town and county government with credit to themselves and their constituents.

CO-OPERATIVE PRINCIPLE.

Perhaps, before closing this article, it would be well to endeavor to give an idea of how the Bank fishing industry is conducted. All the essential elements of co-operation exist in the way the business is

8

carried on. The owners furnish the vessel's fishing outfit and provisions, and receive one-half the catch. The men fish on shares, the cook and two boys being the only hired hands. The captain, or "skipper" as he is called, receives an equal share along with the men, besides a percentage of from two and one-half to four per cent. commission on the value of the gross stock. The business is fairly remunerative for the time employed, $200 being about the average share per man for the season, $350 being the maximum and $150 the minimum.

All the captains and many of the men are stockholders in the vessels in which they fish, giving them a double interest in the trip. The fleet usually starts about the first of April and continues fishing up to about the 20th of September, although many arrive home with full fares the first part of September.

Winter fishing is not prosecuted from this county, it being considered too dangerous to property and life for the remuneration. The men are occupied when not fishing in various ways, such as shipbuilding, lumbering, farming, fish-drying, seagoing, and shore-fishing.

The total catch for the past season was about 245,000 quintals, valued at about $980,000.   WM. C. ACKER.
Lunenburg, November, 1901.

The educational facilities of this town are a credit to the people. The Lunenburg Academy is one of the finest wooden buildings in the maritime provinces. It was erected in 1895 at a cost of $30,000. It occupies a commanding site and is visible for several miles distant. There are twelve class rooms, separate entrances, halls and cloak rooms for boys and girls, a laboratory, a library, and a large assembly hall. The Smead-Dowd heating, ventilating, and sanitary system gives perfect satisfaction. The laboratory is well supplied with physical and chemical apparatus and all students are required to carry on practical laboratory work. The library contains three of the best physiological and geographical charts published. There is a very creditable cabinet of minerals and a good collection of fossils.

This is a great change in three-quarters of a century. One of the old teachers, Mr. Thomas, who died in 1881, related his experience as follows to Judge Des Brisay:

"I have had, in some sections where I have boarded, nothing but Indian meal, without milk or sweetening; in other families, fish, potatoes, and mangel tops for my dinner. Slept on hay and straw

LA HAVE RIVER, BRIDGEWATER

VIEW FROM BLOCKHOUSE ROAD, MAHONE BAY.

DEEP COVE. TO THE EASTWARD OF LUNENBURG.
(A FAVORITE "PICNIC" RESORT.)

LUNENBURG: WEST END, AND SUBURBS.

beds on the floor where mice, fleas, and bugs could be felt all hours of the night. I have frequently found one, two, and three mice crushed to death lying under me—the straw not even put in a sack, and my covering old clothing. I suffered all this, so great was my wish to give instruction to the poor and rising generation. Yea, many families of poor children have I educated and never received a farthing."

The town of Chester is on the eastern border of the county, and forty-five miles from Halifax by highway. It is quite widely known as a locality of scenic beauties and refreshing climate in the same season. Nothing short of a troubled conscience should prevent a person of leisure and good bodily health from greatly enjoying a vacation in this locality. Unless all indications fail, Chester will rapidly become a famous resort for Americans, who cannot find on their seaboard such a combination of delightful and desirable features. In the spacious bay are 365 islands, and the hills to the water's edge afford admirable opportunities to take in the splendid view, from the empty dories tied and tilting on the ripples, to the glint of a sail on the far horizon. Already tourists have discovered the attractions of this locality, and all accommodations are readily taken up during the summer months. This township was erected in 1760, three years after the beginning at Lunenburg. It was a perilous proceeding to venture even thus far from the main settlement, but there were men and women who took the risk, and a little later some thirty families from New England landed there with cattle and implements of husbandry. Their descendants are residing in this township in goodly numbers.

Within this township are promising gold fields, fine fisheries, good timber and agricultural lands. A railway connection with the outside is now the greatest need, and this bids fair to be soon supplied. Population of this township in 1891 was 3,050.

About twelve miles to the westward of Chester is the delightful village of Mahone. It is situated at the mouth of the Musha-Musha River on tidewater at the head of Mahone Bay of most charming features. The village or town is nestled among trees. The houses are neat and commodious, and a general air of well-to-do people is over everything. Fishing, ship-building, and farming are the principal occupations, outside of mercantile pursuits. Large shipments of cordwood are made from this port. It is reached by the Central Railway, and is rapidly increasing in importance. The population of 1,500 for the most part is of German stock. The settlement was founded in 1754 by Capt. Ephraim Cook, a man who made trouble for Lord Cornwallis in Halifax, commanded one of the vessels that brought out the Halifax emigrants, was captain of a schooner that helped to transport the Acadian French from Grand Pre, lost a leg at Schenectady, N. Y., 1759; settled in Yarmouth; died there in 1821; a native of Kingston, Mass. At any rate, the settlement was located by ·a man who had a keen eye for natural advantages, and the place was assured of distinction from the beginning. Fishing, and farming, and lumbering, and gold-mining, and ship-building, and cordwood trade, all these were centered on that spot in the nature of things. ·Add to these the most charming scenery of the island-studded bay, and the long reaches of lapping waters, the wooded shores, the embowered cottages, and we may well consider Mahone to be richly dowered with the good things of the world. A trip in the little steamer to Chester on a fine day affords a continuous pano-rama of beautiful views. A sail in a boat, a.drive, or a stroll' among the people are enjoyable amusements to those who come to rest and recruit for future labors. Here are good hotels, fast teams, and obliging people.

On the La Have River, about fifteen miles from the mouth, is the town of Bridgewater. It is a close rival of Lunenburg in busi-ness importance. It is at the head of tide, and accommodates ordinary shipping at the wharves. If this town had been built on the eastern side of the river, no other in the Province would outclass it for beauty of situation. It seems impossible that men made choice of the present site. As matters stand, it is a town of wide outlooks. The street commanding the river is especially charming, and there are other fine bits that are somewhat hidden in the rear of the business portion. There are several commodious residences, delightfully situ-ated, and a general aspect of reasonable comfort is readily discovered. There are good hotel accommodations, and opportunities for boating on the river, and very pleasant drives along its banks. This town is the commercial center of a large agricultural district, and one may see in the streets some quaint arrivals from the country where much of usages and fashions of the good old days are still in existence.

The largest lumber business in the Province has long been con-ducted by the firm of E. D. Davison & Sons at Bridgewater. The N. S. Central Railway passes through Bridgewater, making this point easily accessible to tourists and general travel.

NEW GERMANY, LUNENBURG COUNTY.

MAHONE BAY, LUNENBURG COUNTY.

Within a dozen miles of the town are promising gold mines, some of them in active operation. Further developments and better methods of working will doubtless result in much profitable business in this line. Agricultural opportunities are good in the outlying district, and the whole region is provided with natural resources of prosperity. The population is about 2,000. There are six churches, a good court house, three public schools well housed, two banks, and other necessities and conveniences to meet reasonable expectations. The town is incorporated, and has a system of electric lighting, and a collection of interesting and valuable articles collected by the late Judge M. B. DesBrisay, the author of the History of Lunenburg County, that must have been entirely a labor of love on his part, and will continually increase in value. I am indebted to him for items not readily accessible elsewhere, and time will continually add to the value of his public-spirited performance.

Bridgewater is comparatively a new town. The second house was erected there in 1812 by Gerhart and Frederic Wile.

Eighteen miles above Bridgewater, on the river, is New Germany, an agricultural and manufacturing center of growing importance. The N. S. Central Railway passes through this district. Near the depot is a pulp mill and stave manufactory. This point is a stave market and distributing center for the thriving villages of Foster's Settlement, Ohio, and Hemford, and Nineveh. This district was founded about 100 years ago by John Feindel; being a remote point from markets, the growth was slow until the coming of the railroad a few years ago. Since then the increasing of population and business has been quite rapid. Church of England, Baptists, and Methodists have suitable places of worship, and the schools are well ordered.

Lunenburg County was from the earliest times famous for its fine fisheries. The French settled at Lunenburg, Fort Point, Petite Reviere, more than a century before 1753, and sent shiploads of fish to Europe. The German settlers were mostly agriculturists, and were obliged to gradually learn the business and handicraft of harvesting the ocean.

It is not the purpose of these sketches of county history to describe all the villages, and one must regretfully pass over interesting and pleasing localities with little or no mention. New Dublin, on the western shore of La Have River, near the mouth, is a place of great natural beauty that eventually will make it a conspicuous resort of tourists who will enjoy the drives on Crescent Beach, the surf bathing, and many other strong attractions.

Petite Reviere, adjoining Dublin on the west, is one of the points of early French occupancy, and traces of their habitations are still to be seen, and by some freak of chance their name of the locality has never been exchanged for another.

Blockhouse, on the road between Bridgewater and Mahone, is a pretty, thriving village, and the seat of a promising gold-mining industry.

Northfield is a thrifty agricultural settlement eight miles above Bridgewater. The first settler was Peter Mackay, a Highland Scotchman who had been a British soldier and was paid off in Halifax in 1783.

Riversdale, ten miles above Bridgewater on the N. S. Central Railway, is a well-to-do farming locality on the river. The original settlers were Daniel and Jacob Mossman.

Between Blockhouse and New Germany is New Cornwall, a back district, but not without its abundant charms and excellent resources of soil and forest products, and sportsmen speak well of the region. Andrew Rafuse, Michael Brum, Thomas Hollomere were first settlers.

·To the westward from Bridgewater a post-road runs to North Queens. On this route and its branches are Baker Settlement, Waterloo, Chelsea, all of them thriving farming localities. Lower Pleasant River and the New Germany Road settlements of Nineveh and Ohio bear witness to the industry and courage of these pioneers of the wilderness.

Here I must come to an end of these notices, having already overrun the limits of my space.

As a rule, the people one meets outside the towns in this county have more or less of German accent. It will soon disappear altogether, as the young generation have no liking for this peculiarity of speech.

Many of them are Lutherans, but other denominations have gained much ground among them.

In the outside agricultural districts much attention is given to raising live stock. The best oxen in the Province are found in those localities, where they are well bred and well trained, sleek and clean.

The people are industrious and economical, not greatly given to strong drink. They are tenacious of opinions, and often obdurate.

CHESTER. LUNENBURG COUNTY.

CHESTER.

FRONT HARBOUR, CHESTER.

CHESTER, LUNENBURG COUNTY.

Greatly given to settle their disputes in a court house, seeming to relish the fray of a lawsuit, although it always proves an expensive luxury. This practice has ruined many men, and brought many others from prosperity to poverty. They take a great interest in party politics, and follow their leaders with an unwarranted confidence. One of these old-type specimens, who could neither read nor write, assured me "dat a Liberal and a Luteran I was born, and a Liberal and a Luteran I vill die, because and because!" . Such pig-headed politics is by no means confined to this county, and the more's the pity.

The geology of Lunenburg County is not very complicated. All the western portion, embracing about two-thirds the whole area, is but an extension of the Cambrian slates and quartzites of Queens County, and the whole Atlantic slope, with few exceptions where granite appears. The other third is granite, being an eastern extension of this formation that forms the western watershed from Yarmouth County to Windsor. In these Cambrian rocks of Western Lunenburg are the gold mines of Vogler's Cove, Millipsigate, Pleasant River Barren, Block House, and Gold River. On the northern border, from New Germany to the Annapolis line, there are more or less granite areas along the ragged and uneven contact of the two kinds of rocks.

Very little prospecting has been done on the promising gold-bearing anticlinals, and no one entitled to an opinion in such matters would be surprised if gold mining became an extensive and prosperous industry in this county.

Sir William Dawson is authority for the statement that a patch of carboniferous rocks occurs at Chester and another at Margaret's Bay, an interesting but not a surprising feature. Very likely it is but a remnant of a formation that extended northward to the coal areas of Cumberland.

CHAPTER IX.

THE COAL MINES AND COAL MEASURES.

Before we discuss the coal measures of Nova Scotia it may be of interest to some readers, if a page or two is devoted to the making of coal mines in general.

Beyond all reasonable doubt, coal is the product of vegetation. In considering the manner in which coal mines have been formed, it will aid us to know something of the nature of the vegetation that was finally entombed beneath the rocks. Fortunately we have ample material to fully determine this matter. Not only have whole trees been found complete in the form of coal, but wonderful imprints of leaves, and fronds and bark, and spore-cases have been discovered in profusion. In point of numbers of species, ferns take the first rank; in many mines they include about one-half the coal flora, but did not contribute very largely to the actual production of coal. The main part of the material for coal-making was produced by three orders of trees. These were, first, the Lepidodendrids, or scale trees, that were gigantic relatives of our dainty club-mosses, and like them were propagated by spores; second, the Sigliarids, or seal trees, allied to the former, and the Calamites or rush trees than have dwindled to our puny Equisetum, or scouring rush. These three groups grew to lofty trees, and they, and all their associates in the coal seams are natives of the swamps where they must have flourished under very favorable conditions. On the elevated ground, grew a species of pine, and that was the highest type of vegetable life in the world. No flower had yet bloomed, to shed its fragrance on the air, no bee had yet appeared. Wherever there are coal mines, there were once wide forests covering inland swamps and sea-shore marshes. Vegetation will not decay under water, and it constantly accumulated, as it has done in peat bogs, and even in our common bogs. But there was another factor that was indispensable to coal-making. It must be buried under great pressure. To accomplish that end the ground whereon it grew must be overflowed by waters carrying with them mud and sand in sufficient quantities to form a stratum of rock in the course of time. That was the actual method taken by nature. In those days the crust of the earth was far more unstable than now.

120

The shrinking crust was subject to more frequent movements in the earlier epochs of its development.

The coal forests grew on lowlands not far above the level of the seas and great lakes. Again and again these lands were submerged after centuries and in some instances thousands of years of undisturbed growth and accumulation of vegetable matter. The inflow of waters brought mud and sand that buried the forest growth. In the course of time this new deposit was elevated above the water, and quickly sown by the spores that were borne on the wings of the wind. This process was repeated many times. Every seam of coal represents a distinct submergence. The stratum of rock that over-lays it is the sediment brought in by the overflowing waters and streams. The roots and standing trees of the under-clay are clear proofs of the growth of the material where we find it. In South Wales there are one hundred seams of coal in succession, one above the other, showing that there were as many old forests buried, and new ones grew over the same area. In Nova Scotia there are at least seventy such seams. An average thickness of coal, taking all the seams together in coal mines, would be about one hundred feet, but extremes would take us to 150 feet. Careful computations make it about one million years to one hundred feet of coal. In some mines the coal seams are about horizontal, thus remaining as they were formed. In others the enclosing strata have been more or less folded, with the result that the coal is deep buried in the earth. In some instances coal was probably formed from the accumulation of drifted trees and the like at the mouths of rivers. The coal-making process continues to our own time, as the peat bogs are still in the making, but the great bulk of it was formed during the time known as the Carboniferous Age. It was produced almost from pole to pole. In Nova Scotia grew vegetable forms requiring a tropical climate, and within the Arctic Circle are veins of coal. The atmosphere loaded with carbon dioxide and saturated with moisture must have greatly modified the climate. As the atmosphere became cleared of the excess of this poisonous gas, the climate was cooler and not so favorable to vegetable life, but better adapted to higher orders of animals than reptiles. We are not surprised to learn that when the Coal Age closed there was not yet on the earth a warm-blooded animal; no beast that suckled its young, and no creature with feathers. Reptiles stood at the head of creation. Shakespeare has it that "Nature hath framed strange fellows in her time." Very strange fellows indeed were the creatures that first introduced the backbone and skull upon the dry land. They carried a very distinct smack of the sea in their structures, that in certain aspects pointed to a higher development in a distant future. Any competent person would expect to find in the fossil record of the Carboniferous Age the remains of creatures that were not true fishes, but departed from that type towards a structure adapted to the land. The coal mines of Ohio have furnished thirty species of animals with lizard-like heads, long, limbless bodies covered with bony scales, the whole structure and aspect suggesting both ganoid fishes and lower reptiles. From the Bavarian coal measures we have the fossil remains of a creature of lizard-like general form of body, with four limbs equipped with paddles, strong jaws furnished with ganoid fish teeth, the body covered with bony scales. Professor Owen, the late great master in these matters, named it Ganeocephalus, meaning thereby that its head was like the ganoid fishes. The coal fields of Nova Scotia have yielded the fossil remains of several species of air-breathing vertebrates, all of them belonging to the sub-class of reptiles known as amphibians. They varied in dimensions from one to twenty feet in length; all of them were provided with limbs adapted to walking or swimming, and their backbones were of the bi-concave structure of fishes. Writing of one of these, Sir William Dawson, who had discovered it, says: "This ancient inhabitant of the coal swamps of Nova Scotia was, in short, as we often find to be the case with the earliest forms of life, the possessor of powers and structures not usually in the modern world combined in a single species. It was certainly not a fish, yet its bony scales and the form of its vertebræ and of its teeth might, in the absence of other evidence, cause it to be mistaken for one." All of these animals here mentioned are included in one group, a sub-order of Amphibians, and the name for them is Labyrinthodonts, meaning labyrinth-toothed, because when the tooth is cut across in thin transparent sections, a labyrinth structure is shown. Through all the later portions of the Coal Age our shores and marshes were inhabited by great numbers and varieties of these primitive reptiles. They fed upon each other in a large measure. It was a very different world from what now meets the human eye as it surveys the features of the globe. The great mountain ranges were as yet unborn. Every species of vegetable was different from our own, and the same was true of animal life. All the carbon of all the coal mines and all the existing vegetation was once in the atmosphere, and unless it was withdrawn this planet could not become the home of the human race nor of the higher animals of mammalian structure. In every molecule of carbon dioxide there are two atoms of oxygen and one of carbon. It was not always thus. Those atoms were once free, but later were chemically combined with oxygen by the force of some vast energy, electrical, or in some other form. To tear them asunder, and retire the carbon from circulation, and set the oxygen free, was the problem of Nature. The sun was the only agent equal to that task, and it operated through vegetable organs to that end. So far as the microscope can reveal, this work is done as a rule in the leaves, where the cells of protoplasm are occupied by grains of chlorophyll that play an indispensable part, in conjunction with light and heat, to separate the carbon from the oxygen. The former is built into wood, and the latter escapes to be ready for other activities. If we char the wood and thus drive away the moisture, we get the charcoal as a result, and that is all carbon, excepting a small proportion of minerals that were taken up through the roots. If we burn a bit of this charcoal, that will mean that we give it an opportunity to become oxidized into carbon dioxide gas, and thus set free in the air again. If a tree is left to ordinary conditions to die of old age, it just as surely becomes oxidized. Nature has after her own methods charred immense quantities of the ancient vegetable world in the form of coal mines. We may now see how vast was the work performed through the agency of "nothing but leaves." By their activities this planet became able to support the higher orders of life, and at the same time there was laid up a mighty storehouse of energy for Man who was destined to be the crown of creation. All the energy that was employed to tear asunder the carbon dioxide molecule was somehow lodged in the carbon or coal. Energy is the power to do work, and one cubic foot of hard coal contains sufficient energy, if wholly utilized, to raise a weight of 3,269 tons one hundred feet. It turns out that coal is the identical vegetable product of many million years ago, and its associated energy is the actual product of the sunshine that cast the shadows of those trees and ferns that reared their fluted trunks and spreading fronds through the millenniums that have no record but the "testimony of the rocks."

If it turns out that some who consult these chapters have no interest in the foregoing introduction, it will be an easy matter to skip it altogether. It has seemed to me that so large a bounty of Providence is worth some other attention than may be prompted by commercial values.   A coal miner is a rational being of a high order, and he should know more of the origin of coal than a gopher does of the earth in which he burrows.   The men who are engaged in buying and selling this material should not be ignorant of its history. We do well to remember the dictum of Scripture that "there is gold and a multitude of rubies, but the lips of knowledge are a precious jewel."

If there was no coal in Nova Scotia, still her natural resources would be very great.   Added to her long list of economic values that are not the work of men's hands, there are 685 square miles of known coal fields and many more almost sure to be discovered, and the world may be safely challenged for another area of twenty thousand square miles of equal richness and variety.   All these values are greatly increased by physical features and geographical position that could not be improved on the face of the whole earth.   Almost an island, and everywhere provided with harbors; located in the north temperate zone, stretching far out toward the British Isles, that lie still further northward; out of the range of desolating hurricanes and tornadoes, and the ravages of malaria and other diseases of more southern climes—these are surely no far-fetched values, but are distinctly among first considerations.

There is a great deal of literature on the Nova Scotia coal fields. Before me are the following: Dawson's Acadian Geology, containing 369 pages devoted to the Carboniferous system; The Coal Fields and the Coal Trade of Cape Breton, by Richard Brown, 1871; The Industrial Resources of Nova Scotia, by Abraham Gesner, 1849, several pages on coal; portions of various reports of the Canadian Geological Survey; papers in the publications of the Nova Scotian Institute of Science, and articles in newspapers and other miscellaneous publications.   To get the most needed portions of all this material into a brief chapter is the problem before me.   In such a position no two persons who would undertake it at all, would begin alike or end alike.   I have no intention of writing an essay on the coal measures of Nova Scotia, but it is my desire to bring into a convenient form a body of instructive and authoritative information that will not be out of date and demand during the present generation.

Beginning with the most important of our coal fields, we will take up those of Cape Breton.   It will be a matter of interest to some readers to learn a little of the early history of these now famous coal fields.   To answer this demand I can do no better than to quote from rather a scarce book, "The Coal Fields and Coal Trade of Cape Breton," by Mr. Richard Brown, a recognized authority.

"The first printed notice of the existence of coal in Cape Breton is met with in the 'Description géographique et historique des Costes de l'Amérique Septentrionale,' by Nicholas Denys, published in Paris in 1672. In the preface of his book he says: 'There are mines of coal through the whole extent of my concessions, near the sea coast, of a quality equal to the Scotch, which I have proved at various times on the spot, and also in France, where I brought them for trial.' He adds: 'At Baie des Espagnols (Sydney) there is a mountain of very good coal, four leagues up the river,' and 'another mine near the little entrance of the Bras d'Or Lakes;' also that 'at Le Chadye, on the northwest coast (probably Mabeu)', there is a small river suitable for chaloups, where there is a plentiful salmon fishery and a coal mine.' Being almost exclusively engaged in the fisheries and fur trade, Denys, during his long residence in Cape Breton, made no attempt to work the coal seams, for want, probably, of a market. After his departure, in 1672, it appears that unauthorized persons helped themselves to whatever coal they needed from the cliffs, without permission from his sons, whom he left in charge of his property. Denys' patent seems to have been revoked in 1690."

"The importance of the coal of Cape Breton was fully recognized in a memoir submitted in 1708 to the French Government by M. Raudot, intendant of the finances, and his son, intendant of the marine of Canada, recommending the establishment of an entrepot on the seaboard, open at all seasons of the year, where the productions of Europe and the West Indies could be stored ready for shipment to Canada. The Messrs. Raudot recommended that a port in Cape Breton should be chosen for this purpose, "as the island could furnish old France with coal, codfish, oils, plaster, and timber of its own growth and produce."

The next notice of the coal of Cape Breton occurs in the journal of Admiral Hovenden Walker, who commanded the unfortunate expedition sent to reduce Quebec in 1711. Several ships and nearly a thousand men having been lost at the mouth of the St. Lawrence, owing, as it was alleged, to the ignorance of the pilots, it was decided at a council of war to give up the enterprise and proceed to Spanish Bay (Sydney), which had been selected as the most convenient rendezvous in case of the fleet being dispersed. Admiral Walker says: "The island had always, in time of peace, been used in common both by the English and French for loading coals, which are extraordinarily good here, and taken out of the cliffs with iron crowbars only, and no other labor." The English, who took coal in common with the French, were most likely New England colonists, who fished on the coast in summer and carried away a few tons of coal on their homeward voyage; the same, probably, that helped themselves some years before without permission from M. Denys. The first attempt at mining in anything like a regular form was made upon the ten-foot seam on the north side of Cow Bay in 1720, when it was found necessary to obtain a supply of fuel for the host of officers and soldiers, mechanics, traders, and laborers who went out to lay the foundations of the celebrated fortress of Louisburg. Some relics have been found recently in the old workings, but they may have belonged to a later period. Cargoes of coal were, about this time, exported from Cow Bay to Boston; for although direct trade between the French and English colonists was forbidden by the treaty of neutrality, the New England traders, notwithstanding, carried on an active clandestine trade with Louisburg, receiving French products in exchange for. bricks, lumber, and provisions.

After Cape Breton had been twenty-two years in the undisputed possession of Great Britain there was not yet a regular mine opened. In 1784 the first Governor, Lieutenant Governor, Col. Frederick Wallet Desbarres, commenced mining operations in the "Six Feet" or Sidney Main coal, as it was called, on the north side of the harbor. During the next three years the mines were worked on Government account. To follow the further development of these coal fields in detail is not within the purpose of this chapter, and we will therefore pass over all the ups and downs till the mines were more extensively worked in very recent years, and that portion we leave for the present and take up the description of these measures from the best sources of information. The following is extracted from a publication of the Geological Survey of Canada, entitled a "Descriptive Note on the Sydney Coal Field of Cape Breton, to accompany a revised edition of the geological map of the coal field, being sheets 133, 134, 135, N. S. Summarized from the reports of the Geological Survey of Canada, with the addition of later observations, by Hugh Fletcher, B. A. 1900:"

"The land area occupied by the productive coal measures in the eastern or Sydney coal field may be estimated at 200 square miles, being about 32 miles in length from northwest to southeast by about

6 miles in width. It is limited on three sides by the Atlantic Ocean, and towards the southwest by the outcrop of the subjacent Lower Carboniferous rocks. This area forms the southern extremity of an extensive trough or basin, which is for the most part hidden under the ocean, and which has been corrugated by numerous subordinate folds, bringing the same coal seams repeatedly to the surface along the northeast coast of the island, under the most favorable conditions and circumstances for their extraction and shipment.

The whole coast is deeply indented by bays and channels approximately coinciding with the axes of these folds, and affording in the sea cliffs numerous natural sections of the strata and exposures of the coal seams. Some of these bays also constitute excellent harbors, one of which—Sydney Harbor—situated towards the center of the district, ranks among the finest and most commodious on the Atlantic coast of North America. The cliffs are generally from thirty to eighty feet high, standing perpendicularly, or frequently overhanging the sea. The country inland is of a gently rolling character, the maximum height being about 250 feet. Such advantages, combined with its highly favorable geographical position, point to this district as probably the most important in the Dominion for the supply of fuel to steamships navigating the Atlantic. During the few months of winter, when the more northerly harbors are closed or obstructed by ice, an outlet is afforded by the railway connecting many of the collieries with Louisburg, a fine harbor, open and safe for shipping at almost any season.

The aggregate thickness of coal in workable seams, outcropping on the shore, and for the most part exposed in the bays and cliffs, is from forty to fifty feet; the seams vary from three to nine feet in thickness. They generally dip at a very low angle, and appear to be very little affected by faults or disturbances. As the strata all dip seaward, much of the coal will be available in the submarine as well as the land areas. From experience at the Sydney mines it has been fully established that, with due caution and care, these submarine areas may be worked to a large extent.

The coal is of the bituminous, or soft, variety, with comparatively little diversity in the quality of the different seams, all of which yield a fuel exceedingly well adapted for general purposes, while that of some of them is especially applicable to the manufacture of gas. As compared with the Pictou coal, it is characterized, on the whole, by a greater proportion of ash, but on the other hand it usually contains a greater amount of sulphur.

. The rocks of this district are affected by three anticlinal and four synclinal folds, approximately parallel to one another, the latter named respectively the Cow Bay, Glace Bay, Sydney Harbor, and Bras d'Or basins. The several folds are, as already stated, marked by the occurrence of bays and channels running in a direction nearly parallel to their axes. The subdivisions are thus geographically, as well as geologically, well marked.

The strata associated with the coal seams may be described under the following heads: (1) Argillaceous shale; (2) Arenaceous shale; (3) Red and green marl; (4) Sandstone;. (5) Under-clay; (6) Limestone; (.7) Black shale; (8) Coal. Detailed sections of the alternations of these beds in the various basins are given in the report for 1874-75.

(1) Argillaceous Shales.—These strata, together with the arenaceous shales (2), into which they pass by insensible gradations, and red and green marl (3), from which they differ chiefly in color and in the general absence of lamination in the marls, constitute upwards of one-half of the total thickness of the measures. They no doubt originally consisted of fine mud, with more or less sand intermixed, and are of a gray or bluish-gray color. Some of the beds contain much iron pyrites, and nearly all are charged with argillaceous ironstone, sometimes in thin, regular layers, but generally in spherical or ellipsoidal nodules or concretions. They generally contain a great variety of fossil plants, chiefly ferns, the most delicate and fragile fronds and stems of these being often beautifully preserved.

: Many trunks of erect and prostrate Sigillariæ, in some cases with their Stigmaria roots attached and penetrating the coal seams, are found in the shales; and these appear to be confined to no particular horizons. The largest observed trunk was nearly five feet in diameter, but the usual size is from two to three feet, the bark being converted into coal matter. Some of the beds are very copiously charged with a small bivalve shell of the genus Naiadites associated with plant remains. The argillaceous shales are not always persistent, but often become arenaceous and sometimes pass into sandstone. Occasionally the change is so sudden as to give to the beds the appearance of being faulted.

In taking a general view of the mode of occurrence of the coal seams in this field, it appears that, although local variations are neither few nor small, their similarity of conditions and persistency over great areas is very remarkable. The disturbances which the strata have undergone are not of such a nature or amount as to occasion any great uncertainty in regard to the equivalency of the various seams at different points. In a few instances the coal seams are split by the gradual thickening of their clay partings. Some seams which are of workable thickness and good quality at one place become from similar causes unworkable at no great distance. Taking the average of all the sections measured, the total number of seams in the productive measures is twenty-four, of which six are three feet and upward in thickness, and the total average thickness of coal may be stated at forty-six feet.

The Cow Bay Basin.—On the north side of this basin the strata dip at a low angle. On the south side the angle of inclination is $35°$ to $42°$. The entire series of strata (which does not, however, include the upper portion of the productive measures developed in other parts of the field) is exposed within a distance of three miles and a half measured along the north side of the bay. The average breadth of the basin at the shore, between the outcrops of the lowest seam, does not exceed two miles and one-third, and it terminates to a point less than nine miles from the shore. Two seams, the Blockhouse and the McAulay, have been worked in this basin.

The Sydney Harbor Basin.—In the further extension of the coal measures westward, the next basin which comes under notice includes the Lingan, Low Point, and Sydney mines district, and extends from Indian Bay and Bridgeport Basin as far as Point Aconi, embracing all the coal seams in the field. An anticlinal axis that skirts the north shore of Bridgeport Basin, and runs thence westerly to the vicinity of South Bar on Sydney Harbor, divides this basin from that of Glace Bay. On the north side of this axis the rocks dip at angles varying from $12°$ to $16°$ at Lingan, increasing to $40°$ at the Victoria Mines. The sea-coast follows the fold of the strata in such a manner as to bring the entire volume of the coal measures upon the cliffs in several fine sections. From Low Point lighthouse to Lingan the strike of the rocks is nearly parallel to the shore.

The Bras d'Or Basin.—A little to the west of the Little Bras d'Or a low incline, running from Point Aconi to Saunders Cove, deflects the strata to the south to form the Bras d'Or Basin, which includes on opposite sides the Bouladerie and Cape Dauphin districts.

Mr. Robb has estimated that the total quantity which this field

9

is capable of yielding, exclusive of any that may be obtained from seams of a lesser thickness than four feet, is probably not less than one thousand million tons."

It is well understood that this coal field extends beneath the ocean, where in all probability the greater portion exists. Mr. Poole, in his report to the Commissioner of Mines for the year 1877, discusses this submarine area in a very interesting way as follows: "Assuming for the present a contour line three miles from shore to the boundary of profitable working, and four thousand feet the available depth, and that no seam under three feet will be worked, then taking into consideration the minimum cover of solid measures required by our present law, the reduction to be made on account of known anticlinals, and the average thickness of the seams along their shore crops, the submarine coal field of Cape Breton, from Mira Bay to Cape Dauphin, will yield 1,866,000,000 tons. This estimate assumes that after allowing one-fourteenth for unavoidable loss and waste in working, 1,400 tons may be obtained from each foot acre, as was assumed in the inquiry by the Royal Commission to ascertain the quantity of coal remaining unwrought in Great Britain. What proportion of the submerged field will be worked can only be roughly conjectured, for so many unknown quantities enter into the calculation. The thickness and quality of the seams, the faults and troubles to be met with in the workings, the cover to be left for security, the proportion of salable coal obtained, the increased cost, the engineering difficulties to be surmounted as depth and distance from the operating centers increase, the relative value of labor to that of fuel produced, these and other considerations have to be better known before an approach to accuracy in any estimate can be made. But basing a calculation on our present knowledge and our prospective ability to meet the anticipated difficulties within a reasonable limit of distance and depth, some idea of the future value of our sub-marine coal fields may be deduced, and the necessity demonstrated even now so conducting all inshore mining, that ultimate deep-sea mining may be safely prosecuted."

The Sidney coal field has become of so much importance and is destined to become a factor of dominating interest in the business affairs of Nova Scotia that it seems worth while to add the excellent description given by the late Richard Brown in his Coal Fields and Coal Trade of Cape Breton:

"The coal field of Sidney—the most extensive and, it may be safely asserted, the most valuable in the Province of Nova Scotia

—extends from Mira Bay on the east to Cape Dauphin on the west, a distance of thirty-one miles, being bounded on the north by the sea coast and on the south by the millstone grit formation. This tract of country, occupying an area of 200 square miles, is intersected or indented by several bays and harbors affording exposed sections of the coal measures in the cliffs, which, with the exception of a few sand beaches, extends along the whole coast from Mira Bay to Cape Dauphin. From these cliffs, varying from twenty to one hundred feet in height, the land rises gradually towards the interior, rarely attaining a greater elevation than 150 feet at a distance of one mile from the shore. Viewed from the sea, the general aspect of the country is undulating, low valleys proceeding inland from the bays and harbors, separated by gently swelling hills, terminating in headlands on the coast. There can be no doubt that at no distant day (in geological time) the coal country extended far to the northward, and occupied a considerable area now covered by the sea, as the scarped cliffs, composed of alternate beds of sandstones and shale, present but a feeble bulwark against the incessant attacks of the waves of the Atlantic. When the island last emerged from the sea, a low gravelly beach—not a cliff—naturally constituted the coast line; this beach, exposed to the abrading action of the surf, soon gave place to an incipient cliff, which has been steadily and gradually receding inland from that day to the present time. If not arrested in its progress by artificial means, in the course of time the whole of the coal lands will become the prey of the restless ocean. In some cases this wasting of the land must have proceeded at a more rapid rate than at others.

The Sydney Mines District, lying between Sydney harbor and the Little Entrance of the Bras d'Or Lakes, occupies an area of about ten square miles. Partial sections of the coal measures are visible at many places in the interior and on the borders of the district, but nowhere in such perfection as in the cliffs on the northwest shore of Sydney harbor, which exhibits a complete section at right angles to the line of strike three miles in length and 1,860 feet in depth, extending from Cranberry Head, at the entrance of the harbor, to Stubbert's Point, where the lowest beds of the coal measures may be seen lying conformably upon the millstone grit. All the principal seams of this district, except that at Cranberry Head, which runs into the sea, can be traced across the country from Sydney Harbor to the Little Entrance of the Bras d'Or Lakes. The Lloyd's Cove seam certainly is not quite continuous, as it crops out on the coast a quarter of a mile to the westward of Cranberry Head and runs into the sea, but owing to undulations in the measures at right angles with the strike the seam is deflected to the west, and rising out of the sea again appears above high-water mark near Bonar's Head, from whence it has been traced running nearly due north to Plant's Point. It maintains a tolerably uniform section until it nearly reaches Plant's Point, when, owing to a rapid increase in the thickness of the clay-parting, it is split into two distinct beds, separated by fifteen feet of shale. The two beds forming the lower seam at Chapel Point, sixteen and four inches thick, were both met with in sinking the Queen Pit three-fourths of a mile to the westward. They are visible in the cliff at Black Point, and also at Oxford Point. At the latter place the upper seam is four and the lower two feet six inches in thickness, separated by fifteen feet of shale.

The "six-foot," or main, seam maintains its full thickness as far as the "Big Pond," gradually bending round to the northward as it approaches the undulation in the measures in that locality. It has been traced by means of boring and sinking from Cox Hill on the north side of the Big Pond, as far as Kidd's Point on the Little Entrance of the Bras d'Or, or a distance of three miles, but between those two places its thickness nowhere exceeds four feet; at Kidd's Point it is only three feet six inches. The quality of the coal, however, shows no signs of deterioration. The Indian Cove seam has been worked at a pit one mile to the westward of Indian Cove, and at a place about one mile further in the same direction. It has also been proved at a trial pit and boring near the Little Entrance.

There is little variation of thickness at all these places. Its roof of bituminous shale, containing *Modioloe, Cyprides,* fish scales, etc., clearly establishes its identity from Indian Cove to the Little Entrance. On the shore of the Little Entrance there is another bed of coal four feet ten inches in depth, lying 200 feet below the preceding, which is probably the equivalent of the Stony seam of the Sydney mines section.

The inclination or dip of all the seams is about seven degrees, but its direction gradually comes around from the northeast on the shore of Sydney Harbor to nearly due east at the Little Entrance. The amount of dip has, however, been found to decrease rapidly toward the northeast in the underground workings at Sydney mines, where at the distance of one mile from the outcrop of the seam it does not exceed five degrees.

The Boulardrie District, bounded on the east and west by the Little and Great Entrances respectively, and on the south by the millstone grit, occupies an area of about eight square miles, containing several valuable seams of coal. Though separated from the Sydney Mines District only by the narrow channel of the Little Entrance, where it is not more than one hundred yards wide, the connection of the coal seams on each side of this channel cannot, owing to serious disturbances caused by faults, be satisfactorily determined. On the northwest side of the island of Boulardrie, fortunately, there is less disturbance, and a continuous section is visible in the cliffs from Point Aconi to the millstone grit, a distance of about six miles, interrupted at only two or three places by low shingle beaches. The three upper seams have been clearly traced by borings and trial pits across the northern end of Boulardrie Island, but those below have only been seen at the place marked on the map by black lines. There is, however, every reason to believe that they continue without interruption from the northwest shore in a southeasterly direction.

The Cape Dauphin District, at the northwestern extremity of the Sydney coal field, is separated from that of Boulardrie by the waters of the Great Entrance of Bras d'Or Lakes. Though occupying an area of little more than two square miles, all the formations of the Carboniferous series are here found between the southern flank of the Syenitic Hills of St. Ann's and the Great Entrance, perfect sections of the members of each formation being visible at Cape Dauphin and Kelly's Cove, the northern and southern ends of the district. At both of those places the strata are inclined at an angle of sixty degrees, dipping to the east, but midway between them the strata are nearly vertical, being squeezed or compressed within very narrow limits at their outcrops by the upheaval of the Syenitic rocks. The coal measures, as shown in the map, occupy an area of one square mile, in the form of a segment of a basin or trough similar to that of Cow Bay, at the eastern extremity of the coal fields. Two seams of coal in a vertical position have been discovered midway between Cape Dauphin and Kelly's Cove—one four feet, the other six feet in thickness, separated by eighty feet of strata. The six feet, which is the lowest seam, has also been discovered in a vertical position half a mile to the eastward, and the four feet, or upper, seam in a deep ravine half a mile to the southward, dipping easterly at an angle of twelve degrees.

THE GLACE BAY DISTRICT.

As the coal measures in the eastern division, between Mira Bay and Sydney Harbor, are most fully developed in the vicinity of Glace Bay, it will be best to describe them in the first instance; we shall then be better prepared, taking the Glace Bay series as a starting point, to define the mutual relations and establish the identity of the seams in the adjoining district. The coal seams are disposed in the form of an elliptical basin or trough, of which the longitudinal axis runs in a nearly east and west direction from Table Head towards the town of Sydney. By far the greater portion of this basin lies under the sea; the western end only, extending from the coast to the mill-stone grit, being available for mining purposes, though workings may at a future day be continued some distance under the sea. This contingency, however, is not likely to occur very shortly, as the coal measures of the Glace Bay basin, bounded on the east and west by the seacoast and the millstone grit, and on the north and south by the anticlinals of Lingan and Cow Bay, underlie a land area of at least sixty square miles.

The Hub seam, the highest in the series, is followed in succession by the Harbor, Three Foot, Back Pit, Phelan, Spencer or Ross seam, McRury seam, Lorway seam, Gardener seam, Not Named, Martin's seam.

The Hub and Harbor seams are confined to the promontory bounded by the shores of Glace Bay and Indian Bay, where they run under the sea and do not reappear. All the others, down to the McRury seam, continue to the eastward as far as the north head of Cow Bay, where they also run under the sea.

The Cow Bay basin is separated from that of Glace Bay by an anticlinal axis formed by an undulation in the coal measures, running in a westerly direction from the north end of Long Beach to its termination at a point three miles to the westward of Sand Lake, where it runs out. Its course is indicated by opposite dips of the strata on its north and south sides, and, occasionally, by blocks of weather-worn sandstone scattered along the surface, which probably have been detached from a thick bed of that material cropping out at Long Beach and along the line of the undulation or upheaval of the strata."

Without the diagrams and maps of Mr. Brown one cannot follow his description further, and it would be of but little satisfaction to do so because many of his remarks are given as conjectures. We may say that the description already given here by Mr. Fletcher covers the ground very well in a general way, and the same is true of the Lingan and Low Point District.

These magnificent coal fields have been worked in a small way, comparatively speaking, until they attracted American capital and enterprise, and then a new order of things began over a large portion of the district. It was officially reported as follows in the Report of the Department of Mines for 1893: "Since the date of my last report negotiations have been concluded by which a company called the Dominion Coal Company, Limited, has acquired the properties known as the Gowrie, Ontario, Caledonia, Reserve, International, Glace Bay, Sword, and Gardener collieries, embracing an area of about forty square miles. This leaves the Sydney Mines and Victoria as the only independent collieries working in Cape Breton County. The collieries of the new company have been connected with Sydney Harbor by extension of the International Railway, and the railway is being extended to Louisburg with the intention of utilizing the harbor as a winter port. The general manager of the new company is Mr. D. Mackeen, M. P., well known for his successful management of the Caledonia colliery."

By this new arrangement there were left but two coal-producing concerns in the Sydney coal field. The other was the General Mining Association. In 1892 the total output of nine collieries was 922,869 tons. The mines report for 1900 contains this important item: "The property of the General Mining Association of London, generally known as the Sydney Mines, was acquired by the Nova Scotia Steel Company. By this sale the General Mining Association has disposed of the last of its lease properties, and now disappears from the mining record of the Province. It is a matter of common knowledge that the acquisition of the mines of this Province by this company led to the first practical development of our coal resources. About the year 1827 they opened the collieries at the Joggins, New Glasgow, and North Sydney. Their operations, conducted on a large scale, contributed materially to the prosperity of the country, and set a high standard of business integrity. It is understood that the Nova Scotia Steel Company has in contemplation the erection of blast furnaces at North Sydney." The Report of the Department of Mines for 1901 informs us that the production of the Dominion Coal Company was for that year 2,352,567 tons as compared with 1,930,425 tons in 1900.

In connection with the coal industry these two powerful companies are large producers of iron and steel. It would require a daily bulletin to keep abreast of their progressive movements, and in view of this fact it would seem desirable to publish here an authoritative expression of their plans and aims, and this we are able to do by extracting two contributions from the Cape Breton edition of the Halifax Herald of August, 1901. Here then follows an article entitled, "The Hopes and Aims of the Dominion Coal Company, by Cornelius Shields, Second Vice President and General Manager."

"Briefly stated, the aims of the Dominion Coal Company are three-fold:

"(1) To develop the Cape Breton coal field, one of the largest and best in the world.

"(2) To give profitable employment to an ever increasing number—now 5,500—Canadian miners and workingmen.

"(3) To aid in the industrial growth of the country by the economical production of fuel, and to add to the importance of the coal trade itself by exporting the surplus to foreign markets.

"With these objects in view the collieries have been equipped with the best and most modern mining machinery. The machinery installed for the automatic handling of coal, from the time it leaves the miner until it is loaded into the ship's hold, is up to date and equal to the best in the United States.

"The Sydney & Louisburg Railway, owned by this company, has been modernized by the addition of steel coal cars of 50 tons capacity, which are hauled by the largest type of consolidation locomotives, capable of moving a train of 1,500 tons of coal, over a solidly built road bed, with all the structures of steel and masonry, and laid with 80 pound steel rails.

• "The shipping piers are situated at Sydney and Louisburg. These piers have a larger capacity than the present requirements, and were constructed to handle a largely increased output. On a single day this season the shipments from the piers reached 16,095 tons, and when the necessity arises the shipping facilities already provided are sufficient to ship 40,000 tons daily.

"Sydney Harbor has a world-wide reputation, and naval authorities are agreed that it is one of the finest harbors in the world, and that it shares this proud distinction with its Australian namesake. Situated at the entrance of the Gulf of St. Lawrence, it is singularly free from fog, and has an established reputation as a cheap and convenient coaling station for trans-Atlantic steamers. No port can be approached and entered with greater ease and security by soundings, and unchartered ships leaving Europe are usually addressed to Sydney for orders. The Dominion Coal Company has made provisions at the International Pier to supply ocean steamers with bunker coal promptly on arrival The despatch given in this respect is equal if not better than that obtained at any other port in the world.

Apart from its historic interest, Louisburg Harbor is also safe and easily accessible. The pier is now used chiefly by steamers carrying coal to Boston and other United States ports. The loading facilities for giving despatch to steamers are similar to those at the International Pier, and in addition there is a conveyer, or belt, for loading small coal from storage bins. This conveyer has a loading capacity of 750 tons per hour. The Black Diamond Steamship line is owned by the Dominion Coal Company. The fleet now in commission consists of seven ships, which are owned by the company, and fourteen operated under charters. The capacities of these steamers varies from 1,700 to 6,000 tons gross. The company also owns and operates several barges. At Montreal, discharging towers for the rapid unloading of ships, have been erected. These towers have a maximum capacity of 10,000 tons per day, thus giving prompt dispatch to steamships.

The Cape Breton coal field, comprising an area of 500 square miles, is already known to contain five workable coal seams, varying in thickness from five to nine feet. Only two seams are now worked; the other three are practically undeveloped. At a time when economists are discussing the rapid exhaustion of the coal reserves of Great Britain, and the impetus thus given to American coal and iron industries, the great coal resources of this part of the British Empire have been overlooked. Already, the policy adopted by the Dominion Coal Company, has made possible the creation of an iron and steel industry, which is capable of further expansion, will prove a rival of the great corporations of the United States. The interests of both the steel and coal companies here, as elsewhere, are closely allied. The success of these valuable properties is now assured. With the present output of the collieries of 10,000 to 12,000 tons daily, the yearly production should exceed 3,000,-000 tons. To utilize the present workings to the best advantage, a further increase may be gradual. Though the Canadian market may be expected to absorb an increasing quantity of coal from year to year, the geographical position of the western inland provinces, bordering on the coal producing states of the neighboring republic, will in a large measure exclude us from that territory. With our collieries situated on the Atlantic seaboard, at the door of a waterway reaching all parts of the world, and with cheap transportation, we expect to export large quantities of coal to the markets of Europe and the Mediterranean. To do this successfully, however, a new business must be created, and another fleet of steamships of large coal-carrying capacity will be required.

Within the past year American coal has gained a foothold in the European market. Sydney is 1,000 miles nearer Europe than either Norfolk or Newport News, the principal shipping ports for American coal and the quality of Cape Breton coal is equal to that of American coal. We should therefore, in time, be successful in building up a large export trade. Our coal is, however, yet unknown abroad, and it may be pointed out as an instance of the prejudice existing in Great Britain and fostered by the British coal owners, that the warships of the British fleet on the North Atlantic Station, continue to import and use Welch coal at double the price for which Nova Scotia coal, equally serviceable, can be bought.

When the class of ships required has been supplied, probably by ' shipyards in our own province, and with Cape Breton coal better known, and its excellent qualities appreciated abroad; and when the iron, and kindred industries are more firmly established, the coal trade of Cape Breton should enter upon an era of substantial prosperity and provide employment for a large population of prosperous and contented workmen."

The following article entitled "Hopes and Aims of Nova Scotia Steel and Coal Company," is by Mr. John F. Stairs, President:

"The Nova Scotia Steel and Coal Company, Limited, have purchased the properties and business of the Nova Scotia Steel Company, Limited, and they will carry on the business in all its branches, including the coal mines of Sydney ·Mines, C. B., a brief account of the business recently purchased and what the company purpose doing in the near future may be of interest to your readers. For the purposes of this letter the business of the company may be divided into four principal branches—mining and selling iron ore, mining and selling coal, smelting pig iron and making steel. For some years past iron ore has been shipped from the company's mines at Wabana, Conception Bay, Newfoundland, and a good demand exists for it in Germany, Great Britain, and the United States, besides what the company uses in its own operations at Ferrona, Pictou County. The output of the mines during the shipping season is about 300,000 tons. The efficiency of the plant is evidenced by the fact that over 3,500 tons have been mined in a day, and that a steamer carrying 7,300 tons has been loaded in five hours, and as much as 21,000 tons have been loaded within thirty hours. Shipments are now being made to Germany, the United States, and Scotland. About 270,000 tons have been sold for shipment this year, and 125,000 tons have been sold for delivery each year up to 1905.

"The company now operate the coal areas lately owned by the General Mining Association at Sydney Mines. It is estimated that these areas contain upwards of 200,000,000 tons of coal—a sufficient supply, even with a largely increased output over that proposed, to last for many generations. The reputation of the coal shipped from Sydney Mines is so well known that it only need be referred to. The output of the mines for some years averaged about 250,000 tons per year, and about this quantity is now being taken out. It is expected that 100,000 tons of this coal will be made into coke yearly at the coke ovens, which are now being erected at the Sydney Mines. This coke will be used at the company's blast furnaces, at Ferrona. The coal from these mines has been proved to be very suitable for making coke for cold blast furnace use. The company having tried many of the coals produced in Nova Scotia and Cape Breton, has not found any so well suited for making coke as that which is taken from the old Sydney Mines. In fact it is largely because this coal was found to make coke so much superior to that from any other of the Nova Scotia or Cape Breton coals that the company purchased the property. Those who purchase old Sydney Mines coal for household and other purposes may depend upon getting a thoroughly screened coal, as the slack is all retained at the mines for coke making. The company also own coal areas near Trenton which are now being opened up, the output of which will supply the coal required for steam and heating purposes at the Trenton Steel Works. The other two branches of the company's business, viz., smelting pig iron and making steel, are carried on at Ferrona, and with the iron ore from Wabana, and from the company's other mine in Nova Scotia, the limestone from Pictou County, and the coke from Sydney Mines, the pig iron is produced.

"Some of this is sold as foundry pig iron throughout the Dominion, but the largest portion is used for the manufacture of steel at Trenton.

"The business of the various works and mines now owned and operated by the company has been very successful and profitable. The Nova Scotia Steel Company paid a dividend of 8 per cent. upon its preference stock, and frequently paid dividends varying from 8 per cent. to 16 per cent. upon its common stock. A dividend of 8 per cent. for 1899 and 10 per cent. for 1900 was paid upon the common stock; and for many years past the Sydney Mines as operated by the General Mining Association paid large dividends to its shareholders. For the past three years the average profit of the business now carried on by this company was $512,215 per year. It is the intention of the company to improve the plant at North Sydney and New Glasgow as experience may show to be expedient, so that the production of iron and steel may be increased and the cost reduced. It is the intention of the company to open up immediately further seams at Sydney Mines. The present working will also be developed and the plant improved by the addition of machinery for increasing the output and reducing the cost of mining. When the improvements contemplated are effected and the new seams opened up, the mines will give an output of 1,000,000 tons per annum. As a large portion of this coal will be shipped by water, and as dispatch in loading is one of the vital points in connection with cheap transportation, a new shipping pier, equipped with the very best rapid-loading facilities, will be built. The commercial manager of the company last winter visited all the principal Mediterranean coal-importing ports of France and Italy, where last year a considerable quantity of American coal was sold, and the company are now in possession of reliable detailed information relative to that trade. With large steamers, designed for rapid discharging, it is not unlikely that "Old Sydney Mines" coal may soon be exported in considerable quantities to these markets. When the company undertakes this business the experience already gained by its officers in rapid loading, transporting, aand discharging of large shipments of iron ore to Great Britain, Germany, and the United States will be of the greatest service to the company."

We will now turn to Inverness County and give a description of the coal outcrop on the gulf shore of the island. The account given by the late Mr. Richard Brown of the general features runs as follows: "Although the lower Carboniferous rocks extend, without interruption, along the western coast of Cape Breton, from Seal Cove Bay, at the southern end of the Gut of Canseau, to Cheticamp, on the shore of the Gulf of St. Lawrence—a distance of eighty miles—small patches of the productive coal measures have only yet been discovered at Port Hood, Mabou, Broad Cove, and Chimney Corner in the county of Inverness, and at Seal Coal Bay in the county of Richmond. At all of these places the measures consist of sandstone and shale, similar to those of the Sydney coal fields, resting upon the millstone grit, and containing several seams of coal of considerable thickness, but of small extent, being evidently detached portions of a large coal field lying under the waters of the Gulf of St. Lawrence, separated from each other in most cases by the undulations of the Carboniferous rocks projecting into the sea. As the lower member of the Carboniferous series extend from the coast at least ten miles inland towards Margarie River and Lake Ainslie, it is very probable that small basins of the coal measures may some day be discovered in the interior. Two thin seams of coal have indeed been discovered on the eastern flanks of the conglomerate hills near the mouth of the Middle River, which runs into the Bras d'Or Lake, but they probably are of older date than the coal measures on the Gulf shore, being apparently members of Carboniferous formation. They are of no economic value."

To follow Mr. Brown further here would be misleading, for the reason that explorations since the date of his writing have thrown new light on the coal areas he discusses. Dr. E. Gilpin, in his Report on the Mines and Mineral Lands of Nova Scotia, 1880, mentions this region in· the following terms: "From Cheticamp to Judique, on the western shore of Cape Breton, there extends a narrow and broken line of productive measures, forming the edges of great basins of coal which have long ago disappeared beneath the Gulf of St. Lawrence.

"At Chimney Corner Professor Hynd reported two groups of seams, nothing being known of the lower. The upper gave the following section.

	Feet.	Inches.
Thin seams	1	6
Strata	300	
Coal	3	
Strata	88	
Coal	5	
Strata	200	
Coal	3	8

"The measures here form a sharp synclinal, about three-quarters of a mile wide, giving an estimated land area of about five square miles. However, but little is yet known of the extent of the seams of the lower group.

"At Broad Cove, about ten miles to the southwest, the following section of seams, contained in about 2,000 feet of strata, is said to exist, and is given on Mr. A. Wright's authority:

First seam	2 feet.	
Second seam	2 feet.	
Third seam	3 feet.	McKinnon Brook.
Fourth seam	4 feet.	McKinnon Brook.
Fifth seam	12 feet.	
Sixth seam	7 feet.	Seam now worked.
Seventh seam	4 feet.	Big River.
Eighth seam	3 feet.	

"The extent of the productive measures here is not yet known positively, but areas embracing about twenty square miles, believed to hold workable coal, have been secured by various parties.

"Another of these small but valuable coal fields occurs at Mabou. Here the outcrop of the following beds are reported, namely, a 4 foot bed, a 13 foot bed about 20 feet above the first, a 7 foot seam 120 feet higher, and a 5 foot seam. There are also several other, seams, the size and extent of which are unknown. The usual basin shape is presented here with an area somewhat smaller than at Broad Cove.

"At Port Hood one seam only has been definitely tested, although the presence of several others has been proved. Here the strata run more nearly parallel with the shore and extend along it about two miles. The seam opened has a thickness of about 6 feet. Workings were pushed a short distance under the sea, but are discontinued. The outcrop of another 6 foot seam is known at low water. Coal occurs again at Little Judique, in close proximity to gypsum and limestone."

In a Summary Report of the Canadian Geological Survey for the Year 1900 occurs the following mention of these coal areas: "Nearly eight weeks were spent in Cape Breton, principally in re-examining the coal measures of the western or Inverness coal field between Margaree Harbor and Little Judique, to the development of which an impetus has been given by the construction of a line of railway from Port Hastings to the Broad Cove mines. At Port Hood mines the slope is now down about 1,150 feet, the dip being throughout about twenty-four degrees and the coal about 7 feet thick. Levels have been turned away north and south and balances and crosses begun. The manager, Mr. Johnson, is of the opinion that the present output of one hundred tons a day can be increased to four hundred tons by the first of June.

"Active work on a large scale has also begun at Broad Cove mines. The coal seams all border on the shore and are not known to extend far inland. Both at Port Hood and Broad Cove the workings will be largely under the sea, and the question of the conditions under which the sea areas can be won becomes one of great importance."

The Report of the Department of Mines for the Year 1902 shows a good deal of activity in the way of preparation for work on a large scale, both at Broad Cove and Port Hood.

THE RICHMOND COUNTY COAL FIELD.

This area is well described by Mr. Richard Brown as follows: "It is situated at the southern extremity of the island, between the river Inhabitants and the Gut of Canseau. The Carboniferous rocks in this district cover an area of about twenty square miles, and contain several workable seams of coal. In the cliff on the western shore of Seal Cove Bay, close to the southern end of the Gut of Canseau, there is a seam eleven feet in thickness, composed of alternating layers of coal and bituminous shale; another, four feet thick, clear coal; and a third, five feet and a half thick, including a fifteen inch layer of shale in the middle. All these seams occur within very narrow limits, dipping to the southwest at an angle of eighty degrees.

"At Little River, a small stream running into Seal Cove Bay, two miles and a half to the northeast of the preceding locality, there are two seams, one three, the other four feet in thickness, nearly in a vertical position, separated by 154 feet of sandstones and shales. Traces of coal have also been seen at two places to the eastward, near the mouth of the river Inhabitants. The measures in this coal field are, however, so much disturbed by faults that the extent and relative position of the several seams cannot be made out. Any attempt to ascertain the true position, extent, and consequent value of the seams will be attended with much expense, as the country is low and there are few cliffs or natural sections. The outcrops of the strata are also concealed by a thick deposit of boulder clay. The seams all occur in situations favorable for shipment." We now take leave of the Cape Breton coal fields, and proceed to give some account of the valuable deposits in the peninsula, beginning with those in Pictou County. For this purpose we will quote from Dr. Gilpin's Government Report on the Mines of Nova Scotia, 1880:

"The Pictou coal field lies immediately south of the town of New Glasgow. The area of the field may be estimated at about thirty-five square miles, and it extends from a point near Sutherland's River to the Middle River of Pictou. This area, although comparatively limited, contains a large amount of coal, owing to the unusual size of the beds and the good exposure of the crops. The district may be roughly described as forming a main east and west synclinal, disturbed and shifted by minor north and south undulations, which expose the outcrops of the seams in irregular curves and basins.

"The former extent of this coal field must have been very considerably larger. It now forms an irregular basin, let down on all sides among rocks of an older age. When we consider that in the Albion mines district there is a section of measure 2,450 feet in vertical thickness, holding one hundred feet of coal, lying at an angle eighteen degrees denuded to a horizontal plane, it is evident that this great mass of sediments, when lying undisturbed, must have stretched a considerable distance over what are now the boundary rocks.

"From the information at present available, the seams of this district may be divided into an upper and lower group, all included in 5,567 feet of measures, according to Sir William Logan. The upper group contains the following beds:

> Captain seam ....4 feet thick.
> Millrace ....,.4 feet.
> Geo. McKay ....4 feet 10 inches.
> Seam ....6 feet.
> McBean seam ....8 feet thick.
> Pottery seam ....2 feet 9 inches thick.
> Stewart McLennan ....4 feet thick.

"The first three mentioned seams occur as a small basin, in the eastern part of the district, and they are also believed to occur again as a small basin immediately in the rear of New Glasgow, while it is not yet settled whether the six and eight foot seams crop in the interval between the two basins, or reappear only near New Glasgow. This uncertainty is owing to the fact that little exploratory work has been done in this part of the coal field.

"The upper group is represented on the western side of the East River by the small seams lying along the axis of the Albion Synclinal and not at present considered as occupying an area requiring extended notice.

"The lower group, hidden in the eastern district by the measures

holding the seams just described, has been extensively worked to the
west of the East River, and present the following section:

Main seam	34 feet 7 inches.
Deep seam	22 feet 11 inches.
Third seam	5 feet 7 inches.
Purvis seam	3 feet 6 inches.
Fleming seam	3 feet 3 inches.
McGregor	12 feet.
Stellar seam	5 feet.
Seam A	11 feet.
Seam C	10 feet.

"There are other underlying seams.

"The general form of the main seam is that of an irregular
synclinal, the north edge of which has been proved on the Montreal
and Pictou area, opposite New Glasgow. The seam opened at Culton's
Mill Pond, to the southeast of the Intercolonial Colliery, is believed
to represent the extreme southerly extension of the main and other
seams in that part of the district. The coal from this seam at the
Albion Mine is well known as a very good steam coal, and also yields
a coke of good quality. There are within the limits of the district
several large and valuable undeveloped areas; and in the event of an
extension of trade the output of this coal field could be largely increased. No complete estimate has yet been made of the coal contents
of this district, as there is so large a portion of it untested. An idea
of the immense quantity of coal contained by the thick seams of this
field in a limited space may be gathered from the fact that the area
of the Halifax Company is estimated to contain 67,365,000 tons of
available coal, after making every deduction for faults, lost pillars, etc.

"The northern extension of this coal field is cut off at New Glasgow
by a bed of conglomerate believed to have been brought up by a
fault from the upper part of the millstone grit. This is succeeded to
the north, in the district between New Glasgow and Pictou, by the
upper non-productive measures. It is the opinion of Dr. Dawson and
others that the true coal measures are beneath this covering of new
strata. Attempts were made to prove this by a bore hole some years
ago, but the operation was not carried far enough to allow of a
decision. The truth of the opinion, which certainly is based on good
grounds, should be carefully tested. If the anticipations proved correct, an immense coal field would be opened up under and around
Pictou Harbor, the value of which could scarcely be estimated."

The production of the Pictou County coal mines has been limited by the demand, and not by the opportunities to obtain the coal, which are equal to an immense output. Says Prof. Leslie: "The Albion Mines beds are very extraordinary deposits; they form an exception to all the phenomena of coal in the British provincial coal regions. Nothing like them has ever been discovered in the Provinces. The thickest beds discovered in Cape Breton, East Coast, are never over twelve feet thick, and usually under nine feet; but here we have one bed—the main seam—thirty feet six inches thick, of which twenty-four feet are good coal, the other portion poor coal and black shale in intermediate layers. The enormous quantity of coal here presented can only be estimated properly by those who have been used to the vast operations on the gray ash part of the anthracite, where the regular thirty feet vein yields at least twenty millions of tons to the square mile after all deductions have been made."

The total coal production of Pictou County for the year 1901, as given in the Report of the Department of Mines, is 490,168 tons, against 538,884 tons in 1900. The Acadia Company raised 271,145 tons, and the Intercolonial Company raised 219,023 tons. During the summer the Nova Scotia Steel and Coal Company opened a colliery on one of the seams of the marsh group between New Glasgow and Thorburn.

To describe in any detail the fine equipments of the companies operating the coal mines of this district would require not only a good deal of space, but in these days of rapid changes resulting in the amalgamation of large concerns my story might easily become a bit of ancient history before it got out of the publisher's hands. Before me lies a finely illustrated circular setting forth the management and many merits of the Drummond Colliery, that in the last thirty-two years of its operation the proprietors have paid out in wages $3,544,000, for goods purchased $1,090,000, and for royalty on coal to the Government of Nova Scotia $239,000. Here too before me is no lack of material descriptive of the great works of the Nova Scotia Steel and Coal Company at Ferrona and Trenton in this county. Something of the history of this huge concern may be found in the chapter on iron in this volume. In connection with the "Stella" and other measures has sprung up the thriving community of Stellarton, where large mining operations are carried on at the Albion Mines. Whoever desires to see a detailed history of the various companies and their operations in this county will find much in that line in Dr. Patterson's excellent History of Pictou County. Enough has been set down here to show the vast quantity of coal that is lying within the limits of this district. The early settlers there, who suffered great hardships, little thought that under their feet were national bonanzas and kings' ransoms that had been getting into conditions suitable for human use during some twenty million years. The Pictou collieries have been very unfortunate in destructive fires and fatal explosions. Owing to many causes, during the last twenty years there has been but little gain in the amount of output, but the prospect is now very encouraging for a notable enlargement of the business. This county long stood at the head of our coal producers, but in 1881 Cape Breton County forged ahead by a long distance, and ever since has made competition for first place entirely hopeless.

We come now to consider the coal fields of Cumberland County. The total output for the year 1901 was 478,226 tons, a little falling away from the production of 1900. It should be borne in mind that the output in all cases is mostly governed by the amount that can find a market, and in this respect is unlike the metallic mines that are generally worked to their full capacity.

We will refer now to Dr. Gilpin's Government report made in 1880 for general information concerning the coal areas of this county.

"Cumberland County has only recently begun to take its place among the coal-producing districts. The first openings were made at the Joggins by the General Mining Association on two seams four and six feet thick. The extension of these seams inland forms what is considered the northern edge of the coal field, and openings have been made at several points on seams considered their equivalent. The identification of the seams, however, is not yet settled, as the continuity of the measures is broken by faults. At the River Herbert a five-foot seam has been opened, holding two partings, sixteen and ten inches thick, of shale. At Maccan only two seams have been found of workable size, the lower being four feet four inches thick, and the upper two feet four inches thick."

A dozen years before Dr. Gilpin made his report from which I have quoted, some small discoveries of coal had been made at Spring Hill, that has since become a famous mining locality. In the Report of the Chief Commissioner of Mines for 1868 there is the following mention made of this locality: "No new coal operations of any moment have been begun in this county, with the exception of some explorations at Spring Hill on the areas held by Mr. Black, by whom six shafts have been sunk, varying in depth from twenty to forty feet. These have been put down at intervals over a distance of about three-quarters 'of a mile, and have proved a very fine seam of coal, the thickness of which is eleven feet three inches; it is being worked for land sale purposes. Other seams have also been found on the property, which have 'not yet, however, been fully opened. They appear to be of a workable thickness. Total expenditure, $1,438. The settlement of the Intercolonial Railway, which is now understood will pass within three or four miles of the mines, and more particularly the speedy commencement of its construction, will tend to hasten the development of this district; and a very important addition to the coal-producing capabilities of the Province, it may be reasonably expected, will in no long time ensue. The position of this coal field in relation to the seaboard, and the facility of transmission thence of its produce, must give it some advantages over more distant localities.'

It may be of interest to note from year to year the progress of this prospect to a mine of great importance, producing nearly one-half million tons annually. The report of the next year, 1869, remarks that "the operations at Spring Hill have been chiefly of an exploratory character. On the same seam opened last year by Mr. Black, levels have been driven a short distance from one of the shafts, and coal has been worked for land sale purposes. Eastward from the shaft, explorations have for some time been carried on for the purpose of proving the positions of the beds of coal before fixing on a site on which to establish works of an extensive and substantial character. These explorations have been made both on the property of Mr. Black and also on the areas belonging to the Hon. A. McFarlane; and although not yet completed, they have proved an uninterrupted range of the seams for some distance in an easterly direction. The openings have been made both on the crop of the seam in which mining has been carried on, and on that of one to the north of it, the thickness of which is thirteen feet three inches. Other seams have also been struck, the coal in all of them being of excellent quality. The subjoined analysis of the coal from the eleven foot three inch seam, the one at present worked, was recently made by the Geological Survey of Canada:

"Volatile matter, water included 35.39
Fixed carbon 60.46
Ash ....:.......................... 4.15
The expenditure for prospecting.......$ 807.34
A joint expenditure is returned of...... 1,711.22"

In the Commissioner's Report for 1873 he says: "Important additions to our knowledge of the resources of the Spring Hill district have been made. The Black or eleven-foot seam has been proved to the westward to lie in a straight line as far as Miller's Hotel, where it bends somewhat suddenly around to the southward. The continuation appears to be further deflected until at a distance of one mile from the Spring Hill Colliery, it, or a seam very similar in character, is found trending still more to the eastward and with a southerly dip. Should subsequent explorations prove the correctness of this surmise, and determine the lay of the seam, untroubled by serious faults, a rapid development of the coal trade in this county may be anticipated. The thirteen-foot seam, originally discovered on the General Mining Association's property, has been proved to be an overlying seam, but has not yet been traced beyond the bend. In anticipation of the facilities of transit which the trade of this county must require when the collieries now being started are fully developed, and when the output exceeds the local demand along the line of the Intercolonial Railway, a company has already begun to build a railway from Spring Hill to Parrsboro. By this branch road the mines will be put into communication with the tidewater at the nearest and most convenient point of shipment, and the operators be enabled to compete in the market of New England, at present chiefly supplied from Cape Breton."

Passing over several years during which there was a continuous verification of the good predictions made for this property, we find that the report for 1886 has this item of interest concerning Spring Hill: "The Cumberland Railway and Coal Company have greatly enlarged their operations during the year. The output was 416,769 tons, compared with 335,955 in 1885."

We come now to consider the Joggins coal field on the Chignecto Channel. They are not remarkable for their output of coal, but they are famous in the world of science. Nowhere is there known such a section of coal measures exposed as the shores of this district present. Sixty years ago the greatest geologist, in the person of Sir Charles Lyell, visited and examined this locality, and thereby contributed very largely to a better understanding of the more difficult problems involved in the structure, and directing attention abroad to our coal measures by his own published accounts of his observations. He was accompanied by Mr. John William Dawson, afterwards Sir William Dawson, who was then a young man of great promise, and later on published a most exhaustive account of this locality. With them was Dr. Abraham Gesner, whose account of this section published in his "Geology and Mineralogy of Nova Scotia," had first of all directed Lyell's attention to the place. Writing in 1828, Haliburton gives some account of this shore and its remarkable display of the coal seams. Dawson is the best guide and interpreter in this region, and we will follow his description as it occurs in the first edition of his Acadian Geology, 1855: "This remarkable section, well known to geologists as the South Joggins section, extends across almost the whole north side of the Cumberland trough, and exhibits its beds in a continuous series, dipping south twenty-five degrees west at an angle of nineteen degrees; so that in proceeding along the coast from north to south for a distance of about ten miles, we constantly find newer and newer beds, and these may be seen both in bold cliff and in a clean shore, which at low tide extends to a distance of 200 yards from its base. We thus see a series of beds amounting to more than 14,000 feet in vertical thickness, and extending from the marine limestone of the Lower Carboniferous series to the top of the coal formation. In the cliff and on the beach more than seventy seams of coal may be seen, with their roof-shales and under-clays, and erect plants appear at as many distinct levels; while the action of the waves and of the tide, which rises to the height of forty feet, prevents the collection of debris at the foot of the cliff, and continually exposes new and fresh surfaces of the rock."

Probably no other coal section in the world affords at the same time such ample evidence of its origin and such an exhibition of vegetable and animal life of that age. The section may well be compared to the leaves of a mighty book on which are inscribed in one way and another the records of succeeding events that covered more than a million years, when as yet there was no higher creature in all the world than an imperfect lizard. In these strata one may see fossil trees rooted in the under-clays, turned to coal where they stood. One may see the unmistakable proofs of the submergence of forest after forest, to be covered with sand and mud that formed another soil when it emerged above the waters again. The once hollow stumps of those coal trees have yielded reptilian remains of great interest, and in fact they were the first of their kind discovered in American coal measures when found there by Dawson and Lyell.

Sir Charles Lyell, in his "Travels in North America," remarks that "I was particularly desirous, before I left England, of examining the numerous fossil trees alluded to by Dr. Gesner as imbedded in an upright position at many different levels in the cliffs of the South Joggins, near Minudie. I felt convinced that, if I could verify the accounts of which I had read of the superposition of so many different tiers of trees, each representing forests which grew in succession on the same area, one above another, if I could prove at the same time their connection with seams of coal, it would go farther than any facts yet recorded to confirm the theory that coal in general is derived from vegetables produced on the spots where the carbonaceous matter is now stored up in the earth. At Wolfville I hired a schooner which soon carried us across the Basin of Mines to Parrsborough. At that place I was joined by Dr. Gesner, and we went together to Minudie." I cannot, for lack of space, follow Sir Charles into the details of his examination, but it may be remarked that his own eyes confirmed the written accounts of Haliburton and Gesner, and he felt himself well repaid for this tedious detour from his main journey.

From the year 1862 there has been issued regularly a report of the Commissioner of Mines, and the first mention of the coal mines occurs in that of the year 1866, and therein is the first and earliest item within my reach of the operation of the Joggins Colliery, and it runs in this way: "Joggins Colliery.—Notwithstanding the well-deserved fame to which the extensively developed section of the coal measures on this coast has given rise, and the presence in it of over seventy beds of coal, only two seams are worked; the others being too thin to be worth opening. The principal workings are in the seam opened some years ago by the General Mining Association, and locally known as the King's seam. It dips to the southwest at an angle with the horizon of 19 degrees. On the surface the erections consist of a small steam engine of nine horse power for drawing the coal up the shaft, screens for cleaning the coal, and thirty-five workmen's houses and workshops, etc. The coal is taken in wagons carrying one and one-half ton to the shipping wharf near the adit. Situated 1,500 yards to the north of the crop of the King's seam is the other seam worked by this mine, and locally termed the 'Hard Scrabble' or 'Cumberland seam.'"

From the date of this report work has been continuous at this colliery, but at no time a large producer. Through the courtesy of Robert Archibald, Esq., the late manager of the Canadian Coals and Railway Co., Limited, that operates the Joggins Mines, I am enabled to give the following items of interest: "Our property is twelve

square miles in extent. The seam varies in thickness, and its present
working face is from four feet and a half to five feet and a half.
The economic working of the seam is hindered somewhat by a band
of fireclay situated in the center of the seam, varying from one foot
to four feet in thickness. There are two slopes in operation, each
sunk to a depth of 2,500 feet, and one of them is being sunk an
additional depth of 600 feet. The coal is of good quality, and finds
a ready market, principally in St. John, N. B. The property has
been much improved lately. The mine is situated about twelve miles
from Maccan on the Intercolonial Railway, and one mile from the
shore, where a wharf and breakwater have been built; and schooners
carrying from 70 to 200 tons of coal are loaded there for Bay of
Fundy ports. The average daily output at present, 1902, is about
350 tons, and is being rapidly increased. The coal is practically
limitless."

The other small collieries of this district, according to official
reports, are irregular producers. Their locations and interelations
are described by Dawson as follows in his second edition of Acadian
Geology, 1878: "Since the expiry of the exclusive privileges of the
General Mining Association attempts have been made to obviate this
disadvantage by opening mines on the Herbert and Maccan Rivers.
Six companies have opened works in this part of the district, under
the names of the Victoria, Maccan, Chignecto, Lawrence, St. George,
and New York and Acadia Mines. The beds which they work seem
to be of a similar character with those of the Joggins, of which they
are the direct continuation."

It is very evident that Cumberland County is exceedingly rich in
coal, and we may be sure that the small amount of prospecting has
not yet revealed what the future investigator of the carboniferous
system will yet bring to light.

In Antigonish County there is a small area of coal measures
where several seams have been discovered varying in thickness from
three to six feet, accompanied by beds of oil shale. No collieries are
in operation there, but the future, with other economic conditions,
will doubtless make this district of value.

Here we come to an end of the chapter on coal, that has already
outrun its assigned limits. I hope it contains something that somebody will like to consult. At any rate, here is the proof that Nova
Scotia contains vast stores of a form of wealth that must always be
in demand. At no point is it possible for a colliery to be far removed

from a seaport. It may be confidently expected that the productive area of Cape Breton coal measures will be greatly extended when the millstone grit formation has been thoroughly prospected. It may be a matter of interest to know that during twenty-five years ending in 1900 the total output of the coal mines of Nova Scotia was forty-three million tons, an average of 1,720,000 tons per annum, but this amount has since been far exceeded, as I have already shown. If the Provincial Government will take an interest in bringing to light the vast deposits of iron ore, especially in Cape Breton, it will be an intelligent policy almost sure to be followed by great economic results.

CHAPTER X.

This county has an area of 736 square miles, and this is within two counties of being the smallest in the Province. The population of 21,884 is not far behind the foremost in that respect. It is triangular in shape and bounded by Digby, Shelburne, and the ocean. The physical aspect is not strikingly different from the Atlantic Counties of the Province. Fishing, farming, lumbering, ship-building, and mercantile business of one kind and another are carried on in this region. Yarmouth was visited by De Monts and Champlain in the summer of 1604; the latter named the entrance to the harbor Cape Forchu, a designation that it still bears. He says of the harbor: "It is very good for vessels as regards its entrance, but further up, it is almost dry at low tide, with the exception of a small river all surrounded by meadows which render the place very agreeable." His own words are: "Ce port est fort bon pour les vaisseaux en son entree, mais au fond il asseche presque tout de basse mer, hors le cours d'une petite riviere, tout environnee de prairies qui rendent ce lieu assez agreable." Campbell, in his history of Yarmouth, says: "This is certainly a highly flattering account of our mud flats, to describe them as meadows, and as rendering the place very agreeable. No doubt to the casual visitor in the spring of the year, and when the long fresh eel-grass was undisturbed by the keels of vessels and the hoe of the clam-digger, it would present a much more pleasing object than it does now, although it requires some exercise of imagination to speak of the flats as meadows."

There was an older discovery of America than that of Columbus; almost 500 years before, the Scandinavians of Iceland, who were fairly in league with the sea, drove their venturous prows into these strange waters when they had neither compass, quadrant, nor chart. The account of their voyages is preserved in Icelandic writings. That they somewhere landed in Nova Scotia as they coasted from Greenland is a very reasonable expectation; that they made the port of Yarmouth seems to be indicated by the narrative. As if to confirm this latter conjecture, there have been discovered two inscribed stones within the limits of the harbor. One of them was found nearly a hundred years ago, the other only four years ago. They were about

VIEW OF YARMOUTH AND HARBOR.

WILLIAM STREET, YARMOUTH.

YARMOUTH. STREET VIEW, WITH THORN HEDGES.

one mile apart and several hundred pounds in weight. The writing is cut into a hard quartzose rock in straight lines, and seems to be in the old Runic characters employed by the Scandinavians. An expert in such matters, Mr. Henry Phillips interprets the brief record as follows: "HARKUSSEN MEN VARU" (meaning "Harko's son addressed the men"). This may not conclusively settle the matter of their origin and import, but it raises a strong presumption that they are genuine records of those intrepid voyagers. More light is desirable and it would be no matter for surprise if other records are forthcoming.

The first white settlers of Yarmouth County were French. I find no exact date of their coming, and very likely there is none outside of France. In 1625 Charles de la Tour was living not far to the eastward on a harbor that still bears his name, where he had built a fort; very likely that his people began to make them homes in Yarmouth County about that time. Before the general expulsion of the Acadians in 1755 there were evidently several points where these people had made small settlements—at Chebogue, Chegoggin, Eel Brook, Tusket, Pubnico, and Vaughan's Lake. As a rule they shared the fate of the other Acadians, and their old cellars long remained as grim and yawning monuments of the old days and their pathetic hardships. A half dozen years later New Englanders began to arrive for permanent settlement. The history of Yarmouth County may be said to have then its beginning. The older occupancy came to a tragical end, the details of which had better be forgotten than kept alive by any persons or publications. The present generation is not responsible for the provocation nor the punishment. We can never mend the past. What's done is done, but we can improve upon the record. Given now such a choice, the Acadians would take some other course, and given such a problem the Government would employ a less drastic remedy for its solution. Many of these unfortunate people were able to return not long afterwards under a better understanding and make them new homes. How well they have succeeded in becoming an important element in the county we shall see later on.

In 1759 Governor Lawrence by proclamation invited desirable people to come here and settle in the Province where the Acadians had made improvements, or anywhere they desired. It had become evident that there must be an English population if the country was to be held for the English. There were several grants issued on the application of New England people before an actual beginning was

made to settle the locality.   On Tuesday, the 9th day of June, 1761,
the first vessel arrived, having on board three families who all came
from Sandwich, Cape Cod.   These were Sealed Landers, Ebenezer
Ellis, and Moses Perry.   On the following Thursday Jonathan Crosby
and Joshua Burgess arrived with their families; they came from
Connecticut.   During the summer eight other families arrived, and
they all returned within a year.   Eighty people passed the first winter
in this new home, and it was a sad and memorable one to them all.
An expected vessel that was to have brought supplies failed to make
her appearance, and the result was very serious.   Almost half of
them returned within a year.   However, there were not lacking others
more stout of heart to step into the breach, and the next summer we
find these names added to the list and apparently all new arrivals, viz.:
John Crawley, Captain Ephraim Cook, Josiah Beal, Seth Barnes,
Josiah Tinkham, Benjamin Darling, Patrick Gowen, Samuel Harris,
Phineas Durkee, Hezekiah Bunker, Richard Rose, Ebenezer Corning,
Samuel Wood, and Ebenezer Moulton.   Among these men Captain
Ephraim Cook is a figure of more than ordinary interest, and a sketch
of his career may well find a place in this connection.   In the course
of my reading, this vigorous character has turned up here and there.
Murdoch says that Cook commanded one of the transports that
brought out the emigrants to Halifax in 1749, and became a settler
there.   He appears to have been a man of means, spending many
thousands on his lots in the new town, and becoming a magistrate
and a judge in the Court of Common Pleas.   In the course of a
couple of years he had fallen under the displeasure of Governor
Cornwallis for insulting the judges and persisting in exercising the
powers of a magistrate.   He was twice imprisoned a few days; on
one occasion he made an apology, on the other the case went to trial
and a jury acquitted him.   Five years after the beginning at Halifax
we find Cook engaged in making a settlement at Mahone Bay, where
he erected a blockhouse, secured grants of land and a guard of soldiers.   So far as I know he did not do more than make a beginning,
for he was the next year in command of a transport engaged in carrying away the Acadians.   He was in Capt. Gamaliel Bradford's company in 1758, and lost a leg at Schenectady by an accident and received
a pension.   In 1762 he turns up as one of the pioneers of Yarmouth.
Almost twenty years later he was still there, as the following interesting documents will show.   They are extracted from a book entitled
"The Annals of Yarmouth & Barrington," by Edward Duval Poole,

GRAND HOTEL, YARMOUTH.

YARMOUTH. LOOKING DOWN THE HARBOUR.

YARMOUTH, FROM ODD FELLOWS' BUILDING, LOOKING NORTH
(THE GRAND HOTEL IN THE MIDDLE DISTANCE)

1899. The author copied the contents of this volume from the archives of Massachusetts, where they have remained almost unknown and altogether unnoticed. Mr. Poole deserves much praise for. his intelligent interest that has given us this interesting and instructive book, by which we can gain a true view of the condition and the political sentiment of the settlers during the stirring period of the War of the Revolution.

"To the HONble the Senate and HONble House of Representatives of the Commonwealth of Massachusetts, in General Court Assembled at Boston June 1781

"The petition of Ephraim Cooke, Esqr. of CaperSue in the Province of Nova Scotia, Humbly Sheweth

"That your Petitioner formerly belonged to Kingston within this Commonwelth where he now owns a Real Estate: from whence he moved to Nova Scotia some years since, and he was a pensioner to this Government having lost his Leg in their service, but has never received his pension since the Commencement of the present War. That your pet'r lately came up to settle his affairs and take care of his estate in Kingston. And is now about returning home if he can obtain a permit from your Honors.

"He therefore humbly prays your Honors would be pleased to grant him a permit to return back to CaperSue and that he may have liberty to carry with him two barrels of sugar, one barrel of Rum and a barrel of Cyder. And also that he may be permitted to return here again & bring with him Fish, Beaver and other Furs.

"Boston June 15 1781   Ephraim Cooke"

The result of the petition was that he might take the provisions, liquid and solid, and go home, but he should not return. At any rate, he got on in the world. I notice that he was Registrar of Deeds in 1784, and the first captain of militia; always a man of influence, the founder of the fishing trade. He knew the locality of Yarmouth well before he came there to make a home. From his name, the place of his birth, and his marked traits I take that he was a descendant of Francis Cooke, a Mayflower Pilgrim. There was a strong dash of fighting blood in his stock. Ephraim died in 1821, leaving many descendants. He had nine children in 1763.

During several years the settlers struggled with many hardships and difficulties that were not unexpected. There were no roads; the soil was rocky and stingy; the winter season required stores of provisions to meet its demands. A small grist mill and a rude saw mill were built, the former by Sealed Landers, the other by Ephraim Cooke. According to law a return of all the settlers in the township of Yarmouth was made in June, 1764, three years after the beginning. These names will always be matters of interest to people in and from that locality, and that is reason enough for their appearance in this place.

John Crawley, Ephraim Cooke, George Ring, Benjamin Darling, Ebenezer Haley, John McKinnon, Consider Fuller, Roger Merithew, Timothy Merithew, Wells Moreton, Samuel Wood, Moses Perry, Joshua Burgess, Sr., Joshua Burgess, Jr., Jonathan Crosby, Benjamin Crosby, Seth Barnes, Peleg Holmes, Samuel Godfrey, Prince Godfrey, Ebenezer Ellis, William Curtis, Edward Tinkham, Benjamin Robbins, Cornelius Rogers, Moses Scott, Samuel Aderton, Nathan Nickerson, Patrick Gowen, James Robbins, David Hersey, Moses Gowen, David Hersey, Jr., Lemuel Churchill—total at Chebogue.

Samuel Harris, Joseph Sanders, Sealed Landers, Joseph Pitman, Eleazar Butler, Phineas Durkee, Samuel Oats, Jonathan Woodberry, James Philpot, William Haskell, Eben Moulton, Joseph Stewart, Jonathan Baker, Elishama Eldridge, Judah Agard, Benjamin Brown, John Perry, Robert Haskell, Robert Durkee—total on Cape Fochue River.

In the whole township there were 246 people, and their live stock was as follows: Cattle, 267; sheep, 161; hogs, 195. Three schooners were owned among them. By some mischance there were several names omitted in this return; among them belong the following:

John Richardson, Andrew Durkee, Levi Horton, Eleazar Hibbard, Josiah Beal.

In three years after this return is dated, the township grant was drafted, and during that time there had been seventy new arrivals, very likely all of them from New England. Such a group of Puritans would not be long without public worship, and for the most part they were of the old Congregational faith. It is said that Eleazar Moulton was the first preacher and Samuel Wood the next. Their meetings were held in private houses till 1776, when a meeting-house was built in the township of Yarmouth. They had cause to remember the verse of garbled Scripture that runs in this way:

> "Unless the Lord doth build the house
> The builders work in vain;
> Unless the Lord doth finish it,
> 'Twill tumble down again,"

for it was seven years from the time it was boarded before the outside was finished and the pews were built. This indicates their lack of means, and not their want of interest in religious affairs.

Haliburton in 1828 said in his history that "Yarmouth has always been in a state of steady improvement, and from its local advantages, and the enterprising spirit of its inhabitants, it promises to become a most flourishing and wealthy place."

In 1790 there were 1,300 souls.

In 1808 there were 2,300 souls.

In 1822 there were 4,000 souls.

In 1827 there were 4,350 souls.

Of these, there are forty families belonging to the Church of England, amounting to 200 souls, and families of Catholics amounting to 40, and 720 families of Dissenters of different denominations.

The historian's prediction was verified touching the future prosperity of Yarmouth. It has become second only to Halifax in commercial importance. Even when there were no railroad connections, still there was the sea, and Boston only distant but a short run of a day or two. The stage lines kept them in touch with the other portions of the Province. Fishing and ship-building were prosecuted with remarkable intelligence and energy by these transplanted Yankees. Later the railway communication gave a new impulse to business and prosperity. The Yarmouth Steamship Company during several years, and until within a few months, provided the public of the whole Province with first-class steamship accommodations between their own port and Boston. This concern deserves to be held in grateful remembrance, not only by the people of Yarmouth, but by the thousands who were given safe passages and comfortable accommodations by their efforts. The present steamship service by the Dominion & Atlantic Railway is the successor to the old line. The railway, that now extends to Barrington, has proved to be rightly located, and therefore contributes not a little to the prosperity of Yarmouth. That it will soon be extended to Shelburne and eastward to Halifax is almost a certainty.

To give a good idea of the present condition of the fishery business in this town, which has become of more importance than any other, I can do no better than insert some portions of letters that were written for the Halifax Herald, November, 1901, by A. W. Eakins, President of the Yarmouth Board of Trade, and W. A. Killam, Secretary of the Harbinger Steam Trawling Company.

Mr. Eakins says: "During the last twenty years the fish export business of Yarmouth has undergone a complete change. At the beginning of the period named, and for a decade or more previous to that, a fleet of about twenty-five brigantines and schooners was employed in carrying cargoes of dry and pickled fish, and lumber, to the different markets in the West Indies and British Guiana; today there is but one vessel in the business. Yarmouth still exports a good many thousands of quintals and barrels of fish, but the business is done in a safer and more profitable way. Whereas formerly the cargoes were sent out on shippers' account and placed in the hands of commission merchants to be sold for what buyers chose to pay—frequently netting shippers a heavy loss—today the fish are nearly always sold before they are shipped, and at prices made by the sellers. Some of the orders are from the West Indies direct, but much the greater part are from New York dealers and exporters, the fish going though the United States in bond for export to Cuba, Hayti, San Domingo, Porto Rico, and elsewhere. The improvement in steam communication between Yarmouth and Boston which has been going on during the period mentioned has greatly favored the change noted. A direct line of steamers between here and New York would, of course, be of the greatest advantage to the business, and would with the tourist business develop a paying business on its own merits. It is to be hoped we may have such a line in the not too distant future.

"The export of fresh fish to Boston—with some shipments to New York—has developed with the shipping facilities. This is more especially true of the item of live lobsters, commencing with a half dozen barrels packed in wet moss and shipped once a week in the 'Old Dominion,' back in the seventies, and growing to a total of fifteen thousand crates of 140 pounds each during a season. Mackerel are in some years shipped to Boston in ice by the thousand barrels; other years the catch is almost a total failure. The fish come up the Atlantic coast of the United States in the early spring, and about the tenth of May in each year they strike across from Cape Cod to Nova Scotia; they skirt the shore from Black Point around Cape Sable and east to the Straits of Canso, thence through to the waters of Northumberland Straits to the Bay of Chaleur and that region, where they stay and grow fat. During the months of May and June, and sometimes July, while passing this shore, they are taken in nets and traps, but the business is uncertain and sometimes a losing one.

"A new departure has just been taken in the fresh fish business

YARMOUTH, FROM BAY VIEW PARK.

YARMOUTH. STEAMER LEAVING THE WHARF FOR BOSTON.

YARMOUTH. CEMETERY ENTRANCE.

by a Yarmouth company in the building of a couple of fine steam trawlers for fishing on these shores. The first of these steamers, the 'Harbinger,' has been about a month in service, and seems to be doing well. The fish are landed every day or two and sold fresh, the buyers converting the haddock into 'finnan haddies,' for which there is a large and growing Canadian market, and salting or shipping the rest fresh, as may be deemed best. The second steamer, the 'Messenger,' has just been launched, and is being fitted with her machinery. If this venture proves to be the success that is hoped for it, it will be the means of making Yarmouth the most important fish-distributing port in the Province, because, without doubt, other steamers will be added as the business warrants."

Mr. Killam writes as follows: "In compliance with your request, I will give you my views of the fresh fish industry of Yarmouth. Yarmouth today ships more fresh fish to the United States markets than any other county in the Province; including their Canadian shipments, from six to seven million pounds, including shell fish, annually for the past few years, would be a fair estimate. This includes half a million pounds from West Port and St. Mary's Bay ports, and one million pounds from Shelburne County, chiefly Cape Island.

"It is not because we have better fishing grounds, but it is because we have such splendid freight service to Boston and New York, our best markets. We can put our fish on T wharf, Boston, in sixteen hours, and at Fulton Market, New York, in thirty-six hours. This is why we are ahead of the South Shore counties in fresh fish. Let the South Shore have railroad service to Yarmouth and you will soon see that one boat a day to Boston will not do the work.

"The fishing grounds from Cape Sable to Sambro are among the best. But there is no encouragement for fish people to strike out unless they have facilities for shipping fish fresh, and that means railroad or daily steamship service to Yarmouth."

With this notice of the town of Yarmouth we must pass on to other localities within the county that space forbids an extended mention. We pass on to notice the township of Argyle. On the 6th of July, 1771, it was resolved by the Council that the lands lying between the townships of Yarmouth and Barrington be erected into a township to be called Argyle. The name was given by Captain Ranald McKinnon, a soldier pioneer of that locality. Had he been a Campbell one could better account for his choice. The region had

11

been sparsely settled by the French before the general expulsion. Preacher John Frost and several other families settled there in 1771. Haliburton three-quarters of a century ago gives this account of the township: "Argyle lies between Yarmouth and Barrington, and is bounded on the south and west by the several courses of the sea coast. It includes all of the islands in front of it, and contains altogether 120,000 acres, or about 187 square miles. This township affords many good situations for farming, and contains extensive marshes, particularly on the Tusket River at Abutic, Pubnico, and the harbor of Cobuiquit. The upland is somewhat inferior to that of Yarmouth. At the mouth of the Tusket River there are about three hundred islands, called the Tuskets, many of which are well cultivated and afford good shelter and anchorage for schooners. There are two French settlements in Argyle—one at Pubnico, the other at Eel Brook; and at both of which places the people bear the reputation of being temperate, industrious, and hospitable. They keep good stocks of cattle, and are in general very comfortably settled."

A correspondent of the Yarmouth Herald in 1875 says: "In the township of Argyle, except the traders and office-holders, every man almost is a shipwright or a fisherman. Every able-bodied Frenchman there can handle a broad-axe or a fishing line with equal skill. They can build or repair their fishing craft in the winter and man them in the summer season." Writing again in May, 1882, he says: "Yarmouth County in her fishery product already holds a foremost place; and that portion of it known as Pubnico is not surpassed by any settlement in Nova Scotia in the thrift and independence of its people, whose neat and cheerful cottages, trim enclosures, and well-cultivated farms greet the visitor upon either side of their beautiful harbor; and be it remembered this happy condition has been attained through a persevering prosecution of the fisheries, undaunted by an occasional failure and disappointment." Brown, in his history of Yarmouth, says: "The steady growth of Yarmouth in commercial importance, and the increase of her foreign trade, during the last half century have been largely due to the industry and enterprise of the people living upon the banks of the Tusket and Argyle Rivers, at Eel Brook, and at Pubnico. They themselves built the fishing vessels from the timber their own lands supplied. The fish these vessels brought to market. enabled the port of Yarmouth to maintain and extend her commerce with the West Indies, and in a lesser degree with the United States."

During the American War of the Revolution there were many

arrivals at Yarmouth of persons known as Loyalists. Some of them were doubtless for King and country, and true British; but many of those who fled to Halifax and other portions of the Province were desirous of getting out of a region where there was something more than a mere scrimmage. It was not loyalty in many instances. It is a very noticeable fact that during the war the American settlers in Nova Scotia, and nearly all of English blood were of that nationality, were largely in favor of the American cause. This may readily be seen by referring to the letters of Governor Legge written from Halifax in those times.

Writing to the Earl of Dartmouth, Secretary of State, date of July 31, 1775, he tells him: "Our inhabitants of Passamaquoddy and St. John's River are wholly from New England, as are a greater part of the inhabitants of Annapolis River and those of the townships of Cornwallis, Horton, Falmouth, and Newport, some of which are not forty miles from this town; that by reason of their connection with the people of New England little or no dependence can be placed on the militia there to make any resistance against them; that many in this town are disaffected, on whom likewise I can have no great dependence." He furthermore tells his Lordship that the House of Assembly was composed of several persons disaffected to the Government. We also know that in the counties of Cumberland and Colchester most of the able-bodied men refused to serve in the militia and declared in a petition that it was a great hardship to demand "their services against their own countrymen and relatives." They refused to take the oath of allegiance when magistrates were sent there from Halifax to swear them. However, there were many true Loyalists who made sacrifices for what they believed to be a good cause and became valuable additions to Nova Scotia and other portions of Canada. There was a good deal of whining over the treatment they received at home, and considerable sympathy has been shown for them by writers hereabouts ever since. Let it be remembered that, had the revolutionists lost their cause, that the British heel would have rested hard on the necks of the rebels. I am not yet an old man, but can well remember when English soldiers blew rebellious Sepoys into fragments from the mouths of cannons; and we need not go so far away in date, when reconcentrado camps on the African veldts are repeating the horrors of Weyler in Cuba. "War is hell"—we can afford to repeat it—and the old Loyalists had more than a taste of that article. Their cause was lost in the nature of things; there was no other reasonable solution of the problem. The great American Anglo-Saxon nation could not be longer delayed in its birth; nothing could overlay it. Destiny makes very cheap a good deal of simpering stuff that gets into books as historical studies. Men who find themselves on the wrong side of political or religious questions in all good conscience must learn, like St. Paul did, that a conscience may be a mighty poor guide on some occasions. The loss to the Americans of good material for national purposes was a gain to these northern provinces in more ways than one. These very people had been, from time out of mind, when at home, great sticklers for personal liberty; even in religion they must worship after Congregational fashion, and did not relish the touch of any kind of a harness.

We owe the Americans who came before the Loyalists a debt of gratitude for their sturdy insistence of the enjoyment of privileges that were reluctantly granted by English Governors in Halifax.

The original center of Loyalist population in this county was in Tusket, and thence they finally spread into the surrounding districts. They arrived there about 1785, and first consisted of twenty-five families, viz.: Hatfield, Lent, Blauvelts, Sargents, Smith, Andrews, Tooker, and others whose names are now household words. Many of them brought their negro slaves with them. At the time they settled, there were vestiges of the Acadian homes in the locality.

The coast of Yarmouth County is rugged and picturesque, and wherever there is a settlement a tourist will be sure to find during the milder months a cool and delightful resting place beside the surge of that "old mother ceaselessly rocking." Where all these quiet resorts are so healthful and pleasing, one does not care to point out particular localities, and to describe them all is beyond my limit of space. Port Maitland, Chebogue, Tusket Islands, Argyle, and Pubnico are important points. Milton and Hebron, near the town of Yarmouth, are thriving and pleasing localities. In the more central region are Carleton, Kemptville, Deerfield, and Canaan, where lumbering and farming are the principal occupations. The whole county to an unusual degree is diversified with beautiful lakes and streams that in the remoter districts make a sportsman's paradise that we hear about now and then. He who desires to know more of this county from books can get his fill of "endless genealogies," and they are not to be despised, and details of early days and ancient people in the two histories written by Rev. J. R. Campbell and George S. Brown, Esq., the first in 1876, the other in 1888. I am indebted to both

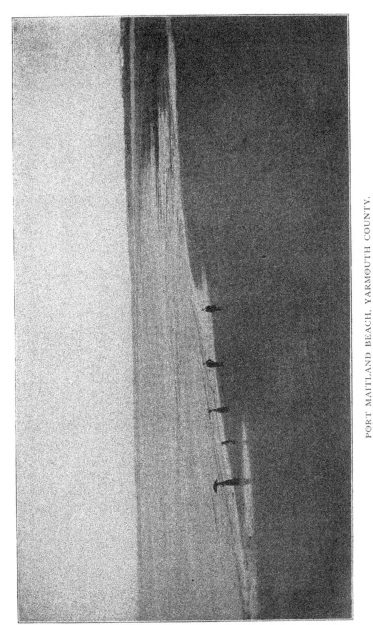

PORT MAITLAND BEACH, YARMOUTH COUNTY.

ABORIGINES, QUEENS COUNTY NATIVES.

authors, who deserve credit for their work, that will increase in value as the years pass away.

The geology of this county is very like that of Shelburne in general features, as one might expect with nothing but an arbitrary line between them. About one-fifth of the area is granite; it occurs in a long tongue extending from Shag Harbor up the county line more than half its length. At the extreme northeastern point of the county there is another area of some sixty or seventy square miles, and Tusket Wedge is also granite. All the other portions belong to the Cambrian formation, and include quartzites, slates, gneisses, and schists. Gold-bearing strata occur at Cranberry Head and Kempt and other localities, but paying mines have not yet been operated. The prospecting has been very inadequate to test the discoveries already made, to say nothing of coming upon new finds; but it may be safely said that the sea is the best gold mine this locality will ever enjoy, and unless this magnificent heritage is despoiled by greed and ignorance, the supply of riches will last as long as men will be there to need them.

CHAPTER XI.

Said a pagan Roman, "Nothing that is human is foreign to me." Surely the earliest inhabitants of Nova Scotia deserve to be noticed in a large book devoted to that Province. They were not only human, but interesting and instructive. Their history ought to furnish something worth knowing, something from which to draw lessons of moral worth, or educational value. The mounds of Palestine are ransacked with pick and shovel for some fragment of the Hittites, who have been extinct almost as long as the mammoths. Books are written to describe their crude writings, and in vain attempts to interpret their meaning. All this is well, but it is equally wise to acquaint ourselves with the history of the people who were first to enter our land after the glacial period had reconstructed its surface, and wild beasts and birds had made their homes in this northern retreat. The white pioneers called them savages—French, sauvage—meaning people who dwelt in the woods, as the word heathen referred to people who lived on the heath, and pagans, to those who dwelt in villages. To Christian ears, these terms have now a new significance, detrimental and degrading, and by no means deserving. Thus the Indian was not only a savage, but a heathen, and pagan, besides. Let us briefly pass in review the aborigine of Nova Scotia as he was before the touch of degrading tendencies reduced him to basketry, and beggary, to shanties, and cook-stoves.

If it is worth while to reconstruct the ancient brutes from their fossil bones, and show what were their appearances, and habits, then it is surely more desirable to get a correct idea of these people who greeted the white strangers, and welcomed them to the land that had been theirs beyond the limits of all traditions. Let us get a definite notion of the situation. Here was a country during half the year subjected to cold and snow. Beyond a few nuts, and berries, the land was fruitless. There were wild animals in the forest, and food fishes in the rivers and sea. The problem was to get food and shelter out of this environment, with no tools but sharpened stones, no weapons but bows, and arrows, and clubs, with which to get clothing from the backs of wild creatures, and sew it into garments. This people contended with these and many more difficulties, and came out ahead.

166

They built beautiful boats of bark; they made comfortable houses of the same material. They fashioned needles and fish-hooks of bone, and to have thus equipped themselves with material implements they could not have been slack in mental endowments. In a close contest of that kind neither idiots nor sluggards could survive. Add to these requirements the demand for protection against his own species who prowled in these distant forests on the war path, and we must see that the Indian needs be hunter, fisher, and fighter. He must know something of distant tribes and their country, and he did know from the mouth of the St. Lawrence to the Great Lakes, and southward to the Hudson River. The adult Indian must have known this Province as but few white men know it today. He could map its coast, and lakes, and streams, and canoe carries. He knew how to find his way through forests without a compass, and even in the cloudy night could feel his course by the moss on the south side of the trees. He knew when and where to fish and hunt, knew when the wild beasts brought forth their young, and when the fishes spawned. All four-footed mammals and all birds were his intimate acquaintances, and he was familiar with their haunts and dispositions and instincts as one brought up with them. The moose in their winter yards had no habits of lying down, and going hither and yon, that this keen-eyed man had not learned to a nicety. The caribou on the open bogs and high barrens had inventories made of all their timorous tactics that turned on the acuteness of their noses and the fleetness of their limbs. The beavers working on their dams and houses under cover of darkness had not eluded the observations of this silent spy, who jotted down every item of their practical doings and domestic economy. Thus it ran through the whole range of natural history. Every living thing, from insects to whales, he knew and appropriately named. His life depended upon the superiority of his wits when measured with the wild creatures about him. He must have their skins for clothing and bedding, and their flesh for food, and these could only be gotten by skill in hunting and dexterity with bows, and spears, and fish-hooks, and canoes. The Indian boy began his nature studies early. He would have a stern demand for all he could learn from his elders and from the use of his own eyes and ears. There were no school houses, but there were pupils without books or slates who could have shamed the high school youth by their proficiency in knowledge of natural things. It is very true that they did not know the dimensions of the moon and sun and their

distances from the earth, and had no knowledge which planet was
Jupiter or Saturn, or what were their dimensions; and neither do
the first fifty white men we meet in our streets today.

All the trees, and plants, these stone age people had named, and
their uses, and properties, and virtues were matters of common information. The lakes, and streams, and harbors, and headlands were
appropriately designated in a language so soft and liquid that it
seemed to be borrowed from the notes of the hermit thrush and the
far-away tinkling of woodland brooks. People like these, who contended successfully against such odds of circumstances, were no
weaklings in body or mind. Their language bears ample testimony
to their mental superiority. Says Dr. Rand, the author of the Micmac
Dictionary, Reading Book, and other related publications: "The
Micmac, like most if not all the North American languages, is remarkable for its copiousness, its regularity of declension and conjugations, its expressiveness, its simplicity of vocables, and its melliflu-
ousness. In all these particulars and others it will not suffer from a
comparison with any of the most learned and polished languages of
the world. A language which contains, besides the tens of thousands of forms in their inflections and conjugations, forty thousand
ground forms and more."

These Stone Age men had not only observed and named the
objects about them, but they had lifted up their eyes to the heavens
and noted the constellations and named them. The conspicuous
planets had also their proper designation, as Ganoose, the leader of
the host, for Venus as evening star; Ootatadabun, the herald of dawn,
for the morning star. Beyond all question these people were not
lacking in healthy curiosity and its accompanying intelligence. Had
they discovered the art of smelting iron ore, and of writing, a thousand
years before the coming of their pale-faced conquerors, then their
historical libraries would have lacked nothing of interest that others
of the kind now possess. That they did not make these discoveries
does not argue against their intellectual vigor. For thousands of
years, from the Euphrates to the Pillars of Hercules, there were
people with great nations in their loins who had not gotten beyond
the picture writing of North American Indians. We have no more
than a mention of them by Cartier in 1534 until Marc Lescarbot in
1609, who had lived in Annapolis a year or two at that period, gives
us some account of them. During this interval nearly a century
had passed, in which they had been more or less in contact and trade

with French, Portuguese, and Biscayan fishermen and fur traders. They had then thrown aside their bows and arrows, and stone weapons, and fur clothing for the superior arms and cheaper garments of their foreign friends. These would seem to have been great advantages, but they were not. It was a sudden liberation from the ancient bondage imposed by necessity to be ever at work in some directions. No more slow fashioning of stone tools, no more long tasks of chipping and cutting with such wretched implements. More game could be secured in one day with a musket than in many days with bows and arrows and traps. The skins of a few beavers and otters readily taken could be exchanged for clothing that would have required weeks of labor to tan and soften for wear. A man could make several canoes with the use of steel knives and axes while he had been constructing one of a ruder build with his old contrivances. All of these apparent advantages gave him more leisure which he could not employ in any way to his profit. His idle brain sought out undesirable channels for amusement. The men who sold him useful inventions also introduced him to the deadliest enemy of mankind, to that to which he had been heretofore an entire stranger. They made him acquainted with firewater, and he took to it as if it had been his mother's milk. He had been for at least three generations under the agencies of degradations that came with white men before we have more than the merest mention of him. Had he discovered and invented the better conveniences of life, and slowly given place to them in the natural way, the result would have been sure improvement; but it was a very different result when into their hands and arms dropped knives, and axes, and firearms, and tools, and cloth, and leather, and jewelry, as if the apron strings of some overgracious Providence had suddenly given way over their heads, and deluged them with unheard-of riches. Such a surfeit of good things was sure to operate to their degradation. The firm fiber of their old energies slackened and grew flabby. The keen senses of sight and hearing falling out of sharp demand, lost their fine edge that once vied with the fowls of the air and the brutes in their coverts.

However, after he had been nearly a century on the down grade, let us see what are the glimpses we get of him. Physically he was of medium size, high-shouldered, light-limbed, well-arched instep, fleet of foot and long-winded as a moose. Jet black hair, cut square across the forehead, and the other portions of it suffered to grow to considerable length. Ochre-red skin, black eyes, obliquely set under an intelligent brow and connected with goodly brain dimensions; nostrils wide, high nose, especially among adult men; beardless faces, square jaws, and lips that well expressed determination, but were no strangers to smiles. The testimony is all to the effect that they were very fond of their wives and children, took care of the helpless, and were hospitable almost to a fault. They had no system of religion, but held to some vague beliefs in spirits of various kinds. Of a future life there was no definite faith, but apparently a general belief in a ghost world, where this life had a shadowy continuance. They readily became attached to Roman Catholicism, as they had nothing to give up nor turn away from, for there was no priesthood, no temple, no sacred books, no venerated altars, nor any trace or tatter of a religious creed. Their French friends had brought them many very useful things, and what more natural than the supposition that this religion was equal to the rest of them. In fact it was admirably suited to them. It had been long before adjusted to such needs as theirs. It was picturesque and authoritative, appealed to the moral sense and religious sentiment, and they became what they have always been ever since, adherents of the Roman Church, and all attempts to separate them from that faith have been deservedly futile.

We must not suppose that the Indians who greeted the first white men were a lot of cruel wretches unrestrained by any sense of duty or any sentiments of natural affection. It is true that they were sometimes at war, just as Christian nations are today and were then. It is related that an Indian rebuked Captain Argall and Biencourt when they were quarreling over the right to Annapolis, that the former had just laid in ruins, telling them that "such superior nations should be ashamed to be engaged in quarrels that were not becoming even to savages." They had no law books and no law courts, but they had unwritten laws and public sentiment sufficient to punish offenders. Theft and murder were almost unknown among them. The women behaved with modesty, and the men had a respect for the common proprieties of life. They lived, and loved, and had a fair measure of enjoyment, as one may infer that their Maker intended they should. They were not overlooked in the large order of things. Scarcely a vestige of them is left but their inferior descendants, who are disappearing as a degraded remnant. The same resistless fate that stifled with sand the glories of hoary Egypt, and buried the splendors of Babylonian dynasties under shapeless mounds, has left us no record of the people who lived and died by hundreds of thousands during their long occupancy of our land. Their graves are hidden away in forest solitudes, by the shores of lonely lakes and streams. In such localities were their "God's acres," where they were laid to rest in their garments of fur and their birch-bark coffins. The white men were not above robbing these graves for the peltry that wrapped the dead.

Many years ago a friend of the writer, and also a friend of an Indian who accompanied him, chanced to be encamped for the night on an island in a lake that lies far from the haunts of men in the western border of Queens County. The Indian was a man of middle life. When the fire was kindled and supper was done he told his companion that he had not been on that place since he was a small lad, when he landed there one afternoon with his father and mother and younger brother, who was taken sick in the night and before morning was gone forever. The next day his father made a grave and fashioned a bark coffin, and the dead child was pillowed on moss, the grave covered with flat stones, and left to the care of Him who marks the sparrow's fall. While he told the story of this gray tragedy his emotions choked him to almost inaudible speech. The next morning the Indian led the way to a low hilltop that overlooked the lake, and after several adjustments of himself with old trees and rocks on the main shore he said, "We buried him here." And he was right. Covered deep under leaves were the stones, and a ring of smooth, pretty pebbles from the beach encircled the small grave. They had been placed tenderly there by hands that could not see their work for tears, and this untutored Indian wept, after all the lapse of years, for the lost playmate of his boyhood. And thus we see one "touch of nature makes the whole world kin."

From the first, the Indians and the French were on excellent terms. They often intermarried, and there was no interruption of their friendly relations. When it became evident, as it did in a half dozen years after the settlement of Annapolis in 1605-6, that the Englishmen were disputing the claims of Frenchmen to this land of Acadie, and carried fire and sword into their settlements, then the red men stood by their friends, as might have been expected. When in 1749 Halifax was founded, and it was thus clearly the intention of the English to do something more than keep a Governor and a squad of soldiers at Annapolis, the Indians became a weapon in the hands of the French at Louisburg and Quebec. The French population of Acadie could not, and dared not make an uprising against the English treaty rights, but the Indians could be used as instruments of death and destruction. They were instigated to commit depredations and paid for their atrocities. They were told that this was legitimate warfare. Their religious teachers, especially in the notable instance of La Loutre, fortified their courage with approval that held good for more worlds than one. There were raids and scalpings at Dartmouth, and Chester, and other localities, till successive Governors placed a cash bounty on Indian scalps and prisoners. These natives were not the kind of men that more than two hundred years before greeted Cartier. It is easy to go down hill. They had been on a toboggan slide of degradation for six generations. They had been men without a country, without chiefs, without organization. They had dropped into the condition of mere hangers-on to the French conquerors. They had lost their arts and their manners. They had no cause at heart, no land to defend, no homes to guard, for no one threatened them at the beginning.

After the French expulsion in 1755 they were joined by fugitives who had escaped the general deportation. For a time this combination was harassing, but in 1761 a treaty was signed at Halifax and peace declared. Louisburg was in ruins, Quebec had fallen to the English arms, and all was over for France in this New World. The Indians then numbered about 2,000. The Government assisted them with provisions, ammunition, and clothing. They hunted, trapped, and made baskets. They lived in birch-bark wigwams, dressed in their own fashion, that had more than a touch of barbarism in it. An observer in Halifax in 1779 says: "Lieutenant Governor Franklin had many Indians in his train arrayed in all their tinsel finery, amongst whom was a sachem who wore a long blue coat adorned by a scarlet cape, and bound closely about his loins by a girdle." During the American-English war of 1812 some of these Indians actually got quite into fighting trim, and so far as sentiment went took sides with the Americans. It was only big talk among restless spirits who still chafed over the loss of their hunting grounds. Within thirty-five years an aged Micmac told me with no little show of spirit that "all these lands belonged to his people, who had been robbed by white men." Within the last forty years they have rapidly adopted the usages of other people around them. Small houses and shanties have taken the places of the picturesque bark wigwams, their campfires have given way to old stoves, and men and women are largely clad in the cast-off garments of their white neighbors. Some of them try to farm a little; others act occasionally as guides, or build canoes, or catch salmon and trout; a few of the younger men are employed at times in the lumber woods and on the timber drives. They are not successful in the occupation of white men. They are lacking in steadiness of purpose and proper ambition. The old fiber and energy that belonged to their forefathers centuries ago is no longer in them. The blood of white men circulates in the veins of many of them, but such commingling of races has not been attended with happy results; the pure-blooded Indian was a better man. All the less desirable traits of the Caucasian seem lost in this amalgamation. There are now about 1,500 of these people in this Province, distributed over its whole extent. They are so thoroughly communistic in their usages that no one of them is much better off than another. Whoever claims hospitality among them must have it; that is the unwritten law. They are well informed about their family connections, even to remote degrees of kinship, and a windfall of luck will be very likely to secure a visit from some of them. There is no hope of any great improvement among them. A well-devised educational plan might rescue a remnant, but that is out of the question in these times when larger interests are clamoring for attention. The leopard cannot change his spots nor the Ethiopian his skin, nor can these people change their natural characteristics. It takes more than a dash of white blood to make one of them walk and run like a white man. A certain limberness of the knees, and gliding softness of step are characteristic touches wrought into their muscles and geared into their joints by their hunter's mode of life that goes back through tens of thousands, perhaps hundreds of thousands of years, to the beginning of the human race. He walks stealthily on the broad highway in daylight. He speaks in subdued tones in his board shanty because his language was evolved in the presence of game that he needed and human foes that he feared. He laughs in silence, for the most part, because a loud indulgence would have betrayed his presence to animals that he hunted or enemies who hunted him. Much of their ancient usages and history are still to be seen in their bodies and their movements and manner of life. For a long time we have not treated them very well, and now they have been handed over to the "tender mercies," which are "cruel," of the Indian Department at Ottawa. No provisions are made for them in the poorhouses. No pauper's aid is extended to them in any way. A sick or otherwise disabled Indian must either perish or throw himself on the charity of his people, who are always on the verge of want. The department will neither feed nor clothe him, and this to the shame of white Christians who taught him by word of mouth, and printed book that all men are brothers, and then proceeded to give him a practical illustration of the parable of the man who fell among thieves, with the part of Good Samaritan left out.

The following verses on the Indian names in the Province were written by Mr. Richard Huntington of Yarmouth and will be appreciated by all who take an interest in this brief account of the aboriginal inhabitants:

" The memory of the red man,
    How can it pass away
While their names of music linger
    On each mount, and stream, and bay?
While Musquodoboit's waters
    Roll sparkling to the main;
While falls the laughing sunbeam
    On Chegogin's field of grain.

While floats our country's banner
    O'er Chebuctos' glorious wave,
And the frowning cliffs of Scatarie
    The trampling surges brave;
While breezy Aspotogon
    Lifts high its summit blue,
And sparkles on its winding way
    The gentle Sissibou.

While Escasoni's fountains
    Pour down their crystal tide;
While Inganis's mountains
    Lift high their forms of pride;
Or while on Mabou's river
    The boatman plies his oar,
Or the billows burst in thunder
    On Chicaben's rock-girt shore.

The memory of the red man,
    It lingers like a spell
On many a storm-swept headland,
    On many a leafy dell;

Where Tusket's thousand islets
Like emeralds stud the deep,
Where Blomidon a sentry grim
His endless watch doth keep.

It dwells round Catalone's blue lake,
Mid leafy forests hid—
Round fair Discouse, and the rushing tides
Of turbid Pisiquid.
And it lends Chebogue a touching grace
To thy softly flowing river,
As we sadly think of the gentle race
That has passed away forever."

CHAPTER XII.

The Island of Cape Breton has not lacked for historians. We have the following in English: "A History of the Island of Cape Breton, by Richard Brown, Esq., London, 1869," now out of print and scarce; "Cape Breton, Illustrated, Historical, Picturesque, and Descriptive, by John M. Gow, Esq., Toronto, 1893"; "Historical and Descriptive Account of the Island of Cape Breton, and of Its Memorials of the French Regime, with Bibliographical, Historical, and Critical Notes, by J. G. Bourinot, Montreal, 1892." About all there is of much historical interest can be learned from these sources.

Cape Breton enjoys the distinction of containing within its boundaries vast commercial interests of world-wide importance, and the historic ruins of Louisburg.

Who among white men first discovered this island will never be known, and perhaps that knowledge, if we possessed it, would not be of more service than the gratification of fruitless curiosity here and there. Very likely the Norsemen sighted it a thousand years ago. There is a strong probability that Basque and Breton fishermen crossed the Atlantic before Columbus, and drew their catch of cod or "baccalaos," as they called them, from Cape Breton waters, and sold them in the European market. The Cabots, in 1497, must have made some acquaintance with the coast, even if they never set foot upon the shores. Early in the sixteenth century Basque fishermen were there, and with them a little later French, Spanish, Portuguese, and English were fishing and fur-trading in Newfoundland, Cape Breton, and Nova Scotia. Anthony Parkhurst, a merchant of Bristol, in 1578 reported that he had made four voyages to that part of the world, or more particularly to Newfoundland, and he has this to say of the latter place, that there were generally more than 100 sail of Spaniards taking cod, and from twenty to thirty killing whales; fifty sail of Portuguese; 150 sail of French and Bretons, mostly very small; but English only fifty sail. From 1600 to 1700 there was on the island a great deal of clashing of rival concerns engaged in fishing and fur-trading, but no serious attempt to found a colony. In 1690 there were only 806 white people in the peninsula of Nova Scotia, and in Cape Breton not a single family of European descent. The fishermen frequented the island as usual,

FREDERICK WALLET DESBARRES.
(FROM A MINIATURE.)

CALEDONIA COLLIERY, CAPE BRETON COUNTY.

and fur traders swapped their hatchets, and knives, and glittering gewgaws for valuable pelts that found a ready market in the Old World.

By the terms of the Treaty of Utrecht the English had undisputed possession of the whole Atlantic coast from Florida to Hudson's Bay, including Newfoundland, and the only exception was the island of Cape Breton. It had become evident that France was losing her grip on this great domain that she had with proper pride named New France. Too late did she awake to the value and importance of these coast possessions. It become evident at last that it was absolutely necessary to hold this island for the protection of her fisheries and for maintaining communications with the St. Lawrence. The most direct and portentous menace came from that fringe of English colonies to the southward called New England. They were a sturdy race, that did not stick at trifles, and very early discovered that North America, north of the torrid zone, was to be either English or French, and it fell to their lot, as they understood the problem, to be no feeble factors in furthering the plans of Providence. It was very evident that this island would not long remain a French possession when it stood thus alone. The first appearance of a quarrel between the parent States would be the signal for these New Englanders to seize Cape Breton. They had not suffered Port Royal or Annapolis to exist as a stronghold, and now with Nova Scotia and Newfoundland under the British flag Cape Breton was fair game on the first excuse. The Treaty of Utrecht, 1713, was the visible sign that France had met with serious reverses at home; it was the beginning of the end that saw her driven from this continent in less than a half century from that date. Thenceforth the destiny of the English in this quarter of the globe became manifest. A half dozen years after this treaty was concluded the French had perceived that nothing short of a vast effort on a national scale could prevent the red cross of England from floating over this Isle Royal, that in spite of a fine name had been shamefully neglected. In order to hold it there was not much choice of means. The natural suggestion was a fortified town that should be both a military post and a naval station, and after some casting about for a proper locality they hit upon the Havre à l'Anglois, but not without considering the claims of St. Ann's and Sydney. In 1720 the work was begun, and for more than twenty years the French Government devoted great energy and immense resources to this one object, the completion of the work, that cost

12

thirty millions 'of livres, or about six million dollars, or, taking into account the greater value of money in those days, over ten million dollars of our money, and even then the fortifications were never completed. The New Englanders were not in the least averse to taking advantage of the brisk times that resulted from such a great outlay of hard cash so near their own doors. They found a ready market for boards, timber, brick, and other products of their country. They knew the work would go on whether they furnished the material or not, so they pocketed all the French coin they could get in exchange for their cargoes. Twenty-five years after the founding of this fortress town, these audacious New Englanders—farmers, mechanics, sailors, and traders—appeared before Louisburg with a demand for its surrender. There was to be no more trading, but stubborn fighting. These fellows had turned soldiers with wonderful readiness, and were not long in securing this focal point of mischief, that was nothing less than a constant menace to their peace and prosperity. Some of the leading features of this expedition I have written out in the brief history of Nova Scotia in another portion of this volume. Three years later, in 1748, Cape Breton was restored to the French by the terms of the Treaty of Aix-la-Chapelle, in exchange for Madras, on the other side of the globe. The next year the British founded Halifax in order to more securely hold the Province of Nova Scotia in a future struggle that was not far under the horizon at that time. Within eight years war was declared, but not till after Braddock's defeat and the fall of Beausejour and other bloody hostilities had taken place without this formality. On the 27th of July, 1858, the British flag floated once more over the ramparts of Louisburg, where Amherst, Wolfe, and Boscawen had distinguished themselves. To prevent further trouble from that source the famous stronghold was destroyed, with the exception of a few residences. Three years later Cape Breton, with all other French possessions in this region, were ceded to the English by treaty, and this island domain by royal proclamation was annexed to the Government of Nova Scotia. Two years later, in 1765, the population was only one thousand, consisting of French and half-breeds for the most part, scattered here and there, camping with the Indians, or in some other way picking up a precarious living. In 1783 another change was made and Cape Breton was made a distinct province. The first Governor was Major Frederick Wallet DesBarres, an English officer who had won his spurs at Louisburg and Quebec. He fixed his abode

GLACE BAY HARBOUR, CAPE BRETON COUNTY.

COMMERCIAL BANK, SYDNEY.

at Spanish River and renamed it Sydney, in honor of Lord Sydney, who had been instrumental in making this separation. The next year a number of persons styling themselves "Associated Loyalists" sailed in three vessels for Sydney with about one hundred and forty passengers who were in search of a locality where they could make new homes and be happy, if possible, under the old flag, on short rations and in rude shanties that were neither protection against the winds of winter nor the rains of all seasons. After some looking around they concluded to remain at the seat of government, where the Governor himself was making the best of the situation and living in a mere hut. The town was laid out by Mr. Taite, and barracks erected for the soldiers. That year settlers came in rapidly. Loyalists who had fought on the losing side in the Revolution were swarming over Nova Scotia, New Brunswick, and Canada in search of some goodly land, and they did not overlook Cape Breton. The first year of the Governor's residence was very encouraging, and he fancied that the authorities in Nova Scotia were looking on him with the green eye of jealousy. His troubles soon came thick and fast, and most of them arose from his own tactless proceedings. His glory was short-lived, lasting only three years, and he was then dismissed from office and his place filled by another. His temperament did not agree with the position. He appears to have been a humane man in dealing with his inferiors, but withal a captious martinet who enjoyed the distinction of commanding, and carried a high hand in many directions. He was succeeded by Lieutenant Colonel Macormick, who remained in office till 1795, and much of the time involved in distressing quarrels with members of his Council and others with whom he came in contact. He was glad to get away to England, and never returned. At that time Sydney had but eighty-five houses, and a large portion of them were deserted, and the entire population was only 121 persons, among whom were many so ill content with their lot that they were packing to go away. It is not my purpose to follow up the petty squabbles of those who thought themselves somewhat in that infant province. Human nature shows at a disadvantage amid such greedy scrambling for pelf and power.

Affairs became so bad that the island was reannexed to the Government of Nova Scotia in 1820 as one county, with the privilege of returning two members to the House of Assembly, who were duly elected for the first time in the persons of Richard John Uniacke and Lawrence Kavanah.

Later the island was divided into four counties. Of these, Cape Breton is most associated with matters of historic interest and economic importance. It has an area of 1,169 square miles and a population of 48,361 for the year 1901, but the new works of various kinds that have recently started up on a large scale have greatly increased the number of people since that census was taken. In the vicinity of the Sydneys and the coal mines a new face is put upon the localities almost every day, and any description I might give here for the present would not answer for tomorrow. The coal mines of this county have received considerable notice in the chapter devoted to that subject, and in the portion treating of iron ores there are descriptions of the smelting industry, that is continually assuming larger proportions. The indications certainly point to a great future for this district, that has been so vastly enriched by nature. The full extent of its wealth is not yet revealed, but enough is known to found immense industries and sustain them for generations.

The island of Cape Breton is pre-eminently Celtic or Highland Scotch, and I will here quote Mr. Richard Brown at the point where he tells how it all came to pass:

"On the return of peace in 1763 a great number of troops were disbanded, among the rest some of the Highland regiments which had seen service in America. Many of the Highlanders, with that prudence and foresight peculiar to their countrymen, who had noted with observant eyes the fertility of the provinces in which they had served, in every respect so much superior to the bleak and barren hills of their native land, determined to make them their future home. Those who settled in Canada, Nova Scotia, and St. John's Island, sent home to their friends such glowing accounts of their new homes, about the year 1773, that the latter prepared to join them as soon as possible. It so happened that just at the time these accounts reached Scotland from the colonies many of the Highland chieftains, who had discovered that the raising of cattle and sheep afforded greater profits than the letting of their lands to miserable tenants, were dispossessing the latter of their farms and holdings. This harsh treatment, of course, gave a great impetus to the emigration, and thousands left almost every district in the Highlands to join their friends in the colonies. In the course of twenty or thirty years following 1773, whole baronies were turned into sheep-farms, and hundreds of families were driven across the Atlantic to look for a home in the backwoods of America. Many of these who had friends in the colonies, and knew what to

THE SYDNEY HOTEL, SYDNEY

BLAST FURNACES AND ELECTRIC POWER HOUSE, SYDNEY.

CHARLOTTE STREET, FROM WENTWORTH TO PITT—SYDNEY, C. B.

(SHOWING THE BLOCKS THAT ESCAPED THE FIRE, OCTOBER 19, 1901.)

expect, emigrated at once, but thousands, who had no such desire, on the contrary, the greatest repugnance to leave the land of their fathers, the familiar hills and the green slopes of Lochabar, were heartbroken at the idea of being separated from them by a thousand leagues of sea. Many, it is true, especially the young men, gladly embraced the offers of their landlords to assist them in emigrating to a country where labor was abundant and remuneration ample, and where they could with common industry soon acquire a comfortable subsistence; but the old people, who had passed all their lives in their native glens, clung to their birthplaces with a tenacity known only to the Celts.

"The 'Hector,' the first ship that arrived in Pictou with emigrants in 1773, was followed by others in such rapid succession that in the course of eight or ten years not only the country bordering on the harbor and rivers of Pictou, but also the coast to the eastward as far as Merigomish, was taken up and occupied. So far all the emigrants who had arrived at Pictou were Presbyterians, but two ships having arrived there in 1791 with Roman Catholics from the Western Islands, they were persuaded by the Rev. —— McEachern, of St. John's Island, to leave Pictou and settle along the gulf shore towards Antigonish. Some of these, dissatisfied with that location, crossed over to Cape Breton and settled upon the northwest shore at several places between the Strait of Canso and Margaree, where they found a more congenial soil and greater facilities for prosecuting the sea fisheries, in which they had been engaged in the Western Islands. The favorable accounts of the country, sent home by these wanderers, induced many of their countrymen to find a passage to the western shores of the island, where they settled chiefly about Judique and Mabou. There were, of course, no roads, not even a blazed track through the forests, from the seacoast to the Bras d'Or Lakes, at that time; nevertheless some stragglers were not long in finding their way to the fruitful, sheltered shores of the lakes, whose innumerable bays, arms, and creeks offered such desirable places for settlement that the emigration agents who had furnished ships for conveying the people hitherto to Pictou or Canso were induced to send their vessels direct to the Bras d'Or Lakes. The pioneer ship on this route arrived at Sydney on August 16,1802, with 299 passengers, of whom 104 were heads of families, the remainder children. From this time the tide of emigration gathered strength as it advanced, until it reached its highest point in 1817, when it began gradually to decline. The last emigrant ship arrived in 1828. The great influx of Scottish emigrants (said by some authorities to have exceeded 25,000 souls) gave quite a new complexion to the population of Cape Breton, if it can with propriety be said that it was, before their arrival, distinguished by any complexion whatever. The island is now decidedly Scotch, with every probability of its continuing so to the end of time."

The following extract is taken from the Cape Breton edition of the Halifax Herald of August, 1901, being a portion of an article contributed by G. H. Dosson, Esq.:

"The nearest first-class harbor to Europe is Sydney, which comprises the ports of Sydney and North Sydney. It is one of the most spacious and safest in the world. Its arms are five and seven miles long respectively, and the average depth of water is fifty feet. At Sydney are the coal piers of the Dominion Coal Company, which are of the largest and most modern type, fully equipped with machinery and chutes, with a loading capacity of 20,000 tons per day. In addition to the facilities provided for rapid loading of large steamers, there is also an auxiliary equipment of buckets which are worked by hydraulic towers, and are so placed that ships of any height or draught are loaded at any time of the tide. These piers have been so planned as to meet the requirements up to a capacity of 40,000 tons per day, whenever the output of the collieries will warrant the increase of force and the additional machinery. In fact the International piers are among the largest in the world, and with one exception the largest on the Atlantic seaboard. Steamers of 6,000 tons capacity are loaded within twenty-four hours of docking. At North Sydney are the piers of the Nova Scotia Steel and Coal Company. Here new piers of modern equipments for the largest class of shipping are being designed. The Dominion Coal Company has also splendid shipping facilities at Louisburg, which is used for shipment to the United States, and also for Southern trade during the winter months. The Louisburg pier is also of the largest and most modern type, and has a conveyor and storage bins for loading slack at the rate of 750 tons per hour, or 18,000 tons per day. Steamers drawing twenty-four feet of water carry this coal to Boston, making two trips per week.

"The Sydney & Louisburg Railway, which is owned by the Dominion Coal Company, has a total length, including branches, of forty-six miles. This line connects Sydney and Louisburg with the six large collieries now in operation."

From the same edition of the Herald the following paragraph is

ST. PETERS.

STEAMER PASSING THROUGH THE ST. PETERS CANAL INTO THE
BRAS D'OR LAKES.

A PARTY OF AMERICAN TOURISTS AT ST. PETER'S, CAPE BRETON.

extracted: "North Sydney is centrally situated, with a splendid harbor in front, and the agricultural sections of Bras d'Or and Boulardarie in the background. Only two miles away are the famous Nova Scotia Steel and Coal Company properties. The shipping piers of the coal company are in the center of the town, which is connected with the railway system of the continent by the Intercolonial Railroad. It is the Canadian terminus of the Newfoundland railway and steamship system. North Sydney has advanced in trade and population more rapidly than any other town in the Province which has not experienced a boom. The census figures, showing an increase of 84 per cent. in ten years, speak for themselves. The assessor's books show a corresponding increase."

Glace Bay is the name of a place that is central to the mining operations near Sydney, and within a very short time has grown to comparatively large dimensions. The following extract from the Glace Bay Gazette of January 18, 1901, gives an idea of the prosperity of this town that has come to stay: "It is the town's first birthday. One year ago we were a struggling, straggling, muddy village. To-day we are a town of at least 10,000 people, with streets, sidewalks, electric lights, a fire department. We have our own town government, we have a board of trade, we are to have a water supply.

"Apparently there is nothing the matter with Glace Bay, and it is bound to grow by virtue of natural laws. It is the headquarters of the Dominion Coal Company in Cape Breton, the center of the extensive collieries of that concern. In the vicinity are the Bridgeport, Reserve, Caledonia, Dominion and other mines, employing several thousand men. The pay roll of the company has amounted to $125,000 in one month. The town is located on the Sydney & Louisburg Railway. It is impossible within my limited space to even mention the localities beyond a few of the most importance. Scores of places might be described that are either beautiful for the eye to rest upon or inviting as points of economic interest. Cape Breton County, by virtue of its mineral wealth, its geographical position, and scenic beauties, has no equal on the American continent within the same area. It was first discovered four hundred years ago, but within ten years it has been rediscovered by capitalists, and henceforth it will be heard from throughout the civilized world."

GEOLOGY OF CAPE BRETON COUNTY.

About three-quarters of the area of this county is included in the Carboniferous system. The other quarter is made up of Silurian and pre-Silurian measures that are not very exactly determined so far as classification is concerned. A comparatively small portion is of the so-called "productive" coal formation, according to the maps of the Geological Survey. Dr. Gilpin has conclusively shown (see paper in the Proceedings and Transactions of the Nova Scotia Institute of Science, Volume IX, Part 2) that the "millstone grit" contain workable seams of coal; for instance, the Mullins Gardener, Long Beach, and Tracey seams in the Sydney district. With this understanding, the really productive or possibly productive area is vastly enlarged, and will doubtless eventually be much extended.

This county is now attracting a great deal of attention among capitalists, and prospecting for coal, iron, and copper is carried on with rapidly increasing energy. Nothing I can say here, within this brief space, will be needed to call attention to that now famous locality.

To describe all the various areas that are laid down on the maps of the Survey would answer for this locality, at present, no practical purpose. Those who desire more information in this direction need not be at a loss for aid. The ground is all covered by geological maps drawn on a scale of a mile to the inch, and there is enough explanatory text to throw additional light upon them. However, a few good calyx drills well located would be of great practical value in this promising field.

OLD LOUISBURG.

THE MARCONI TOWERS.

COMMERCIAL STREET, GLACE BAY.

CHAPTER XIII.

This division of the Province, together with Antigonish, was at first included in the bounds of Halifax County, but in 1784 the area now included in them was erected into the county of Sydney, and later this name was dropped and the region formed the two counties of Antigonish and Guysborough. The later, now under consideration, contains 1,656 square miles, being exceeded in extent in only one instance, that of Halifax. It is bounded by the Strait of Canso, the open sea, and the counties of Antigonish, Pictou, and Halifax. The population is 18,320. The figures are from the census of 1901, and show a steady gain over other returns, an item that is not true but of only one-half the counties in the Province. A notable feature of this division is its relation to the Strait of Canso, one of the remarkable waterways of the world, a natural canal of immense importance to the commerce of a wide region; not only giving a safe entrance by a short cut to the gulf waters, but affording a secure shelter at various points within its limits. Such a locality was not likely to be long passed over by the white men who were first to invade its waters with sail and keel. It would be quite easy to make word-pictures of this beautiful locality, which abounds in views of striking features wherein sea and shore, passing ships, and fisher folk in tossing boats, and sun and cloud furnish ample materials. We must pass over this inviting field and leave it to the imagination of the reader, till he sees for himself; and even then what he perceives of beauty will depend upon what he has in him that is responsive to what his eyes behold. Deep answers to deep.

From its convenient location at the entrance of the strait, the harbor of Canso was sure to be taken advantage of by the earliest European fishermen, who appear to have been either there or in the vicinity only a dozen years after Columbus "crossed the ocean blue." Since then it has passed through a varied experience that would require a sizable volume in which to relate it, and tell of the deeds of Indian scalping parties, the capture by French forces, and the raiding by privateers, its building, and its burning, and other tales of long ago. At this point it is convenient to draw upon Haliburton, who wrote as follows:

"Canseau is situated at the southeastern extremity of the county, about twenty-five miles from Guysborough. It has an excellent harbor, accessible at all seasons of the year. The strait is called Little Canseau, and is navigable for the larger ships, and affords safe and commodious anchorage. The town plot of Wilmot is situated on its southwestern side. It was laid out during the administration of Governor Wilmot. A great proportion of the district bordering on Canseau, and indeed the whole of the promontory that terminates at this place, is a naked granite rock, with the exception of a few solitary hills of good land, that appear to have been left us as monuments of the general deluge, while the surrounding country has been swept to its foundation."

Canso is an important place in connection with the fishing business. The population numbers about 1,500 people, who are looked upon as a prosperous community.

Guysborough is the shire town, situated at the head of Chedabucto Bay. The population is in the vicinity of 1,500 people, who are engaged in the various occupations that the locality suggests. One does not read very far in Nova Scotian history before coming upon the name Chedabucto, and with it scenes of violence in which Indians, French, and New Englanders have in turn had their parts.

It would be a long story to relate the recorded doings of all these parties, with a pirate ship now and then thrown in to enliven the scene. Here was settled Nicholas Denys, a notable character of the early days of sixteen and thirty-six and later; a man of great enterprise and probity, admirably suited to the needs of a new country, and deserving of marked success, but far otherwise did it fare with him; he was beset by rapacious scoundrels of his own nation, who thwarted his industrial efforts, destroyed his property, imprisoned his body, and drove him from the Province. Among his enemies the chief was the detestable D'Aulnay, who executed Madame La Tour's little garrison, and forced her to witness the atrocity with a rope about her neck. There is some consolation to know that an Indian whom he had wronged upset him from a canoe in the mouth of the Annapolis River, amid the swirling mud and racing eddies of the great tides that bore his carcass to some fitting resting place, to either feed the crows that patrol the beaches, or stay the hunger of the scavengers of the deep! We all feel that the death of Quilp was just the taking off that he deserves after his course of heartless brutality. Dickens relied upon a wholesome indignation in his readers when he told the story of his frightful death. Nicholas Denys de Fronsac, pioneer, man of business, author of an interesting book concerning this part of the world, deserves a monument in this Acadian land, and old Chedabucto is just the place for it to stand. Perhaps the future will thus commemorate him.

About 1690 Sir William Phipps, in command of some armed vessels that had recently captured Annapolis, called in at Chedabucto one fine morning early in June and demanded of Montorgieul a surrender of the place. He was given to understand that nothing short of a fight would be required to gain what he wanted. Sir William was a man of spunk, and energy, and combativeness, who did not mind a little blood-letting and the chances of getting a scratch or two himself. He was one of a family of twenty-two children, more or less, all dependent upon the efforts of a blacksmith father in New England to provide for their needs, who apprenticed William to a shipbuilder, where he acquired the trade of constructing vessels, and then he took to the sea to learn the art of sailing and navigating them. He was determined to get on in the world, and having observed that money was the key that unlocked the way to great places and preferments, he set about to get it by the ton and not by the dollar. He learned that Spanish ships bearing great treasures in precious metals had sometimes gone to the bottom in the shallow West Indian seas, and he undertook to locate one or more of them. Twice he failed; the third time he won the prize, and more than a million dollars fell into the hands of himself and his associates, some thirty tons of silver. It never rains but it pours, so the next thing William knew he was Sir William, and finally became Governor of his native State of Massachusetts; got into great trouble through his bad temper; went to England to defend himself, and before he had made an end of that business death made an end of his life in 1693. Well, this was the man, just then forty years of age, who dropped into Chedabucto Bay on the King's business, and that was, to get possession of Nova Scotia, and having already done up Port Royal, there was no other settlement worth a cannon shot but the one he was now before. The Frenchman acted the man, and put up a stiff fight, and then Sir William resorted to the old Norman fashion that lingered in his blood, and applied the firebrand, and then it was either "turn or burn," as the old conditional offer of salvation went, and a surrender on honorable terms was effected. The little garrison of a score of men was sent to Newfoundland, the valuable stores seized, and the place de- .

stroyed. Twenty-three years afterwards the Province by treaty fell to the English and has ever since remained there, and it is not known that the French ever attempted to rebuild the establishment at this point. Three-quarters of a century afterwards, when great efforts were made to settle the Province with English subjects, old Cheda-bucto was not forgotten, and in 1765 a grant of land was issued to Richard Smith, and in 1780 another to Joseph Hadley, and in 1790 others to Benjamin Hallowel, the Cooke brothers, etc.

Here we can follow Haliburton again, who says: "The township of Guysborough reaches from Crow Harbor to the northern bounds of the district, and contains, according to the original patent, 100,000 acres, 53,850 of which were granted to Nathan Hubbel and 278 other persons. These people belonged to the Civil Department of the Army and Navy, and at the evacuation of New York were settled in the year 1783, at Harbor Port Mouton, in Queens County, under the superintendence of Colonel Molleson, wagon-master general to the forces. Having suffered much at that place, 200 of them with their families, were removed during the ensuing spring, at the expense of the Government, to the shores of Chedabucto Bay, where they found a part of the Duke of Cumberland's Regiment, that had been landed there about one month. The town and township of Guysborough were laid out soon after the arrival of these Loyalists, and were thus named in honor of Sir Guy Carleton, the then Commander in Chief of his Majesty's forces in North America. To each of the settlers both a town and farm lot were assigned, and also a share in the rear division. At first they all erected houses and settled on the town plot; and during the succeeding winter cut down the adjoining timber. In attempting to burn the wood the fire spread with such violence and rapidity that most of the houses were destroyed, and they were compelled to seek refuge from its fury in the water. Notwithstanding this disastrous occurrence, they were still unwilling to separate and settle upon their farm lots, but rebuilt their houses and remained together until the Government allowance of provisions ceased, when many, appalled by the difficulties of subduing the wilderness, removed from the Province.

"Those who remained were compelled to make the attempt, after suffering the severest privations, in consequence of the difficulty of procuring supplies from Halifax, and in a few years the town was nearly deserted. In this derelict state, inhabited by only a few merchants and mechanics, it continued until within the last ten years,

RESIDENCE OF A. J. MOXHAM, THE KING'S ROAD, SYDNEY.

BANKHEAD, DOMINION NO. 2, CAPE BRETON COUNTY.

during which it has partaken of the general growth of the county. Guysborough harbor, or Milford Haven, is situated at the head of Chedabucto. This extensive bay is formed by Cape Canseau on the west and Cape Hogan on the east. It is fifteen miles in breadth, from Fox Island to the southern end of the Gut of Canseau, and about twenty-five miles in length from Canseau to Fort Point, at the entrance of Guysborough harbor."

Here follows an interesting account of the fisheries of this locality seventy-four years ago, and surely nothing short of human greediness and stupidity are responsible for the great falling off that has taken place in the quantity of these valuable articles of food supply.

"The fisheries of Chedabucto Bay are perhaps as productive as any in the known world. Codfish, and pollock or scale-fish, are taken early in the season near the shores and even in the harbors. In Milford Haven they are sometimes caught in great quantities in and about the narrows, a distance of about five or six miles above the entrance of the harbor. Herring of a superior quality are abundant in summer and in early part of autumn. They are found in all parts of the bay, and in small quantities in the harbors. But the shoals of mackerel that traverse the coast in spring and autumn are immense. In May and the early part of June they reach the northern shores about St. Peter's and the River Inhabitants, and sometimes enter Guysborough harbor in such quantities that several thousand barrels are caught in one day. But at this season there is no appearance of fish along the southern shore; nor do they begin to arrive on that side until about the first of August. From that time to the end of October or the middle of November is generally the season of fall fishing, and so abundant are the mackerel in some years that from 800 to 1,000 barrels are often taken by a seine at one draught. In the years 1824 and 1825 the catch at Fox Island amounted to upwards of 20,000 barrels; and including Crow harbor and Canseau Island, which comprise only a space of twelve miles of coast, it is probable 50,000 barrels were taken in each of those years. They are either sold fresh to traders, who resort thither in great numbers with supplies for the fishermen, or are cured and sold to the merchants, or shipped to Halifax and the West Indies."

The historian continues this account with some minor details we need not repeat, and closes by relating a state of affairs that reflect no credit upon the Government of the day, and giving us a glimpse of a pack of greedy rascals, reaping where they had not sown, that is far from pleasant reading, but not to be left out in this connection, so here it is:

"In former years the occupation of the lands adjoining Crow harbor and Fox Island were for all necessary purposes connected with the fishery alike free to all his Majesty's subjects, but these lands were subsequently granted by Government to certain individuals, who thereupon claimed a percentage of all fish hauled upon the shores of their respective locations, and also a ground rent for fishing huts, yards, and places to spread seines, etc. This claim was at first resisted by the fishermen, and in consequence thereof a suit was commenced and tried at Guysborough, before one of the judges of the Supreme Court, in the year 1811, and determined in favor of the proprietor of the soil, since which decision the claim has been recognized and the restrictions in some instances greatly increased. At the commencement of the season the fisherman generally obtains permission from the proprietor or his agent to erect his hut; and if he is a seine owner, to occupy a certain space for his boats and sheds, etc. At the end of the season, or before he leaves the ground, he pays a barrel of cured mackerel, or its value, for the rent of his hovel, and an additional quantity or price, in proportion to the ground he occupies. For every hired man he pays five shillings; and if he has either a partner or associate in his hut, he pays an additional barrel of mackerel for each of them. Besides these exactions the proprietor not only claims, but enforces, the right of sending two free "dippers" into every seine that is hauled; and has also one-tenth part of the seine's share after the fish are dressed— that is, one-twentieth of the whole draught—the sharesmen or assistants being entitled to one-half for their trouble. In 1825 Patrick Lanigan, Esq., received 1,200 barrels of mackerel for rent from Waterloo beach and a portion of Fox Island."

A portion of the shore between Crow harbor and Guysborough was settled or assigned to the Sixtieth Regiment, Hessians, disbanded about 1785.

Manchester, opposite the town of Guysborough, was called for the Duke of Manchester, father or brother of Lord Charles Greville Montague, who was patron of a corps called the "Montagues," who settled the backlands of this section. Benjamin Hallowell had a large grant here in 1765, before referred to. He had been an official in the Boston Custom House.

That portion known as "The Intervale" was in part allotted to the Seventy-first Regiment in 1785.

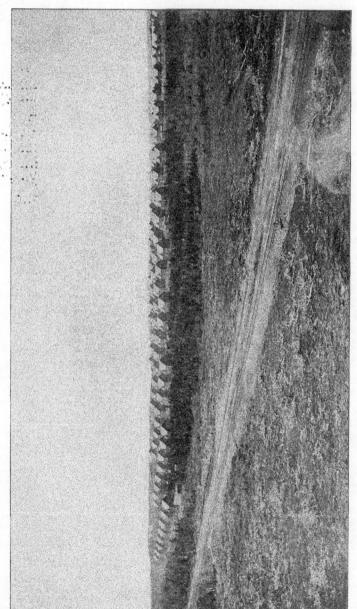

DOMINION NO. 2, GLACE BAY, CAPE BRETON COUNTY, C. B.

On the Atlantic coast are numerous harbors and settlements on them.

Next to Canso is Whitehead, a fine port that seems to invite some large enterprise that has never materialized.

Around the shores of Tor Bay there are the following villages: Coal Harbor, Charles Cove, Larry's River. The inhabitants are mostly Acadian French engaged principally in fishing. Isaac's Harbor has come into some local prominence during the last forty years on account of some gold discoveries that were made by white men and Indians. The first settler was Isaac Webb, whose name is perpetuated in that of the place.

Country Harbor occupies a central position on the county coast. It is a fine port, navigable for eight miles. In 1785 the King's Carolina Rangers, some 300 in number, were settled there. Gold mines are worked thereabouts.

Wine Harbor is another locality best known for its gold mines, that were discovered in 1861. A Portuguese vessel laden with wine was cast away on this place, and hence the name that commemorates the disaster.

St. Mary's River is one of the largest in the Province, being navigable for ordinary vessel to a distance of ten miles. The mouth opens out to the dimensions of a bay. Early as 1654 there was a French fishing and trading establishment at the head of navigation where now is the village of Sherbrook. It was a few years later destroyed by the English. There are good farming lands in this vicinity, and Goldenville and Cochran Hill are important gold-mining centers. A large timber district is tributary to this river, and lumbering has been one of the leading industries of the St. Mary's District. This river was once noted for its valuable salmon fisheries. In 1765 Jonathan Binney and others received a grant there of 150,000 acres. This is our old acquaintance who figures largely in the early history of Halifax.

Liscomb River is noted for its fine timber district and excellent water power. Melrose is eleven miles inland from Sherbrooke, where there is a scattered farming community.

On the far northeastern corner of the county is Port Mulgrave on the Strait of Canso, the land terminus of the Intercolonial Railway, that is resumed in Cape Breton.

GEOLOGY OF GUYSBOROUGH COUNTY.

A line drawn from the mouth of the Salmon River to the vicinity of Trafalgar, near the southwestern corner of the county, will have on the southern side the Cambrian slates and quartzites, with granite intrusions here and there. On the northern side appear the later formations of Devonian and Carboniferous, with patches here and there of trap or dolorite. The Salmon River has its channel almost continually along the contact of Cambrian and Devonian formations. The slates and quartzites of this Atlantic slope contain the gold mines of the county that have been already mentioned.

The principal granite areas are at Canso, Forest Hill, Ingersoll Lake to the Strait vicinity of Tor Bay, a little back from the coast, Sherbrook and Cochoran Hill, making in all about one-quarter of the county. The gold never occurs in this rock throughout the Province. The northern portion of the county, from the line of the Salmon River contact, has been the scene of considerable controversy among geologists. When all the needed facts are brought together, doubtless there will be a substantial agreement among them. The tattered and distorted record is not readily arranged in the natural order.

From the Survey Report of 1887, Fletcher and Faribault, I take the following items: "Lower Devonian strata run from Guysborough Harbor to South River Lake, and are also found about Cape Porcupine. A broad belt of rocks, similar to those regarded in New Brunswick and Newfoundland as Devonian, extends from the Strait of Canso to Lochaber, thence keeping south of the East River of St. Mary's and of the East River of Pictou to strike the Intercolonial Railway near Glengarry, to form the high land south of Truro, and pass unconformably beneath the Carboniferous of the Stewiacke River. A second belt of the highest member of this series extends from the Arisaig trunk road westward to Bailey's Brook. The strata of the first belt are separable into three distinct groups, corresponding closely with those of New Brunswick, as follows:

"Lower conglomerate group, equivalent to Bloomsbury conglomerate.

"Middle gray sandstone and slate group, equivalent to Dadoxylon sandstone and Cordaite shale.

"Upper red slate and sandstone group, equivalent to Mispeck group.

"A zone of the lowest group, five or six miles wide, runs due west from Guysborough Harbor to South River Lake, keeping south of Roman Valley to the Strait of Canso, Upper Tracadie and Merland, to the westward of Lochaber, where it is only a half mile wide, increasing, however, to four miles at Kerrogware, and still more to the westward. The upper group, nowhere exceeding six miles in

GUYSBORO FROM EAST SIDE OF HARBOR.

CHURCH STREET, GUYSBORO.

MAIN STREET, GUYSBOROUGH TOWN, FROM THE NORTH.

COMMERCIAL CABLE COMPANY'S STATION, HAZELHILL,
GUYSBOROUGH COUNTY.

width, runs from Merland to the westward of Lochaber. At the base of this, or at the top of the preceding group, or possibly forming an independent subdivision, is a belt of greenish and red slates and rusty weathering, flinty, gray sandstone containing iron ore which has been worked at several places."

The following paragraphs descriptive of the scenery in certain parts of this county are extracted from the same report from which I have just quoted

"The coasts of Canso, Dover, and the islands in the vicinity are wild 'and romantic, presenting to the ocean rough bold cliffs, mostly granite, the surface being either barren or supporting a few scraggy spruces, cranberries, and other low-growing plants. The most northerly of the Cranberry Islands, called the 'Frying Pan,' is the home of innumerable sea-gulls. Extensive barrens lie between Canso and Tor Bay; but hay marshes fringe some of the brooks, and small spots of cultivable land are found on the shore. Towards the head of New Harbor mossy spruce land, interspersed with clumps of birch and maple, occupies the valleys and also some of the hills, on which, however, much of the timber is blown down.

"The valley of New Harbor River to the head of tidewater is very beautiful, the hills on either side being high. Above the salt water, it is wide and easy to follow. On Isaac's Harbor River fine meadows and marshes occupy a narrow belt about the lakes, while higher up the river flows through a well-wooded valley from which a large quantity of timber for ship-building has been obtained, but which is otherwise unproductive.

"The scenery of the St. Mary's River at Melrose is picturesque in its well-cultivated meadows and numerous small lakes enclosed by rough woody hills. Many of the lakes which empty into this river are rocky and beautiful, bordered with hardwood and evergreens."

CHAPTER XIV.

IRON MINES AND IRON PROSPECTS.

The human race could have become civilized, and made a conquest of the material world without the precious metals of gold and silver. In fact, if the preciousness depends upon the intrinsic value, then iron is the most precious of all metals. It has been the greatest economic factor in bringing about the civilization of mankind. When we consider that there could be no proper keen-cutting instrument without it, then we may the better realize how indispensable it was to human progress. The quantity used by any nation to-day is considered as an index of its grade of civilization. The total product of the world, China excepted, reaches the enormous figure of forty-three million tons of pig iron in 1900, and out of a portion of this there is made twenty-eight million tons of steel. Of this vast amount the United States produced 13,941,842 gross tons of 2,240 lbs. of pig iron. , and 27,650,285 tons of steel; only so far back as 1870 the total product of pig iron for that country was 1,665,179 tons, by comparison we may perceive at a glance how rapidly this industry has assumed its immense proportions. Great Britain produced in the same year, 8,959,691 gross tons of pig iron, and 5,050,000 tons of steel; and Russia's contribution was 16,137,736 tons of pig iron and 1,830,-260 gross tons of steel. Germany reports 8,520,390 gross tons of pig iron, and 6,365,529 tons gross of steel. These figures furnish the reasons for calling this the Age of Iron. The Golden age is in the future, we will have reached it when steel and iron are no longer used to construct ships of war, and cast black-lipped cannons. The existence of iron ore in such inexhaustible quantities to furnish means of human conquest over natural obstacles, seems surely to more than suggest that a providential Forethought had us in view, when as yet we were being made "in secret, and curiously wrought in the lower parts of the earth." We do not know when iron was first melted from its ores by the art of man. The most ancient tombs of Egypt contain tools and weapons of stone, but no trace of iron. Their date is about 0,000 years ago. Mankind has probably looked upon Sun, and Sea for a period remotely beyond ten thousand years, and all this weary while, up to within four or five thousand years ago, he was fighting the battle of life at an immense disadvantage, with weapons and tools of stone and wood and bone. It was a pathetic struggle with wild beast and elemental forces. The thing he needed was at his hand, but it must be mixed with brains before it could be used. Copper, and gold, and silver could be sparingly found in nuggets, but iron as metal uncombined with other elements did not exist. The exception would be that stones falling out of the sky, sometimes in pieces weighing hundreds of pounds, are in many instances very largely composed of metallic iron. These may have furnished the first bits of this metal used by mankind; at any rate they have been found in the possession of savage people. We may readily see that a fiery body falling out of the heavens, and striking the earth in the presence of witnesses, would provoke their curiosity to the extent of examining its make-up and securing any detachable portions. But this would not lead to the discovery of smelting iron from its ore. Metallic iron in lumps and nuggets has been found in the ash of a burning coal seam accidentally on fire. A find like that would be a very broad hint that a man might get the ore and melt it himself. That mankind should have remained so long in ignorance of this most useful and common metal is difficult to explain. Up to within the memory of living men it remained a scarce article, and steel of good quality was so dear that it was used with the greatest care and economy. We are safe in assuming that mankind knew the art of making iron five thousand years ago. The discovery of a process to convert it into steel was made at a date beyond all historical knowledge. The human mind five thousand years ago was acute, strong, and curious, and has been ever since. Yet the manufacture of iron and steel during all this time, almost to this generation, never got beyond primitive methods. There could not be much progress until the advent of the steam engine and the science of chemistry. In order to have cheap iron it must be made in large quantities. So long as charcoal was the only fuel for smelting, the price must be high and the product very limited. The iron furnace for the production of pig iron from the ore demands three materials—ore, coal, and limestone. These are never assembled by Nature within gunshot or carting distance of each other on a scale calculated for large operations. There are iron deposits in the coal measures, often enough, but their percentage of metal is either very low or the coal is not well adapted to become coke to be used in smelting. Nevertheless these mines have been, and in several places are still worked, but they do not produce on a large scale, and will be sure to drop out of the business in the stress of competition with great concerns that are placed with nice discrimination where vast amounts of the raw material can be assembled at the cheapest possible rate, and shipping facilities are favorable. At these focal points of 'the iron-smelting business is the best opportunity for the production of steel. So long as this material was made by a process that no one could explain, there was little or no advancement in its mode of production during thousands of years. Chemistry at last penetrated to the cause of its hardness and strength, and therein lay the way to new inventions that have given us steel rails, steel ships, steel bridges, steel frames for great buildings, and other steel structures in almost endless variety. The demand has led to the discovery of new iron mines, and competition in the United States among producers ended in a billion-dollar trust, wherein warring interests are extinguished in a policy designed to be profitable to all within the gigantic combination. The demand for iron and steel has increased with marvelous strides. No seer of the business world a generation ago could have foreseen this new order of things. "It is the unexpected that happens.' There has always been recognized the presence of certain elements in iron ore that were either detrimental or fatal to its utility. These are sulphur, phosphorus, and titanic acid. They were devils that refused to be cast out, even by the ordeal of the fiery furnace; they turned up in the pig iron product as ruinous ingredients, even though the percentage was less than one. Science has grappled with these enemies and largely overcome them. Phosphorus was the most objectionable, as an extremely small quantity rendered the pig product useless for Bessemer purposes, wherein the object is to make a grade of steel for structural uses at a cheap figure. Human ingenuity has been equal to the problem, and ores that very recently were worthless are now profitably treated, and the phosphorus is driven into the slag, that at once becomes valuable for fertilizing purposes, where it enters the farm products and reaches the brains of men who dislodged it from a position hostile to human interests and turned a curse to a blessing. Surely this was a marvelous circuit. The ability to treat successfully those hitherto undesirable ores is no small item in dealing with the value of Nova Scotia iron mines. So rapid have been the improvements in the last few years in connection with the making of iron and steel that we may be confident that other important discoveries and inventions within the next decade will make some of the present methods and machinery mere back numbers in this wonderful story of human triumphs over the obstacles of Nature. An iron mine in Nova Scotia in the nature of things cannot be remote from coal and limestone, nor have a long haulage to a harbor; the country is too small for that.

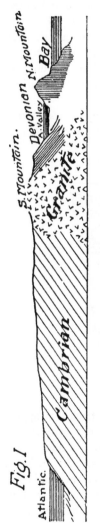

Fig. 1.

The counties of Yarmouth, Shelburne, and Queens are the most distant from the coal measures, and they are occupied by Cambrian slates, quartzites, and granite areas, in which there are no iron mines. The geography of the Province makes it impossible to get beyond forty miles from the coast and shipping facilities. The great iron and steel plants in Sidney have for the present thrown somewhat into the shade the claims of Nova Scotia iron mines, but it can be scarcely more than a temporary eclipse. That anything here in this line can compete with the advantages of the ores of Bell Island treated in Sidney may seem an extravagant estimate of our iron deposits. They will doubtless need to come up to severe exactions to match the favorable features of this new iron and steel metropolis. The increasing demand for these products of varied qualities can scarcely fail to draw upon iron resources so favorably located and so enormous in metallic contents that they are national bonanzas awaiting skill, and capital, and energy to send their abundant riches into the business circulation of the country.

We come now to a notice of such mines and prospects, and make a beginning with the Nictaux and Torbrook deposits. These for the present may be considered as different outcrops of the same system of veins. The locality is in Annapolis County, through which from east to west runs an elevation known as the South Mountain, with a general altitude of about 600 feet; it is parallel to what is called the "North Mountain," a low ridge of sandstone and igneous rock of Triassic times, forming the southern coast of the Bay of Fundy and reaching an altitude of some 600 feet. These mountains are some ten miles apart, and between them is the fruitful Annapolis Valley. The South Mountain alone concerns us here. It is in reality the rather abrupt northern border of the granite upraise and axis of the Province. On the southeast it forms a contact with Cambrian slates and quartzites of the Atlantic slope. On the opposite side the contact is with Devonian slates and quartzites that are melted and otherwise metamorphosed at the junction, and lie along the valley side of this great granite uplift. In this Devonian formation are the iron mines under discussion. The situation will be made clearer by the slight diagram, No. 1, showing a section from the Bay of Fundy to the Atlantic, not strictly to scale. The actual distance is 70 miles; of this, 40 is Cambrian, 8 is granite.

The following map of Annapolis County, showing the rock structure, on a scale of eight miles to an inch, is taken from the Government Geological Survey.

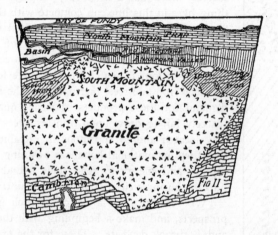

The iron mines occur as veins in the Devonian strata that appear as the upturned edges of synclinals. These veins run conformable to the course of the strata, or, in other words, they are mineralized zones or beds that were once in a horizontal position, and the profound folding and denudation have exposed them as nearly perpendicular veins, with a strike or course northeasterly and southwesterly, thus roughly corresponding to the trend of the mountain. These veins are either of red hematite or magnetite, and vary in width from two to twenty feet at the outcrop, and several of them have been traced about six miles, from Torbrook to Nictaux. At the former locality about twelve years ago the Torbrook Iron Company was organized and began work on one of these hematite veins. This new work was reported on as follows in the report of the Department of Mines of Nova Scotia for the year 1891:

"About the beginning of March last, active operations were first commenced at Torbrook, Annapolis County, on the bed of red hematite ore discovered there during the previous year. The ore extends along the base of the South Mountain, the strike being about north 60 degrees east, and has been traced on the surface from Nictaux Falls eastward to the Kings County line, a distance of four miles. The lead has an average thickness of 5½ feet, clear ore, and is tilted up, to dip at an angle varying from 70 to 80 degrees. Both the hanging and foot walls are of a variegated talcose slate, very light in color, and between 18 to 24 inches thick. These walls form a fairly good support for the time being, although slightly soft. The country rock is of a dark bluish slate, probably of Upper Devonian Age. A fair sample of the ore yields about .60 per cent phosphoric acid, 0.3 per cent sulphur trace. All the ore is shipped via Windsor Junction to Londonderry, N. S. Last month 1,650 tons were shipped."

The next year 27,114 tons were mined and smelted at Londonderry. The Government report of mines for 1895 was as follows:

"The Torbrook Iron Mining Company worked steadily during the season, its output being divided between Ferrona and Londonderry furnaces. The vein was found on the Holland property, about three-quarters of a mile to the westward of the mine, to be uniform, of good quality, and four feet thick. The main shaft at the Torbrook mine is now 350 feet deep. The angle of inclination of the bed of ore, which was about 80 degrees at the surface, is now 45 degrees, and the vein has increased in thickness from 6 to 12 feet."

In 1897 the mine was closed, but not for lack of ore. The Government report for that year says: "The Torbrook mine worked up to July, producing 19,944 tons, which was sold to Londonderry and Ferrona. When closed down the mine was in good working order, with a large amount of available ore." Since that date there has been considerable activity in that locality, and the Mines Report for 1900 informs us that "The Torbrook areas in Annapolis County have received a good deal of attention. A large bed from 6 to 10 feet thick has been traced from Black River, near the county line, westward, and passing a short distance south of the Leckie lead, is believed to represent the well-known 'shell bed.' "

Several other leads of workable dimensions have been opened;
the horizon represented by this bed is over a distance of between
five and six miles. The ores run from 48 to 55 per cent of metallic
iron. Late in the fall the five-inch-core calyx drill was secured, and
the bed drilled through at a depth of 300 feet beside the Torbrook
road. At this depth the bed was about nine feet thick. The drill
has been working in almost vertical slate and quartzite, and has given
satisfactory results. These explorations have shown a wonderful
regularity in the measures at Torbrook, and there is no doubt of a
large amount of ore in the properties tested, running into many million
tons. Near the western portion of this district, in the valley of
Nictaux, are outcropping beds of iron ore. One of these attracted
attention in the first decade of this century, when a small Catalan
forge produced some bar iron from the ores of Nictaux. It is even
said that the French had forestalled this undertaking. This ore bed
was remarkable for the fossil shells that it contained. Dr. Gilpin
describes it as "a highly fossiliferous peroxide of iron, associated
with dark slates."

In 1855 a company erected quite extensive works, and during a
few years continued operations with the ores from this shell bed.

In 1858 the quantity of iron exported was 744 tons, value $2,375,
and in 1859 1,125 tons of the value of $14,790 ("How's Mineralogy
of Nova Scotia").

This must have been nearly the last output, for the writer recalls
that he saw these furnaces in 1860 closed down for good and all.
In the report of the Department of Mines, 1877, there is a quotation
from Dr. Jackson, 1855, State Assayer for Massachusetts, relating
to the Nictaux ores, as follows:

"One cannot fail to be surprised at the enormous quantities of
ore already exposed by the numerous openings which have been made.
There are several distinct and parallel beds of iron ores which we
examined, from 4 to 10 feet in width, extending certainly no less
than five miles continuously. The supply of iron ore at Nictaux is
inexhaustible."

The quantity of ore in this district is very great; all whose opinions are of value are agreed upon that point. Dr. Gilpin, than whom
there is no better authority, says: "As to the quantity of ore there
can be no question. The amounts above the water levels of the
Torbrook and Nictaux Rivers must be enormous." Another vital
question is the cost of getting ore and its transportation to a proper

locality for treatment. On this Dr. Gilpin remarks: "The mining and transportation of these ores would be cheaper than from almost any other district in Nova Scotia, and the preliminary outlays for machinery, drills, wire tramways, etc., be reduced to a minimum by the facilities available for utilizing water power for generating electrical power."

These extracts are taken from a paper published in the transactions of the Nova Scotia Institute of Science, Vol. 9, part 1, to which I am also indebted for the following analyses of ores from this district:

MAGNETITES.

	No. 1.	No. 2.	No. 3.	No. 4.
Metallic iron	54.22	39.11	53.14	54.96
Silica	14.97	11.64	.....	11.12
Sulphur	.069	.09	.....	trace
Phosphorus	.36	.17	.172	.192
Alumina	5.53	.....	.....	.314
Lime	2.70	.....	.....	5.88
Magnesia	.41	.....	.....	2.01
Manganese	.86	.....	.....	.....

RED HEMATITE.

Metallic iron	58.05	57.93	18.47
Silica	.....	17.21	33.50
Sulphur	.....	.03	.....
Phosphorus	.....	.....	.....
Alumina	.....	.....	.....
Lime	.....	.....	.....
Manganese	.....	.....	.980
Magnesia	.....	.....	.....

This Devonian formation outcrops again some thirty miles west of Nictaux on the south side of the Annapolis Basin, at Moose River. Dr. Gilpin describes it thus: "At Clementsport there are two beds of ore running nearly east and west, and underlying to the south at angles of 75 to 80 degrees. The highest of these, the Milner bed, varies in thickness from two to four feet. It is specular ore metamorphosed with magnetic properties and still retaining casts of Virelebite, Spirifers and associated mollusks. The ore, which is of a fair quality, yields about 33 per cent of metallic iron. The Potter bed is a magnetite (?) and presents the following section where worked:

	Feet.	Inches.
Ore	3	0
Slate	2	6
Ore	3	6

It is stated to 'yield 15 per cent more iron than the Milner bed. (See "Mines of Nova Scotia," page 55.) In 1828 Messrs. Jackson and Alger, very competent American gentlemen, contributed to the American Journal of Science an article on the mineralogy and geology of Nova Scotia, the result of very able pioneer work in this Province. The next year they visited and re-examined the ground, and enlarged their essay, and communicated to the American Academy, and it was printed in book form in 1832. These men had an intimate acquaintance with the Clementsport and Moose River iron ores, and their account is interesting and instructive, and in the main it is here reproduced:

"Having thus far described the appearances and productions of the South Mountains, we shall now advert to ore beds at Clements, the last place along the range where it is known to appear. This bed is three miles from the mouth of Moose River, and several extensive openings having been made into it during the past season from which many hundred tons of the ore have been removed, peculiar facilities are afforded for its examination. Its width is about 6 feet, but from the intimate union of the ore with the contiguous slate it is very difficult to discover the line of separation between the one and the other. By the assistance of the compass this ore may be traced for the distance of two miles towards Bear River, so powerful is its magnetic influence on the needle. This ore is fine-grained, of a bluish gray or steel gray color, and possesses a glistening metallic luster; when reduced to powder its color is similar. It is highly magnetic, as we have before observed. Its specific gravity is 4.5, and it yields by fusion in the assay furnace 65 per cent of soft cast iron. But when reduced in the smelting furnace it has hitherto yielded less, owing to its admixture with the slate, from which it is difficult to separate it. The cast iron obtained from this ore is a good quality for strength and softness, while that of a harder nature containing less carbon is readily converted into malleable iron, which, to give it the praise it deserves, is equal to the best of this description made in the United States. The pure iron has been also converted into blistered steel, which on trial was found equally as useful for the purposes to which the foreign article had been applied." The Mr. Alger of this report had an ample opportunity to know whereof he wrote, as he was one of the gentlemen largely interested in the iron works at Moose River. The report of the Department of Mines, 1874, has, what I take to be a sort of "dying declaration" about these works, and runs as follows: "The Annapolis iron mines at Clements-port have passed into the hands of the New York & Nova Scotia Iron & Coal Mining & Manufacturing Co., who have employed some eight men only, during the year, mining ore. The furnace is out of blast undergoing repair." Dr. Gesner, in his "Industrial Resources of Nova Scotia," 1849, says: "At Clements, in the County of Annapolis, and three miles from the mouth of Moose River; brown hematite outcrops and may be traced a mile on the surface, with an average thickness of 9 feet 6 inches. It yields from 33 to 40 per cent of cast metal, and the quality of the iron is superior. The river affords abundant water power to propel machinery, and the harbor at its mouth communicates with the beautiful basin of Annapolis."

On the North Mountain, that long upraise of sandstone and trap that stretches unbroken from Blomidon to Digby, there are veins of iron ore of good quality, but thus far the quantity discovered is not sufficient to attract capital. In various parts of the Province there are small deposits of iron ore, but from an economic point of view do not come within the scope of this chapter.

So far as known the Cambrian slates and quartzites are destitute of iron mines. For this reason the counties of Digby, Yarmouth, Shelburne, Queens, Lunenburg, and Halifax are not to be reckoned among present or probable producers of iron. We pass on to the county of Colchester, where geological conditions have changed, and the extensive Londonderry deposits occur. Sir William Dawson, in his Acadian Geology, 1855, gives a detailed account of this iron mine, and Prof. How, in his Mineralogy of Nova Scotia, 1868, has abridged Dawson's account and added some notes of his own, and I will quote from How: "The iron worked (at Londonderry) is found in a vein of ferruginous magnesian limestone, a variety of magnesia which extends along the south slope of the Cobequid Hills, and which has been most carefully explored in the vicinity of Folly. and Great Village, Rivers. At the site of the Acadia mine furnace, in the western bank of the Great Village River, at the junction of the carboniferous and metamorphic rocks, a thick series of gray and barren sandstones and shales, dipping to the south at an angle of 65 degrees and 70 degrees west, meets black and olive slates, nearly vertical and with a strike north 55 degrees east. The vein is well seen in the bed of the stream, and also in the excavations in the western bank, which rises abruptly 327 feet above the river bed. In the stream bottom it presents the appearance of a complicated network of fissures penetrating quartzite and slate, and filled with ankerite, with which is a smaller quantity of red ochery iron ore and micaceous specular ore. In ascending the stream the vein appears to increase in width and in the quantity of the ores of iron. In one place it showed a breadth of 20 feet. In some parts of the vein the ankerite is intimately mixed with crystals and veinlets of yellowish spathose iron. The red ochery ore occurs in minor veins and irregular masses dispersed in the ankerite. Some of these veins are two yards thick, and the shapeless masses are often of much larger dimensions. Specular iron ore also occurs in small, irregular veins and in disseminated crystals and nests. At one part of the bank there appears to be a considerable mass of magnetic iron ore mixed with specular ore. The general course of the vein at the mine and further east is south 98 degrees west, the variation being 21 degrees west. At the mine the course deviates about 33 degrees from the containing rock; elsewhere the deviation is less, and there is an approach to parallelism between the course of the vein and that of the rock formation of the hills as well as that of the junction of the carboniferous and metamorphic systems. The vein for a space of seven miles along the hills is always found at the distance of from 300 yards to a third of a mile northward of the last carboniferous beds, and always in the same band of slate and quartzite. Westward of the Acadia mine the course of the vein is marked by the color of the soil for about a mile, as far as Cook's Brook, where the outcrop of the ore is not exposed, but large fragments of specular iron have been found, and a shaft sunk on the course of the vein has penetrated more than 40 feet of yellow ochre, containing a few rounded masses and irregular layers of ankerite. Specimens of specular ore and ankerite have been received from the continuation of the same metamorphic district as far west as Five Islands, twenty miles distant from the Acadia mine. On the east side of the west branch of the Great Village River the vein is not so well exposed, but indications of it can be seen on the surface as far as the west branch of the river, in the bed of which it has been found to continue. Further eastward, on higher ground, between the Great Village and Folly Rivers, indications of iron ores have been found, especially near the latter, where in two places small excavations have exposed specular and red ores, and where numerous fragments of brown hematite are found on the surface. On the elevated ground east of the Folly River the vein is again largely developed. At one point 10 feet of red iron ore were seen without exposing the north side of the vein. The width here exposed was 15 feet, and neither wall was exposed. Still further east, on the property of C. D. Archibald, Esq., on equally elevated ground, three excavations have shown a still greater development of the vein. One trench fifty-three feet long, nearly at right angles to the course of the vein, shows in its whole length a mixture of red and specular ores with ankerite. In the bed of the Mill Brook, about two miles east of Folly River, the vein attains a great thickness in the eastern bank. Here it consists of a network of fissures filled with ankerite. It was found in the bank of another brook still further to the east, and, though not traced further, there was no doubt entertained of its continuance to a great distance in that direction.

I visited the mines in 1861 and saw with great interest the admirable arrangement by which a large amount of work was being done, and, having requested E. A. Jones, Esq., the manager, to favor me with some descriptive details, I received the following valuable account of the history, progress, and nature of the establishment: "The Acadian works were commenced in 1849, and the first iron was made by the Catalan forge in 1850. In 1852-3 a blast furnace was erected for the manufacture of pig iron, the Catalan forge being abandoned. Up to the time of my arriving in the Province, in the summer of 1857, there had been made altogether about 1,000 tons of iron, from about 4,000 tons of ore.

"Since that time to the present, 1861, we have made about 4,000 tons of iron, using about 9,000 tons of ore. Our present make of bar iron is at the rate of 1,200 tons, of an economic value of about 24,000 pounds per annum. The ores we use are a hematite yielding about 48 and a brown and red oxide yielding about 40 per cent of iron.

"The ores are somewhat refractory; this arises mainly from the presence of a stone mechanically mixed through the ore, which is very difficult to act upon in the blast furnace. It requires about 160 bushels, imperial, of charcoal, and 200 bushels of limestone (this is found in the vicinity), used as a flux, to smelt one ton of pig iron, and about 3½ cords of wood to convert the pig into bars. The wood used is required to be perfectly dry. We have one blast furnace and three puddling furnaces, with one reheating furnace. The pressure of the blast is about four ounces to the square inch. We now employ about 230 men; our expenditure for wages, etc., at the works will average about £1,200 a month. The iron made compares very favorably with the best brought to market from any part of the world for the same purpose, namely, the manufacture of steel."

Writing in 1868, Prof. How says: "In all, there have been made at the Acadia works 15,000 tons of pig iron and 7,000 tons of bar iron, of tne aggregate value of $1,000,000." In the report of the Department of Mines, 1874, we have this record: "The Acadia iron mines at Londonderry have changed hands and become the property of the Steel Company of Canada (Limited), having a capital of £500,000 sterling. According to the prospectus, the property consists of fifty-five square miles of freehold lands, together with the mines thereunder and the works and buildings thereon. It was purchased for £82,000 in cash and £120,000 worth of fully paid up founders' shares."

From this date to 1897 the company is reported by the Department of Mines from year to year as a producer. Without quoting in full, here are a few items. Report for 1890: "The Steel Company have continued their operations the past year, and reached an output of 50,696 tons of iron ore mined, against 28,889 tons in 1879. There were also 4,773 tons of ankerite quarried for flux." This seems to be the high tide of operations. In 1892 the report gives 37,223 tons of ore mined, 27,114 tons of ore treated from Torbrook.

In 1894 the report gives 9,214 tons of ore mined and some "supplies" from Torbrook. Since that date very little work has been reported from Londonderry; but now in January, 1903, these mines are being opened up again.

It is not within the design of this book to relate the particulars of business concerns, but to describe the natural resources, together with general facts connected with the work done in connection with them. We now proceed to give some account of the iron deposits of Pictou County. In Dr. Gilpin's Report on the Mines and Mineral Lands of Nova Scotia, before referred to, is the following description:

PICTOU COUNTY—IRON ORES.

"The iron ores of this district are probably more varied and of greater extent than elsewhere in the Province, and from their relation to fuel, flux, and shipping are destined to play an important part in its future development.

Although the existence of iron ores on the East River of Pictou was known for many years, it was not until 1872 that any systematic attempts were made to test their extent. As early as 1828, or shortly after the General Mining Association of London opened their Pictou collieries, a blast furnace was erected at the colliery and a small quantity of red hematite and limonite smelted; but the expense of hauling the ore twelve miles soon put a stop to the work. Nothing was then done until in 1872-3 extensive explorations were carried on under the supervision of Dr. Dawson and continued for several years from that date by the writer. Taking the ores in descending geological order, the first to be noticed are the bog ores. These are scattered over many parts of the county, notably on the West Branch and the headwaters of River John. Several small deposits have been found near French River, of which an analysis by the writer is given below. They also occur north of New Glasgow, and are apparently derived from the conglomerate already referred to as limiting the coal field. . We have next to notice the clay ironstone ores of the Pictou coal field. ҳ They form irregular beds from 5 to 40 inches thick, and are found everywhere in the coal measures, in some cases forming part of the seams. But little attention has yet been paid to them. From the writer's analysis given below it will be seen that they are of good quality, and it is considered that they will prove an important addition to the older ores. .

At French River, in the marine limestone formation (?), are numerous beds of clay ironstone carbonates and hydrated peroxides on beds from 6 inches to 4 feet in thickness. The discovery is a recent one, and little is yet known about the deposits. The following analysis is by the writer:

	Bog Ore, French River.	Clay Ironstone, Pictou Coal Field.	Black Band, Pictou Coal Field.	Clay Ironstone, French River.
Moisture	5.500	2.132	.732	. . . . . .
Water of comp..	6.100	. . . . . .	. . . . . .	. . . . . .
Sulphur	.208	.612	.214	.022
Phosphoric acid . .	.384	Trace	.586	Trace
Manganese	5.886	. . . . . .	4.450	. . . . . .
Lime	Trace	Trace	3.780	. . . . . .
Magnesia	Trace	1.655	.783	Trace
Alumina	3.106	16.962	3.180	2.718
Silica	12.325	.780	16.546	58.800
Carbonic acid	. . . . . .	. . . . . .	27.589	3.370
Iron protoxide . .	. . . . . .	45.361	36.000	35.942
Iron peroxide	66.510	. . . . . .	. . . . . .	. . . . . .
	100.019	67.502	100.000	99.852
Metallic iron. . .	46.557	35.000	28.000	25.160

Passing to the westward, a large deposit of spathic ore is found at Sutherland's Brook, held by the Pictou Coal & Iron Company. The containing strata were formerly considered of millstone grit age, but from the proximity of gypsum and limestone they would seem rather to belong to the marine limestone formation. As far as can be judged from a rough survey, this ore is found at a horizon 800 feet lower than the ironstone of French River.

The bed dips south at an angle of 60 degrees, and varies in thickness from 6 to 10½ feet, and has above and below a small bed of the same, 6 to 10 inches thick. The ore is a sparry carbonate of iron, holding peroxide in places, with a variable proportion of manganese and very little sulphur and phosphorus. Superficially it is rusted, but where unweathered of a pearly gray color. From surface indications it appears probable that this ore extends over a considerable district, and the writer is inclined to consider it characteristic of a horizon low down in the marine limestone.

From Springville for several miles up the East River the line of contact of the Marine limestone and Silurian follows closely the course of the river. At several points along this line a fine deposit of limonite has been proved. On the property of the Halifax Company, some years ago, the writer proved it to have a thickness of 21 feet 6 inches, and recent researches have proved it to be 15 feet thick on the Saddler area of the Pictou Coal and Iron Company, and an equal development at other points. The ore is compact, concretionary, and fibrous,. with considerable quantities of gravel ore. At two points ore has been proved to rest on the Silurian clay slates, and has limestone on the hanging wall, usually with a gouge of red clay, frequently holding concretions of manganite and pyrolusite intervening. The ores are very pure, and appear to be much more free from phosphorus than the Londonderry limonite, the average of five analyses of the East River ore giving .118 phosphoric acid, or .083 phosphorus, in 100 parts of iron.

These ores in places hold notable quantities of manganese, and resemble closely the Spanish limonites imported into England. The following analyses of large averages by the writer will show the great purity of these ores, and their manganese contents:

ANALYSES OF EAST RIVER LIMONITES.

Water	7.702	12.530
Iron peroxide	87.925	48.223
Alumina	trace	
Silica	3.000	25.130
Manganese binoxide	trace	14.410
Lime	trace	.015
Magnesia	.500	trace
Sulphur	trace	.480
Phosphorus	trace	.020
	97.127	100.908
Metalic iron	65.54	33.826

The belt holding ore is 600 yards wide at several places, as shown by surface indications, and it appears probable that there is a large amount of it in the valley. The limónite may have been derived, like the limonite of the Cumberland district and other localities in Pennsylvania, as a residual precipitate from disseminated iron sand grains of the Upper Silurian strata as well as a deposit from the gradual dissolution óf the Marine limestones. In view of this it may be stated that in this district the rocks of both ages contain considerable quantities of iron as carbonate and peroxide, and that the erosion has been on an enormous scale. This has been fully treated by the writer in a paper read February, 1879, Institute of Natural Science, Halifax.

, · It may be mentioned here that some of the East River limestones may be found valuable iron ores. An analysis of a bed 12 feet thick near Springville giving the writer the following results:

```
Moisture ...............................    .400
Lime carbonate .........................  55.280
Magnesia ..............................   10.150
Iron  .................................   24.110
Manganese .............................    1.835
Alumina ...............................    4.300
Sulphur ...............................     .168
Phosphorus ............................    none
Residue ...............................    5.000
                                         _____
                                         101.243
```

The district extending from Sunny Brae nearly to the Spathic ore on Sutherland's Brook is occupied by gray and brownish quartzites, olive and gray slates with calcareous bands, usually coarse and unevenly bedded, and containing the fossils of the Arisaig group, a series considered equivalent to the Lower Helderberg of American geologists, and perhaps in its specific forms more related to the English Ludlow. The following are among the more common fossils of this district: Favosites, Zaphrentis, Chonetes tenuistriata, Spirifer rugoecosta, Strophomena profunda, Rhynchonella spirata, Atrypa reticularis, Athyris didyma, Megambonia striata, trilobata, Orthoceras sev. sp., Cornulites, Dalmania Logani, etc. The chief ore of this formation is bedded in red hematite found in four principal deposits. The most northerly of these is known as the Mc-
14

Kenzie red hematite. It appears from the surface indications to be of large size, but no work has yet been done to test it.

The next bed, known as the Webster ore, has been carefully trenched and tested at several points, and extends about three miles. Its thickness varies from 15 to 30 feet, its dip being generally north at angles varying from 25 to 60 degrees. This ore follows the crest of a hill, cut transversely by the valley of Sutherland's River, and admits of adit drainage to a depth of 300 feet. The ore is compact, non-fossiliferous, and brick-red when weathered. The third exposure is known as the Blanchard great bed. No attempts have yet been made to trace it beyond the natural exposures, which extend about half a mile. It varies in width from 20 to 100 feet, measured across a dip nearly vertical. It is also situated on elevated ground, and would yield a large amount of ore.

At a geological horizon about 700 feet higher than the last mentioned bed is a conformable range of red hematites forming the fourth series. This ore appears to form a synclinal trough. On the west side the ore is 12 feet thick; at the apex there appear the outcrops of two other beds 8 and 3 feet in thickness, the larger possibly representing the great bed at Blanchard. On the east of the synclinal only one bed has been opened, varying in width from 3 to 5 feet. Underlying this bed, and on a line where the great bed would show its eastern outcrop, are large boulders, precisely similar in appearance to the ore on its western outcrop, and it is expected that it will shortly be found here. It is considered by some geologists that the large single beds were originally one, and owe their present disjointed condition to faults and erosion; no detailed survey, however, has been made to prove the correctness of this opinion, and at present it can only be said that they are apparently contained in a limited vertical range of strata. The outcrops of other red hematites have been detected, but no work has yet been done to allow of details. These red hematites are all of the same class, being of a red color, with earthy to steely luster, compact or laminated, sometimes oolitic, owing to the peroxide forming minute concretions around grains of sand. In places these ores contain fossils, but the larger proportion are quite free from them. They are excellently adapted for mining, being on high ground, with good roof, and requiring little or no dead work. Similar ores, called fossil red hematites, are found in Pennsylvania, in strata of the Clinton age, and extensively worked near Tyrone, for mixture with red hematites and magnetites. The following analysis will show its relation to the Pictou ores, of which analyses are given further on:

Sesquoxide of iron 38.48
Peroxide of iron 4.37
Silica 37.99
Alumina 9.56
Lime 1.08
Alkalies 2.89
Phosphoric acid 1.48
Sulphur .... trace
Volatile 4.50
Metallic iron 30.34

Passing to the west side of the East River, the carboniferous is found resting on a broad belt of black and olive slate, with bands of quartzite, dipping almost vertically to the south. In these measures considered by Dr. Dawson the equivalents of those holding the Londonderry ores is a large vein of specular ore. The exact relation of these measures to those holding the red hematites is not easily ascertained, as no fossils have yet been found in them, but they appear to occupy a lower position.

The vein shows ore varying in width from 5 to 20 feet; in places there are intercalated masses of quartzite and ankerite. The Pictou Coal and Iron Company own over two miles of this vein, in addition to large and well selected areas on the Limonite, and the Webster and other red hematites on the east side of the river. At two points a vein of a mixture of specular and magnetic ore, one to two feet thick, has been met, but no work has been done to test its value. The main vein is cut by several ravines, and for some distance runs close to the brow of a hill 200 feet high, which would be found advantageous in mining. About two and a half miles to the westward, and nearly on the strike of the specular ore, a large body of reddish quartzite is found in similar black slates, and holds several veins of limonite from 1 to 3 feet in thickness. The bed rock has been traced for some distance, and is capable of yielding a considerable quantity of ore above water level. The ore is compact, of a chocolate color, with small cavities lined with crystals and plates of the same mineral. Near Glengarry specular ore is again met in small veins, in a yellowish-gray quartzite, but no work has yet been done to test its extent.

At numerous other points in the county, rocks of Silurian and Carboniferous age, and some of the traps, contain crystals and veinlets of specular and magnetic ore, as traces of metamorphic action, as well as indications of permanent deposits; but little attention has been paid to them beyond the district described.. The following analyses, by the writer and others, will show the very high character of the ores just described:

	Specular.		Limonite.		Red Hematite.	
	I	II	I	II	I	II
Oxides of iron	92.01	97.52	93.09	81.19	70.00	65.26
Oxides of magnesia	2.16	.....	1.10	.20	.....	trace
Alumina	.21	.....	.....	.....	.....	5.59
Carbonate of lime	1.27	.....	.91	.63	3.03	1.88
Carbonate of magnesia	.43	.....	.....	.....	.....	1.05
Phosphoric acid	.08	.....	.....	.15	.20	.....
Sulphur	.16	.06	.04	.....	.....	.....
Silica	3.68	3.20	4.80	4.26	25.83	25.68
Metallic iron	64.41	68.33	.....	56.83	45.47	43.40

On the St. Mary River are reported large beds of limonite. . At Arisaig, in the Upper Silurian strata, a bed of red hematite, 3 feet thick, has been found. From specimens that the writer has seen, it appears similar in character to the bedded hematites just described, but less silicious. This bed is found at the eastern end of the Lower Helderberg strata just referred to, and in the long range intervening new discoveries may be confidently anticipated. A large amount of money has been expended in testing the iron ores of Pictou, and it is to be hoped that at no distant date smelting operations will be started. Every visitor to the iron beds is astonished at their extent and value.

A half dozen years later than the date of this report prospecting operations were begun on these properties, and some 342 tons of ore shipped to Londonderry smelters.

After the formation of various companies from this date onward, large plants were constructed, a railway built, and smelting carried on at Ferrona. In 1895 the Ferrona plant owned by the New Glasgow Iron, Steel and Railway Company, was amalgamated with the Nova Scotia Steel Company of Trenton, in the same county of Pictou, and thenceforth this Nova Scotia Steel Company became a leading business enterprise in Canada. They purchased Bell Island, Newfoundland, where the experts reported 6,000,000 tons of ore of a superior quality and cheaply mined. This company has now valuable properties in Pictou, Cape Breton, and Newfoundland. A brief history and a list of the properties now owned by this concern is here extracted in full from an official statement published Nov. 21, 1901:

HISTORY.

"The Nova Scotia Steel and Coal Company's undertaking developed in the following way:

"In 1872 a business was established at New Glasgow, Nova Scotia, under the name of the Nova Scotia Forge Company, for the manufacture of railway and marine forgings. The enterprise prospered, and in 1882 the proprietors decided to establish another concern to engage in the manufacture of steel. The Nova Scotia Steel Company was therefore formed to manufacture steel from imported pig iron and scrap steel, by the 'Siemens-Martin Open Hearth' process. Seven years later, namely, in 1889, to insure economy in working, these two concerns were amalgamated as the Nova Scotia Steel and Forge Company, Limited, and extensions and additions were subsequently made to the plant. In 1891 a company was incorporated called The New Glasgow Iron, Coal and Railway Company, which built a' blast furnace for making pig iron at Ferrona, near New Glasgow.

"In January, 1895, the Nova Scotia Steel Company acquired the interests of the New Glasgow Iron, Coal and Railway Company and of the Nova Scotia Steel and Forge Company, and carried on the business previously conducted by these companies until the present year.

"In the year 1900 the Nova Scotia Steel Company purchased as a going concern the business and property of the General Mining Association. The general Mining Association was formed by deed of settlement in 1829, and (inter alia) took over the lease of the Duke of York's extensive coal areas in Nova Scotia. In or about 1858, by arrangement with the Provincial Government of Nova Scotia, the association released some of its rights and secured the exclusive right to all coal seams in certain areas. The leases have been renewed, and are now held under the general law of Nova Scotia. Th association had disposed of some of these coal areas before the property was purchased by the Nova Scotia Steel Company, but had retained the Sydney mine and Point Aconi areas, which contain a superior quality of coal, with good facilities for shipment. The Nova Scotia Steel and Coal Company, Limited, has

acquired the whole business, property and assets of the Nova Scotia
Steel Company, Limited, as a going concern.

PROPERTY.

"The properties now owned by the Nova Scotia Steel and Coal
Company, Limited, consist of:

"1· All the lands, shafts, buildings, plant and railways used
in connection with the coal mines, together with the leases of the
coal areas which were acquired by the Nova Scotia Steel Company
from the General Mining Association. These areas extend from
Sidney Harbor to the entrance to the Great Bras d'Or, and comprise:

"a. The Point Aconi and Sidney Mine areas of 11,700 acres,
which contained in 1871, according to the estimate of the late Mr.
Richard Brown, 155,000,000 tons of coal.

"b. The Sidney Mine submarine areas of 3,200 acres, estimated
by the same authority, in 1871, to contain 66,000,000 tons of coal.
Since 1871 about 5,000,000 tons only have been worked out of the
Sidney mine and Sidney mine submarine areas. The Point Aconi
have not yet been worked.

"2. About 7,824 acres of freehold land in Cape Breton.

"3. A freehold iron ore mine situated at Bell Island, Conception
Bay, Newfoundland, and several deposits of iron ore held by the
company in fee simple or by lease in Nova Scotia.

"4· Leases of coal areas containing two coal seams of good
quality, one of which is now being opened up, situated within six
miles of the steel works at Trenton.

"5· A standard gauge railway, 12½ miles in length, with 3.87
miles of siding, with rolling stock, in Pictou County, Nova Scotia.

"6. About 160 acres of freehold land at Ferrona, Nova Scotia.

"7. A blast furnace, coal washing and coking plant, built in
1892, at Ferrona, with a capacity of 100 tons of pig iron per day.

"8· About 50 acres of land at Trenton and New Glasgow, on
which are the steel works, consisting of four steel melting furnaces,
together with the rolling mills, forges, and other plants, capable of
turning out 100 tons of finished steel per day. Over 4 acres are
actually covered with buildings, and the tramways in and about the
works aggregate about 4 miles in length.

"9· Large limestone and dolomite properties of excellent quality in the County of Cape Breton.

"10.   Net assets represented by cash balances, book debts and stock in trade, these amounted to $635,789.48 on the first day of January, 1901."

COAL DEPOSITS.

The coal deposits owned by the company in Cape Breton alone are estimated to contain 216,000,000 tons of coal.

STEEL AND IRON.

The iron and steel produced by the company has always found a ready market in Canada, large quantities being shipped to the Provinces of Ontario and Quebec.   It is expected that the Canadian market will in the future continue to take the larger part of the company's output, but if any surplus should be produced the company is in as good a position to sell in the foreign markets as any other company in Canada.

A good deal of work has been done on these Pictou iron mines by the Pictou Charcoal-Iron Company.   This concern, according to the report of the Department of Mines for 1891, have located themselves at Bridgeville, on the line of the New Glasgow Company's railway, and the object of their work may be gathered from the following remark of Mr. E. J. Spotswell: "Our object is to establish a charcoal-iron plant here at Bridgeville, and to use the brown ores principally, and to produce a charcoal iron especially adapted for car wheel making and also for specially strong machine castings.   With this object in view we have purchased mining rights of iron ore, of limestone and manganese ore, and some 6,000 acres of hardwood land.   The size of our furnace will be 11 feet bosh, and 50 feet in height, and the estimated output for the first few years 5,000 tons per annum."

"The Mines Report for 1892 says this company started their furnace late in the fall.   They report having mined about 3,000 tons of ore and 459 tons of limestone.   They smelted 415 tons of iron ore, with 56 tons of limestone and 33,461 bushels of charcoal, and made 211 tons of iron.

"After operating a half dozen years, I find this item in the Report of the Department of Mines for 1899: 'The Mineral Product Company worked for some time with the Bridgeville Charcoal furnace, making ferro-manganese.   It was stated, however, that operations would be continued next year.'   But the 'next year' there is no report on this concern."

IRON DEPOSITS OF WHYCOCOMAH, CAPE BRETON.

From Gilpin's report on the mines of Nova Scotia:

"At Whycocomah, on the Bras d'Or Lake, on the property of the Inverness Coal and Iron Company mine, deposits have been exposed, and proved to form beds in measures of the Laurentian Age. They were traced some hundreds of yards, when further explorations were stopped by the heavy covering of soil. The ore appears to be a mixture of red hematite and magnetite in varying proportions. From the analysis of the late Dr. How and Prof. Hays the ore appears to be free from all impurity except silica, the proportions of sulphur and phosphorus being small. A great point in favor of these deposits, and what are supposed to be their continuations in the district, is the presence of deep water within a few hundred yards of the ore, which would allow vessels of large burden to load for distant markets, while it can be carried in scows or barges to any part of the Bras d'Or Lake."

In the report of the Department of Mines for 1900 occurs the following paragraph:

"Mr. Neville reports visiting Whycocomah at the close of the year. A number of pits and trenches have proved sound during the season, and have the extension of the iron ore on the property of the Cape Breton Iron Company for a distance of nearly two miles. Previous reports have stated that a number of beds have been opened in this district. The additional work done this year has been on a bed of very good quality running from 5 to 7 feet in thickness. It is to be desired that this locality should at an early date be thoroughly prospected. The deposits are very large and of a good quality. Should the explorations turn out as anticipated, this district would furnish a cheap and valuable source of iron ore.'

IRON ORE OF GEORGES RIVER LOCALITY.

I take the following extract from a paper read before the Nova Scotia Institute of Science, 1899, by Dr. Edwin Gilpin, Jr.:

"The district lying between Little Bras d'Or Lake and East Bay in Cape Breton County is traversed diagonally by lower Silurian strata, and by felsite and limestone divisions of the pre-Cambrian, which are flanked by lower Carboniferous strata. The presence of iron ore near the junction of the Georges River limestone and lower Carboniferous has long been known near Gillie's Lake, and outcrops are known at Upper French Vale and near the mouth of the

Barosois River, emptying into the Little Bras d'Or Lake. At the latter place the Silurian slates are literally soaked with iron oxide, and at several points they present deposits which may on further investigation prove of economic value. To the southwest of the railway bridge at Barosois, on a line running towards Eskasonie on the East Bay, are several large outcrops of magnetite. As yet but little work has been done to test the value of these deposits. Should they prove free from titanic acid, they should, judging from the following analysis, be available for the operation of the miner:

Oxide of manganese and aluminum..........	.600
Lime	.110
Magnesia	.100
Sulphur	.050
Phosphoric acid	.040
Silica	2.120
Volatile	.840
Metallic iron............................	67.298

The existence of iron ore at many points in Cape Breton is already known. The attempts made to find deposits, and to test them, are scarcely worth noticing. In the forest and swamp-covered tracts there may be masses of iron ore worth an empire's ransom. It must, however, be remembered that these deposits, to be of any value, must be pure, extensive, and capable of cheap mining and shipping. The output must be large and the expense low to enable the Cape Bretoner to enter the world's competition in selling iron ore in the markets of the world."

LIMONITE ORE OF BROOKFIELD.

At Brookfield, in the Township of Truro, is a bed of iron ore, described as follows in Gilpin's Report on the Mines of Nova Scotia:

"At Brookfield, ten miles south of Truro, in measures of the same age, viz., Carboniferous, and near the contact of the older strata, are extensive surface indications of limonite. As yet but little has been done to test the deposit. An engineer of some repute said, in reporting upon the property: 'I consider that the indications of an extensive deposit are greater than even at the Londonderry mines.' This deposit is very favorably situated, being only two miles from the Intercolonial Railway and about forty-five miles from the Pictou coal field. The ore is of an unusually good quality, as will be seen from this analysis of Dr. How, of Kings College:

```
Water ...................................  11.36
Silica and gangue .......................   1.54
Phosphoric acid .........................  trace
Sulphuric acid ..........................  none
Magnesia ................................  trace
Peroxide of iron ........................  87.00
                                          _____
                                          100.00
Metallic iron ...........................  60.00"
```

The report of the Mining Department for 1888 has this record:

"The limonite deposit of Brookfield was worked by Mr. R. E. Chambers, who took out about 1,000 tons. The vein was cut and proved to be from 18 to 20 feet wide. The ore hitherto extracted has been smelted at Londonderry. It is of excellent quality and very accessible, being within two and a half miles of the railway."

Other shipments followed, but all is closed down now. At Arisaig, in Antigonish County, are extensive deposits of iron ores that have been worked to some extent. At present the locality is attracting considerable attention of capitalists engaged in the iron business in Sydney.

There are many other deposits of iron ore in this province, but so far as known are not of great magnitude and purity. Further developments will doubtless sooner or later show some of them to be of economic value. The ever increasing demand for iron and steel will bring to light our available resources. The vast bodies of superior ore obtained in Michigan and Newfoundland have made it impossible for many smaller smelting concerns to continue operations. It would be no surprise to those best informed if the Island of Cape Breton came to the front with an iron mine to match the rich stores of coal that are now so largely used in the treatment of Newfoundland ores.

The London Economist in the issue of Nov. 10, 1901, discusses the coal and iron resources of Nova Scotia, and has this to say of iron:

"The general result of our inquiry is the conviction that Nova Scotia is seamed throughout with some of the most valuable iron deposits in the world. It follows that with coal and limestone also at hand, this province should become one of the world's chief sources of iron supply. The question which, however, presents itself to our mind is whether Nova Scotia should not be our resort for sup-

⸮ plies of mineral iron in place of the diminishing supplies and deterio-
rating quality of the Spanish mines.   This matter of ore supply is
the great problem which faces the British iron industry at present."
Greater progress has been made in 1900 and 1901 in the development of the iron and steel industries of Canada than in all previous years.   Complete statistics for 1900, and in part for 1901, are
herewith given in sufficient detail.

PRODUCTION OF PIG IRON IN CANADA.

The production of pig iron in the Dominion of Canada, as ascertained from the manufacturers by the American Iron and Steel
Association, amounted in the calendar year 1900 to 86,090 gross
tons, as compared with 94,077 tons in 1899, 68,755 tons in 1898,
53,796 tons in 1897, 60,030 tons in 1896, 37,829 tons in 1895, and
44,791 tons in 1894.   Our statistics do not go back prior to 1894.
Of the production in 1900, 70,349 tons were made with coke and
15,741 tons with charcoal.   The production of Bessemer pig iron in
1900 included above amounted to 3,781 tons.   Neither spiegeleisen
nor ferro-manganese was made in 1900.   On Dec. 31, 1900, the
unsold stocks of pig iron in Canada amounted to 12,465 gross tons,
as compared with 9,932 tons at the close of 1899 and 9,979 tons at
the close of 1898.   Of the unsold stocks on Dec. 31, 1900, 6,900 tons
were coke pig iron and 5,565 tons were charcoal pig iron.

On Deç. 31, 1900, there were 10 completed furnaces in Canada
and four furnaces were in the course of construction.   During 1900
one new furnace was completed at Midland, Ontario, by the Canada
Iron Furnace Company, Limited.   It was blown in on Dec. 4, 1900.
The other furnaces referred to were all being erected by the Dominion Iron and Steel Company, Limited, at Sydney, Cape Breton,
Nova Scotia.   One of the furnaces was completed early in 1901
and was blown in on Feb. 4 of that year.   Two additional furnaces
have since been put in blast.   ⸤

The production of pig iron in Canada in the first half of 1901
amounted to 95,024 gross tons, exceeding by nearly a thousand tons
the production in the whole of any preceding year.   Of the total
production in the first half of this year, 17,577 tons were Bessemer
pig iron and 13,292 tons were basic pig iron; the remainder was
foundry and forge pig iron.   No spiegeleisen or ferro-manganese
was made.   Of the total production 86,430 tons were made with

coke and 8,594 tons with charcoal. The unsold stocks on June 30, 1901, amounted to 28,711 tons, of which 21,367 tons were coke pig iron and 7,344 tons were charcoal.

PRODUCTION OF STEEL AND ALL ROLLED PRODUCTS IN CANADA.

The steel industry in Canada may be said to be to-day in a state of preparation for important results. The fulfilment of great expectations would seem indeed to be near at hand. Several steel-making enterprises are in a more or less forward state of completion at the present time, the most advanced of which is the open-hearth plant of the Dominion Iron and Steel Company, which is erecting at Sydney ten 50-gross-ton open hearth furnaces of the Campbell tilting type, at which both acid and basic steel will be made. It is expected that a part of this plant will be in operation early in 1902. Its rolling-mill products will embrace blooms, slabs, billets and rails. Early in 1900 William Kennedy & Sons, Limited, of Owen Sound, Ontario, erected at that place one 2-ton Tropenas converter for the manufacture of steel castings. Steel was first made in May, 1900. The total production of steel in Canada in 1900 was 23,577 gross tons, against 22,000 tons in 1899, 21,540 tons in 1898, 18,400 tons in 1897, 16,000 tons in 1896, and 17,000 tons in 1895. Both Bessemer and open hearth steel ingots and castings were made in 1899 and 1900. Of the total production of open hearth steel in 1900 about one-third was made by the acid process. The production of open-hearth steel rails in 1900 amounted to 700 gross tons, against 835 tons or open-hearth and iron rails in 1899; structural shapes, 4,674 tons, against 2,899 tons in 1899; cut nails made by rolling mills and steel works having cut nail factories connected with their plants, 117,186 kegs of 100 pounds, against 235,981 kegs in 1899; plates and sheets, 2,100 tons, against about 2,220 tons in 1899; all other rolled products, excluding muck and scrap bars, blooms, billets, sheet bars, etc., 87,984 tons, against 94,153 tons in 1899. Changing the cut nail production from kegs to gross tons, the total quantity of all kinds of iron and steel rolled into finished products in the Dominion in 1900, excluding muck and scrap bars, billets, and other intermediate products, amounted to 100,690 tons, against 110,642 tons in 1899, 90,303 tons in 1898, 77,021 tons in 1897, 75,043 tons in 1896, and 66,402 tons in 1895. The number of completed rolling mills and steel works in Canada on Dec. 31, 1900, was 18.

We now present a chronological record of the leading events in the development of the iron and steel industries of the United States and Canada down to the close of the nineteenth century.

THE SEVENTEENTH CENTURY.

1619—In this year the Virginia Company sent to Virginia a number of persons who were skilled in the manufacture of iron to "set up three iron works" in the colony. The enterprise was undertaken in that year and the works were located on Falling Creek, a tributary of the James River.

1620—In this, as stated by Beverly in his History of Virginia, "an iron works at Falling Creek, in James River, was set up, where they made proof of good iron ore." In this and the following year the enterprise languished. On March 22, 1622, the works were destroyed by the Indians and all the workmen were massacred. The works were not rebuilt.

1642—In this year "The Company of Undertakers for the Iron Works" in the Province of Massachusetts Bay, consisting of eleven English gentlemen, was organized with a capital of £1,000.

1643—In his History of Lynn (1844) Alonzo Lewis says that in 1643 "Mr. John Winthrop, Jr., came from England with workmen and stock to the amount of £1,000 for commencing the work. A foundry was erected on the western bank of Saugus River," at Lynn, in Massachusetts. This foundry was a small blast furnace, completed in 1645. It was the first successful iron enterprise in the thirteen colonies. Bog ore was used. For a hundred years after its settlement in 1620 Massachusetts was the chief seat of the iron industry on this continent.

1645—A small iron pot, holding about a quart, which is still preserved, was cast at the Lynn foundry in 1645. It was the first iron article made from the native ore in America.

1658—In 1658 Captain Thomas Clarke, in company with John Winthrop and others, put in operation an "iron worke" at New Haven, Connecticut. This enterprise embraced a blast furnace and a refinery forge.

1675—Rhode Island made iron soon after its settlement in 1636, certainly at Pawtucket and elsewhere as early as 1675, when a forge at Pawtucket, erected by Joseph Jenks, Jr., was destroyed by the Indians in the Wanpanoag war, as well as other iron works and infant enterprises.

1679—In the Statistics of Coal, by Richard Cowling Taylor, published in 1848, it is stated that the earliest historic mention of coal in this country is by the French Jesuit missionary, Father Hennepin, who saw traces of bituminous coal on the Illinois River in 1679. In his journal he marks the site of a "coal mine" above Fort Crevecoeur, near the present town of Ottawa, Illinois.

1682—In an account of the province of East Jersey, published by the proprietors in 1682, it is stated that "there is already a smelting furnace and forge set up in this colony, where is made good iron, which is of great benefit to the country." This enterprise was located at Tinton Falls, in Monmouth Co., New Jersey. Other authorities definitely establish the fact that the Shrewsbury works, as they were called, were established before 1676. They were the first iron works in New Jersey.

1692—In 1692 we find the first mention of iron having been made in Pennsylvania. It is contained in a metrical composition entitled "A Short Description of Pennsylvania," by Richard Frame, which was printed and sold by William Bradford, in Philadelphia, in 1692. Frame says that at a "certain place about some forty pound" of iron had then been made. This was doubtless an experimental enterprise.

THE EIGHTEENTH CENTURY.

1703—Abraham Lincoln's paternal ancestry was identified with the manufacture of iron in Massachusetts. The head of the American branch of his father's family, Samuel Lincoln, emigrated in 1637 from Norwich, England, to Massachusetts. Mordecai Lincoln, son of Samuel, born at Hingham on June 14th, 1657, followed the trade of a blacksmith at Hull, from which place he removed to Scituate, where he "built a spacious house and was a large contributor toward the erection of the iron works at Bound Brook" in 1703. These iron works made wrought iron directly from the ore. Mordecai Lincoln had two sons, Mordecai, Jr., and Abraham, who settled in Berks Co., Pennsylvania. Mordecai, Jr., was the great-great-grandfather of Abraham Lincoln.

It is worth noticing in this connection that in 1732 Augustine Washington, the father of George Washington, was engaged in making pig iron at Accokeek furnace in Stafford County, Virginia, about fifteen miles from Fredericksburg, when his famous son was born. This furnace had been built by the Principio Company, composed of English capitalists, as early as 1726, on land owned by

Augustine Washington, aggregating about 1,600 acres and containing iron ore, Mr. Washington becoming the owner of one-sixth of the furnace property in consideration of the transfer of his land to the Company.

Connecticut was probably the first of the Colonies to make steel. In 1728 Samuel Higley of Simsbury, and Joseph Dewey of Hebron, in Hartford County, represented to the Legislature, that the first named had, "with great pains and cost found out and obtained a curious art, by which to convert, change or transmute common iron into good steel, sufficient for any use, and was the very first that ever performed such an operation in America." It was doubtless cementation steel.

The first iron works in New York were "set up" a short time prior to 1740 on Ancram Creek, in Columbia County, about fourteen miles east of the Hudson River, by Phillip Livingston, the owner of the Livingston manor, and the father of the signer of the Declaration of Independence.

The iron industry of New Hampshire probably dates from about 1750, when several bog-ore bloomeries were in existence on Lamper Eel River, but were soon discontinued. About the time of the Revolution there were a few other bloomeries in operation in New Hampshire.

I have extracted these statistics, and items on the early history of the iron industry in America, from The Annual Statistical Report of the Iron and Steel Association, Philadelphia, 1901.

CHAPTER XV.

This county, like Kings and Annapolis, was settled by the French at an early date, before the founding of Halifax. It was an inviting field to these Acadians, where they found fertile lands, fine rivers, and abundance of timber. What is now called Windsor was then known as Pisiquid, an Indian word signifying the junction of two rivers. Furthermore, as a matter of great convenience, this point was readily reached by water from the old settlements of Minas and Port Royal, and the trail from across country to Halifax Harbor, or Chebucto, as it was then called, was the shortest and most accessible from this place. It was a route well known to the Indians, and often used by the Acadians as they journeyed to and from the small settlements on Bedford Basin and Musquodoboit.

The area of the county is 1,179 square miles, and the population is 20,066. Between 1749 and 1755 the English established a military post at Windsor, and by the name of Fort Edward it figures in the annals of the Province. One reads much of it in the dark days of the French Expulsion. Here is an item that vividly recalls the past. It is from the Journal of Col. Winslow, who was in charge of the forces that removed those unfortunate people from the region of Grand Pre. He and his men had embarked at Amherst, or Fort Cumberland as they called it then.

"1755 August 17th came to sail, stood down Chignecto Bay & dobled the Cape of that name, stood up the Bay of Mines, anchored near the mouth of the river Pisiquid. 18STH 18TH 18th came to sail and stood up the river Pisiquid to Forte Edward at which we arrived at Eleven o'Clock in the Forenoon, Found it to be a Fine, Pleasant Scituation. The Forte of Great Strength, waited on Capt Murray and Dined with him & the Gents the officers, and from Whome I received the following Minnets Directed to Captain Murray viz." These "minnits" were directions from Governor Lawrence, instructing Capt. Murray how to deal with the Acadians in his vicinity, and also containing instructions for Col. Winslow when he came to deal with the Horton and Cornwallis communities. They show Lawrence to have been a man of "blood and iron," firmly determined that Nova Scotia from that date should be British in fact as well as name. Here

WINDSOR FROM CHAPEL HILL.

GIRLS' SCHOOL, WINDSOR.
"EDGEHILL."

is a specimen of his instructions: "Show these Memoranda to Col Winslow as Soon as he arrives, take an opportunity of Acquainting the Inhabitants that if any attempt by Indians or others to Destroye or otherwise Molest his Majesty's Troops, you have my orders to take an Eye for an Eye, a Tooth for a Tooth and in Shorte Life for Life from the nearest Neighbours where such MIschief is Performed."

We have not the space to enter into details of the Acadian settlement or their complete uprooting. With the exception of those who escaped to the woods and lived with the Indians, all were sent away—a sharp remedy for a sore evil.

The English occupancy naturally grew up around the fort, and from that starting point extended to other localities. Writing of Windsor in 1828 Haliburton says: "This place is distant from Halifax forty-five miles, the road to which, by many late alterations, is level and in an excellent state of repair. This locality was held in great estimation by the French, on account of its extensive and fertile meadows, which they enclosed with dykes, and brought into a high state of cultivation. The crops of wheat which they raised were so superabundant, that for many years previous to the war of 1756 they exported a great quantity to the Boston market. Although immediately occupied by the English after the removal of the French, it underwent no material changes until within the last twenty years. The most valuable lands were granted to gentlemen residing in Halifax; among them were many of His Majesty's Council. That portion of it which fell into the hands of resident proprietors, was divided among a few individuals, and thus was introduced a system of tenancy in Nova Scotia, which neither contributed to the improvement of the soil, nor the profit of the landlord. Under these circumstances the appearance of the place remained stationary for several years, until in the progress of time, the transfer of property, and the increase of population gradually worked a change in this defective system. The dyke lands, of which there are 2,544 acres, are decidedly the best in Nova Scotia, the deepest, richest, and most productive. The rise and fall of the river at Windsor is about twenty feet at neap, and thirty at spring tides. The whole of the salt water flows and reflows, and the bed of the river at times is totally exposed. The whole of the neighborhood of Windsor is extremely beautiful. The luxuriance of the meadows, the frequent changes of scenery, the chain of high hills

15

on the south and west, clothed with trees of variegated foliage, and the white sails of vessels passing rapidly through the serpentine windings of the Avon and the St. Croix, are some of the leading features of this landscape. There was a small military post at Windsor, named in honor of his Royal Highness the Duke of Kent, which is much out of repair, and now scarcely tenable."

From the days of Haliburton the growth of this town has not been by "leaps and bounds," as the politicians describe their kind of progress; but it has been steady and healthy. It has long been in railway communication with Halifax and other localities. Recently it has suffered most severely from a fire, that perhaps in the long run will not be looked upon as altogether a calamity, although it has fallen with great severity on many people of this generation. The oldest college in Canada is to be found in this town, King's College was founded in 1787 and chartered by King George III. in 1802. A more extended notice of this institution occurs in another portion of this book devoted to educational matters.

The Township of Newport lies on the eastern side of the River St. Croix. It was granted in the year 1761 in seventy shares, and consists of 58,000 acres. It abounds in gypsum, and has valuable freestone quarries. It is a well cultivated district, and was peopled at first by New England settlers.

The Township of Falmouth lies between Horton and Windsor. The grant bears date July 21st, 1759, and contains 50,000 acres. It contains a good deal of diked lands, and altogether is a delightfully located and thriving community.

The Township of Kempt is situated on the Basin of Minas, between the Kentecook River and Cobequid Bay. It consists mostly of upland, a great portion of which is productive. Chiverie, Cambridge, and Pembroke are thriving communities along the shore.

Walton is a small township containing six or seven square miles, and was formerly a portion of Douglas, and lies between that division and Kempt. Within its bounds have been worked some very promising deposits of manganese, a metal much in demand.

Douglas embraces a region on the south shore of Cobequid Bay, and west of the Township of Shubenacadie, that has also been clipped from its ample bounds since 1828, for Haliburton included both it and Maitland, and Walton in the Township of Douglas. As it stands it is a large district of excellent farming lands, and contains vast supplies of gypsum, limestone, and freestone. The new Midland Railway crosses the entire width of this section and opens up a fine country. The Acadians were settled at Noel, as one may guess from the name, which has not been displaced by something less pleasing, as it often turns out in this Province.

Maitland township includes the western shore of the mouth of the Shubenacadie River, and extends westward to the Douglas line. Maitland village is a place of some shipping trade, and a commer-' cial center for the region round about. The eastern boundary of the county is the Shubenacadie River, a strong tidal stream arising in a large lake from which there is a connection with the Atlantic coast by way of the Dartmouth lakes. About seventy-five years ago there was a great effort made to construct a canal along this spindling waterway that would admit of the passage of schooners and other crafts, but after a large sum of money had been squandered on the childish project it was abandoned, and the present generation hardly knows that such a work was ever begun by our fore-fathers. In his history Haliburton has much to say of this scheme, that was just then a topic of great interest. He gives us a map of the whole distance, showing all the lakes and streams, and altitudes, made from the notes of a careful survey, and tells us that a "Chain of lakes in this township, connected with the source of the Shubenacadie River, suggested the idea of uniting the waters of the Basin of Minas with Halifax harbor, by means of a canal. Of these Lake Charles, or the first Shubenacadie Lake, is distant from Halifax about three miles and a half. It extends from north to south 4,300 yards, and occupies the higher portion of a valley, which reaches, with irregular breadth, and elevation, from the Basin of Minas to Dartmouth, dividing the province by a well-defined line of separation into two parts of nearly equal extent. The project having been decided by a competent engineer to be not only practicable, but attended with fewer obstacles than usually accompany works of that description, an Association was formed, denominated the Shubenacadie Canal Company, and on the 1st of June, 1826, it was regularly incorporated. As it was supposed that the resources of the Province would be developed by this work, and that the public would also, in the event of a war, be much benefited by this internal navigation, the Legislature granted to the adventurers the sum of fifteen thousand pounds. Thus encouraged the company commenced the work upon a scale adapted to schooners. According to the plan finally agreed upon, the canal will be sixty feet in width at the water level, and thirty-six feet at the bottom, the slopes being one and a half horizontal to one perpendicular, and the depth sufficient to admit vessels drawing eight feet of water. The locks will be ninety feet within the chambers, nineteen feet and a half in width, and 125 between the extremity of the wing walls.—The artificial communication is confined to a few places, advantage being taken, when practicable, of navigating the lakes and the channel of the river; when completed, small steamboats, of twelve or fourteen horse-power, will be employed for towing, each boat performing the passage from Halifax harbor to the mouth of the Shubenacadie in fifteen hours, and carrying each four trade boats of thirty tons' burden. The whole distance of this inland navigation will be fifty-three miles and 1,024 yards, and will be completed, according to the estimates, of 75,000 pounds."

The canal was commenced on Monday, the 24th of July, 1826, with great ceremony in the presence of a notable assembly. His Excellency, the Earl of Dalhousie, then on a little visit, was pressed into the services of the occasion, and with him were also the Governor, Sir James Kempt; Sir Howard Douglas, Sir John Keane, the members of the Council and officers of the army and navy, a number of citizens, and the Masonic lodges. His Lordship, the Earl of Dalhousie, broke the ground and made the following hopeful little speech:

"Mr. President and Gentlemen:

"It is to me a most pleasing compliment to have been called upon to assist here to-day, in the first operation of this public work, so long desired—so important to this province. Persevering inquiry has now overcome all doubts of the practicability of this work, and the spirit of enterprise and improvement has contributed the funds on which to make a beginning. The Legislature has afforded that liberal support which, I trust, will encourage, and lead to a speedy and successful accomplishment of this great undertaking. I am happy, Sir James, to see such convincing proof as this affords of the progress of improvement in Nova Scotia. I have always thought that the advancement of these young countries ought not to be forced, but leaving the march to the increasing of time and rising spirit, a few years comparatively would bring changes far out-doing what we can anticipate in human foresight. I think I have

THE WINDSOR BRIDGES OVER THE AVON RIVER.

OLD BLOCKHOUSE AND OFFICERS' QUARTERS
FORT EDWARD, WINDSOR.

RESIDENCE OF JUDGE HALIBURTON, WINDSOR.
(AUTHOR OF "SAM SLICK.")

been right as regards this work, for now I feel convinced that we not only commence the canal, projected so many years ago, but in this act we also lay the foundation of many and various improvements that will spring up in connection with it.

"Mr. Wallace' permit me to congratulate you personally on this occasion, for you are amongst the first whose public spirit suggested this work, and whose constant pursuit of public improvement has never permitted the subject to be dropped, until it has been brought to this point."

"The best laid plans of mice and men" often come to naught. Dalhousie's fine predictions proved to be based on his hopes, rather than on his knowledge of the enterprise. The Government with judicious prudence agreed to pay in small installments as the work went forward, and private subscriptions never reached much more than one-quarter of the whole estimated cost of the work, and so the project died a natural death at an early stage.

The Shubenacadie River has some historical connections that are not without interest to those who find pleasure and profit in turning over such matters. The region about the lower portions of the river was a favorite camping ground of the Indians, who found there a central location in the midst of good hunting and fishing. To them was sent a missionary from France in the person of the Abbe Louis Joseph de la Loutre, who reached them in 1740 after having been three years in the Province. During a portion of each year for fifteen years he remained with them, and in his communications calls it "my mission," although it seems that his principal residence was at Missiquash, near Fort Lawrence, in Cumberland County. In Shubenacadie his residence was about a mile below the railway bridge in the village of the same name and in Hants County. This man was the evil genius of the Acadians. Beneath the garb of a priest beat the heart of a vain, cruel adventurer, the moral inferior of almost every savage he met. It is quite probable that there would have been no expulsion of the French peasants had it not been for the advice and tireless activities of this deadly enemy of the English interests. He was in Fort Beausejour during its besiegement in the fall of 1755, and escaped in disguise before its surrender. The Bishop of Quebec bitterly reproached him for meddling with temporal affairs, and charged him with being the cause of serious misfortunes. The next year, after the deportation of the Acadians, when he saw that his occupation was gone, he made ready to leave the scenes of his varied misdoings. A half dozen years before Lord Cornwallis was so exasperated with him that he offered a reward of £100 for his head, and sent after him the redoubtable Captain Silvanus Cobb, who had seen no little of the rough side of life, and was yet to take an important part in the capture of Quebec. Here is the order:

"To Captain Silvanus Cobb: .

"Having certain information that one Le Loutre, a French priest at Chignecto, is the author and adviser of all the disturbances the Indians have made in this Province, and that it is he as their chief, excites, directs, and instructs them, and provides them from Canada with arms and ammunition, and everything necessary for their purpose.

"You are hereby ordered to apprehend the said Priest Le Loutre wherever he may be found, and deliver him up to me at Halifax or into any English fort, where he may be secured, that he answer the crimes laid to his charge."

However, even Cobb could not secure this desirable prize, and he was reserved for further mischief. When all was over, and having some concern for safety, he embarked for France in 1756, but was unlucky enough to be taken by a British ship and carried to England, where he found there was already a knowledge of his career, and he was accordingly imprisoned in the Isle of Jersey, where he remained eight years, and narrowly escaped assassination at the hand of one of his guards, who declared that when he was a soldier in Nova Scotia and was taken prisoner by Indians, that this priest ordered him to be scalped, and even marked the circle on his head with a knife, but he escaped the cruel fate by some fortunate turn of affairs. Le Loutre finally returned to France, where, of course, he had friends, and died in obscurity.

The Township of Uniacke evidently perpetuates the name of a notable man in the early history of the Province. There is a station on the railway between Halifax and Windsor in this township called "Mount Uniacke," and from that point one may see across the small lake, and near its margin a large old-fashioned house that was built by Richard John Uniacke as a quiet retreat in his autumn of life. He was born in Castletown, County of Cork, Ireland, son of a country gentleman of some means, with whom he had a serious falling out when he was but twenty years of age. He had begun the

WATER STREET, WINDSOR.

BLOMIDON KINGS COUNTY.

study of law, but he impetuously ended that arrangement and soon put the Atlantic Ocean between himself and his father. After a brief tarry in the West Indies, he landed in Philadelphia to seek his fortune in some way yet to be discovered. Before he left the wharf, as the story goes, he met Mr. Moses Delesdernier, a Swiss gentleman, whose home was in Amherst, N. S. They by chance got into conversation, with the result that the fine-appearing young Irishman went home with his new friend to become useful in some capacity suitable to his ability. He had not been many months with his employer before he married his daughter, who was not yet thirteen years of age, and he not yet one and twenty. This was in 1775, when the American Revolutionary war was simmering in the early stages. The next year Uniacke was suspected of being concerned in the toy rebellion, led by Jonathan Eddy, and placed under arrest and brought to Halifax, where he seems to have in some way avoided a trial and got away to Ireland, where he studied law three years and returned in 1781 and began the practice of his profession in Halifax, in which he met with great success from the very first. The next year he was commissioned Solicitor General, and a year later he was a member of the House of Assembly from Sackville, now in New Brunswick. He soon became a leading spirit in that body, where there was need of his trenchant tongue and honest purpose to correct abuses. He had not long to wait for another turn of the wheel of fortune, and he was commissioned as Advocate General in the Vice Admiralty Court, a lucrative office. In 1797 he was appointed Attorney General, and remained a member of the House of Assembly till 1808. His wife had died three years before, greatly to his sorrow. She was the mother of six sons and six daughters, eleven of whom were living at the time of her death. The family was remarkable for the even dozen, the equal division of sexes, and the bodily excellence and exceptional talents of several of its members.

It was an object of ambition with Mr. Uniacke to become Chief Justice of the Province, but in this he was not to succeed; a disappointment that he bore with no very good grace when a Boston Loyalist lawyer secured the coveted prize.

When he was sixty-two years of age he was devoting a large portion of his time to his estate at Mount Uniacke, where he had grants covering 5,000 acres. He had an inherited tendency to become a country gentleman after the manner of his fore-fathers, so in 1813 he built the large house I have mentioned, and in which he resided till his death in 1830.

Little did the old Attorney General think as he walked over his broad acres of stones and ledges, that there were gold mines under his feet, and nuggets of the yellow metal on the surface, scarcely hidden by the leaves and brush. People are most likely to discover what they are seeking, and while it was gold that the proprietor wanted, yet he never looked for it in any other shape than a coin of the realm, and so he never saw what was in sight for him who had the eye for that sort of thing. Thirty years after Mr. Uniacke's death prospecting licenses were taken out, and in a year later the roar of a stamp mill broke in upon the sylvan quiet of the locality. Since then the miners have had a variety of experiences, as usual with them; some have been good, and some quite the reverse. At present there are on the spot parties full of hope, assaulting the ledges and veins in search of bonanzas that may or may not be there to reward them for their efforts. Very likely that the prospecting has been quite inadequate to secure the best prizes, as no great depth has anywhere in the Province been reached to penetrate the saddles of the productive anticlinals.

GEOLOGY OF HANTS COUNTY.

It would require a bulky volume to contain the details of the rock structure of this county. If a few of the general features can be here set down it will be quite within my present purpose.

Here are granite, Cambrian slates, Devonian or Horton series, and carboniferous shales and other sediments of that time, each one representing great epochs in the history of the globe. Here are gold mines in the Cambrian slates, manganese mines in the carboniferous limestone, and gypsum quarries on all sides. The granite is an extension of the outcrop of that rock that appears along the divide of the Province, reaching out here and there to the Atlantic coast. It makes a contact on the southeastern side of the county with the Cambrian slates on the county line, then in a long deep fold it meets the Horton series to near the Avon River, where its contact is with the carboniferous formation for a distance of five or six miles, where it again encounters the Cambrian slates and quartzites that extend over the southern side of the county, and include the gold-mining district of Rawdon. All the rest of the county has for its surface rock the carboniferous formation, with the exception of a patch of the Horton series that extends across the Avon between Avonport and Horton Bluffs, and continues to the eastward and northward, forming the shore line nearly to Walton, with the exception of a carboniferous exposure west from Chivere Creek to near the coast in the direction of Indian Point.

CHAPTER XVI.

HISTORY OF KINGS COUNTY.

It is rather surprising that no one has yet written a history of this county. In the first place, it has been the scene of events that will live long in the annals of the British Empire, and in the second place, a college has long existed in this locality, and one might naturally expect that some scholarly graduate from that institution, and that section, would have taken up this inviting theme, and got it into print long ago. For my own part, I have levied on Haliburton, and Murdoch, and Winslow's Journal, Herbin's Grand Pre, and other sources here and there, that have amply furnished me with material for my present purpose.

In the matter of area, Kings is among the small counties, having but 811 square miles within its lines. The population is 22,389. It is bounded by the Bay of Fundy, the Basin of Minas, the Avon River, and Hants, Lunenburg, and Annapolis Counties. It will be readily seen by reference to the map that Annapolis Valley is extended through Kings, and the North and South Mountains maintain their characteristics through both counties. To the southward of the South Mountain there is a considerable area of timber land, and some agricultural facilities, but the fruit-growing industry, the dyked lands, and the delightful scenery, are the leading features in this division of the Province. They are permanent values. The apple-raising business, although large, is yet but in its infancy. The day cannot be distant when the land that is suitable for that purpose will all be covered with orchards. The dyked lands should support a large dairying business. The scenery is so happily arranged by Nature that the hand of man can scarcely deform or deface it. It is not dependent upon forests that can be chopped away, nor on rivers that may be largely diverted from their courses, or on any other feature within the vandal tendency of human nature, and thus its fine views are safe while the present order of the world endures. In fact, it has turned out in this instance that mankind in their ordinary operations have heightened the beauties of the landscapes. Fine orchards, and fine houses, and wide dykes, are suggestive of comfort, and order, and thrift, and they give a pleasing variety as material objects. The outlooks from many of the most elevated points are admirable pictures of rural loveliness. Notable among them is the

234

CANNING HARBOUR, WITH THE TIDE OUT, KINGS COUNTY.

"Lookout' on the North Mountain, from which portions of five counties are visible, and the eye ranges some ninety miles westward till it reaches the shores of the Annapolis Basin, and the whole intermediate distance. When seen in the early October haze of a beautiful day it is a panorama of unforgetable charms. One has but to turn his head from this view of the valley in order to take in the historic Basin of Minas framed in green and azure, fretting the wide curves of its shores with far-famed tides that race over the tawny flats, back and forth from age to age. Another turn of the head from this Lookout and we have in view the Minas Channel, and on its farther shore the bold hills of Greville Bay and Spencer's Island and the frowning cliffs of Cape D'Or. We must not tarry to describe the fine scenery of this county, although it is no small item in its attractions.

The history, of course, begins with the earliest French occupation, and thereby hangs a tale of woe that I have treated at some length in the pages devoted to the history of Nova Scotia in this volume, and need not be repeated here at length. The French settlements were in Horton, Cornwallis, Gaspereaux and Grand Pre. In the fall of 1755 there were no houses nor barns, and unclaimed cattle roamed over the desolate scene. The New England men who removed the Acadians saw these forfeited lands, and knew they could soon have them at a mere nominal cost; but they were evidently not greatly pleased with the prospect, or they would have taken early steps to have secured them. Men who had very humble homes in New England might well take a second thought before leaving them for the chances of bettering their condition in this remote district. Houses and barns must be built, live stock must be brought over, together with all tools and farming implements. There were no saw-mills, nor grist-mills, and they had no experience with mending the mud walls that kept at bay the unrivalled tides. No wonder that for six years there was no one induced to grapple with these difficulties for the sake of the prize there was in view. Unreasonable partizans have sometimes said that the Acadians were rooted up because the New Englanders coveted the rich lands that their skill and industry had won from the sea. This is a mere idle surmise. The people were taken away because it was determined by Lawrence and Shirley that Nova Scotia should remain a British colony, and that it was not likely to do unless some vigorous measures were employed beyond keeping a few soldiers in Halifax, An-

'napolis, Windsor and Fort Lawrence. There seemed to be no other way to secure this end than to clear the Province of those who could not be trusted as British subjects while their countrymen were in possession of all Canada, Cape Breton and Newfoundland. Had every Acadian been a Britisher true blue, still it would have been problematical if this Province could have held out against the enemy if a well-directed effort had been made to seize it. Much greater was the uncertainty when the Acadians kept in touch with Quebec and Louisburg, and suffered themselves to be guided by the treacherous and fanatical Le Loutre. It was very hard and dreadful for these poor Acadians to be caught in the storm center of such warring interests, and however much we pity them and regret any measures of needless cruelty, still it must seem to many of us the only way out of a difficult position.

After a half dozen years settlers came from Connecticut at the expense of the Government, bringing with them cattle and furniture, and made a beginning in Horton and Cornwallis. Haliburton says: "From the removal of these Acadians, in 1755, the country remained unsettled until the year 1760, when two hundred emigrants from Connecticut were invited to remove thither and take possession of it. They found the dykes very much dilapidated and most of the meadows under water. As they were ignorant of the manner of rebuilding these embankments they contented themselves for many years with gathering salt grass and such other herbage as the higher parts of the Grand Prarie still afforded. As they increased in population and acquired experience they at length succeeded in shutting out the tide from all the land that had been formerly enclosed. But it was not till the year 1810 that that extensive meadow which is bounded by the Grand Prarie on the east and Wolfville on the west was finally encircled by a substantial dyke." This account is in a measure misleading, for the fact is that there were a number of Acadians in the vicinity, wandering hither and thither over the desolate acres, who had fled to the woods in the general expulsion, and were employed by these Yankees to take charge of repairing and rebuilding the embankments and aboiteaux. We may learn this from a letter written by Governor Belcher to Colonel Foster under date of June 18, 1761, in which he says:

"Sir,—By representations made to me from the new Settlements in this Province, it appears Extremely necessary that the inhabitants should be assisted by the Acadians in repairing the Dykes for the

BERWICK, STREET VIEW, KINGS CO.

BERWICK, KINGS CO.

SCENE IN WESTON.

VIEW OF ANNAPOLIS VALLEY, FROM BERWICK.

preservation and recovery of the Marsh Lands, particularly as on the progress of this work, in which the Acadians are the most skilfull people in the country, the support and subsistence of several hundred of the inhabitants will depend."

Three years from the beginning of the settlements the following returns were made:

Horton—Families, 122; persons, 689; wheat, 991 bushels; rye, 172 bushels; Indian corn, 1,070 bushels; potatoes, 4,613 bushels; horses, 99; oxen, 159; cows, 302; young cattle, 469; sheep, 369; swine, etc., 395.

Cornwallis—Families, 125; persons, 656; wheat, 1,759 bushels; rye, 368 bushels; oats, 2,900 bushels; potatoes, 12,569 bushels; horses, 123; oxen, 195; cows, 395; young cattle, 469; sheep, 495; swine, 395.

This is a good showing that indicates the thrifty quality of this Anglo-Saxon stock that loves to get rooted in the soil; they can fight, but prefer to farm.

The present inhabitants of Kings County are very largely the descendants of New England settlers. Their lines fell in pleasant places, and they have given a good account of themselves, at least from an industrial point of view, and such persistent workers were reasonably safe from moral delinquencies, for have we not learned that "Satan finds some mischief still for idle hands to do?"

The three principal towns are Kentville, Wolfville and Canning. They are all charming localities, and a stranger likes each one best as he visits them one after another. Kentville is the shire town and therefore has an official importance over the others. Haliburton says: "At the upper part of this township, and near its junction with Cornwallis, is situated the village of Kentville, containing several well-built private houses, the Court House and jail. It is distant from Halifax about seventy miles and from Annapolis sixty, forming the central point at which the stage coaches meet that run between these two towns. There is a good grammar school at this place, and it is said that the Baptists of Nova Scotia have it in contemplation to found an academy within a few miles of it, which shall be open for the reception of the youth of every denomination, but under the particular control of the General Association. The views in this neighborhood are remarkably fine, and the formation of the land such as to present a great variety in the landscape."

This was written seventy-five years ago or thereabouts, and

has a smack of ancient history about it. The town has now a population of 1,781, and is a railway station of considerable importance,
where there are repair shops and the head office of the Dominion
and Atlantic Railway, and also a terminus of the Cornwallis Railway that extends to Canning and Kingsport. There are good hotel
accommodations and most delightful drives in all directions. The
town is also a commercial center of a large district devoted to farming and fruit raising in a very profitable way. The streets are
shaded with fine trees, and the Cornwallis River adds a charm to the
locality that only a lake or a stream can give.

Wolfville was named after the De Wolfs of that locality, of
whom Nathan was one of the first, if not the only pioneer of the
family. The town is situated on a small tributary of the Cornwallis
River, entering it near the mouth on the basin of Minas. Small
vessels come up this creek or stream to wharves in the vicinity.
The population is 1,412, and it would be difficult to find that number of people in any other part of the world settled down amid more
of the comforts and delights of life. The climate is not severe;
there are no malarial diseases to rack a poor body with chills and
fevers; tornadoes are unknown; turn where it will the eye is pleased
with the prospect, whether it be across the wide dykes and the
brown Basin to the hills of Parrsboro, including the bold bluffs of
Blomidon, or whether it takes in the long stretches of the embowered streets and cosy cottages, or looks down upon the beautiful
valley of the Gaspereaux.

Wolfville is not only a trading center to a considerable district,
but it has the distinction of being a college town; caps and gowns,
and grave professors and retired clergymen are the commonplaces
of the locality. Since 1829 the Horton Academy has been in operation, and since 1838 Acadia College, starting with small beginnings,
has continued to disseminate the higher learning. The Ladies'
Seminary has long been another feature of academic life in the place,
and recently a Manual Training School and a School of Horticulture have been added to the list of useful institutions, of which more
is set down in another portion of this book where educational matters are treated at some length.

Canning is a surprise to one who drives for the first time across
the Cornwallis region from Wolfville or thereabouts, especially in
the summer or autumn, when the orchards are in fruitage. One
comes abruptly upon pretty streets, shaded with fine trees, stores

and wharves and tall spars, and flapping sails almost in the shade of overhanging branches. The schooners with their hulls hidden in the narrow channel appear to be sailing on dry land through dykes and fields as they follow the great tides that follow the moon around the world.

This place is readily reached by rail from Kentville, or by steamer from Kingsport at the mouth of the river, or by wagon roads from many directions. My own chief experience suggests the apple-picking season, on a fine day, going by team from Wolfville, with the drive continued to the Look-off. Nothing short of some acute malady should prevent one from a keen enjoyment of the whole journey.

Port Williams is a station on the D. A. R. line between Wolf-ville and Kentville. It is about one-half mile from the railway, on the Cornwallis River, a place of some trading importance, where vessels freely enter on the high tides and depart on the ebb.

Berwick is a beautiful and enterprising village about a dozen miles west of Kentville, in the midst of a fertile region well adapted to farming and fruit-raising, and the people are alive to the natural advantages of the locality.

The county is divided into three townships, Horton, Cornwallis and Aylesford. The latter extends in a belt across the entire western end of the county, and a village of the same name is a station on the Dominion and Atlantic Railway. On the Bay of Fundy side of the county there are precarious shelters known as Harborville and Hall's Harbor, where there is some shipping trade carried on in small vessels. There are many other villages and hamlets scattered over the region under discussion, for which there is no room for extended description. These are Waterville, Cambridge, New Minas, Greenwich, Gran Pre, Hortonville, Avonport, all of them on the line of railway, and each one with points of interest and excellence worthy of attracting the attention of tourists, and persons in search of a place to make comfortable homes.

I have not forgotten that here is the land of Evangeline, the heroine of Longfellow's famous poem, but it seems to me that our Province has been overmuch advertised by means of this mythical maiden in "cap and kirtle." When it is well understood that a poet is drawing on his imagination for his characters and incidents, then he is not likely to deceive any one, but when he mingles truth and fiction in such a manner that all seems to be true, then he deceives while he delights, and kindles our indignation over fancied wrongs. In the main features "Evangeline" is taken to be true by the great majority of its readers, and therefore it places British subjects either in the attitude of defense or apology. The author intends to make his readers angry, he hopes to make them weep, therefore he tells all the affecting hardships for which he can find any warrant in history, or furnish from his fancy, without a word of the culpabilities of the sufferers that ended in such tragical results. The motif of the poem would not have been weakened had he given a few lines to the causes that led up to this expulsion, and a few more introducing us to the officers and men who carried out the order that separated his Evangeline and Gabriel. In that case his readers might have learned that this wholesale banishment is far from being indefensible in view of all the circumstances, and whatever we may now think of it, or feel about it, the fact remains that there must have been a sore evil to have called for such drastic treatment by men who were not considered monsters in their day. The poet very skilfully keeps out of sight the fact that Governor Shirley of Massachusetts not only sanctioned this expulsion, but he originated the remedy that Lawrence also had hit upon as the only means of holding the Province for the English.

When the poet relates that—

"Then uprose their commander and spake from the steps of the
        altar,
  Holding aloft in his hands, with its seals, the royal commission,"

Why not have given a little piquancy to the personality of the commander, who is made to stand on the steps of the altar, although in his journal he says otherwise, by adding:

And this was none other than Colonel John Winslow of Marshfield,
But third in descent from Edward, the Mayflower Pilgrim,
Who enobled his family by virtues both public and private,
Till the name seemed like a title bestowed for high service,
And marking the owner with certain distinction.

These lines may or may not have as many poetic feet as the verse of Longfellow, but they show that much light might have been thrown on the situation in a few words, and he could have consistently gone somewhat further and told his readers that every armed man who came on those transports was a volunteer, and a New Englander who enlisted for the distinct purpose of capturing

GRAND PRE, KINGS COUNTY.

THE OLD CHURCH. GRAND PRE.

KENTVILLE.

KENTVILLE

Beausejour and inflicting other damages on the French at adjacent points, in a manner not specified in detail, for the period of one year for the sum of "fifteen pounds old Tenor pr Man." Surely if there was anything infamous in these proceedings then the blame belongs with those who were willing for a very small money-consideration to carry them out; and allowing that neither Colonel Winslow, nor one of his men, knew they were expected to be the direct instruments of expelling the Acadians, still there is not a word in that officer's journal indicating that he, or any of his volunteers, objected to the business as no part of what they considered a soldier's duty. To heighten the atrocity of the expulsion, the poet gives us a description of the Acadians that reads very smoothly in this fashion:

"They dwelt together in love, these simple Acadian farmers,
Dwelt in the love of God and man. Alike were they free
From the fear that reigns with the tyrant, and envy the vice of
    Republics.
Neither locks had they to their doors, nor bars to their windows,
But their dwellings were open as day and the hearts of their
    owners.
There the richest was poor, and poorest lived in abundance."

There is proof in plenty that these people were neither better nor worse than other peasant folk of their nation, and in fact there is no reason why they should exhibit any special virtues. They had seen enough of human blood not to turn pale at the sight of it. They had entertained and shielded over and over again the Indians who came with English scalps in their belts, and their tomahawks dabbled in the color of their murderous work. They had long listened to the brutal harangues of Le Loutre, who had himself wielded the scalping knife to gratify his revenge. From childhood they had been accustomed to scenes and recitals that could do no less than dull the keen edge of sympathies and blunt the finest affections. By their hearthstones had slept the swarthy savages who had beguiled the evening hours with the tales of their murderous affrays in Dartmouth, and Lunenburg, and elsewhere, wherein neither babes at the breast, nor white-haired matrons, escaped the fierce ordeal that secured them a dripping trophy as evidence of their courage. They had harbored traitors to their sovereign; proved false friends to the flag under which they were born, and one that secured to them such rights and privileges as no other nation pre-

16

tended to grant, much less to defend. We shall not readily believe that these people were the guileless innocents the poet portrays.

If these Acadians were so amiable, loving and pious in 1755, then they seem to have lost all trace of such saintly dispositions a half dozen years later, according to official records of our Province, that are not fairly to be taken as hysterical memoranda of mere alarmists. Here follows an extract from an address of the House of Representatives to Governor Belcher in 1761:

"The lenity with which these people (the Acadians) have been treated by the Government, since they have been prisoners, in allowing them the liberty of working at high wages, furnishing them with provisions and retaining them so long in the province, we conceive has been done on a presumption, that these measures would show them the sweets of the English Government and incline them to become real good subjects; but we had reason to be convinced that this can never be effected, at least while they remain in the province; for no sooner was the Spanish war declared, and the junction of Spain with France known, than they assumed fresh courage, and began to be insolent to the Settlers in the Townships where they were at work, telling them that they should soon regain possession of their lands and cut every one of their throats! At a meeting of the Council holden at Halifax the 26th of july 1762, they were of the opinion that, Some late threats and Insults of numerous bodies of the Indians, assembled in various parts of the province to the Terror of His Majestys Subjects in the New Settlements, has been occasioned by the Stimulations and artful Insinuations of the Acadians. That the Council apprehend that there cannot be any hope of a sincere Submission of the said Indians to His Majestys Government while the said Acadians are suffered to remain in this Province, they being connected by intermarriage with them, and thereby maintain a considerable Influence over them at all times. That it had lately been discovered that the said Acadians had collected and Concealed in Secret Places in Kings County in this Province a considerable Quantity of Ammunition for Small Arms. That at this Time the necessity of drawing all the troops together at Halifax, had stripped the new Settlements so effectually of Protection, that, except the very small Garrisons at Annapolis, St. John's River, and Fort Cumberland, not amounting in the whole to one hundred men, there was no protection to any of the Settlements. The Interior Part of the Country being entirely destitute of any, and the Garrison at Fort Edward wholly occupied by the Militia of that County to the great detriment of the Inhabitants, who are forced to neglect their husbandry; and so much to their Terror that not only one hundred and fifty of the Settlers have on this Alarm quitted one of the new Towns in the Country, but others are preparing from other parts to follow them."

There is an old Latin maxim to the effect that no one suddenly becomes very bad. Had these Acadians been the community of saints, as the poet represents them, dwelling in the love of God and man, and found themselves through some dark dispensation of Providence called upon to suffer the loss of home and friends they would have said, "The Lord giveth, and the Lord taketh away, Blessed be the name of the Lord!" Instead of striking back, they would have turned the other cheek to the smiter; they would have exclaimed, "Whom the Lord loveth he chasteneth," and remembered that "the meek shall inherit the earth," as the promise runs. Had they been so pious and simple of heart they would have "hung their harps on the willows" and cried "The Lord is good unto them that wait for him, to the soul that seeketh him, for the Lord will not cast off forever: but though he cause grief, yet will he have compassion according to the multitude of his mercies, for he doth not afflict from his heart nor grieve the children of men."

Quite otherwise was their conduct. They fled to the woods in great numbers and there joined hands with the Indians for no peaceful purposes. Many of them came from their banishment to their old homes, but no one molested them, but quite otherwise they were given remunerative employment by the new settlers, but they were still in hopes that a turn of national affairs would restore them to the land they once occupied but never owned. In June, 1762, the French made a spasmodic effort and captured St. Johns, Newfoundland, and the news inspired the Acadians with fresh hope that the day of their deliverance was nigh, and they began to make the threats that resulted in their confinement in Halifax and Windsor, and finally many of them were again sent away to Boston to be ultimately scattered here and there.

In all this they conducted themselves very much like ordinary mortals, but not in the least like people whose proper home was Heaven, and not earth! Says Sir Adams G. Archibald in a paper read before the Historical Society of Nova Scotia:

"There is not a doubt that these Acadians were a very quarrel-

some and litigious people.   Their commercial transactions were too
trifling to occasion many disputes.   But they had, to be sure, but
little personal property to fight about.   But they had in the titles
and boundaries of their lands, material for numberless quarrels.
They did not hold their lands by grant from the British Crown.
They claimed under French absentees who were supposed to have
grants from the King of France; but these absentees were themselves aliens, and could not own lands under the treaty.   The occupants claimed under oral agreements, without definite descriptions
or boundaries.   When these lands descended to heirs, and became
divisible among children, whose shares were held without division
or description, the boundaries necessarily became still more complicated.   Under these circumstances there could not but be an
infinite number of disputes, and we hardly need the assurances of the
authorities of British and French officials and travelers of both
nations to be certain that the people of every Acadian village were
in a state of chronic quarreling about their lands.   But the position
was made still worse by the reluctance of the British courts to take
cognizance of these disputes.   In the eye of the law the occupants
were all squatters together, and the courts did not care to give a
quasi legal title by deciding in favor of either claimant.   This work
therefore fell to the priest, who spent most of his time in mediating,
and if that failed, in adjudicating between the parties.   It was an
imperfect jurisdiction, and judgment could be enforced only by
spiritual weapons.   The erring party was deprived of the sacra-
ments; and if that was not enough, the terrors of excommunication
were held over him.   Even these were not always successful.   In
some cases the litigant braved the threats of eternal punishment,
rather than submit to a loss of temporal rights.   Is it any wonder
that quarreling and litigation were rife in every Acadian village?"

So long as people are made to believe that the Acadians were
an ideal community of blameless souls, just so long will they see the
Expulsion in a false light.   It was all sad and terrible, but let us
remember that it was a mere fly-bite compared to some of the outrages within the range of Christian history.

GEOLOGY OF KINGS COUNTY.

The rock record of this county is particularly varied and accordingly instructive and interesting.   Much has been written about it,
and yet the last word explanatory of the formations remains to be

said. The students of geology, and its most closely allied sciences, can all find in this small area ample field for valuable work. Here are the granite, slates, sandstones and trap, representing several of the great primary divisions of the earth's crust; here are beautiful specimens of amethysts, agate, jasper, chalcedony, zeolites, magnetite, selenite and many other desirable finds in this direction. Here are fossil shells, fossil rain-print, fossil ripple-marks and other instructive and curious mementoes of the ages left behind us by millions of years.

Much has been written on the geology of this county. Before me are the following: "Jackson and Alger on the Mineralogy and Geology of Nova Scotia, 1832;" "Gesner's Remarks on the Geology and Mineralogy of Nova Scotia, 1836;" "Gesner's Industrial Resources of Nova Scotia, 1849;" "Dawson's Acadian Geology, Editions of 1855 and 1878;" Dr. Honeyman's paper on "Nova Scotian Geology" in Nova Scotia Institute of Science, Vol. V, Part I; paper by Prof. Ernest Haycock, entitled "Records of Post-Triassic Changes in Kings County, N. S.;" in publications of the Nova Scotia Institute of Science, Vol. X, Part 2; Summary Report of Geological Survey Department 1901, with map. These sources of information are mentioned for the possible benefit of beginners in this field who would wish to avail themselves of the services of those who have already gone over the ground, a matter never to be neglected without regret. In the summary report just mentioned there is a geological sketch map of portions of Kings and Hants Counties, and this will largely be my authority for the distribution of the formations.

The extreme southwestern portion of the county is occupied by the intrusive granite axis of the Province, to which no definite age has been assigned, mutually agreeable to all who have looked into the matter. Not unlikely that it is an highly metamorphosed sedimentary formation that was once continuous with our provisionally called Cambrian slates and quartzites: in that case the granite is the core of a vast alpine uplift that has disappeared by the operations of denuding agencies continued through many million years, and left us but the tattered and ragged edges of the strata that once rose to form the now vanished arch. If this is a guess, then it adds not greatly to the varied speculations about this interesting outcrop of granite. This granitic area makes a contact with the lower Cambrian gold-bearing series of slates and quartzites near Meadow

Brook and Little River. This latter formation is not very extensive, embracing about forty square miles, almost reaching the
Gaspereaux River, and coming in contact there with the Silurian
formation, and to the eastward bounded by the newer, Horton
series. These latter are set down on the map as "Devonian," and
very likely with good reasons, for Mr. Hugh Fletcher is responsible
for the classification. At any rate it is an interesting outcrop that
may be roughly bounded as follows: Beginning on the county
line next to Hants, at a locality known as "Halfway," and continuing to the Avon River, and thence down the stream to a mile below
the Horton Bluffs, and thence westward crossing the Gaspereaux
near the railway bridge and running nearly parallel with the railway
a mile to the southward up to Wolfville; thence southward to the
place of beginning. Sir William Dawson has described these Horton Bluffs that are rich in fossil fish scales and fish teeth and fine
plant impressions. He has placed this formation in "the very lowest
part of the Carboniferous System." Since that position would be
inseparable from the highest or most recent of the Devonian, it
becomes a very delicate question as to where one ends and the other
begins. How delightful to think that we are not going to solve all
the problems of nature in a hurry, and leave nothing for intellectual
research along those lines.

From Hants County extends down the River Avon a narrow
wedge of Carboniferous limestone that almost reaches Blue Beach.
Triassic sandstones occupy the valley from the Silurian border, or
contact, near Wolfville, Greenwich, and Kentville on the southern
side, to the North Mountain, where they underlie the igneous overflow of trap that extends over the summit area where it has acted
like a protective shield against the erosive agencies that scooped
out the valley from the softer sandstones. On the bay shore near
Broad Cove there occurs a remnant formation of limestone that
may by further study turn out to be a tattered leaf from the
Cretaceous times, an interesting item, if it can be thus identified.

These are the naked generalities of a region deserving more
attention than it has ever received from students, although college
classes have long been graduated in the midst of this tempting field.

AYLESFORD, KING'S COUNTY.

CAMP-MEETING GROVE, BERWICK.

CHAPTER XVII.

For a certain class of tourists, Nova Scotia has no attractions. It is destitute of such human antiquities as may be found in most other portions of the globe. Here are no buried cities, nor feudal castles, and blood-stained battlefields. Professional globe-trotters will find here but little to tickle their jaded appetite for wonderful things.

Having thus made a clean sweep of all lofty pretensions, we may honestly bring out our wholesome attractions for ordinary mortals who are seeking a good locality for a vacation, and we confess to a sense of modest pride in the variety and abundance of good things at our disposal. We have twenty thousand square miles of country. While this is not of startling dimensions, still there is ample room for natural features in great variety. It equals in area Massachusetts, Connecticut and New Jersey combined, and these are no mean Commonwealths at present, with room for large expansion in population, property, and influence. This territory is in the shape of a narrow peninsula about 350 miles in length, and over 50 in average breadth. The whole circuit of the coast might have been made with a uniform line of 1,000 miles, but owing to its great irregularity, it is 2,500 miles in length; wherein there are 100 harbors to say nothing of sheltering coves. Every one of these places offers to the tired and over-heated people of American cities a delightful, cool, and healthy retreat. The rock formation from Canso to Yarmouth, 250 miles, in a direct line, meets the ocean in naked ledges of Cambrian quartzites, broken here and there by intrusions of Granite.

The Bay of Fundy shore lacks the savage surge of the wide sea, but makes ample amends in view of matchless tides, and the quiet charm of land-locked basins. On all this coast, in every harbor and at intervals between, dwell hospitable people. They are fishers, shipbuilders, farmers, traders, mariners, and lumbermen; and not infrequently several of these vocations are followed by one person. No handier people can be found anywhere. They are resourceful to a remarkable degree. There are highways not far from the coast, around a large portion of the Province. Persons desiring a bit of seclusion where none intrudes, within sight and sound of "the sand and the sea" and the "wild uproar," can readily find free accommodation in such localities where they may pitch their tents on unclaimed lands, and yet within easy reach of telegraph, telephone, and stage accommodations. The whole south shore of the peninsula proper, from Shelburne to Canso, is adapted to such purposes.

People who prefer the towns will find one or more in all the eighteen counties, and always one situated on tide-water and offering comfortable accommodations at reasonable rates. There are churches, and schools, cultivated people, and pleasant drives with many other enjoyable features. No matter what town in this Province that a tired, overheated refugee from an American city happens to reach, he would be deliciously cooled and tenderly ministered to by natural agencies around him.

From the Atlantic coast there is a gradual ascent for about forty miles where the watershed or "divide" is reached at an average elevation of some 600 feet. This may be looked upon as an inclined plane of slates and quartzites, folded into great waves until the once horizontal beds are now standing on their edges at various angles, and the crests of the waves have been scored and denuded by agencies that have operated upon them during some fifty million years. For the most part this surface is covered with vegetation. There are extensive forests of spruces, pines, and firs; there are large areas of exposed ledges and broken rocks, known as barrens, where small shrubs and scrub oaks and pines manage to live. Other portions are occupied by tracts of hardwood hills, and meadows, and bogs, and lakes. There are hundreds of squares miles in which there is not a human habitation, and the moose and caribou and bear are its most important inhabitants. All this interior region is very inviting to those who are pleased with beautiful lakes, and quiet streams, and fine old forests where they may sleep within earshot of the loon's weird cry, and the owl's "Too Whoo," as if the night itself had found voices in these wild things of flood and forest. People with enthusiasm for natural sciences will find in these inland districts many things to gratify their taste and curiosity.

The botanists will not be unrewarded for their "walks abroad." The bogs and meadows and barrens that will have but little interest to others will contribute to their knowledge and their pleasure at the same time. They will find the Rhodora spreading its "leafless bloom" over wide areas of rocky lowlands, and the rose pogonia making the boggy meadows blush with their abundant blossoms. The twinflower finds in these cool forest solitudes a congenial home, where it luxuriantly carpets the ancient aisles with a living green, and fills all the air with an incense befitting the gods.

The student of birds, coming here from the southward, will congratulate himself for being in the midst of so many pleasant experiences. It would be a pleasure to give in some detail the delights that await him, but space forbids more than a glimpse of all of these good things. He may watch the *solitary vireos* weave their pendant cradles of birchen strands, and hear them scold him for intruding upon their privacy. He may listen to the wondrous notes of the ruby-crowned kinglet, and perhaps will find his snug warm nest in the covert of thrifty fir or spruce. He may find prizes in the nests of yellow-bellied flycatchers, mourning warblers, and three-toed woodpeckers. He can make close acquaintance with the Hudsonian chickadees, the pine grosbeaks and crossbills, and many other feathered creatures of forest, lakes, and shores.

On this southeastern watershed, stretching from Canso to Cape Sable, the geologist will discover many features of great interest in the ancient Cambrian rocks, now tilted and pushed into anticlinal waves and synclinal valleys, but denuded to the heart of mighty folds in which are stored the gold mines of the Province.

He will find on these naked areas, the scratches, and grooves, and polishings of glaciers that about a score of thousand years ago covered all this peninsula, and far beyond, a mile or more in depth in solid ice that crawled down this low incline to the sea and floated away in towering icebergs to be melted in warmer seas, return to the air, and perhaps fall again on the ice-cap of Nova Scotia, and repeat a former experience. The trained imagination can reconstruct the Age of Ice, and the educated eye will see its footprints in hills, and lakes, and rivers, and boulders, that are eloquent with this ancient story of death and desolation, that was more than once enacted, and may again overtake all temperate eastern North America. Tourists with likings for geology will be gratified to a greater extent in the counties of Annapolis, Digby, Kings, Hants, Colchester, Cumberland, Pictou, Antigonish, and portions of Cape Breton. Rocks of other ages, existing under other conditions, with vast contents of iron and coal, and interesting fossils will engage their attention and enrich their stores of knowledge. They can saunter anywhere to advantage with open eyes, a hammer and a note book. There are features of special interest to sportsmen of rod and rifle, and these are treated in another chapter, but the naturalist *at large,* the lover of the various fields of living things, people who are not making collections of birds, or butterflies, or beetles, but still have a keen interest in nature, will find this northern peninsula far richer in forms of life than many a tropic region. The great Congo forest yielded to Stanley's starving company hardly more than fungus for food. Brazilian forests over great extents are sparsely populated with beasts and birds and insects. True there are creatures new to northern eyes in their native haunts. There are monkeys and parrots, and great serpents, and gorgeous trogons, and toucans, and creepers, and flycatchers. Of all these brilliant birds not one is gifted with musical ability. This delightful talent is withheld from all birds of prey, from *professional* flycatchers, from woodpeckers, from butcher-birds and crows, and ravens and vultures and jays. No ravenous creature red in tooth and claw can yield a musical note. Thrushes, warblers, finches, these are the principal groups that are truly vocal, and our northern woods and pastures, and shores and waysides are rich in these delightful creatures. We can add to these, the vireos, and the ruby-crowned kinglet, and somewhat rarely the marvelous winter wren.

Rabbits, squirrels, porcupines, muskrats, minks, woodchucks, beavers, and moles are the principal small mammals that contribute an agreeable interest to those who love the woodland walks, or find delightful retreats in old pastures, and by the plashy brinks of meadow brooks, and shores of lonely lakes. Let no one despise an intimate acquaintance with these fellow-mortals who live so close to the bosom of nature, who have not sought out many inventions to their hurt, who art not toothless, and bald, and bespectacled, and dyspeptic, and drugged, and slashed with surgeons' knives, and besotted with opium and alcohol; but every one of them fitting into his place and acting his part with reasonable contentment and admirable foresight. No wonder that Job of old exclaimed, "Ask now the beasts and they shall teach thee, and the fowls of the air, and they shall tell thee, or speak to the earth and it shall teach thee, and the fishes of the sea shall declare unto thee."

Says Walt Whitman:

" I think I could turn and live with animals,
They are so placid and self-contained,
They do not sweat and whine about their condition,
They do not lie awake in the dark and weep for their sins,
No one is dissatisfied—not one is demented with the mania of
owning things."

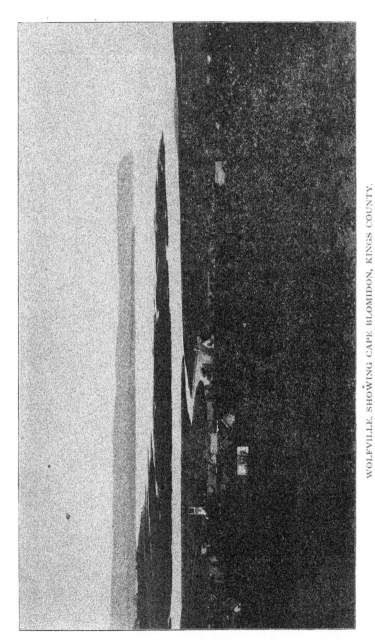

WOLFVILLE, SHOWING CAPE BLOMIDON, KINGS COUNTY.

SUMMERSET.

It is a sad reflection that so many people are more desirous of wantonly taking the lives of these innocent creatures, than they are to learn from them the useful lessons they are competent to teach. In these days a large percentage of tourists and vacationists take along with them a camera. No one coming to Nova Scotia with that outfit will be likely to regret the trouble. There is to be found a great variety of scenery if one cares to zig-zag here and there to find it. Many forms of industries are open to the photographer and may be captured in full action. These are to be found on the farms, and in the shipyards, and sawmills and pulp mills, and quartz mills, and smelters, and gold mines, and coal mines, and other localities too numerous for recital. Bits of charming landscapes with all the adjuncts of rural life are of common occurrence. There are villages of Acadian French, hamlets of fisher folks, and encampments of Indians. All of them with some phase of special interest.

The artists of pencil and brush will not be at a loss for subjects that will demand all their skill. In the Cape Breton portion of the Province they will discover that Scotland, at her best, cannot out-rival the rugged beauties of her namesake. One of the pleasing and assuring aspects of this region is the fact that no venomous creatures are to be found within its limits. The serpents are small and harmless, and not numerous. Even New England has its rattlesnakes on the Blue Hill and Mt. Thom, and great black snakes that climb trees, and get under foot and scare people half to death, if they do not bite them. There are here interesting turtles and salamanders, but with neither desire nor capacity to harm man, woman, or child, unless a turtle might be tormented into taking a justifiable nip in self-defence. The very fact that he lives in a shell is a glaring notice to all comers that he does not intend to fight. He pulls into his shell, head, and tail, and legs, on the appearance of danger. He is as toothless as a babe, and bites with the sharpened edges of his shell as best he can in a hard cutting grip that no one need feel if the animal is not tortured by them.

Porcupines are quite numerous, but are unable to "shoot their quills," as the popular notion goes. In fact their whole make-up assures us that they do not intend to pick a quarrel with anything. They are very confident of safety from such attacks as ordinary animals can make. Wild-cats, foxes, and bears have a wholesome fear of their barbed quills, and well they may, for they are so constructed with numerous curved hooklets at the tip, that once they are stuck

on the skin of an animal, they will by aid of the muscular motion
go anywhere through him. In fact bone will not always turn them
aside, as I have seen for myself. Porcupines are quite aware of their
safety, and do not take much trouble to get out of the way of man
or beast. In case of a movement that looks like close pursuit, he
stops, and with a rustling sound his quills stand on end, his head
drawn down, his tail clad ferociously in spines, twitches and jerks
from side to side, and if one brings a stick within reach it receives
a smart blow, and a lot of quills are left sticking in it, that a living
thing would have received in place of it. He can bite, and will,
with a vengeance, if cornered by some human action, but he has no
fear of man. All his inherited habits have been formed without
reference to this strange new animal on two legs who carries a bow,
or a bludgeon, or a gun. He humps himself for defence against a
man with a rifle as he would before a hungry wolf or lynx that was
tempted to make a meal of him. Mankind came upon the scene of
his activities hundreds of thousands of years after his instincts had
been formed with reference to other creatures. A very interesting
animal he is, dead or alive, and it is greatly to be regretted that so
many people are ready to murder this innocent aborigine whose
claim on the land and its native products, antedate by thousands of
years the earliest of red men. I had only meant to say a word for
the benefit of timid people, but have been tempted to overrun my
intention, with such a suggestive and delightful topic for discussion.
At any rate the presence of such a real native reasonably common
is one more reason why a person who came here to rest may not
be without profitable diversion. There are bears in the Nova
Scotia woods, and village skirts, but they are far more desirous of
getting out of reach than coming in contact with people. They are
very intelligent and in this unlike the porcupine which are stupid in
the extreme. The reasons for this difference is largely to be found
in their food and the means of procuring it. Porcupines live on the
bark of trees, of which there is always a plentiful supply; a clump of
hackmetacks will afford plenty for weeks together. The ability to
climb trees and gnaw and digest the bark is all required of them.
There are no long journeys and varied experiences. Add to this the
feeling of security against enemies who dread their quills and the
result will surely be a stupid creature. The same great law holds
in the world of human life. Mental inactivity ends in mental
incapacity. Too easy conditions of life result in degradation.

Bears are suggestively human. They not only can walk on their hinder feet on their soles, and use their forefeet and legs like arms, but they are large-brained and think in a manner and measure like ourselves. The following instance is easily verified. I received it from a man as truthful as George Washington, and the bear and the hunter were natives of this Province. It was a warm sunny day in the last of March. A party of moosehunters set out from Port Jolie on the snow crust; after a few miles they came to an open spot strewn with bits of broken ferns, the tall bracken species. The snow was trampled with bear tracks, and beneath the trunk of a wind-fall that formed a roof was a fine bed of these ferns, that had been taken out the day before and dried in the sun, and then carried back again. The bear was soon espied sitting on her haunches not far away, watching the movements of these men who actually killed this intelligent fellow creature. I had as soon taken deadly aim on my grandmother! The bear is among animals what the crow is among birds—an all around creature. His teeth were formed for eating flesh and capturing large animals. The time came in his history, as a family, that there was not meat enough to maintain them, within their ability to get it. It was a question of extermination or adaptation to new circumstances, and the bears rounded that critical corner, and their brain cells multiplied with their new demands. See now our fine fellow with a mouthful of teeth that suggest meat and blood and struggling moose and deer, contenting himself in the early spring with black-ash sprouts, and later with blueberries and chokecherries, and suckers from the brooks, and sheep, or heifer, or calf moose, if he can have the luck to secure the thing. He will even descend to tickle his palate with ants, tearing up their mud nests and their houses in old trees. There is formic acid to be had from these insects, from which it gets its name, and bears find therein a fine relish worth the trouble of securing. He discovers the honey of bumble bees in deserted mouse-nests. He comes upon nests and eggs, and young of birds, and makes a tooth some meal on beechnuts and oaknuts. From all these "going up and down in the earth" and to and fro in it, searching out his food, there has resulted a larger and better brain than his distant ancestors possessed. He plans now and thinks like the rest of us. He will avoid by one artifice or another a whole rural neighborhood for weeks together armed with guns and provided with traps, and all the while help himself to cattle and sheep. He knows the dangers of a steel trap and understands how it operates. This knowledge he shows by avoiding the spot where it is covered in leaves, or taking it up out of the way, that he may secure the bait hanging over it, or by actually springing the trap *under* the jaw. The occasional presence of such an intelligent animal on all fours, with no disposition to encounter mankind, is a pleasurable feature to many people who like the prospect of seeing such a true native of the Province.

People who would pitch their vacation tents in the outer wilds for a few weeks will hardly be able to miss the sight of moose that are still fairly common in such localities. Such parties would be provided with canoes, and by that means, in a very pleasing way explore large areas of country along the streams and over the numerous lakes. The best region of this kind is the interior of Queens, Shelburne, Yarmouth and Digby Counties, as they unite to form a natural game preserve of one thousand square miles, in which there are no human habitations, and the land is barren, and meadows, and bogs, and swamps, and cone-bearing forests, and lakes, with occasional hills of hardwood, and will therefore always remain in this wild state.

The moose and caribou are protected by law during a portion of the year. Their better protection should be the reluctance of people to kill these noble animals, in time, or place, or manner, or number unbecoming the best sportsmen; and when the man of the Stone Age is evoluted out of our constitutions there will no longer exist a desire to kill them at all, but I greatly fear that all the game will be exterminated before the last sportsman dies.

Before closing this chapter something must be said about the climate. In the United States it is eminently respectable to be ignorant about all that pertains to Nova Scotia. A writer in "Recreation" not long age designated it as an "island" although he had been here on a hunting trip. The average New Englander, although college-bred, knows next to nothing of this neighboring Province with which the early history of his State is bound up in battle, and blood and military exploits—a Province very largely settled by Yankees, and where I can name Mayflower descendants by the hundreds within the limits of a single county.

Considering the population of about four hundred thousand, one may safely say that no community of equal number within the limits of the United States has produced more men of commanding talents, and unusual ability, than this land of the "Blue-noses" has to its credit. Several thousand citizens of New England who had minds of their own and courage of their convictions, were expelled from New England at the close of the War of the Revolution, and took refuge beneath the British flag in this Province. Like many other transplanted stock, it rather improved by the new conditions. There was no taint of criminality in their conduct at home, but it was, as it turned out, an unfortunate affair to be on the losing side, among a people who had so narrowly escaped defeat of their cause that they failed to be magnanimous enemies, although they had been rocked in the same cradles. In one generation came Joseph Howe from the loins of John Howe, a Boston loyalist printer, and New England will needs be ransacked to find a fellow for that statesman, orator and poet, who left the indelible mark of his genius on the political institutions of his Province. In three generations was born Sir Charles Tupper, Bart., whose distinguished career in the political field has made his name familiar over all the British Empire. Scores of conspicuous examples could be given of the fertility and superior quality of this Pilgrim and Puritan stock, that has taken firm root in this ancient colony. There is a prevailing belief among Americans that Nova Scotia is within the Arctic Circle, either literally or figuratively, and the result is continuous cold, fog, and almost constant snow. After a residence of more than twenty years of adult life in the United States, in various localities, I am confident that the following statement is true. The fact is about what might be expected from our latitude and almost insular position. The worst thing to be said of the weather is that it does not exceed in disagreeable qualities the same article in New England, and during the summer months is much to be preferred. There is considerable difference in the length and intensity of the cold season at Yarmouth, on the southwest extremity, and northern Cape Breton. In the former locality the spring vegetation is about two weeks behind the vicinity of Boston, at the northeastern extremity it is at least four weeks later.

If one desires to spend a vacation amid the finest scenery of the Province, then go to Cape Breton in the vicinity of Bras d'Or waters, or drive to St. Ann's Bay, the North River, and on by the wild shore to Ingomish, and Aspy Bay. Railway communication is direct to Sydney, and steamers are run in various directions to accommodate the public.

There is plenty of room for all who care for the advantages

offered. At present there are but twenty people to the square mile, so there is no immediate danger of tumbling over each other. There are so many advertisements and folders describing routes and rates that anyone with gumption enough to come without a guardian can find out the best way to make a landing, and the most desirable localities to visit.

DIGBY.

BEAR RIVER, DIGBY COUNTY.

CHAPTER XVIII.

HISTORY OF DIGBY COUNTY.

Whoever desires to prepare a brief history of this county need not be at a loss for material. This is not true of several other counties. There are two published histories of Digby, one by Isaiah Wilson, Esq., the other by the Rev. Allen Massie Hill. The former is by far the fuller work. The author deserves more thanks than he will ever receive. It is fortunate that men can be found to voluntarily perform such tasks, wherein there is neither cash nor compliments for all their pains. The latter book is intended to preserve some bits of history, and some local incidents and genealogy not to be found in the other.

This county is bounded as follows: On the northwest and west by the Bay of Fundy, on the south by Yarmouth County, and on the east by Annapolis and Queens. The area is 1,021 square miles, and the population is about twenty thousand.

In point of picturesque features, this county is not excelled in all the Province. Nature has lent her varied charms of sea and land to beautify the locality. The historic and ᵥdelightful Annapolis Basin swings its great curves for many miles for boundary lines, and invites the eye by its ample dimensions, that are set round about with hills, and meadows, and villages, and orchards. During many thousand years no human eye rested upon all this; no light canoe of dusky savage, nor white sail of his conqueror disturbed the placid waters, that reflected only the natural aspects of sky, and land. The graceful gulls screamed, and laughed in storm, and shine, and the wild creatures of wood, and wave, came and went, and no human beings had appeared to make them afraid. "Beauty is its own excuse for being," and so we may understand that through the thousands of years before the coming of man to this region there was no lack of lovely scenes, no stinting of autumn's gorgeous foliage, no faltering notes of feathered songsters; but the maples hung out their flaming banners, and the hermit thrush, from his hidden retreat, sung down the sun, and sung in the dawn. Had the scene been clustered with human eyes and ears, the leaves would have been decked with no richer colors, and the bird-notes had no added charms. Such is Nature's amplitude, such her incalculable wealth, that she arranges her magnificent landscapes,

17   257

introduces her delectable dainties of flowers, and songs, and sunsets, where there are none to admire and none to praise.

> " Mysteries of color duly laid,
> By morn and eve in light and shade;
> And sweet varieties of chance,
> And the mystic seasons dance,"

all these in affluent measure, are never withheld but

> " The harp at Nature's advent strung
> Has never ceased to play,
> The songs the stars of morning sung,
> Have never died away."

But we will get back to the "sea, and the sand, and the shore, and the wild uproar" that lies outside the narrow gateway that leads to the tempestuous bay, where the great tides chase each other up the far-famed waters, where the fishers are tilting in the frail crafts, praying "Him whose ocean is so large to care for them whose boat is so small."

Turning from this gateway southward, we have for nearly fifty miles a rugged and storm-swept coast. Unless the most competent people who have visited the locality have been far astray in their estimates this strip of land abounds in such attractions as no other portion of North America sea-board of the same extent is likely to equal. To the artist, the naturalist, the geologist, the tourist, it offers no ordinary inducements. If I were to extract from the writings of eminent men the passages that treat of this noted "Neck" there would be no space for further notice of this county here. However, it is but justice to the locality to lay before my readers somewhat of the descriptions from competent hands. Let us begin with Sir William Dawson, who says, "This long promontory, though only from two to three miles in width, consists of two ridges, one forming the cliffs that front St. Mary's Bay; the other sloping toward the Bay of Fundy; while between them there is a narrow and almost level valley, with several little lakes and ponds arranged in a line along its bottom. The rock in this valley appears to be amygdaloid, and it is probably owing to this circumstance that the valley has been scooped out, while the edges of the beds of more compact trap remain as ridges. This at least is the explanation which appears most probable from the structure of all parts of the ridge that I have visited, except the very singular and romantic spot named Sandy Cove. At this place a deep cove penetrates about one-fourth across the ridge from the south, between precipitous cliffs of trap resting on amygdaloid, and apparently with a southerly dip; or at all events without that decided dip to the north which prevails over the greater part of this trappean ridge. Opposite the southern cove there is on the north side of the ridge a shallower cove, and between is a little lake, on either side of which rise lofty beetling cliffs of basaltic trap, which appear to be a part of a thick bed dipping to the northward. Can this be a volcanic crater? Whatever the cause of its present appearance, Sandy Cove is more like something a poet or a painter might dream of than like an actual reality in our usually tame Province of Nova Scotia."

Writing long since Dawson, only a half dozen years ago Prof. L. W. Bailey, of the University of New Brunswick, and long time on the geological survey of Canada, has this and much more to say of the region: "Of the more readily accessible portions of Nova Scotia there is probably none less frequently visited, or of which less is known by ordinary travelers, than the peninsula commonly known as 'Digby Neck.' Thus while hundreds, or thousands, are, in the course of every summer, whirled along the rails from Yarmouth to Digby, and vice versa, or are forced into expressions of admiration as they steam through the wonderful passage of Digby Gut, few ever think it worth while to visit and study the long curious neck of land whose eastern end forms one of the pillars of that famous gateway, and which stretching thence to the westward as a narrow, and yet almost mountainous ridge, separates the waters of St. Mary's Bay from those of the Bay of Fundy. Even professional naturalists and geologists, usually upon the alert for whatever is new or instructive in the world of nature, would seem in but few instances to have visited Digby Neck, except that portion immediately adjacent to the town of Digby, and observations upon its structure, physical features, mineral contents, or floral characteristics, are alike few. And yet it may be safely said that, with the exception of Blomidon, no area of equal extent is to be found in Nova Scotia, and probably not in eastern America which presents such peculiar features of scenery, geological structure, plant distribution, or mineral associations, as are here met with. The total length of this belt of high land, from the Gut to the extremity of Briar Island, is forty-four miles; and for much of the distance the breadth varies but little from a mile and three-quarters. The maximum elevation of the hilly range is about 350 feet. As regards its physical features it is a district of bold contrasts, including long and prominent ridges, separated in some places by broad and open valleys, in others by narrow troughs, while across both at intervals stretch transverse depressions always relatively deep, and in some instances sinking far below tide level. In these latter cases especially at Sandy Cove, and in the Petite Passage, the whole structure of the peninsula is admirably exposed, and in the craggy bluffs that border them is discovered scenery which in many respects may well be compared with much of that in the vicinity of the Giant's Causeway in Ireland. So high indeed, and so steep is much of the shore, particularly upon the southern side, that a safe descent to the beach, if beach there be, is often hard to find, and in some places quite impossible."

These extracts are taken from the Transactions of the Nova Scotia Institute of Science, Vol. IX, Session 1894-95, wherein the locality is treated in a very instructive manner. This paper has been published separately, and doubtless could be furnished to those who care to have it, by Prof. Bailey himself.

In 1832 there was published in Cambridge, Mass., a book entitled "Remarks on the Mineralogy and Geology of Nova Scotia, by Charles T. Jackson and Francis Alger.' These American gentlemen were the pioneers in this field in Nova Scotia, and were well equipped for their work, especially in those early days of geological science. They made themselves well acquainted with this region, and here follows a very small part of what they wrote about it:

"Digby Neck is a continuation of the North mountain from Annapolis Gut, and extending thirty miles to the westward, is bounded on the north by the Bay of Fundy, and on the south by St. Mary's Bay, which separates it from the main territory. At its western extremity are situated Long Island and Brier Island; the former separated from the latter by Grand Passage, and from the main peninsula by Petit Passage; but geologically considered, they are a continuation of the neck of land, with which, though separated from it by these narrow channels, they are identical in structure and composition. They are composed of trap, under its different modifications, to the entire exclusion of every other rock; and, like most islands of a similar nature when freely exposed to the ocean, they present scenery of unrivaled grandeur and magnificence. On the south side of Brier Island near the entrance of the channel, the cliffs present a very striking assemblage of neat and regular columnar masses, which sometimes descend in lofty and continuous ranges of steps for many hundred yards into the sea; their serrated ridges rising up here and there from beneath its surface, and appearing at first sight like so much pierwork reared in defence of the island."

Space forbids further quotation, but we trust enough has been said of this interesting and instructive portion of Digby County to add a little to its deserving reputation. The area of this county is not the largest in the Province, yet it has 135 miles of coast and over the whole length there is no lack of variety of scenery, occupations, and people.

It would be difficult to tell who was the first white man to settle within the limits of this county. We know by various indications that here and there near the basin the Acadians had made themselves homes. They were always on good terms with the Indians, and had nothing to fear from their visits in the remotest locality. A cloud of disaster was forming over their heads that burst in 1755 in the general expulsion. From that date till 1764 these exiles wandered hither and thither, and many perished in various ways; but by this time they were at liberty to return to their native land, but to find their old homes occupied by New England settlers. In 1768 a remnant of them finally reached St. Mary's Bay in Digby County and began the settlement that grew into the thrifty District of Clare, which has grown into a chain of villages that for more than a half century has been a separate municipality. Its extreme boundary is a little below Weymouth, and extends westward along the coast to Beaver River, with this as a baseline, its southward extension very nearly forms a triangle, one side touching the Yarmouth County line, and the other bordering on the municipality of Digby. Its water front is a little more than thirty miles, and its greatest breadth south is about fifteen miles. Within these limits is a population of nearly 9,000 souls. The great majority are French, and their everyday speech is the language of their fathers. They are engaged in fishing, farming, and lumbering. Meteghan, Salmon River, and Church Point are fair-sized villages. A newspaper, printed in French, at Weymouth, finds the most of its patrons in this region. These people were greatly favored during many years by the presence of Father Sigogne, who came there from France in 1799, having lived two years in England immediately before his arrival in Clare. He was a man of noble spirit and many parts, and became their spiritual guide, their lawyer, historian, and referee; and, he left the mark of his character in these people, whose fathers would never have figured in a tragical expulsion had they been under the guidance of such as he, instead of the fierce and cruel Le Loutre, the principal author of their woes.

The Town of Digby is of first importance in the county. After the expulsion of the French the first settlers in that vicinity were a small company of Americans, who came in 1776, led by William Mac Dermott; but they were greatly harassed by privateers a few years afterward, and were scattered here and there. The settlement of the locality from which the present state of affairs is in unbroken succession, began with the coming of the Tories, or Loyalists, from New England and adjacent regions in 1783. It was a fortunate thing for them that Nova Scotia had not been included in the new Republic, as might readily have been the case, for there was scarcely any organized resistance to oppose them, and sympathizers with their cause were in a majority in the Annapolis Valley, in Colchester, Cumberland, and Yarmouth Counties.

These Tories, as they were called at home, or Loyalists, as they were termed abroad, had in them excellent material for colonizing purposes. For the most part they were men of convictions, and of good Anglo-Saxon stock. They had taken sides in a great question and lost. It was fixed in the nature of things that the Revolution should end in that way. When Quebec surrendered to Wolf, and French dominion on this Continent came to an end, a long stride was taken toward American independence although the great question lay yet beneath the historical horizon.

This congenery of lusty young colonies, peopled with British blood, and animated with the spirit that had been forged in the contests of centuries of British history, were not to accept the humiliating terms imposed by a narrow-minded King and incompetent advisers. If an attempt of that kind could be made with the present generation of Canadians, they would spring to arms as one man.

When the war closed in 1783 there was no mistaking the temper of the victors toward those among them who had helped to draw out the struggle through years of acutest suffering. The Northern Colonies offered a refuge and opportunities to make new homes under pioneer conditions. Digby County was favorably situated for settlement, where many of their countrymen were already to be found in the Annapolis Valley. The name of the county and town is in honor of the Honorable Robert Digby, a British Admiral, who superintended the transportation of many of these Loyalists.

The Town of Digby, situated on the west side of the Annapolis basin, possesses one of the best harbors in the Province, and attracts many tourists by its fine scenery, delightful drives and cool summer climate. It is doubtless destined to become a famous resort for overheated multitudes to the southward of us. The town site was selected with excellent judgment. The locality was known as Conway, and the grant from the Governor bears date of February 20, 1784, and runs to some three hundred persons whose names would appear in this place but for the fact that more than one-third of the grantees failed to occupy their lands, and a large number arrived who were not named in the patent. Great confusion prevailed over the distribution of lots, and very soon there was a cry of hunger went up from the multitudes because the promised rations had been delayed.

In the spring of 1784 they petitioned the Government for assistance, and Mr. John Robinson was appointed to enumerate all these settlers. He reported in July of the same year, and this document informs us of the names of all the heads of families so far as the men are concerned, and the number of each family. This record has a real interest to those who desire to look into their ancestral lines, and one may find it complete in Wilson's History of Digby County; it is too long a list for insertion here.

The township grant of Digby covered one hundred thousand acres and included Long and Brier Islands. The growth of this town has been slow to within a few years. The present population is 1,100, and the prospect for the future is very good. Railway and steamboat services make it easily accessible to Americans, who already are becoming favorably acquainted with the many attractions of all this region.

To write even a very brief notice of this country and not make special mention of Bear River would be scant justice to a charming locality. Not only has nature been lavish with scenic attractions, but the people have not marred her fine effects. One must take it for granted that visitors will have the good taste to go there in the warm season when the beauty of the foliage contributes so much to the many attractions. The drive from the railway station affords a succession of pretty pictures, and when the village is reached it

turns out to be in excellent keeping with the locality. The houses
are neat and tasteful, embowered amid giant cherry trees that have
found there a most congenial home. The main street swings up
the high hill with curves that please the eye however much they demand strength and wind from the climber. Here come staunch square-
rigged vessels to load with lumber, almost poking their yards into
the cherry-orchards, and when the tide is out they lie naked in the
mud like stranded whales, but within a few hours they will be floating like swans, or standing down the river under a bit of sail on their
voyage to some distant port. The best way to get acquainted with
this choice bit of the Province is of course to go and see for yourselves, gentle readers.

WEYMOUTH, DIGBY COUNTY.

CHAPTER XIX.

THE SEA FISHERIES.

The Province of Nova Scotia may be considered richly endowed by nature, even if we confine ourselves to the land, the mines, and quarries, and timber, and fruit-growing, and agricultural facilities, are of themselves phenomenal in variety for one small province, but in addition to all of these, the sea is an added domain of unfailing wealth on a great scale.

It might seem at first glance that any part of the sea would be inhabited by fishes, but the truth is very far from that state of things. Expeditions from England and America first, and afterwards from other countries, have spent years in dredging the sea bottoms. They have trailed their drag-nets across the widest oceans, sounded their abyssal depths, taken their temperatures miles deep, and secured specimens from all the forms of life that could be found in those localities. The results of these expeditions have been to open up a new realm of research, a dark continent of wonders whose immensity has only been skirted by the pioneers of these researches. Already the great museums of the world have been vastly enriched by the new specimens captured by the English ship "Challenger," and the American ship "Albatross." We have learned from their work that the sunlight is very feeble at a depth of 1,200 feet, and ceases altogether not much beyond that point. The deepest soundings reach almost six miles, and that is in the Pacific ocean. Plant life has not been found deeper than light extends. Sixty-two per-cent of the sea area is somewhat more than two and a half miles in depth. Deep dredging shows that most of the sea bottom is a region of cold, the temperature of the water even at the equator being sometimes below the freezing point of fresh water. This is due to deep currents from the polar·zones creeping to the equatorial latitudes. The pressure at the deepest known soundings is six tons to the square inch. As a rule from the shore outward to a depth of 600 feet and an average distance of 200 miles from the shore, there are deposits of sand and gravel, worn from the land by the action of waves and rivers. On the vast sloping plains beyond this shore margin, the bottom is covered with dull blue, green, and red muds, clays, and organic ooze. In medium depths these muds and oozes are made up of the shells and skeletons of minute animals

which once lived in the waters above. Descending these plains of
the sea into greater depths where the bottom is from two to six
miles from the surface, these shells disappear, and there succeeds an
immense stretch of soft red clay, covering fully half the entire ocean
floor. There the shells have fallen so far through the water that
they have been crushed and dissolved, and the bottom deposit is
made up of volcanic ashes that have sifted through the depths in the
course of millions of years, having been first thrown high in the
atmosphere through the volcano's throat. Mingled with this
material there is meteoric dust, the ashes of shooting stars, like we
may see any clear night, but in reality these bits of mineral, mostly
iron, are all the time coursing through our atmosphere, where they
are heated by the friction of the air, and oxidized to dust, and this it
is that has fallen upon the sea and from age to age accumulated on
the undisturbed floor. There also are found the ear-bones of whales
and the teeth of huge sharks, covered with a deposit of manganese.
Some of these remains are from extinct species, but they are dredged
up with those of living forms.

Even in the depths of two, three and four miles, where the water
pressure is so great and the temperature is nearly ice cold, and
darkness, so far as the sunlight is concerned, is complete, there are
hordes of living creatures. Fishes and crustaceans abound, and the
eye of man never rested on them or their kind till they came up
entangled in the dredge that had dragged through their domain, that
man alone could find means to invade. Many of these fishes are
equipped with living lights of different colors. When brought to
the surface they are already burst asunder and dead; once the pressure was largely removed the result was fatal. Our fishes of the
upper waters would fare no better if they were taken to even the
two-mile limit where pieces of tarred rope used on the make-up of
the dredges are compressed to half their previous diameter.

In the sharp struggle for existence in the ocean there has been a
natural selection of individuals from many species that could live
at greater depths than others. When pursued they escaped into the
·deeper water, where the pursuer could not follow them. There they
were safe from many of the marauders of the upper region. In this
way the great deeps must have been invaded, and became the home
of many forms of life, that for the most part are yet unknown to
science. In order to live they must turn upon one another there
as elsewhere and enact the old tragedies over again. We find that

many of them are toothed and jawed in fiercest fashion. The largest of them yet taken was five feet in length; but with suitable dredges there may well be brought to light huge creatures of startling aspect. When these fish are handled they are soft and flabby objects composed more largely than usual of water, and thus adapted to withstand the pressure of their haunts, where they are not lacking in firmness. We can readily see that even if it were feasible to fish in waters a mile or more in depth, still the flesh of such fishes as one might secure would be of little or no value for food.

It is a matter of common knowledge that all the fisheries of these regions are within the areas of certain localities called Banks. In other words the food-fishes and their enemies frequent the shallow waters that do not much exceed in depth one-quarter of a mile, while for the most part it is very much shallower, for all species but the hallibut, that are partial to about 1,200 feet.

To get something to eat, and to get away from the eater, are the problems of fish existence. Every scale is a visible notice of onset or defence, or both. To swallow, and to be swallowed, with that understanding the game of life is played, and it is very certain that not one of them will ever get a chance to die of old age. The sea is a tremendous battlefield, where there is never a cessation of hostilities, never a truce. There, all visible living things at once find themselves in the midst of great dangers that threaten their existence. In such circumstances every advantage of color, of form, of swiftness, of spines, of scales, of ability to exist on certain foods, all counts for something vitally important. To be colored like lobsters to match the rockweed of their haunts, or to mimic the sea floor like flat-fish, or resemble the gulf-weed like the mouse-fish and the pipe-fish, and hundreds of others, are all of them advantages in the never-ending struggle. The prodigious fecundity of fishes announces the dangers and fatalities that beset the eggs and young. The progeny of a single codfish, if they could find enough to eat, and escape being eaten themselves, might within a few hundred years brim the Atlantic from surface to bottom. Out of a half million eggs of one of these fishes produced in a season, less than one on an average comes to maturity; all the others are for the most part devoured either as eggs or young. To provide against this onset of rapacious jaws, in which the parents take a part, is the meaning of the multitude of eggs—there is no sentiment in the sea. Any failure on the part of these creatures to keep themselves adapted

to their surroundings will surely be a fatal step, and thus we find in
the rocks that were once sea-bottoms, hundreds of fossil fishes that
have no living representatives; their names have been "blotted from
the book of life." The spiritual law holds good in the natural
world, and the promise ever is "to him that overcomes" more life
shall be the reward. It is well for mankind to know that they hold
these food-fishes on precarious conditions, even though no devices
of their own were employed to capture them. They might go the
way of so many other species that had their day long before the
human race appeared. Now that we have interfered and thrust our
greedy, clumsy hands into the problem, the danger of extinction is
vastly increased.

It is only within recent years that there has been an adequate
realization of the great value of fishes. Indeed they are almost
indispensable as a portion of the world's food supply. The rapidly
increasing population of the globe, and the widespread interest in
natural history have resulted in fishery commissions and biological
stations, and extensive hatcheries, and through their investigations
and operations very much has been learned of the habits and
instincts of the food fishes and their enemies that prey upon them,
and the creatures that the food fishes need for their subsistence.
We have learned that these fishes we so much value do not roam
here and there for thousands of miles as the old belief held, but
each species has its own local area, that includes different depths
of water over a few thousand square miles. Indeed the practiced
eye of our fishermen will distinguish a fish from a particular locality,
especially of certain species. The best authority, like Professor
Prince, Dominion Fish Commissioner, tells us that it is not difficult
to tell the difference between a St. John River salmon and one from
the Miramachi and one from the Restigouche if we have the
examples to compare. Even the herring on the Scottish coast are
in most cases easily distinguishable. A menhaden caught on the
coast of Maine can with facility be distinguished from a Long
Island menhaden, a Chesapeake, or a Florida one, by certain indescribable characters, easy to perceive but difficult to define. That
the same species present these subtle variations is complete proof
that they do not roam very far from the environment that has in the
long run effectually put its mark upon them. There are doubtless
instances in which an unusual shortage of food, or an unusual number of enemies, or some other phenomenal occurrence, may cause

them to wander far outside of their native haunts. Similar causes
are in operation on the land. A notable instance among birds is
found in the snowy owl, whose native haunts are within the Arctic
Circle, but in the year 1876 they appeared in great numbers in Canada and the New England and Middle States, and this has occurred
again the present winter 1902, and two of their number, shot on the
Grand Pre dyke, have fallen into my hands. Although fish can see
no further than a few yards, yet they are able to find their way to
spawning places and feeding grounds with great accuracy. It seems
that they are endowed with a sense of direction that governs their
movements. It must be something akin to the power exercised by
migrating birds that enables them to accomplish feats almost beyond
belief, as for examples the snipe-like tattler, *Heteractitis incanus,* and
a sanderling *Calidris arenaria* that nest in islands in the Bering Sea,
and spend the winter in the Fanning and Hawaiian islands, distant
some 2,000 miles; and as the birds are not swimmers they must make
the distance without resting.

Another bird, the American golden plover, *Charadrius dominicus,*
breeds in arctic America and then flies the entire length of North
and South America to its winter home, and we must remember that
this journey is made by young birds as well as old ones. While our
fishes do not go so far, still they doubtless cover two or three hundred miles in exchanging their feeding-grounds and seeking their
accustomed spawning-places, and in this feat they cannot be aided
by their eyes, so far as the course is concerned, which may not be
true of birds that do not go very far at a flight, like our robins and
sparrows, except when they cross from the western end of Nova
Scotia to Boston which is a common practice. I have seen them
come aboard the steamer in quite thick weather, and after a rest
start out again as true on their course without a compass as the ship
held her way with the aid of that instrument. On the land they
very likely have no need to use this directing sense; but out to sea
they are guided by it in some way we have not learned. At any
rate the last word of science on this fascinating subject has offered
no other explanation.

It is considerable satisfaction to know that the fishes of our
region are our own, that they are as much at home as the birds
of our woods and fields, that they have no inclination to stray into
strange depths, nor wander wide from their native haunts. On this
point we have a clear statement from the late Prof. Spencer F. Baird,

a most competent authority, and one to whom we owe much for his intelligent energy used for the protection, preservation and study of our valuable fishes. He says: "In all discussions and considerations in regard to the sea fisheries, one important principle should be borne in mind, and that is, that every fish that spawns on or near the shore has a definite relationship to a certain area of sea bottom: or in other words, as far as we can judge from experiment and observation, every fish returns as nearly as possible to its own birthplace to exercise the function of reproduction, and continues to do so, year by year during the whole period of its existence. It is an established fact that salmon, alewives and shad, both young and old, have been caught on certain spawning beds, and after being properly marked and allowed to escape, have been found to reappear in successive years in the same locality. The principle is rather more difficult to establish in regard to marine fishes, but experiments have been made by competent men on our coasts and elsewhere which prove the existence of the same principle in relation to them."

Several factors have contributed to the making of our superior fishing grounds. They have been for ages in the process of formation and are most largely the result of the ceaseless action of the waves on the shore lines that once extended far out to sea. At present the relative geographical positions of the peninsula of Nova Scotia, the Island of Cape Breton and New Foundland, and the gulf stream and Bay of Fundy tides have each and all a part to play in the making and preservation of these fishing banks. It is well to know that our fishermen who seek the cod and hallibut go off to the "Banks" for that purpose. Now it will be desirable for the general reader to know something about these ocean areas where baited hooks bring up the vast supplies that are derived from this source.

If we unroll a mariner's chart of these coasts and waters it will throw a flood of light on the subject, for thereon we will find marked the various depths and soundings and the "Banks" outlined and named. In order to better understand this portion of the ocean floor that so much concerns our welfare, let us imagine that the water is withdrawn to a depth of 250 feet over all this region from Long Island Sound to Labrador. By this occurrence the dry land would be extended into the Atlantic Ocean from our shores about fifteen miles on an average. We would find the new territory for the most part a sandy surface strewn with more or less rocks that had been carried there by the agency of the ice. The new coast line would fall off quite rapidly to three or four hundred feet depth, where it would reach the bottom of a muddy valley running roughly parallel with the present coast-line. On the eastern side of the valley the ascent continues till the bottom emerges at one point eighty-five miles from Canso in the bit of land now known as Sable Island, which in reality is but the crest of the great Sable Island Bank, that is exposed by this imaginary subsidence of the sea, and shows its area of 14,000 square miles. To the eastward we would see the island of Newfoundland, vastly enlarged by the emergence of its costal sea-bottom, and a narrow channel off Cape Race would show a southern border formed by a portion of the Grand Banks of Newfoundland. That would be out of water here and there over its whole area of about 25,000 square miles. Between the Grand Banks and Cape Breton is an area of about 5,000 square miles, known as Banquero; this would be all under water, a desert of sand. To the northeast of its border would be seen a narrow channel separating it from St. Pierre Bank, an equally large area near the coast of Newfoundland, that would no longer be hidden under the waves. This narrow channel would extend northwest between Cape Ray and Cape North, and open into the Gulf of St. Lawrence. To the southwest of Cape Sable about 100 miles, a large area of some 4,000 square miles, known as Georges Banks, and now famous fishing grounds, would be in place sixty feet above water, and the dry land would extend with but slight interruptions to Nantucket Shoals, and the mainland of New England.

Suppose that there was a further falling of the waters of 750 feet, making 1,000 in all. We might then walk from the northeastern extremity of the Grand Banks to Boston; the Bay of Fundy and the Gulf of St. Lawrence would be dry land. From this new shore line fronting the Atlantic, the sounding lead would abruptly sink into profound depths of from 1,000 to 7,000 feet, and even 12,000 feet. A vast ocean desert, so far as the needs of man are concerned.

With this study of the locations and relations of these fertile "Banks," we can go further, and show that the sandy materials of which they are composed is a shore product. It has come from the washing of the rocky coast lines that have been lashed and buffeted by the waves through untold ages. The tides and ocean currents have carried the sand away and every grain of it has found its lodging place through the action of great natural forces, and the resistance of the various coast lines, and contours of sea-bottom. They will remain till the sea has devoured Newfoundland, Nova

Scotia and Prince Edward Island, an event on the great program that will come to pass if the present order of the world is maintained, in about a million years. By that time we may not need fish for a subsistence. At any'rate we have the fishing grounds, and if we act like rational creatures we are not likely to be deprived of the fish. It is not to be anticipated that their existence is seriously threatened by any agencies but those of human contrivance. But before we look into that aspect of the case, let us get a proper estimate of the value of these fisheries not only to ourselves, but to those who procure their products. The Canadian fisheries are the largest in extent of area, the most prolific, and the most varied in the world. They comprise an immense extent of maritime coast, and almost innumerable lakes and rivers in the interior of the provinces which form the Dominion. It is the good fortune of Nova Scotia to lead all the other Provincial divisions in the value of her fisheries.

The annual report of the marine and fisheries departments shows the total value of the catch in Canada for the year 1900 was $21,-557,639. The Provinces shared as follows:

Nova Scotia	$7,809,152
New Brunswick	3,769,742
British Columbia	4,878,820
Quebec	1,989,279
Ontario	1,333,294
Prince Edward Island	1,059,193
Manitoba and N. W. Territory	718,159
	$21,557,639

It will be seen that Nova Scotia stands for over one-third of the amount.

These figures speak for themselves in a brief, but instructive manner. We will now take up the matter in somewhat of detail. The branch of this great industry that is the most remunerative, curiously enough has nothing to do with fish, but refers to the lobsters that are crustaceans, pure and simple, and are no closer related to fishes than they are to birds. In saying that the lobster catch is the most remunerative I have not agreed with the Government figures. The explanation for this will be found in the following contribution to the Halifax Herald of November 22, 1902, special South Shore Edition, by M. H. Nickerson, Esqr., of Clarke's Harbour, Shelburne County, a member of the late Government Commission to investigate the conditions of the lobster fishery, and a gentleman entitled to serious consideration on any subject which he chooses to treat seriously. The entire article is interesting and instructive reading, and it is given here complete:

"Forty years ago lobsters were canned on a very limited scale at points widely separated from each other on the South Shore of Nova Scotia. That was the humble beginning of a business which has spread and flourished to a wonderful extent, reaching out everywhere; that also was the real start of a fishery almost wholly neglected till then, a fishery whose expansion both in product and values has indeed been remarkable. No other resource of our coast-waters has been so rapidly developed, or yielded better returns to nearly eighteen thousand fishermen engaged in it steadily or for the most part along the whole Atlantic seaboard from Westport to Scattarie. It is the staple industry within that range. It has created good, wholesome activity in trade over the same territory, and as a natural consequence it has brought a fair degree of prosperity, which otherwise would have been quite impossible to many of the shore settlements.

"The two divisions of this industry are canning and the live export trade. The latter began scarcely twenty years ago. It was at first carried on with little regularity, for the American sail-smacks, which visited these shores to buy lobsters in the shell, made trips far between. They bought at prices slightly above the factory rate, so the fishermen were not greatly in pocket by the new departure. At present by means of rapid transportation afforded by lines of steamers to Boston, the business not only rivals in value the work of the canneries, but since 1896 has actually surpassed it, with the exception of one year—on the part of coast now under consideration. In the official report for 1899, the latest returns available, the total value of the lobster industry for the whole Province is put down at $1,639,790, (a considerable drop, by the way, from that of the previous year), of which the live export counts, according to the same authority, $672,310. But the year before the whole amount was $2,673,623, of which more than half was realized from live sales, all but a very small portion of which is credited to the South Shore. Besides, it must be remarked that in all government returns for recent years, lobsters exported alive are estimated strangely enough, at only $5 per hundredweight. Now that is altogether too low.

18

"The Boston market, to which live shipments chiefly go, fluctuates, of course, at certain seasons, but the top figures have sometimes been $25 a crate, and they seldom went below $12 last winter. It would be entirely within bounds to place the average at $10 per hundredweight through the season, which would rightly add another million of dollars to the lobster yield of the Province, mostly that of the South Shore. This fact is worth bearing in mind, and it certainly should appear in the statistics if the same rate is maintained in the future. It places the annual yield from lobsters ahead of all of that of any other fishery in Nova Scotia, not excepting the shore and bank cod fishing combined, although the latter is now prosecuted more vigorously than ever, especially in Lunenburg county, whose fleet of schooners—fine as ever rode the billows, manned by stalwart and active crews—now number well on to two hundred, and bring in an immense quantity of fish every season.

"This comparison may help one to realize what a source of wealth lies almost at our very landings, and what possibilities there are in it for future generations if only due caution is observed in exploiting it. The lobster man's gains count up fast. A crate contains the bulk of say two quintals of codfish. That quantity of lobsters, put on the market right, often nets $20, and the cash return is prompt. That quantity of codfish with all the labor of curing, may be worth $6, and the proceeds from delayed shipments and other causes is of necessity somewhat slow. This is the difference which makes itself apparent in some places at the conclusion of the respective seasons. There were some instances among us last year where a lobster fisherman cleared over $1,000 from his season's work.

"The canning business in some respects has kept pace with the general advance. Improved methods of packing are to be seen in most factories. Almost every year has witnessed an increasing number of men engaged in fishing and using more effective gear than formerly. A wider European market for the canned article created a brisk demand and prices' abroad have until quite recently been extremely good. These things were tempting enough to allure capital in big or small blocks, and of late there has been a tendency to overcrowd the business. Factories have sprung up almost at every available spot, so that the number which stood at about 100 on the South Shore some few years ago is now increased to fully 220, and still there is a planning for more, especially in the western counties. As might be expected, some inferior packing is the result, which has been found slightly detrimental to the trade. To remedy this and put the industry on the basis of genuine enterprise is the object of the convention shortly to be held by the packers of recognized standing from as wide a territory as may be practicable. If their views are carried out, there is still an ample field and a hopeful future awaiting this division of a great industry.

"The growth of the lobster fishery has led to many improvements in connection with it, and given a lively impulse to traffic of various kinds. The boats now owned by the more pushing fishermen are models of beauty and marvels of seaworthiness. They cost about $200 each, and resemble a yacht in lines and rig more than anything else. They safely weather the winter gales and play over the waves like a duck. No other style of craft of that size could be used in the stormy season.

"A numerous class of small coasting steamers has been called into existence by the requirements of the lobster trade. Many of them combine general freighting with the carrying of lobsters to the ports of shipment abroad—chiefly Yarmouth and Halifax. They collect the catches, crated up for transport at the different stations along the shore, and the regularity with which they make these trips to and fro is not the least wonderful part of the vast system by which that special product of the sea is forwarded with all dispatch to the American markets. At the busiest periods those boats have been known to carry to Boston 2,000 crates per week as the aggregate shipment from both the above named ports. At $10 per crate, such export would bring $20,000 to be distributed in cash among the fishermen of the South Shore.

"This brief survey may afford some idea of the importance of lobster fishing to the shore population of Nova Scotia. It is already the leading factor in their commercial and industrial activity. As a branch of productive labor, it calls for as much attention as farming or lumbering, if not more. There has been a question as to whether the supply would continue, considering the enormous drain from year to year, and it must be said, the persistent violation of laws intended to preserve it. It is evident that overfishing and indiscriminate slaughter must work some mischief, but the area exploited, especially in the west, is exceedingly prolific. Every care should be duly taken by all concerned to husband and protect the resource on which the economic welfare of so many thousands of our people is dependent.   M. H. NICKERSON.

"Clark's Harbor, November, 1901."

This much for the lobster industry of the southwestern end of Nova Scotia, and in order that we may have a fair opinion of the other extremity, I have extracted complete the following contribution by H. Harris, Esq., of Gabarus, Cape Breton, to a special Cape Breton edition of the Halifax Herald of August 31, 1902. The article was prepared at the request of that journal:

"When the limited extent of our coast line is considered, the lobster fishery of Cape Breton is probably the most valuable one in the world. The annual crop is about seven and one-half million lobsters, preserved and canned, worth $12.50 per case for 25,000 cases, $312,500, to which may be added about 350,000 of 10½-inch ones exported alive to Boston and valued at $50,000 or more. Every harbor and cove along the coast is studded with factories in which, during the fishing season, several thousand men, women and children are employed.

"During the season of 1899 seventy-four factories were in operation and turned out 1,200,000 pound cans, equal to 25,000 cases.

"The fishing season is limited to three months out of the year. No spawn or berried lobsters are supposed to be taken and none under eight inches in length.

The canneries are visited several times weekly during the season by experienced officials whose duty it is to see that the law is enforced. In addition to these officers, speedy cutters patrol the coast, the commanders of which unexpectedly appear on the scene of operations and make things very uncomfortable for any packer caught violating the regulations. The impression among many is that the lobster is doomed to early extinction, but no indication of depletion or even scarcity of the supply is noticeable in Cape Breton.

"Here the size is well maintained, no falling off in the pack occurs, and it is safe to say that with the legal season as at present, there is no possibility of destroying this valuable article of food in our waters. In fact, if some more efficient method than that now in vogue were adopted for protecting the spawn lobsters, it would only be a question of a few years when the supply would greatly increase. The necessity for protecting the lobsters carrying eggs is emphasized by the fact that the eggs of one of such represent ten thousand young ones. Yet I regret to say that.thousands of these egg carrying lobsters are taken from the traps, the eggs washed off and the lobsters sent to canneries in apparently legal condition. If returned to the water when caught these lobsters would restock the ground with millions of young. The only way to restrict this wholesale destruction of these mother lobsters is to license the fishermen, and to have each man so licensed made a sworn official of the law to the extent that he will return to the water the berried or spawn ones that may come to his trap, and will report to the inspector of fisheries any violation of this law on the part of others that may come to his notice. There should be no charge for the license and no charge for the services of the fishermen. Any man desirous of fishing lobsters could do so by simply taking out a free license from the local fisheries official, in return for which he must become an officer of the fisheries to the extent above referred to. Let any violation of the law be punished by cancelling the offender's license. Now let us see how this would work.

"Say twenty men leave the shore in the morning to haul their traps, and that these men are licensed as suggested. Any one of them is in sight of the remaining nineteen, and any attempt on the part of one to wash the eggs off a lobster would be detected by some of the others. It is, I am sure, safe to figure that out of twenty men some would respect the oath of office. Under the present system only one officer is appointed to look after over a hundred men, and the washing of the eggs occurs at sea, far beyond the reach of this official. Under the system suggested every fisherman would be an official and no washing could be done without being detected by several of the other officials. In the United States the Government purchases the egg lobsters and hatches the eggs by artificial means. It is, however, doubtful whether these young lobsters ever mature, and the safer way would be to return the egg lobsters to their native grounds to hatch their eggs in the natural way.

. "The inspector of fisheries for Cape Breton is putting forth every effort to enforce the laws, and the good he has done is well known to all. The adopting of the license system as suggested would so strengthen his hands that I venture to say in five years the supply in Cape Breton waters would increase 50 per cent, and those of the fishermen who might for a time consider the license as severe would in a short while be the first to recognize its merits.

"Some 1,500 fishermen in Cape Breton are engaged to catch the lobsters, while 2,000 to 2,500 hands are employed in the factories to can them; 150,000 traps are used, to make which 60,000,000 of laths are required, 60,000 pounds of nails, 18,000 pounds of twine

and 10,800,000 feet of rope. About 1,200 boats are used, while
in a few instances steam smacks convey the lobsters from the fishing grounds to the canneries or connect with the steamers of the
Plant line from Sydney and Hawkesbury to Boston, in which the
live ones are forwarded to that city.

"The material for making and sealing the 25,000 cases of cans
annually packed consists of 3,300 boxes of tinplates, 50,000 pounds
of solder, 15,000 pounds of nails and 300,000 feet of pine lumber.

"The cost to place these 25,000 cases of lobsters in Halifax may
be estimated as follows:

```
7,500,000 lobsters at $2.50 per 100........$187,500
Labor and smacks .......................   50,000
Cans, solder and linings..................   40,000
Freight, insurance, fuel and sundry expenses  15,000
                                            _____
    Total ..............................$292,500
```
or $11.70 per case.

"These figures are based on last season's work. The markets
for the present season are lower by about 75 cents per case, which
has necessarily caused a small reduction in the prices being paid for
lobsters along the coast.

· "The pack in Cape Breton is about the same as last season's to
this date.   H. E. BAKER.

"Gabarus, C. B., June 14, 1901."

The following extract is taken from a booklet entitled "Shooting and Fishing," issued by the Dominion of Canada, 1900:

"It is hardly more than a quarter of a century since the birth of
the lobster industry in the Maritime Provinces of Canada, partien-
larly in the Bay of Chaleur and in many of the rivers of the Canadian Labrador, and at that time one could procure, in most of these
districts, lobsters of medium size for five cents each. About 1870
an enterprising citizen of New Brunswick came to Prince Edward
Island and founded a factory for the preserving of lobsters. The
investment succeeded from the first year, and was soon followed
by other capitalists, who invested considerable money in the industry, which progressed from that time with astonishing rapidity.
Prince Edward Island in 1871 had an output of 67,000 boxes of
lobsters, but four years later there were packed 151,248, and in
1882 the number of boxes had increased to 6,300,000. This same
province, which in 1871 possessed only one factory, now has 120

in full activity. The same increasing progress is apparent in New Brunswick and Nova Scotia. In 1870 the proprietor of the only lobster factory then existing in New Brunswick placed upon the market some 20,000 boxes of lobsters; twelve years later, in 1882, about 6,000,000 boxes left New Brunswick for the United States and Europe, and Nova Scotia, which in 1870 could only offer 30,000 boxes, exported in 1883 nearly 5,000,000. Today 740 lobster factories can be counted in the Maritime Provinces, and the value of the output in 1897 was estimated at 17,500,000 francs, the Province of Quebec only accounting for little more than 1,000,000. The lobster industry employs, according to the last statistics, 15,165 persons, of whom 1,870 are in the Province of Quebec. The value of lobsters canned was 11,130,000 francs, which represent an average of 15,000,000 pounds contained in 11,130,554 boxes. England is the best market for the Canadian lobster. She buys three-quarters of the canned lobster, the other quarter going to France, Germany, Brazil and the West Indies. Besides this export, enormous quantities of lobsters are shipped in the natural state to the interior and the United States."

I am fortunate to have at hand several of these letters from very competent men who discuss the various items of the fishery business from an up-to-date standpoint. The next communication is from A. W. Eakins, Esq., President of the Yarmouth Board of Trade. It was written by request of the Halifax Herald for the Special South Shore Edition, 1902:

"During the last twenty years the fish export business of Yarmouth has undergone a complete change. At the beginning of the period named and for a decade or more previous to that a fleet of about twenty-five brigantines and schooners was employed in carrying cargoes of dry and pickled fish and lumber to the different markets in the West Indies and British Guiana; today there is but one vessel in the business. Yarmouth still exports a good many thousands of quintals and barrels of fish, but the business is done in a safer and more profitable way. Whereas formerly the cargoes were sent out on shippers' account and placed in the hands of commission merchants to be sold for what buyers chose to pay— frequently netting shippers a heavy loss—today the fish are nearly always sold before they are shipped, and at prices made by the sellers. Some of the orders are from the West Indies direct, but much the greater part are from New York dealers and exporters,

the fish going through the United States in bond for export to
Cuba, Hayti, San Domingo, Porto Rico and elsewhere. The improvement in steam communication between Yarmouth and Boston
which has been going on during the period mentioned, has greatly
favored the change noted. A direct line of steamers between here
and New York would, of course, be of the greatest advantage to
the business, and would, with the tourist business, develop a paying
business on its own merits. It is to be hoped we may have such
a line in the not too distant future.

"It may be of interest to note in passing some of the reasons
why the quantity of dry fish shipped from Yarmouth has diminished
in recent years. Probably the cause contributing most to this result has been the enormous increase in the production of beet sugar
in France and Germany and other European countries, such increase having been brought about by the artificial stimulus of Government aid. Cane sugar that sold at from $4\frac{1}{2}$ to 5 cents a pound
dropped in a few years to $1\frac{1}{2}$ to 2 cents. Such a depreciation in
the market value of its chief article of export could but have the
effect it did have on many of the West India Islands. Planters
were impoverished and in many instances ruined, estates were sold
under foreclosure of mortgage, and many of them abandoned as
sugar producing estates. All this, of course, meant the loss of
employment for laborers and others, and the general stagnation
and business paralysis usually resulting from such a condition. A
lessened purchasing power made it necessary to do with less imported foodstuffs, and to buy in much smaller quantities at a time.
Another cause operating in the same direction was the closing
against us in the year 1893 of the large fish consuming markets of
the French islands of Martinique and Guadaloupe. In that year
a protective duty amounting to absolute prohibition was adopted
by those colonies under pressure from the home government. The
object was to give the French fishermen of St. Pierre, Miquelon, the
exclusive supplying of these markets, and this object has been attained. When it is considered that the two islands named consumed
about 10,000 quintals of dry fish a month, and that Nova Scotia
used to furnish the most of the supply, it will be seen what a serious
blow this was.

"The export of fresh fish to Boston—with some shipments to
New York—has developed with the shipping facilities. This is more
especially true of the item of live lobsters. Commencing with half

a dozen barrels packed in wet moss and shipped once a week in the "Old Dominion," back in the seventies, and growing to a total of 15,000 crates of 140 pounds each during a season. Mackerel are in some years shipped to Boston in ice by the thousand barrels; other years the catch is almost a total failure. The fish come up the Atlantic coast of the United States in the early spring, and about the 10th of May in each year they strike across from Cape Cod to Nova Scotia; they skirt the shore from Black Point around Cape Sable and east to the Straits of Canso, thence through to the waters of Northumberland Straits to the Bay of Chaleur and that region, where they stay and grow fat. During the months of May and June, and sometimes July, while passing this shore they are taken in nets and traps, but the business is uncertain and sometimes a losing one.

"A new departure has just been taken in the fresh fish business by a Yarmouth company in the building of a couple of fine steam trawlers for fishing on these shores. The first of these steamers, the 'Harbinger,' has been about a month in service, and seems to be doing well. The fish are landed every day or two and sold fresh, the buyers converting the haddock into 'finnan haddies,' for which there is a large and growing Canadian market, and salting or shipping the rest fresh, as may be deemed best. The second steamer, the 'Messenger,' has just been launched, and is being fitted with her machinery. If this venture proves to be the success that is hoped for it, it will be the means of making Yarmouth the most important fish distributing port in the Province, because, without doubt, other steamers will be added as the business warrants.

"Since the abrogation of the fishery clauses of the Washington Treaty, and the re-imposition by the United States of a heavy duty on our fish, many of our best fishing skippers and men have gone to Gloucester each season to fish in United States vessels, and thus get the benefit of the higher prices ruling in that market by reason of the exclusion of foreign caught fish.

"Indeed, so large has this annual exodus become, it has been asserted that fully half of the Gloucester cod fishing fleet is manned by Nova Scotians. As far as concerns these fishermen and their families, they are probably making a better living by this change of base than they could make at home, but other interests on this side suffer—we lose the building and outfitting of the vessels, the curing and packing of the fish, and the profit of selling them. We lose also the other advantages which result to a community from having its members remain at home and take part in the industrial and social life.

"In this connection it is worthy of passing notice that the people of the United States tax themselves 84 cents per quintal on codfish, $2 a barrel on mackerel and $1 a barrel on herrings, in order that a few thousand fishermen—half of them Nova Scotians—may be assisted in making a living. Seventy odd millions of the people pay the tax, either directly on imported fish, or indirectly in the increased price of domestic caught, and probably less than a quarter of a million get any benefit from it. It has apparently not yet occurred to the politicians who make the tariff that it would be much cheaper to board these few beneficiaries of the fish duties at hotels, and furnish them with clothes and pocket money, than thus to tax the whole nation to help them get a poor living by fishing. But there are even now some encouraging signs that the .people are becoming aware of the absurdity of the situation and that a change is not far off.

"It is undeniable that a treaty of reciprocity between the United States and Canada, which, while giving American fishermen equal privileges with our own in our waters and ports, would give us the freedom of United States markets for our fish, would be an excellent thing for this Province, but it would also be an excellent thing for consumers of fish in the United States. It would be particularly beneficial to the trade of the cities of Portland, Boston and New York by putting these cities in a position to act as distributors of our fish to the millions of consumers who look to them for supplies. New York, under free trade in fish, would become the great depot for the supply of dry fish to the West Indies and Central and South America. Its facilities for shipping by steam, frequently and in small lots, as wanted by dealers, would put New York in the best position to do the business. At present the custom house expenses, bonded warehouse charges and red tape generally are a great drawback and hindrance.

"It may also be safely asserted that even Gloucester—the very cradle of the protected infant fishing industry—would be benefited by the change. Her fish curing, cutting and distributing firms are now limited to the fish caught by their own fishing vessels, and, as frequently happens, by reason of a short catch (the present season is an instance) they have to pay high prices for their supplies, and

charge a correspondingly high price for the marketable product, thus curtailing consumption and lessening both percentage and amount of profit. With the door open to provincial caught fish, millions of pounds of our green fish would be sold in Gloucester for her dealers to cure and market.   A. W. EAKINS.
"Yarmouth, November, 1901."

The next letter was written for the same edition of the Herald by W. A. Killam, Secretary of the Harbinger Steam Trawling Company, Yarmouth, N. S.

"In compliance with your request I will give you my views of the fresh fish industry of Yarmouth. Yarmouth today ships more fresh fish to the United States markets than any other county in the Province; including their Canadian shipments from 6,000,000 to 7,000,000 pounds, including shell fish, annually for the past few years, would be a fair estimate. This includes half a million pounds from West Port and St. Mary's Bay ports, and 1,000,000 pounds from Shelburne county, chiefly Cape Island.

"It is not because we have better fishing grounds, but it is because we have such splendid freight service to Boston and New York, our best markets. We can put our fish on T wharf, Boston, in 16 hours, and at Fulton Market, New York, in 36 hours. This is why we are ahead of the South Shore counties in fresh fish. Let the South Shore have railroad service to Yarmouth and you will soon see that one boat a day to Boston will not do the work.

"The fishing grounds from Cape Sable to Sambro are among the best. But there is no encouragement for fish people to strike out unless they have facilities for shipping fish fresh, and that means railroad or daily steamship service to Yarmouth.

"The American markets are what we have to cater for, and fresh fish is what they want. Give the South Shore shipping facilities. Get a reduction on fish duty, do away with the license fee of $1.50 per ton on American vessels, and allow the American fishing fleet free access to our ports for shipping fares and refitting, and the money and business this fleet of four hundred sail vessels would leave along our shores would make this one of the best countries on earth.

"Canada is a large country, but not a very large market for salt water fish, outside of finnan haddies; New York City alone uses more fresh fish yearly. Digby leads the finnan haddie business at present. Last year's output amounted to one and a half million pounds, mostly to Canada. Give Shelburne and Queens a chance of shipping and they can better this as they have bettered haddocking along their shores, and there is no danger of overstocking the American markets with this article.

"If our government would substitute a few fertilizer factories and give our fishermen a small bounty on dog fish it would benefit the fishermen much more than the bait freezers will, as you will find many of the latter will not be of any benefit, as they are not in the right localities. Dog fish, unless they are made a marketable fish, will in a few years ruin our Bay of Fundy fishery, as they are increasing very fast, and during the summer season hinder fishermen from fishing more than the scarcity of bait does. A bounty of one cent on each dog to the fishermen and factories to buy them, with the oil and jelly, would make them as valuable as our scale fish.

"The same subsidy at each fishing port for a factory that they are giving the freezers, would induce people to go into the business; it would give lots of employment on shore and be a paying business and no doubt would in a few years clean out the dog fish nuisance.

"W. A. KILLAM.

"Yarmouth, November, 1901."

The following brief letter is well worth reading in this connection. It was written by W. H. Troop, Esq., of Halifax, for the South Shore Herald:

"How many people in Nova Scotia, aside from those directly interested in the business, realize that a splendid fleet of schooners, of the most modern type, sail from our coast every spring to prosecute what is known as bank fishing? Yet hundreds of thousands of dollars are invested in this business, thousands of men earn a living, and a catch of considerably over a million dollars is annually marketed. Surely an industry such as this is worth much to the Province, and especially to the ports where most of the vessels outfit.

"Lunenburg harbor, for from that port a large portion of the fleet fits out, presents a busy scene from about the middle of March till the vessels get away.

"The importance of this business can be realized when the supplies needed to prosecute the voyage are taken into consideration. Each vessel, and there are about 200 sail, carries a crew of fifteen to seventeen men, and .requires in provisions alone from $800 to $1,200 for the season. To these are to be added hawsers, trawl gear, cordage, lines, hooks, salt, (a most important item, usually Liverpool or Trapani), and the thousand and one things needed for the vessels and men.

"The fleet usually makes two trips, one called the spring, and one, the more important, the summer. A catch of from 300 to 500 quintals per vessel would be a fair average for the spring trip, and for the summer from 1,000 to 1,400 quintals, though some vessels hail for as high as 2,000 quintals.

"The crews are all young men, and well it is so when the hardships and exposure endured are taken into consideration. The work on the Banks is very hard, but the men are well fed, well clad, and of a sturdy build, well able to withstand the exposure to wet and cold so unavoidable in such a calling. The loss of life from our fleet is surprisingly small when the risk involved is considered. The vessels are of good model, well found, not oversparred, and handled with great skill by their skippers, as the captain is usually called. He, by the way, is usually part owner of the vessel.

"The general custom among the 'trawlers' is that the crew takes one-half the proceeds of the catch, the other being taken by the owners, who pay all the bills, save such as may be contracted by the men for their personal use.

"Nova Scotia has reason to be proud of her fishing fleet and the men who man them and whose toil helps to enrich the province by the sea.   W. H. TROOP.

"Halifax, November, 1901."

From booklet "Fishing and Shooting," issued by the Dominion of Canada, the following is extracted:

"The infinitely numerous species of fish have, in general, two characteristics in common, namely: fecundity and voracity, and it is necessarily so, because the different species incessantly devour each other; and man also performs his part in the consumption of incalculable numbers of the fish which form such a large factor in his daily wants. The cod is amongst the number of those species whose reproductive powers are greatest. A Dutch naturalist counted as many as 9,334,000 eggs in one female. The cod is often called the 'bread of the sea.' Certain it is that the cod takes the place of bread in countries too cold for wheat growing purposes. If there is an article of food that may be called inexhaustible, it is fish. Far from failing, the demand grows every year, and the production will doubtless finally become three or four times greater than it is today, and if southern countries, such as Brazil, Spain, the West Indies, etc., could be supplied with cold storage facilities, the cod and other fish exporting industries would be considerably benefited thereby. The inhabitants of warm climates regard dried codfish as an indispensable article of diet, while pickled fish has an enormous sale in Europe; the United States and West Indies, and the quantity of dried cod exported to these countries is placed on an average of 35,000,000 francs. The cod fishing industry gives employment to a vast number of persons, and without taking into consideration the millions of pounds consumed on the spot by the 20,000 families of fishermen occupied in the capture of these fish, or the enormous quantities disposed of in the markets of the interior, the cod occupies first place in the list of food fish, as well as for the oil, which is known the world over. This oil, which is extracted from the liver of the fish, is used for many industrial purposes, lubricating machinery, preparing skins, etc., and it is also largely utilized medicinally in the treatment of scrofula and other diseases of a debilitating nature. The swimming bladder furnishes a glue which is quite equal to that of the sturgeon. The eggs also are preserved for the table, unless they happen to be in a bruised condition, when they become an object of commerce, like the intestines, and are used as bait in the sardine and anchovy fisheries. Finally the bones and entrails of the cod, submitted to certain chemical processes, are converted into a fertilizing manure, the qualities of which resemble the celebrated guano of Peru.

"Yet, in estimating the value of the codfish, the tongues and livers are often overlooked. These are by no means unimportant details of the economy of this fish, for the livers yield as much as 350,000 gallons of oil, which, added to the number of pounds of pickled tongues, bring in about 1,000,000 francs per annum. Further, the price of codfish bait represents each year a sum equal to a quarter of the value of the codfish yield. The sale of the salted intestines forms another article of commerce which it is well to study. For instance, in France and Spain, where the sardine and anchovy fishing is carried on, 50,000 barrels of cod intestines are consumed every year. Now Norway in the best fishing years can only furnish 35,000 barrels, and generally she exports 25,000, there remain the 25,000 barrels which Canada can supply, and from which the Dominion can extract another million of francs, each barrel of cod intestines being estimated at 50 francs. Cod is found in all the seas of the northern hemisphere comprised between the 40th and 60th degrees of latitude. Since the fourteenth century cod has been the object of an extremely active fishery with all the maritime nations; nevertheless, there is not the slightest apprehension that the supply can ever diminish. The general rendezvous of the cod seems to be on the great Banks of Newfoundland, which is a submarine projection of 300 miles in length and 180 in breadth.

"Cod fishing lasts till the end of November, and is pursued on the great Banks either in decked vessels, varying in dimensions from 60 to 100 tons, or in small open boats at a short distance from the shore. From ten to twelve hands generally man the decked vessels fishing on the Banks. The Bank codfish is much larger than the cod nearer the coast; they are, besides, a better quality, and on an average thirty codfish from the Bank when dried are sufficient to make one hundredweight. The fishing done in open boats is carried on off the small Banks, distant from the shore some ten to thirty miles. These boats, perhaps the best of their kind in the world, are made by the fishermen themselves, and their dimensions vary from 20 to 30 feet in length. Two of these boats were shown at the International Fisheries Exhibition of London in 1883, where they attracted the attention of connoisseurs. Canada consumes a large quantity of haddock, a small variety of cod, for which the taste is more marked than for the real cod, and which, like it, does not bring satiety."

The following letter, also written by request for the Cape Breton edition of the Herald, deserves careful perusal by those who are interested in our fisheries:

"The value of the Island of Cape Breton for cod fishing was well known to the Spanish and Portuguese, as well as to the French fishermen, as early as the latter part of the fourteenth century. When in 1714 the removal of the French settlers of Placentia to Louisburg took place the conclusion arrived at by the official reports sent to Paris was that the value of Cape Breton for fishing and commercial purposes far exceeded that of Newfoundland, and St. Anne's Harbor is described as possessing great advantages, easily fortified, and codfish abounded there more plentifully than at any other part of the island.

"A writer in 1719 speaks of the French in Cape Breton as 'improving rapidly in wealth and in numbers, being very prolific, and in a few years likely to become very numerous;' and the writer adds: 'It is by all accounts the best and most convenient fisheries in any part of the King's dominions.'

"According to a report sent to the Lords' Commission of Trade in 1740 there were 48 schooners and 393 shallops and 2,443 men employed in the fisheries of Cape Breton. Of these 54 shallops were fishing at Ingonish. The total catch for that year was 117,050 quintals. The cod store houses were full of fish by the time the ships arrived from France laden with provisions and other goods sold by the merchants to the fishermen in exchange for their fish. Vessels from the French colonies of St. Domingo and Martinique brought to Louisburg tobacco, sugar, coffee, rum, etc., and returned loaded with fish. To such an extent had this industry grown when Louisburg was taken in 1758 that the previous year 15,000 men were employed in fishing, scattered all over Cape Breton. There were 726 decked vessels and 1,335 shallops, and the number from each station fully given from Egmont Bay, now Cape North, to Canso. Ingonish Bay and Cove sent out 245 shallops with a crew of from six to eight men in each. From St. Anne's went out to the Banks close to Bird Island 100 decked vessels, and the total catch exported from Cape Breton was 974,700 quintals. No wonder it was a great loss to France when Cape Breton became a British colony, and the catch of fish and the whole trade connected therewith never again reached anything like what it was under the industrious rule of its French inhabitants.

"What an object lesson have we here for the people of St. Anne's and Ingonish, when even today the ruins of houses and the stone foundations of their fish piles can be seen in abundance! French people have settled in Richmond, Cape Breton and Inverness, where they still follow fishing for a living and with varied success. Contrast Cape Breton, with its extensive and expansive fisheries under French rule, with results under the English protection, when in 1757, 974,700 quintals were exported and in 1770 the exported quantity was only 26,020 quintals. In 1785 there were several enterprising firms prosecuting the cod fisheries, as the export for that year was 30,580 quintals.

"Coming to more recent times and to the early recollection of the writer, codfish and mackerel were abundant closer to the shore than found now. As soon as the drift ice moves from the lakes and coast the spring herring in large bodies frequent the whole coast of Cape Breton and up into every creek and corner of the Bras D'Or Lakes, where they remain for only a short time to spawn and then disappear again. Spring herring are suitable for bait, and are used by the bankers for that purpose. They are generally followed by the codfish that come closer to the shore in May than at any other season of the year. From the 26th of May until the middle of June is the spring mackerel season full of spawn and poor, thin quality. Halifax papers speak of No. 1 mackerel in May and June, but October and November are the months for fat No. 1 mackerel. Until very recent years mackerel used to trim the shores of Richmond, the southern coast of Cape Breton County, then striking along the north shore, Ingonish, Neil's Harbor, and then to the Magdalen Islands, where they deposit their spawn.

"By causes not yet explained the movements of the spring and fall mackerel for the last fifteen or twenty years have changed, and they pass north in as large bodies as ever without coming near the shore in the places regularly frequented before now. Various reasons are assigned, such as being frightened with purse seines or regulated by the action of the wind. In bright, clear weather, with westerly winds, they may be seen passing outside the range of nets, and if the weather should be dark and foggy, with easterly winds, they usually hug the shore closer. My theory is that mackerel follow the small fish on which they feed. Summer mackerel, now so uncertain on the Cape Breton coast, used to be seized in large quantities in and around St. Anne's harbor, but with the exception of a few taken with hooks, very few summer mackerel are secured now in any part of Cape Breton. The mackerel going north in the spring return rolling in fat in the fall, and used to be caught in large quantities in Aspy Bay, Ingonish and around Scatarie and other fishing stations, but of late years they appear to pass outside of their former ports of call, so that very few of these valuable fat mackerel are secured by our fishermen. After the disappearance of the spring mackerel comes the large fat July herring, usually striking the northern shore of Victoria and gradually working southward towards Richmond County. From causes unknown the quantity and quality of these excellent fish, for which a market was found in all parts of the Province, has not been for the last ten years equal to what it used to be before that time. Last year there was con-

19

siderable improvement. Soon again they may attain their former
standard of being the highest quality of herring coming to the
Halifax market. July herring are too fat for export except to the
northern States, where there is always a good demand for fat herring. In September large sized herring are taken along the Cape
Breton coast, but the quality is not equal to those fished in July.

"Salmon, the king of fish, frequent the large creeks and river entrances of the whole coast, and are noted for their fine flavor and
superior quality compared with those of British Columbia. As a
rule they are larger in size and considered better quality than those
coming from Newfoundland. Cape North Bay, Ingonish and St.
Anne's are stations where salmon are yearly taken. The United
States market has been so well supplied with British Columbia salmon that prices have fallen to half the value obtained there a few
years ago. The great object now is to supply the Canadian and
United States markets with fresh salmon packed in ice. This trade
is increasing, and to follow it up successfully, rapid transit by
steamer and by rail is necessary to secure the salmon reaching the
best markets in good condition. Salmon run up the Bras D'Or
Lakes later than they do along the outer coast. The rivers they frequent to spawn are Salmon River, Bay St. Lawrence, the three Cape
North Rivers, Clyburn Brook and other streams in Ingonish. Indian
Brook, Barrachois, North River, St. Anne's, Mill Brook, Big Bras
D'Or, then Baddeck, Middle River and Washabuckt River, streams
near Cheticamp and other places in Inverness, and particularly the
Margaree River, are places where salmon work up to deposit their
spawn in the uppermost parts of these streams, and as far as possible from the disturbance of man.

"There are several Cape Breton streams, such as Mira River,
where salmon ascend to spawn, but the local knowledge of the writer
is unable to give particulars. With the large expenditure of money
on river guardians in the Island of Cape Breton there should be a
marked yearly increase in the catch of salmon, but it is to be feared
that in some cases these guardians, whose duty is to see the salmon
ascend to their respective spawning resorts, are not as watchful and
alive to their duty as they should be. Even some of themselves require careful watching.

"It is impossible in the short space allotted me to write of haddock, pollock, hake, alewives, etc., etc., which form part of the Cape
Breton fisheries, and to touch upon the proper method of curing

pickled and dry fish, more than to say that inferior prepared fish in ˌbarrels or in bulk are not fit for the Halifax or other markets, Fish, particularly the best quality, will always meet a fair market. Next to our codfish catch comes the lobster business, and there is no vacant place now around the whole island of Cape Breton where lobster traps are not set, and Cape Breton well packed lobsters find a market equal, and in many instances better than some parts of the Province that might be mentioned. So particular are they in London and other markets that the quality readily sold a few years back cannot now find a market. Never before was it so necessary to attend to careful packing in order to find a fair market as it is now. The highest prices have been reached last year, and the tendency will be to lower prices.

"Next to our codfish export comes the lobsters, and the continuous drain of fishing from the middle of December until the 1st of July must in time largely reduce the catch. The season in most parts of Cape Breton is from May to August 1, and there being no winter fishing, there will be lobsters there when other parts of the Province are depleted. The number of men and boats employed in lobster fishing has tended largely to reduce the catch of codfish; still the cash circulated for lobsters has proved a rich blessing to poor people in all parts of the island of Cape Breton.

"A very industrious class of fishermen from Newfoundland have settled in Ingonish, Neil's Harbor and New Haven, who confine their time to cod fishing and have succeeded in having comfortable homes and make a good living. Of recent years winter cod fishing has been sucessfully followed in Ingonish, Neil's Harbor and New Haven, from November until sometimes the 10th of January. These large fat fish are salted down in kenches and washed out and dried in the spring, when the market is generally better than at other seasons. The winter cod fishing is extending, as there is no other fishing followed at that season.

"With the south harbor of Ingonish open, the breakwater at North Bay and the breakwater under contract at Neil's Harbor, a larger class of fishing boat will be successfully used. Under proper management fishing vessels from 20 to 30 tons should be built and manned by our fishermen. It is doubtful if a large export trade of dry fish can be successfully carried on in Cape Breton, the quantity not being large enough without banking being prosecuted. This trade requires heavy capital to begin with, business men of experience to conduct it, with perfect knowledge of the fish suitable for the different markets. Bankers from Lunenburg, Lockeport, etc., can fit out earlier than it could be done in Cape Breton, with no drift ice to obstruct them, and exporting every month in the year. Fishing banks in and out extend along the whole coast from Scatarie to Ingonish, and inner banks now frequented by our fishermen prove beyond question that no part of the Province can excel Cape Breton in the value of its fisheries, which could certainly be extended with industrious fishermen uniting their interests and building during the winter months a larger and better class of boats and schooners than are now used.   W. ROSS."

It is very evident that Nature has dealt very bountifully with us, and whether we are long to enjoy what she has provided or whether our portion is to be cut off forever will depend upon our conduct. If greed and stupidity are to direct our actions, instead of unselfishness and intelligence, then there will be an end to our portion at no very distant day. We have seen in one generation the immense herds of bison almost disappear from this continent before the rifle bullets of men who shot them down by the hundreds of thousands for their hides and the mere sport of killing such noble creatures, as if they were not far more interesting as splendid living animals than they could be as dead hulks of carrion. If a few men who love the wild creatures had not interfered there would not be a living bison at this moment. Even the few small bunches that are wards of the nation are not safe from prowling pot-hunters, who would pick off the last survivor without the least hesitation. The last moose in the state of Vermont was shot a year or two ago, and the miscreant who did the deed was never punished. The moose in our own woods are doomed to speedy extinction, unless some effectual steps are taken to prevent their destruction. They are not only hunted with rifles, but are set upon by dogs and also caught in snares; by this latter means many are killed every season by people who will not take the trouble to look after their snares, and the animals are often allowed to starve and rot.

The same kind of men who do that mischief will strip the eggs from the female lobster and throw her into their catch for a male, without a care for the result, that must surely be a reduction in the number of the very creatures they wish to catch.

Nothing short of eternal vigilance will preserve our fisheries. The following is what Prof. Pierce has to say of the destruction of

FISHING VESSEL TAKING ICE, CANSO.

FISHING BOATS LEAVING THE HARBOR, CANSO.

FISHING VESSEL READY TO LAUNCH. MAHONE BAY.

mackerel by an invention calculated to line the pockets of a few hundred people at the expense of a great and needed industry:

"The decay of the mackerel in the North Atlantic, and esp cially in the Gulf of St. Lawrence, can be traced to the use of most destructive gear, precisely when the fish were schooling for spawning purposes. In spring and early summer an examination of specimens of schooling .mackerel shows how near ripeness these myriads of fish are. When the eggs are perfectly translucent they are cast out on the surface of the waters of the open sea, where they are fertilized and float for a week or two until the young fish are formed and burst out of the thin, transparent shell. Every female mackerel produces not less than 750,000 eggs on an average and as the purseseiners were able to enclose entire schools of these breeding fish, numbers of eggs beyond human computation were destroyed, and the mackerel cut off more or less completely. Other methods of fishing—gill-nets, inshore traps, jigging, hooks and lines—though formerly remunerative enough, were comparatively harmless compared with the completely exterminating character of the purse seine which was used out in the open sea precisely where the mackerel finds the appropriate conditions; clear, rippling sea-water of some depth, absence of rocks, hurtful objects, pollutions, etc., access to sunlight and the necessary modicum of heat, all necessary for the incubation of these most delicate floating ova."

No doubt but there are disturbing natural causes that produce considerable irregularity in the appearance of fish at certain localities. They are exposed to diseases peculiar to each species, that doubtless on occasions takes a violent and widespread form. Then again if their natural enemies are reduced in numbers by disease or any other cause, there will be an unusual supply of food fishes, but in the long run Nature will take care of these affairs if left to herself; but this long-headed fellow who invents purse seines and builds weirs, and saw mills, and quartz mills, comes along and thrusts his greedy hands into this nice problem and brings destruction to eggs, and young, and adults, and then drops his lip and grumbles if the catch is not up to his expectations. It is surprising that such an intelligent inventor should be so short-sighted about many affairs that are of the most vital interest to himself. A most aggravating feature in these matters is the fact that the innocent suffer with the guilty. Nature has gotten into operation in many animals an instinct by which they are moved to lay up something against the winter, but man is the most improvident of animals—he scarcely needed to be seriously reminded that he was not to take thought for the morrow, for as a rule he is quite content to live a day at a time. If he can get his quota of fish this year, though it is gotten by the most destructive means, there will always be found some way to justify his conduct in his own eyes. As another instance of this reckless greed I quote the following from Professor Prince:

"The disappearance of that small smelt-like salmonoíd, the caplin, from considerable stretches of the coast of Canada may be attributed to destructive methods of capture. The cod regularly came close inshore along the Labrador and northern coasts of the maritime provinces, in order to feed on their favorite food, the caplin. When the caplin no longer appeared the schools of cod disappeared, too. Now along the shores in question, especially along the estuary of the River St. Lawrence, traps or weirs built of brush or fine wickerwork were placed at every available point. These became filled to excess with hosts of caplin which crowded in with the flowing tide, and were left high and dry when the tide receded. These valuable little fish were used for manure to some extent, but visits to these weirs or *Peches* showed that for one ton of dead fish thus utilized twenty tons were left to rot and waste away. Masses of decayed caplin several yards deep were thus piled up, day by day, involving not only the grossest and most criminal waste of fish, but the production of widespread pollution in the neighborhood and the cutting off of the supplies of natural food which brought the valuable cod almost up to low water mark. So eager were the schools of cod in their quest of caplin that large fish were continually running on shore and were left stranded when the caplin were moving along. It may be added that the caplin came close inshore for the purpose of spawning, as an examination of caplin from the Labrador coast showed. A great run of cod, usually called the "caplin school," as a rule touched the Labrador coast about the middle of June, near Natashquan, and moved east to disappear from the shore a month later. In 1898 no sign of this school was apparent, and the total absence of the caplin may be regarded as a sufficient explanation.

"The gaspereaux (also known as alewives or kiaks) attracted the cod inshore in western Nova Scotia in a way similar to that of the caplin schools referred to, and the disappearance to a considerable extent of the cod from the littoral waters south of the Gut of Canso is no doubt largely due to the destruction of the gaspereaux, a destruction due to causes described on another page."

The Dominion Government is dealing with this great industry in a commendable manner that looks to its protection and perpetuation. For the regulation of the business Nova Scotia is divided into three districts, namely: No. 1, comprising the four counties of Cape Breton; No. 2, including the Counties of Cumberland, Colchester, Pictou, Antigonishe, Guysboro, Halifax and Hants; No. 3, covering Kings, Annapolis, Digby, Yarmouth, Shelburne, Queens and Lunenburg.

Inspector A. C. Bertram, North Sydney, controls the first named of these divisions; Inspector Robert Hokins, Pictou, the second; and Inspector L. S. Ford, Milton, Queens, the third. Each of these head officials is assisted by overseers, but the number assigned to them respectively does not appear to depend upon extent of territory, or volume of business, since Mr. Ford has in his jurisdiction only about fourteen of the sixty-two overseers in the Province. These again are reinforced by an army of special guardians—167 strong—located for the most part in the eastern and middle divisions. The table which follows is for the year 1901, the latest official returns to hand. We have put the counties of each inspectoral district in a separate group, with their earnings; also the totals for the divisions, and the grand totals for all. In this manner the reader can see at a glance the comparative value of the fisheries in the different parts of the Province:

DISTRICT NO. 1.		Counties.	Amount.
Counties.	Amount.	Hants	5,987
Cape Breton	$260,106	Pictou	118,914
Inverness	225,081	DISTRICT NO. 3.	
Richmond	456,444	Annapolis	808,064
Victoria	130,455	Digby	1,341,884
DISTRICT NO. 2.		Kings	29,231
Antigonish........	74,648	Lunenburg	1,563,071
Colchester	44,135	Queens	208,105
Cumberland	128,799	Shelburne	804,689
Guysboro	711,117	Yarmouth	470,802
Halifax	1,028,423		

Total $7,809,152

FROM THE BANKS.

The following lines from the gifted pen of Moses H. Nickerson could be written only by one who has hauled a line, and knows at first hand the ways of fisher folk:

It haunts them yet—that autumn day
   Of moaning seas and leaden skies;—
That schooner beating up the bay
   And watched by scores of eager eyes.
The last arrival from the Banks
   For which she sailed three months before:
An absence filled with fears,—but thanks
   To pitying Heaven, she comes once more!

With thoughts that common toils inspire,
   Troops down the mingled village train;
The glow of many a cottage fire
   Lights up the cold and cruel main.
As fast as flies the snowy gull,
   Still onward stands the gallant craft,
With all her towering spread of full
   And flowing canvas sheeted aft.

The curving waves are sharply cleft
   And stream astern in swirling foam;
She rode them lighter when she left
   The port than in returning home.
She brings a fare, but does she bring
   Her hardy crew in safety back?
'Twas answered when they saw her swing
   Quick-rounding on the starboard tack.

What evil news did ever lag?
   It wanted none to give it tongue—
It trembled in the drooping flag
   That half-way down the topmast clung.
The burly north wind, keen and strong,
   That with the angry surges shid
Had kept the dreaded signal long
   Behind the white gaff-topsail hid.

Each anxious moment seemed an hour,
   But when the vessel reached the pier
The pallid captain had no power,
   Or need to say, "He is not here."
And she who stood among the rest,
   With tearless eye and bloodless cheek,
And lips in agony compressed—
   What voice could like that silence speak?

CHAPTER XX.

Shelburne County is bounded by Queens, Yarmouth and the Atlantic Ocean. It has an area of 948 square miles, and a population of 14,000. This county has two points of especial historic interest, viz., Port Latour and Shelburne Town. The first locality is connected with stirring events of French occupancy; the latter has a unique and tragical record of English settlement. Among the very early French adventurers who came to this Province and settled at Port Royal, or Annapolis, were Claude Turgis De St. Etinne Sieur de la Tour, and his son Charles, a boy of fourteen years. They were here in 1606, and seven years later Annapolis was destroyed by Captain Argall of Jamestown. The young man took refuge with the Indians in company with several of his countrymen, among them young Biencourt, son of Jean de Biencourt, Baron de Poutrincourt, who held a grant of Annapolis. This young man died in 1624 and bequeathed all his rights inherited from his late father to Charles. At this date we find young La Tour at Cape Sable, or Port La Tour, as we call it, and his father Claude with him. The French interests in Acadia were seriously imperiled not long after, in 1627, and Charles wrote to Louis XIII. and requested to be appointed commandant in all the coasts of Acadia. His father undertook to deliver this letter, but before he reached France, Kirk had taken Port Royal and threatened Quebec, and returning to England, by chance fell in with the vessel on which the elder La Tour had taken passage for the return trip to Acadia. Everything was fish that got into Sir David Kirk's nets. La Tour was made a prisoner and carried to England. He was a Protestant and a nobleman, and soon met influential friends of his own religious faith, who presented him at court. He married one of the maids of honor, and both he and his son were made baronets of Nova Scotia. He renounced all allegiance to the French King, and for substantial considerations received from Sir William Alexander he agreed to serve the English interests and win over his son to the new arrangement. He was provided with two warships and, taking his wife, sailed for Cape Sable. He was doomed to bitter disappointment by the unexpected manliness of his son, who refused all his fine offers, and declared he would stand for his country and King to the last breath.

This was an awkward dilemma for the father. He dared not return to England, and he could not remain there without his son's permission unless he could drive him out of the fort. Thus he was reduced to the necessity of making war on him or accept his terms of remaining near him, but outside of the fort. He chose the attitude of war, and the ships opened fire and were met with such resistance that several men were killed on the part of the English, and they withdrew from the encounter. The elder La Tour was glad to accept an offer to remain, and his wife most dutifully shared his lot in adversity. Charles La Tour had married before going to Cape Sable. He had chosen Frances Marie Jacquelins, who twenty years later defended her husband's fort on the St. Johns River during his absence with such valor as to win a place for her among the heroines of history.

A few French settlers were located at, or near, the present town of Barrington, but in the general expulsion of the Acadians in 1755 the whole region was left to the Indians and quite a number of young Acadians who had escaped the general "round-up" cast in their lot with the red men. Not without cause they became a desperate element over all the Province.

The French had early made a settlement near the entrance of Shelburne harbor, but between the pirates and hostile New Englanders life became too wretched for endurance, and all was deserted. Years afterward, in 1765, Col. Alexander McNutt, who was a very active agent in procuring settlers, secured a grant of a large tract of land at Port Raizor, as Shelburne harbor was then called. He named the place New Jerusalem and induced some Scotch-Irish families to come there and make it a place worthy so fine a name.

Haliburton says that McNutt having wholly failed to comply with the conditions of his grant, it was escheated to the Crown. Doctor Smith, in his account of the Loyalists at Shelburne, says the grant was escheated "just before the arrival of the Loyalists." Murdoch, in his history, says this New Jerusalem was "the site of Shelburne." The impression conveyed by all other writers is to the effect that the locality was deserted when the Loyalists came to Shelburne. There is apparently some new light thrown on this point by the publication last year of the "Annals of Yarmouth and Barrington, by Edmund Duval Poole." The book is made up of papers copied from the Massachusetts Archives. Among them is the following document:

"State of Massachusetts Bay, In The House of Representatives June 22 1780 On the memorial of Alexander Mc Nutt Praying Leave to carry Certain Articles to Port Roseway in Nova Scotia.

"Resolved that Alexander McNutt be & he is hereby permitted to export from the State to Port Roseway in Nova Scotia for the benefit of fourteen families residing there, Sixty Bushels of Grain, One hogshead of Molasses, 1 barrel of Rum one loaf of Sugar and several small articles of crockery ware such as Milk pans Porringers and Butter pots for said families.

Sent up for Concurrence.

John Hancock Spkr.

In Council June 22 1780

READ and Concurred John Avery D, Secty."

It is reasonable to suppose that there were at least one hundred people in these fifteen families. It is not probable that they all disappeared in less than three years, and if they had not, then the Loyalists had something of this New Jerusalem to begin with, and all was not a howling wilderness.

In 1783, at the close of the long struggle for independence by the American colonists, there were a great many people who had favored the English in the desperate encounter, and when all was over they were considered very undersirable persons to have in the new nation that had "come forth out of great tribulation" and "escaped by the skin of the teeth." New York City had during these years of war been in the possession of the British, and thousands of their sympathizers had flocked there for protection till the end would come. On the surrender of Cornwallis their hopes were crushed. After two years of distressing delay, caused by the slow movement of those who were negotiating treaties, it became evident that their old homes would shelter them no longer. They had become exceedingly obnoxious to the new nation that was preparing to treat them with needless harshness, as we see matters now.

At this crisis was born the movement that ended in the building of the town of Shelburne. One hundred heads of families in New York bound themselves by an agreement to settle in Nova Scotia. This was in the autumn of 1782. Joseph Pynchon and James Dole were selected to act as agents for this association, and they were sent to Halifax to confer with Governor Parr and secure the best terms possible. They were instructed to secure lands at

or near Port Roseway. The agents were met more than half way
by the Governor, who promised substantial assistance on a generous
scale. They returned home with visions of a city that would soon,
as they believed, become the capital of the Province. At this time
the leaders in this movement had been directed and advised to
settle on the shores of the Bay of Fundy. They distrusted the
motives of their true friends and went forward with their rosy
project that in the nature of things must end in disaster. When
spring opened in 1783 no less than 470 heads of families in New
York were included in the association and preparing for a movement. There was a general break-up and separation among the
Loyalists there, who numbered about thirty thousand. They were
scattering in all directions over the British colonies. No less than
eighteen brigs and many schooners were loaded with those destined
for Port Roseway. They entered the harbor on the 4th of May,
five thousand in all. They were soon actively at work on the townsite, under the directions of professional engineers. The location
was of the finest, the harbor was unsurpassed on the Atlantic coast
of America. There were salmon, and trout, and alewives, in the
river, and cod, herring, mackerel, lobsters and other good things to
eat in the sea. The flag of England was over them, the ground
was theirs by royal grant, and altogether this seemed more like the
founding of a New Jerusalem than the dream of McNutt. On the
sightly town lots handsome residences were built by men of means.
Marble mantels and fine furniture adorned them.

These people were all respectable, and some of superior social
rank. No family had been admitted unless some member could
vouch for its good reputation. After four months this satisfactory
state of affairs was rudely disturbed by the unexpected arrival of
five thousand Loyalists from New York, who had tarried there till
the eve of embarkment of the British troops, when they made haste
to get away lest a worse thing befall them from the hands of their
angry countrymen. Among these were not a few undesirable
characters—mere- camp-followers in search of free rations. However, with Government aid, much exertion and hardships, the people got through the fall and winter, but not without an ominous
graveyard. Rations were issued during this time to about nine
thousand people by the British Government. Great dissensions
arose over the allotment of lands; the imposition of heavy duties

VIEW OF SHELBURNE, LOOKING WEST.

SHELBURNE, MAIN STREET.

SHELBURNE, FROM THE HARBOR.

OLD FIRE ENGINE, SHELBURNE.

by the Provincial Government was another sharp grievance. Open riot was the result.

Within a brief period three newspapers were successively printed in the town, and the last issue of the last of the lot was in 1787. Some of the numbers are yet in existence. The names were as follows: "The Royal American Gazette," published by James Robertson. The second was the "Port Roseway Gazeteer and Shelburne Advertiser," published by J. Robertson, Jr., and T. & J. Swords. The third was the "Nova Scotia Packet and General Advertiser," published by James Humphrys.

Shelburne was built on a boom and it soon gave way. Natural laws in the business world are as unavoidable as they are in all other directions. It is one thing to build a town by means of capital derived from outside sources, but it is quite another matter to obtain a livelihood after the houses are built, unless there are opportunities for remunerative labor. Shelburne was wrecked by natural laws. Here I cannot follow her rapid decline, but it corresponded with her artificial rise. There were good houses for sale within two years after the beginning, and after four years Government rations ceased, and then there was a stampede of people who could not live without them. After seven years nearly all the families of means had deserted their fine houses. Sell them they could not at any price. After thirteen years there were on the rate rolls but 125 names out of 710 that were there ten years before. In a quarter of a century, that is in 1808, it was a town of deserted, dilapidated houses, and ten years later there were living there but 300 people. This was about the lowest tide. A few of the oldest families remained, notably that of Mr. Gideon White of the Mayflower Pilgrim stock, whose sons, Thomas and Cornelius, were long its respected representatives. Haliburton, writing in 1828, says: "Shelburne is at present in a most dilapidated state. It is said within these few years past it seems to be emerging from the obscurity into which it had fallen." The emergence was very slow, but in thirty years after that paragraph was written the place was quite a prosperous shipbuilding center. Old buildings had largely disappeared and there was an air of prosperity in the locality. In 1864 a commodious academy was erected and the writer of these lines may be pardoned if he here recalls the incident that he was the first teacher to open the school in this new building with the encouraging presence of Rev. Dr. White, Rev. G. M. Clarke, Rev.

T. Watson Smith, who has since published an admirable account of the founding of Shelburne, to which I am indebted, and all of them have gone to the "land of no return." To this very moment the town bears the marks of deliberate construction. There are none of the ordinary irregularities indicating that streets were evolved from cow-paths and from short-cuts across lots to neighbor's houses and stores. That imaginary old lady Mrs. Partington, who had a genius for saying the wrong thing on purpose, remarked that she "had often been impressed by the goodness of Providence arranging that large rivers should run through great cities." There must be natural advantages if there is to be a great city properly founded. There are dead cities built by ancient kings who had enriched their treasuries with the plunder of nations. But the great capitals like Rome, Alexandria, London, Paris, New York, will last while the world endures.

At present Shelburne has about one thousand inhabitants. Shipbuilding, fishing and trade with the outlying country are the principal industries. A railroad is expected soon, and if that expectation is realized there will be a large increase of business. The safe and beautiful harbor, the fine location of the town, and opportunities for fishing trips, pleasant drives, and many other diversions combine to make the locality an ideal resting-place for people who wish to escape from heat and city turmoil.

Of the Township of Barrington, Haliburton has this to say in his History, written in 1828: "Barrington lies between the Township of Shelburne and Argyle and includes Cape Sable Island. It was granted in 1767 to one hundred and two persons and contains fifty two thousand acres, one-third part of which is covered with barrens and bog. The remaining portion is clothed with spruce and fir, intermingled with maple and birch and occasionally with red and grey oak. Barrington, like Yarmouth, was originally inhabited by French, although there were but few families in this township. In the year 1761, 2 and 3, it was settled by about eighty families from Nantucket and Cape Cod, Massachusetts. The former were induced to settle to carry on the whale fishery, but being disappointed in their object, some returned at the commencement of the Revolution, and others removed into the District of Maine; so that in a short time Barrington was abandoned by nearly one-half of its inhabitants. The latter were attracted by the cod fishery, and finding it equal to their expectations, continued to remain there.

The population of the township now amounts to 2,186 souls. Formerly almost every male was employed in the fishery, and the catch for many years amounted to over twenty-two thousand quintals, but latterly many of them have quitted this branch of business and engaged in other pursuits. There are now owned in Barrington sixty-nine vessels, whose united tonnage amounts to 2,780, exclusive of four square-rigged vessels on the stocks. Two brigs and four schooners are employed in the West India trade, fifteen as coasters, eight in the Labrador, and forty-one in the shore fishery. The latter business employs besides these vessels sixty-two boats. The village of Barrington consists of an inconsiderable cluster of houses, the inhabitants of the township being dispersed throughout the whole coast for the convenience of carrying on the fishery. Barrington River, which falls into the harbor, takes its rise in a lake about nine miles distant, called Sabim."

Since the above was written Barrington has become a thriving place of about one thousand inhabitants, very neat and pretty of aspect, where the people are engaged principally in fishing and the coasting trade. The recent arrival there of the locomotive from Yarmouth will doubtless do much to increase the population and prosperity of the locality. It is a very desirable place for a vacation among excellent people and picturesque surroundings of land, and sea, and river, and lakes.

In the old burying ground rests in an unmarked grave the remains of Mrs. Israel Doane, who was the maternal grandmother of John Howard Payne, the author of "Home, Sweet Home," and she, too, was the great-great-grandmother of our own poet and scholar, Moses H. Nickerson. This woman was a daughter of the Rev. Dr. Samuel Osborne, of Glasgow, a Congregationalist minister.

Burchtown is a settlement of colored people between Shelburne and Barrington. These people for the most part originated from the slaves who escaped into the English lines in New York during the war of the American Revolution. At its close they were sent to this unpromising spot, where it must often have been difficult to keep soul and body together. Many of the first arrivals were sent by the British Government to Sierra Leone in Africa, where they very largely went to the bad. With the Loyalists of Shelburne came several hundred black servants, who were in reality slaves. Some of them and their descendants have lived in and about the town even since. By hook and by crook they managed to get along

when white people, with pride and dignity to maintain, were obliged
to go away to either hide their poverty or mend it as best they
could. There is, as we may see, some advantage·of being at the
lower end of the scale, where, as Burns says, "we can no further
fa." Many of these negroes have been honest and useful persons.

Haliburton says: "Port La Tour is separated from Cape Negro
by a peninsula and is only capable of sheltering small craft. The
tide leaves a great part of the head of it dry. The lands in the
neighborhood are barren, but a small portion of the marsh enables
the settlers to keep a few head of cattle. The remains of the fort
erected at this place previous to the Treaty of St. Germain in 1632
are still visible.'

The locality since that was written has not changed in natural
features, but there is a thriving village, a good school, and churches
and other evidences of prosperity. It will always be a spot of historic
interest, and if it were not somewhat outside of the beaten
track of travel there would be more visitors to view the scenes so
intimately connected with stirring and romantic incidents of our
early history.

Port Clyde, between Barrington and Burchtown, is a small settlement
of thrifty families in the midst of interesting and pleasing
surroundings. It is at the mouth of a beautiful river that extends
about forty miles into the interior, and connects with many lakes.
On it there are settlers with good homes, and the region is famed
for its excellent fishing and hunting opportunities.

In front of the township, and southwest of Barrington harbor,
is Cape Sable Island. It is seven miles long, and from two to three
miles wide, and separated from the mainland by less than a mile.
About 1786 a few settlers from Barrington made a beginning in
the wilderness of stunted firs. The French had been there long
before, but beyond one or two cleared spots they had left no trace
of their occupancy. Shortly after the Barrington pioneers had
gotten a precarious footing they were joined by a few straggling
Loyalists, probably from Shelburne, but they did not remain long,
and went in search of a more pleasing and promising locality. No
wonder they were discouraged at the prospect where the savage
sea alone promised an existence to those who would dare its dangerous
moods. The original settlers who remained were made of
sturdy stuff, and fought the battle of life at a great disadvantage.
They were not only obliged to contend with natural obstacles, but

were unjustly dealt with by human regulations that originated in
the old Court of Sessions. During almost a century there was but
a slow progress. A new dispensation of prosperity began about
twenty years ago and dates from the beginning of the lobster industry, and has kept pace with the development of that business, which
by putting in circulation a large amount of money has brought about
many salutary changes both in the way of trade and in the manner
of living. The nearness to the United States' market and the fine
transportation facilities for the catch are great advantages. As a
rule the fishermen transport live lobsters on their own account, get
prompt returns, and have nothing to do with the middle men.

Cape Island has now a population of 2,570, of which 1,534 are
in the Clarke's Harbor District. The island is divided into six
school sections. The school of Clarke's Harbor has four departments, and is overcrowded at that; of the others one is a graded
school, with two departments. There are nine regular postoffices.
Clarke's Harbor is a common landing port, and the bulk of the
business is transacted there by about ten general stores. There are
excellent hotel accommodations, 'coasting steamers call several
times a week, and a steam ferry is is operation between the island
and the mainland. The locality is noted for its extensive and beautiful beaches, affording the finest of wheeling for teams and cycles
almost within touch of the sounding sea. In the proper seasons
sportsmen find the best of shooting among the shore birds.

Eastward from the Town of Shelburne, about twenty-five miles
by wagon, is Ragged Island Harbor, at the head of which is a village of about four hundred inhabitants, engaged in fishing and
farming. On the west side of the harbor is Lockport, a place of
considerable activity in the fishing business. In recent years there
has been a decline from the hustling days when the little town was
distinguished for its energy and prosperity. It is still the residence
of about eight hundred people, who do a considerable business on
the old lines, exporting about seventy thousand quintals of fish a
year, and carry on a general trade with the outlying villages. I
have no exact dates for the first settlement of this locality, but it
was about 1763. At any rate there were some permanent residents there in 1779 during the war of the Revolution, and they
were in sympathy with the uprising, although they were supposed
to be patriotic subjects of the King. They felt the more aggrieved
therefore when a crew of American privateers from their native

20

land came ashore and looted their premises in spite of all protestations of sympathy for their cause, and declarations of actual services to escaping prisoners of war. Thinking that there must be some remedy for such an outrage, they laid their case before Col. Alexander McNutt, who was then in Boston, and he brought the matter to the notice of the Honorable Council of the State of Massachusetts Bay. Here is their letter, lately copied from the Massachusetts archives:

Raged Islands Sept W 25 1779.
These lines comes with my respect to you & to acquaint you of the Robery done to this Harbour, there was a guard of men placed upon every house and the houses stript, very surprising to us, they came here early in the Morning on the 20th day of August last and said they were from Penobscot and were tories bound for halifax, they come to my house first and wanted some refreshments accordingly we let them have what they wanted; and they then went away and stayed on an island till the tide run so that they could Come at my Boat, then they come and took by Boat and put a guard upon my house and went a Robing they took about 19 quintals of Codfish and Four Barrels of Salt, three Salmon Netts 60 lbs of Butter, one Green Hyde, five dressed Skins and some Cheese and a Great many other Things. The Boat Cost me fifty pounds Halifax Currency. then they went to Mr Matthews and there Robed him, then went to Mr Haydens, and Robed him, then went Mr Locks and Robed him. these things are very surprising that we in this Harbour that have done so much for America, that have helped three or four hundred prisoners up along to America and Given part of our living to them, and have Concealed Privateers & prizes too from the British Cruisers in this Harbour. All this done for America and if this be the way we are to be paid I desire to see no more of you without you Come in Another Manner, but I hope the America gentlemen that Grants out Commissions or are Bondsmen would take these Notorious Rascalls in hand for this Robery. Sir be so kind as to Inform some of the Council of the affair, that we might have some restrictions, otherwise we shall not be able to help the American prisoners any more Sir, if you find out who these be, and whether we are like to have anything, be pleased to write.

Signed

William Porterfield
John Matthews
Thomas Hayden
Jonathan Lock

Colonel McNutt ascertained the names of these "Robers" who came in three whale boats from Coakset River, near New Bedford. It is very doubtful if they were punished for making this raid in the enemy's country, but it is quite probable that the victims received some substantial redress for their grievance as that had been done in other instances since the war began. McNutt resided near them on an island at the entrance of the harbor that still bears his name, and as he had been "held up" the year previous he knew how it was himself. These American privateers whom he called "armed ruffians" had robbed him of "superfine Scarlet, and Blew cloth, books, Silver Spoons, Silver Buckles, Gold Lace, Diamond Rings, and other articles of much value," as he stated. This he had suffered in spite of the fact that he had been an active friend of the rebellious Yankees, that is, as active as he dared be, considering that he had been the recipient of several royal grants of land of no mean value and on very favorable terms. He had caused the authorities in Halifax to distrust his loyalty, and in Massachusetts had been arrested as a possible spy. Defending himself in a memorial to the Council of Massachusetts Bay, he says: "How I can be Justly Considered in a Double Capacity and treated as both Whig and tory seems a Paradox to me. I have always spoken my sentiments Clearly, and would have readily added Actions to words had I had a call in providence so to do, being well convinced that the cause of God will admit of no neutrality, and I Challenge even enmity itself to produce one single Instance in which I have deviated from the Resolves of Congress Since 1774."

All of which goes to show that the Colonel was having an eye to the main chance of advancing his own interests and keeping his skin whole.

Another brief word about Lockport: The town is built on an island and connected with the mainland on the east by a fine crescent-shaped beach about three-fourths of a mile long, and at the nearest point by an iron bridge. The main beach, which lies just below the town, is admirably adapted for bathing purposes. In the immediate vicinity there are a number of pretty country places where many visitors would find delightful retreats for summer rest. These are Brighton, Osborne, Allendale, and Bay Head, all within five miles of Lockport. A little to the eastward of Ragged Island Harbor is Jordan Bay, where there is a scattered settlement of farmer-fishermen living in reasonable comfort as a result of industry and sobriety. The Jordan River enters the head of this bay and up the stream a few miles is the village of Jordan Falls, where for many years there has been conducted a flourishing lumber business and considerable shipbuilding. ' Extensive forests on this river and its tributaries will long continue to supply a great amount of material for manufacturing purposes. The mills are operated by means of a fine water-power that has been largely the making of the village. To the eastward of Jordan Bay is Sable River, where there is a settlement of farmers, fishers, shipbuilders, and lumbermen, the same men often doing good service in all these industries. The post road from Liverpool and all points eastward runs through the head of this settlement, as it also does that of Jordan Falls.

About one-quarter of the area of this county is granite. It includes the upper portion of Shelburne Harbor around to Churchover and across to Burchtown, and up the river about ten miles in a narrow strip. It occurs in Barrington, following the shore and reaching up in a wedge shape on the county line half way to its junction with other lines. An area of some seventy square miles is found at the extreme inland point of the county. Between Jordan Falls and Sable River is a small outcrop of granite, and another between Sable and Port Herbert. All the other rock may be considered as more or less altered portions of the Cambrian slates and quartzites of the Atlantic coast, and water shed. The quartzites greatly predominate. Profound metamorphosis or alterations have taken place with these ancient sediments that were deposited in the ocean many million years ago. At Jordan Falls the rock abounds with staurotide crystals that are an assemblage of silica, aluminum, iron and magnesium. Gneisses, that are stratified granite, occur at various localities, as Green Harbor and lower Jordan Bay. No gold mines have been discovered in Shelburne County, and very likely for the reason that there are none.

LIVERPOOL.

LIVERPOOL.

CHAPTER XXI.

Queens County has an area of 1,065 square miles and a population of about 11,000. It is reckoned among the western counties of the Province. It is bounded by Shelburne, Annapolis, and Lunenburg, and the ocean. The coast is very rugged and rocky. There are three harbors, viz., Liverpool, Port Medway, and Port Mouton. Into each a considerable river is discharged. These streams take their rise in the unsettled back country, where lakes are very numerous, the largest in the Province, Rossignol, being among them. From the coast to the northern boundary the distance in a straight line is about thirty miles, and a gradual elevation reaches at that point some 500 feet. The southern portion of the county, embracing about one-half its area, is rather flat, and where fires have not run is covered with "softwoods," or cone-bearing trees. The extreme northern part of the county is diversified with "hardwood" hills, meadows, bogs, barrens, brooks, and lakes. How long the red men had made their homes in these solitudes before they were disturbed by the coming of Europeans, we shall never know, but it was long enough to give names to lakes and streams and harbors. In 1604, Rossignol, a Frenchman, had his vessel in Liverpool harbor, and conducted a trade with the natives for their furs. His name is borne by the large lake on the Liverpool River. Thirty years later there was a fishery established on Liverpool harbor by a French concern. No settlement was made of any importance by Frenchmen, although for a long time they were acquainted with the locality. The history of the county, so far as its occupation by white men is concerned, begins in 1759, when Liverpool was founded by New England pioneers of the Pilgrim stock. They came principally from Plymouth, Kingston, Eastham, and Chatham, and adjacent townships. They were a rugged people, who had been accustomed to contend with a stingy soil and a tempestuous sea for the means of a livelihood. There was no better material in the world to undertake such an enterprise as they entered upon at Liverpool.

At that date Nova Scotia was a particularly lonesome place; five years before the Acadian French had been expelled, and the ruins of their homes formed a line of desolation from end to end of the Annapolis Valley, and extended far eastward and westward. Halifax had been founded ten years. Annapolis was a small military post, and Windsor another. At Lunenburg the wretched Germans had been a half dozen years contending with great difficulties; and more than these, there were hostile Indians, and refugee Acadians who lived with the savages, and all eager to pay off the old score of revenge.

Work must have gone forward rapidly, for in August of 1760, only one year, Governor Belcher visited Liverpool, and reported of that place: "They are now employed in building three vessels for the fishery, and have laid in hay for the winter fodder of their cattle, and have raised a considerable quantity of roots, and erected a grist and saw mill. They have sixteen sail of fishing schooners, and although several of them came late in the season, they have caught near 400 quintals of fish, the principal owners of which have gone back to the Continent to dispose of it, and will return in the spring for a further supply of stock for their lands. From these circumstances I flatter myself your Lordships will entertain a favorable opinion of this settlement." The population is not given, but in the township grant that was issued four years later, there appear the names of 142 proprietors, and the number of inhabitants was 500. In 1762 the book of records was begun in these words: "Liverpool, February 20th, 1762. These births, deaths, marriages, to be mentioned or to be registered by me, Elisha Freeman, Proprietors' Clerk."

It is a matter of deep regret that this book was not kept in a more orderly manner, as to dates. People dropped in and told of their marriage, or of a birth in their family, or a death, and the item was recorded when convenient. However, that was better than no record at all. In the course of five months from the beginning, Mr. Freeman, the clerk, registered his own marriage to Mary Waterman, widow of Elkanah Waterman, and daughter of Silas West. The men who settled in Liverpool could have had for the asking rich, cultivated lands of Grand Pre and Annapolis. One of their leaders, Capt. Sylvanus Cobb, knew that country well. He had been master and owner of a vessel that had assisted in deporting the original proprietors. At any rate their choice of a new locality indicated that they were men of courage and natural resources. Some of them had visited this region on their fishing trips and their voyages to Lunenburg. Even the aspect of Nature was stern and forbidding, with rock-bound coast, boulder-strewn shores, overhung with somber forests of spruce and fir.

LIVERPOOL.

LIVERPOOL (WINTER SCENE).

LIVERPOOL (WINTER SCENE)

• Still there were fishes in the sea and river, game in the woods, and chances of one kind and another to wrest a livelihood from the locality. To men less sturdy and less inured to hardships, there would have been no visions of prosperity in these uninviting features before them. Not without many hardships and fatalities was a footing gained. They could not live on fish. The land was covered with woods, that must be chopped, and burnt, and cleared before hay and grain could be raised. The soil was very poor and filled with stones. Flour was so dear that it was almost prohibited by the price.

Haliburton is authority for the statement that one winter "they were compelled to subsist wholly upon wild rabbits." I fancy the menu was varied with fish, and dried blueberries, and portions of moosemeat, and a little bread for the weaker members of the community. For the most part they built comfortable houses, and evidently had come to stay as long as the "wild rabbits" held out. Quite a number of the faint-hearted returned when called upon to face the discomforts of the situation, but the great majority held their ground and mastered the obstacles. Twenty-seven years after the arrival of the pioneers, on May 7, 1787, Col. Simeon Perkins wrote in his journal: "I finish my return of the inhabitants and militia. There are 283 men, 234 women, and 449 children in Liverpool, making a total of 966 white inhabitants; and 19 men, 10 women, and 19 children, making a total of 48 black inhabitants. In the county there are 449 white men, 320 women, and 615 children, making a total of 1,384. There are 20 black men, 11 women, and 19 children, making a total of 50 in the county. The militia of Liverpool, officers included, 249; militia in the county, officers included, 414." These "black people" were not slaves, although they might have been, so far as the law of the land was concerned, and several of their race were in actual bondage at this date in Nova Scotia. There is preserved a lot of names of the proprietors of the Township of Liverpool, but all of them did not cast in their lot with the community. Here follows the list, and it is interesting to note how the English element overruns all the rest. There is a portion of the best of New England yeomanry, one hundred and fifty years after the landing of the "Mayflower," and many of them were lineal descendants of that illustrious band of Pilgrims who landed on Plymouth Rock, and defied the stern obstacles, and cruel elements that laid half their numbers in their graves in that first winter, while the courageous survivors proceeded to lay the foundation of a great commonwealth:

Elisha Freeman, John Dagget, Nathan Tupper, Samuel Dogget, the heirs of Jas. Godfrey, the heirs of Jno. Young, the heirs of Joshua Harding, the heirs of Elkanah Waterman, Ebenezer Nickerson, Joseph Headley, Cornelius Knowles, Ebenezer Dogget, Benjamin Cole, Samuel Dolliver, Samuel Freeman, John Hopkins, Joseph Collins, Jabez Gorham, John Mathews, George Fancy, `Peleg Dexter, Prince Snow, —— Nickerson, Thomas Brown, John Peach, Barbara Cuffy, Theodosius Ford, Benjamin Parker, Thomas West, Robert Slocomb, Henry Young, Nathaniel Godfrey, William Murray, Jonathan Crowell, Wm. K. Cahoon, Stephen Smith, Jacob Cobb, Peter Coffin, Samuel Hunt, Thomas Padderson, Elisha Nickerson, Elisha Kenney, Jeremiah Nickerson, the heirs of Samuel Cobb, the heirs of Elkanah Nickerson, Joseph Feebk, Edward Doten, Joseph Dryeter, Zephaniah Eldridge, Benjamin Holmes, John West, Paul Doten, John Wall, Acus Tripp, Howes Stewart, Jonathan Brerer, Elisha Freeman, Prince Knowles, Simeon Freeman, Barnabas Freeman, Robert Placeway, Luther Arnold, Joseph Bartlett, Edward Foster, Jonathan Locke, John Giffin, Robert Hebest, Isaac Tinkham, Samuel Battle, John Ryder, Israel Tupper, —— Gorham, Stephen Paine, Stephen Gullison, Richard Kempton, Samuel Hunt, Timothy Burbank, William Mitchell, Thomas Foster, Joseph Whitford, Abraham Copeland, Thomas Gardiner, Enoch Aleyter, Samuel Eldridge, George Briggs, Thomas Gordon, Ebenezer Thomas, Jeremiah Nickerson, Thomas Brehant, Thomas Burnaby, Seth Drew, Hezekiah Freeman, Smith Freeman, John Foster, Jonathan Godfrey, Daniel Torry, Ebenezer Dexter, Obadiah Albree, Robert Harlow, John Lewin, Jonathan Darling, Nathaniel Toby, Cyrenius Collins, George Winslow, William Gammon, John Waterman, Jesse Warner, Lemuel Drew, Joseph Burnaby, John Dolliver, Joseph Woods, Abner Eldridge, Simeon Perkins, William Foster, Alden Sears, Benjamin Godfrey, Thomas Osgood, Thomas Bee, Osgood Hilton, Samuel Crowell, Thomas Hayden, Nathan Hetly, Abner Doaty, Nathaniel Freeman, Nathan Tupper, Jr., Robert Millard, James Nickerson, Elisha Nickerson, Jr., William West, Wire Morton, John Peach, Nathaniel Knowles, Joseph Collins, Jr., Enoch Randall, Nathan Sears, Ebenezer Simmons, William Tripp.

Many of these names do not appear in the county records. Quite a number of those who came went away from the dreary outlook. By a kind of natural selection the fittest remained, and fought it out with hard conditions and secured some of the humble comforts of life

SOUTH BROOKFIELD, QUEENS COUNTY.
(SITE OF FIRST HOUSE IN NORTH DISTRICT.)

LOCKEPORT BREAKWATER. SHELBURNE COUNTY.

LOCKEPORT BEACH

out of the struggle. Thus matters went on with them till the War of the American Revolution broke out, after they had been a quarter of a century settled in their new homes.

All of them had near relatives and friends in New England, and even there the people were by no means of one opinion and Loyalists were everywhere. "It's an ill wind that blows no one any good," and the thrifty Yankee of Liverpool concluded to make hay while the sun shines. So in due time they had a fine fleet of privateers harrying the New England waters for the spoils of war, and the practice was returned, but these Nova Scotians got the better of the game, and several families, who were very plain people before, became persons of consequence on this money that had been taken from their own flesh and blood. "All was fair in love and war," was a maxim that quieted tender consciences, if there were any. The town shared in the prosperity in some measure, and the War of 1812 proved another blessing, for privateering was the order of the day. Since those times they have had their ups and downs, but the mark of a superior lot of men and women for pioneer work was impressed on the town early in the last century. Haliburton, writing in 1829, says: "Liverpool is the best-built town in Nova Scotia. The houses are substantially good and well painted, and there is an air of regularity and neatness in the place which distinguishes it from every other town in this Province." The locality is well chosen at the mouth of a goodly river, where Nature offered a townsite not readily excelled for business accommodations, home conveniences, and picturesque surroundings. Very early after their arrival these pioneers explored the adjacent country and began other settlements at Brooklyn, on the eastern side of the harbor; at Milton, two miles above Liverpool, on the river; at Port Mouton, ten miles to the westward; at Port Medway, eight or nine miles to the eastward; at Mills Village, on the river that enters the Medway harbor. All of these are now thriving communities. Milton was for a long time noted for the manufacture of lumber. Of late years the supply of timber has been limited, but two pulp mills are constantly in operation, giving employment to many people and making a demand for a class of wood not hitherto utilized. This village is pleasantly located on the head of tidewater, and the inhabitants are prosperous. Mills Village is a pretty little town built up around saw mills, and has an air of thrift in its make-up that commends it to the eye of a stranger. It is noted for salmon fishing, and the river for a dozen

miles attracts the lover of the rod and fly,˙ for trout and salmon.
Port Medway has the best harbor in the county. With the decline
of lumber manufacture on the river, business has somewhat fallen
off. Within sixteen miles there are 1,400 horse power running to
waste in the falls. Chances are that enterprising capital will transmit that energy electrically to some point near Port Medway where
it can be used in the manufacture of pulp. A nice, quiet, pretty
place is the "Port," where one can find rest and pleasant walks,
drives, and sails, and sniff the caller air, and listen to the surf in
the offing.

Port Mouton has a history in the old French occupation, and
later, in 1784, when an attempt was made to settle a lot of disbanded
soldiers at that point. A fire devoured the beginning of a town; the
inhabitants were scattered, many of them going eastward near Caso
to Guysborough,˙ a name they had bestowed upon their Queens
County township in honor of Sir Guy Carleton. Port Mouton is
now a fishing and farming village, a picturesque locality. Brooklyn
is older than Liverpool, if one reckons from French occupancy. It
is a thriving and attractive locality, where the inhabitants are engaged in various pursuits. Some are captains, some are ship-builders,
others are occupied in lumber and mercantile enterprises.

Forty years after the founding of Liverpool a move was made to
occupy the northern end of the county, distant from twenty to thirty
miles through the forest. The pioneers of this movement were well-
seasoned men, the pick of the southern district in pluck and energy.
William Burke was the first settler. A succession of pretty villages
extend over this region, that is known as the "Northern District."

The Medway River and many beautiful lakes contribute very
much to the interest and attractiveness of that locality. Fine farms,
orchards, and mills, and good houses are everywhere in evidence of
the fair prosperity of the inhabitants. The whole region is convenient to excellent hunting grounds of moose and small game, and
streams for trout fishing. Caledonia, South Brookfield, North
Brookfield, Westfield, Pleasant River, Molega, Harmony, and Kempt
are the names of the villages. To these must be added Greenfield,
at the foot of Ponhook Lake, distant from Mills Village about twelve
miles. This is a delightful locality, and famous for its salmon fishing.

There are several gold mines in the Northern District. Some of
them have been in successful operation on a large scale for seven

MILTON.

PULP MILL DAM, MILTON

or eight years, and it is safe to say that this industry is but in its infancy.

From a letter contributed to the Halifax Herald by C. U. McLeod, November, 1901, this extract is clipped:

"This is essentially a farming, lumbering, and gold mining district. The majority of the inhabitants are farmers, possessed of good lands and capable of working them in an intelligent manner. The 'upland' soil is well suited to raising hay, grains, root-crops, apples, grapes, plums, and quinces. Currants, gooseberries, strawberries, blueberries, raspberries, and cranberries thrive with little attention.

"Of late years attention has been turned to apple culture with gratifying success. This fall three thousand barrels of marketable fruit has been gathered, experts pronouncing them as second to none produced in the Province. Much of our lowland is available for cranberry raising, and doubtless this will some day become a profitable industry. In the manufacture and export of lumber lies a goodly share of our future prosperity. To give exact figures is next to impossible, but an approximate estimate is conservative at four hundred thousand acres of green woods north of the 'Hervey line,' to this one can well add one hundred thousand acres of growing timber on the farming lands. Hemlock, spruce, and pine predominate, much of it first class pulp wood.

"Oak, beech and birch grow in abundance. This is the best material for shipbuilding, stave making, and the numerous articles manufactured from these hard woods. The northern district alone has an area of one hundred and twenty-five square miles of fresh water, vastly more than any other portion of the Province. It is a network of lakes, rivers and streams. Here are innumerable facilities for driving timber, and the requisite water powers for converting it into finished product ready for the market."

Along the shores are settlements of farming fishermen, where the tourist will find pleasure in the people and their surroundings. Such are Black Point, White Point, Hunt's Point, Summerville—all westward of Liverpool—while to the eastward are Beach Meadows, Eagle Head, West Berlin and Ragged Harbor.

After this general survey we return to Liverpool, the shire town, as the natural center of attraction to outside parties. The town is lighted by electricity and supplied with water by a good system of works. There is a marine slip, operated by electric power derived from a waterfall in Milton. There are several ship yards, and wharves, and a lighthouse, and another on Coffins Island at the entrance of the harbor. The shipping registered in the port is:

	No.	Tons.
Barquentines	2	595
Brigantines	3	688
Schooners	68	4,282
Steamers	4	160
	77	5,725

A line of railway about three miles in length, built by the people of the town for the most part, is in operation from Liverpool to the upper pulp mill above Milton. There are good schools of different grades and church accommodations for everybody. Episcopalians, Congregationalists, Methodists, Baptists, Roman Catholic and Salvation Army, all are represented. Hotel accommodations have thus far proved ample. Steamers call at this port that ply between Halifax and Yarmouth and intermediate ports. Mail coaches are run daily eastward and westward and northward, and railroad connection will soon be accomplished. Two banks, a board of trade, an iron foundry, and a fine machine shop are evidences of life in this town that has been on the increase steadily during the last ten years. Ship building, shipments of lumber and pulp, fishing and general trade with the outlying country are the principal industries of the town.

The geology of the county is the key to its surface appearance, its land products and coast line. The seaboard is a frowning rampart of granite and allied schists. Passing inland they rapidly but gradually change to quartzite and slates, and belong to the Cambrian formation, or perhaps older still, the Laurentian, the oldest of the known rocks. They were once sediments eroded from an ancient shore, and if there was any life in the ocean of that time it must have been so small and delicate that no impression of it could be preserved in these beds of mud and clay, for these rocks are destitute of fossils, although they were several miles in depth. They are no longer in level beds, but have been thrown by lateral pressure into great folds and corrugations, and these folds were worn away by the elements as they arose, and we have the rocks now on edge at various angles. This formation extends from

PORT MEDWAY, QUEENS COUNTY.

MILLS VILLAGE, QUEENS COUNTY. PORT MEDWAY RIVER.

Canso to Yarmouth on the Atlantic slope of the peninsula and constitutes the gold-bearing rock of Nova Scotia.

On the northern border of Queens County these Cambrian slates came into contact with the granite axis of several miles in width, forming the divide of western Nova Scotia. Over all the county is the covering of sand, and gravel, and mud, and rocks. All of it the ruins of the underlying slates and quartzites and adjacent granites. In many localities the bed-rock crops out in ledges. The depressions are swamps and lakes, the naked portions are "barrens," where blueberries grow in abundance. This in brief is the small County of Queens, about which much more could be said with truth and to its credit.

CHAPTER XXII.

The following paragraphs are from Gilpin's report to the Government on "The Mines of Nova Scotia:"

"The trap of the Bay of Fundy has, as already noticed, from the earliest days of our history yielded grains and lumps of metallic copper, sometimes weighing fifty pounds. Attempts were made, some years ago, to mine it near Margaretsville, on the shore of the Annapolis County. The copper occurred associated with zeolites and other infiltrates, but it proved to be too irregularly scattered in the matrix to permit systematic mining. It is found at many other places, among which may be mentioned Cape D'Or, Spencers Island, Five Islands, Briar Island, etc.

"The trap of this locality is considered to differ widely in age from that associated with the Huronian copper-bearing strata of Lake Superior, which has yielded the metal from pre-historic times. But when it is found in the Bay of Fundy trap, at so many localities, there will always be a strong inducement to test the more promising exposures; and it may be found in places to be scattered in the trap in fine grains, in quantity sufficient to allow of its being profitably extracted.

"It may be mentioned in this connection that I have observed metallic copper in dendritic forms in the copper ores of Antigonish County, and Mr. Barnes reported finding it near Cheticamp, Cape Breton.

"The upper and lower coal measures of Pictou, Cumberland and other counties frequently show outcrops of nests and layers of the vitreous sulphuret and green carbonate of this metal, associated with jet-like coaly matter. These deposits are believed to have originally consisted of accumulations of vegetable matter in the swamps and estuaries of that age, and afterwards when the strata became solidified that the ores of copper were deposited from the aqueous solutions through the not yet clearly understood medium of the carbonaceous matter they have now partly or completely replaced.

"Such deposits have been observed and tested at many points in the Province, among which I may mention the East River of

318

Pictou, near Hopewell, and below Springville, West River, near Durham.

"In Kings County, at East Dalhousie, a lode of quartz associated with granite in pre-carboniferous measures has been sunk on during the past year to a depth of about ninety-five feet. The ores are vitreous and gray, sulphurets, and blue and green carbonates. Assays show the presence of silver up to twenty-five ounces per ton of two thousand pounds. At many points through the district strong indications of copper ore are found, and should the present prospecting show workable deposits they would probably also receive attention.

"Mr. Poole, in his report on the Western Gold Fields, in 1862, mentions finding copper pyrites in slates at Blanford Cove, Lunenburg County, Hillsboro Brook, Westville Brook, Geyser's Hill, Jebouge Point. It is also a common mineral in the gold-bearing lodes of the Province.

"In the vicinity of the Garden of Eden several localities have been observed holding veins of spar up to several feet in thickness, with crystals of copper pyrites. The only deposits which have been tested to any extent are those of Antigonish County, where large sums of money have been spent and a considerable tract of county proved to be cupriferous. At Lochaber, on the property controlled by Messrs. McBean, Fraser and others, of New Glasgow, the explorations so far as carried show a series of veins, cutting at oblique angles black and red shales and quartzites, and thrown for a short distance 30 degrees out of an east-and-west course by a dyke, apparently a diorite containing talc and serpentine.

"The quality of the Lochaber ore is unusually good; the chief variety met is copper pyrites, with a small admixture of carbonate of copper and erubescite. The gangue at Lochaber is chiefly micaceous iron ore, with a little spathic ore; at Polson's Lake, exclusively the latter.

"In Cape Breton a large number of places are noted in the reports of Mr. Fletcher, of the Geological Survey, as holding copper ores, as traces and deposits possibly of workable extent. Thus he mentions the metal as occurring in traces as copper pyrites in the crystalline rocks of Benacadie, the White Granite Hills; in quartz veins in the Lower Silurian felsites of Gillis' Brook, as green carbonate; in Lower Carboniferous Conglomerates, Spruce Brook, Bras d'Or. In his report 1867-77, he says: 'Mention has already been made of a number of places showing traces of copper glance, oxidized to carbonate, impregnating a conglomerate often as its contact with an overlying bed of limestone, as at Irish Cove, East Bay, Washaback, Middle and North Rivers.'

"Three assays of samples from the Washaback Conglomerate, near Crow Point, are said to have yielded Dr. Hayes:

"1.   5 dwts. of gold per ton.

"2.   3-10 of copper, and 19 dwts. 4 grs. of gold per ton.

"3.   16 dwts. 8 grs. of gold, and 6 dwts. 12 grs. of silver per ton.

"Although in some cases these deposits may be the remains of plants replaced by metallic ores, as.pointed out by Professor Hydn, in a report on the district, the mineral often forms the matrix of the conglomerate.

"Yellow copper pyrites occurs on the farm of Angus McDonald, on the French Road, near Garbarus, as nodules and layers in a compact felsite, occupying a considerable tract of country.

"Copper pyrites occurs at Eagle Head, in Gabarus Bay, in a belt of laminated quartz, some twenty-five feet thick, intermixed with soft felspathic rock. The quartz layers are of various thickness and carry the ore in irregular quantities. Associated with the band is a whitish green soapstone with arsenical pyrites, bismuth glance, iron pyrites, molybdenite, and traces of gold. The copper is also met in a light colored felsite, containing vugs lined with crystals of quartz, and appears to be generally distributed through the neighboring felsites. Shafts have been sunk at the Eagle Head and French Road deposits by Mr. F. Ellershausen, and it is understood that well defined and promising veins have been found.

"On the Gillis Lake road an excavation made by Mr. J. McKenzie, of Sydney, disclosed a soft, Sectile, soapy rock, impregnated with calcspar, drused with a talcose hematite, and holding iron and copper pyrites and green carbonate in a compact grey and pink felsite. Similar ores occur at other places, as at Boisdale and Coxheath Hills, but have not yet been tested sufficiently to allow of estimates of their value.

"At Cheticamp, about fifteen years ago, a good deal of work was done on a vein five inches thick, holding chrysocalla, blue and green carbonates and grey ores, but the results were presumably unsatisfactory. During the fall of 1879 fresh discoveries of a number of small veins holding copper pyrites were reported from this locality;

but owing to the prevailing neglect displayed in making returns by those holding licenses from the crown, I can give no details. At numerous other points in the vicinity of Cape North, the northern part of the island, specimens of copper ore are found, but no work has been done to test their value.

"Although in this Province no copper mines have yet been systematically worked, and many of the deposits have not repaid the prospectors' labor, the indications are so widespread, and many parts so well adapted, geologically speaking, for workable copper lodes, that we may reasonably expect to see it form a regular article of export before many years. And so long as so many promising indications are met there will always be an inducement to test their adaptability for working."

In the annual report of the Canadian Geological Survey is the following item concerning a copper mine in Cape Breton County:

"Traversing the country in a northeasterly direction and constituting the great mass of the Coxheath hills is a large body of felsitic rocks very much broken and fissured, carrying large and small masses and veins of copper, and iron pyrites containing small quantities of gold and silver, and, it is said, entirely free from antimony, arsenic or any other refractory materials. Small quantity only of quartz and calcite is noticeable in the ore in the dumps. The belt of cupriferous felsite is about 1,500 feet wide following the general trend of the hills, about northeast and southwest. Six distinct veins from two to twenty feet wide are said to have been located and exploited, work having been carried on to a depth of 176 feet in No. 1 shaft, and 320 feet in No. 2, and a considerable extent of ground opened up by means of cross-cuts, levels, winzes, etc."

COPPER MINES OF CAPE D'OR.

At Cape D'Or, Cumberland County, is the finest mining plant and the best constructed mining work both on the surface and underground to be found in the Province, coal mines excepted. The purpose of it all is to mine and mill copper ore and otherwise treat it for shipment in the form of metallic copper, and this on a very large scale, from a locality whereon the first prospector ever went in search of the precious metals in Nova Scotia. That event takes us back to a day in June, 298 years ago, when the first sail ventured into these waters, and Sieur De Monts, Samuel Cham-

21

plain, Baron Poutrincourt and a motley crowd of adventurers might
have been seen scrambling over the tide-washed sand and boulders
in search of gold.   In spite of the fact that they never saw a grain
of it, they left the name that still survives of the "Golden Cape.".
They found pieces of bright metallic copper and seem to have taken
them for some kind of alloy of gold.   From time to time ever since
people have reported their finds' of copper in this locality; and whoever has written about the mines and minerals of this Province has
told us something of this promontory that defiantly breasts the savage tides and turmoil of the sea.

We read as follows from Dawson's Acadian Geology, 1878,
"Beyond Cape Sharp, with the exception of the isolated mass of
Spencers Island which I have visited, we see nothing of the trap or
red sandstone till we reach Cape D'Or, the last and noblest mass
on this coast.   At Cape D'Or as at Five Islands, a great mass of
trap rests on slightly inclined red sandstone and this again on disturbed carboniferous rocks, while from beneath these last still older
slates rise into mountain ridges.   Cape D'Or thus forms a great
salient mass standing out into the bay, and separated from the old
slate hills behind by a valley occupied by the red sandstone and
carboniferous shales.   The upper part of the cliff consists of
amygdaloid and tufa, often of a brownish color, while beneath is a
more compact trap showing a tendency to columnar structure.

"Cape D'Or derives its name from the native copper which is
found in masses varying from several pounds in weight to the most
minute grains in the veins and fissures that traverse the trap.   'It
is sometimes wedged into these fissures, along with a hard brown
jasper, or occupies the center of narrow veins of quartz and calcspar.   At first sight these masses and grains of pure copper appear
to have been molten into the fissure in which we find them.   On
more careful consideration of all the circumstances and those of the
associated minerals it seems more probable that the metal has been
deposited from an aqueous solution of some salt of copper, in a
manner similar to the electrolytic process.   Why this should have
occurred in trap rocks more especially does not appear very obvious;
and indeed when we take a piece of native copper from Lake Superior or Cape D'Or, with the various calcareous and silicious min-·
erals which accompany it, nothing can be more difficult to account
on chemical principles for these assemblages of substances, either
by aqueous or igneous causes.   The valuable   discoveries which

have been made on the shores of Lake Superior have in late years
caused increased importance to be attached to the appearance of
copper in trap rocks, and .perhaps this and other cupriferous localities in the trap of Nova Scotia may deserve a more careful examination than they have yet received."

About two years ago this copper region was brought to the
notice of certain American capitalists who were induced to send
experts on the ground who made favorable reports. The outcome
of these and further investigations was that the Colonial Copper
Company took hold of the property. In order that I might learn the
truth or falsity of current reports 'concerning their operations I
spent a couple of days on the ground last October. Beyond all
question they had shown that this native copper was almost entirely
confined to certain strong, well defined veins from fifty to seventy
feet in width that had been exploited by blasting for the most part
at low tide, at considerable distance from the perpendicular wall
of lofty cliffs that form the shore line. These veins extend out
under the sea in one direction and backward under the Cape in the
other. The cliffs are more than two hundred feet high and are
formed of stratified rocks about which there is considerable diversity
of opinion touching their mode of formation. The stratified planes
showing as lines on the face of the cliffs are not level, but somewhat inclined, forming synclinal depressions where the rocks are
more or less broken in the axis of deepest depression, and at these
points the copper appears. It is very evident that these two features, the synclinal trough and the concurrence of copper there, are
of no small significance in ascertaining the manner and means by
which this metal was mingled with the rocks. Since this work of
the Colonial Copper Company is the only serious attempt to mine
copper in Nova Scotia on a large scale and because Cape D'Or is
the only place on the continent that native copper is to be found
with the exception of the far-famed Keewana Point in the State of
Michigan, I have thought proper to devote considerable space to
the enterprise.

CHAPTER XXIII.

There are but three larger counties than Colchester. It has an area of about 1,308 square miles, and a population of 24,899, a surprisingly small number for a district so advantageously situated, and with distinct advantages of natural resources and delightful resorts. It is bounded on the south by Cobequid Bay and Halifax County, on the west by Hants County, on the east by Pictou, and on the north by Northumberland Straits and Cumberland.

It was early settled along the shore of Cobequid Bay by the Acadian French. On the present site of Masstown, then called Cobequid, was a considerable village, with a church building of dimensions that indicated quite a numerous population. At Onslow and Truro were other settlements. They were all destroyed in 1755, when the Acadians were expelled from the Province.

In writing these county histories the greatest difficulty is found in deciding what shall be left out of the material at hand.

Taking up the townships, towns, and villages for brief notice, we may properly begin with Truro.

Since Haliburton's History is not a common book, it will be of interest to read his description of the locality, written in 1828. It runs as follows:

"Truro is nominally divided into upper, and lower, villages, but the designation of village belongs with more propriety to the former, the latter being merely a continuation of farm houses at moderate · distances, situated on the uplands that rise gently from the marshes.

"The upper village consists of about seventy dwelling houses, and these are in general compact enough to merit the appellation. Both are situated on the south side of Colchester Bay, near its head, with no evident separation but a small creek, near which stands a Presbyterian meeting-house, placed intentionally to accommodate the inhabitants of both. The upper village is built upon what may be called tableland of about a quarter of a mile in width and three-quarters in length, and is laid out in two parallel streets; running east and west. These terminate on the west by a square surrounded with houses two stories in height, in which are also the court house and jail. From this square diverge the Halifax, Pictou, and Lower Village road. In pursuing the road leading to Pictou, the whole front street is traversed, and near its head stands the Episcopal Church, a very beautifully proportioned building with a spire and bell. Near this place the street terminates in two roads, the Eastern, leading directly up the Salmon River, and its rich interval toward Pictou; the Northern crossing Salmon River by a new and most ornamental bridge toward Cumberland, and a division of the village denominated from its situation 'the Hill,' which is exactly one mile from the court house. No doubt the alluvial lands which here extend between the Salmon and North Rivers for nearly two miles, first led to the erection of dwelling houses on this part of the village, the number of which is now twenty, and daily increasing.

"The situation is one of the most consummate beauty. From the hills another road, and the most frequented, leads to Pictou, and from it also the Cumberland road may be said to commence through the township of Onslow and Londonderry. Whether originating in accident, taste, or convenience, this is the place where public business is transacted, all the law offices, the custom house, postoffice, the Masonic Hall, and the two principal inns being situated here.

"In this township there are four grist mills. One of them is in the center of the upper village, and the second, which is not far from it, has also a carding machine and a fulling mill attached to it.

"Independent of these, all of which have kilns for drying oats, there are nine saw mills.

"The aspect of Truro, when neared from the elevated land on the northeast, is highly pleasing. The whole sweep of the Basin of Minas, as far as Cape Blomidon, embracing a space of more than sixty miles, is distinctly visible, while the two villages into which the township is mainly divided, with their level marshes relieved by finely swelling upland, and backed with woods and undulating hills, compose the foreground of this beautiful landscape."

The town was incorporated in 1875, when there were about 3,500 people within the lines proposed to enclose the municipality. At that time the assessed value of real and personal property was $185,150; now there are 6,500 population, and the taxable property valuation is $2,440,257.

The water supply is of the best and abundant, the reservoir containing 31,000,000 gallons, and located 200 feet above the rails in the depot.

Streets, dwellings, and stores are lighted by electricity. There are eleven churches and two superior hotels. Victoria Park is one of the attractions of Truro that deserves to be seen. I have before me an elaborate description wherein the writer can hardly keep his feet for the tendency to take flight. Here, too, at my hand are half-tone views of rustic summer loveliness as they were caught by the camera, and they fill me with "longings for spring." Here are driveways following the cycloidal sweeps of a curve system that has delved under the sheltering hillside, where it frets the roots of ancient trees, and gets itself tented under their friendly branches.

It is very evident that the spell of the place is on me also, and to stop while I can is prudent. But surely this park is a feature of justifiable pride to all the good people of Truro.

Here is an educational center of excellence and interest. In 1855 the Government established in Truro a normal school for the training of teachers. During the first thirteen years of its existence Rev. Alexander Forrester was the principal. He was succeeded by J. B. Calkin, M. A., who held that position till June, 1900, when David Soloan, B. A., was called to preside over this institution, that had not only maintained an existence, but had grown in dimensions and efficiency from the beginning.

In 1878 new quarters were provided in the way of a handsome and convenient brick building, erected at a cost of $40,000. New departments have been added from time to time to meet the new demands. At present the faculty is adequate to all reasonable expectations. Teachers are provided for the following studies: Principles of Pedagogy and Method in Language, Psychology and Practical Mathematics, Chemistry and Natural Science, Drawing and Calisthenics, Manual Training.

The attendance of students has increased from an average of about sixty during the first twenty-four years, to that of 153 during the last twenty years, the enrollment during the session of 1899-1900 being 220.

The annual cost of maintenance has increased from $3,200 in the earlier years to $12,000 at present.

This is really a very small outlay for an institution of the kind. There seems to be something niggardly about its dimensions when one considers the object and work of the school. While it is quite true that to a large extent teachers are like poets, born, not made, still there are not enough of the natural kind to go around, so there

STREET VIEW, TRURO.

VICTORIA SQUARE, TRURO

VICTORIA PARK, TRURO.

should be a systematic attempt to train from slender aptitudes a respectable efficiency for this responsible and vital work of teaching in the common schools.

The County Academy building is a credit to the town, and its equipments are of a high order. It has a staff of seven teachers, and an annual enrollment of about 250 students. Of these about one-half are from beyond the town and represent almost every county in the Province. The course of study embraces English, Mathematics, Science, History, Classics, and Modern Languages.

The academy has a good laboratory and is well equipped with apparatus for scientific work. A Conservatory of Music is among the later institutions of the town, and is reported to be in a flourishing condition.

Included in the public school is a kindergarten and the McDonald-Slayd School of Manual Training. The work of the common school is carried on in four buildings under the direction of eighteen teachers.

Situated at the head of Cobequid Bay, Truro is a seaport, where there is carried on some fishing and shipbuilding.

Quite a number of manufactories are in successful operation. There is the Truro Foundry Company, the Truro Knitting Mills Company, the Truro Condensed Milk and Creamery Company.

This town is also a railway center of considerable importance, being on the Intercolonial Line, also the point of departure for Pictou and all points in Cape Breton. Recently the Hants Central Railway has been opened to Truro, and it will doubtless add not a little to the business importance of the place.

We will now go back to the forefathers and foremothers of the town.

Alas that the mothers are so often overlooked in the records of people, and often in the written lives of illustrious sons. John Stuart Mill wrote his life and never once mentioned his mother, who was a worthy woman, and did more for him than his father, whom he never tires of admiring. From Mr. Thomas Millar's "Historical and Genealogical Record of the First Settlers of Colchester County," I have taken the following names and connected data in a somewhat abbreviated form. They are the names of the earliest and principal permanent settlers of Truro and vicinity:

Alexander Miller, of New England. His father of Belfast, Ireland.

Anthony Elliot, a soldier with Cornwallis at the founding of Halifax.

Matthew Staples, a blacksmith with Cornwallis.

David Archibald, Esq., of Londonderry, Ireland.

Matthew Taylor, Sr., of New England.

John Taylor, son of Matthew.

James Dunlop; no mention of his birth.

Janet Logan and two sons from Londonderry, Ireland.

Hugh More; came with his brothers, sisters, and their husbands 1760.

George Scott, James Rutherford, Alexander Nelson, of Ireland.

James Wright.

Captain William Cock; born in Scotland.

Captain John Morrison, of New Hampshire; came with first company in 1760.

Captain William Blair, of New England, of Scotch ancestry.

Francis Blair, a brother of William.

Robert Barnhill, of Donegal, Ireland, came with Colonel McNutt's settlers, 1761.

Alex. Deyarmond, of Ireland.

James Crow and six sons from Londonderry, Ireland.

William Corbett, a Scotchman with General Wolfe at the taking of Quebec.

John Smith, of Scotland, not an early settler, 1776.

Eliakim Tupper, of New England, probably from Sandwitch, came to Truro 1773.

Colonel Thomas Pearson, an English officer, came in 1784.

Dr. John Harris, of Philadelphia, came 1767.

John Christie, of Roxburyshire, Scotland.

David McCullum, early settler of Onslow, 1775.

John Dickson, an early settler of Onslow, born in Scotland.

John Oughterson, early settler of Truro.

Colonel Jonathan Blanchard, of New Hampshire, came to Truro 1785.

Samuel Fisher, of North of Ireland, but of Scotch ancestry.

James Johnson, of North of Ireland, came with six sons and four daughters, 1761, settled in Lower Village of Truro.

James Yuill, of Clydesdale, Scotland, came in 1761 to Nova Scotia; settled at Clifton, then called "Old Barns," because there were two old French barns in the field at the east of Mr. Ebenezer

Archibald's house, and an old grist mill standing on the bank near John Yuill's shop; for more tthan eighty years this village was called Old Barns, and had no other name.

Robert Hunter, of Ireland, one of the first settlers.

Andrew Gammell, a first settler.

William Kennedy, came with the first settlers.

Charles Cox, first settler.

Adam Dickey, of New England.

Charles McKay, came from New England; returned there after a brief period.

John Fulton, of Ireland, who came from New England.

John McKeen, born in Londonderry, Ireland.

William McKeen, son of John.

John McKeen, son of John.

William Fisher, of Londonderry, Ireland, early settler.

John Jeffry, among the first settlers.

James Gourley, of New England.

Samson Moore, of Ireland, came in 1762 from New England.

James Downing, of New England.

Joshua Lamb, a grantee of Onslow Township, returned to New England.

James Whidden, a first settler, born in New England.

James Kent, of Scotland.

Robert Hamilton, of Armagh, Ireland.

James Fulton, of Ireland.

Samuel Creelman, of Ireland.

Jacob Synde, early settler in Cobequid, native of Ireland.

Charles Dickson, from New England, among first settlers.

Mr. Miller has not in all cases given the birthplace with the name.

These appear to be good material for a new country. It is quite certain that no coward or laggard would volunteer for such service as this pioneer work demanded. It appears that during the Revolutionary War these people were largely in sympathy with the Americans, and caused no small amount of worriment to Governor Legge, who managed between imaginary ills and needless quarrels to have his cup of distress running over all the time. From Sackville, Amherst, Truro, and Onslow were sent up to the Governor strongly signed petitions asking that they be excused from the operations of the militia law.

From Amherst the petitions said: "Those of us who belong to New England being invited by Governor Lawrence's proclamation, it must be the greatest piece of cruelty and imposition for them to be subjected to march into different parts in arms against their friends and relations."

From Onslow a petition of a like import was signed by fifty-six men, and from Truro by sixty-three, and Samuel Archibald heads the list, as Joshua Lamb did in Onslow.

Legge sent these memorials to the Secretary of State, and wrote in connection: "The same spirit of these petitioners subsists in all the out-settlements, and that it will require the most diligent attention to prevail upon them and *prevent their joining with the enemy in case of invasion."* ·

A year later, "in 1777, two justices of the peace were sent from Halifax to Truro, and Onslow, and Londonderry, to tender the oath of allegiance, and there were but five persons willing to take it.　`

"When their Representatives went to the House of Assembly the next session, they were not allowed to take their seats on account of the people being suspected of disloyalty." This from Murdoch. It looks very much as if the suspicion was well founded in reason.

Meantime, in 1776, Lieutenant Governor Arbuthonot visited these three settlements and reported home to England that they: "Were a strong, robust, industrious people, bigotted dissenters, and of course great levellers. But, my Lord, how can it be otherwise, for to my astonishment no Governor had ever visited these poor people, or sent any person among them, so as to form a judgment of the necessary steps to make these men useful subjects; but, on the contrary, they have been left the parents of their own works. I found full 500 men capable of bearing arms, the finest men in the Province, settled on the best land, and the most flourishing, because they are the most industrious."

This much for a glimpse of the old times and the old spirit; and we pass on to other points.

A post road runs west from Truro, between the Cobequid Mountains and the tide water of the Bay and Basin, passing Masstown at ten miles, Folly Village at fourteen miles, Great Village at eighteen miles, Highland Village at twenty-one miles, Port Au Pique at twenty-three miles, Bass River at twenty-seven miles, Upper Economy at twenty-eight miles, and Five Islands at forty-five miles.

SCIENCE BUILDING AND PROVINCIAL NORMAL SCHOOL, TRURO.

PROVINCIAL NORMAL SCHOOL, TRURO.

This is a delightful region, pleasing to the eye by its natural beauties of scenery and the evidences of prosperity. From the Town of Truro the post road runs down the shore of the bay, through a pleasing and thrifty country of Lower Truro, Clifton, Beaver Brook, and Princeport, the latter on the Shubenacadie River. The Township of Onslow is an important part of the county. I am indebted for my information here set down to a chapter in the "History of the Township of Onslow, Nova Scotia," by Israel Longworth, Q. C., of Truro, published in the collections of the Nova Scotia Historical Society, 1893-95; a valuable contribution to local history, of which only a few items can be used here.

"It is believed that the Government of the day named the Township of Onslow in honor of Arthur Onslow, an English statesman, who was born in 1691. The erection of the township was ordered by Governor Lawrence in Council, 24th July, 1759. The formation took place upon the application of Joseph Scott and Daniel Knowlton, for themselves and fifty others of the Massachusetts Bay, for a tract of land at Cobequid. Several were of the Port Cumberland expedition of the previous year. The fifty-two proposed grantees with their families represented 309 souls. A grant of fifty-two shares or rights in the township to these persons passed the Governor and Council 26th July, 1759. The township was stated as being at the head of Cobequid Basin, to extend upon the north side of said Basin, and to run westerly six miles, from thence northerly about twelve miles, thence easterly about twelve miles, thence southerly twelve miles, thence to Cobequid Basin, six miles. All to be laid out on the north side of Cobequid River. Scott and Knowlton and their associates were to have twenty-six acres; half were to settle in October, 1760, and the remainder in May, 1761. The names of the first settlers in the order they appear in the township grant are as follows:

"Richard Upham, William Hamilton, Anthony Elliot, Thomas Stephens, James Lyon, John Steel, James Wilson, Francis Blair, Jonathan Higgins, Joseph Scott, John Carter, William Tackles, Hugh Tackles, Jacob Stephens, William McNutt, and the heirs of Jacob Lines, Nathaniel Gallop, Edward Brooks, David Hoar, Martin Brooks, William Blair, Ephraim Howard, Joshua Lamb, David Gay, David Blackmore, Abner Brooks, Carpenter Bradford, George Howard, Ephraim Scott, John Poly, Samuel Nichols, Peter Richardson, Ephraim Howard, Jr., Robert Crowell, Abijah Scott, David

Cutting, Isaac Ferrel, Daniel Knowlton and Mary Knowlton, Eliz-
abeth Blackmore, Abigail Upham, Caleb Putnam, Nathan Upham,
Richard Upham, Jr., Nicholas Blanchard, James Tackles, John
Cutting, Solomon Hoar, William Blair, Jr., William Whippy,
Peter Wilson, James Brown, the heirs of Jabez Rude, Joseph
Pierpont, John Howard, Daniel Calf, the heirs of Samuel
Whippy, the heirs of Joel Camp, the heirs of Benjamin Brooks,
Asa Scott, Francis Harris, John Barnhill, Samuel Bencraft,
John Hewett, John Polly, Jr., Reuben Richardson, William Crowell,
Jonathan Higgins, Jr., Mercy Brooks, Hugh Acton Tackles, Chris-
topher Stevens, Jacob Stevens, Jr., Abner McNutt, Jacob Lines, Jr.,
Silvanus Brooks, Edward Brooks, Jr., Ebenezer Hoar, John Blair,
and Deborah Wright.

These settlers were called upon to endure great privations,
especially the first few years in their new home. It is related that
one man actually died of starvation, although we must believe
that in a new country abounding in fish and game, that there was
no need of great hunger. The Government came to the rescue,
and supplied them with corn. Within a reasonable time these
people took root and prospered. Haliburton says that on the arrival of the settlers they "found the country laid waste to prevent
the return of the Acadians, but 570 acres of marsh land was still
under dyke, and about forty acres of upland around the ruins of
houses were cleared, though partially overgrown by young shrubs.
Remains of French roads are still visible, as also parts of their
bridges. Near the sites of their buildings have also been found,
at various times, farming implements and kitchen utensils, which
they had buried in the hope of being permitted at some future
time to return to their possessions."

Mr. Joshua Lamb was the first Registrar of Deeds, and he
was in 1770 returned a member from the Township of Onslow to
the House of Assembly. Later on by a half dozen years he became
a notable figure thereabouts for his expressed sympathy with the
Americans, and he left the Province altogether and returned to his
own country, where he was at larger liberty to aid the cause of
independence. One might very well expect that among these men
and women so recently removed from New England, where many of
their relatives still resided, and had doubtless enlisted in the Revolutionary service, that there would be more or less of them whose
hearts were with the men who believed they had a grievance that
ustified taking up arms against the mother land.

There was no little dissatisfaction in Onslow over the terms of their grant, that were not up to the promises of Governor Lawrence, and far less liberal than that of Truro. That fact, no doubt, had its effect in creating some measure of disloyalty. It is worth remarking that Lamb was an intelligent and influential man, and Colonel MacNutt was another who expressed most earnest sympathy with the Americans. See his recently published letters in Mr. Poole's book on the Annals of Yarmouth and Barrington; see also the history of Shelburne County in this volume. In the heat of the conflict in the Colonies the inhabitants of Onslow refused to take the oath of allegiance, every one of them, thirty-nine in all. This is good evidence of spunk and independence of spirit that had done well to outlive such grinding hardships as fell to their lot. This township is well watered by the North River of the Salmon and its tributaries, and the Chiganois and its branches. On these streams are extensive settlements in charming localities.

The Township of Londonderry, or the larger part of it, was granted to James Fulton, Esq., and nineteen others; five shares each, and to Robert Barnhill and forty-eight others, certain rights or shares. This grant was for 53,000 acres, and bears date of March 6, 1775. Mr. Fulton was born in Belfast, Ireland, in 1740, and married Mary Campbell of the Folly in 1771. Robert Barnhill came from the north of Ireland with his wife in 1761 with Colonel McNutt. Haliburton says of Londonderry: "This township lies between Onslow and Parrsboro. It extends twenty miles in length, and is bounded in front by the Basin of Minas, in the rear by the county of Cumberland. This part of the Province was originally settled by the French, who were attracted by its extensive marshes, its facility of communication by water with the other settlements, and the superior quality of its upland. Some idea may be formed of the extent of their population by the size of the chapel, which was one hundred feet in length and forty feet wide. This spacious building, together with their dwelling houses, was destroyed by the Provincial troops, on the dispersion of the Acadians in 1755. It was subsequently settled by the exertions of Alexander McNutt, Esq., an enthusiastic adventurer from the north of Ireland, to whom and his associates there were granted in different parts of Nova Scotia upwards of a million acres. The first attempt at settlement was in 1761 by twenty families, who gave it the name of the place of their nativity. Londonderry contained

2,000 acres of dyked lands, and 1,000 acres of salt marsh. The upland consists of two varieties of soil, which bear an equal proportion to each other, one half being clay, the other light and dry loam, and both generally free from stone. The upland produces birch, beech, maple, and elm, and a small quantity of pine."

The iron deposits of Londonderry are described at length in this book under the head of Iron Mines. The scenery, especially along the shore of the Basin, is very picturesque and interesting, as indeed it is from around the entire coast line from St. John to Brier Island.

Brookfield was first settled by families from Truro in 1786. Prominent among the first of these were William Hamilton, Daniel Moore, William Downing, and John Hamilton. The first church erected there was Presbyterian, and was built in 1833, and there was no other till 1857, when the Baptists were numerous enough to provide accommodations for separate worship. This is a prosperous farming community, and a station on the Intercolonial Road. A very promising iron mine has been prospected here and the ores sent for treatment to Londonderry.

The Shubenacadie River forms the western boundary of Colchester County. This is a turbulent tide-swept stream almost to its source. About twenty miles from the mouth is the thriving village of Shubenacadie, on the Intercolonial Railway. It is central to a large farming and dairying region, in a fertile district, noted for its productive hay lands. This is a point of departure for the stage line to Upper and Middle Musquodoboit, and Sheet Harbor and other eastern points.

Some twenty miles of the northern boundary of Colchester is formed by the Straits of Northumberland. This portion is included in the Township of Tatmagouche. The town of the same name is situated at the head of a large harbor, and has about 1,500 inhabitants. Some shipbuilding and shipping traffic, together with farming, make up the principal occupation of the community. In 1775 Governor Lawrence wrote to Colonel Monckton as follows: "I would have you give orders to the detachment you send to Tatmagouche to demolish all the houses they find there, together with all the shallops, boats, canoes, or vessels of any kind which may be lying ready for carrying off the inhabitants and their cattle, etc.; by this means the pernicious intercourse and intelligence between St. John's Island and Louisburg and the inhabitants of the interior part of the country will be in a great measure prevented."

We see by these words that the French had settled at this place in considerable numbers, and what their miserable fate would be is easily read between the lines of this grim 'message. Within a year from this date, the place that had once known them knew them no more, and within a few years their conquerors began to resettle the locality.

Within this township is Erule Harbor, a large village, picturesquely situated, where one may cool in dog days, and find much on sea and land to employ his leisure in restful diversion.

Between Tatmagouche and Truro is the Township of Sterling on the more elevated region, where most of the streams arise.

Earltown and New Annan are the principal villages of a distriet that has attracted attention by its promise of economic resources and pleasing natural scenery.

About one-third of the area of this county is included in the Stewiacke District in the southern portion; through it runs the Stewiacke River; it is for several miles a tidal stream. Rich and extensive interval lands are characteristic of this region. There are but few finer agricultural tracts in the Province. It is well settled with thrifty and enterprising people, who are very largely the descendants of Truro, Onslow, and Londonderry pioneers. In this Stewiacke District are several villages that we can do no more than mention: Upper and Lower Stewiacke, Fort Ellis, Gays River, Coldstream, South Branch, Meadow Vale, Goshen, Wittenberg, Newton Mills, Pembroke, Eastville, Greenfield, Boisdale, Southfield, Otter Brook, and Cross Roads. On the heads of Salmon River is the township of Kempton, a farming district quite well settled in the vicinity of the Pictou branch of the Intercolonial Railway. The iron and coal deposits of this county are described in the chapters dealing with these metals.

The gold-bearing slates and quartzites occupy but a small area on the southern border, and with but a few unimportant exceptions are not productive of gold.

At Coldstream, near Gays River, there is a notable deposit of conglomerate that has attracted attention and capital by its gold contents. It is the bottom of a dead river that flowed millions of years ago, over the Cambrian formation of slates, that even then was thrust into anteclinal waves and penetrated with auriferous veins. 'In fact there is no indication that these Cambrian rocks have undergone any change of position since the river bed was formed either in or near the Carboniferous Age. This deposit of conglomerate is formed of sand, gravel, smooth boulders, and rough fragments of slate that have been detached from the banks and bed of the stream. It varies in depth from a few inches to fifteen feet; the inequalities of the bottom determines the thickness. Gold in particles, varying in size from a grain of gunpowder to a large bean, is scattered throughout this deposit in the shape of smooth, flattened grains, to the average value of $4 to the ton of rock. Richer deposits have been found in the joints or seams of the ledges that run across the current; these forming natural riffles, or stops, when occurring on the up-stream side, and the gold slid down the slant of the crevice and there remained packed in the fine sediment that has become stone, that can be extracted in pieces several inches in area and from one-quarter to an inch in thickness, inlaid with particles of gold. Some of the best of these crevices yielded $2,000 dollars to a half dozen men, in as many weeks. This form of gold mine when found in a living river, or in loose sand and gravel of their beds in dry seasons, or after the water has been turned aside by dams, is called a "placer mine." In this instance it is a fossil placer. A change of level, due to extensive oscillations, caused the river to disappear. We cannot here follow the vicissitudes of its history; but at any rate, over this ancient river bed, at present, there is, first, a stratum of coarse sandstone, from a few inches to several feet in thickness. Upon that is another layer of conglomerate, in places thirty feet thick, and this is spread over the adjacent district, but it carries no gold. Upon that again is a stratum of gravel, sand, and stones, varying from nothing to twenty feet in depth. Thus far no gold-bearing quartz veins have been discovered in the bedrock of this old placer, and it has been a rare occurrence that a bit of quartz with gold in it has been found. Thus the indications are that the source of the precious metal is not in that immediate vicinity. It is very evident that somewhere in its course, at no very distant point, rich veins of quartz were encountered, broken up by the action of moving stones, and thus the gold was set free as the mere sport of the current. More than probable that the veins were very thin, or the gold would not have been so completely released from the quartz. It may be a long time before the bonanzas of this mine are discovered, but in the nature of things there must be places where the gold was brought together by the force of the stream in favoring cavities and eddies. Every attempt to prospect this interesting and promising field has ended in failure. It is very easy to misunderstand the geological problems it presents, but enough has been done now to make it plain, and some day, not likely to be distant, this mine will be opened at the right spot. It may be the result of chance, or it may be the reward of skill.

Among the good things claimed for this county is a lead mine at Smithfield. An attempt to smelt galena there in 1883 and '84 ended in failure. In 1894 the Dominion Smelting and Refining Company took over the property on the strength of some favorable reports, and after considerable prospecting all work came to an end. Mr. John Hardman, S. B., a very competent expert, in a published paper describing this deposit that he had examined professionally, concludes in these words: "The mode of occurrence of these small and scattered patches of ore, their irregularity, and the failure of any of the deep bore-holes to locate any deposit at depth, led to the conclusion that the property does not possess lead ore in quantities for a commercial venture. The similarity of this occurrence of galena with the deposits of lead ore in southwestern Missouri, might lead one to expect larger and perhaps profitable deposits along the lines of these mineralized strata, and it is possible that extended explorations may yet discover them, and form the basis of a lead industry.

GEOLOGY OF COLCHESTER COUNTY.

The oldest rocks in this county are the extensions and outcrops of the Cambrian strata of the Atlantic slope. Overlying this formation are various areas of Devonian, Carboniferous, Permian, and Triassic strata. There are outbreaks and intrusions of granite and other igneous rocks. This is the barest general view. We will consider the matter in brief detail.

Carboniferous limestone occupies a considerable portion of the basin of the Stewiacke and Shubenacadie Rivers. Devonian fossiliferous strata are largely developed south of the East River of Pictou, and thence without interruption run far to the westward of Truro, on the south side of Cobequid Bay and the Basin of Minas. They appear again in Water's Hill and MacCulloch's Brook and Mount Thom, and form with the series of igneous rocks which are everywhere found to cut and alter them, the axis of the Cobequid Hills. They include the iron ore series of Londonderry, and are

22

similar to the metamorphic rocks of Antigonish and Guysboro
Counties. A considerable area of Carboniferous rocks skirt the
south side of the Cobequid Hills.

On the southern border forming the county line there is a
narrow area two or three miles in width of the gold-bearing slates
of the Lower Cambrian series forming a contact with the Carboniferous limestone, where there are many deposits of gypsum.

The upper beds, of the Upper Devonian, are most widely distributed in a tract which lies north of Stewiacke River, and south
of the railway between Riversdale and Truro stations, and in the
country south of Cobequid Bay.

Devonian rocks are well exposed in all the streams flowing into
Cobequid Bay from the north. Beginning with the North River,
and ending with the Parrsboro, this formation is continuous, although the variety of rocks are many, and Carboniferous and Tri-
assie formations are represented, and igneous dykes are numerous.

Carboniferous limestone occupies the Stewiacke from its mouth
to the top of the settlement at Eastville. The rock structure of
this county is complicated, and much careful work by competent
men must yet be done before the "ifs and buts" and "probables"
will disappear from the Government Geological Reports.

I have quoted here and there from these reports by Mr. Hugh
Fletcher, B. A., and some portions, particularly at Gay's River, are
the results of my own experience on the ground.

CHAPTER XXIV.

To write about apples seems a goodly theme to one who was a country boy in a locality, and at a time when they did not greatly abound, as they do now. There must have been something about them that stimulated the imagination, for they managed to get themselves packed away with many a pleasing fancy and long-lived incident. They had a subtle charm for the youthful eye, with their varied tints and shades, where green and gold kissed each other as they met from opposite sides, and rich color schemes in pink and red came out to find the waiting leaves to give them the advantage of harmonious setting. Then we remember the very forms and dimensions of the fruit of each tree in a small orchard; we could have selected, and placed these ungrafted mongrels in the dark, by their flatness, or roundness, or longness, or bigness, or smallness; but above all, for the endurance of impression of them, outlasting a half century, comes the smell of the plump, firm, unctious beauties, that got furtively hidden away in the hay mow, where the exact location was supposed to be known only to him who had stowed them there, till the evidences of a high-handed raid became beyond all question.

Like all our grains, and roots, and fruits, the apple has been captured, and tamed, and improved for the use of mankind. Nature had, through long processes of evolution, surrounded the seed receptacle with an edible pulp, that was an invitation to birds, and squirrels, and other animals to help themselves, and thus get the seed distributed; for they can stand the passage of the digestive tract, and fare all the better in the way of planting by that experience. Man took what was intended by nature for other creatures. He cooked the fruit, and thus ruined the seed. The very device that worked to perfection with other animals was the means of destroying the seeds in the hands of this firemaking fellow, who took it for granted that everything was made for his use. However, in this case his gumption came to his rescue; he knew enough to plant the seed, and raise the trees at his convenience. He must have very soon discovered that there were varieties of taste, some sour, others sweet, and some were larger than others; but the embarrassing difficulty lay in the fact that they could not bring forth "after their kind"; the seeds of the sweet apple were not likely to produce a tree of that variety, but in a seeming whimsical obduracy Nature did as she pleased. This order of things was a serious drawback to primitive apple culture, and it was doubtless a stretch of many thousand years before it was discovered that a scion could be cut from a desirable tree and successfully grafted into the stock of a healthy but undesirable one, and by this simple process the scion would grow up to a tree and yield after its kind and not after the stock that supplied the sap. Had the scion taken root in the ground, like a slip of willow, then one might well expect the fruit would be like the tree from which it was taken; but to be nourished on the very life blood of the stock, and then show no trace of this operation would be contrary to general expectation, and it is difficult to imagine how the discovery of grafting was made. As proof that it did not lay on the surface to be readily found out we may mention the Indians of the Northwest who from time immemorial have eaten the wild crab-apple *Pyrus rivularis,* taking pains to keep them by one means and another for seasons of scarcity, in winter, and yet no attempts at grafting were made among them. The art was practiced in the region of the Mediterranean more than two thousand years ago.

St. Paul mentions the process of grafting, but singularly enough seems to be in error of the true nature of it, "and if some of the branches be broken off, and thou being a wild olive tree, wert graffed in among them, and with them partakest of the root and fatness of the olive tree." The illustration would have been capital had the facts been different; at all events he knew there was an operation by which one tree was made to be nourished by another and that seemed near enough for his purpose, and so it was. Nearly a century before his time Virgil said: "Often we see the boughs of one tree transformed with no disadvantage, into those of another, and a pear tree, being changed, bear ingrafted apples, and stony cornels grow upon plum stocks."

The Old Testament Scriptures in English are made to mention apples more than once as "the apple of the eye," "comfort me with apples," and "apples of gold in pictures of silver," and "as the apple tree among the trees of the wood." Very likely a citron well-known thereabouts is the fruit referred to in these passages. "Apple of discord" is an expression one reads often enough, as if there was some discreditable story tacked to this beautiful fruit, but the fact is, the saying has a complimentary origin, inasmuch that the Greek myth set forth that Eris, the goddess of strife, at a gathering of the celestial four hundred, flung among them a golden apple on which was inscribed "To the Fairest," and in the scramble Venus secured it, to the great jealousy and displeasure of the others. It was sacred to this goddess whose statue sometimes bears an apple in one hand and a poppy in another. For this reason a present of these orchard beauties was considered a mark of affection, and so it was considered a tender expression to throw them at friends; hence Virgil in his Bucolics says, "What I could I sent to my boy, ten golden apples gathered from a tree in the wood." And again he says, "Galatea, wanton girl pelts me with apples, and flies to the willows, but wishes first to be seen." Was it because the apple was sacred to the goddess of love and beauty that Milton represents it as the forbidden fruit "of fairest colors mixed, ruddy and gold," and so firmly did Milton's genius weld this assertion into the Genesis account that there is a current belief to the effect that the forbidden tree was no other than our orchard favorite. We need not resent the poet's selection; he did not make it without due consideration we may be sure. There was no other fruit tree that he knew so likely when bending under its burden to catch the eye and salute the olfactories with appetizing odors, hence the Tempter says: "I nearer drew to gaze; when from the boughs a savoury odor blown, grateful to appetite, more pleased my sense, than smell of sweetest fennel."

Thus much to introduce our notable orchard product, and if any reader does not care for the introduction, then he can pass on to facts and figures of a more practical nature, but we must not neglect the poetical elements of nature and life; man cannot live by bread alone. "Consider the lilies how they grow" is imperative as the Golden Rule, and yet it has in it no hint of practical material reward: consider the apples how they grow is a fair exchange for the lilies, and he who is not moved in deep and holy places by the splendor of blooming orchards, the mysteries of growing fruit, and bounties of gracious gatherings, has missed the very best there is to apple culture!

Although our apple orchards are derived from European stock and represent many varieties secured from natural variation and grafting yet there are at least four species indigenous to temperate North America, viz.: *Pyrus angustifolia, Pyrus coronaria, Pyrus soulardi, Pyrus rivularis*. Besides these there are many family connections, not to be included in this real apple genus of crabs, for that they all are to begin with. The Almighty did not make an apple fit for anyone to eat, but he made a beginning and gave us the intelligence to do the rest, and surely that was good enough. Also at large in the woods of many portions of the United States are the descendants of orchard trees now but little better than crabs. It is easy to go down hill by running back to almost the original crab condition. So it is everywhere among plants and animals, man included. Dogs allowed to interbreed result in the yellow, jackal type, from which have been probably derived all the varieties from the great mastiffs to the tiniest lap-dog. The different varieties of domesticated pigeons, pouters, fantails and all, if permitted to freely interbreed, arrive at the parent stock, viz.: the blue rock-pigeon species. Domestic cattle soon become wild in habits and aspect; with cultivated fruit trees the same great law holds. Only one of our American indigenous crabs has been improved and turned to economical account, and this "Soulard" crab is rated an hybrid, a cross between a common apple and a wild species, and this was an accidental occurrence. The fruit is sometimes two inches in diameter, and is prized for preserving purposes.

Although apples have been so long known and appreciated, still their cultivation on a large scale, with due attention to selecting and improving the best varieties, is of quite recent date. Many causes operated to restrain any tendency to get beyond a small orchard for home use. Not until railroads and steamboats became common was it possible to market this fruit at a profit beyond a few miles, and there would be little or no sale for them near where they grew.

In the United States a great impetus was given to apple raising when means were provided to land their orchard product in good condition, at a cheap rate, at points where none were raised. Very soon all over the Union orchards were planted, and old trees were grafted and cared for as never before. In spite of the apparent advantages of the older Eastern States they have been far exceeded in yield by Missouri, Texas, Kansas, California, Oregon and Washington.

The aggregate of these States for 1901 was twenty-five million barrels, against the forty million average yearly product. These figures give us a proper idea of the great magnitude of this business. From Texas to Nova Scotia is a long cry across the lines of latitude, and yet at both extremes, and all between, this fruit in some of its many varieties finds congenial soil and climate. I have seen them in the Republic of Mexico doing as well as could be expected with no care, within a half mile, and at the same altitude, of a prosperous orange grove. The Tarhumar cave-dwellers of the Sierra Madre Mountains of that region raise apples enough for family use, and have a few to spare. So once a year, in March, a scarce time for fruit, the men take each a bushel on their backs and travel an hundred miles over mountains and gulches to make a sale at the rate of one dollar and fifty cents a backload of small, shrivelled fruit, and this money is used to purchase needles, pins, thread, knives, hoes, and other small articles. These apple farmers are quite contented, and perhaps get as much enjoyment out of life as some of our people who have acres of orchard and a railway depot at their doors.

Taking into consideration the great adaptability of the apple tree and its large number of varieties, one might fairly expect that here in this Province some kinds would prosper better than elsewhere, and this turns out to be the case. Writing recently to the Maritime Homestead, Mr. J. W. Bigelow, President of the Nova Scotia Fruit Growers' Association, gave some account of his experience at the Pan-American Exhibition. He says: "I must first note the fact that in each State and Province, and in different localities in each, apples of certain varieties will reach greatest perfection if adapted to the different soils and climate. The Ben Davis, Wealthy, Wolf River, Jonathan and others are grown in the west, perfect in flavor, size and color, and compare favorably with our Gravesteins, Blenheim, and Nonpareil, which reach their greatest perfection in Nova Scotia, and experience proves that each locality must grow fruit best adapted to it to insure success. * * * The standard varieties of English apples are grown to perfection here."

Surely nothing within reasonable expectation has been denied us in this line, when "standard varieties of the most desirable apples can be grown to perfection here." All through life we have so often to regret that there is something the matter with everybody to prevent perfection, and it is difficult to find a perfect crystal or a perfectly symmetrical leaf; but there certainly can be perfect apples where the imagination cannot create them more shapely in contour, more beautiful in colors and tints, or more delicious to the taste. Having been proved that such goodly fruit can be produced here with ordinary care, the next question that comes up is, how many of them can we raise?

Within forty years it has been discovered that this Province was enriched by Nature with extensive areas of land admirably adapted to apple orchards. In a pamphlet prepared by the Fruit Growers' Association of Nova Scotia, and widely circulated, is a good deal of valuable information from a reliable source, some of which may be properly introduced at this point.

"The favorite fruit region of Nova Scotia is the Annapolis Valley. This "garden of the Continent" is protected from the cold north and west winds which blow from Maine and New Brunswick, by the North Mountain, a range composed of trap rock resting on a sandstone formation. The valley is about one hundred miles long, and the soil consists of sand, sandy and clayey loam, based on the sandstone formation, sandy loam predominating throughout. At its eastern extremity the rise and fall of tides from time immemorial have worn away soil and rocks and have produced those rich and extensive marshes and dyke lands; these produce from year to year, hay, grain and pasture, without any renovating substance or manure of any kind, and still continue productive even after the lapse of one hundred and fifty years; the Grand Pre, as in the days of Longfellow's poem, is still covered with abundant crops, and in the autumn months with numerous herds as in the days of Gabriel and Evangeline. On the south side of the valley, and distant six or eight miles from the North Range, is the South Mountain; the valley between is comparatively level, and throughout its whole extent of one hundred miles, is of good soil, easily cultivated, well watered by streams and rivers, and is one of the most fertile and productive belts of land in the world. Here the apple, pear, plum, cherry, grape and peach grow and attain perfection. In other parts of the Province, in Lunenburg, Yarmouth, Queens, Pictou, in fact in every county in the Province, apples and other fruit are produced in favored localities in great abundance. Near the coast as a rule apples are not a great success, but plums and cherries and other small fruit grow and produce large crops near the sea coast, where the salt breeze is daily felt.

The apple attains a large size in Nova Scotia, and is of fine flavor, well ripened and colored. This is owing largely to the beautiful autumn months of September and October—the heat of the sun and the warm dry weather being a peculiarity of our climate at this season of the year.

In the Annapolis valley there are about 250,000 acres of land adapted to the cultivation of fruit. Probably not more than 5 per cent of this area is already set with trees, while tens of thousands of acres of choice orchard land wait the incoming of capital and labor.

Orcharding in Nova Scotia is yet in its infancy. True we have trees bearing an annual crop of apples that are over one hundred years old, and thousands of trees are annually planted, but it is only within a few years that the people even of this favored district have become alive to the immense possibilities of apple culture. During the past five years the acreage of young orchards has doubled and in five years to come will quadruple in extent. There is no investment open to capitalists that will yield such abundant returns for a period of fifty or one hundred years, and there is nothing to hinder any industrious man from having an orchard of ten acres that will yield a fair income in ten years, while for capital a hundred acre orchard means uncounted wealth.

To prove the truth of these assertions we will place before you a few figures based upon actual experience to show the possibilities in orcharding. We will present an estimate prepared by Mr. J. W. Bigelow, of Wolfville, President of the Nova Scotia Fruit Growers' Association:

COST OF AN ORCHARD OF ONE THOUSAND APPLE TREES AND REVENUE THEREFROM IN KINGS COUNTY, NOVA SCOTIA.

25 acres of land @ $30 per acre	$750
1,000 apple trees @ 20c each	200
Setting out 1,000 trees @ 10c each	100
Fertilizing	100
Fencing and Sundries	100
8 years' interest on $1,250 at 5 per cent	500
Cultivating 8 years at $100 a year	800
Manuring, mulching, replacing dead trees, etc	450
Total cost till 8 years old	$3,000

All expenses after eight years are paid by other crops and value of apples over net sales.

REVENUE.

Yield 9th and previous years, say 500 bbls. @ $1 net	$500
Yield 10th to 15th years, average 1,000 bbls. @ $1 net	5,000
Yield 15th to 45th years, average 2,000 bbls. @ $1 net	60,000
Total income in 45 years	$65,500

This orchard will produce same results for one hundred years. This estimate was presented to the Association in 1888, published in the annual report and in five years past has never been contradicted.

When we consider that the fruit belt of the three counties, Annapolis, Kings and Hants, contains over four hundred square miles of the best orchard land in the world, and that of this area not 20 per cent has been cultivated and not 5 per cent has been set in orchards, and as is shown by the following statistics that no other investment will give such profits when reckoned over a term of one hundred years, it is to be wondered at that labor and capital have not long since secured this rich inheritance, and it will be a greater wonder if in this age of large combines and the inquiry for profitable investment this vast territory is not immediately acquired, and on business methods be made to yield as it can, an income of from twenty to thirty millions of dollars per year. No other country in the world can offer more favorable inducements to the settlers with moderate means. With lands at from five to one hundred dollars per acre, intersected with railway and navigable rivers, affording the cheapest outlet to the markets of the world the healthiest and most invigorating climate, the soil best adapted to fruit culture, with an inexhaustible supply of fertilizer brought to our doors by every rise of the Bay of Fundy tides, and the most desirable social and religious conditions, the seeker for a home finds the most desirable conditions for a happy and prosperous development of human life.

But some may ask why it is that if orcharding in the Annapolis Valley is so enormously profitable, more and larger orchards have not been planted, or why indeed the whole Annapolis Valley is not one continuous orchard. The reply is as stated before, that this industry is yet in its infancy here. It is only within a very few years that even our most progressive farmers have come to realize the great importance of this industry, and it is only within a comparatively few years that the supreme adaptability of the Annapolis Valley to the raising of apples and other fruits has become thoroughly recognized even by the more progressive fruit growers.

Now, indeed, our more advanced and enterprising farmers *are* devoting all the attention possible to this branch of their business, and it may be confidently asserted that before the end of the first quarter of the next century every available acre of this remarkable fruit belt will be clothed with orchard.

"Will not the increased production lower the price?"

Our most experienced fruit growers think not. Prices are better now on the average than when our product was only one-tenth of what it now is, and with the increasing demand for our fruit in the English and Continental markets, and with the enlarging demand for canned and evaporated fruit, it is not probable that with the fulfilment of our largest possibilities in the way of production in this valley present prices will be permanently lowered.

As we have already stated there are thousands of acres of land in Nova Scotia as well adapted to fruit growing as the best of this which yields such abundant returns; and the fruit growers of Nova Scotia will gladly welcome tens of thousands of intelligent inhabitants to utilize the vacant lands.

We have a magnificent climate, beautiful scenery, and a most charming country, and nowhere in the world do men and women live more comfortably and happily than among the orchards of Nova Scotia.

Any information will be gladly supplied on application to J. W. Bigelow, President of the Nova Scotia Fruit Growers' Association, Wolfville, Nova Scotia, or S. C. Parker, Secretary, Berwick, Nova Scotia.

Professor Saunders, Director of the Dominion Experimental Farm at Ottawa, says: "In Nova Scotia you have some of the finest apple orchards in the Dominion. Indeed, I know of no locality where trees bear so abundantly and continually as in your favored Annapolis Valley."

Professor Hind, of Kings College, Windsor, an eminent authority on fruit growing, says: "This valley with its soil and climate, particularly adapted to the development of this great industry, meets with no successful competition on the American Continent."

Judge Weatherbee, of Halifax, who has found time amid his professional duties to plant and superintend one of the largest orchards in the valley, says of our possibilities in the line of apple culture: "We have a belt containing about four hundred square miles, capable of producing an annual revenue of thirty million dollars. There is no land in the world that will yield like this valley, and we should plant the whole of it. There is no fear of raising more apples than are required. We can raise them more profitably than in any part of the world."

Mr. C. R. H. Starr, of Wolfville, writes in the Maritime Homestead that in 1880 the total export of apples from Nova Scotia to England had not reached 25,000 barrels, but five years later records show the export to have doubled, and in 1886 were exported 121,-000 barrels. The following season, however, the crop was small, and the export dropped to 57,000. The next five years the variation in quantity was not so great, averaging about 103,000 per season, and not exceeding 120,000 any season." In 1896 there were shipped 369,000 barrels and this figure has not yet been repeated. The crop for 1901 is estimated by Mr. Bigelow at 300,-000 barrels, that will yield nearly one million dollars."

While this favored region has been recently awakened to a sense of its great advantages for apple raising, it is by no means the only portion of the Province to be aroused to an effort in this direction. The movement has been general and the results most encouraging. In "ye olden time," not so far back but some of us can remember, it was considered the proper thing to plant a few apple trees on a new farm, and after a year or two they were expected to very largely, or altogether, shift for themselves, and whatever they yielded, sweet or sour, big or small, many or few, was received as the natural product of each tree, a sort of "manifest destiny" of the thing, and it could not do otherwise "so help me!" Sometimes the branches were gingerly lopped away, if they were dead for sure, and no thought was given to the cause of death. Woodpeckers tattooed the bark in long vertical lines of holes as if they were working out a pattern in their brains for amusement, and nothing else. That these trees must have a favorable position of sun and soil and fertilizer did not seem to be entertained. Some people *live* in this world, and many there are who simply hang on, merely exist, and the same thing may be seen with trees. There is a great difference between thriving and holding on by the "skin of the teeth." The poorer the care of the apple tree the more they were set upon by mosses and fungi and insects, like vermin that most abound on ill-fed, badly wintered calves. Determined to get something for nothing, the first sign of awakening interest was manifested in grafting the old tree-tops, with a view to make these monuments of neglect and abuse furnish the sap and substance for the goodly fruit of the new scion, but the great law holds everywhere, that you shall not take out of anything riches and power without giving an equivalent. Apple trees are long lived and hardy, but like everything else that lives, there comes an end at last. To profitably maintain grafted tops they must be ministered to in a way new to all their past experience. The next move has been to set out grafted stock sent out from the nurseries, and this has been done all over the Province. The result is that the apple belt that once was supposed to be confined to the area between the North and South Mountains, has been extended over all the peninsula, even to Cape Breton. All the Bay of Fundy counties are coming forward with good reports, and what was not expected, the Atlantic shore region produces apples second to none. In Yarmouth, North Queens, Lunenburg, are fine orchards, yielding good returns in fruit sold in the English market.

The gold mines of Nova Scotia have excited more interest than apple culture, but that is due to the fact that fortunes are sometimes quickly accumulated from that source, but whatever the economical value of these mines, it is far exceeded by the natural advantages afforded for raising apples in Nova Scotia.

CHAPTER XXV.

The county of Pictou lies on the southern shore of the Straits of Northumberland, along which it presents a length of about fifty miles. It extends into the interior to a distance of over twenty miles, being bounded on the south by the county of Guysborough, on the east by the county of Antigonish, and on the west by the county of Colchester. It was set off from the county of Colchester in 1792. It is divided into three townships—Pictou, Egerton, and Maxwelton. Their areas are as follows:

Pictou Township .... 215,360 acres
Egerton .... 239,600 acres
Maxwelton .... 222,400 acres

Pictou harbour is the largest and best on the northern shore of Nova Scotia. There is a bar at its mouth, but even at low tide, vessels drawing twenty feet can pass over in safety to the capacious basin. It is generally frozen over from the middle of December till the last of April. A few miles to the westward is the small harbour of Caribou, that has two principal entrances. About fifteen miles further to the westward is the only other harbour on that side of the county; this is the estuary of the River John, where there is some shelter from easterly and southerly winds.

Proceeding to the eastward from Pictou, we pass other harbours, known as Chance, Boat, Little, and Merigomish. The coast is generally low, scarcely in any place forming cliffs. The nature of the sandstones causes them to yield readily to the buffeting of the waves, that are rapidly changing the aspect of this whole shore. Even within the memory of aged people the inroads of the sea are very readily pointed out. The French made some small attempts at settlement in the eighteenth century, but when the American pioneers came, in 1767, all their belongings had long since been deserted. A few cellars and apple trees at the head of French Channel, and at the mouth of French River, together with rusted and broken implements, afforded the only visible evidence of their former occupancy.

The history of the people of this county begins with these settlers, whose descendants form a large proportion of the present population. After the peace of 1763, when there was no longer French posses-

NEW GLASGOW AND BRIDGE.

. OLDEST LOCOMOTIVE IN AMERICA, NOW AT NEW GLASGOW.

NEW GLASGOW. TEMPERANCE STREET.

sions to contend with, there was a determined effort made by the Government to settle the Province, and Pictou was not neglected. There was a good deal of granting land to speculators, in which Col. Alexander MacNutt took an active part, as he had done in Colchester, but his activity did not help the settlement, and his grant was escheated. Parties in Philadelphia organized into a company that dispatched a vessel in May, 1767, with six families of settlers. They were Dr. Harris and wife; Robert Patterson, who came as a surveyor for the company, his wife and five children; James MacCabe, with wife and six children; John Rogers, wife and four children; Henry Cumminger, wife and four children; and as sixth a family whose name is uncertain.

They reached Pictou Harbor on the 10th of June. These people endured many hardships, far more than they expected, as it most always turns out. After some delay they got into communication with the settlers of Truro by cutting a road through the woods, a difficult operation for a few persons.

Slowly arrived other venturesome men from Philadelphia and Truro, and after a half dozen years but little progress had been made, and it was not for lack of sturdy courage of those who began the work. In 1773 arrived the ship Hector with a number of Highland Scotch emigrants, and this was a notable event in the annals of the county. There were thirty-three families, making in all about two hundred people. Most of them had come from Rossshire. After a voyage lasting ten weeks the vessel dropped anchor in Pictou Harbor on the 15th of September. This was the beginning of Scotch immigration to these lower Provinces, that has proved of the greatest importance to their progress. These Highlanders who came in the Hector had been deceived by the agent, who had painted in glowing terms the advantages of the new country. They were not looking for the soft side of things, but were not adapted to the work that must be done. They were not axemen, but here was the forest to be cleared, before a crop could be raised. The lands assigned to them lay two and three miles from the coast, and the way to them was over a trackless wilderness. Squire Patterson and Dr. Harris, the agent of the Company, lived near Brown's Point, almost a half mile above the town site, and there they had erected a small store in which they kept the supplies of the Company. At this place the Highlanders were landed without provisions and without shelter, other than the rudest camps. Many of them wept, and all were sorely tried by hunger and exposure. They refused to settle on the lands of the Company, and for that reason were denied rations from the store. Their mountain blood was challenged and they took by force what they most needed, and could not be had by milder means. The Government came to the rescue of these people, but many of them went away to Truro and other parts. The other portion wintered as best they could and became the principal factors in the settlement of the county.

About seventy years ago there was a list of those passengers of the Hector drawn up by the late Mr. William McKenzie, of Loch Broom. It is not complete, but it runs as follows:

SHIPPED AT GLASGOW.

Mr. Scott and family. Unknown.

George Morrison and family. Settled on Barney's River.

John Patterson. Settled at Pictou.

George McConnell. Settled at West River.

Andrew Main and family.

Charles Frazer. Descendants at West River.

John Stewart. Unknown.

Andrew Wesley. Unknown.

FROM INVERNESSSHIRE.

William McKay and family. Settled on the East River, where he died March, 1828.

Roderick McKay and family. Settled on East River.

Conlin McKay and family. Settled on East River.

Hugh Fraser and family, from the parish of Kiltarlity. Settled on East River.

Donald Cameron and family. Settled on East River. Removed to Antigonish.

Donald MacDonald and family. Settled on Middle River.

Colin Douglas and family. Settled on Middle River.

Hugh Fraser and family. Settled on West River.

Alexander Fraser and family. Settled at Middle River. Said to be a relative of Lord Lovat, Chief of the Clan Fraser.

James Grant and family. Settled finally on East River.

Donald Munroe. Settled on west branch of East River.

PROVOST STREET, NEW GLASGOW, LOOKING NORTH.

POSTOFFICE, NEW GLASGOW.

HIGH SCHOOL, NEW GLASGOW.

FROM LOCH BROOM.

John Ross, agent. History unknown.

Alexander Cameron and family. Settled at Loch Broom. Died 1831, aged 103 years.

Alexander Ross and family.

Alexander Ross, son of the above Alexander. Settled on East River. Said to have reached the age of 104 years, and his child Duncan was on board the Hector, and died in 1871, the last of the passengers.

John Munroe and family. History unknown.

Kenneth MacRitchie and family. Unknown.

William McKenzie, a schoolmaster. Settled at Loch Broom.

John McGregor. History unknown.

John McLellan. Settled on a brook of that name.

William McLellan, a relative of the last. Settled at West River.

Alexander McLean. Settled at East River above Irishtown. One son settled on McLellan's Mountain.

Alexander Falconer. Settled near Hopewell.

Donald McKay. Settled at East River, just above the mines.

Archibald Chisholm. Believed to be the same person who settled at East River.

Charles Matheson. History unknown.

Robert Sim. Never married.

Alexander McKenzie. History unknown.

Thomas Fraser. History unknown.

FROM SUTHERLAND.

Kenneth Fraser and family. Settled first at Londonderry, but afterwards on Middle River.

William Fraser and family. History unknown.

James Murray and family. Settled in Londonderry. Descendants are there.

Walter Murray and family. Settled in Merigomish.

David Urquhart and family. Settled at Londonderry.

James McLeod and family. Settled at Middle River.

Hugh McLeod and family. Settled on West River.

Alexander McLeod and family. He was drowned in the Shubenacadie River. His descendants are at West River.

John McKay and family. History unknown.

Phillip McLeod and family. Uncertain.

23

Donald McKenzie and family. Probably settled at Shuben-acadie.

Alexander McKenzie and family. History unknown.

William Matheson and family. First settled at Londonderry, but afterwards came to Pictou. Settled at Roger's Hill.

Donald Grant. History unknown.

Donald Graham. History unknown.

John McKay, piper. Unknown.

William McKay. Name changed to McCabe.

John Sutherland. Settled at the mouth of Sutherland's River.

Angus McKenzie. Settled finally at Green Hill.

From 1776 to 1783 was the period of the American Revolutionary War, and the settlements of Pictou, although far away from the scene of the conflict, were nevertheless not a little disturbed. Most of the American settlers strongly sympathized with their countrymen at home who had taken up arms against England, while the Scotch maintained their attachment to the British Government. But one may well believe that there was no great heartiness about their allegiance, since it had been only a trifle over thirty years since Highlanders on Culloden's disastrous field had tried conclusions with the Duke of Cumberland's forces, and some of these pioneers were on that bloody field where the last blow was struck for king and country by the kilted mountaineers.

Rev. Dr. Patterson, in his History of the County of Pictou, an excellent work, to which I am largely indebted, says: "From the facts that have come to my knowledge regarding these people in Colchester, and the few settlers in Pictou who had come from the old colonies, we can positively assert that they generally sympathized with the Americans, and that a number were ready to take up arms to manifest their sympathy if there had appeared a favorable prospect of serving their cause."

Some of those who had come to Pictou, as well as to other parts of the Province, had brought negro slaves with them, and as a matter of interest here is a copy of a document to be found on the records of Pictou County:

"Know all men by these presents that I Archibald Allardice, of the Province of Nova Scotia, mariner, for and in consideration of the sum of forty pounds currency to me in hand paid by Dr. John Harris, of Truro, have made over, and sold, and bargained, and by

STELLARTON, PICTOU COUNTY.

WHITMAN'S FISHING ESTABLISHMENT. CANSO.

CANSO FROM LIGHTHOUSE ISLAND.

CANSO HARBOR AT SUNRISE.

these presents do bargain, make over, and sell to the aforesaid Dr. John Harris, one negro man named Sambo, aged twenty-five years or thereabouts, and also one brown mare, and her colt now sucking. To have and to hold the said negro man, and mare with her colt, as his property, for and in security of the above sum of money until paid with lawful interest. And at the payment of the above mentioned sum with interest and expenses, the aforesaid Doctor John Harris is by these presents firmly bound to deliver up to the aforesaid Archibald Allardice the said negro man, named Sambo, with the mare and colt, (casualities excepted). But if the said negro man, mare, or colt, should die before the said money should be paid, then in such proportion, I, The said Archibald Allardice, promise to make good the deficiency to the said Dr john Harris. In witness whereof I have hereunto set my hand and seal in the year of our Lord, one thousand seven hundred and eighty six, and in the twenty sixth of our Sovereign Lord, George the Third's Reign.

Archibald Allardice, L. S.

Signed, sealed, and delivered in presence of
James Phillips,
Robert Dunn."

Immediately after the close of the American war in 1783 the County of Pictou received considerable accessions to its population from disbanded regiments. These men for the most part were Highlanders of the Eighty-second or Hamilton's Regiment and the Eighty-fourth, known as the Royal Highlanders. Many of them came and looked over the prospect, or made some half-hearted attempt at settlement, and then went away to try their luck in other quarters. They were unmarried men, for the most part, and there were no opportunities to secure wives among the settlers, who had demands for all their girls.

A small number of families from Lunenburg, not well pleased with their outlook, had been induced by Colonel Des Barres to settle in Tatmagouche, where he had a grant of land, but he did not treat them well, and the sons of these pioneers and their families settled on the River John in Pictou County.

After a score of years a Presbyterian minister was secured in the person of Rev. James McGregor. He landed in Halifax, went to Truro, and rode over a path to Pictou. He says: "When I looked around the shores of the harbor I was greatly disappointed and cast down, for there was scarcely anything to be seen but woods growing down to the water's edge. Here and there a mean timber hut was visible in a small clearing, which appeared no bigger than a garden compared to the woods. Nowhere could I see two houses without woods between them."

We will get a good idea of the state of things by reading Dr. McGregor's account of his first religious public services as follows:

"Squire Patterson gave orders to lay slabs, and planks, in his barn for seats to the congregation; and before eleven o'clock next morning I saw the people gathering to hear the Gospel from the lips of a stranger, and a stranger who felt few of its consolations, and had but little hope of communicating them to his hearers. None came by land except certain families who lived a few miles to the right and left of Squire Patterson's. Those who came from the south side of the harbor, and from the river, had to come in boats or canoes, containing from one to seven or eight persons. The congregation, however was not large; for numbers could not get ready for the notice was so short. I observed that the conduct of some of them, coming from the shore to the barn, was as if they had never heard of a Sabbath. I heard loud talking and laughing, and singing and whistling, even before they reached the shore. They behaved, however, with decency so long as I continued to speak, and some of them were evidently much affected. I endeavored to explain to them in the forenoon in English, 'This is a faithful saying, and worthy of all acceptance, that Christ Jesus came into the world to save sinners;' and in the afternoon, in Gaelic, 'The Son of Man is come to seek and to save that which is lost.' The first words which I heard after pronouncing the blessing were from a gentleman of the army, calling to his companions, 'come, come, let us go to the grog shop;' but instead of going with him, they came to me, to bid me welcome to the settlement, and he came himself at last."

This was surely a field in great need of earnest workers. The good minister made choice of two very comforting texts, that seem to mean that all the lost will be saved somehow somewhere through the operations set in motion by the gospel. This was the beginning of Presbyterian preaching thereabouts in the county, and since that date there has been a goodly array of ministers of that faith. Other denominations gradually got a footing as the population increased. Dr. Patterson, writing twenty-five years ago, gave the following statistics:

STREET VIEW, PICTOU.

POSTOFFICE, PICTOU.

Y. M. C. A. BUILDING, PICTOU.

Presbyterian Church of the Lower Provinces. . . 14,105
Church of Scotland 12,250
Roman Catholics 2,065
Church of England 1,470
Wesleyan Methodists 797
Baptists 345
All others 193

Through much tribulation Pictou Academy was founded in 1817 with the Rev. Dr. McCulloch as President, and instructor in Greek, Hebrew, Logic, Moral Philosophy and Natural Philosophy. This admirable and most useful man came from Scotland in 1803, and died in Halifax in 1843. This institution was the cause of much discussion, as it seemed to the Episcopalians a menace to Kings College, and something to be sternly discouraged by loyal subjects of the king. In one sense it was but a tempest in a teapot, but it is now a matter of some interest to see how much of the old "grounds" of bigotry and intolerance was roiled up to the surface by the commotion that involved bishops, grave councillors, governors and judges. Here is an extract from a speech in the House of Assembly by Thomas C. Haliburton (Sam Slick), who was a member of the Church of England and a graduate of Kings College, but kept his head above the level of sectarian malaria and its deplorable accompaniments: "I will never consent that this seminary of education for Dissenters shall be crushed to satisfy the bigotry of a few individuals in this town, who have originated, fostered and supported all the opposition to Pictou Academy. I do not mean to say that they directly influenced those gentlemen in this house who oppose the bill, but their influence reaches to people who are not conscious of it themselves. They are in a situation to give a tone to public opinion. Few men take the trouble to form just conclusions on any subject, but adopt the sentiments of those whose judgment they respect. In this manner they hint, 'ambitious Scotchmen at Pictou,' 'sour sectarians,' 'disloyal people,' 'opposed to church and state.' Their hints circulated from one to another, men hear it they know not where, adopt it they know not how, and finally give it as their opinion; until you find honest and honorable men, as you have heard to-day, pronounce a judgment evidently tinctured by the breath of poison, which they are wholly unconscious of having inhaled."

Haliburton, in his History of Nova Scotia, written in 1828, says of this institution: "As a dissenting academy, it has encountered

much opposition, and although it has always received the support
of a very large and respectable majority of the House of Assembly,
the Council rejected last year not only the bill for its permanent
endowment, but also the annual allowance of four hundred pounds,
and even a vote to discharge a part of the debt which the trustees
had incurred in its progress.   It is now left to struggle with these
difficulties, and the salaries of its officers are raised by the voluntary
contributions of its friends.   It is foreign to the design of this
work to enter into local politics; we shall therefore not detail the
particulars of the controversy, nor the reasonings of the contending
parties, but it may be permitted us to express a regret that the
opposition of a few individuals should have succeeded in withhold-
ing the funds from an institution that is both useful and respectable,
and one that has always enjoyed the decided approbation of the
representatives of the people."

Says Dr. Patterson in his History of Pictou County: "To
avoid exciting the jealousy of the friends of Kings College, who
were really all powerful in the Government, it was resolved not
to seek the right of conferring degrees or the other privileges of a
college.   Hence the name, Pictou Academy, though from the first
it was intended to impart the education usual in colleges."

Perhaps it will give a keener edge to the enjoyment of our
liberties and privileges if we are not allowed to forget what they
cost to the brave men who fought for them.   To come in contact
with the conduct of those dead lions gives a fillip to the nerves, and
makes the fingers tingle, to tackle some fortified abuse without
gloves.   We read that the dead body of a certain man was hastily
let down into the tomb of Elisha the prophet and when it happened
to touch his bones "he revived and stood upon his feet."   The
bones of our modern Elishas are not without virtue, and to come
in contact with such men as Dr. McCulloch may well cause a thrill
to run through a man who is very much of a corpse, and yet able
to be up and about.   The demand for men of this stamp will never
cease.   We are not face to face with the bigotry that cast its
armed tentacles about his noble efforts, but we are beset with other
dangers to the state that call for valiant service.   We need men who
can stand before a demagogue

"And damn his treacherous flatteries without winking;
Tall men, sun-crowned, who live above the fog
In public duty and in private thinking."

PICTOU ACADEMY.

LIGHTHOUSE. PICTOU.

PICTOU HARBOR R. R. TERMINUS

I. C. R DOCKS, PICTOU.

With this little aside we proceed with a word more about our subject. The town of Pictou occupies a commanding position on a hillside over a small cove on the north side of the harbor, and nearly opposite; the basin is divided into three arms, into which flow the East, Middle, and West Rivers. The population is 3,235.

The town of New Glasgow, situated on the East River in the midst of many natural advantages, is one of the most prosperous in the province. The population is now 4,447, and has been for several years rather rapidly increasing. The coal mines of this county have been described in the chapter on coal to be found in this volume and therefore need not be repeated here. Dr. Patterson says: "Farming is still the leading industry of the country, the number engaged in it, according to the census of 1871, being more than equal to the number employed in all other lines of business. Altogether we may set down Pictou as the first agricultural county in the province, the only one which can compete with it being Kings.

GEOLOGY OF PICTOU COUNTY.

If one follow Sir William Dawson's geological map of 1863 he will find the rock distribution as follows: The Carboniferous area of Cumberland extends over the county line between the coast and the Cobequid uplift, and continues along the shore to the Antigonish line, the latter half of this distance in a belt about five miles wide. With the exception of two shall granite areas all the rest of the county is set down as Silurian.

One of the privileges that a man has over those enjoyed by a donkey is the ability to change his mind, or, in other words, his conclusions as the result of new facts or new feelings. Sir William could do that in every direction but the one where his theological dogmas were involved, and there he seemed to hold that it was so much the worse for the facts if they did not agree with him, thus maintaining with Josh Billings, that "When a feller is right he can't be too conservative." In the third edition of his Acadian Geology, 1878, Dr. Dawson introduces a sketch map that admits an area of the Devonian formation, and this was something to be expected. In 1889 Sir William published his hand-book of Canadian Geology, in which he says of a portion of Pictou County: "Crossing over to Nova Scotia, we have in the Cobequid Mountains a great series of slates, quartzites and volcanic rocks, evidently underlying the Silurian Wentworth series, but destitute of fossil remains. These, with their continuation in the district extending eastward from the Cobequids to the Strait of Canso and into Cape Breton, were characterized by me in 1850 as consisting of various slates and quartzites, with syenite, greenstone, compact feldspar, claystone and porphyry, and were named in the Acadian Geology the "Cobequid group," and their age defined as intermediate between that of the lower Arisaig fossiliferous series and the Gold series (Cambrian) of the Atlantic Coast. As they had afforded no fossils, and as there seemed to be a lithological and statigraphical connection between them and the lower part of the Silurian, they were placed with that series as a downward extension, or, in part, metamorphosed members of it. The arrangement of these rocks in the central part of the Cobequids, and also between the East River of Pictou and the east branch of the St. Mary's River, may be thus stated: There is a central mass of red intrusive syenitic granite, usually having a large predominance of red orthoclase, with a moderate quantity of hornblende and quartz; this sends veins into the overlying beds, and is itself penetrated by dykes of diabase. On this central mass rests a great thickness of felsites, porphyries, felsitic agglomerates, and diorite, evidently of volcanic origin. Upon these are gray, black, and reddish slates and quartzites, with a bed of limestone penetrated by metallic veins. The lower volcanic portion and the upper more strictly aqueous parts might perhaps be separated as a Lower and Upper Cobequid series; but the difference appears to depend rather on mode of disposition than on any great difference of age. Along the northern side of the Cobequids, and between Pictou and Arisaig, these beds are seen immediately to underlie the Silurian rocks, which have been disturbed with them, and are penetrated by the same igneous dykes. I have no doubt of the identity of the greater part of the altered and volcanic beds of the hilly country extending through Pictou and Antigonish Counties, and underlying the Silurian, with the Cobequid series."

The Canadian Geological Survey has extended the formation series by adding the Permian areas, so that we have a portion of the geological order in the Cambrian, Silurian, Devonian, Carboniferous and Permian. Evidently there is yet a fine field for geological work in this county, especially in the oldest outcrops, where more fossils might well give a desirable definiteness to existing tentative classification.

CHAPTER XXVI.

AGRICULTURE.

Nova Scotia is so rich in the products of forests, sea, mines, and quarries, that she might be considered well endowed by Nature, even though the soil were stingy and unproductive of agricultural products; but taking into consideration the practically insular location of the Province, the temperate latitude, the variety of rock-formation, and all the physiographic factors, it follows that there must be valuable agricultural districts where farmers can plant and sow to their profit. No one expects to find here opportunities for raising vast quantities of grains, and roots, in fields of thousands of acres in extent; but it is true that available resources for successful cultivation of the soil have been as yet turned to comparatively small account. The science of agriculture has been one of the latest contributions of the Spirit of the Age. There could be nothing worthy this designation, until chemistry was able to analyze the soils, and fertilizers, and structural botany by the aid of the microscope had penetrated the secrets of plant life, and learned what elements, and combinations of elements, were demanded for their healthy growth. It is now generally recognized that in vital importance no industry can take precedence of the agricultural pursuits, that prevent the human race from starving. Ministers of Agriculture are rather late acquisitions to governmental cabinets. The civilized world with its greatly increasing populations has awakened to the importance of scientific agriculture. Scores of chemical laboratories in Europe and America are now supported by public funds, and are entirely devoted to the problems of agriculture. Farmers as a class have been slow to take up with the discoveries and suggestions that have cost them nothing. They have gone from generation to generation, since man first planted seed, in practices that had in them a good deal of hit or miss, and thus they often laid to bad luck what in reality was the natural results of ignorance of the laws that governed the growth of their crops, or of indolence in supplying the evident means of success. The old practices have passed, or are rapidly passing away. A new dispensation has broken full upon this ancient brotherhood that tilled the soil with crude implements and weary toil, till they urged the artistic genius of Millet to picture him on the rocky acres he does not own, grasping with toil-crooked fingers

361

his rude hoe, over which he painfully stoops, while he gazes vacantly about him. This is the "Man With a Hoe" who moved to immortal verse the muse of Markham, in which he called the world to note this figure as

> " Bowed by the weight of centuries he leans
> Upon his hoe and gazes on the ground,
> The emptiness of ages in his face,
> And on his back the burden of the world."

The poet with the license of his craft overdrew the wretchedness of the class, here and there, but we have only to go to enlightened Germany and Austria and other portions of Europe to see women yoked with beasts, to plows, and harrows, and in the oriental world the lot of the agricultural laborer is even more severe and degrading. Until recently in England, for a thousand years his lot has been one of grinding hardships, and for the most part but little better than slavery. His utmost exertions on his landlord's estate could neither furnish him with the most ordinary comforts of life nor keep him from ending his days as a pauper. To raise rabbits, deer, pheasants and grouse seemed of vastly more importance to English legislators than it did to give the men who raised their bread a chance to make homes on the lands designated by Nature for the use of human beings. Writing in 1821, Robert Owen, the reformer, expressed in the following words the farmer's future, as he saw it, and we are witnessing the fulfilment of his prediction:

"Agriculture, instead of being, as heretofore, the occupation of the mere peasant and farmer, with minds as defective in their cultivation as their soils, will then become the delightful employment of a race of men trained in the best habits and dispositions, familiar with the most useful practices in the arts and sciences, and with minds fraught with the most valuable information and extensive general knowledge—capable of forming and conducting combined arrangements in agriculture, trade, commerce and manufacture far superior to those which have yet existed in any of these departments, as they have been hitherto disjoined and separately conducted. It will be readily perceived that this is an advance in civilization and general improvement that is to be effected solely through science of the influence of circumstances over human nature and the knowledge of the means by which those circumstances may be easily controlled."

This new dispensation is now at our doors: it is being ushered in with all manner of labor-saving devices. The oldest sickles have been found in Egyptian tombs that antedate the use of iron, and they are but crooked curves of wood in which are set teeth of flint; from that implement to the fully equipped harvester of to-day is a vast stride of progress, but the strangest part of it is the fact that our sickles are still hanging about the old barns and attics. The flint sickles gave place to iron about five thousand years ago, and there matters rested until the last decades of the last century. With surprising suddenness agricultural implements made their appearance. With the new inventions have come the new sciences, that contribute to the success of agriculture in a marked degree; in fact they were essential to its success.

The researches of chemists, naturalists and geologists are daily contributing to the elucidation of agricultural principles and problems. The farmer will find ample use for all his intellectual learning that a college course may have secured in an occupation that is at once an art, a science and a business. In every farming community there should be, and there will be, local museums where all plants, insects, birds, rocks, minerals and soils of the region will be collected and preserved as specimens and the new farmer will find that in more ways than one it will pay to "consider the lilies how they grow."

In order to show in a connected manner a general view of the farming resources of Nova Scotia, I have here introduced the official report for 1898 of the Secretary of Agriculture, B. W. Chipman, Esq. It is contemplated that this volume will be largely circulated outside of our Province, where in pamphlet form the report would never reach. This should be read with the chapter on fruit raising and other items related to agriculture in order to get a fair idea of the prospects afforded by this locality for intelligent, industrious people who are looking for opportunities in a healthy climate, under the British flag, to make them homes and a living by cultivation of the soil and its products.

SKETCH OF THE PROVINCE OF NOVA SCOTIA FROM AN AGRICULTURAL STANDPOINT.

"Having in the preceding pages given a general outline of the geographical position, physical features, general resources, population, educational and social advantages of Nova Scotia, I purpose, with the aid of the map enclosed in this pamphlet, to give a bird's-

eye view of the agricultural progress and capabilities of the Province east and west, making Halifax, the provincial capital, the starting point, and following the lines of railway which radiate from it.
One of these, the Intercolonial, pretty well covers the central and
eastern counties of the Province, and the other one, the Dominion
Atlantic, with its connections, covers the larger portion of the
western counties. They both use a common line as far as Windsor
Junction, fourteen miles from the city, and then radiate east and
west respectively. Following the Intercolonial we find the country
rocky, barren and unproductive, but exceedingly picturesque
through the lake region, until we reach Oakfield, where the soil
begins to show evidence of being productive.

At Enfield, twenty-eight miles from Halifax, the farms are all
well adapted for raising hay, grain and all sorts of roots and vegetables. Two miles further on Elmsdale is reached, a village of
about two hundred inhabitants. Here the extent of farm lands
widens, running west into the fertile county of Hants and east in a
good farming region in Halifax County. The land is uniformly
good; farms range in size from seventy-five to two hundred acres,
with comfortable buildings, and in value from $1,000 to $4,000.

Milford, six miles further on, is a small village with a population
of 175 inhabitants. This is about the head of the tide-waters of the
Shubenacadie River, a sinuous stream which has its start in the
Grand Lake and empties its waters in Cobequid Bay. It is enriched
by the tidal waters of the bay, which bring up a rich deposit, peri-
odically overflowing the land and keeping it in a permanent state
of fertility. The dike-lands on this river are as rich as any land
in the world, as are all the lands in Nova Scotia drawing their fertility from the same source. No artificial or other fertilizers are
ever used or needed in these lands, the natural conditions making
them practicably inexhaustible. At Milford there are several fine
farms. Excellent upland farms extend east and west into Halifax
and Hants Counties respectively. The land is of a naturally good
quality, and is susceptible of a high state of cultivation. It can be
purchased at a moderate price.

Crossing over the Shubenacadie River at this point and going
east two or three miles, Gay's River is reached, a fine settlement
of thrifty farmers. Gay's River district embraces Lake Egmont, a
small lake which constitutes its source, Antrim Settlement and
Dutch Settlement. All this region possesses good, cultivable lands,

and on the margins of Lake Egmont, and this river and small tributary streams are fine intervale lands. Farms and lands can be bought in this section at very reasonable rates. The land is admirably adapted for the grazing of sheep and cattle. Continuing east we strike the rich and fertile region of the Musquodoboit Valley, a very fertile belt of land following the course of the river for several miles. This region embraces the˙Lower, Middle and Upper Settlements, the Taylor Settlement and Meagher's Grant. The land in all this section of country is of high class quality, and mostly kept in a fine state of cultivation, though in many instances there is marked room for improvement. There are few more thrifty and attractive agricultural communities in Nova Scotia than the Middle Settlement of Musquodoboit. A railway is projected and route surveyed through this fine section of country, which when built, as it doubtless shortly will be, will greatly enhance the profits of farming in this region. Farm lands and properties can now be bought at prices ranging from $1,000 to $8,000.

Coming back to the Intercolonial Railway at Shubenacadie, four miles east of Milford, we strike a flourishing and prosperous village of 3ʹ50 inhabitants, having all modern conveniences, including electric light. It is situated in the midst of a splendid agricultural district, embracing hundreds of acres of rich dike marsh and fine uplands. The farmers here are mostly engaged in supplying milk for the Halifax market, the abundance of fodder enabling them to keep fine herds of milk cows. Hay is produced here in large quantities, and grains, and all sorts of roots and vegetables grow and mature abundantly. Farms can be bought here for from $2,000 to $10,000. There are several adjoining settlements well adapted for farming, nearly all upland, and much of it well wooded. Farms and lands in these outlying districts may be had at moderate prices, which with intelligent cultivation could soon be brought up to first class condition.

The next station is Stewiacke, in Colchester County, a thrifty and growing village, with a population of 250. It has a foundry and a large steam saw mill, the latter of which gives employment to a large number of men. The dike. land here is of the same quality as at Shubenacadie. The village is on the river of the same name, and the tide flows up three or four miles above the station. The river drains a large and fertile region of country, possessing the same characteristics as the Musquodoboit Valley.

The Stewiacke Valley, about thirty miles in length, is a rich and beautiful section of country, and contains many prosperous and well cultivated farms. The different settlements, Upper, Middle and Lower, Pembroke, Springside, Eastville, and Otter Brook, have all the accessories of advanced agricultural communities. Upper Stewiacke maintains a creamery. A railway is projected, and will probably be in operation in this valley in a few years, which will greatly enhance the value of farms. They can now be bought at prices ranging from $1,000 to $5,000.

After leaving Stewiacke, Brookfield is the next station of agricultural importance on the line of the Intercolonial. It is a community of some two hundred inhabitants, and is a very fine farming section of Colchester, possessing a large acreage of fine bottom lands, and uplands of excellent quality. It is well adapted for dairying, and has a cheese and butter factory, which has been operated for some years with encouraging success. The hay grown on its broad acres is of excellent quality, and all kinds of grains, roots and vegetables grow well. The hills by which it is surrounded form excellent grazing and pasturage for both cattle and sheep. It is only eight miles from Truro, the shire town of the county, and one of the most prosperous and progressive towns of the Province.

Truro is situated in the heart of the fine agricultural County of Colchester, at the head of Cobequid, is an important railway center, and possesses foundries, carriage factories, a hat factory, a peg factory, furniture factories, and several smaller manufacturing industries, and also the largest milk condensing factory in the Dominion. It is an educational center, being the seat of the Provincial Normal School, where the great bulk of the teachers of the common schools of this Province, and a great proportion of the teachers of the other Maritime Provinces, receive their training. The Provincial Government maintains a farm quite near to the town, in connection with a school of agriculture, where young men are fitted for practical and scientific farming without any tuition fees. Truro has a population of about six thousand, and affords a ready market for farmers within its radius. It is surrounded on three sides by magnificent farm lands, the most of which has been brought to a high state of cultivation. It is on the Salmon River, which empties its waters into Cobequid Bay, the tides from which have formed the rich dike lands containing many hundreds of acres which lie along its banks. The districts of Upper and Lower

Onslow, and Fort Belcher and Clifton, all of which may fairly be called outlying portions of Truro, are all illustrations of prosperous husbandry carried on under the most favorable conditions. The places named lie to the west and south of Truro. Their broad dike lands and marshes are most prolific in the production of hay, and of hay of the very best quality. As before mentioned, these dike lands never require any artificial fertilizers, and produce a most luxurious growth from generation to generation, without exhibiting any signs of exhaustion. To the north and east lie the North River and the Salmon River districts, both of them fine agricultural districts. The farmers in all these sections are thrifty and prosperous, and have comfortable homes, big barns and out-buildings for stock, etc. Prices range from $2,000 to $10,000.

Following down the western shore of the Cobequid Bay from Truro, we find an excellent farming country for many miles, where rich dike lands and undulating upland and hills abound. First, Masstown, a good agricultural district; next, Folly Village; then, Great Village. All this region presents a splendid field for raising stock for either beef or dairy purposes, while farming can be and is conducted with a degree of success fully equal to the efforts put forth. Masstown has a population of 150; Folly, of 400; and Great Village, 600. Below Great Village are Economy and Five Islands, both good agricultural districts, but where a good many of the inhabitants lead a mixed life of farming, and fishing in the bay. Farm prices, $1,000 to $3,000.

Three or four miles northeast of Great Village lies Acadia Mines, the seat of a large iron industry, with a population of 1,800, and thus affording a good local market for the surrounding country. Not far from Acadia Mines, on the borderlands of Colchester and Cumberland Counties, chiefly in Cumberland, are the Westchester Mountains, where there is an immense section of grazing lands, capable of maintaining many thousands of sheep. It is a magnificent forest region, as well, and these lands can be bought very cheaply.

Lying to the north of Truro are Earltown, New Annan, Waugh's River, Tatamagouche, and Brule. Tatamagouche is a village on the Northumberland Straits, which separate this Province from Prince Edward Island, and is in the midst of a fine agricultural section, famous for its hay, grains, and capital grazing lands. Waugh's River possesses many good farms, as does Earltown and

New Annam. Apples and plums are successfully cultivated in this region of Colchester. This is what is called the northern section of the county, and embraces an area of many thousands of acres, large portions of which only wait the hand of industry to make it blossom as the rose. Where the land is occupied and tilled the people are thrifty and prosperous, with good dwelling-houses and outhouses. In all the districts named there are stores and churches, and excellent common schools. Farms range in prices from $1,000 to $5,000. Farm and forest lands, without buildings, may be bought at exceedingly low prices.

Again coming back to Truro and following the line of the Intercolonial as it proceeds into Cumberland County, after passing Belmont, Debert, East Mines, Londonderry, and Folly stations, all of which are in Colchester County, we will pass all intermediate stations in Cumberland until we reach Amherst, the chief town of that great agricultural county, and near the border line between this Province and New Brunswick. Amherst has a population of 3,981. It contains foundriés, machine shops, car works, boiler and engine works, a boot and shoe factory, and other factories, giving employment to a large number of people, and furnishing a good local market. Amherst lies in the midst of a splendid agricultural distriet, having vast stretches of dike marsh land embracing thousands of acres. The districts of Nappan and Maccan, lying four and eight miles, respectively, east of Amherst, are made up largely of these prolific and exhaustless dikelands, and the adjoining uplands are of a very rich quality. At Nappan is situated the Dominion Experimental Farm for the Maritime Provinces, where tests are made of roots, vegetables, fruits, grains, stock, etc., best adapted for our soil and climate. The Maccan River, west of Amherst, eight miles, is bordered by dikelands of great value, and proceeding westerly we strike River Hibbert, also a dikeland region of considerable extent. A few miles further west is the Minudie River, with the "Elysian Field," as the great dike of Minudie has been called. The Maccan, the Hibbert, and the Minudie Rivers all empty their waters in the Bay of Fundy, from whose rich tides they draw the fertilizing element which makes the lands on their margins of such exhaustless quality. The sections enriched by these streams are all thickly settled and prosperous farming communities. From Minudie, going westerly, we reach Southampton, West Brook, and Half Way River, and thence to Parrsboro, a town of 1,900 inhabitants, about thirty-six miles distant from Amherst. The country along this route is dotted with excellent farms, good buildings, and supports a thrifty population generally. Farms range in value from $2,coo to $10,000.

Following the shore from Parrsboro, through Diligent River, Spencer's Island to Advocate Harbor, we pass through a section of country, forty miles in extent, somewhat hilly, but containing a great deal of good farm land and a large quantity of excellent timber land. In the days of wooden ships a great many vessels were built along this shore.

Pugwash is an important town of Cumberland County, about thirty miles from Amherst, following the line,of the post road, which carries one through the thriving agricultural settlements of Shinimicas and River Philip. This is all a good farming country, mostly upland, with good interval lands along the margins of the streams, comfortable farm houses and outbuildings, and prices ranging from $1,000 to $3,000.

Following the Amherst shore to Pugwash, we take in the settlements of Tidnish, Northport, and Linden, a distance of about forty-five miles, thickly settled with good farms all along the route.

Pugwash has a population of 700. For many years it has been noted for the shipment of immense quantities of deals to the Old Country, and it still continues to do so. A large amount of business is transacted in this town. It is surrounded by admirable farms, which cut vast quantities of hay and carry a considerable quantity of stock. The River Philip runs into the harbor at Pugwash.

Continuing along the gulf shore for ten miles, Wallace is reached, another important shipping place, noted for its extensive freestone quarries, and surrounded by splendid farm lands. Passing Wallace and continuing along the shore, through a fertile and productive country, Tatamagouche is reached, before mentioned in our brief sketch of Colchester County.

I may here add that a branch of the Intercolonial, called the Short Line, shoots off at Oxford Junction, crosses through a fairly well settled section of Cumberland County to Pugwash, on to Wallace, Tatamagouche and Brule, and thence to River John, in Pictou County, and on to Pictou, the chief town of that county, about twenty miles from River John. River John is a pretty village, where formerly an extensive shipbuilding business was carried on. When, owing to the introduction of iron ships, the business of building

24

wooden ships declined here as elsewhere in Nova Scotia, the people
of this section of the country turned their attention to farming and
to lobster-fishing. The farm lands in this section are good, and with
proper tillage could be brought into excellent condition, but, as
the people have never made a special business of agriculture, farms
with comfortable and useful buildings may be purchased at very low
prices. Pictou town contains a population of 3,000. It is a town
of considerable wealth, and is a shipping place of importance, having
daily steamship connection with Prince Edward Island and other
maritime Province ports.

A few miles from Pictou lies the lively and bustling town of New
Glasgow, being the principal trade center of the county. New Glasgow had population in 1891 of 3,776. It has grown considerably
since that date. Within a radius of eight miles of New Glasgow are
the thriving towns of Ferrona and Hopewell, Stellarton, Westville,
Trenton, and Thorburn, the combined populations of which reach
about 10,000. These towns have been largely built up through the
coal and iron mines and the steel industries which have grown out
of the production of the mines. They furnish, in conjunction with
New Glasgow, a capital local market for the farmers of the county.
Pictou County has long been an important seat of the great coal-
mining industry of the Province. The production of iron is a later
growth. Of the country generally as an agricultural field it may
be said to take high rank. It is intersected in every direction with
rivers and streams, along the margins of which are fine interval
lands. It is filled with hills and valleys, the soil of which is generally
fertile and much of it very productive. It is admirably adapted for
grazing, and is capable of keeping immense flocks of sheep. The
population is distinguished for thrift and intelligence, and the county
is dotted all over with comfortable homes and good farms. It is
a large county, and much of it remains still open for settlement.
It is quite capable of sustaining in comfort three or four times its
present population. Prices of farms, with good buildings, range
from $1,500 to $8,000, according to size, quality, and location.

From New Glasgow, following the Eastern Branch of the Intercolonial Railway, and passing through a section of fine farming lands
and more or less prosperous districts, the beautiful town of Antigonish is reached, a town of 3,000 population, and the shire town of
the county of the same name. Antigonish is a fine agricultural
county, but the inhabitants—a considerable section of it lying on

the sea—combine fishing with farming as a regular employment. Antigonish has a splendid acreage of good uplands, and stretches of magnificent intervals. It is one of the best grazing counties in the Province, and is capable of producing large numbers of cattle and sheep. It is noted for the excellence of its dairy products, and has now in operation several cheese factories. Farms range in value from $500 to $4,000.

Adjoining Antigonish County is the County of Guysboro, chiefly noted for its extensive and rich gold mines and its valuable shore fisheries. Yet there are two very fine farming sections in the county, capable of much greater development. The west end of the county, known as St. Mary's District—not many miles from Sherbrooke, a town of 1,000 inhabitants—contains farm lands of great fertility. Along the St. Mary's River are stretches of splendid intervals, and the farmers are generally thrifty and prosperous. The section lying east of this, and covering about forty miles to Guysboro town, can hardly be ranked as first-class farming land. Sheep-farming could be profitably conducted on a great deal of this part of the county: It is pretty well settled, and prices range low. Guysboro town is the capital of the county, and has a population of 1,800. It is a seaport town and is devoted to general trade. Opposite Guysboro, a magnificent harbor lying between, is the village of Manchester, surrounded by a fine section of country similar in quality to the beautiful lands of St. Mary's District.

CAPE BRETON.

Following the Intercolonial Railway through Antigonish County and a small portion of Guysboro, the Strait of Canso is reached, which separates the Island of Cape Breton from the mainland. The strait is about a mile wide and is crossed by steamers run in connection with the Intercolonial. Landing at Port Hawkesbury, which is situate near the dividing line between the counties of Inverness and Richmond, and proceeding by rail and passing by River Inhabitant, West Bay, River Denis, crossing the Grand Narrows, following the shore of the Bras d'Or Lakes to North Sydney, thence following the North West Arm, we reach Sydney Town, the terminus of the Intercolonial Railway in the Island of Cape Breton.

The island is divided into four counties, namely, Richmond and Cape Breton, lying to the northeast and Inverness and Victoria, lying to the southwest. Of these Inverness is the largest, and beyond all doubt the best agricultural county. If we start from Port Hawkesbury, we soon reach River Inhabitant, River Denis, and the head of West Bay. River Inhabitant and River Denis traverse fine agricultural districts, containing many excellent farms, having large stretches of fertile interval lands. Prices are exceedingly low, considering the intrinsic value of land from an agricultural standpoint. Farms with more or less comfortable buildings can be had at prices ranging from $800 to $2,000. If we follow the strait from Port Hawkesbury, passing Port Hastings and continuing the shore, we reach Port Hood, the capital of the County of Inverness, and containing a population of 1,500. Proceeding thence, we come to Broad Cove, where coal mines of vast extent are now being opened up, and which in all probability will soon be the seat of a mining town. At Broad Cove and Strathlorne excellent farms are found, with splendid intervals, capable of producing great crops of hay and grain, and all other farm products. Prices range from $1,000 to $3,000.

Ten miles from Port Hood is the village and farming settlement of Mabou, an exceedingly rich and fertile district; in fact, taking it for all in all, and barring fruit, it cannot be surpassed by any other district in the Province. And even the cultivation of fruit might, with proper attention, become a profitable pursuit in this district, as apples and plums are grown to some extent, and I have seen fairly well-matured grapes on vines at Mabou that were grown and ripened in the open air. Leaving Mabou and passing Hillsboro and Brook Village, both fine farming districts, we reach picturesque Whycocomagh, at the head of a section of Bras d'Or Lake. The scenery is magnificent, the farms are good, and recent gold discoveries have drawn great attention to the district. Continuing east about twenty-five miles, we come to Baddeck, in Victoria County. But continuing Inverness, through the best farming districts, we would touch Lake Ainslie. Along the margin of this lake for about fifteen miles on either side are excellent farms, and to be had at very low prices.

Passing Lake Ainslie, we come to South West Margaree, a beautiful stream which we follow quite a number of miles to Margaree Forks, where the waters of the North East Margaree join the waters of the South West and thence they flow onward until they enter Margaree harbor. These two branches of the Margaree River are noted for the beautiful scenery through which they flow, and also noted for the trout and salmon which abound in them. They constitute a veritable paradise for sportsmen, who fiock there in great numbers in the fishing season, not only from Halifax, but from the United States as well. The beautiful intervals and fine upland farms to be found along their banks are the admiration of all who taken an interest in stock-raising or dairy-farming. Farms may be had from $1,000 to $4,000.

The entire shore of Inverness County from Port Hawkesbury to Cheticamp constitutes a valuable fishing ground.

As this county possesses large sections of valuable agricultural lands, and is not thickly settled, it offers a capital field for the thrifty, industrious, and intelligent agricultural emigrant, who at the cost of a very moderate outlay would soon find himself in the possession of a comfortable and prosperous farm with pleasant and picturesque surroundings.

From North East Margaree, in this county, before referred to, we drive for several miles, through a section of country in which there are not many farms to note, but which is characterized by very beautiful scenery. The road passes between two forest-clad mountains and skirts the margins of a lovely chain of lakes until we reach the head of Middle River, in Victoria County. Following down the river, the valley between the mountains widens and the fertile intervals expand. For upwards of fifteen miles prosperous farming settlements are found on each side of the river. The valley of the Middle River presents a charming picture to the eye by virtue of its bewitching scenery, and the excellent farms attest to the comfort and prosperity of the farmers. It is a favorite resort of tourists from the United States, the excellent trout-fishing in the river forming an extra attraction. Farms in this valley range in price from $1,000 to $2,000.

Leaving Middle River valley and driving about eight miles through picturesque scenery, Big Baddeck is reached. The farms on the Big Baddeck are good, the soil is rich, with large stretches of intervals. Crossing another ridge of good upland we reach the beautiful town of Baddeck, the capital of the county, with a population of 1,700. It is a shipping port, beautifully situated in the Bras d'Or Lakes, and is surrounded by hills. There are many fine farms in the vicinity of Baddeck, and much good land that could easily be brought into a state of excellent cultivation. Baddeck

is a center of summer tourist travel from the United States from
which searchers after health, sport, and romantic and picturesque
scenery spread all over the Island of Cape Breton. Going west
from Baddeck and passing many fine farms, we again come to
Whycocomagh, in Inverness County, before described. Thence going east fifteen miles, the headwaters of St. Ann's, in Victoria
County, are struck. St. Ann's is an arm of the sea, noted for its
excellent fisheries. Boularderie, an island in the Bras d'Or Lake,
part of which is in Victoria County, is covered with capital farms,
and the waters by which it is surrounded are excellent fishing
grounds. It is twenty-two miles long and seven miles broad.

A large coal mine is being operated in this county near the shore
of the Bras d'Or Lake.

Cape Breton County, which lies southeast of Victoria, is noted
chiefly for its immense coal deposits. It is the seat of the operations
of the General Mining Association, a wealthy corporation, mostly
controlled by British capital, which has been carrying on coal-mining
in this county for a great many years, and also the Dominion Coal
Company, which in 1893 acquired leases of many valuable collieries
in the county, and having an immense capital, is conducting the
work on a very extensive scale. This company last year, 1897,
raised 1,262,484 tons of coal, and gave employment to 20,196 men.
The company is composed of United States and Canadian capitalists,
and since its organization has displayed great energy and enterprise in carrying on its business. The great coal-mining industry
has been the means of building up in Cape Breton County many
flourishing towns and villages, chief among which are Sydney
Mines, Sydney, and North Sydney, the two latter towns being shipping places of considerable importance, and they constitute the
termini of the Intercolonial Railway in the Island of Cape Breton.
Cape Breton contains the historic town of Louisburg, and other
towns of importance are Little Glace Bay and Port Morien. There
are several smaller villages, and all these communities combined
constitute a valuable market for the farmers of the county and the
island generally. There are several good agricultural districts in this
county. The land in close proximity to Sydney and North Sydney
is of good quality. There are good stretches of interval lands
at Sydney Forks, and also at East Bay, on the Mira River especially,
and at other points. The fishing industry of Cape Breton County
is quite an important one. The eastern end of Boularderie Island,

before referred to in the brief sketch of Victoria County, as an island of fine agricultural fertility, belongs to this county. As the mining and fishing industries of this county give employment to a large number of men, it will be seen that the farmers have the advantage and stimulus of a home market for their products.

The remaining county in the island is Richmond, which lies south of Cape Breton County, and with the Atlantic and the Strait of Canso on its southwestern shores. It is largely a fishing county, although along the shore of the Bras d'Or Lakes on its northern side and along the Grand River, and that portion of the county adjoining Inverness County near West Bay, there are some good agricultural settlements. Here farms are cheap, and as the land is of good quality, much improvement can be made in its agricultural production. Arichat is the capital, with a population of 2,000.

In closing this bird's eye description of the Island of Cape Breton, I cannot do better than to quote from an interview with Professor Macoun, naturalist, of Ottawa, who visited and spent some months on the island during the past summer.

Professor Macoun, naturalist to the Geological Survey for Canada, returned last evening from Cape Breton Island, where he was investigating plant life. Mr. Macoun says: "I went to Cape Breton with a view to establishing the relationship to the plants of Newfoundland and Labrador. I did not find one plant which indicated low temperature in summer. I consider Cape Breton the gem of Canada. The climate is grand. During the summer it ranges from 60 to 80 degrees; never too hot, never too cold. A large number of Americans spend the summer there, but very few Canadians. Agricultural developments are very meager, while the soil and climate are such as to make it become one of the grandest of Canada."

THE WESTERN COUNTIES.

Having completed our sketch of the eastern and central sections of the Province, including the Island of Cape Breton, we now return to the place of beginning on the Intercolonial at Halifax, and will proceed to give a sketch of the western counties from an agricultural standpoint. At Bedford, at the head of Bedford Basin, the Sackville River, which traverses a fairly good agricultural section of country, though somewhat limited in extent, empties its waters. Following the line of the railway to Windsor Junction and branching to the west, we pass through an exceedingly sterile

and rocky section, including Mount Uniacke, where gold mining on a fairly extensive scale, and with intensely varying
results, has been conducted for 'nearly thirty years, and reach
Hartville, formerly called Ellershouse, where the land on this
route first begins to show evidence of fertility. The land improves
in quality until we reach Windsor, the capital of Hants County,
forty-five miles from Halifax. Windsor is one of the oldest towns
in the Province, and is in the midst of a magnificent agricultural
country. The town was almost totally swept away by fire last year,
but the pluck, energy, and substantial wealth of the community is
attested to by the fact that rebuilding immediately began, and it
is now assuming its normal condition, with a complete outfit of new
and improved buildings. This town is the seat of King's College,
one of the oldest colleges in British North America, and the only
one possessing a Royal ·charter, it having been granted one by
George III. There is also a ladies' seminary at Windsor, the college and seminary drawing their chief support from the adherents
and members of the Church of England. Windsor was formerly
famous 'among Provincial towns for its shipbuilding industry, which
there flourished greatly in the days of wooden ships. It has always
been and still continues to be largely engaged in the shipment of
gypsum from the immense, and apparently inexhaustible, quarries
which lie contiguous to it. It is situated on the Avon, a tidal river,
along the course of which are thousands of acres òf diked marsh
lands, the finest in Nova Scotia. The upland is light and easily
tilled, and well adapted for the growth and cultivation of fruit. The
dike marsh lands extend up the Avon, and if we go in the opposite
direction we cross the St. Croix and Kennetcook Rivèrs, which
contribute their waters to the Avon, both streams being noted for
the fertile lands through which they flow. There are large stretches
of diked marsh land on each side of them. Many fine and well cultivated farms dot the course of the Avon and its tributary streams.
Following the shore and along the headwaters of the Bay of Fundy
into Maitland, excellent farms are .found, ranging in value from
$1,000 to $4,000. If we take a central course from Windsor, we
pass through Newport, with its excellent farms and dikelands. Next
are the Rawdon Hills, where there are fine grazing lands, especially
for sheep. Then there are Gore and Nine Mile River, both fine
settlements for general farming, and several other fine farming settlements in East Hants.

Returning to Windsor, following the Dominion Atlantic Railway, and crossing the Avon, we reach Falmouth, a rich agricultural district, with abundance of diked marshed land, and then Hantsport, formerly a seat of the shipbuilding industry, surrounded by excellent farms and having fine orchards.

Adjoining Hants County on its western limit is Kings, and next to that again Annapolis, which counties, with the western part of Hants, contain the great fruit valley of Nova Scotia. For a distance of upwards of eighty miles in length, and ranging from four to eight miles in breadth, lying between what are called the North and South Mountains, this great and fruitful valley extends. It possesses the requisite soil and climatic conditions which easily place it first among the fruit-growing districts of the Dominion of Canada, and unsurpassed in the United States for such fruits as obtain their most perfect development in the temperate zone. The apple production is not confined to the valley, for on the slopes of the mountains, both North and South, splendid orchards are found. The annual production of apples in this valley is now about three-quarters of a million barrels, which, with the new trees now rapidly coming into bearing, and others being planted every year, will soon be very largely increased. It is estimated by careful and conservative authorities that within the next two decades the production of apples and other fruits in this valley will reach twenty-five or thirty million barrels. Though apples are the principal fruit crop, large quantities of plums, pears, and cherries, and in a lesser degree quinces and peaches, are cultivated, together with an infinite variety of small fruits, such as strawberries, raspberries, gooseberries, currants, etc., all of which grow in great abundance.

This valley also possesses large quantities of excellent land for general farming. Kings County has vast stretches of dike marsh on the rivers which flow into the Basin of Minas. It is admirably adapted for stock-raising and dairying. In the western section of the county, hitherto waste bog lands are rapidly being utilized for cranberry culture. Those who have engaged in this industry have found it to be quite profitable.

Kings is noted for the superior quality of its potatoes, and their prolific growth, running from 200 to 350 and even 400 bushels to the acre. All kinds of roots grow well in its rich and fertile soil. It is dotted over with thriving towns and villages, and the scenery is varied and picturesque. Taking into account its many advantages,

I do not consider the price of farms in this beautiful county at all high. . Good farms may be purchased at prices varying from $3,000 to $15,000.

Kentville is the shire town and a center .of business activity, with a population of 1,700. Wolfville is the next town of importance, being the seat of Acadia College and the Nova Scotia School of Horticulture; Canning and Berwick may also be mentioned as busy and beautiful little towns. All of these towns are centers of prosperous agricultural districts.

Annapolis County, like Kings, is noted for its fruit and general agricultural capabilities. The eastern section of the county has the same characteristics as the western part of Kings, which it adjoins being well watered with rivers and streams coming from the mountains, along whose courses are rich interval lands, and as we follow down the western part of the county we find rich dike marsh bordering the Annapolis River. Farms through this valley, in addition to their immense fruit production, are especially adapted for dairying, almost every farm having an excellent stream of pure water running from the mountains. The principal towns are Annapolis (the shire town), population 2,000; Bridgetown, population 1,400; Paradise, population 350; Lawrencetown, population 600, and Middleton, population 700. Over the North Mountains, about eight miles from the center of the valley, is the Bay of Fundy, the tidal waters of which wash the northern shores of Annapolis and Kings. There are shipping ports every few miles along the coast, and formerly large quantities of wood were shipped, the mountain forests being the source of supply. The range of mountains, all the way from Blomidon in the east to Digby Gut on the west, present excellent opportunities for sheep-raising. These lands can be purchased remarkably cheap. Cultivated farms in the better portions of this fine country range in price from $3,000 to $10,000.

From Annapolis going west we pass into Digby by crossing Bear River, which is the county line. If we follow up the river a few miles from its mouth in Digby Basin we pass through beautiful scenery, the immense 'hills being dotted with a most luxurious growth of cherry trees.' The village of Bear River was formerly an extensive shipping port, and is still a place of considerable business activity. Following the line of railway along the shores of Digby Basin the town of Digby, population 1,800, is reached. It is placed nearly opposite the Gut, as the passage which forms the outlet to the Bay of Fundy is called. Digby is the capital of the county and is prettily situated; it does a flourishing business, and is a fashionable resort for summer tourists from the United States. Continuing west by rail about twenty miles along St. Mary's Bay, we come to Weymouth, a beautiful village on the Sissiboo River. Here cherries abound in their season, as well as in Digby, Bear River, and intermediate places. St. Mary's Bay divides the county proper from Digby Neck, a long strip of land, bounded on the north by the Bay of Fundy, settled by a thrifty and industrious population. The railway from Digby to Yarmouth passes a few miles south of the shore of St. Mary's Bay. New farms are being brought into cultivation along the line of railway, but the most populous part of the county lies along the shore of St. Mary's Bay. This part of the county is settled by a very thrifty and intelligent population, nearly all French Acadians. For almost thirty miles the settlements constitute a continuous village. The people are progressive and well-to-do, with comfortable homes and surroundings. Every eight or ten miles there is a large church. On Church's Point is situate St. Anne's College, a valuable institution of learning in connection with the Roman Catholic faith, which is the religion of the French Acadians. There is also a convent here.

Digby County, although not strictly speaking an agricultural county, has, nevertheless, many well-to-do farmers. Farming, fishing, and lumbering constitute the chief employments of the inhabitants, and between these three occupations a good living is assured and enjoyed.

From Digby by rail, we soon reach the beautiful and enterprising town of Yarmouth, the capital of the county of the same name, and the terminus of the Dominion Atlantic Railway; or if we follow the shore of St. Mary's Bay, we find thickly settled villages all the way to the town. The town of Yarmouth has the largest population of any town in the Province, with the exception of Halifax, and has always been noted for its enterprise. It is wealthy and prosperous to a remarkable degree, and its people have fostered and illustrated a most enlightened public spirit. Whatever Yarmouth undertakes to do, it accomplishes on broad lines, having a clear and distinct light of the definite ends in view. In the heyday of wooden shipbuilding, Yarmouth was the leading town in the Province in this industry. Yarmouth ships and Yarmouth captains were found on every sea and every port in the world. In those days were laid the foundation of its wealth. When that industry declined, while still retaining a great interest in shipping, under changed conditions, Yarmouth turned its attention to manufacturing, and factories, foundries, etc., take the place of shipyards. Yarmouth is also largely interested in the fisheries, and does a flourishing business in general merchandise. It is noted for its beautiful and costly private residences, surrounded by well-trimmed lawns and hedges, graperies and fruit trees, which make them exceedingly attractive and pleasing to the eye, and give assurance not only of comfort, but of luxury. Although Yarmouth is not one of our best agricultural counties, farming operations are conducted in several sections of the county with signal success. It is noted more especially for dairying, sheep-raising, and fruit growing. Farmers are particular about their stock, generally insisting on pure breed, and in this way they attain the best results. Farms are well tilled, and many of them are brought into a high state of cultivation. The town affords a good local market all the year around.

While Yarmouth town is the terminus of the Dominion Atlantic Railway, it is also the terminus of the Shore line now in course of construction, part of which is now in operation, on the south shore. It is surveyed through Shelburne, Queens and Lunenburg to Halifax, and will no doubt be completed and in operation within a few years. In addition to its railway facilities, present and prospective, Yarmouth has lines of steamships with Halifax and intermediate ports, with Bay of Fundy ports and with Boston.

Shelburne County is the next county to Yarmouth on the south Atlantic coast, lying towards Halifax. The shire town, Shelburne (population 2,000) has one of the finest harbors in the Province, being ten miles long and three in width, offering a perfect shelter for vessels, and surrounded by scenery of the most picturesque character. It formerly took high rank for shipbuilding, and still continues the construction of fishing vessels. Fishing is the great industry of Shelburne County, taking first rank in this calling in the Province, after Lunenburg, the adjoining county east. The fish catch of this county last year was upwards of $800,000 in value. Agricultural pursuits are not followed to any extent in this county, although in the intervals from fishing the people in favored localities raise considerable farm products for their own use. The settlements and towns are chiefly along the shore, the principal of which are Shelburne, already mentioned, Barrington, Clyde River, Jordan

River, and Lockeport, all of which are places of considerable importance. Lumbering is carried on to a considerable extent on the Jordan River.

East of Shelburne lies Queens, of which Liverpool is the shire town, with a population of 2,700. Milton, population 1,000, is close by, and to the east are Port Medway, population 600, and Mill Village, population 400, all coast towns. The coast line, like that of all the shore counties, is rocky and ill-suited for farming. Fishing and lumbering are the chief industries. Pulp mills have been established recently near Liverpool, which is the chief port of shipment · for the product of the mills. This industry, together with fishing and lumbering, make the shore ports places of considerable importance. If we drive north from Liverpool over some twenty-five miles of barren and rocky country we come to Caledonia and Brookfield, two good farming sections in the northern part of the county, where apples and other fruits are successfully cultivated, and farmers are making forward steps in advanced agriculture. In this section gold mining is carried on to a considerable extent and with fairly satisfactory results. This belt of fair farming lands extends east through the greater part of Lunenburg, the adjoining county east, and lying between it and Halifax.

In Lunenburg County gold mining is conducted to a more or less extent, while fishing is conducted to a greater extent than in any other county in the Province. The River La Have, which has its source in Annapolis County, runs through Lunenburg, and along its course are good farming lands and large lumber forests. The lumbering industry is conducted on an extensive scale on the La Have, whose banks are dotted with gang saw mills at several points. The La Have is one of the largest and most important rivers in Nova Scotia, and is navigable for steamers and other large craft as far as Bridgewater, population 3,500, fifteen miles from the coast. The scenery along the La Have is so grand and picturesque that it has been called the "Nova Scotia Rhine." Bridgewater is the great lumber shipping port of the county, and is otherwise a busy, go-ahead town. Twelve miles from Bridgewater is Lunenburg, population 4,000. Here, also, a large shipping business is conducted, especially in fish to the West Indies. It is the outfitting port for many fishing vessels, and having a good agricultural country to the back of it, is a good town for general business. Taking the Nova Scotia Central Railway, which passes by Mahone Bay and Bridge-

water, and runs across the country to Middleton, in Annapolis
County, connecting with the Dominion Atlantic Railway system,
we take in New Germany, in the northern part of the county,
which is a fine agricultural district. From New Germany station
a long belt of rich farming lands runs both east and west, and
farmers with modern notions and appliances are bringing up old and
worn-out farms to a high state of cultivation. Adjoining this region
are Springfield and Albany, two thriving and prosperous settlements
in Annapolis County not previously noted.

Mahone Bay is situate seven miles east of Lunenburg. It is a
thriving town and was formerly a large shipbuilding place; it still
owns and builds fishing vessels, and does a flourishing business with
the farmers of the fine agricultural country by which it is surrounded.

A drive of thirteen miles through beautiful scenery, round Chester Basin, with its numerous islands, brings us to the old town of
Chester, picturesquely built upon a peninsula, and having a superb
view of the scores of island gems which dot the surface of the magnificent basin. Chester was early laid out for a large town, but has
not grown up to the full expectations of its founders. It is, however,
very much admired for its splendid scenery, and is a favorite health
and pleasure resort in summer, not only for the people of Halifax,
but for tourists from the United States, who come every year in
increasing numbers. Following the shore a distance of forty-five
miles, and passing through the beautiful districts of Hubbard's Cove
and St. Margaret's Bay, both in Halifax County, we reach the city
of Halifax, the place of beginning, having made the circuit of the
Province of Nova Scotia, and noted its agricultural resources and
capabilities."

In view of all that is here set forth by a competent hand, it is
evident that Nova Scotia affords opportunities for many thousand
farmers to make comfortable livings here on their own lands, and
have homes that belong to themselves and their children. The
home is the unit of the nation; it must be an aggregate of homes or
it cannot be at all. No place becomes so truly a home as a farmer's
house. Men and women born and bred therein never lose their
interest and love for the buildings, the trees, and all local surroundings. A homing instinct is begotten there that brings back the
wanderers from the ends of the earth, if it be only to take a last
look of scenes that are interwoven with earliest and tenderest recol-
lections, and sacred to memories of dear hearts and hands that are

still, and clasped forever. The solution of the slums problem is to be found in settling up the country till there are no slums. With the means we now have for rapid transportation there is no necessity for poor people being huddled in festering masses in the filthy and loathsome tenements, where poverty begets rags, and rags beget degradation of every wholesome sentiment. The city must ever be replenished by the brains and brawn of the country or it would soon come to an end. A cottage of logs in a Nova Scotia hamlet, removed as far as possible from a town, is endowed with riches compared with a one-room tenement in a city. Fresh air, clear water, the fields, and forests, and flowers, are worth all the wealth of baronial castles, and cheapen every contrivance of man for the betterment of his race. We do not greatly need large cities, but we do need more farm-homes, and our invitations can well afford to bring us large numbers of industrious, sober people, who will not look in vain hereabouts for opportunities to get in touch with the soil, where there are no cyclones, no pestilences, no drouths, no venomous reptiles, nor any enemy to make them afraid.

CHAPTER XXVII.

HISTORY OF ANTIGONISH COUNTY.

This is the smallest county in the province, and I believe the last one to be erected, but it is proverbial that "good things are done up in small parcels," and this holds true of the division now under consideration that has but 552 square miles within its borders. The population is 13,617, or 24 to the square mile, which is above the average of the counties, Annapolis having but a fraction over 14, and Hants but 16, both of them old and exceptionally favored regions. In the earliest division of the province the county of Halifax included the whole eastern section of Nova Scotia proper, but in 1784 the eastermost part was formed into the county of Sydney, whose eastern boundary was set at the River St. Mary, but in 1822 the line was extended westward to the Ecum-secum River. This new county of Sydney contained the townships of Arisaig, Dorchester, St. Andrew, Tracadie, Manchester, Guysboro, and St. Mary's, that was afterwards divided into the Upper and Lower Districts, and these eventually became the counties of Antigonish and Guysboro.

Haliburton in his history describes as follows the "Upper," or what is now the Antigonish division: "This district forms a triangle, its south side being 36 miles long, its western 25, and its seacoast, including the circuit of St. George's Bay, about 50 miles. The first settlement was made by the English in the year 1784, by Lieut.-Colonel Hierlihy, Major Monk (afterwards Judge Monk) and other officers and soldiers of the Nova Scotia Regiment. At that period there were no inhabitants in this district but a few families of Acadians at Pomquet, Tracadie, and Harbor Au Bushee, whose descendants now occupy the principal part of the front lands on St. George's Bay. The first material addition to their numbers was made in the years 1795 and 6, by the arrival of emigrants from the Highlands and isles of Scotland, who were, with a few disbanded Highland soldiers, located by the Government along the coast from Meregomish to Antigonish. In 1801 the settlement was greatly extended into the interior by the arrival of a numerous body of the same hardy race, with those whose labors had already made many inroads upon the forest, and converted a large portion of it into

ANTIGONISH CATHEDRAL.

ANTIGONISH, FROM GREGORY'S HILL.

fertile fields. By subsequent arrivals of emigrants from Scotland, Newfoundland and New England, every part of this important district is now filling up with an industrious and hardy population the amount of which already exceeds 7,000. The interval, or alluvial, soil of this district is equal, and the upland is superior, to that of any other portion of the Province." ·

This Highland population prospered and multiplied till in the year 1881 the population was 18,000. In ten years afterwards it fell to 1,614 and in 1901 it was still further reduced to 13,617. This record goes to show that more people were reared there than cared to remain when the way out in the wide world of opportunities was open and inviting them. The great law expressed in the formula of "greatest gain for least effort" operates continually everywhere that there is life in any form. This great sociological factor both elevates and degrades, both builds and destroys; it operates to found great nations and produce that night-side of Nature, the world of parasites. It is responsible for the leafless dodder that winds its snaky coils about its kindred and sucks the ready-made juices that cost but the slightest effort: it started on the down grade the bugs and beetles that now infest birds, beast and people; a wretched community of fallen structures! Obedient to the workings of the same law started the Angles, the Saxons, and Jutes from the shores of the Baltic to harass the strange coastlines of Britain and seize the fertile acres that never cost them a blow with their mattocks that they wielded with skill when occasion required. I throw this remark in by the way, in hope that it may reconcile some people who are much inclined to grumble over the fact that our young men and women will not all stay at home, instead of going away to the United States. They have simply acted under the influence of a great law, and when we have sufficiently made known our natural resources and varied attractions there will be a reversal of the migrating stream and then outsiders will come here to see if peradventure they may not secure "the greatest gain for the least effort." Already this very movement has made a strong beginning in the far western portion of the Dominion. The Town of Antigonish is the county seat and has the reputation of containing many attractions for people who enjoy natural scenery and the wholesome comforts of a small town. The population is 1,528, very largely of Highland Scotch origin. The arrival of the Intercolonial Railway that extends to Sydney and passes through this place, at once put it in closer relations with the out-

25

side communities from which it had been a good deal isolated, except by water. The town is situated at the head of a long and shoal harbor, near St. George's Bay. One of the additional attractions of the locality is the excellent institution of learning, St. Francis Xavier's College, that has grown from small beginnings in 1855 to be an object of justifiable pride to the community and the Province at large. In another section of this book one can find an extended account of this college. The Cathedral of St. Ninian is counted among the objects of interest that reflect credit on the people whose religious zeal made it possible. "It is in the Roman Basilica style, 170 by 70 feet in area, and is built of blue limestone and brick. On the facade, between the tall square towers, is the Gaelic inscription, 'Tighe Dhe' (the house of God). The arched roof is supported by fourteen Corinthian columns and the interior has numerous windows of stained glass. There is a large organ, and also a chime of bells.'

Here is a bit from Warner's "Baddeck and that sort of thing." "The sun has set when we come thundering down into the pretty Catholic Village of Antigonish, the most homelike place we have seen. The twin stone towers of the unfinished cathedral loom up large in fading light, and the bishop's palace on the hill, the home of the Bishop of Arichat, appears to be an imposing white barn with many staring windows. People were loitering in the street; the young beaux going up and down with the belles, after the leisurely manner of youth in summer. Perhaps they were students from St. Francis Xavier's College, or visiting gallants from Guysborough. They look into the postoffice and the fancy store; they stroll and take their little provincial pleasure, and make love, for all we can see, as if Antigonish were a part of the world. How they must look down on Marshy Hope, and Addington Forks, and Tracadie. What a charming place to live in is this."

Haliburton's history affords us this account of the locality, written three-quarters of a century ago: "Antigonish is a shire town of the district, and the largest and most flourishing in the county. It is situated about a mile above the head of the navigation on Antigonish River, and a short distance beyond the junction of the north and west branches, on a spot of ground that is elevated but a few feet above the streams that environ it. It is one of the prettiest villages in the eastern section of Nova Scotia, and the neatness and simplicity of its appearance amply compensates for the absence of bolder scenery. It has but one principal street, which is serpentine, extending half a mile from east to west, and containing about forty-five dwelling houses, exclusive of other buildings. The court house is built on a hill of moderate ascent and commands a pleasing view of the whole village, the adjacent intervals, the harbor and the mountains of the gulf shore. The Roman Catholic Chapel stands on the same side of the street with the Court House, and only a short distance from it. It is by much the largest and most respectable looking building in the county, and perhaps in the eastern division of the Province. The length of this edifice is 72 feet, its breadth 45, and the height of its spire 110 feet. It is capable of accommodating eight hundred people. There is also in the center of this village a small Presbyterian meeting house, and another of larger and more convenient dimensions (54x36) is now erected and partly finished. In this vicinity is a small Baptist meeting house, in which missionaries of different denominations of dissenters occasionally preach, and where a part of the inhabitants meet regularly every Sabbath for religious worship. Dorchester Village (meaning Antigonish), from its central situation, is the principal trading place in the district, having roads of communication to Guysborough, Morristown, the Gulf Shore, St. Mary, Addington and Merigomish. The entrance of the harbor which is eight miles from the village, is narrow and rather difficult of access, there being only nine feet of water on the bar at high tides. Two miles from its mouth are the gypsum rocks, which afford employment for the vessels of Arichat and the adjoining ports. At the first settlement of the district an attempt was made to build a town on a spot of ground near the harbor, which is still designated as 'Town Point,' but which failed, like every other attempt to make the formation of villages precede the cultivation of the land."

Haliburton's History has become a scarce volume, and it has seemed to me that it would be a matter of interest to see the place as he saw it so long ago. The natural features have, of course, remained the same, and those who are familiar with the locality will in reading these extracts have an opportunity to note the changes that have been wrought by the hand of man. With this word of explanation, we will continue a little further with the historian's description: "Twelve miles westward of Cape George, and twenty-one eastward from the entrance of Pictou harbor, is Arisaig Pier, which was projected by the late Rev. Alexander McDonald, for the purpose of affording shelter to boats and small vessels from the

sudden and violent gales of wind that prevail upon this coast during the spring and autumn. It forms the only harbor from Antigon-
ish to Merigomish, and is of infinite service to the trade of Canseau,
Cape George, Pictou, and the intermediate coast. The principal
roads in the district are the Gulf road, Manchester road, Canseau,
St. Mary's, and Morristown roads. The former is the post road to
Malignant Cove and Pictou. It passes through the settlements on
the coast for several miles, and presents an extensive view of the
Northumberland Strait, parts of Cape Breton, and Prince Edward's
Island, and the Highlands of Pictou and Mount Tom. The Manchester road traverses a part of the elevated land that lies between
the north and south branches of the Pomquet, affording splendid
views of the valley of the South and West Rivers, and the country
bounded by the Highlands between St. Mary's and the Merigomish.
This chain bounds the view to the northwest, and terminates with
majestic boldness at St. George. Eastward of the cape St. George's
Bay is seen over the gently declining lands in the rear of Pomquet
and Tracadie, and beyond are the Highlands of Cape Breton,
stretching northward until they are lost in the distance. The St.
Mary's road leads through nearly the centre of the tract that lies
between the south and west branches of the Antigonish, or College
Lake, and along the margin of that beautiful body of water, for six
miles. The land on both sides of this lake, particularly toward its
upper extremity, rises from it with abruptness to a considerable elevation, but without rocks or precipices. The water is nearly as pure
as a spring and of great depth; it is never frozen, with the exception
of a small piece at its head, until after several weeks of severe frost.
In addition to these lines of communication, there are several other
main roads, all of which are again intersected by cross roads. This
county is now very readily accessible, and the great enterprises now
on foot in Cape Breton have very much increased the passenger
traffic through this highly favored region. There will not be lacking
men among them who will have an eye to the advantages of one kind
and another of the natural resources of the county in iron, plaster,
copper, agricultural lands, fisheries, grazing and other openings for
business.

GEOLOGY OF ANTIGONISH COUNTY.

Dawson, in his "Acadian Geology" edition of 1878, has given
quite an extended paragraph to the rock structure of this county.
It can hardly be misleading to any extent, and more detailed ac-

counts can be found in the reports of the Geological Survey. It is here introduced as follows:

"The Pictou district is bounded on the south by an irregular tract of slaty and syenitic rocks, forming the hills of Merigomish and those extending toward Cape George. In the coast section, the last and lowest rocks of the Pictou Carboniferous district are seen near McCara's Brook to rest unconformably on slates to be subsequently described, and which are of Silurian age. Passing these, towards Malignant Cove, the Lower Carboniferous conglomerates and sandstones are again seen, but very much disturbed and altered by heat. It is a very instructive study to compare the soft conglomerates and their interstratified trap at McCara's Brook with the continuation of the same beds eastward of Arisaig Pier, where they appear fused into hard quartzose rocks, in some of which the original texture is entirely obliterated.

"The conglomerate and sandstone seen at Malignant Cove conduct us through a gap in the metamorphic hills, or round by Cape St. George, to the gypsiferous rocks of the neighborhood of Antigonish. These run along the south side of the metaphoric hills with general southerly dips, from Cape St. George to the western extremity of this district, and exhibit a very large development of the gypsums and limestones, the latter containing some of the fossils already noticed in other localities.

"At Cape St. George the Lower Carboniferous conglomerates appear to be largely developed, and associated with these are sandstones and shale containing fossil plants, and also a bed of gypsum. The shale and the fossils are precisely similar to those of Horton Bluff. Similar scales occur farther to the westward holding the same fossils, and are stated to be so rich in bituminous matter that hopes are entertained of utilizing them as a source of coal oil. In the vicinity of Morristown there are red sandstones, conglomerate, and gray sandstone, the latter containing *Calamites Sternbergia,* and other coal formation fossils, and no doubt higher in the series than the beds last mentioned. Near Morristown these beds dip to the northeast, and have been disturbed by a spur of trappean or altered rock, containing kernels of epidote, and associated with contorted dark shales, probably Lower Carboniferous. Beyond this interruption, the coast shows soft reddish sandstones and shale, with some beds of gray sandstone and conglomerate, dipping to the S. S. E. at an angle of fifty degrees, and on these rests a bed of limestone nearly one hundred feet thick; in its lower portion laminated, the laminæ being occasionally broken up so as to give it a fragmentary or brecciated appearance; in its upper part compact, and penetrated by small gypsum veins. On this, limestone and gypsum, above which is a great thickness of pure flesh-colored gypsum; on this again white fine-grained gypsum with minute grains of carbonate of lime. The whole thickness of the gypsum is about 200 feet and it forms a beautiful cliff fronting the sea. This gypsum and limestone can be traced with scarcely any interruption to the village of Antigonish, about five miles distant, where the same beds are seen in the banks of Right's River. Near the mouth of this river, at the head of Antigonish harbor, is a thick bed of white gypsum, dipping to the southwest. Succeeding this in descending order, after a small interval, is a bed of dark-colored limestone, in which, at different points where it appears I found *Productus semirectulatus,* with other shells occurring in the East River; and *Productus Cora,* a shell not yet met with in the East River limestones, but very characteristic of the Gypsiferous formation in other parts of the Province. Below this limestone there is another break, also showing traces of sandstones and a bed of gypsum, and then a thick bed of dark limestone, partly laminated and partly brecciated, without fossils, and containing in its fissures thin plates of copper-ore. Beneath this limestone is a great thickness of reddish conglomerate, composed of pebbles of igneous and metamorphic rocks, and varying in texture from a very coarse conglomerate to a coarse-grained sandstone. In one place it contains a few beds of dark sandstones and shales. These are succeeded by red, gray and dark sandstones and dark shales in a disturbed condition, but probably underlying the conglomerate. They contain a few fossil plants, especially a *Lepidodendron,* which appears to be identical with the species already mentioned as found in a similar geological position at Horton and Noel.

"On the west side of the Ohio River, about fifteen miles from Antigonish, this Carboniferous district terminates against the metamorphic hills, which here occupy a wide surface, and send off a long branch to Cape Porcupine in the Strait of Canseau. This branch consists in a great part of slates older than the Carboniferous system, but it also appears to contain altered carboniferous rocks. It bounds this district on the south. Along its northern side, the Lower Carboniferous limestone and gypsum appear at the north end of Lochaber Lake, at the South River, and at the northern end of the Strait of Canseau, that are probably continuous, or nearly so, between these points. In the coast between the places last mentioned and Antigonish, carboniferous rocks, principally sandstones, appear in several places; and toward Pomket and Tracadie, in the ceneral part of the district, the coal formation, probably its lower portion, is seen; and small seams of coal have been found in it. I have had an opportunity of examining them, but have no doubt that they form the southern edge of the coal field underlying St. George's Bay, and the eastern side of which appears at Port Hood in Cape Breton.

"The Antigonish area thus appears to be of triangular form, with the Lower Carboniferous beds extending along its western and southeastern sides, and the coal formation occupying a limited space on the northern side. It is rich in limestone and gypsum, and has that fertile calcareous soil which so generally prevails over the rocks of the gypsiferous series.

"Until recently it was supposed that all the carboniferous rocks in the vicinity of Antigonish harbor were referable to the Lower Carboniferous; but I learn from a manuscript report of Mr. J. Campbell that a limited, though productive, coal-field has been discovered in the vicinity of South Lake Brook, extending northeasterly from the road to Malignant Cove."

CHAPTER XXVIII.

INTRODUCTORY NOTE.

The following papers on the educational institutions of Nova Scotia were contributed by the writers who were in close touch with their subjects.

The Rev. Dr. Trotter, the President of Acadia, prevailed upon the Rev. Dr. Saunders to speak for that college.

Inasmuch that Mt. Allison of Sackville was largely supported and patronized by the Methodists of Nova Scotia, and being located almost on the line between this Province and New Brunswick it was deemed proper to include it among our colleges with the understanding that it was by no means all ours. Mr. Archibald was the choice of that institution when selecting a proper person to represent its history and equipments.

Rev. Dr. Thomson, Rector of St. Francis Xaviers, has made a brief contribution for his college that might have been extended, had he cared to take up the space accorded to him for that purpose. In fact, I am persuaded that he has been far too modest in the matter. This institution, founded as a theological school, has very much widened the scope of its work, and has in fact given itself to secular education with much earnestness and ability.

Dalhousie College has been represented by Professor Walter C. Murray, who has given somewhat more of a detailed account than I had purposed for this book, but it is the result of much painstaking work, and has a local historical value that should make it a welcome contribution.

Professor De Mille of Kings has spoken for the oldest of Canadian colleges and doubtless has done her ample justice.

The Superintendent of Education, Dr. A. H. Mackay, has given us a valuable paper on our common schools that, after all, are the most important educational institutions upon which the great mass of our people must depend for their book learning.

Superintendent Fraser has given us a lucid account of the School for the Blind to which he has given the labor and devotion of his life these many years.

Mr. Patterson of the Acaciaville School has given an account of their work and their ability to continue it.

St. Andrews School at Annapolis would have had a fuller notice but for the absence of Head Master Bradford.

Lack of space has prevented a notice of all the deserving schools in our Province. The Halifax Ladies' College, in connection with the Presbyterian Church, is well worthy of honorable mention. It is under the control of twenty-one Directors, and the President of that Board is Rev. R. Laing. The Principal of the college is Miss Ethelwyn Pitcher, B. A. (McGill) with whom is associated a staff of twelve teachers.

Another opportunity for the fair sex to obtain educational advantages is afforded by the Church School for Girls, Edgehill, Windsor. It was established by the authority and under the patronage of the Synod of the Diocese of Nova Scotia, and the Synod of the Diocese of Fredericton, Incorporated (Limited) 1891. Lady Principal, Miss LeFoy, from Cheltenham Ladies' College, England, and with her are associated ten excellent teachers.

Under the direction and patronage of the Roman Catholic Church is the Academy of The Sacred Heart, Spring Garden Road, Halifax, for boarders and scholars. The community numbers forty, of whom fifteen conduct classes each day in various branches. The French and German languages are taught by natives of both countries, as well as all the branches of an English education. A school with an excellent reputation.

A school for the education of the deaf and dumb has been forty-three years in operation in Halifax. It provides for the education of the deaf and dumb of all the maritime Provinces. Pupils from the Province of Nova Scotia between the ages of six and eighteen are admitted free. Both the manual and the oral methods are employed in the institution.

James Fearon, Esq., is the Principal and the President is Hon. D. McN. Parker, M. D.

My thanks are due to all who have so readily responded to my invitation that placed a space at their disposal. I am thinking that their work in the following pages will long remain a source of reference to students of our educational affairs.

HISTORY OF DALHOUSIE COLLEGE AND UNIVERSITY, ITS AIMS AND EQUIPMENT.

Written for Markland by Professor Walter C. Murray, of Dalhousie College.

On the 26th of August, 1814, Lieutenant Sir John Sherbrooke, Governor of Nova Scotia, and Admiral Griffiths sailed out of Halifax with a small force to take part in the war between Britain and the United States. On September 1st they captured the port of Castine. Subsequently that part of Maine between the Penobscot and New Brunswick was in the possession of the British. When peace was declared and the British left in 1815 they brought with them to Halifax £11,596 18s. 9d., the amount of the duties collected at Castine.

In a letter to Sir John Sherbrooke, written on the 10th of October, 1815, Lord Bathurst, the Colonial Secretary, requested him to suggest any improvement which it might be deemed expedient to undertake in the Province, and to which these funds might be devoted. Sir John seems to have found it no easy matter to determine which objects were the most important and beneficial to the Province. At a meeting of the Council, held on the 22d of June, 1816, he recommended that the matter be left over for his successor.

The Earl of Dalhousie, after distinguishing himself in the Peninsula campaign and again on the field of Waterloo, was appointed Governor of Nova Scotia on the 24th of July, 1816. Exactly three months later he arrived at Halifax and took the oath of office. Apparently he also found it difficult to decide upon the best object for the appropriation of the fund. But, as befitted a son of Scotland, his thoughts turned to education. On the 11th of December, 1817, the Council unanimously approved of his proposal to use the funds for the establishment of a seminary for the higher learning, and for the Garrison Library. On the 17th of the same month he wrote to Lord Bathurst for the Prince Regent's approval.

There were present at the Council, that day, the Lieutenant Governor, Chief Justice Blowers, Justice Stewart (all Governors of King's College), Justice Halliburton, Chas. Morris, Surveyor General; Mr. Wallace, Provincial Treasurer; Chas. Hill, "an opulent and respectable merchant": Thos. Jeffrey, Collector of Customs, and P. Wodehouse, Dockyard Commissioner. Of these the Governor and Messrs. Wallace and Hill were members of the Church of Scotland. Bishop Stanser, who was ill in England, Attorney General Uniacke, and J. Black, a Scottish merchant, were absent.

Through all the vicissitudes of its fortunes, save one, Dalhousie has remained true to the principles laid down by Lord Dalhousie in his communication to the Council. So important is his statement of the objects of the college that it deserves to be quoted:

"I wish again to call the attention of his Majesty's Council to the subject of the Castine duties which still lay unappropriated. I have given it the most anxious consideration. I do not agree with Sir John Sherbrooke in his suggestion of a House of Industry, nor with that of almshouses. I think these rather offer a retreat for the improvident than encouragement to the industrious part of society. "The Shubenacadie Canal would prosper better as the work of a private company. These works are always done by that means.

"I formerly thought that it might be applied to the removal of Kings College to a situation here more within our reach, but I am better informed now and I find that if that college were in Halifax it is open only to those who live within its walls, and observe strict college rules and services.

"A seminary for the higher branches of education is certainly wanted in Halifax, the capital of the Province, the seat of the Legislature, the courts of justice, the military and mercantile members of society. It has occurred to me that the founding of a college or an academy on the same plan and principle as that in Edinburgh is an object more likely than any other I can think of to prove immediately beneficial to this young country.

"The Edinburgh College provides for the higher branches or classes of Greek, Latin and mathematics. Professors are appointed on small salaries, having privileges of lecturing in open class to students who take their admission at one, two or three guineas for the whole course or term.

"Their classes are open to all sects of religion, to strangers passing a week in town, to the military, to young men of the law—in short, to all who choose to devote an hour to study ih the forenoon. The professors are able and diligent, as on their personal exertions depends the character of the class and of the individual who presides in it.

"Such an institution at Halifax, open to all occupations and sects of religion, restricted to such branches only as are applicable to our present state, and having the power to expand with the growth and improvement of society, would, I am confident, be found to be of important service to this Province.

"The amount of Castine duties, after deducting a payment made to General Gosselin, is £10,750 currency. From that sum I would set aside £1,000 for another purpose.

"I would apply £3,000 for a building of stone and sink the remainder for the support of the professorships. I am aware that this would be scarcely sufficient without an annual vote of the Legislature.

"As a situation for this institution I would suggest that area in front of St. Paul's Church, now the Grand Parade.

"As trustees of the institution I would suggest officers ex officio, the Lieutenant Governor, the Chief Justice, the Lord Bishop of Nova Scotia, the Speaker of the Assembly, the Treasurer of the Province."

The minister of the Scotch Church in Halifax was added to the Trustees by Lord Dalhousie in his letter to Lord Bathurst, but his name does not appear in the Act of Incorporation.

On the 6th of February, 1818, Lord Bathurst wrote in reply that his Royal Highness the Prince Regent had been "pleased to express his entire approbation of the funds in question being applied to the foundation of a seminary in Halifax for the higher classes of learning and toward the establishment of a Garrison Library."

What reasons induced Lord Dalhousie to found another college? Akins in his brief account of King's College says that when the House of Assembly made provision in 1788 and '89 for the establishment of a college at Windsor, "The dissenters in the House cheerfully united with the Churchmen to make the requisite provision for this undertaking under the impression that the college would meet fully the existing requirements of the people and would raise the character of the Province." When the Governors were drawing up the statutes for the government of King's College in 1804, Judge Croke induced a majority, in spite of the vigorous and continued protests of Bishop Charles Inglis, to require "every student in his matriculation (or joining the seminary) to subscribe his assent to the XXXIX Articles of Faith of the Church of England," and also to adopt the following by-law: "No member of the university shall frequent the Romish Mass or the meeting houses of Presbyterians, Baptists or Methodists, * * * or shall be present at any seditious or rebellious meeting."

The Bishop appealed to the Archbishop of Canterbury, who altered the statutes, but "did not go far enough," so Bishop Inglis wrote to Dr. Cochran. (Hind's King's College, p. 44.) Candidates for degrees were required to sign the Thirty-nine Articles, and the obnoxious by-law was not withdrawn.

The altered statutes were, however, not published. After the foundation of Dalhousie had been sanctioned, but before building was begun on the 8th of May, 1818, Lord Dalhousie induced the Board of King's College to repeal "such parts of the statutes of the college as required a subscription to the XXXIX Articles of the Church of England to be made by candidates for degrees, and also the statutes which direct the oath of supremacy to be taken, and inhibit students from frequenting the Romish Mass, the houses of Presbyterian and other Dissenters from the Church of England." But the Archbishop refused his sanction, although at the request of Bishop Inglis he had previously sanctioned the removal of the subscription to the Thirty-nine Articles from the time of admission to the college to the time of conferring degrees. His letter of refusal was dated January 1, 1819. (Hind, p. 50-4.) Thereafter Lord Dalhousie energetically hastened the building of a college in Halifax to be "open to all sects of religion."

Pictou Academy was started in 1805, the year after Croke's miserable statutes. Through the energy and ability of the Rev. Dr. Thomas McCulloch, and the generosity and loyalty of the people of Pictou, it had prospered greatly. In 1816, it sought incorporation. The Council, notwithstanding the opposition of the House, inserted a clause requiring the "Trustees and teachers to be members of the English or Presbyterian churches:" Pictou became almost as exclusive as King's. It was at a greater distance than King's from the capital of the Province, the centre of the political, military, and commercial life of the colony.

Lord Dalhousie had two objects in view in founding the college—"to provide a seminary for the higher branches of education," *open to all occupations and sects of religion,* "and to have *this seminary at the capital* of the Province, the seat of the Legislature, the courts of justice, the military and mercantile society.

When the union of King's and Dalhousie under the constitution and government of King's, without the restrictive statutes, seemed probable in 1824, Lord Dalhousie wrote thus to Sir James Kempt, Governor of Nova Scotia: "If these proposals (i. e. the removal of the institution to Halifax, open lectures in college, instruction and honors, with the exception of Church degrees, free to dissenters of all classes) be finally approved, I think the very character and name of Dalhousie College should at once be lost in that of the other, so that the style of King's College should alone be known and looked up to." (Akins, pp. 41, 42.)

At the first meeting of the Trustees Lord Dalhousie proposed St. Paul's for the name of the college. No decision about the name was reached until 1819, when the Earl applied for a Royal charter for the "Halifax College.' But when it was found that a Royal charter would cost £600 the canny Scot concluded that a Provincial charter would do as well. After Dalhousie left for Canada the Provincial Legislature was asked to incorporate the Governors of the college in Halifax to be called "Dalhousie College." This was granted January 13, 1821. On the 19th of December, 1818, the grant of the Grand Parade was made to the Trustees for a site for the college.

On the 22d of May, 1820, Lord Dalhousie laid the corner-stone of the new building in the presence of the officers of the garrison and the Navy and the members of the Legislature. This was his last act before leaving for Canada, where for eight years he was "Governor in Chief."

As early as 1818, plans for the new building had been prepared, but had been set aside. In 1819, the Legislature granted £2,000, and building was begun. When Lord Dalhousie left Nova Scotia the House voted him the usual grant of £1,000 given to retiring Governors. This he declined, and the Legislature granted it to the college that had been named in honor of him. In 1823, a loan of £5,000 was made to the college by the Legislature. This loan gave rise to many bitter debates then and in every succeeding decade, until the courage of Dr. Tupper and the loyalty of Joe Howe united in delivering the college from its enemies in 1864.

Two rooms of the building were ready for classes in 1822. Up to June of that year the total cost had been £11,806 2s. This old building, bearing the likeness of the Provincial building, stood on the north end of the Grand Parade until 1887. At different times it held within its walls the Bank of Nova Scotia (in 1832 and until the Governor took the college for a hospital during the cholera outbreak), the Post Office (1852-72), the Provincial Museum, the Mechanic's Institute (1853-58), the Literary Society, and an infants' school. When the college was dormant its rooms were used by private teachers. Rooms in the basement were let for commercial purposes.

UNION WITH KING'S.

Four attempts were made to unite King's and Dalhousie. In 1823, at the suggestion of Sir James Kempt, King's College appointed Dr. Inglis, Rector of St. Paul's and afterward Bishop, and Dr. Porter, the President, a committee to confer with the Hon. Mr. Wallace, Provincial Treasurer, and S. G. W. Archibald, Speaker of the Assembly, a committee from Dalhousie College, about terms of union. A bill was drafted whereby the colleges were to unite under the name of "the United Colleges of Dalhousie and King's." King's was to withdraw the restrictive clauses, add the Treasurer of the Province, the only member not on both Boards, to its Board of Governors, and come to Halifax. Dalhousie was to retain its name and location. The constitution (without its restrictive clauses), the officials and staff of King's were to be those of the new institution. Chief Justice Blowers, a Governor of both King's and Dalhousie, and Dr. Cochran, the Vice-President of King's, bitterly opposed the union. The veto of the Archbishop of Canterbury was successfully invoked. Meanwhile Dr. Inglis secured contributions in England for the use of the college in Windsor, and its friends now became indifferent to union.

Four years after, in 1829, the question of union was again discussed. This time Sir George Murray, the Colonial Secretary, urged union, and later the Imperial Parliament was induced to withdraw the annual grant of £1,000 to King's in order to compel that college to enter the union. Twice, in 1832 and in 1836, the Boards of King's and Dalhousie conferred and practically agreed upon a basis of union. The Colonial Secretaries had been troubled with representations and counter-representations about disputes between the Council and the Assembly, principally about grants to Pictou Academy and King's College and the loan to Dalhousie. The Assembly supported Dr. McCulloch and Pictou Academy; the friends of King's and Dalhousie were in a majority in the Council. Apparently the union of King's and Dalhousie would remove the grounds for separate grants and build up one strong institution. King's resisted as a unit, when the surrender of the Royal charter was demanded in 1835. The Archbishop of Canterbury again intervened and the agitation ceased.

Nearly half a century passed before the question was revived. Again the Governors decided upon union, but this time the alumni intervened and consideration was defeated in 1885. In 1901, King's made overtures; the Governors adopted a scheme; the alumni resisted; the synod divided; and the question was deferred until 1903.

THE MC'CULLOCH REGIME.

As early as May 15, 1820, the Governors of Dalhousie wrote to Professor Monk, of Cambridge, asking him to recommend a suitable man for Principal. Three hundred pounds, with class fees, was offered to one qualified to teach mathematics and classics. Chill penury nipped the scheme in the bud.

Again, in 1830, the Governors offered the position of Principal, with a salary of £300, to Dr. J. S. Menus, of Ayr. He accepted and intended to leave for Nova Scotia in October, 1821. Nothing more is known of him; with him, the Rev. Thomas Atkin, who had a private school in the college, was to have been associated.

Dalhousie and King's could not work together. However, Pictou and Dalhousie might. So, on the 6th of August, 1838, the Rev. Thomas McCulloch, D. D., Principal of Pictou Academy, was appointed President "for the present," and Professor of Logic, Rhetorie, and Moral Philosophy of Dalhousie College. Apparently the forces of these two institutions were united. A month later the Governors appointed the Rev. James Mackintosh and Alexander Romans to the chairs of Mathematics and Classics respectively. The Rev. A. Crawley, a distinguished Baptist clergyman of the city, a graduate of King's College, a man of unquestioned ability and scholarship, had applied for the position two months before at the suggestion of the Governors of the college and had been promised the support of a majority two or three days previous to the appointment. To-day there is no difference of opinion about the justice or wisdom of the rejection of Mr. Crawley. It led to the unfortunate denominational system of collegiate education which has crippled the Province for the best part of a century and bids fair to continue its blighting influence on university education. Mr. Crawley, as he asserts in his letters to the *Nova Scotian,* was an earnest advocate of a single university until bigotry excluded him from Dalhousie. His rejection led to the development of Horton Academy into Queen's College, afterward called Acadia. Then followed grants to the denominational colleges. These grants stimulated denominations without colleges to start them and prevented those with colleges from uniting. To-day the system has produced governmental paralysis so far as university education is concerned.

MAIN STREET. ANTIGONISH

MT. ST. BERNARD CONVENT. ANTIGONISH.

ST. FRANCIS XAVIER'S COLLEGE. ANTIGONISH.

What produced the sudden change of mind of the Governing Board of Dalhousie College? There were three members present at the meetings—the Governor, Sir Colin Campbell, who was then fighting Howe and the popular party in their attacks on the Council; S. G. W. Archibald, the Speaker of the House, Mr. Crawley's loyal supporter; C. W. Wallace, Treasurer of the Province, son of the late Michael Wallace, late President of the Council and Treasurer of the Province, once a bitter opponent of Dr. McCulloch. When Queen's College applied for a charter Mr. Crawley stated before the House that Sir Colin had told him that he would have been appointed had he been a Kirkman. Speaker Archibald dissented from Sir Colin's view that Dalhousie had intended his college to follow its model at Edinburgh to the extent of appointing to its chairs only members of the Church of Scotland. Wallace had promised to support Crawley, but at the last moment he voted for Romans, because, so he stated before the House, he thought it unfair to appoint another dissenter with Dr. McCulloch.

When Dr. McCulloch was transferred to Dalhousie with £200 of the Pictou grant the Kirkmen were furious. The *Pictou Observer* declared it to be an imperious duty to dissuade all parents and guardians from placing their children or wards in contact with what they honestly believed to be dangerous and unconstitutional tenets. It urged as reasons against the appointment of Dr. McCulloch the tenor of his past life, his sectarian bitterness, his political bias, his advanced age, his little success as a public teacher, his malignant hostility to the Church of Scotland, and finally it implored the Governor, "by the intentions of the founder, by the interest of the people, by the virtues of the noble dead * * * by the claims of your children * * * by the demands of decency, * * * to cancel the appointment of Dr. McCulloch and to postpone the appointment of the professors for six months." The synod of the Church of Scotland in Nova Scotia, in a memorial to Sir Colin, urged delay until better men could be secured. It is said that they privately insisted that the professorships should be filled by members of the Church of Scotland.

Sir Colin and Wallace were either strengthened in their prejudice or frightened for the future of the college. If the Kirkmen—the loyal supporters in the past—were to turn against the college, as the *Observer* advised, ruin seemed inevitable. Crawley's appointment would put the dissenters in control, and at that time

26

the Church of Scotland felt more at home with the Church of England than with its Presbyterian sister. It was not because they loved the Baptists less, but that they hated the Seceders more that Mr. Crawley was rejected.

. Lord Dalhousie had founded the college as a protest·against the exclusiveness of creed and of class. It was for the people—"open to all occupations and sects of religion." The democratic ideas of its founder won for it the life-long devotion of Joe Howe and William Young. Lord Dalhousie was a soldier, not a statesman. He placed the people's college in the hands of the official class. Its Governors were the Governor, the Chief Justice, the Bishop, the Provincial Treasurer, and the Speaker (the only representative of the people). He had fought the exclusiveness of King's, yet he placed his new college in the hands of the Governors of King's. For only one member (the Provincial Treasurer) of the Dalhousie Board was not on the King's Board.

Joe Howe, in 1839, the next session after Crawley's rejection, introduced a bill to liberalize the trusts for Dalhousie College by appointing a non-sectarian and popular board. In another debate he thus spoke of Dalhousie's evil fortune:

"It appears to have been the fate of this institution to have had foisted into its management those who were hostile to its interests, whose names were in its trusts but whose hearts were in other institutions. These, if they did nothing against, took care that they did nothing for it; their object was to smother it with indifference. Surrounded by such men, and clothed with a sectarian character for twenty-three years, it stood a monument of folly."

The one comforting thing in this sorry business was the fact that Lord Dalhousie was spared the pain of seeing his democratic designs frustrated by the men whom he had trusted. He had died six months before.

The college opened on November 1st with sixteen or seventeen students. Its prospects were black indeed. Dr. McCulloch was broken in health, and his enemies forgot nothing. Romans was a man of little force of character. His resignation was accepted in 1842. Mackintosh had conducted a fairly successful school in St. Matthew's and was assistant minister of that church; but his fondness for society and its pleasures drew him away from his work. The hopes of the college collapsed with the death of Dr. McCulloch on the 9th of September, 1843. Classes were still conducted within it, but its life was gone.

DALHOUSIE DORMANT.

The denominational grants kept the college question before the public. Dalhousie's board was reorganized with William Young for chairman and Howe as one of the members. They abandoned the college idea in despair, and opened a high school in 1849, with Thomas McCulloch as head master and three other teachers. Again in 1856 they made another attempt with Hugo Reid, a man of some ability and energy, as principal. He remained for four years.

NEGOTIATIONS FOR UNION.

The union of the Congregational College at Liverpool, N. S., with Dalhousie resulted in a renewal of college work, with Professors Frederick J. Tompkins, M. A. (Lond.), and George Cornish, B. A., of New College, London, both of Gorham College, in the chairs of mathematics and classics. Within a year the college relapsed into a high school. Meanwhile negotiations with the Presbyterians had been going on at odd intervals. The union of the Free and U. P. Churches, and the movement in the Church of Scotland, headed by the Revs. G. M. Grant and Allan Pollok brought matters to a crisis. In 1862 Dalhousie agreed to appoint three professors at $1,200 each. The Presbyterian Church of the Lower Provinces agreed to support two, and the Church of Scotland one. The churches were given one representative on the governing board for each professorship endowed or supported to the extent of $1,200 per annum. The college was to be non-sectarian and the Board of Governors was to continue independent of any denominational control. The college as thus reorganized was opened November 1, 1863, with forty regular and twenty occasional students.

DALHOUSIE REDIVIVUS.

There were two periods in the history of the college when hopes were high and the stimulus of new movements left deep their impress upon professors and students. The first was in the early sixties, when a band of able and enthusiastic professors entered upon their duties. Professor Johnson, whose merits have not yet received their due share of recognition, came to the chair of Classics from Trinity College, Dublin, imbued with its passion for thoroughness and exactness. Professor Macdonald, one of Aberdeen's most distinguished students in the fifties, by his brilliancy as a public lecturer and by his great power as a teacher, made the name of Dalhousie known and respected throughout Eastern Canada. Professor Lawson, who had been trained in Edinburgh and Germany, and had been professor in Queens College, Kingston, brought to Dalhousie an enthusiasm for scientific work that made him a leader in the application of scientific methods to agriculture, and placed him at the head of the botanists of Canada. When Professor Lyall was appointed he was regarded as the leading metaphysician in Canada. The name of Professor DeMille is too well-known to require words of mine to reveal the manner of man he was. Nor need I speak of the large-mindedness and broad humanity of the venerable principal, James Ross.

The Rev. John Pryor, D. D., formerly President of Acadia, was offered the chair of Classics by the Governors, but he declined it. Professor Thomas McCulloch came from Truro to the chair of Natural Philosophy. Within two years he died. At his death the Presbyterian Church of the Lower Provinces undertook the support of Professor Lyall, and the Governors appointed James DeMille, a graduate of Acadia and professor of Acadia, to the chair of Rhetoric and History. M. Pujol was appointed Tutor of Modern Languages in 1863. The next year he was succeeded by Mr. James Liechti.

The Arts Faculty has always been the strength of the college. In 1868 a Medical Faculty was organized, although as early as December, 1863, at the suggestion of Professor Lawson, the medical society was approached with a view to the establishment of a medical school similar to that at Kingston. In 1870 the Medical Faculty began work with Hon. M. B. Almon, M. D., as president and Dr. A. P. Reid as dean and secretary. Dr. Farrell was one of the active supporters of the school. Insufficient accommodations and the inability of the Governors to provide a building, led to a movement of the medical men to build on their own responsibility; and in order to do this they secured an act of incorporation in 1873, which made them independent of Dalhousie. In 1874 all connection with Dalhousie was severed, though the medical school was anxious for the college to grant the degrees. The Halifax Medical College has to this day remained an independent and distinct college, conferring degrees in medicine. Under its present president, Dr. M. A. Curry; secretary, Dr. A. Halliday, of Glasgow; registrar, Dr. L. M. Silver, it continues to enjoy great prosperity. In 1885 Dalhousie organized

ACADIA COLLEGE AND SEMINARY. WOLFVILLE.

DALHOUSIE COLLEGE.

an examining faculty of medicine, which confers degrees after examination upon students trained in any recognized medical school. Upon Dr. Lindsay and Dr. Lawson much of the work of this faculty has fallen.

In 1877, under the presidency of Dr. Lawson, with Dr. Bayne as secretary, and Drs. Somers and Honeyman as officers, an ambitious Technological Institute was organized. In the second year of its existence it had 127 students.

In 1878 Dalhousie organized a Faculty of Science, but the want of funds caused it to lapse until 1891, when it was re-organized by Dr. J. G. MacGregor.

In 1874 the Rev. G. W. Hill proposed that the Governors of the different universities be invited to confer about the establishment of one central university. His suggestion was unanimously adopted May 14th by the Dalhousie Board; and he, Sir William Young, Judge Ritchie, S. L. Shannon, Rev. G. M. Grant and Mr. Robson were appointed to represent Dalhousie. The original project was to "concentrate the talents of the different faculties" and let the denominational colleges confine themselves to the teaching of theology. Two years later the University of Halifax, on the model of the University of London, was incorporated. Its Chancellor was the Rev. G. W. Hill. This university was expected to become the Provincial university, so far as the power of conferring degrees was concerned. The teaching was to be done in Acadia, Dalhousie, Kings, Mt. Allison, St. Francis Xavier's and St. Mary's Colleges. These colleges refused, however, to surrender their degree conferring powers. Examiners in the faculties of arts, science, law, and medicine were appointed. A small number of degrees were conferred in each faculty, but with the withdrawal of the annual grant of $2,000 the university ceased to exist in 1881.

Dalhousie held aloof from the first. Her professors bitterly assailed the "paper university," and held that what was wanted was not more examining, but more teaching. They believed that the effect of an Examining University would be to hamper the teacher, whose best work is done, not according to the rigid lines of a prescribed syllabus of study. These objections apply with the greatest force to such subjects as philosophy and literature. Yet granting the strength of these arguments, there is another side. The central examining university was a means of bringing the colleges together. It could have become the means of establishing something better. Its model, the University of London, and its sister, the University of Manitoba, have become teaching universities. Today the University of Halifax might have had teaching faculties of law, science, and medicine, as well as an examining faculty of arts. The greatest credit is due to the far-sightedness of Mt. Allison for the part which she took. While the other colleges were neutral or hostile she was friendly.

The financial history of Dalhousie in the pre-Munro era is distressing. In 1864 Avard Longley proposed that the House require Dalhousie to repay the loan of £5,000 received forty years before. The leader of the Government, Dr. Charles Tupper, was threatened with the loss of the support of Mr. Longley's following if he resisted. Joe Howe, the leader of the opposition, had an opportunity to score a victory. But the courage of Tupper and the loyalty of Howe routed the enemies of the college in their last serious attack.

In 1871 the college was threatened with the loss of $700 of its revenue through the removal of the postoffice. A committee of the Governors, consisting of Sir William Young, Judge Ritchie, and Rev. G. M. Grant, was appointed to raise a sustaining fund of £300 per annum for five years. They succeeded. But in 1875 the college was in a serious state.

When the Presbyterian Church of the Lower Provinces joined forces with Dalhousie they transferred to the college £250, their share of the denominational grants. Dalhousie received directly no part of the Government grants until 1875, when the Governors appealed to the Government for a due share. They had been denied a grant because they were not under the control of a denomination; they were unfairly accused of being Presbyterians and therefore denied the support due to a non-sectarian institution. At the same time the Church of Scotland, in Nova Scotia, received no grant because it had no college. The Hill government increased the grants, and gave to Dalhousie $3,000; Kings and Mt. Allison, $2,400 each; to St. Francis Xavier and St. Mary's, $1,500 each. At the end of five years these grants were to cease and not be renewed. About 1879 Dalhousie's finances were in a desperate condition. The salaries of Principal Ross and Professors Lyall and Macdonald were paid by the Presbyterian Church. Professors Johnson, Lawson and DeMille were receiving from the college funds $1,500 each, while Mr. Liechti, Tutor in modern languages, was receiving about $500 a year from the same source. The invested funds, so a Governor of that time has said, did not exceed $50,000. It requires little computation to see that the withdrawal of the Government grant of $3,000 a year left the college in a poor position to meet an annual expenditure of at least $6,000. So black was the prospect that the Governors felt unable to grant the usual $400 to supplement the fund of $350 a year, raised in the first instance by Rev. G. M. Grant, for the lectureship in physics first held by Dr. McGregor, and later by Dr. J. J. MacKenzie. Again in 1880, when Professor DeMille died, it was decided not to fill the chair of Rhetoric and History. The night is darkest just before the dawn.

GEORGE MUNRO.

George Munro had taught mathematics in the Free Church Academy in Halifax from 1852 to 1857, before going to New York, where he established a publishing business and made a fortune. Ill health forced him to seek rest and strength in Nova Scotia. Naturally he was deeply interested in the fortunes of the educational institutions in Halifax. From the Rev. John Forrest, then a Governor, he learned of the despair of the college. One beautiful afternoon, as they rowed over the Arm, and were talking of the college, Mr. Munro asked what chair was most needed, and when told that Physics was the greatest immediate need, he said, "If you will find the man, I will find the money." An endowment of $40,000, yielding a salary of $2,000 a year, was promised, and Dr. James Gordon MacGregor was appointed August 21, 1879. In rapid succession Mr. 'Munro established the Exhibitions and Bursaries, and endowed the chairs of History, Law, English and Metaphysics, gifts exceeding $320,000. Mr. Munro's liberality was then unparalleled in Canada. Without doubt it stimulated the wealthy men in Montreal to come to the rescue of McGill, and it set the wealthy men of Halifax thinking about the wisdom of giving to the colleges. It not only saved the college, it made it strong.

In 1883 Alexander McLeod, one of Halifax's most successful merchants, died at the patriarchal age of 92 years, and left to the college about $100,000, the residue of an estate valued at $210,000. With this sum the Governors endowed the chairs of Classics and Chemistry and Modern Languages.

Sir William Young became a member of the Board of Governors in 1842 and chairman in 1847. He had always been very active in the interests of the college. He was one of the leaders in securing the five years' fund of $6,000 in 1871, and the fund for scientific apparatus in 1878. In 1886 he offered $20,000 to the new building, and at his death he left $4,000 for a prize, and the residue of his estate, about $35,000. From him the college received loyal and devoted service as a Governor for forty-five years, and gifts amounting to over $62,000.

John P. Mott, one of the ablest business men, and the most liberal philanthropist that Halifax has even seen, bequeathed the college $10,000 in 1890. Other bequests were received—$500 for a prize from Dr. Avery, £1,000 from Mrs. MacKenzie for a bursary, and $2,000 as an endowment for the library from Professor Macdonald in 1901.

From 1891 to 1896 the college was in receipt of a sustaining fund of $20,000. Within recent years considerable gifts for scientific apparatus, for the Law and Arts libraries, have been received. The Alumni association has given over $1,700, the graduating classes in Arts and Science since 1894 have given over $1,000 for the purchase of memorial collections of books for the Arts library, while the Law faculty has given and supported an excellent law library.

The expansion that followed the Munro gifts made a new building imperative. In the seventies the medical faculty left for want of room. The new law faculty and the science classes of the college could not be accommodated in the old building on the Grand Parade. For many years a most disastrous quarrel had been raging between the city and the college over the right to the Parade. As long as the title was in dispute neither party was willing to spend money in making the spot an ornament to the city. The Parade became a reproach and a civic disgrace. The city claimed that at the founding of the town the parade had been set aside for a Common, for the use of the town, and therefore that it could not be used for any other purpose without the town's consent. The college maintained that Cornwallis had intended it for military purposes, as its name, the Grand Parade, indicated, and therefore Lord Dalhousie was well within his rights in setting aside by grant, as he did in 1818, a portion for the college, and in driving the military nearer the barracks. A test case was carried to the courts. Justice Weatherbe charged in favor of the college but the jury disagreed. A compromise was agreed upon whereby the college relinquished all rights to that part of the Parade south of the line fifteen feet from the college, and received in return an annual grant of $500 from the city. This compromise was ratified by an act of the Legislature in 1883. Later the city wished to build a city hall, and the college wanted a larger building. The college offered its building and site for $25,000 and a site on the Common, its present site. Sir William Young subscribed $20,000. The city accepted the offer, and the cornerstone of the new college building was laid April 27, 1887, by Sir William Young.

The educational history of this period is most important. Mr. Munro's princely gifts brought a brilliant band of professors and students to the college. J. Gorden MacGregor, then a D. Sc. of the University of London, became professor of Physics in 1879, and continued building up a strong department in Physics until his work brought him a Fellowship in the Royal Society of London; an Honorary Doctorate from the University of Glasgow, and the appointment to the chair of Natural Philosophy in the University of Edinburgh. Prof. J. Gould Schurman, a D. Sc. of Edinburgh University, came to the chair of Metaphysics in 1882, and reformed the teaching of Philosophy. After four brief years he was called to take charge of the Sage School of Philosophy, and later of the Presidency of Cornell University. Dr. J. W. Alexander, a graduate of London and Johns Hopkins, filled the English chair from 1884 to 1889, when he was appointed to Toronto University. Mr. James Seth succeeded Professor Schurman. After six years of service here he went first to Brown, and later to Cornell, and finally to the chair of Moral Philosophy in the University of Edinburgh.

The Munro endowments brought to the college the Rev. John Forrest, who became Professor of History in 1881 and President in 1885; and Dr. Weldon, who became Dean of the Law Faculty in 1883. The Law School gathered about it an enthusiastic band of volunteer lecturers, among whom were Sir John Thompson, Hon. R. Sedgwick, Justices Graham and Townsend and J. Y. Payzant.

The Munro Exhibitions and Bursaries had a most stimulating effect upon the schools. The candidates for these prizes were well trained, mature, and able students, several of whom attained high distinction in Dalhousie, and afterward went abroad for further study, and so highly distinguished themselves in the larger universities of the United States that Dalhousie, in spite of mean buildings, meager equipment and a small staff, was regarded as one of the best of the smaller colleges. In the *Halifax Herald* of April, 1896,

Dr. MacGregor showed that while Dalhousie had only 7 per cent of the college students of Canada during the six years preceding, its graduates won 21 per cent of the scholarships awarded to Canadian students by the larger universities of the United States.

Important changes were introduced into the course of study. The work of the third and fourth years became largely elective, and the best students were permitted to take honor courses in special subjects. These honor courses had been instituted in 1871, but had not become very useful until the eighties.

On the 9th of July, 1881, in response to a letter of inquiry from Principal Calkin of the Normal School of Truro, the Governors agreed to admit young women to all the privileges of the college, "so that hereafter there shall be no distinction in regard to college work between male and female students." Principal Ross, Dr. Lawson and Mr. Munro strongly supported the application. The following September Miss Lillie Calkin and Miss Margaret Newcomb, the daughter and niece of Principal Calkin, entered Dalhousie and captured Munro Bursaries. Miss Newcomb, after a distinguished course, took the degree of B. A. with honors in 1885. Miss Calkin did not finish her course. Since then several young women have taken degrees with honors, and afterwards distinguished themselves in other colleges. Last session there were over fifty young women attending classes.

During the nineties the college passed through a period of consolidation. The lines laid down by the expansive movement of the eighties were followed, and the strength of the staff was devoted to filling up the details. Several important changes in the staff took place, and with the death of Professor Macdonald in 1901, and the departure of Professor MacGregor for Edinburgh, the ties binding the college of to-day with the traditions of the Dalhousie of the sixties have been severed. The new century finds the college with a young staff, new problems and an assured reputation, thanks to the excellent work of its former teachers.

The rapid industrial development of Nova Scotia, and the prospect of great wealth, indicate the need for a new movement. The college must meet the new problems or cease to claim to be discharging its duty to the state.

At present the new movement centres around the scientific departments. A School of Mines has this year (1902) been established with good prospects of success, and the Governors are actively engaged in raising an endowment. The Alumni is active and loyal.

This year they raised over $20,000 for a memorial to the late Professor Macdonald. The success of the movement is assured.

The bitterness between the colleges which once was too prominent, has practically disappeared. The confederation movement of the eighties, which sprung from a series of events of which the founding of the University of Halifax was one, was defeated by a slight majority by King's in 1885, and came within a short distance of being successful so far as Mt. Allison was concerned in 1881 or 1882 The latter college was willing to surrender its degree conferring powers, but not to come to Halifax. Dalhousie declined the proposal of the Provincial Government to surrender its degree conferring powers in 1881. The recent movement to unite King's and Dalhousie is meeting with some success.

To-day, Dalhousie has an endowment of over $340,000, buildings, books and apparatus worth at least $125,000, an income from all sources of over $27,000, and no standing indebtedness. She has faculties of Arts, Science, Law, and Medicine. Her staff is made up of eleven professors, including the recent appointments, one professor emeritus, twenty-two lecturers, and twenty examiners. She has 245 students on the register, 671 graduates in Arts, 36 in Science, 258 in Law, 121 in Medicine, and 14 Honorary Doctors of Laws, in all 1,100. The college has always been non-sectarian and must remain so, or forfeit over $100,000 which have been given subject to that condition. Lord Dalhousie designed the college for the use of the people. She must continue doing everything in her power to meet the people's needs for technical as well as for literary and scientific work, and she must keep this education within the reach of any lad of ability, whether he be rich or poor.

To the men who have given their money and their services to the college, the Province is under very great obligations. To Lord Dalhousie, Sir James Kempt, and Hon. Michael Wallace, who cherished the college in its infancy; to Sir William Young, Joe Howe and Sir Charles Tupper, who defended it in its hours of sorest need; to George M. Grant, who threw himself with great enthusiasm into its work; to George Munro, who saved it from extinction; to Alexander McLeod and John P. Mott; to the men who have so fearlessly fought the battle of non-sectarian education; to the professors now gone, whose zealous devotion to duty and high ideals of scholarship and manhood gave to the college its reputation; all Dalhousians owe deep and lasting debts of gratitude.

ACADIA UNIVERSITY, LOCATED AT WOLFVILLE, NOVA SCOTIA.

Written especially for "Markland" by Rev. Edward M.
Saunders, D. D.

Acadia University is a general term, used in an accommodated
sense, and includes Horton Collegiate Academy, Acadia College
and Acadia Ladies' Seminary, a residence school for young women.
The attendance is about as follows: College, 140; Academy, 70,
45 being residents and the rest day pupils; Seminary, 130, this
year (1901-02), 78 being residents, the rest day pupils. Total, 340.

The Baptists at the beginning were very few in numbers, and
only by the most heroic and self-sacrificing efforts was the work
inaugurated and carried on. So deeply, however, have our own
and other voluntary institutions rooted themselves in the educational life of the country that the higher education is still conducted
almost entirely by them.

The institutions at Wolfville, while controlled by the Baptists,
are not sectarian in aim or spirit. They are avowedly and thoroughly Christian, and have been characterized throughout their
history by a fervent Christian life.

The founding of the Horton Academy and Acadia College was
brought about by the concurrence of a number of noteworthy circumstances. In the first quarter of the nineteenth century, the
minds of the leading men in the Baptist denomination were exercised about the matter of an educated ministry, as well as about
education in general. In this matter they received inspiration from
the Baptists in the Northern States who were earnestly engaged
in educational work. The Presbyterians also were deeply interested in the same subject. Dr. James McGregor of Pictou advocated the establishing of an academy for the Presbyterians of the
Maritime Provinces. The coming of Dr. McCulloch from Scotland in the early years of the century solved this problem for the
Presbyterians. He was a man distinguished for his talents, attain-
ments and self-sacrificing labors. Led by him, the Presbyterians
established an academy at Pictou in 1817. It was opened with
thirty-three students, a number of whom became Presbyterian ministers. The Provincial Council, at that time having both legislative
and executive powers, rejected a grant of £500, voted by the
House of Assembly for this academy, notwithstanding the recommendation of the grant by Lord Dalhousie, a Presbyterian, and

CONSERVATORY OF MUSIC AND LINGLEY HALL, LADIES' COLLEGE, MT. ALLISON.

OWENS MUSEUM, MT. ALLISON.

UNIVERSITY BUILDING, SACKVILLE, N B

MT. ALLISON UNIVERSITY, SACKVILLE.

at the time Lieutenant-Governor of the Province. The Episcopalians and the adherents of the Church of Scotland combined to
defeat the vote.   •

Dr. McCulloch desired to have the Baptists share in the benefits of Pictou Academy; but its great distance from the part of the
country where the larger portion of the Baptists lived, and the
necessary expense of attending that institution, made it impracti-
cable for them to patronize it to any large extent.

The college and academy at Windsor, the county grammar
schools, Pictou Academy, the schools taught by the S. P. G.
masters, the private schools which had sprung up in some places
and the common schools which had greatly multiplied, quickened
the intellectual life of the people and increased the demand for a
well-trained ministry. Kindred institutions in New Brunswick had
produced similar results. Other denominations were. prepared to
meet these charges and to take foremost and influential places in
all the departments of life. The process of evolution and construction was everywhere apparent. Vital. questions touching the civil
and religious rights of the people, the principles of representative
and responsible government, the separate spheres of the church
and the state, the equality of all denominations of Christians in
civil life, the duties of the state in matters of public education, and
many other questions were discussed in and out of Parliament.
It was emphatically the period of destruction and construction.
Order was everywhere coming out of confusion. Men of talent
and education were needed for leaders, teachers and preachers.
The demand for men to uplift and mold society increased with the
passing years.

Ignorance and lack of culture in the ministry became more
and more a stigma and a reproach. Baptists and Baptist ministers
were branded as ignoramuses; and, of course, were compelled to
represent all that involved in this disgrace.

The man in the Maritime Provinces, who at that day towered
above all others in the Baptist ministry, and who discerned the
signs of the times, and examined them with searching analysis, was
the Rev. Edward Manning of Cornwallis. His endowments were
of the highest order. He had the qualities necessary to· make him
a leader of men. He had also the love of leadership, an element
of character essential to a leader's success.

It was clear to him that in the onward march of the denominations the Baptists, without an educated ministry, would be left in the rear, and would lose the power and influence they had already obtained. The discussion of this subject with ministers from the United States, where the denomination was engaged in founding institutions of learning for the education of both the people and their ministry, confirmed his views on this subject. But the mass of the people did not see this. Some of the ministers were in the same state of mind. Lacking discernment, this condition of the Provinces, so clear to Mr. Manning and other ministers as well as to some laymen, was hidden from their eyes. In looking into the future they saw no danger; they felt no discouragement.

Among the Baptists the work of evangelizing and church building went forward with a good degree of success; but nothing especially noteworthy took place until the year 1828. Then a vision of grand possibilities came above the horizon. It arrested the attention of the Baptist churches and their ministers. They prayerfully studied it as a new and important problem. During the last nineteen years they had not been blind to their surroundings, their advantages and disadvantages. They clearly saw that other bodies, especially the Presbyterians, had a great advantage over them in the matter of an educated ministry.

In 1827 a Baptist church was organized in Halifax composed chiefly of seceders from St. Paul's Episcopal Church. Among its members were the Hon. J. W. Johnstone, J. W. Nutting, Lewis Johnstone, M. D., E. A. Crawley, John Pryor and others. The organization of this church was an event charged to the full with promise of great things to the Baptists of the Maritime Provinces. In this respect it was not a deceptive vision. In that company were men and women of devout piety, talent of high order, culture and learning. Filled with new joy and inspired with a great purpose, they cast about them to find how large the sphere of labor and influence was into which they had entered. They saw that it was grand and called for self-sacrificing toil. This was in harmony with their consecrated ambition. The ordeal, in the circumstances, of leaving the old church had been a painful one; but after it was over they were ready for heavy, humble work for their Master. New openings and great possibilities of usefulness beckoned them on to labors on a large scale.

At this point the attention of the Baptists of the Maritime Provinces was arrested; and the current of their denominational life and history was turned into new channels. With a single bound they came out of obscurity, and, no longer embarrassed by the charge of ignorance, took a foremost place among other religious denominations. To accomplish this was the vision of the future which filled the new converts with a sacred ambition and a noble purpose. These men found room as well as need for the employment of all their gifts and acquirements. Edward Manning, Charles Tupper and others like minded, both in the ministry and among the laymen, were prepared heartily to co-operate with the new converts in founding a school for higher education.

In projecting a plan for an academy, the young men of the church in Halifax naturally looked to Mr. Caswell, who had become their pastor, for advice. Most willingly did he render them this service. Very cordial also were the fathers, Manning, Dimock, Harding, Crandall and others, in their sympathy and co-operation. In the prospectus which was published may be seen the combined wisdom of all the leading men of that day. The plan was submitted to the association at Horton, in June, 1828. Great preparations had been made for this yearly meeting of the denomination. Word had gone abroad that delegates from Halifax would be present, and would place before the Association a scheme for an institution of learning. Lawyers and other learned and highly cultured men would be there. The stigma of ignorance and fanaticism was about to be effaced. Baptists could now hold up their heads and with an air of importance say, we have among us people of learning and culture as high as can be found in the Provinces. The vanity of the denomination was flattered. All were on tiptoe of expectancy. Perhaps some might have feared that genuine piety would suffer by the coming of these cultured gentlemen and ladies into the humble Baptist fold. But all such fears were vain. J. W. Nutting, Alexis Caswell, Lewis Johnstone and Edmund A. Crawley were present at the Association as delegates.

A prospectus for an academy was submitted to this body and unanimously accepted. An education society was formed; and the grounds now occupied by Acadia College and its associated schools were purchased. Early the following spring the academy was opened in the farm house then on the land secured for the site of the school. The aim was to give the people of the country an opportunity to educate their sons at a moderate cost. The education promised was to be thorough and adapted to the times. The intellectual and religious elements in the training about to be given were rightly related, the latter having the first place. This was one of the forces of that early time turned upon the people of the Maritime Provinces, the tendency of which was to level up the people and to level down the classes and cliques which by inheritance found themselves occupying all the positions of influence and emolument, controlling and directing the social and civil affairs of the country. The aristocracy fancied their rights unquestionable and almost divine. Far removed from this principle of conduct were the aims and efforts of the men who led in founding Horton Academy. They embraced and acted upon principles purely democratic. The genuineness of their motives was proved by their life-long labors.

At this time two strong currents had met in Nova Scotia. The democratic force, originating in England, had been deflected in part from Puritan New England to these Provinces. Here it was opposed by the exclusive class then in power, and which had been transferred directly from Britain to the City of Halifax. The latter had gathered volume and strength from the Loyalists who had taken refuge in these British dominions. The conflict was irrepressible. It was not always alike active. By truce, hostilities were sometimes suspended. In the department of public education the two policies had found expression, the one for the classes at the academy and college at Windsor and Fredericton; the other for the people, at Pictou and Horton. Windsor was from the first in the sunshine, because Toryism was in the ascendant. The one at Pictou was fighting for justice and fair play. Its founder, a seceder from the state church of Scotland, sought in the matter of education an alliance with the Baptists of the Provinces. Among those who had resisted the ecclesiastical Toryism in St. Paul's church, and had been carried, against their natural inclinations, across the line to those who stood for the rights of the people, were three graduates of King's College. Now they appear as the founders of a second people's academy located in the picturesque country of "Grand Pre."

At the end of the second year Horton Academy reported an attendance of fifty pupils. Windsor Academy, which has never been able to rid itself of the flavor of class distinction, saw the popularity of its neighbor; but continued its mission of teaching the few. The work of the higher education, begun by Dr. McCulloch for the masses, was greatly enlarged by the founding of Horton Academy.

Since Dr. McCulloch opened the Pictou Academy, and Asahel Chapin began the work of Horton Academy in the old red farm-house at Wolfville, until the present time, the number of such institutions has steadily increased. Had the colleges and academies at Windsor and Fredericton given the advantages of the higher education to the masses of the people they would have been the leaders in this grand work. The failure of Episcopacy to undertake popular education compelled other denominations to engage in it. Dr. Mc-Culloch and Dr. Crawley, filled with holy zeal for the education of the masses, raised their voices and wielded their pens in its behalf. Every generation has a claim, unquestionable and divine, for an education to prepare it for the duties of life. The pressure of this claim was the secret of the founding of Pictou and Horton Academies.

It was found that, at the completion of the course in the academy, some of the students wished to pursue their studies further; but there was no college in the Province to which, if they were not members of the Episcopal church, they could go and maintain self-respect. The only course open to them was to go to the United States. But the openings for advancement were so much greater there than in the Maritime Provinces it was feared that but few of them would return. This would leave nearly all the places of emolument and responsibility to be occupied by the Episcopalians, who had their colleges at Fredericton and Windsor. If the young men did not go to the United States to complete their preparation for life, they would have to take inferior positions at home. This led to the consideration of the necessity of founding a college in connection with Horton Academy. Frequent references were made to the matter in the reports of the Education Society organized in 1828; but the great expense of founding a college seemed to make the undertaking impossible. The academy was heavily in debt, and the interest awakened in foreign missions was about to be a further tax on the resources of the churches.

The demand for the solution of this educational problem became more and more urgent with the passing years, and rested heavily upon those men who, having withdrawn from the Episcopal church, had become the leaders of the Baptists in the founding of Horton Academy. Indeed, the prospectus for the academy which they presented to the association in 1828 foreshadowed a college as the ultimate aim of its founders.

27

Another element was introduced into the subject of collegiate education. During the War of 1812 the English, while holding Castine in the State of Maine, collected the duties on the goods received at that port. Some years afterwards the amount collected was put into the hands of the Earl of Dalhousie, then Lieutenant-Governor of Nova Scotia, to spend as he might think best for the benefit of the Province. After applying a part of it for the purchase of a library for the soldiers in the Halifax garrison, and to the academy at Windsor, he decided to use the balance in founding a college free to all denominations of Christians. The corner stone of Dalhousie College was laid in 1821 on the north end of the Grand Parade in Halifax. The Province lent the governors $20,000, without interest, to aid in erecting the fine stone structure, which was completed in 1823. But from that time until 1838 it remained unoccupied; no classes were formed within its walls, except some private classes in the higher branches, taught for a time by the Rev. E. A. Crawley. At this time Pictou Academy had through political entanglements became so weak that its very life was threatened. This state of that institution led to a scheme for opening Dalhousie College, which it was proposed to conduct in accordance with the principles laid down by Earl Dalhousie.

After the subject had been well discussed both in the Legislature and among the people, it was announced that Dr. McCulloch, who stood high in the esteem of the Baptists, would be appointed President and the Rev. E. A. Crawley Professor of Classics. For these positions they were the equals, and, perhaps, the superiors of any other two men in the country.

About this time Dr. Crawley wrote a series of articles for the public press in which he outlined and advocated a plan for the public education of the Province crowned with a provincial university.

At the suggestion of the governors of Dalhousie, Dr. Crawley applied for a professorship in that college. Each of the governors promised him the chair of classics. In discussing in the Legislature the opening of the college, his name was mentioned as one of the professors about to be appointed. The public fully expected his appointment; but when the names of the professors were gazetted, to the utter astonishment of all who were not in the crafty scheme, the staff consisted of the Rev. Thomas McCulloch, D. D., Principal; the Rev. Alexander Romans, Professor of Classics, and the Rev. James McIntosh, Professor of Mathematics and Natural Philosophy

—three Presbyterians—two of the established church of Scotland, and the other a member of the Free church.

It would not be an easy matter at this day fully to appreciate the cruel keenness of this act of deception. To a man of Dr. Crawley's high sense of honor and sterling integrity, it was a wicked breach of faith and a public insult. These feelings were shared by all his friends, especially by those who, with him, having seceded from St. Paul's, had united in founding the Granville Street church.

In this act of folly and injustice the perpetrators did not take into account the character and resources of the men whom they undertook to suppress. Among those who took in the full measure of this sudden exhibition of bigotry in 'the department of higher education was the Hon. J. W. Johnstone, Solicitor-General and a member of the Legislative Council. Had the rebuff been to himself it would not have stung his spirit more keenly. Among the many distinguished men in Nova Scotia at the time, and there were some great men, none could be found superior to J. W. Johnstone and E. A. Crawley. Compared with their contemporaries in any respect, they stand the test. Were others eloquent, so were they. Had others indomitable wills, tireless perseverance; so had they. In fortitude and courage none exceeded them. They were great, and belonged to the highest class of Christian gentlemen. They were too noble, they understood too well the principles of Christianity to indulge in any plan of retaliation. Get the facts, was the advice of Mr. Johnstone. The reasons for the rejection of Dr. Crawley were obtained. He went personally to each one of the governors. Sir Colin Campbell, as Lieutenant-Governor, was a member of the Dalhousie Board. He regretted the act. Each in turn acknowledged Dr. Crawley's superior ability and qualifications. The weak excuse was put forward that Lord Dalhousie intended the college for the Kirk of Scotland, at that time only a small part even of the Presbyterian population of the Province. But the very opposite was the expressed purpose of the Earl. The college was intended for all creeds, all classes, without any distinction. But when hard pressed to give the reasons for this breach of faith, it was finally admitted that the sole reason was that E. A. Crawley was a Baptist.

The Rev. Edward Manning was now heavily weighted with years and was, therefore, disqualified for taking much responsibility in settling this new trouble—in solving the college problem. But among the men in the ministry there were two young pastors who, in view of their talents and influence, were specially qualified to co-operate with Dr. Crawley and his friends in meeting this emergency, and in saving the Province from the further evils of sectarian bigotry in the work of collegiate education. They were I. E. Bill, pastor of the Nictaux church, and Charles Tupper, pastor of the church at Amherst. Mr. Bill was the popular preacher at that time, and a great favorite with the people. His location in the midst of a thickly settled part of the country, where most of the people were Baptists, afforded him a good opportunity to take an important part in the impending campaign. The Rev. Charles Tupper was the best trained intellectually among the young ministers of that day. His position at Amherst made it favorable for him to influence and lead the Baptists in the eastern part of Nova Scotia.

After fully discussing the subject with his friends in Halifax, and acting on their advice, Dr. Crawley went to Horton and consulted Dr. Pryor. Then they went as far as Nictaux, to confer with Mr. Bill and others in that part of the country. One hundred miles by carriage was as nothing in such a cause at that day. Of that meeting Dr. Bill says:

"We spent a portion of the night in talking and praying over the matter and as the morning light dawned upon us we resolved in the strength of Israel's God to go forward."

Immediately after this, Dr. Crawley again discusses in the press the burning question of the higher education.

The older ministers feared, and their experiences justified them in it, that in a union college Baptists would not get fair play. Their apprehensions were soon realized. They, shaking their wise heads, had silently acquiesced in Dr. Crawley's plan, but when he was rejected they were not disappointed. They were, therefore, prepared to enter at once into a plan to have a college for the Baptists. In closing a series of letters published in the press Dr. Crawley said:

"I am not endeavoring to imbue you with a spirit of feverish excitement. But permit me to strongly urge you to consider. Weigh thoroughly the thoughts presented in these letters with the utmost prudence and caution; view the whole ground again and again; attempt nothing rashly; and regard what I have written simply as the language of an individual who, in his judgment, beholds you brought to an important crisis in your affairs. If you deem it so, you will act; you will of course permit no burst of excited feeling, and especially no sentiments of partiality towards an individual, to whom nothing you could do in the matter would be any personal favor, to hurry you into measures you might eventually consider yourselves not warranted to attempt."

Shortly after Dr. Crawley's rejection by Dalhousie, a meeting of the Education Society was held at Horton. It met on the 15th of November, 1838. At this meeting it was unanimously resolved to establish a college at once. The Rev. John Pryor was appointed Professor of Classics and Natural Philosophy, and the Rev. E. A. Crawley Professor of Moral Philosophy, Rhetoric and Mathematics.

The Presbyterians, by political combinations, succeeded in defeating the purpose to appoint Dr. Crawley to a professorship in Dalhousie College. While for this disgraceful and unjust act the Kirk of Scotland was especially responsible, yet the seceders, with whom the Baptists had co-operated in their prolonged efforts to get justice for Pictou Academy, either concurred in what was done or took no active measure to defeat it. In founding Acadia College, the Baptists had a good opportunity to retaliate and they did not fail to improve it. Dr. Pryor, having resigned his principalship of the academy to take a professorship in the college, Mr. Edward Blanchard of Truro, N. S., a decided Presbyterian, was chosen to take his place. This was a noble offset to the narrow, ungrateful treatment of Dr. Crawley. They employed the most effective weapons with which to fight supercilious bigotry. For narrowness they returned generous treatment, and large-hearted Christian dealing for cunning and sectarianism.

Queen's College was the name adopted for the institution to be established at Horton. The academy buildings were utilized for college work. An appeal published on the 30th of the same month in which it was decided to have a college was made to the denomination for funds to meet the increased expense. Three weeks after this meeting was held the necessary arrangements had been made and notice given that classes would begin on the 20th of the following January. On the 21st of that month twenty students and a large and enthusiastic audience assembled in the academy hall to listen to the first inaugural address delivered at Queen's, now Acadia College. Both professors spoke at this meeting, and the college forthwith commenced work. In the two insti-

tutions there were over seventy students. About the time Dalhousie started on its career Acadia College, as if by magic, sprung
into existence, having more students in its classes than either Dalhousie or King's. On the 2d of the following October, Isaac Chipman, M. A., a graduate of Horton Academy and Waterville College, in the State of Maine, was made Associate Professor of
Natural Philosophy and Mathematics.

Nothing short of Spartan courage and Abrahamic faith could
have carried the Baptists forward in the face of such apparently in-
surmountable obstacles. But they were equal to the emergency
and went on heroically. This undertaking of the Education Society
received the hearty approval of the Association at its session in
1839. It also co-operated with the society in petitioning the Legislature to make Queen's College a chartered institution.

The application for a charter· was defeated in the House of
Assembly by a majority of one. In the following year, 1839, petitions from the Education Society, the Assocation, Baptist ministers
and laymen were sent to the Legislature renewing the appeal. This
claim for collegiate privileges was made on the grounds of common
justice and the merits of the college. The Association at which
the resolve was taken to renew the application for a charter was
held at Wilmot. Large numbers attended it and great unanimity
prevailed. Men of extraordinary ability were there to take part in
the discussion. The second petition for a charter was successful.

Giving the reasons for establishing institutions of learning, Mr.
Johnstone in a speech in the Legislative Council said:

"We were not blind to the fact that a new era is breaking on
our country,· that literature is extending, science advancing, and
that this little Province, where a man, by continued toil, could
once scarcely secure sustenance for his family, is becoming a
field of some importance in the intercourse of the world. We saw
that the character of the country was changing, and we felt that
our ministers ought not to be behind the general progress of
intelligence in society. To obtain a cultivated ministry, education
must be diffused generally throughout the denomination."

Four years after the founding of the college, a scheme was
introduced into the Legislature to have the colleges then in existence superseded by a Provincial university. The debate which
followed the introduction of the one college scheme into the House
of Assembly was prolonged and vehement. As it touched the

heart and appealed to the judgment of the denomination, it soon became the subject of discussion wherever there was a Baptist minister or a Baptist church. The public was deeply moved; the whole Province was concussed. Soon the one college scheme eclipsed the subject of party government.

Late in the autumn of 1843 Lord Falkland, advised by Mr. Johnstone, dissolved the Legislature, and an appeal was made to the country. Mr. Johnstone resigned his seat in the Legislative Council, and offered himself to Annapolis County for the House of Assembly. Howe, Uniacke, and McNab opposed the dissolution of the House, taking the ground that it should run to the end of the four years' term; but the Governor took the advice of Mr. Johnstone. For the time being the subject of responsible and party government was thrown into the shade by the college question. The great majority of Baptists, of course, supported the policy advocated by Mr. Johnstone; but, in doing so, they did not leave Mr. Howe or abandon their politics, as both Mr. Howe and Mr. Johnstone were in Lord Falkland's cabinet. The result of this struggle seems to have settled for all time to come the policy for collegiate education for Nova Scotia. The one college scheme then vanished, and has since been flitting about in the dreams of enthusiasts, like some weird ghost that has no certain dwelling place.

A number of ladies' boarding schools which had done very good work in different parts of the country gravitated toward Acadia College. Finally, in 1879, a large building was erected for this purpose on the grounds of the college. A large extension was subsequently made to this building, which makes it the finest for one of its kind in the maritime Provinces.

Acadia University has six buildings—the college building, containing lecture rooms and class rooms for the college and academy, library, museum, chapel, assembly hall, and President's office; Chipman Hall, the college dormitory, with accommodations for about fifty-five students—the rest of the students board in the village; the Gymnasium; the Ladies' Seminary building, a large, admirably appointed building; the Academy Home, a dormitory for about forty-five students; the Manual Training building, connected with the academy. In addition to the buildings there are ample college grounds, and a field for athletics, also forty or fifty acres of farm land, mostly pasturage. The whole plant, with furnishings, is worth probably $140,000.

The seminary has no endowment, but is dependent solely upon fees and an occasional appeal to the constituency for special help. The academy has no endowment and is dependent upon the same sources of income as the seminary.

The ideals of the college are sound and true and noble, both on the intellectual side and on the side of Christian influence and character-building. All the members of the faculty are Christian men. Hundreds of young people have been converted here. A high degree of educational efficiency within the limits of the work attempted has already been attained. A sufficient proof of this is found in the fact that an Acadia graduate of good rank is admitted to the senior year of Harvard without examination. Every year we send a group of men there, who in one year receive the Harvard degree.

Together with its affiliated schools, the college has exerted a wide and beneficent influence upon the life of these Provinces. Its graduates and those who have come under its influence are in every walk of life. Its influence upon the Baptist denomination has been simply incalculable. It has largely created and unified the denomination as it exists to-day. Through its influence the churches have been imbued with the spirit of missions, their intellectual life has been stimulated, their tastes refined, their influence increased, and all their life ennobled and enlarged. It has made, and is making, a large and valuable contribution to the life of the United States. Half of our living graduates are in the States to-day, filling positions as educators, lawyers, physicians, ministers, and business men. As specimens of those who have labored, or are laboring, in educational work alone, I might mention Professor McVane and Professor Benjamin Rand of Harvard, the late Professor Hartt of the Brazil Geological Survey, the late President Corey of Richmond College, Professor Seaman of Vermont University, and Professor Read of Colgate. President Schurman of Cornell was also an undergraduate here, and did his first professional work as a professor at Acadia.

Acadia is a constant feeder to the student ranks of American universities and professional schools. Half of the members of every graduating class proceed at once to post-graduate work in the United States, most of them investing their lives afterwards in the life of that great country. The theological schools at Newton, Rochester, Hamilton and Chicago always have Acadia graduates upon their registers. At the present time Acadia has more graduates in attendance at Newton than has any other single American college or university. Harvard, Chicago, and the Massachusetts School of Technology always have our graduates upon their registers as post-graduate students in arts, science, law, medicine, philosophy, or pedagogy.

SAINT FRANCIS XAVIER'S COLLEGE.

By Rev. Dr. Alexander Thomson. Written for "Markland."

St. Francis Xavier's College, the principal educational institution in Eastern Nova Scotia, was opened at Antigonish in 1855. A Catholic college had been started in 1853 at Arichat, C. B., but was closed upon the establishment of St. Francis Xavier's at Antigonish. Most of the students and professors of the former institution entered that latter in their respective capacities.

The object of the founders of the college was to provide the Catholic body with a school for the training of teachers and the preparing of young men for the ecclesiastical and other learned professions, all of which scopes have been attained to an eminent degree. In more recent years, the work of the college has been extended so as to include engineering. The comparative neglect of applied science in the schools of Nova Scotia, a country of great mineral wealth and other natural resources, seemed such an anomaly that the college authorities decided to make a move in order to supply what they regarded as a long-felt want. The opening of a scientific school necessitated a great expenditure in providing a building and plant. A large addition was made to the college buildings, and equipped for practical work in the various departments of engineering. The lecture rooms have seats arranged in theatre form, and are provided with experimental tables supported by brick piers built on heavy concrete foundations in the cellar, in order to secure perfect stability and freedom from vibration. The college has a complete electric plant, testing sets, apparatus and supplies for courses in physics and chemistry, assaying outfits, lathes, drills, tools for steam fitting, etc.

The nucleus of the College Library was a collection of books from the estate of John Ryan, a student of the Propaganda College, Rome. It has been increased chiefly by donations from friends, among whom special mention must be made of the Right Rev. Dr. Cameron, Bishop of Antigonish, who has during the last two years enriched it with gifts amounting to about $2,000. It contains at present about 5,600 volumes, besides pamphlets and other papers, comprising works on history, literature, theology, and science. The library is in the eastern wing of the university buildings.

The educational work of Saint Francis Xavier's College now embraces courses in Art and Philosophy, Engineering, and a partial course in Law. The School of Divinity has been discontinued, students of Theology for the Diocese of Antigonish being now trained chiefly in the Grand Seminary of Quebec and the Propaganda College, Rome.

St. Francis Xavier's is a residential college, and has large and commodious buildings with all the furnishings and accessories necessary for such schools. The excellent water system of the town has been taken full advantage of by the college authorities in installing a complete system of baths for students in residence. The college buildings are situated at the west end of the town, extending in a line east and west about 300 feet, the depth from north to south being about 200 feet.

The institutions in affiliation with St. Francis Xavier's College are Mt. St. Bernard's Convent for young women, and the Collegiate School of St. John the Baptist. The more advanced pupils of the former attend the lectures of the college professors. The Collegiate School is attended by boys preparing for the courses in Arts and Science, and has attached to it a school of manual training.

ACACIA VILLA SCHOOL.

Acacia Villa School, the oldest private boarding school for boys still running in the maritime Provinces, situated at Hortonville, Kings County, was founded in 1852 by J. R. Hea, D. C. L., who ran it till 1860, when it was purchased by Arthur McNutt Patterson, at that time a teacher in the Mt. Allison Male Academy, Sackville, N. B.

Mr. Patterson was born in Aylesford, Kings County, December 14, 1829, of Irish Protestant parents. His father moved to Horton in 1832, and his son thus received the groundwork of his education from Thomas Soley, John Laird, and Rev. Wm. Somerville, three of the strongest intellectual men then in the valley. Mr. Patterson taught his first school in Horton when only seventeen years of age, and had the honor of teaching one of the first grammar schools in Nova Scotia when the late Sir Wm. Dawson was Superintendent of Education. After teaching three years he went to Sackville, N. B., and studied under Dr. Pickard, from whom, he says, he obtained his ideas of order, discipline, and thorough training. He taught in the Sackville Academy for eight years prior to taking charge of Acacia Villa School.

Although offered the principalship of some of the best schools in the Province, he chose to remain where he could conduct a school along lines he believed best, untrammeled by the often erroneous ideas of school boards. He is "a born teacher," has devoted his life to his school, and has brought Acacia Villa from being a school with one teacher and an attendance of from twenty or twenty-five resident students, to what it is to-day—six teachers, all college graduates, on the staff, and sixty names on the roll. New buildings have been added as circumstances required, until now there are several, well arranged and adapted to the work, while new additions are contemplated.

The establishment works like a piece of machinery, every half hour in the day having its own work or recreation. The general good health of the school is a matter of comment. Only two deaths have occurred since Mr. Patterson took charge. The only explanation seems to be that some one is always with the boys, and great care is taken to prevent them from contracting colds, or running any risk in regard to health. The table fare, unlike that of the proverbial boarding school, is at all times first class. It has sometimes been called a "family school," which name is significant of its design and management. The aim is to educate boys and young men in the fullest sense of the word, keeping ever in mind their moral and physical as well as their intellectual development. The home comforts, parental care, and social intercourse of the school are distinguishing characteristics. The pupils are under the care of the principal or his teachers at all hours. The boys prepare their lessons under the supervision of a teacher whose duty it is to see that the work is attended to, and to help any who need assistance. His presence is a constant stimulus to the pupil, who is taught how to go about his work, and how to study, and is not allowed to waste time in a blind, unintelligent, fruitless endeavor to acquire knowledge. The course of study is practically the same as that of the collegiate academies of the Province, embracing the usual branches

of a commercial, classical, and general education. Special attention is, however, given to laying a correct and thorough foundation in the English branches. Mr. Patterson believed in securing a
good groundwork, and requires all to spend a considerable time at
reading, spelling, arithmetic, and English grammar. Advanced
subjects must be postponed till a boy learns to speak and write good
English. Every boy may also become a good penman, and with
constant attention the school has been very successful in this
department.

The commercial department of the school is in charge of a
thoroughly competent and most successful teacher; the course pursued and the instruction given is equal to that of any business
college in the Province. Shorthand and typewriting are also
taught, as well as piano and violin instruction. The course is continually being widened and modified to suit existing circumstances
and the ever-changing demand of the times. Over one thousand
boys and young men have passed through the institution, and many
have atttained to honorable positions in life.

**THE MOUNT ALLISON INSTITUTIONS—THEIR HISTORY AND THEIR
WORK.**

By Raymond Clare Archibald, M. A., Ph. D. Written for
"Markland."

Synopsis.

Methodist Academies prior to the establishment of the one at
Sackville, N. B.

The founding of the Academy, 1839-43—Charles F. Allison.

Progress of the Academy during the next twenty years.

The death of the founder in 1858.

Founding of the Ladies' Academy (female branch), 1847-54.

The University of Mount Allison College.

Founding of the "Mount Allison College," 1857-62.

Students and graduates in 1863 and 1902.

Name changed by an act of 1886.

Courses of study offered and the number of graduates from the
opening of the college to the present.

Government aid prior to 1881. The Educational Society's aid.

Relations with the University of Halifax, 1876-81.

Various University buildings, 1862-1900.
University societies, associations and clubs.
The faculty.

Mount Allison Academy and Commercial College.

1862-1902.

Mount Allison Ladies' College.

Principals.
Courses of study.
Number of graduates.
The music department.
The fine arts department.

An account of the Mount Allison institutions appears not inappropriately in a history of Nova Scotia, in spite of the fact that they are situated just across the boundary line—in New Brunswick—because for many years the Legislatures of both Provinces made grants for their support and because at least half of their students are drawn from Methodist homes in Nova Scotia.

The Methodists of the Maritime Provinces entered upon Educational work at a later period than did the adherents of some other sections of the church. Nothing had been done by them till 1828, when the ministers of the Nova Scotia district "resolved to establish a seminary competent to afford a thorough classical education; and in the following year circulars on the subject were forwarded to all parts of the country; but the popularity of the scheme proved the cause of its failure. Gentlemen from Halifax, Horton, Bridgetown and Amherst claimed for the proposed school a location in each place, and by the urgency of their claims perplexed the committee which sought refuge•in delay."*

In 1833 a proposal for the establishment of an academy in both the New Brunswick and the Nova Scotia districts received the sanction of the Missionary Committee. Especially were efforts made to carry out this plan at Fredericton, where a lot of land was purchased, but the subscription list did not justify their proceeding further than the purchase of the land.

In 1839—the Centenary year of Methodism—however, a letter dated St. John, N. B., January 4, was addressed by Charles Fred-

T. W. Smith. Methodism in E. B. America, II, 389.

erick Allison to Rev. W. Temple and laid before the annual distriet meeting of the Wesleyan Methodist Ministers held in St. John
in May of the same year. In this letter we find the prolific germ
of the institutions which now stand on the elevation of ground in
Sackville, N. B.,* called *Mount Allison*. A portion of this letter†
reads:

"I now propose through you, to the British Conference, and to
the Wesleyan Methodist Missionaries in the Provinces of New
Brunswick and Nova Scotia to purchase an eligible site and erect
suitable buildings in Sackville, in the County of Westmoreland, for
the establishment of a school . . . . in which not only the elementary, but the higher branches of education may be taught; to be
altogether under the control and management of the British Conference, in connection with the Wesleyan Missionaries in these
Provinces.

"If my proposal should be approved of, and the offer I now make
accepted, I would proceed at once to make preparation, so that the
buildings may be erected in the course of next year; and I will, as
a further inducement, give, by the blessing of God, £100 per annum
for ten years. . . . . "

This munificent offer was gratefully accepted and the corner-
stone of the main building was laid in July, 1840, by the founder
of the institution. Money being subscribed to provide the necessary furniture, library, "philosophical apparatus," etc., the building
was ready for occupancy early in 1842. It was not, however, till
the 19th of January, 1843, that the educational work was begun.
On that day seven students presented themselves. This number
increased during the first term to thirty-four, and during the second
term to eighty. That the school steadily grew in favor is indicated
by the following figures regarding the attendance: During the
first seven years the different names on the record amounted to 381,

---

*It was in this locality, too, that Methodism was first introduced into Eastern
Canada and the first Methodist Churches in Canada erected.

†The letter is given in full in *J. W. Lawrence's* Foot Prints, 1783-1833, pp. 43-44.
C. F. Allison was descended from an Irish family which emigrated to Nova Scotia
in 1769 and settled at Horton, N. S. He was born in Cornwallis on Jan. 25, 1795,
moved to Sackville, N. B., in 1817, and entered into partnership with Hon. Wm.
Crane in mercantile business, which continued till 1840. In 1851 the Government
of N. B. appointed Mr. Allison to a seat in the Legislative Council, a position he
declined. He died in Sackville, Nov. 20, 1858. For more detailed biographical
information see "A Cyclopædia of Canadian Biography," II, 50-52, 1888; "History
of the Alison, or Allison, Family," by *L. A. Morrison*, pp. 194-5, etc.; Lawrence,
l. c.; "A History of Methodism in Sackville;" The Borderer, Oct. 5, 1876; The
Mount Allison Academic Gazette, No. VIII, Dec. 1859, pp. 5-16.

while the annual attendance was 119; during the second seven years 445 new names were placed on the records and the average attendance was 142, and during the seven years ending in 1864 with the celebration of the twenty-first anniversary of the institution 399 new names had been added, giving an average annual attendance of 157. The average attendance for the first twenty-one years was then 139.

This success was due not only to the constant oversight, interest and help of Charles F. Allison up to the time of his death in 1858, but also to the great energy and zeal of Humphrey Pickard, M. A., D. D., who was principal of the academy from the time of its foundation till 1869.*

At a united meeting of the Wesleyan ministers of New Brunswick, Nova Scotia and Prince Edward Island and several of the lay members of this church, held in Sackville in the summer of 1847, a resolution was unanimously adopted declaring "That an academy for females, similar to the one in existence for the other sex, was a necessity."

Early in the following year Mr. Allison intimated his willingness to contribute a thousand pounds toward the establishment of such a branch institution.† Several years elapsed before the additional amount deemed necessary was available. But in August, 1854, "The Female Branch" of the Mount Allison Academy was opened for the reception of students. During the first term there were 118 in attendance, making a total of 230 students at both "branches."

This was the *first permanent Methodist academy for girls* in Canada.‡

At the close of the year 1856-57 both Dr. Evans, who had been at the head of the ladies' branch of this institution since its opening, and Miss Adams,‡ tendered their resignations.

---

*Dr. Pickard's forefathers moved. from Massachusetts to Fredericton, N. B., where he was born June 10, 1813. He was educated at Wesleyan University, Middletown, Conn., where he received the degree of M. A. in 1839 and D. D. (honorary) in 1862. He was editor of the *Provincial Wesleyan*, 1869-81, and died at Sackville, N. B., Feb. 28, 1890. For further biographical information see "Alumni Record of Wesleyan University, Middletown, Conn.," third edition, 1886, pp. XXXIX 31; "Obituary Record of the Alumni of W. U. for the year 1889-90," 1890, p. 6; "A Cyclopædia of Canadian Biography," II, 140-142, etc.

†Dr. Pickard. "Historical Address," Argosy (Cl., p. 8), Oct., 1884.

‡In an illustrated account of other academies for girls in "The Canadian Methodist Magazine," 1879, IX, 399-408, this honor is claimed for the Wesleyan Female College of Hamilton, Ont., which was opened in Sept., 1861, through the instrumentality of Rev. S. D. Rice. This erroneous statement was repeated in a biography of Dr. Rice (who, by the way, took a very active part with Dr. Pickard in organizing the Mount Allison Male Academy) in *H. J. Morgan's* Dominion Annual Register for 1884, p. 242. The first chief preceptress of the Wesleyan Female College, Mary E. Adams, was also the first preceptress of the Mount Allison Ladies' Academy, 1854-57.

Hitherto, although there had been a collegiate department in both branches of the institution, and systematic instruction had been given therein in most of the studies embraced in a regular college curriculum, yet no provision had been made for conferring the usual University degrees. This had for some time been felt to be a want which ought to be met.

THE UNIVERSITY OF MOUNT ALLISON COLLEGE.

At the annual meeting of the Wesleyan Conference of Eastern British America in 1857 a series of resolutions respecting the Mount Allison Academy was adopted, among which was the following (Minutes 1857, p. 18): "That the Conference earnestly requests the Board of Trustees for the ensuing year to direct attention to the important question, to the consideration of which God in His Providence seems to be now calling our church, i. e., what measure should be adopted for the establishment of a college proper, to comprise a theological department, etc."

By an act of Legislature in April of the following year,* "the Board" was "authorized and empowered [under certain conditions] to found, establish, maintain and manage a collegiate institution at Sackville to be designated and known as 'The Mount Allison Wesleyan College.'"

The death of Mr. Allison, the founder of the institution, in the fall of this year doubtless tended somewhat to delay the accomplishment of the purpose to establish the college, although in his last will and testament he made provision to aid in the work. "Mr. Allison thus continued to evince his unflagging interest in the great enterprise which he had originated for eighteen years. By his unwearied devotion of personal attention to its business, and by his many additional contributions, and ever ready subscription whenever any effort was made to carry it forward, or in any way to strengthen and extend it; and, finally, by his last will and testament, to aid in the establishment, he, beyond the possibility of any question, entitled himself to be regarded the founder of the institution in all its departments—academic and collegiate."†

But in July, 1862, the required conditions having been duly fulfilled, a collegiate organization was effected and the work of instruc-

---

*Not 1861, as stated in the University Calendar, 1901, p. 6.
†Dr. Pickard. "Historical Address," l. c. Mr. Allison's total contributions to the Institutions which bear his name amount to at least $30,000.

tion regularly entered on. During the first year there were but twelve students, the graduating class consisting of two members; there are now about 130 students, and the class of '02 numbers fourteen.

By an amendment of the original charter in 1886 the corporate name of the college was changed to "The University of Mount Allison College." At this time also the name of that part of the institution known as the Mount Allison Academy, Female Branch, or the Mount Allison Ladies' Academy was changed to the Mount Allison Ladies' College.

The regular courses in the university are now: The Arts course leading to the degree of Bachelor of Arts (B. A.) and Master of Arts (M. A.); and the Divinity course, leading to the degree of Bachelor·of Divinity (B. D.). Honor courses are provided in Classics, Mathematics, Science, Philosophy and in English Languages and Literature. Furthermore the university is affiliated with the Dalhousie Law School in such a way that graduates can, under certain conditions, finish the course in Law at Dalhousie in two years. A Manual Training department will be started at an early date.

During the period 1864-78 the Degree of Bachelor of Science (B. S.) was conferred on six students, one a lady, Miss Grace Annie Lockhart, '75· Mount Allison University was thus *the first in Canada to confer a degree on a lady.* It was also the first to confer a B. A. degree on a lady in the person of Miss Hattie Starr Stewart, '82· The degree of Bachelor of Philosophy (Ph. D.), first offered in 1879, was twice granted, in 1882 and in 1887. The requirements for both of these degrees differed from those demanded for the B. A., in the extra work taken up in science, and in the substitution of modern languages for Latin and Greek.

In each of the school years 1879-81 a twenty weeks' course in Agriculture was offered. It was designed especially for farmers, although opened to the students. A course of twelve free lectures along the same lines has been delivered in the university during the winter of 1902.

From the inception of the college up to 1875 the Theological department was distinct from the collegiate organization. It was under the sole management of the Professor of Theology, who was neither appointed nor maintained by the college corporation. The Wesleyan Conference appointed him and provided for his support

28

independently of the college funds. In 1875, however, by the appointment of a Theological Faculty from among the members of the Faculty of Arts, arrangements were made for giving the necessary instruction to complete a full course in Divinity. Nine have completed this course for the degree of Bachelor of Divinity (B. D.) —the first in 1883.

An extensive course was for many years (1884-94) outlined in the College Catalogue, for those who wished to receive the degree of Doctor of Philosophy (Ph. D.); but no one has ever completed this course.

Up to the present the university has conferred 462 degrees on 367 persons, 38 of whom are ladies. Besides the 17 above mentioned, 327 have received the degree of B. A., 47 that of M. A. in course. The remaining 413 were honorary.

When the Legislature of Nova Scotia in 1876 passed an act establishing the University of Halifax as an examining board, Mount Allison College modified her Arts curriculum so as to promote the convenience of students preparing for its degree examinations. This board was done away with in 1881. The only lady undergraduate was Canada's first lady bachelor above mentioned and the sole graduate in Arts was Mr. S. D. Scott (editor of the St. John Sun), who was a student at Mount Allison for some years in the seventies and eighties, and who there received the second degree in Arts in 1890.

For thirty years the Mount Allison Institution enjoyed the unique distinction of receiving financial aid from the Legislatures of both New Brunswick and Nova Scotia. These grants which latterly annually amounted to $2,400 each, were withdrawn in 1872 and 1881, respectively. An endowment fund was therefore established in order to carry on the work.

Further, in 1874 the Educational Society of the Methodist Church of Canada was organized "(1) to assist in maintaining our universities and theological schools, (2) to aid theological students in their education." The grants from this source to Mount Allison now average annually about $1,500, although the grant was as small as $150 in 1879 and as large as $1,970 in 1889.

The first university building was a wooden structure erected in 1862. This was wholly adapted to the needs of a students' residence in 1884 when "The Centennial Memorial Hall,"* containing chapel, library, museum, laboratory and class rooms, was opened.

---

*So named because it is a memorial of the centenary of the establishment of Methodism in the Maritime Provinces.

The structure of 1862 became inadequate for student accommodations and a large brick residence was opened in 1894. This was destroyed by fire in June, 1899, but replaced shortly after by a building of stone. Great losses had been previously sustained by the institutions through fire. In January, 1866, the original building was burnt to the ground. Work was, however, carried on without interruption till a new building on the same site, was ready for occupancy at the beginning of the year 1867-68. But this building was also destroyed by fire, in January, 1882. There seems to be a fatality connected with January, for in this month of the following year the fine college gymnasium was burned. This was replaced in 1887.

Of societies in connection with the university perhaps the most important is "The Alumni Society of Mount Allison Wesleyan College and Academy," established in 1864, incorporated in 1874, and empowered to elect two members to the Board of Regents.* By an act of 1895 the number of its representatives on the board was increased to six.

Since 1870 the society has annually (with few exceptions) awarded fifty dollars in prizes to matriculating students for proficiency in classics and mathematics. It also contributes annually about $100 for the purchase of reference books for the University Library which contains about nine thousand volumes, and which is the best working library in connection with any university in the Maritime Provinces.

At present the society has about 170 annual members.

In 1899 "The Eurhetorian Society of the University of Mount Allison College" was incorporated. It was founded by a band of students of the Old Academy in 1861. Its object is "literary culture, improvement in public speaking, social advancement and the furnishing of an acquaintance with the rules of procedure and debate in deliberative assemblies."† The regular members are those who are "male students of Mount Allison University."† For twenty-eight years this society has published monthly during the college year a magazine called *The Argosy*, devoted chiefly to the interests of the institutions. It has also been the means of bringing to Mount Allison many eminent lecturers.

---

*A bill will be introduced into Legislature in 1903 to have the corporate name of this society changed in accordance with the change in 1886 of the name of the university.

†Constitution and By-laws, etc., VII ed., 1900, p. 3.

In a similar way "The Alpha Beta Society of the University of Mount Allison College," organized in 1893, has as its object "the cultivation of eloquence and sound literature and of an acquaintance with the rules of procedure and debate in deliberate assemblies."* The regular members are "lady graduates or undergraduates of Mount Allison University."*

The Young Men's Christian Association of Mount Allison College, organized in December, 1886, has for its object "to associate for Christian effort the young men who from year to year attend the university and academy." The association publishes each year for gratuitous distribution a hand book containing information for new students about Mount Allison.

A corresponding association (Y. W. C. A.) was organized by the ladies at the same time. These societies are of great assistance to new students.

Of religious societies there are, further, "The Mount Allison Students Missionary Society," organized in 1870, a society for the benefit of theological students by means of the discussion of essays, exegetical papers and oral discussions, which stimulate inquiry as to the best methods of ministerial efficiency; it was founded in 1878, the same year as "The Theological Union of the University of Mount Allison College." This Union has as its object "to serve as a connecting link between the theological students and ministers laboring in the three conferences of the Maritime Provinces, as well as to promote among the latter a spirit of theological and ministerial culture." It meets at the close of each collegiate year, and, in addition to the consideration of topics of interest belonging to their work, an annual sermon is preached by one of its members and a theological lecture delivered. These sermons and lectures were printed in pamphlet form from 1878 to 1884.

Then there is the Glee Club, and "Athletic Association," under whose auspices matches in cricket, lawn tennis and lacrosse were arranged in former years in addition to the regular athletics, while latterly the games are chiefly hand ball, foot ball and base ball.

The university faculty consists of ten members two of whom are the Canadian Gilchrist Scholars of 1878 and 1882. David Allison, M. A., LL. D., has been president of the university since 1891. His early education was obtained at Halifax and at the Mount Allison Academy. He returned to this institution to become an

---

*Constitution and By-laws, 1896, p. 3.

instructor in classics in 1859, after graduation from Wesleyan University, Middletown, Connecticut. This position he resigned in 1862 to take a similar one in the College. In 1869 Dr. Pickard resigned the presidency of the college and Dr. Allison was unanimously elected to take his place. He held the office till 1877, when he was appointed Superintendent of Education in Nova Scotia, a position which he only relinquished when he again became president in 1891.

MOUNT ALLISON ACADEMY AND COMMERCIAL COLLEGE.

Since 1862, the collegiate department in the academy has been done away with, and the course of study largely adapted to the requirements of students preparing for the university. The Commercial College was organized in 1874 and its course, which is now very complete, embraces the following subjects: Bookkeeping, Business Papers and Practice, Business Penmanship, Correspondence, Arithmetic, Phonography, and Typewriting.

The most marked progress in connection with the institutions has however, been displayed in the development of

THE MOUNT ALLISON LADIES' COLLEGE,

with the "Owens' Art Institution and Conservatory of Music."

Following Dr. Evans (page 3), Rev. John Allison was principal of the Ladies' Academy 1857-64; J. R. Tuch, LL. D.,* from 1864 till 1878, when he was appointed President of the university to succeed Dr. Allison. This office he retained till the return of Dr. Allison to the presidency in 1891, when he became Superintendent of Education in New Brunswick. David Kennedy, S. T. D., was principal of the Male Academy 1874-78, and of the Ladies' Academy 1878-85; and in 1885 Byron C. Borden, D. D.,† was appointed to this

---

*Dr. Tuch is the youngest son of Nathaniel Tuch, who emigrated to New Brunswick in 1824 from Ireland and settled in Queens County. Here the doctor was born in 1835. Educated at the Gagetown grammar school and Mount Allison College, he received the degree of B. A. in 1864, of M. A. in 1867, and in 1878 (*honoris causa*) that of LL. D. For further biographical details see *Morgan* Canadian Men and Women of the Time, 1898; *Rose*, Canadian Biography, Vol. II, p. 332, 1888.

†Dr. Borden is a native of Kings County, Nova Scotia, and was born in 1850. He is descended from Perry Borden, who emigrated in 1759 from Fall River, Massachusetts, to Cornwallis, Nova Scotia. Educated at Mount Allison College, he received the degree of B. A. in 1878, of M. A. in 1886 and in 1891 (*honoris causa*) that of D. D.

office, a position which he has filled with conspicuous ability ever since.

The Ladies' College now provides nine courses of study: The Primary Department, the University Preparatory Course; the Gradnating Course for the degree of Mistress of Liberal Arts (M. L. A.); the Regular Course for the degree of B. A.; Courses in Shorthand and Typewriting; the Course in Elocution; the Courses of Instrumental Music (Piano, Organ, and Violin), and Vocal Culture; the Courses in Harmony, Counterpoint, and Musical History; and the Course in Drawing and Painting.

As already noted, prior to the establishment of the university in 1862 there was a collegiate department in the Ladies' Academy. From that time on, however, classes in the university were open to ladies as well as gentlemen, so that, already, the degree of B. A. has been conferred by the university on thirty-seven ladies. The course of study required for the degree of M. L. A. covers three years and is roughly equivalent to that for the degree of B. A. in the university to the end of the sophomore year. This degree has been conferred on 135 students; the first graduates being those of 1866.

The music department has made great progress, especially during the last fifteen years. There are now nine members on the staff. The violin department was organized in 1886 and there have been three students who have received diplomas as certificates of completion of the course. The first graduates in the piano department were in 1874; they now number 93. Six have completed the course in Pipe Organ, the first in 1895; and seven have received a teacher's diploma in Voice Culture since the first in 1895. The school possesses a fine three-manual pipe organ, two vocalions, forty pianos for practice and teaching purposes, and two Steinway grand pianos for concerts. One of these grand pianos was the gift of the Alumnæ Society when the conservatory building was erected in 1890.

The Alumnæ Society of the Ladies' College corresponds to the Alumni Society of the university, and is a most important factor in the institution's progress. Almost ever since its organization in 1871 it has annually contributed about $45 for distribution in prizes. Its members were largely instrumental in the erection of the Conservatory, to the cost of which they contributed about $3.000; the society contributed $500 toward the erection of the large pipe organ above mentioned and $1,000 to defray a portion of the debt on the magnificent stone building, the Owens' Museum of Fine Arts, which was erected in 1895 at a cost of $25,000; and finally the society has already raised over $2,000 for the "Mary Mellish-Archibald Memorial," which is "to take the form of a fund to assist worthy and ambitious young ladies in obtaining a higher education."

The four hundred works of art in the Owens' Museum of Fine Arts were secured in the summer of 1893 from the Trustees of the Owens' Art Gallery in St. John and transferred to Sackville, N. B. They had been purchased by the Trustees with the proceeds of a foundation of John Owens, a citizen of St. John who died in 1867. Of the English school the collection contains original works by Morland, Sir John Gilbert, W. H. Hunt, Constable, Landseer, Sir Joshua Reynolds, Cooper, Elizabeth Thompson, Millais, Sir A. Calcott, etc., etc. There are works, also, from the hands of Gasper and Nicholas Poussin, Carlo Dolci, Sir Peter Lely, Rembrandt, Horace and Claude Vernet, Bouvier, Jean Francois Millet. Canadian art is represented in examples by Blair Bruce and John Hammond,* who has been director of the museum at Mount Allison since 1893.

During the year 1901-2 there were 197 students in attendance at the Ladies' College; fifty were students in the art department, 150 in the Conservatory of Music, and 172 in the literary department.

THE UNIVERSITY OF KING'S COLLEGE, WINDSOR.

By Prof. A. B. DeMille. Written for "Markland."

"Old King's" is the center of much historical interest. Beginning work in 1790, the college has continued in active service well over a century. It is associated, by origin and tradition, with the Old England and the New, with the great University of Oxford and the younger institution of Columbia (formerly also King's), New York. During many years it was the most important educational establishment in the Maritime Provinces. Indeed, had the early

---

*Mr. Hammond was born in Montreal in 1843, and began life as a miniature painter, being intimately associated with Wyatt Eaton and Henry Sandham before success came to them. He studied in England, France, Holland and Italy, and is a great admirer of the French School of 1830, whose methods he endeavors to perpetuate. He exhibited in the Paris *Salon* in 1885 and in the Royal Academy in 1886, and was elected a member of the Royal Canadian Academy in 1884. His pictures are more sought after than those of any other Canadian artist. He excels as a landscape painter, and of late produced some paintings of Rocky Mountain scenery, which have been widely noticed. For further biographical details see *W. Blackburn Hart* in The New England Magazine, 1891, and *Morgan*, Canadian Men and Women of the Time, 1898.

settlers adopted the wise plan of its founder, it would to-day have been in all probability the only university in that part of Canada. Educationalists will readily understand what this would signify in the economy of men, money, and means.

It is typical of the Anglo-Saxon pioneer that as soon as he gets foothold in a new country and has time to breathe he begins to provide for his mental advancement. Thus Harvard College was founded only sixteen years after the landing of the Pilgrim Fathers. And the early settlers of Nova Scotia were no exception to the rule. In 1768—as soon as might be after the establishment of English rule—there was an attempt made to start a public school. As the Church of England was the most powerful of the religious bodies at that time, the proposal naturally emanated from that denomination. As to locality, it was thought that "in consideration of the example to youth in the capital from a mixture of troops and navy, a seminary or college could be more safely and usefully established at Windsor, the nearest country town, ... where the youth to be trained up would have less avocations from their studies and pursuits in learning." This plan, however, was postponed for various reasons, of which lack of funds appears to have been the chief.

The war of American Independence and related events forbade any further steps being taken towards higher education in Nova Scotia during the next few years. In 1783 eighteen Church of England clergymen met in New York to formulate a "plan of a religious and literary institution for the Province of Nova Scotia." They also looked to found a Nova Scotian Episcopate. Brave men, these, who under stress of persecution and loss could still think of the welfare of their church. Most important of the divines was the Rev. Charles Inglis, afterwards Bishop of Nova Scotia. Consecrated in 1787, he was the first Colonial Bishop of the Church of England. His jurisdiction extended over the Provinces of Upper and Lower Canada, New Brunswick, Prince Edward Island, Newfoundland, and Bermuda. Immediately upon entering on his new field, Bishop Inglis began working for the establishment of a public grammar school. He brought the matter before the House of Assembly and obtained a grant of £400. The members were also recommended to consider the propriety of founding a college, and to consult their constituents on the subject. The academy was duly opened at Windsor on November 1, 1788, a governing body having been appointed by the House. The "academy" is now called the Collegiate School, and is still (1902) doing valuable work after a useful career of over one hundred years.

The agitation for the college went forward zealously. The value of an institution for the higher branches of learning appears to have appealed strongly to the Nova Scotians of the day. The population of the Province at that time was about 32,000—some 18,000 being refugee Loyalists. What this handful did for education is worthy of the highest praise. In 1789 there was passed by the Legislature "an Act for founding, establishing, and maintaining a college in this Province." The preamble stated their belief that the "permanent establishment and effectual support of a college at Windsor may, by the blessing of God, become one of the greatest public utility to this Province, and to His Majesty's neighboring Colonies." This Act provides grants of £400 a year for the maintenance, and £500 for the purchase of a site. The Governors were the Governor of the Province, the Bishop, the Chief Justice, the Secretary, the Speaker of the House, the Attorney-General, and the Solicitor-General. The Act remained in force until 1853, and is an interesting historical document.

The efforts of Bishop Inglis were thus crowned with success. He was the first to recognize the liberal spirit in which the matter had been treated. "The Legislature," he says, "has great merit in this business. No other British colony in North America ever did so much to promote literature. The Province has gone to the utmost of its ability, and we must now look to the parent state for help to complete the design. The institution will be . . . . the means of diffusing useful knowledge, virtue, and loyalty among the mass of the people." The "parent-state" responded liberally—as indeed she generally does. The House of Commons voted a goodly sum towards the Nova Scotian College, and His Majesty declared his intention of granting a Royal Charter. An estate of some sixty-nine acres was bought near Windsor in 1790, to be held in special trust "to the proper use and behoof of the said college forever." The Royal Charter was granted in May, 1802, after having been delayed owing to matters of more pressing importance at home. It is preserved in the College Library handsomely engrossed on parchment with the Great Seal of His Majesty King George III attached—and a very imposing document it is.

The first step after receiving the charter was to frame a body of statutes for the college. It is not too much to say that upon the judicious management of this hinged the measure of success which the future held for the new university. Yet the statutes adopted were sadly at variance with the real needs of the time and country. To mention but two points: They were modeled upon those of the University of Oxford, and they required that all matriculated students should sign the XXXIX Articles of the Church of England. Bishop Inglis, the head of that church, used his strongest influence against the adoption of such a clause, but in vain. The clause was adopted and Dissenters were shut out from participation in the benefits of the college. Ever since that time King's has been reaping the harvest of that most ill-advised step. To exclude those who did not belong to the Church of England when they formed a majority in the Province and had taken a deep interest in the foundation of the college, was little short of suicidal.

In time the statutes were modified, and finally all restrictions were removed. By 1829 the whole of the obnoxious rules had been repealed after much struggle. The college was now thrown open to students of all denominations, and no limitations of any sort were imposed. But the harm was done. The chance of a single university—the dream of Bishop Inglis—had for the time gone by. Other denominational colleges gradually appeared.

The history of King's College is marked by three attempts to remove to Halifax. The first was inaugurated by the Earl of Dalhousie, Lieutenant-Governor from 1816-1820. His views of King's were founded on the original statutes, and he did not see the amended regulations until after he had determined to form a seminary at Halifax. He desired a "college on the same plan and principle as that of Edinburgh," as "more likely than any other to prove immediately beneficial to this young country. . . . . These classes are open to all sects of religion, to strangers passing a few weeks in the town." In pursuance of this plan, Dalhousie College was founded, 1821 (though not going into operation until 1838). Two years later the question of union came up before the Governors of King's. Their committee handed in a detailed report (1824) accompanied by certain observations, one of which is worth while quoting because of its wise statement of circumstances:

"It is considered that several sacrifices will be necessary for both, but an ample return will be obtained by putting an end at once to all rivalry, the tendency of which would inevitably be to keep

KINGS COLLEGE,

both in poverty and insignificance, because it 'must be evident that one college will be ample for the literary wants of Nova Scotia, and perhaps of the adjoining Provinces for several centuries; and it is equally evident that it is scarcely possible to obtain funds that are essential to the competent and liberal support of one college."

Lord Dalhousie warmly commended the plan, suggesting that the very name of Dalhousie should be changed in favor of King's. The scheme failed, however, chiefly through the difficulty that was thus stated at the time: "It is proposed to effect an union by means approaching to a breach of trust, in which a present and acknowl-edged good is to be sacrificed for uncertain and future advantage."

The next attempt to bring about union originated with the Imperial Government, and very strong pressure was brought to bear. But methods of correction seldom effect that which gentler means have failed to achieve. After a struggle extending over seven years (1830-7) King's College was left once more to the enjoyment.of those principles and privileges which the Governors thought a *sine qua non* of existence.

The withdrawal of both the Imperial and Provincial grants by the year 1851 threw the college completely upon its own resources. The Alumni had been incorporated in 1847. To them, and to private individuals, the college looked afterwards for support. In 1853 an Act was passed incorporating a new Board of Governors in place of the old "Political Board," which had never been satisfactory. A Provincial grant was made to place the college on an equal footing with the other colleges, and it was left to work out its own destiny. For some ten years it progressed favorably. The American war of 1860-4, however, caused loss, and in 1881 the Government grant was permanently withdrawn from all the colleges in Nova Scotia.

In 1885 a third attempt at federation was made. A preliminary resolution passed the Board of Governors, but the Alumni voted down the proposition. The time was, perhaps, inopportune. Five years later the college celebrated its centenary.

This was observed with appropriate ceremony, and, indeed, the record of King's was one that called for high praise in the faithful persistence of its teachers. It had kept continually at work for a hundred years in the face of all discouragements.

During the next fifteen years the opinion seems to have gained ground that interests of education would best be served by a single university for the Maritime Provinces. This, of course, was a'

return to the view expressed by the joint committee in 1824: "One
college will be ample for the literary wants of Nova Scotia for
several centuries." In 1901 this opinion came to a head. At the
semiannual meeting, December 12th, two resolutions were passed
looking towards the union of all the Maritime universities. The
following extracts will indicate the nature of the resolutions:

"*Resolved,* that in the opinion of this Board, the time is ripe
for promoting the federation of the higher educational institutions
of the Maritime Provinces.

"*Resolved,* that the governing body of Dalhousie University be
asked to appoint a committee of fourteen to confer with a like committee from this Board, as to the feasibility and probable terms of
. . . . federation with Dalhousie.

"*And that said committee* from this Board consider the subject
of Maritime college federation, by conference with the authorities
of other universities or colleges, or otherwise."

The realization of this plan would be of very great value to education in the Maritime Provinces. It is fitting that the movement
in its best and wisest form should have emanated from the ancient
university just on the turn of the new century.

Of the service of King's College to the Church of England this
is not the place to speak in detail. Her work has been of the
highest usefulness in this regard, and upwards of 250 clergymen have
been trained within her walls.

The instruction given by the college has been remodeled from
time to time in accordance with the demands of the day. In 1857,
for example, the course embraced Classics, Hebrew, Mathematics,
Theology, Science, and Natural History. That the instruction given
was of a high order may readily be seen by a glance at the calendar
of the year. The following classical authorities were read: Homer,
Xenophon, Demosthenes, Sophocles, Æschylus, Aristophanes, Horace, Livy, Cicero, Virgil, Tacitus, Lucretius, and others. Logic
and Rhetoric were taken in connection with Classics. In Mathe-
maties we find Colenso's Arithmetic and Algebra, Goodwin's and
Hall's Trigonometry, etc. In Science the studies were Chemistry,
Mineralogy, Physiology, Geology, Heat, Light, and Electricity, and
field Botany.

At the present day there are six schools open to matriculate
students: Arts, Divinity, Engineering (founded 1872), Science,
Law (in St. John, N. B.), and Medicine (examining Board). Vari-

ous scholarships and prizes are offered, among them eight "Divinity," three "Stevenson," "McCawley" Classical and Hebrew, "Cogswell," not to mention several others. Residence is required for the most part. A handsome chapel is used for daily services. It was erected in 1877, in memory of Dr. Hensley, nineteen years Professor of Divinity.

The University Library is well housed in a large stone building near the college. It was catalogued in 1892 by Mr. Harry Piers, who says: "It must be considered one of the most valuable collections of bibliographical treasures that the Dominion of Canada holds." Among these treasures may be noted no less than thirty-eight volumes from the very famous Aldine and Elzevir presses. At present the library contains about 14,000 volumes, exclusive of manuscripts and pamphlets.

A goodly number of King's men have obtained a fame wider than Provincial. Best known of all is Judge Haliburton, author of *Sam Slick,* etc. He attended the college from 1810-1815, graduating in the latter year. Some other distinguished men follow: Sir John Eardly Wilmot Inglis, of Lucknow fame; Chief Justice Cochran, of Gibraltar; Judge R. J. Uniacke; Rev. Dr. Pryor, first President of Acadia College; Rev. Dr. Crawley; Judge Bliss; Sir Edward Cunard; Hon. J. Boyle Uniacke; Chief Justice Jarvis, of Prince Edward Island; Senator Almon; P. C. Hill, Esq.; Bishop John Inglis; Bishop Suther, of Aberdeen; Hon. F. W. Borden, D. C. L., Minister of Militia and Defense.

PRESIDENTS OF KING'S COLLEGE, 1790-1902.

1790-1804, Rev. W. Cochran, D. D.
1804-5,   Rev. Thomas Cox, D. D.
1806-36,   Rev. C. Porter, D. D.
1836-75,   Rev. G. McCawley, D. D.
1875-85,   Rev. John Dart, M. A.
1885-89,   Rev. I. Brock, M. A.
1889-1902, Rev. C. E. Willets, M. A., D. C. L.
           A. B. de Mille, M. A., King's College.

ST. ANDREW'S PRIVATE BOARDING SCHOOL FOR BOYS AT ANNAPOLIS ROYAL.

The head master of this excellent school is Mr. H. M. Bradford, M. A., a late scholar of St. John's College, Cambridge: 21st Wrangler, 1886: Honors London University.

The master is ably assisted by—

Mr. O. M. Glasspole, B. A., of St. John's College, Oxford.

Mr. C. E. Hodson, M. A., of Trinity Hall, Cambridge.

Miss Lillian Johnson, Piano.

Miss M: A. Chipman, Drawing and Painting.

Mr. George Wells, Carpentry.

This school is heartily commended by a long list of gentlemen well known in both public and private life all over Canada. During the last ten years over thirty of Mr. Bradford's pupils have matrieulated at King's College, Windsor; fifteen at the Royal Military College of Canada, and several at McGill, and Dalhousie, the Queen University, Harvard Medical School, Nova Scotia Barrister's Society, and St. John Law School.

The senior course is based on the requirements of the McGill matriculations and the Royal Military College of Canada; but the pupils are prepared also for other professional matriculations, or for business life.

The religious affiliations of the school are with the Church of England.

CHAPTER XXIX.

This is one of the largest counties in Nova Scotia, having an area of 1,612 square miles, and a population of 36,000. This is but a small fraction of what the region could support if the resources were developed by competent hands and this remark holds good for the entire Province that now has a population of only 459,116, and in the last ten years made a gain of but ten thousand.

Cumberland is rich in varied resources: in agricultural lands of superior quality, in coal measures on a large scale, in grindstone and building-stone quarries, in valuable fisheries, and extensive timber and pulp-wood resources. Add to these the favorable opportunities for shipbuilding and the fact that the county has about 175 miles of coast, and several harbors, and what bids fair to be a copper mine of great value at Cape d'Or, and we may see that this division of the Province is a fine domain of itself, and should have a population of at least one hundred thousand.

The Acadian French, as usual, soon discovered the portions of Nova Scotia best adapted to their purpose of farming. They selected such localities as afforded salt marshes that could be walled off from the ocean, and cultivated ever after without manures. We find these early settlers at Parrsboro, Advocate Harbor, and Chigneeto or the region about Amherst. They were not inclined to win farms from the forests, but were well calculated to make conquest' of their needed acres from the grasp of the sea, a business that their forefathers had learned on the shores of the Bay of Biscay.

Cumberland County prevents Nova Scotia from being an island. Geographically it is happily situated, being in communication with both the Northern waters of the St. Lawrence Gulf and the Bay of Fundy and its connections.

In the vicinity of the isthmus the Indians had long been accustomed to gather in' considerable numbers, as it was a convenient crossing-place from Bay Verte to Cumberland Basin, and by following the rivers the "canoe-carry" was a very short one. In that vicinity were ample opportunities for dyking the marshes and there the Acadians early settled in considerable numbers on the southern side of the Missiquash at a place they called Beaubassin. So far as natural features were concerned, there was nothing lacking. The beautiful scenery was noted in the name of their village, and the fertile meadows responded to their industry, but the conflicting interest of nations far beyond the sea extended to this remote hamlet destroying their humble homes and scattering the inmates in many directions.

When the French owned Acadia they said it comprised not only the peninsula, but all the vast tract of country now known as Quebec, New Brunswick and a portion of the State of Maine, but now that the ownership was in other hands they claimed that its proper boundaries did not include even the whole of the peninsula, but only its southern portion of rocks and wilderness. The truth is that Acadia at all times and in many ways in which documents were concerned, had been held to include the Province of Nova Scotia as it is at present delimited, and the Province of New Brunswick and a portion of Maine. After Cape Breton was foolishly restored to the French in 1748 they became very insistent upon their claims and fixed the limits of Acadia at the banks of the Missiquash River and built the strong fort of Beausejour on the northern side and garrisoned it amply for its purpose although it was a time of peace. Halifax was founded in the summer of 1749, and the next year Governor Cornwallis was obliged to protest by means of an armed demonstration against the conduct of the French military at that point where they were fast driving the Acadian peasants from their homes to a miserable exile in Cape Breton. To this end he despatched Major Lawrence with four hundred men to Beaubassin to prevent further abuses of that kind. Beyond dispute this settlement was within the limits of Nova Scotia and the inhabitants were British subjects for the most part by birth, and the remainder by terms of treaty. News of the coming of Lawrence was in advance of him, and the infamous priest Le Loutre, who lived there a portion of the time, was determined that the English should not have these Acadians within their boundaries, and to carry out that purpose he set fire to the church with his own hands, while his Indian converts under his direction applied the torch to one hundred and forty houses, and thus compelled the inhabitants to cross over to the French side of the river where they suffered more from their friends than they did from their enemies, even in the general expulsion five years later. Unable to cope with a superior force, Lawrence withdrew to Halifax, but returned in the following September with seventeen small vessels and seven hundred men. Before the end of autumn Captain Edward Howe, while carrying a flag of truce, was shot dead by Le Loutre or his Indians under his directions and in his presence. The French officers were indignant at this villainy and charged it upon the priest, but after all did not attempt to punish him for the outrage. These Indians under the same evil inspiration soon turned up in the vicinity of Halifax, where they murdered about thirty people and carried off eight or ten prisoners. Lawrence set to work on a fort within the limits of the village-site as the answer to the fortifications under construction by the enemy at Beausejour. The Acadians had been burned out of their homes in April and led a precarious existence through the summer, but when the cold weather came on their sufferings were greatly increased. Parkman, writing of this affair, says: "How the homeless Acadians from Beaubassin lived through the winter is not very clear. They probably found shelter at Chipody and its neighborhood, where there were thriving settlements of their countrymen. Le Loutre, fearing they would return to their lands and submit to the English, sent some of them to the Isle St. Jean. They refused to go, says a French writer, but he compelled them at last, by threatening to make the Indians pillage them, carry off their wives and children, and even kill them before their eyes."

There need not be a shadow of doubt but every available means both fair and foul were employed to keep the Acadians all over the Province in a state of expectation for a turn in the national affairs that would result in France regaining her ancient colony of Acadie. It was now clearly perceived that this peninsula was of vast importance if the domain of New France was to be retained. Every Acadian was to be kept French at heart till this day of deliverance, that in the nature of things could not be far distant. It did not require a great statesman to see that the present time of peace was but a truce, a mere apparent cessation of hostilities, and meanwhile the contestants were preparing for the oncoming struggle that would determine whether England or France was to be entrusted under Providence with this North American domain. The formalities of a declaration of war did not seem to be of much importance on this side of the ocean, and meantime neither party would allow an interest to suffer that might be rescued by a hostile demonstration. While Halifax was getting into a station and town of some consequence, and Fort Lawrence at Beaubassin was built, the

29

French had made Beausejour a formidable stronghold and strengthened the defences of Louisburg, and in the attitude of conquest
entered the Ohio Valley from the Lake Erie Shore when they knew
that the territory belonged to the King of Great Britain. In the
spring of 1755, when as yet war had not been declared, the English
had made their plans to effectually restrain this growing appetite
for more land that their French neighbors were displaying. The
enemy at four points were especially aggressive and dangerous.
These localities were Fort Duquesne, on the present site of Pittsburg; Fort Niagara; Crown Point, on Lake Champlain, and Fort
Beausejour, at Chignecto, in Acadia. At each of these places a
blow was to be struck, and they were all to be delivered in the
spring and summer of 1755. When completed the arrangements
provided that General Braddock with his Regulars and Colonials
should march against Fort Duquesne, and after its capture chase the
audacious enemy from the valley of the Ohio. Governor Shirley,
although well past his threescore, was to act in the new capacity
of a military chief and lead the expedition against Fort Niagara.
William Johnson, afterwards Sir William, was to march northward
with a force of colonial volunteers and Mohawk Indians and wrest
from the enemy the Fort of Crown Point that had been for a quarter
of a century a prolific source of mischief. Colonel Robert Monckton
was to be charged with the work of capturing Fort Beausejour and
expelling the Acadians from the Province, where they could no
longer remain without seriously endangering English interests as
the chiefs of that day saw the problem. Monckton was to have two
thousand volunteers from New England, and these were to co-operate with the garrison at Fort Lawrence, who were already on the
ground of action. Monckton was the first to get in motion. On
the 22nd of May he sailed from Boston in forty transports con-
voyed by three frigates, with a regiment of volunteers that had been
raised by Lieut. Colonel John Winslow of Marshfield.

We shall get but a crude understanding of these events in our
history if they are separated from their causes and relations. The
blow designed against the Acadians was not a contemptible piece of
marauding in a time of peace committed by a band of relentless
Puritans, but it was an act of defence against French aggression that
was steadily crowding the English settlers into narrower quarters,
and contemplated nothing short of complete conquest of North
America.

OXFORD, CUMBERLAND COUNTY.

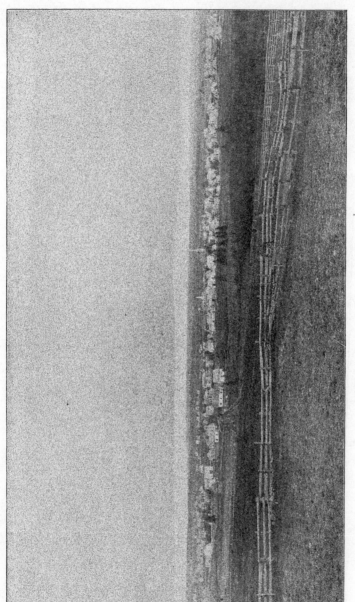

OXFORD, CUMBERLAND COUNTY.

It does not come within my design to enter into the details of this expedition, that reached its destination on the first day of June. They landed the next day, and that night were encamped around Fort Lawrence in sight of the hostile Beausejour. Parkman gives us a vivid glimpse of the locality, the structure, and the life that went on there, and here it is:

"The French fort of Beausejour, mounted on its hill between the marshes of Missaguash and Tantemar, was a regular work, peutagonal in form, with solid earthen ramparts, bomb proofs, and an armament of twenty-four cannon and one mortar. The commander, Duchambon de Vergor, a captain in the colony regulars, was a dull man of no education, of stuttering speech, unpleasing countenance, and doubtful character. He owed his place to the notorious intendant Bigot, who, it is said, was in his debt for disreputable service in an affair of gallantry, and who had ample means of enabling his friends to enrich themselves by defrauding the King. Beausejour was one of those plague-spots of official corruption which dotted the whole surface of New France. Bigot, sailing for Europe in 1754, wrote thus to his confederate: 'Profit by your place, my dear Vergor; clip and cut—you are free to do what you please—so that you can come soon to me.' Vergor did not neglect his opportunities. Supplies in great quantities were sent from Quebec for the garrison and the emigrant Acadians. These last got but a small part of them. Vergor and his confederates sent the rest back to Quebec or else to Louisburg, and sold them for their own profit to the King's agents there, who were also in collusion with him. Vergor, however, did not reign alone. Le Loutre, by force of energy, capacity, and passionate vehemence, held him in some awe, and divided his authority."

The English spent some days in preparing their camp and reconnoitering the ground. At the head of five hundred Provincials, Scott, a New England officer, seized upon a ridge within easy range of the works. The fort blazed away at them but with small results. The next day the besiegers opened fire, that provoked a ready response, but no great harm was done. The Acadians in the fort had no relish for this business and dropped out of sight on the side of the fort that was not attacked. They had been forced into the defence, and now feared that they would fall into the hands of the English, who would hold them to be British subjects in arms against their sovereign. On the morning of the sixteenth a shell fell through the bomb-proof that was not much of a bomb-proof, for it killed six officers and a prisoner. The party was taking their breakfast when this fatal incident took place. In another bomb-proof was the commandant, and with him Le Loutre and other priests and officers. This was a strong intimation that any one of them or all in a bunch might be called to a last account right speedily. Up went the white flag and Vergor showed that he had no notion of holding out when his life was put in serious peril, although some of his officers were not for such a speedy surrender. The besiegers had as yet made but little more than a beginning, and were greatly surprised that the enemy desired to surrender. The terms were soon arranged: the garrison to march out with the honors of war, and to be sent to Louisburg at the charge of the King of England, but not to bear arms in America within six months; the Acadians to be pardoned the part they had just borne in the defence, seeing they had been compelled to take up arms on pain of death. Le Loutre was for holding out even if they were buried under the ruins of the fort; no one ever took him to be a coward. He had been seen by the besiegers in his shirt sleeves with a pipe in his mouth directing the Acadians to strengthen the works: but now he was not to be found, for he had escaped in disguise amid the confusion and made his way to Quebec. In the history of Hants County in this book there is a further notice of him.

Vergor, the commandant, was a descendant of the La Tours of early Acadian history, who were of noble blood, but it seems to have trickled down to a small matter in this individual who was no honor to his line. He was tried by court martial in Quebec for his feeble defence of Beausejour, but managed to get acquitted through the connivance of Governor Vaudereuil and the intendant Bigot. He afterwards turns up discreditably at the capture of Quebec, and finally disappears in France with his pockets well filled.

The fortification was renamed Fort Cumberland, in honor of the brutal duke who ten years before on the field of Culloden was "insulting the slain." The main features of the fortification are still there, although the place has been entirely neglected. The fatal "bomb-proof" can yet be entered by a little crouching, and the accommodations were never more than scanty for a half dozen people. A farmer plants his potatoes on the embankments where once swarmed the motley group of Acadians, Indians, Canadians and New Englanders.

AMHERST, LOOKING SOUTH.

POST-OFFICE AND COURT-HOUSE, AMHERST.

Fort Gaspereaux, at Baye Verte, a dozen miles away on the northern waters, was summoned to surrender by letter, on the same terms accepted by Vergor. The Commandant Villeray accepted without hesitation. The time passed on, week after week, without incident of importance till the sixth of August, and, strangely enough, even Colonel Winslow was ignorant of what further services were expected of him and his men. In his journal he remarks: "Thus have we Got to the End of July the whole of which was Spent In an Indolent Maner and the acquaintance between the Two Camps Greatly Dropt. There being no Cal for a Convention of officers Since the Surrender of Fort Cumberland and No No Partys of the Army Stiring." , On the sixth of August Colonel Monckton sent for Winslow and informed him that he had received a letter from Lieut.-Governor Lawrence, by which he was informed that it was determined to remove all the French inhabitants out of the Province. Winslow remarks in his journal that "This is the First Conference of a public nature I have had with the Colo since the reduction of Beausejour, & I apprehend that No officer of Either Core has been made more free with, that Even these things remain a Secret to the rest."

The Colonel did not forget to express his gratification over the fact that he had been taken into the confidence of the Commander, but it is not set down that he was displeased because he had been so long kept in the dark, neither has he a word of disapproval of the policy about to be enforced against the Acadians: he evidently considered it one of the hardships of war and he was ready to do his part, although, as he said afterwards at Grand Pre, it "was very disagreeable to his natural make and temper."

Passing over the well-known scenes of the uprooting of the French population wherein they did not suffer more hardships in Chignecto from the English than they had already from Le Loutre and his Indians who had burned them out of house and home, we must at once proceed to notice the settlement of the region by other parties more desirable for the safety and welfare of the Province.

There was no end of trouble with the New England men about their pay, and other loud complaints of unfair treatment. However, all this came at last to an end, and after three or four years arrangements were made for settlers to come from the outside and occupy the fertile lands of the Acadian exiles. For the most part the movement was from Massachusetts and adjacent States. The following document, for which I am indebted to Judge Morse, of Amherst, will afford considerable information to those who care to look into the matter of the early settlement by the English.   .

Nova Scotia, S S
To all to whom these presents shall come.
Greeting.

Wheras John Houston, Joshua Winslow, and William Allan, Abial Richardson, Elijah Ayre, Josiah Throop, and Joseph Morse; Committee of the Township of Cumberland, behalf of themselves & others Proprietors in the said Township: apprehending, and being advised that the former Grants made to them, and their associates, would for many deficiencies be insufficient to secure to them their properties therin; and and therefore have requested that a new Grant of part of the said Premises might be made out for the more fully assuring to them and their associates their respective Rights & Shares therin:—

NOW KNOW YE that I Montagu Wilmot Esqr Lieut Governor and Commander in Chief, in and over His Majesty's Province of Nova Scotia, or Acadie; and Colonel of His Majesty's Eightieth Regiment of Foot: by virtue of the Power and authority to me given by His Present Majesty King George the Third under the Great Seal of Great Britain: Have given, granted, and confirmed, and do by these Presents, by and with the advise & consent of His Majestys Council for the said Province, give, grant, and confirm, unto the several persons hereafter named. Thirty Four Thousand, five hundred acres of Land, in said Township of Cumberland: Which Township is situate lying, and being in the District of Chignecto, and is bounded,——Beginning at the entrance of the River, O Lac, on the East side thereof; and bounded by said River, and measuring from the point of said entrance, with the course of the River, till it comes to a marked Boundary on the said River, being four miles in a right line from the said point.——Thence running North Ten miles to a Boundary there marked. Thence South thirty five degrees East, Nine miles and seventy five chains till it meets the Bay of Verte, at the mouth of the River Gasppero, and thence is bounded by said Bay Verte till it crosses the River Tidnish at a fixed boundary, and from thence running up the Country Southwest Nine Miles and Thirteen chains till it meets with the River La Planch. Then on said River till it comes to the Bason of Chignecto, and by the said Bason till it comes to the point at O Lac

GENERAL VIEW OF PARRSBORO.

PARTRIDGE ISLAND, NEAR PARRSBORO

River first mentioned, containing in the whole Eighty Nine Thousand acres exclusive of land heretofore reserved about Fort Cumberland, and on the said Bay Verte: Which said lands are hereby to remain exclusive of this Grant according to a plan hereunto annexed. The said Thirty four Thousand Five Hundred acres of land making Sixty nine Rights, or shares of One hundred and Sixty six Rights or shares, whereof the said Township doth consist, Computing every whole share at Five·hundred acres more or less: With all Rights and Privileges thereunto belonging as now divided. Lettered, Numbered and Described on the margin of the Grant. With all and all manner of mines unopened. Excepting Mines of Gold, and Silver, Precious Stones, Lapis Lazuli, in and upon the said tract of land hereby granted in the said Township. That is to say Unto Joseph Morse, Elijah Ayre, and Josiah Throop: Two shares each, and unto John Houston, and Joshua Winslow, Esqr, Jese Bent Gamaliel Smethurst, Senacherib Martin, James Law, Abel Richardson, and Sara Jones, each One Share and a half, and unto William Best junr, Obadiah Ayer, William Nesbitt, William How, Windsor Eagar, Archibald Hinshelwood, Gideon Gardener, Samuel Danks, Thomas Dixon, Zebulon Roe, John King, Hezekiah King, John Bent, Jonathan Cole, Ebenezer Gardener, Jonathan Eddy, William Huston, Alexander Huston William Chester, Thomas Proctor, Brook Watson, William Allan senr, William Allan junr, Jotham Gay, Martin Peck, John Walker, Henry Mc Donald, Daniel Goodin, Ebenezer Storer, Amos Fuller, Benoni Danks, Samuel Gay, John Allan, Assel Danks, Isaac Danks, Charles Outon, David Burnam, Ebenezer Burnam, David Earl Robert Watson, Anthony Burk, William Welch, John Philmore, William Southard, Samuel Raymond & Nehemiah Ward & John Collins One Share each. and unto Joseph Ayre, Thomas Clews, William Milburn, Abel Richardson, junr, George Allan, Wentworth Allan, Jabez Chappel, Leffy Chappel half a Share each. together with one Share for the First Minister, One for the Glebe, and one for the School, as particularly describes in the margin of this Grant, Forever. Saving always the previous Right of any other person or persons in the said Township, or any part thereof.————To have and to hold the said Granted premises in the said respective rights & shares to each and every of the the said Grantees in manner herein before described, with all privileges, profits Commodities, and Appurtenances thereunto belonging, Unto the said Joseph Morse, Elijah Ayre, Josiah Throop,

John Huston, Joshua Winslow, Jese Bent, Gamaliel Smethurst, Senacherib Martyn, James Law, Abrel Richardson, Sara Jones, William Best junr, Obadiah Ayre, William Nesbitt, William How, Windsor Eagar, Archibald Hinshelwood, Gideon Gardener, Samuel Danks, Thomas Dixon, Zebulon Roe, John King, Hezekiah King, John Bent, Jonathan Cole, Ebenezer Gardener, Jonathan Eddy, William Huston, Simeon Chester, Thomas Proctor, Brook Watson, William Allan senr, William Allan junr, Jotham Gay, Martyn Peck, John Walker, Henry Mc Donnell, Daniel Goodin, Ebenezer Storer, Amos Fuller, Benoni Danks, Samuel Gay John Allan Assell Danks, Isaac Danks, Charles Outon, David Burnam, Ebenezer Burnum, Daniel Earl, Robert Watson, Anthony Burk, William Welch John Philmore, William Sothard, Samuel Raymond, Nehemiah Ward, John Collins, Joseph Ayre, Thomas Clews William Milburn, Absel Richardson, junr, George Allan Wentworth Allan, Jabez Chappel, Leffy Chappel Their heirs and assigns forever,.———Each Right or Share of the said said granted premises to consist of five Hundred Acres according to the Division of the said Township now already made: Yielding and and Paying by the said Grantees their heirs and assigns, which by the acceptance hereof Each of the said Grantees binds and obliges himself his heirs executors, and assigns, to pay to His Majesty King George the Third, His Heirs and Successors, or to the Commander in Chief of the said Province, for the time being, or to any person lawfully authorised to receive the same for his Majestys use, a fee yearly, Quit Rent of One Shilling sterling money, on Michaelmas Day, next after the expiration of Ten Years from the date hereof, and so to continue payable Yearly hreafter forever.———But in case Three Years Quit Rent shall at at any one time be behind, and unpaid, and no distress to be found on the premises Then this Grant to the Grantee so failing shall be null and void, And Whereas the selling or alienating the Right or Shares of the said Township to any person except Protestant settlers, and inhabitants within this Province may be very prejudical to, and retard the selling the said Township. In case any of the said Grantees shall within ten years from the date hereof alienate or grant the Premises, or any part thereof except by Will, without Licence from the Govrnor, Lieut Governor, or Commander in Chief for the time being under the seal of the said Province: For which Licence no fee or reward shall be paid, Then this Grant to him so alienating, or granting the premises or any part thereof

Except by Will, shall be null and void, and moreover the Grant hereby made is upon the express condition: and each of the said Grantees hereby binds and obliges himself, his heirs and assigns, to plant, cultivate, improve, or inclose one third part of the land hereby granted within Ten Years. One other part within Twenty Years: and the remaining third part within thirty years from the date of this Grant, or otherwise forfeit his Right to such lands as not be actually under improvement and cultivation at the time the forfeiture shall be incurred.————And each of the said Grantees doth likewise hereby bind himself his heirs, Executor, and assigns to plant within ten years from the date herof, two acres of the said land with Hemp, and to keep up the same, or a like quantity of acres planted during the successive years.————And for the more effectual accomplishment of His Majesty's intentions for settling the land within this Province. The Grant hereby made is upon this further express condition that if each, and every of the said Grantees shall not settle either themselves or a family on each of their respective share or Right with proper stock and material for the improvement of the said land, on or before the last day of November which will be in the Year of Our Lord One Thousand Seven Hundred and Sixty five, Then The Grant shall be null and void, and of none effect to such of the said Grantees, as shall fail to settle the premises in the in manner aforesaid within the time above limited.————and the Governor, Lieut Governor, Or Commander in Chief for the time being may at his pleasure grant the Rights, and Shares of all and every of the Grantees mentioned in this Deed so failing, to any other person or persons whatever in the same manner as if this Grant had not been made.—

In Witness Wherof I have Signed These Presents, And And Cause The Seal of the the Province to be thereunto affixed at Halifax in the said Province This Twenty Second Day of November in the fourth year of the Reign of Our Sovereign Lord George the Third By the Grace of God, of Great Britain, France, and Ireland King, Defender of the Faith & so forth & in the Year of our Lord One Thousand Seven Hundred & Sixty Three,

By Command of the Lieut Governor, with the advice and consent of His Majestys Council.

Rich Bulkeley Sec

Here and there the same person has his name spelled differently in the repetitions of them: manifestly only one way is correct. If the result was not in some cases to make a different name altogether it would be of small moment, but in some instances that have happened, as in Burnam and Barnam, where it is evident by the given name that the same person is designated, I have inserted them as they appear in the document before me.

The principal town in the county is not within the boundaries of this Grant, for Amherst is situated on the slight elevation to the southward of the La Planche Creek. The present population is 5,000. It is a trading center for a large and prosperous farming district. Of late years several manufacturing concerns have greatly contributed to the business of the place. There are many fine residences, and the general air of a prosperous community is over everything. The schoolhouses and churches are in keeping with other aspects. Delightful drives open up in all directions, where the natural scenery and the historic association furnish a great variety of interesting features. Amherst is on the line of the Intercolonial Railway and therefore readily reached, and should not be neglected by those who wish to see a pretty Bluenose town with something of the old dispensation overlapping the new era that is so hostile to the conservative spirit that desires to live in the way of the fathers to the end of the world.

Leaving this portion of the county we may sail out of the Cumberland Basin into Chignecto Bay, and doubling the rugged Cape of the same name leave the lofty Isle Haute on the right and the bold Cape D'Or on the left and soon pass Cape Split, and land at Parrsborough, a delightful village situated amid a variety of natural charms. About one thousand people are there engaged in the various occupations of lumbering, trading, farming, fishing and other industries. It is distant about ten miles from Cape Blomidon on the western side of the channel. A railway connects the town with the Intercolonial Railway, and with the Spring Hill coal mines. In the year 1776 a grant of two thousand acres was made to Messrs. Avery, Bacon and Lockhart on condition that they run a ferry with a craft capable of carrying passengers and cattle between Partridge Island and Windsor. This arrangement was to meet the demands of a considerable settlement at Parrsborough that was then known as the Parish of Partridge Island, but in 1784 it became Parrsborough, in honor of the Governor of the Province. All this time the present so-called township together with the District of Five Islands was a part of Kings County. In 1840 a change was made and the Five

VIEW OF ADVOCATE, CUMBERLAND COUNTY.

CAPE D'OR, CUMBERLAND COUNTY.
(SHOWING A DUMP FROM SHAFT NO 1, OF COLONIAL COPPER COMPANY.)

Islands cast in their lot with Colchester, and the remainder got included in Cumberland.

On the northern side of Cape D'Or there is a bit of a harbor gouged out of the marshes by the restless waves, where a small stream enters, and the great tides surge endlessly back and forth, now filling the channel with turbid waters, and now leaving it naked and desolate to the sun. Beyond the marshes to the eastward the land is a little more elevated, and extends for miles in a great wide semicircular amphitheater to the base of the forest-clad hills. On this plateau is the village of Advocate with its rectangular streets, and neat cottages, and an unmistakable air of roominess that, unaware, invites one to take a long breath. There is a consoling assurance of seclusion when you know that there is not a railway within thirty miles, and no steamboat calls. A capital resting-place within sight of the sea, and the marshlands, and the lofty bastion of the Cape D'Or, and the sweep of the wide woodlands that still shelter the bear, and moose, and other wild creatures that claim the unwritten rights of sanctuary in these unfenced domains. Here reside a number of master mariners who find their ships in other ports and sail away on long voyages. A wagon road extends northeastward to Apel River and thence on to the Joggins where a connection is made with the Intercolonial Railway at the Maccan Junction.

To the southward there is a post road to Parrsborough, passing through the villages of Spencer's Island, Frazerville, Brookville, Port Greville, Fox River, and Diligence River. This is a delightful drive in the warm season. The scenery from the high hills is very attractive, and the villages are evidently the homes of prosperous people.

On the Cumberland shore of the Northumberland Strait are many interesting and picturesque localities that deserve a more detailed description than can be given them here. Some must be passed over, and others receive the briefest notice. Haliburton says: "Pugwash is the best harbor in the county. It is situated about two miles from the mouth of the bay of that name, and though not more than eighty rods wide, is so bold that a vessel of five hundred tons may lay with safety at all times of the tide within twenty yards of the shore. Just above the harbor a sudden turn of the channel displays a beautiful Bason two miles in length and one in breadth, at the head of which is the Pugwash river, fed by lakes seven miles distant." Doubtless this description holds good to-day.

Statistics give about 3,500 inhabitants to this district, and these people are engaged in shipping, ship-building, fishing, farming, lumbering, trading, and other incidental vocations. The average Nova Scotian can turn his hands to many occupations. Many of them can build a ship and sail her over the seas to any charted country. The same man is often farmer, fisher, and carpenter, harvesting both land and water, building his house and his boat, and knitting his nets, and doing it all with a masterful knack that answers his purpose. To grapple with the difficulties that beset an early settler on those northern coasts required courage and aptitude of no mean order. The climate demanded good shelter and plenty of fuel; markets were far away, roads either did not exist, or were almost impassable with teams. The land was covered with heavy forests that must be chopped and cleared before a crop could be raised. Sheep must be bred, and by industrious use of wheels, and looms, and skilful needles their wool got fashioned into clothing. All these obstacles, and difficulties called for tireless activities, and the application of intelligent courage or there would be no homes in all that region. This work was done by willing hands and strong arms that are now at rest and forever. Others have entered into the rewards of their labors, and are now reaping where the brave sowers won the land and cast in the seed. It is well to see that they are not forgotten, and a frequent commemoration of some kind, of all our pioneers, might do much to perpetuate the sturdy virtues that are critically endangered "in these piping times of peace."

Haliburton has this to say of localities near Pugwash: "The River Phillipp, though not navigable for any extent, is extremely beautiful. The town plot of Wallace is situated at the mouth of the bay of that name, where the harbor is about a mile and a half wide. It was settled by loyalists from the old Colony of New York, who sought an asylum at this place after the Revolution. On the banks of the river there is a large quarry of freestone. On the opposite side of the bay is situated Fox Harbor, which is one mile wide. This place was settled about seventeen years ago by a body of Highlanders who, though they arrived in indigent circumstances, are now comparatively prosperous."

Since the historian wrote these paragraphs three-quarters of a century ago, a great change has come over the region he had in view. Not only has the population increased, but the manner of life has entirely changed, and he would not recognize in the pros-

SPRINGHILL.

VIEW OF COAL WORKS SPRINGHILL.

MAIN STREET, SPRINGFIELD.

perous communities provided with railway conveniences, and telegraph and telephone communications, and the many other inventions of modern life, the obscure hamlets and straggling villages that he set in the best light he could without violating the proprieties.

GEOLOGY OF CUMBERLAND COUNTY.

When Dr. Dawson published his Geological Map of Nova Scotia thirty-five years ago he assigned to the carboniferous formation the whole area north and northwest from a line drawn from Cape Chignecto to Wentworth, a station on the Intercolonial Railway. Since that date there has been some important work done by the Canadian Geological Survey that has resulted in a more detailed classification of this area by which it is divided into upper and permo carboniferous and lower carboniferous. Draw almost a straight line between Minudie and Pugwash and one will have the upper division on the north and northwest, and the lower on the opposite side, the latter occupying a large irregular area stretching entirely across the county and including the narrow strip of coal measures of the Joggins and its eastern extension to Maccan and beyond, and also the Spring-hill mines. Quite centrally through the county extends the uplift of the Cobequid range. In a book entitled "A Handbook of Canadian Geology," published a half dozen years before his death, Sir William Dawson thus describes the Cobequids:

"Crossing over to Nova Scotia we have in the Cobequid mountains a great series of slates, quartzites and volcanic rocks, evidently underlying the Silurian Wentworth series, but destitute of fossil remains.

"The arrangement of these rocks in the central part of the Cobequids may be stated thus. There is a central mass of red intrusive syenite or syenitic granite, usually having a large predominance of red orthoclase, with a moderate quantity of hornblende and quartz. This sends veins into the overlying rocks, and is itself penetrated by dykes of diabase. On this central mass rests a great thickness of felsites, felsitic agglomerates, and diorites, evidently of volcanic origin. Upon these are gray, black, and reddish slates and quartzites, with a bed of limestone penetrated by metallic veins. The lower volcanic portions and the upper more strictly aqueous parts might perhaps be separated as a lower and upper Cobequid series; but the difference appears to depend rather on mode of deposition than on any great difference of age.'

R. W. Ells, M. A., of the Geological Survey, 1885, remarks that "On the south side of the Cobequid range the lower carboniferous formation has a considerable development and apparently extends in a continuous belt from the coast west of Advocate Harbor eastward to the North River in the vicinity of Truro, where our examinations terminated. Sections were made across the measures on a number of the streams between the North River and the Five Islands, including the Chiganois, the Debert Pine Brook, Folly, Great Village, and Economy Rivers. The rocks on all show considerable disturbance, frequent changes of dip indicating the presence of faults of greater or less extent. A thin seam of coal is seen at several places in their lower portion, generally not far from the contact with the older series along the flank of the mountains and has been opened at several points from Kemptown on the Pictou road to the Folly River. The character of the coal seam at all the places where tested appears to be much the same, and it is apparently of but little value."

VIEW OF AMHERST, FROM THE CUPOLA OF NEW ACADEMY, LOOKING NORTHWEST.

IN THE LUMBER WOODS.

CHAPTER XXX.

The area of Nova Scotia is 20,882 square miles. About one-half is forest. The principal trees are spruce, fir, hemlock, pine, maple, birches, oaks, beech and ash. Until within about forty years there were large areas of virgin pine of finest growth. To a very great extent they have disappeared before fire and the axes of lumbermen. With extreme carelessness and stupidity fires were allowed to escape from clearings and left unquenched by campers and teamsters. Owners of fine tracts of this timber land were wasteful in their lumbering operations, leaving large portions of valuable trunks to rot in the woods because they would not take the trouble to trim up the top part of the tree. They took only the cream of all that fell beneath their strokes. Greed 'and ignorance, a precious pair, how have they contributed to the sum total of human poverty and wretchedness, and they never did more execution on a small scale than they wrought in the beautiful pineries of Nova Scotia. Ichabod, signifies the glory has departed, and we are justified in placarding that name at the entrances of our forest domain. Aside from the commercial value of the pine, it has an esthetic worth not to be despised. It is never commonplace; and full grown, and at their best, they are suggestive of lofty qualities. They are sturdy competitors for light, pushing straight up their cone-crested crowns to catch the first rays of the rising sun, and the last beams of the gilded sunset. Their smooth symmetrical trunks suggest a natural architecture:

"Straighter than temples upbuilded by hands,
Tall column by column the sanctuary stands
Of the pine forests infinite aisles."

Very likely my readers will not expect to find poetry when looking for the figures and estimates for lumber. All the more fortunate they to come upon something here and there that does not admit of bread and butter consideration.

I can tell more about the characteristics of a person by knowing his valuation of a tree than I can by hearing him talk about himself by the hour. One who sees no beauty in a tree will scarcely see it elsewhere. The Indians set us a good example; they respected the forests, they never wantonly wounded a tree; they never killed wild animals unless they had need of them, or had reasons to fear them, and they did not allow fires to escape from their camping grounds. When but a lad I heard an aged Indian, who was respected by all, chide his small grandson for making a cut with an axe into a slender sapling birch. He gravely declared that the tree was crying from the hurt, and had the little fellow place his ear against the wound. The fact was that at this season, the spring, the starting sap may be plainly heard in such a cut, in a simmering noise. The boy was convinced, and both of us received a useful lesson.

The government and the owners of timber lands have but recently become aware of the real importance of these forests. There are about six million acres of timber, and none of it more than twenty-eight miles from tide water, and all of it in the vicinity of streams large enough to float it to shipping. This is surely no small item of natural wealth. Some of this timber is suitable for lumber and deals, some of it adapted to shipbuilding, some of it for pulpwood, some for cordwood. To a very large extent the portable steam rotary saw-mills have taken the place of the water-power mills. They are well adapted to the country, readily taken down, and put up again in another locality, and they turn out all kinds of lumber much faster than the old mills. The annual exported output of lumber, including deals, is about two hundred million feet. The home consumption for building and manufacturing purposes must amount to quite a large figure.

A few months ago there appeared in the Halifax Herald a letter written by request of that journal by Mr. E. D. Davison, of Bridgewater, Lunenburg County, and Mayor of that town, and a member of the corporation of E. D. Davison & Sons, Ltd., of that place, one of the oldest and most extensive lumbering concerns in Nova Scotia. The following extracts from his communication seem pertinent for my purpose here:

"Among the first of the exports of the south shore, pine lumber may be classed with fish as the two oldest and most important. Nearly always companions, in the same hold or on the deck of the same vessel, they have wended their way to the West Indies from the harbors of Queens and Lunenburg Counties for a century and a half. The old forest monarchs of former days have almost vanished, however. The axe and the fires—principally the latter— have swept them out of existence. The ground they occupied presents views of bleached stumps and withered skeletons, interspersed occasionally with patches of green where a swamp has prevented fire from spreading, and left occasionally a 'seeder' perhaps to prevent absolute extinction in the next century.

"As time passes, however, lumbermen have been given a substitute, and to-day the chief article of export in the lumber trade of the south shore, as of the Maritime Provinces generally, is spruce, worked up in all the various forms and dimensions suitable for the different markets to which inclination or circumstances may direct the manufacturer, until to-day this wood supplies fully nine-tenths of the lumber exported from this section of the Province.

"Of the 13,750,000 of superficial feet shipped from LaHave in 1899 about two millions were pine, but this is a much larger proportion of the latter article than from any other port of the whole Atlantic Coast. This proportion would hold good for the succeeding year, with its shipment of 14,000,000 feet, and for the ten months of the present year, which shows an export of 11,500,000 feet. This larger proportion of pine shipment from LaHave is due to the fact that the lands on the waters of LaHave have, compared with the timber lands of the Medway and Mersey Rivers, where pine was the prevailing timber, been opened up only recently; and even on La-Have the area is limited compared with the areas drained by the Medway and Mersey Rivers, and which have yielded their best pine years ago. On the whole it would seem, therefore, that the proportion above stated would be fully as much as the forests of this section of the Province would yield at the present time.

"The estimates, made by 'experts,' of the standing timber on the different tracts of land tributary to the various rivers of Nova Scotia have varied so widely, and the tracts so estimated have been 'exhausted' so often, and have increased in value so often afterwards, that it seems idle to make any attempt at any further estimate. Spruce lands are so liable to 'overrun' that it has been said of such attempts that it is pretty safe to multiply one's estimate by two, especially since pulp wood has become such an important item as a raw material.

"There are to-day, roughly estimated, probably half a million acres of forest land on the southern slope of the South Mountain, and trending toward the Atlantic, between Halifax and Yarmouth. which we may call spruce lands. Probably two-thirds of this has been cut over. We may say, however, that this proportion, operated, will yield at least one thousand superficial feet per acre, which would give a cut of, say, 350,000,000 superficial feet. The remaining 170,000 acres would yield, say, 2,500 per acre, or about 400,000,-000 in round numbers.

"Hemlock, the timber of the future, for this section at least, will figure prominently in the customs returns before very many years. Even now attention is being drawn to it by purchasers of lumber, and manufacturers are preparing to respond. New methods of operating will be adopted in order to utilize the bark. Tanneries will be established as near to the forests as possible, or even in the heart of them, and the immense tracts of lands now covered with this valuable and hitherto despised wood, will be reached by cheaply constructed railroads, the hides carried to the tanneries, and the timber, stripped of its jacket, brought to the water powers or manufactured on the spot, and the finished product brought by rail to the seaboard. This wood is found in large tracts on the lands now yielding spruce, and only awaits the enterprise of the manufacturer, who in his turn is ready to obey the universal law of supply and demand. On the lands watered by one river alone, the Medway, there are more than 100,000,000 superficial feet, and the Mersey has for years been floating millions of feet to the mills—cut in forests that have sent these quantities out to indicate what is in reserve—the bark of which has necessarily been wasted from lack of means of transportation or of any way of utilizing it.

"Millions of feet of hardwood, suitable for ship plank, ship frames and timber of various kinds, await the properly directed energy of capitalists and workers. And now that it has been demonstrated that wooden ships have yet profitable work to do, there is good reason to believe that the business of shipbuilding may be revived with a good share of its old-time vigor.

"One thing is certain, that if the great enemy of the lumberman —fire—can be placed under control, the growth of the forests of this section of our Province will keep up the present supply of our forests for an indefinite number of years, or even admit of a considerable increase when the hemlock and hardwood is taken into consideration."

In the same issue of the Halifax Herald appeared a letter by request from Mr. H. W. Freeman, of Jordan River, Shelburne County, a large manufacturer on that river, and the following extracts are from his letter:

"There are not a few important lumbering sections in Nova Scotia, and Shelburne County is not the least important of these. For many years active lumbering operations have been carried on at Clyde, Shelburne, Jordan, Sable River and Granite Village, in this county, and with proper management the day will never come when Shelburne County will cease to be the scene of operations in this line:

"The production of the Shelburne and Clyde is mostly used for' home consumption, large quantities of timber of different kinds being used for ship building purposes at Clyde, Shelburne, Lockeport and Sable River.

"The output of the Jordan, by far the largest, finds a sale in foreign markets, most of it going to the Argentine Republic and Europe. Spruce, pine and hemlock predominate, but other varieties are here in abundance. Fortunately the pulp wood fiend has not yet reached these limits.

"In order to give an idea of the extent of the operations on the Jordan it may be stated the annual cut is eight million feet and employment is given to 150 men. Taking the population of Shelburne County at fourteen thousand, and supposing that each man employed has five persons depending on him, then it will be seen that the lumbering industry on this river alone maintains nearly one out of every family in the county. The total annual cuts of all these mills is equal to 20,000,000 feet, and can be produced annually for many years if fire is kept out of these districts.

"The fire fiend has destroyed vast areas of timber on the Shelburne and Clyde streams, and the only way these lands can be reclaimed is by reforesting.

"Foreign countries for many years have been reclaiming their forest lands by reforesting, and it seems to me that any government that would appoint a commission to look into the matter carefully and reforest land where it can be done, and give ample protection to lands now growing, would be conferring a great boon on generations to come.

"There are vast tracts of hardwood on all the streams in the county that are waiting some means of transportation before any use can be made of the hardwoods suitable for furniture manufacture."

The forest area of this Province could be increased by many million acres if the Government would undertake to plant the burnt country with pines, and see that it was not burnt over again. The

area selected for this purpose could be the very land that once stood
thick in pine as the remains of them would amply prove. If they
grew there a century ago they would do so again with proper protection.   In fact Nature by her own motion and methods makes
some attempt to secure a new forest of pines on these desolated
tracts! but the odds are too heavily against her.   Pine seeds,
although winged, are not calculated to be carried very far beyond a
few hundred feet from the parent tree, and, unlike the seeds of
berries and small fruits and apples, they are never distributed by
birds and other creatures that eat them. A pine forest once fire-
killed is next to powerless to get itself replaced. On the wings
of the wind are numerous seeds of trees and shrubs, and herbs that
are adapted to take long flights and fall everywhere over the
depopulated area.   Then all the berry kind have their seeds carried
by the agencies of living creatures; in fact, that was the intent of the
plant in growing the fruit, and making it palatable, and coloring it
in order that it might not be overlooked by the animals that liked it.
In the ceaseless struggle for existence the most conspicuously colored fruit was surest to be discovered and eaten, and thus the seeds
get planted. We find that pine forest tracts, devastated by fire,
quickly spring up in other kinds of growth, the progeny of wind-
sown or berry distributed seeds.   At this point man could profitably
intervene and take the matter in hand, by planting these fire-swept
areas. The growth is so rapid that a boy of ten years of age who
plants them to-day, at sixty years may cut logs more than two feet
across the stump: this I know to be the truth from the testimony of
several men now living and active, and well able to lumber their
lands if they had them.

CHAPTER XXXI.

By chance this division has come up for consideration last of all the eighteen county histories that appear in this book. Very likely some readers will be looking for items of interest that will not be found in them, but for all that I have been fairly embarrassed with the quantity of material. Some other writer doubtless might have made a better use of it. I have been in every county and consulted all the books that have been written about the Province, to say nothing of articles and papers published by the Historical Society of Nova Scotia, and the Nova Scotian Institute of Science and other sources of information, as the reports and maps of the Canadian Geological Survey, Marine charts, reports of the Department of Marine and Fisheries, etc., etc.

Victoria County is a generous half of that lofty wedge of precambrian rocks, fringed here and there with carboniferous strata, that extends nearly one hundred miles into the Gulf of St. Lawrence. If a line be drawn from St. Ann's Harbor west to the county boundary, and thence northward on that line to Cape St. Lawrence and following the coast eastwardly, and southerly to the place of beginning, an area will be included containing about three-quarters of the county. In this large tract of country there are no settlements in the interior, which is for the most part a great forest domain unspoiled by fire or the woodsman's ax. The population of this northern portion is confined to the shores where the principal industry is fishing. The people thereabouts are for the most part of Highland Scotch origin, and so close up to the original stock that the Gaelic speech will make one at home among them anywhere in that region. Like other portions of Cape Breton, this shore was first sparingly settled by the French.

From Gow's "Cape Breton Illustrated," I abbreviated and adapted the following paragraph to my space:

"Keeping round the head of St. Ann's Bay, and down the west side, you come to the North River. Do not pass that, but drive up the river as far as you can go, which is about five or six miles, and you will be repaid. Here are intervales of intensest green, sentineled by fantastic conclaves of mighty hills, riven by tremen-

dous gorges through which rush the tributary brooklets of the
North River, which winds, and gleams, and glitters between its
emerald banks to the sea.

"Leaving the North River you can drive, if you like, through a
back settlement called Tarbert. Here are some splendid secluded
woodland views. Coming out again to the sea, you presently arrive
at Indian Brook, on which there are bits of rugged and majestic
scenery hidden away from the road that may be followed to Cape
Smokey, twenty miles away, and this is one of the eastern bulwarks
of the north Atlantic. The road winds up the southern side of the
promontory for a distance of a mile or more before you reach the
table-land at the top, and this is a thousand feet or more above the
level of the sea. This proud ocean-mountain has seen many sights
from his lofty watch-tower since he first descried the quaint little
ships of the early discoverers timorously creeping along the far
horizon. From the northern shoulder of 'Smokey,' about half
way down the descent, the settlement and harbor of Ingonish, and
the distant outline of the Cape North range of mountains burst
upon the view. Before leaving you should visit the island. Here
is a lighthouse 237 feet above the sea, near which are tremendous
cliffs rising sheer out of the water. Leaving the South settlement
at Ingonish, you drive around the head of the south, and then of
the north harbor, till you come nearly opposite Ingonish Island,
where you strike off to your left for Aspy Bay, twenty miles distant
over a bad road. Driving around the bay you pass some very beautiful landscapes. This is a variegated district—land and sea, fertile
intervale and grove and meadow, field and stream, gigantic white
plaster cliff, and thrifty farms studded with sleek and beautiful
cattle, and abounding in the richest of milk and Celtic respectability
and gravity and hospitality."

In Warner's "Baddeck and That Sort of Thing" occurs the following notice of this quaint settlement and vicinity, the shire town
of the county: ·

"Although it was Sunday I could not but notice that Baddeck was
a clean-looking village of white wooden houses, of perhaps seven
to eight hundred inhabitants; that it stretched along the shore for
a mile and more, straggling off into farmhouses at each end, lying
for the most part on the sloping curve of the bay. There were a
few country-looking stores and shops, and on the shore three or
four rather decayed and shaky-looking wharves ran into the water,
and a few schooners lay at anchor near them; and the usual decay-

BADDECK, VICTORIA COUNTY.

ing warehouses leaned about the docks. A peaceful and perhaps a thriving place, but not a bustling place.

"Having attributed the quiet of Baddeck on Sunday to religion, we did not know to what to lay the quiet on Monday. But it is peacefulness continued. I have no doubt that the farmers began to farm, and the traders to trade, and the sailors to sail; but the tourist felt that he had come into a place of rest. There was an inspiration in the air that one looks for rather in the mountains than on the sea coast; it seemed like some new and gentle compound of sea-air and land-air, which was the perfection of breathing material. In this atmosphere that seems to flow over all these Atlantic isles at this season, one endures a great deal of exercise with little fatigue; or he is content to sit still and has no feeling of sluggishness. Mere living is a kind of happiness, and the easy-going traveler is satisfied with little to do and less to see."

Within rifle range of this little town is the residence of Prof. Graham Bell, where he can say, "Good-by, proud world," and give himself up to contemplations, without fear of some one "spoiling his afternoon," as Thoreau said, by telling him a great deal that he knew already, and very much of what no one knows. I saw his beautiful and snug retreat at a distance without a pulse-beat of curiosity to enter his domain as a tourist. It is so good sometimes to be securely alone, and the man who fled into that retreat should not be visited even for five minutes, except on invitation or urgent business. I would as soon think of talking to a man while at his devotions, as disturb by a call the lord of such a lonely manor. Perhaps the wireless wizard, Marconi, will find a refuge in this northern paradise, and then the precious pair may rig up their devices for communication between them.

A southwestern extension of Little Bras d'Or runs past Baddeck and forms St. Patrick's channel, a waterway some twenty miles in length ending in a commodious basin at Wycocomagh. Mr. Warner thus describes the road from Baddeck to that point: "From the time we first struck the Bras d'Or for thirty miles we rode in constant sight of its magnificent waters. Now we were 200 feet above the water on the hillside, skirting a point, or following an indentation, and now we were diving into a narrow valley, crossing a stream or turning a sharp corner; but always with the Bras d'Or in view, the afternoon sun shining on it, softening the outlines of its embracing hills, and casting shadows on its woody islands. Sometimes we opened on a broad view Watchabaktehk Hills, and again

we looked over hill after hill, receding into the soft and hazy blue
of the land beyond the great mass of the Bras d'Or. The reader
can compare the view and the ride to the Bay of Naples and the
Cornice road. We did nothing of the sort; we held onto the seat,
prayed that the harness of the pony might not break, and gave constant expression to our wonder and delight."

Wycocomagh is a Scottish village situated at the northwest
angle of the Basin, beyond St. Patrick's Channel, and surrounded
by fine scenery. There are about 400 inhabitants in the neighborhood. The shipment of timber has been one of the principal industries of the place, and the discovery of large bodies of iron ore
suggests a mining business on a large scale at no distant day. A
writer says: "Beyond the Little Narrows is a magnificent basin,
into whose sequestered and forest-bound waters large ships make
their way and are here ladened with timber for Europe. We were
startled on rounding a promontory at seeing a large Liverpool
ship lying here at anchor with her yard arms almost among the
trees. The road runs around the successive spurs of the 'Salt
Mountain,' a massive ridge on the north shore of the Basin, and
many attractive views are gained from its upper reaches."

The Bay and Harbor of St. Ann's must have very early attracted
the attention of French explorers, for it is a beautiful and safe retreat
from the tempestuous seas.

The earliest name for the place was the Grand Cibou; it is
thus designated on maps of 1632. About that time Capt. Daniels
named it St. Ann's, and later it was known as Port Dauphin.
Capt. Daniels in the autumn of 1829, having raided Lord Ochil-
tree's fort Port Balienes, near Louisburg, brought up all hands and
set them at work with his soldiers to build a fort and chapel and
houses at the entrance of St. Ann's. There was a great deal of
flourish and high-handed half-piracy in his conduct, but that was
the fashion of the time. A few years afterwards there was nothing
to show for all his war-like preparations and Nicholas Denys, ever
with an eye to wholesome business, was erecting a fishing and
trading station there, which his envious countrymen did not permit
him to enjoy very long, and he was gone altogether out of the
island by 1660.

In the year of 1634 there resided at the spot Father Julien
Perrault, of the Society of Jesus, one of those worthy men whom
France sent in former years to Christianize the Indians of New
France. In his letters to his principal he says that at that time

Fort Saint Anne stood on the left side of the entrance to the harbor, completely commanding it. The worthy father highly praised the Indians whom he found there, describing them as being gentle and honest, and without guile, deeply deploring at the same time their ignorance of God who created them and of our Saviour Christ. They were a strong and healthy race, for the Father says that he had seen many of them of eighty to one hundred years of age, who had not a gray hair in their heads. At this time the harbor was called Cibou. Father Charlevoix, in 1720, calls the place Port Dauphin. When the French, about 1713, determined on the erection of an important fortification on the Island of Cape Breton they long wavered between Port Dauphin and Havre and Anglais. The latter was, however, finally decided upon on account of the difficulty of entering Port Dauphin, and the fortifications were built there and the name changed to Louisburg.

The morning after our arrival, on going up to the entrance to the harbor, we noticed a ledge of rock several hundred feet in length rising to a height of about twenty feet. On the side towards the sea the slope was gentle, and it was covered by a greensward, the earth having evidently been placed upon it by the labors of man. On the other side it was vertical or nearly so. Immediately in rear of this mass of rock were the remains of an old cellar wall, 120 feet long by 30 feet wide, which marked the spot where the French barracks once stood. The fort must have stood below it, so that the barracks were protected on one side by the ledge and on the other side by the fort, every trace of which, however, had vanished. A 50-pound shot and some broken shells were shown me as mementoes of bygone times, and there were a few pieces of broken crockery scattered here and there over the surface of the ground. On ascending the summit of the ledge a fine view of the harbor was presented. Its length appeared to be about five miles, its shape approaching that of an oval. At its southern extremity a small river empties into it, called formerly La Riviere de Rouville, after Hertel de Rouville, who about 1703 sacked Deerfield, Connecticut. Here and there around the harbor are little cottages. These stand quite thickly at the head where the soil is especially good, and where one sees low cliffs of gypsum skirting the shore."

At North Gut, St. Ann's Harbor, is another deposit of considerable extent from which gypsum has been shipped, more or less, for the past twenty-five years. This deposit is close to deep water. A wharf was built there from which twenty feet of water was reached at low tide, only seventy feet from the shore. At this wharf a steamer has been loaded carrying three thousand tons of cargo. In no year, however, did the output from this quarry exceed seven thousand tons. Besides the quarries above mentioned, this company own by lease or in fee simple an immense area of country containing several thousand acres of gypsum.

The deposit of gypsum at Goose Cove, in St. Ann's harbor, is exceedingly interesting and of great extent.

It is about one mile back from tide water, rises four hundred feet above tide level, and contains millions of tons of gypsum of superior quality. The shipping facilities here are also most excellent, opening as the deposit does on one of the finest harbors in Canada. Shipment has not been made in any large quantities from these quarries, although sample lots have been shipped to Philadelphia for trial purposes, and have proved exceedingly satisfactory.

The Middle River discharges into St. Patrick's Channel and there is a gold-bearing area along certain tributary brooks that has attracted considerable attention, but as yet no paying mine has been located there. Prof. J. Edmund Woodman, in the employ of the provincial government, made a detailed report on this region that appeared in the annual Report of Mines for 1898. The following paragraphs are extracts from his report:

SITUATION AND GENERAL CHARACTER.

The "Gold Brooks" of Middle River are tributaries from the south, the first of them joining the river four miles above the Upper Settlement, near the house of Kenneth McLennan. There are four of these brooks, numbered from one to four, number one being westernmost. The surrounding country is a flat upland, seven hundred to nine hundred feet above sea-level. From this upland, which in many places forms "barrens,' the streams descend in irregular courses, following in general the structure of the rocks. Usually for several hundred yards of their upper reaches they have barely strength enough to clear the surface boulders of organic debris; but they rapidly gain in grade and velocity, and for the lower portions have cut down through six or seven hundred feet of rock. It is in these narrow glens that the best exposures may be found; and prospecting is facilitated by the fact that in their lower parts the brooks cut directly across the strike of the rocks. So far as seen, the glacial drift which mantles the bed-rock throughout the lowland areas does not reach the Gold Brooks. As a direct consequence of this, the prospector is free from the composite "surface" so common elsewhere. Moreover, he can depend upon the

BADDECK.

KIDSTON ISLAND.

WHYCOCOMAGH, VICTORIA COUNTY.

loose fragments, or "float," to give a clue to the distribution of the various formations below, as success in tracing veins for several hundred feet in such a manner has shown me at Middle River.

The main portion of the barrens on the south consists of a complex of granitic rocks, which have not yet been studied. It is certain, however, that they are of diverse ages and show intricate relations. Like all the Archæan areas, they will repay the petrographer well for any study he may make upon them. Against these lies a series of probably Algonkian metamorphic slates and chloritic and sericitic schists. In many places the true slaty nature of the rock is readily distinguishable, from the small amount of alteration which has taken place. From these stages it is easy to follow the series into the condition of schist, and to see that the planes of schistosity are really planes of bedding, which metamorphism has nowhere been sufficient to obliterate. The fissibility of these rocks is due to the presence of secondary muscovite, biotite, actinolite, chlorite, sericite, and possibly talc. That there are several separate series is evident. Yet in the present state of our knowledge the attempt to define these and to give them names would be folly.

Into these rocks have come many veins, chiefly of quartz. A large number are mere lenses, extending only a few feet, and either cut the strata or lie in the bedding-planes. In general, the gangue is rather cellular. I do not consider the fancied resemblance of the quartz in these veins, noted by early students, to that in bedded veins of the metamorphic slates of Nova Scotia as of any weight. The origin of the ore here is different, and the two series have little in common. In addition to the lenses are more persistent veins, most of which lie with the strata; but a few occupy fissures of the ordinary type. Where the veins are most abundant a dike of quartz porphyry outcrops, having the same strike as the sediments, and lying nearly in the bedding planes. The whole series of metamorphosed sediments dips down under the cloak of lower carboniferous rocks which underlies the main valley of Middle River.

After discussing the situation in considerable detail, Prof. Woodman concludes as follows:

Second Brook is the best field for capital as far as known at present. The water power is fair. There is a head of about five hundred feet at the "Lizard Lode," but the stream is not large. However, in

mid-summer it seemed sufficient for such operations as would be necessary in treating any amount of ore likely to be taken from the glen.
Veins which are said to be auriferous, and which in some cases are
readily seen to be so, have been stripped for a total length of 1,400
feet, and a vertical height of at least 700 feet. This should make it
easy for anyone who desires to test the field carefully to procure unprejudiced samples himself, with little labor would yield a small net
income. The gold is largely free, yet so fine as to be only occasionally
visible to the naked eye. It is associated in the "Lizard Lode" with
galena, pyrite, chalcopyrite and other sulphides. Apparently it is never
in pockets, and on the whole is evenly distributed. An amalgamation
assay was made by the analysts, of a combined sample of parts of three
specimens, with the result that 78.7 per cent free gold was saved on
the plates. These statistics will give an idea of the character of the
ore. The gangue is rather dense for crushing, but not too hard to give
satisfactory results. Platinum is said to have been found frequently
in the alluvium, and to have been detected in assays; but a test made
for me failed to bring to light even a trace. Bismuth has been reported
in a few instances.

There is ample room for development here, especially between
First and Second Brooks, and for an unknown distance east of the
latter. The veins have been traced only a few hundred feet in this
direction. But, while proper capitalization would bring success here,
little success would attend divided interests. The manner in which
present ownership of the land is distributed, and the limited field for
operations, make this probable. Transportation down the valley of
Middle River will not be difficult, although a good road is needed if
activity arises.

I have had a number of assays made of the contents of the quartz
veins of the Middle River. As my work was understood to be, as
far as possible, of a general nature, I do not give the names of the
veins, or the nature of the assays. They were of a very encouraging
character, a number running several ounces of gold to the ton. Should
these results be confirmed by larger and more systematic sampling and
assays, it would appear that in this locality decided auriferous values
are available to the miner.

GEOLOGY OF VICTORIA COUNTY.

Nine-tenths of the rocks of this county belong to the Pre-Cambrian
formation: the other tenth is of carboniferous age. This latter formation appears as mere patches and shreds clinging here and there to
the rocks that were old when they were in the making.

Beginning at the northeastern boundary near Meat Cove and thence to Cape North, the shore is carboniferous until within about a mile of the cape, where there is a narrow gap at the point where the Pre-Cambrian reaches the sea. Cape North itself is a mere knob of carboniferous strata, doubtless a fragment not yet swallowed up by the insatiable sea. Around the Bay of St. Lawrence, reaching to the cape of that name, there is an area of some twenty square miles of carboniferous rocks.

The head of Aspy Bay is occupied by carboniferous strata that extend in a narrow wedge southwesterly barely across the county line. From this bay the coast is Pre-Cambrian to Rocky Bay and thence around North Ingonish Bay and South Ingonish Bay in a narrow border often less than a quarter of a mile in width, broken at Archibald's Point and Middle Head by outcrops of Pre-Cambrian. From the narrow entrance of South Ingonish Harbor the Pre-Cambrian has the coast to Pathend Brook, where there is a fragment of carboniferous; after a break of two miles of the older rocks, the carboniferous is continued without interruption as a mere fringe, often less than forty rods in width, till within the narrows at Englishtown, and forming the slender spit at that point whereon stands the lighthouse. St. Ann's Mountain is Pre-Cambrian hump, flanked on both sides with the carboniferous, and only at the point are its strata exposed to the bay. Both banks of the North River to a distance of four or five miles are carboniferous, making in all thereabouts some seven or eight square miles; this is continued around the northwestern shore of St. Ann's Harbor, and across to the Bras d'Or waters by a narrow tongue and then forms continuously the coast entirely around St. Patrick's Channel, extending in irregular area into the county. The extensive point between St. Ann's and the Great Bras d'Or Channel is Pre-Cambrian bordered narrowly here and there with carboniferous. There is a bit of it between Otter Island and Point Jane. From Kelly's Cove to Cape Dauphin is a carboniferous area of workable coal measures. Boulad-erie Island is entirely carboniferous.

CHAPTER XXXII.

PAPER PULP RESOURCES.

From the southern extremity of this Province to the Straits of Canso, a distance of 250 miles, and width of 30 miles to include the Atlantic water-shed, will be an area of about five million acres. Out of this at a moderate estimate there are a half million acres of pulp land that will yield on an average ten cords to the acre. The numerous lakes and rivers afford a cheap conveyance to tide water for the greater portion of this material, where it can either be manufactured or shipped to some mill in the vicinity.

At the present time there are two pulp mills on the Liverpool River in Queens County, near the mouth, at Milton, and one on the Medway River. All of them belong to the Acadia Pulp and Paper Mills Company, Limited, of Halifax. They are run by water power, and their united product is about 150 tons per day.

On the upper waters of the Lahave River, in Lunenburg County, at Morgan's Falls, in New Germany, is a pulp mill in active operation near the Nova Scotia Central Railroad. With the exception of a small plant at Ellershouse, on the Intercolonial Railroad, some miles from Halifax, there are no more mills on the Atlantic slope.

The demand for large water-powers thus far seems to be imperative, and the smaller streams to the eastward of Halifax, and on to Canso could not meet it, although there is abundance of wood on them and their tributaries.

Recently wood is brought to the mills in vessels from various localities along the shore. On the Bay of Fundy water-shed, there is a pulp mill at Sisibou, in Digby County, where there are large quantities of suitable wood. On the Avon River, in Hants County, and its tributaries are extensive areas of coniferous forests, well stocked with lumber-logs, and material for pulp.

Colchester, Cumberland and Pictou can contribute no small share of stock for pulp mills. We may now cross over to the Cape Breton portion of the Province, and in this island so richly provided with other sources of wealth, we find that the supply of pulp-wood is in proportion to the coal measures, the deposits of limestone, gypsum and iron. The County of Inverness contains 1,385 square miles, or 886,-875 acres. It is safe to say that one-half of this area is covered with virgin forests that will yield on an average ten cords to the acre of fir and spruce well suited to the pulp business. The fir is a Northern variety with but little balsam, and grows large, tall, and smooth, even to the dimensions of lumber logs. It has been tested in the Rumford Falls Mills, and proved to be of excellent quality.

The County of Victoria contains 1,198 square miles, or 767,000 acres. Almost the whole of this region is covered with virgin soft-wood forests. The damage by forest fires is too small a fraction to notice. In fact, these Northern solitudes are carpeted with damp moss, and therefore fires will not spread extensively under these conditions. No exact estimate can be made, but from considerable data at hand, and some personal knowledge gained on the ground, it will be within the mark to say there are four hundred thousand acres grown in pulp wood, that will cut on an average ten or twelve cords to the acre. Victoria County is on the Atlantic slope, and there are three streams draining the high lands, running nearly parallel to each other. These are the North River, entering at St. Ann's Bay, the Barasois, further north, and Indian Brook, a few miles more northward. Very competent hydraulic engineers, after careful survey, estimate that 14,000 H. P. can be obtained from the falls on these rivers, and electrically assembled near the mouth of any one of them. These falls are from thirty to eighty feet in height, and all of them within three and five miles of the sea.

On the Gulf of St. Lawrence side of the island the Margaree River will afford ample water-power for pulp mills. The Counties of Cape Breton and Richmond have an aggregate of 1,146,000 acres. It has not been explored with a view to its pulp-wood product, but the forests cover most of the surface and they are largely of spruce and fir. The inference is that a vast quantity of desirable material for pulp pur-poses is now standing upon these lands and awaiting the enterprise that will send their values into the general business circulation of the world.

In reply to a common complaint that the pulp-mills are robbing the lumber mills we may remark that a large portion of the wood used for pulp is not suitable for boards, and never would grow into saw-logs. Along our Atlantic shores are hundreds of thousands of cords of spruce belonging to a variety that never reaches dimensions much above fence poles; until the pulp industry came there was little or no value in them. We must also consider that thousand feet of spruce made into pulp gives a far greater return to the owner, and manufacturer than it does when made into boards or deals. The growth of spruce on well proctected lands will nearly make up for the loss of cutting away the larger trees.

Forest fires have been the great destroyers of our magnificent heritage. The Indians were shrewd enough to see that their lives depended upon the woods that sheltered the game. They carefully guarded against the spread of fires, but our own reckless people will set fire to a meadow, to clear it up, and then allow it to escape and consume thousands of dollars worth of wood and timber. The meadow was never worth clearing. Hunters and fishers, and tourists are often careless about fires, and unless some stringent laws are made and enforced there will soon be no forests in Nova Scotia.

CHAPTER XXXIII.

QUARRIES OF VARIOUS KINDS.

GYPSUM.

This mineral is known in the Province under two forms: as soft gypsum, containing

Lime . . . .'. 32.55
Sulphuric acid 46.51
Water 20.94

and as hard gypsum, or anhydrite, which consists of 41 per cent of lime and 59 per cent of sulphuric acid. The mineral is found in extensive beds, varying in thickness from a few inches up to 120 feet, and also occurs disseminated in fine grains in shales, marls and limestones which are usually associated with it. In the Maritime Provinces it occurs in the lower or marine carboniferous formation, already referred to in connection with the manganese ores, and where the limestones appear it is usually at no great distance. Its appearance is so well known, and it is so widely scattered through the northern and eastern part of the Province, that a catalogue of its exposures would be an endless task and serve no useful purpose. The chief localities yielding it are Windsor, Cheverie, Maitland, Walton, Hansport, Wallace, Antigonish, Mabou, Jubique, Port Hood, Port Hawkesbury and many places on the Bras D'Or Lake, and in Pictou County.

The deposits of gypsum in Nova Scotia are on an unequalled scale; the beds are frequently traceable for miles by exposures presenting faces fifty feet in thickness. In Antigonish it occurs on St. George's Bay as a crystalline cliff two hundred feet high, and similar exposures are met at Plaster Cove, Mabou, and many places on the Bras D'Or. This scale of exposure and the frequent proximity of the deposits to good shipping places has materially aided its output. The facilities for quarrying have allowed its extraction at rates varying from 45 cents to 65 cents a ton and this low price can be maintained for many years to come.

The anhydrite is found as lenticular masses of every size imbedded in the gypsum, and as beds underlying and alternating with it.

81   481

The soft gypsum, however, is the one chiefly quarried. It has been largely exported in the raw form to the United States, where it is ground for a fertilizer, or burned and ground for finishing houses, cornices, mouldings, etc., according to its pureness and color. It is said to be a suitable dressing for tobacco and cotton lands, and large quantities are mined for this purpose in Saltville, Virginia. It may be remarked that at many points in the Province, as Antigonish and Windsor, the transparent, pure variety of gypsum, commonly called isinglass, and known to the mineralogist as selenite, can be procured in large quantity, and almost chemically pure, massive, white gypsum. These qualities are specially utilized for cornices and center-pieces, and when they can be regularly obtained, furnish the best material for the more common applications of the manufactured article. The anhydrite has hitherto been utilized for few purposes; it is quite as well adapted for agricultural use as the soft gypsum, but as it requires stamping for its pulverization, its cost is thereby increased over that of the other, which can be readily ground. It has been used for foundation walls, etc., but is not durable enough for any permanent building purpose. It takes a good polish, and has several times been cut for mantels, tabletops, etc., but has not come into general use, as it is believed not to stand exposure long enough to supplant marble. The following statistics will show the extent of the trade which has been carried on for many years:

	Tons.	Value.
1855	95,301	$80,875
1860	805,431	85,936
1865	56,155	45,088
1870	98,050	75,650
1873	120,693	120,693

Some of the later returns are as follows:

	Tons.
1895	133,300
1896	130,489
1897	125,000
1898	131,000
1899	140,000
1900	122,281

MATERIALS APPLICABLE FOR BUILDING PURPOSES.

The building stones of Nova Scotia are chiefly sandstones and granites. The various grades of the former are supplied almost entirely from the upper coal measures. We accordingly find the quarries in the Counties of Pictou and Cumberland, and parts of Colchester and Hants. In Pictou large quarries were in operation some years ago, at the head of Pictou Harbor, and shipped annually about five thousand tons. Other quarries have been opened at Glenfallock and Middle River. A considerable quantity of stone for the use of the Eastern Extension Railway was quarried at Merigomish Harbor. Every harbor and river from Pictou to Amherst affords building stones, frequently of good quality, as at Wallace and Tatmagouche. Samples were sent to the Philadelphia exhibition from a quarry at Wallace, situated about one hundred and fifty feet above high water mark, and only six hundred yards from a good harbor. The beds are horizontal and for the first fifteen feet from the surface vary in thickness from four inches to two feet. Below this there is a massive bed which, according to Mr. Heustis, is from three to eight feet thick. It is divided into rectangular masses by joints from six to fourteen feet apart, which greatly facilitates the quarrying. The cost of the stone, delivered on board vessels in the harbor, is from forty to sixty cents per cubic foot. At the Joggins, Minudie and River Philip valuable deposits have been opened. Passing to the Basin of Minas: Cornwallis, Johnston's Brook, Horton, Falmouth, Kennetcook and Old Barns are known to contain material adapted for building purposes.

About half of the stone used in the St. Peter's Canal was from the southeast side of Boularderie Island and the vicinity of Kelley's Cove. The Boularderie quarry was abandoned, owing to the heavy capping. There was also much broken stone in the Kelley Cove quarry, and great part of the material used was from boulders. The locks were finally finished with stone from Wallace, as the engineer in charge did not succeed in finding suitable material on the Bras d'Or Lake.

The reports of the Mines Department give the shipments of freestone for the years 1873-9 at 45,814 tons, the value varying from $2 to $20 per ton.

SYENITES, PORPHYRIES AND GRANITES.

Granite is very abundant in the older rocks of the Province. Among localities that have furnished it for building purposes may be mentioned Shelburne, Queens and Lunenburg Counties. It also occurs at Aspotogen and various points, thence to Halifax. As already mentioned in describing the gold fields, it runs almost continuousiy from Halifax to Windsor, and thence westward. It occurs again at Waverly and runs through Musquodoboit, Jeddore, Ship Harbor, Sherbrooke and Country Harbor to Canso. It occurs inland at the headwaters of many of the eastern rivers, and is estimated to cover a large area of the Atlantic district. It* has, however, been quarried only at points accessible to shipping.

At Halifax it has been used a good deal about the fortifications, and a number of houses have been constructed of it, its cost, rough, being from $2.25 to $4.00 a ton. In the Cobequids there are masses of flesh and red colored syenite, which have afforded very handsome polished samples; but, as yet, have not been worked for construction. Porphyries and syenites occur in various parts of Cape Breton, but their economic value has not been tested. The following localities may be mentioned: St. Ann's, Boisdale, and Coxheath. The crystalline diorites of Louisburg were used by the French in building their fortifications.

LIMESTONES.

In Nova Scotia the limestones are confined practically to the lower carboniferous, and are generally associated with the gypsums. There are also beds of this mineral in the Laurentian, etc., of Cape Breton, and in the Cambrian and Silurian measures, but they do not usually form deposits of economic value. The carboniferous limestones are strongly developed in Cumberland, Colchester, Hants, Kings, Pictou, and Antigonish Counties, and at many points in Cape Breton. They occur in beds varying in thickness from a few inches to fifty feet, and in some localities their aggregate dimensions will exceed four hundred feet. Their quality varies from calcareous sandstones and clays to the almost crystalline pure mineral.

. At Windsor, Brookfield, and many other localities beds are found composed entirely of fossils, characterizing the marine limestone formation, and give the following component parts on analysis by Dr. How:

Carbonate of lime......................97.64
Carbonate of magnesia.................. 1.10
Oxide of iron......................... .07
Phosphoric acid ....trace
Insoluble residue .... .68

A limestone similar to the above was extensively quarried at Brookfield as a flux for the Londonderry iron ores, the quantity forwarded for this purpose in 1878 being about 16,000 tons.

In Cape Breton several places are known which afford marbles, believed to be well adapted for building and decorative purposes. The finest deposit of workable limestone yet discovered is on West Bay, Bras d'Or. In variety of color and tint this rock resembles the limestones of the George River series, of which it forms a part, but it contains little or no admixture of foreign materials, and is uniform in texture and in unequalled abundance. The following varieties have been recognized:

1. Fine white statuary marble.
2. Fine white building marble.
3. Coarse white building marble.
4. Blue and white clouded marble.
5. Brocatello marble mixed with six varieties of colored marbles.
6. Fine flesh colored marbles, often striped and variegated.

The locality offers every facility for quarrying and shipping, and blocks of any dimensions can be cheaply shipped to the United States equal in quality to those already admired as samples.

At St. Anne's Mountain, Cape Dauphin, Salmon Creek, French Valley and Escasonie, marbles are also found. At the latter place they usually are too much broken and mixed with other rock to be available for artistic purposes.

At Five Islands, Colchester County, promising marble deposits are known. The carboniferous and other limestones are quarried at all points for lime for building and other purposes. That from East Bay has been extensively burned for lime, as has also that from the George's River beds, which furnished in 1876 about six thousand barrels, invoiced at 80 cents a barrel. The Nova Scotia lime is frequently brown, arising probably from carelessness in selecting and burning. Its price per barrel may be averaged at 95 cents. At numerous points in the Province the limestones contain foreign ingredients, indicating the presence of a certain amount of hydraulicity, such as alumina, carbonate of iron, magnesia, silica, etc.

Our limestone has not been used to any extent in Nova Scotia for building purposes, although it is frequently found to stand exposure well, and to be readily quarried. Among localities yielding it may be mentioned the Shubenacadie River, Kennetocook, Lower, Horton, Thompson Station; Glengarry and Springville, Pictou County. Stones from a quarry here retain, after an exposure of forty years, every trace of the chisel or pick. As before mentioned, the anhydric or hard gypsum has been used to a small extent for walls and foundations, etc. A flaggy arenaceous schist, known as iron stone, was extensively used some years ago for warehouses and walls in Halifax. Many of the metamorphic sandstones of the Atlantic coast would furnish a most durable and pleasing building material.

FLAGS AND SLATES.

A small amount of flagstone has been quarried on the northwest arm of Halifax Harbor, and at Beaver Bank. Slates were quarried to a small extent at Rawdon and various places in Hants County, and the quality and quantity are equal to any demand. Dalhousie Mountain and West River, Pictou, are said to have good slate beds, and it is also reported from the South Mountain, Digby and Yarmouth Counties. At the Provincial Exhibition of 1879 slates were shown from Sackville, River John, and Upper Stewiacke, which although in the rough, were of good material.

BRICK CLAY.

These clays are found in many places, presenting an unlimited supply of raw material to the brickmaker. The best known clay fields are those of Shubenacadie, along the line of the Intercolonial Railway, and many points in the carboniferous districts of Colchester, Pictou, Cumberland and Antigonish.

BARYTES.

This mineral, generally known as "heavy spar," is frequently met with in this Province. It is confined to no particular horizon in the geological sequence, but occurs in the Carboniferous, and all the older strata. It is extensively used as an adulterant for paints and enamels, etc. In England the amount raised in 1878 is put down at 21,715 tons valued at about £21,000. The mineral sells in proportion to its freedom from iron, copper and other ores, imparting a color to the ground material. Other impurities, such as silica, gypsum, etc., are not so injurious. At Five Islands, Colchester County, it occurs in irregular pockets in the Lower Carboniferous. The mineral is frequently in the beautiful characteristic tabular crystals, and is associated with calc spar and copper pyrites. About one thousand tons have been exported to the United States, and a considerable quantity manufactured for home use. Some years ago a few hundred tons were mined from veins in Lower Carboniferous sandstones and shales on the Stewiacke River, near Brookfield. During the last few years this mineral has been intermittently mined at River John, where it occurs in veins, in measures said to be of Lower Carboniferous age. The quantity exported from River John in 1879 amounted to 480 tons, valued at $2,400. It also occurs associated with limonite at the mouth of the Shubenacadie River and Clifton, and at Brookfield, near the iron ores of that locality. Among other localities may be mentioned the Lower Carboniferous of the Avon, Musquodoboit and Wallace Rivers, and Greenville, Cumberland County. It is frequently found with the manganese ores of Hants and Colchester Counties. I have also seen samples from Antigonish County, Cheticamp, Loch Lomond, St. Anne's and other Cape Breton localities. Although occurring in numerous places it is the exception to find the ore holding only traces of impurity.

PLUMBAGO.

This mineral is not uncommon in the Province, although as yet no deposits have been worked. Among the localities affording it may be mentioned: Parrsborough, Salmon River, Musquodoboit, Hammond's Plains, Fifteen Mile Stream, Boularderie Island, Gregwa Brook, and Gillis' Brook, Cape Breton. These deposits are, in many cases, really highly plumbaginous shales, but were attention directed to the subject some might be found of economic value.

INFUSORIAL EARTHS.

The deposits of this material at present known are found chiefly in the lakes of the Atlantic coast, and in some bogs and swamps, which have resulted apparently from filling up or drainage of similar waters. Wentworth, Country Harbor, St. Ann's, Grand Lake, Lochaber, French River, Earltown and Cornwallis may be mentioned as localities yielding it. Beds of it are found eight feet thick in the lakes supplying Halifax with water. It is employed for polishing, etc., and the silicious varieties may be found useful in the manufacture of fire and bath brick.

GRINDSTONES.

At several, points in the Province stones are found admirably adapted for the above purpose. Among the best known localities may be mentioned the Joggins, Pugwash, Glenville, and Pudsleys

Point, where the stones are taken from a reef uncovered at low water, having a thickness of twenty to thirty feet. At Port Phillip both red and gray grindstones are made of all sizes, up to seven feet in diameter. Several cargoes have been shipped from Merigomish and stones are cut for local use at several points in Cape Breton.

Sir William Dawson, in his Acadian Geology, 1878, has this mention of grindstones: "Grindstone is one of the most important productions of the Cumberland coal fields. The principal localities of the quarries are Seaman's Cove and Ragged Reef; the beds at the former being below the productive coal measures, those at the latter above them. In smaller quantities grindstones are obtained from a number of other beds and reefs along the coast, and also from a continuation of these beds on the estuary of the Herbert River, and from the geological equivalents of the beds at Seaman's Cove, where they reappear in New Brunswick. Forty-six thousand four hundred and ninety-six grindstones were made in Nova Scotia in 1861, the greater part in Cumberland. Grindstones are also quarried in the sandstones of the eastern coast of Cumberland, and at Wallace there are valuable beds of freestone."

Doctor Abraham Gesner, in his work entitled "The Industrial Resources of Nova Scotia," Halifax, 1849, has this to say: "Grindstone grits are common, and they are cut at the South Joggins, in the County of Cumberland. During the summer season the manufacture of grindstones employs about five hundred men, who reside in temporary huts scattered along the borders of the cliffs. During the recess of the tide the strata are broken near low water mark, and large masses of rock are secured between boats, which, at high water, are lifted up and hauled to the shore, where the stone is cut into grindstones from four to six feet in diameter, and from ten to eighteen inches thick. These are called 'water stone,' and they are employed in the manufactories in the United States. A smaller kind of grindstone is made from the sandstone situated above high water mark. The principal site of these operations is at a place called the 'Bank Quarry.' The grindstones from this quarry are superior to any other ever discovered in America and besides being generally employed in the country they meet a ready sale in the American market and in England."

MINERAL WATERS.

From Dr. Gilpin's "Mines of Nova Scotia" the following is extracted: "There are numerous mineral springs in Nova Scotia, as would be expected from the variety of its geological formations.

and the deep-seated disturbances that have brought them to the surface. Many of these springs are locally believed to exercise healing or restorative powers, and in some cases it appears justly so. Others again owe their fame merely to an abnormal taste, caused by common salt not present in quantities large enough to exert medical effect. The late Dr. How examined several of these waters. The result of his labors, and a few analyses by the writer and the chemist of the Geological Survey, comprise all that is positively known about them. Among these springs, that of Wilmot, some fifty years ago, had a considerable reputation, but is now seldom visited. On the property of Mr. Bowman, near Windsor, is a spring rising from the Lower Carboniferous Limestones and gypsums and containing, as would be expected, an unusual large amount of sulphate of gypsum. An alkaline spring is known near Chester; on the Salmon River in Cape Breton, another spring is known. Cheticamp, Mabou, and Grand Anse are other localities on that island yielding mineral waters. Gair Loch, Irish Mountain, Sutherland's River, and Salt Springs are localities in Pictou County, where mineral waters of local repute are known. Earltown, Shelburne, Renfrew, and several other places are also noted for mineral springs, said to be useful in many disorders."

The following paragraphs have been extracted from Gilpin's "The Minerals of Nova Scotia, Halifax, 1901."

MANGANESE.

"The exceptional purity of the manganese ore found in Nova Scotia makes them interesting to the mineralogist, and valuable in certain operations of the manufacturer. The attention paid to these ores is by no means proportionate to their value, and to the great extent of the geological formation to which they appear to be chiefly confined.

The least valuable, but the most common of the ores, is wad, or bog manganese. It is found as a superficial deposit in connection with every geological formation known in the Province. Among the localities may be mentioned Jeddore, Parrsboro, Springhill, Ship Harbor, St. Margarets Bay, Shelburne, La Have, Chester, and in several localities in Pictou and Antigonish Counties. On Boularderie Island, Cape Breton County, it occurs as a bed several feet thick, containing from 25 to 44 per cent of manganese peroxide, from 12 to 35 per cent of sesquioxide of iron, and from 10 to 33 per cent of insoluble matter.   At Londonderry, in the iron mines, in precarboniferous strata, the ores have in places been enriched by manganese oxides to the extent of 14 per cent.

Pyrolusite occurs near Mount Uniacke in pockets and veins penetrating granite, and in the quartzites of the auriferous rocks. It also occurs as veinlets in granite as Musquodoboit and Ship Harbor.   In the slates of the Devonian age south of Wolfville, it is found in small masses and stringers.

Pyrolusite and its associated ores occur, however, most conspicuously in the lower horizons of the Carboniferous and in some of the upper divisions of the Devonian.   In the northern part of Hants County a manganiferous limestone belt appears to pass from the mouth of the Shubenacadie River to Tenny Cape, and to Walton and Cheverie.   This appears to underlie the gypsiferous strata. The measures carrying manganese ores reappear again south of Windsor and at Douglas, fifteen miles south of Tenny Cape, and near the junction with the gold-bearing rocks.   In this range of measures the manganese of Tenny Cape appears to be principally connected with a red and gray limestone, dolomite in composition. At the western end of the district it occurs as veins in conglomerate and sandstone, and also in limestone in places magnesian.

The Tenny Cape ore occurs in irregular nests and in seams eroded on the bedding planes and across fractures.   The ore is chiefly fibrous pyrolusite, with splendent luster, based on a compact or granular ore consisting of pyrolusite, psilomelane, and magnatite, the latter not present in large quantity.

Minudie, in Cumberland County, has yielded small quantities of soft, fine-grained pyrolusite giving 97.04 per cent of binoxide of manganese.   Similar ores are found at Onslow and on the Salmon River, near Truro.   Boulders containing a mixture of psilomelane and magnatite are found associated with brown hematite at the Bridgeville iron mines, and in places the ore is heavily charged with manganese.

In Antigonish County similar manganiferous iron ores are found in the drift at several places.

In Cape Breton County, at Salmon River, several shipments of manganese ore have been made from the Mosely mines.   The deposit occurs as beds and irregular layers and nodules in the soft arenaceous shale, and associated with a dark manganiferous limestone, both of lower carboniferous age.   The ore runs as high as 88.9 per cent of binoxide and are very low in iron.

During the last two years a few shipments of ore have been made from the college grant, New Ross, Lunenburg County. The ore extends over a large tract of country and is said to occur as veins sometimes three feet in thickness. The distance to shipping has proved a drawback to mining. The ore is apparently a mixture of psilomelane and manganite, and is said to carry up to 50 per cent of manganese with traces of phosphorus, and to be suitable for ferromanganese. The shipments of these ores have never risen to a large figure, and for many years have ranged from fifty to five hundred tons, principally from Tenny Cape, with small lots from Walton, Cheverie, Truro, New Ross, and Cape Breton County.

ANTIMONY.

The sulphide of this ore occurs at Rawdon, in Hants County. A mine was worked there for some years and about 3,000 tons shipped. Owing to the distance the ore had to be hauled to reach the railway, it was found profitable to ship only the richest, and a fall in the prices caused the closing of the mine. The ore carries considerable gold, and the opening of the Truro Windsor Railway will assist in the development of this district, which is undoubtedly of importance."

CHAPTER XXXIV.

In point of area this County is next to the smallest in the Province, containing but 623 square miles, but within its limits are many places of more than local interest. Its northeastern line runs from Red Cape to Irish Cove, crossing the Grand Lake midway in the course. Its southern boundary is the ocean swarming with islands, and a portion of the Strait of Canso. On this picturesque coast is the Lennox Channel, between the main land and the Isle Madame with one end opening into St. Peter's Bay, and the other into the entrance of the Strait of Canso, near the mouth of the River Inhabitants. The northern boundary is entirely formed by the beautiful arm of the sea, the Bras d'Or. The northwestern line extends from the head of West Bay to the Strait of Canso. This is a greatly cut up bit of country that has been erected into a separate County. A large proportion of its area is made up of islands that bespatter the whole south shore of all dimensions from Isle Madame ten miles in length to solitary rocks of as many feet. The shore is ragged and torn, with deep coves and long headlands and other rugged features of sea and land. ·Here are opportunities for fishing, farming, mining and lumbering. The population is 13,512, and if the natural resources of the region were turned to practical account twenty times that number could be comfortable there. A railroad is now in course of construction that will open up this long neglected district, and the most distant house from the line will not exceed ten miles.

No portion of this Province was earlier known to white men than this locality. Perhaps the Cabots or Cartier, or some other early navigator might have touched here or there in the neighborhood, a trifle earlier than the Basque, and French fishermen, and perhaps they did not.

I have mentioned St. Peter's Bay, but in that locality are the village of St. Peter's and St. Peter's Canal, all of which goes to show that the French pioneers did not forget the names of their saints, although they often neglected the practice of their virtues in that very place. It was the practice of the French, Spanish and Portuguese to give all manner of sacred names to harbours and rivers and mines and mountains, and men and women. If piety could be indicated by such simple

492

"EARNSCLIFFE GARDENS," WOLFVILLE, KINGS COUNTY.

ARICHAT, RICHMOND COUNTY.

proceedings, it would be an easy means to great ends that always lie on the far side of many difficulties. However we will not discuss this matter, the practice must have its favourable aspects or it would not commend itself to so many worthy persons. We will return to St. Peters and the Canal. It is almost a straight line from the head of East Bay, at the Portage, to St. Peter's Inlet; the shore line is at the contact of the carboniferous, and the older Cambrian formations, leaving a narrow fringe of the carboniferous here and there along the coast. At Soldiers' Cove near the Inlet the Devonian rocks take the place of the Cambrian and continue to the coast, merely faced along the line of the canal with fragmentary outcrops of the carboniferous, and at the canal itself replaced by a narrow belt of diorite that is intruded between the two great formations that flank the waterway. Thus we see that this opening is along the line of contact of these epoch-marking rocks. Man was not required to do a great deal in order to mingle the waters of the North and South that had already opened up a tortuous channel for miles along the shattered overlapping of the strata that were not firmly welded at this junction. Long before white men availed themselves of this short isthmus, the Indians had shouldered their bark canoes and passed back and forth at will. We do not know who were the first Europeans to discover this convenient step into the inland waters, but it would not remain long undiscovered in the nature of things. We have, at any rate, the written account of the first settlement at that point, from the hand of the man who made the beginning, and established a thriving fishing and trading business there. This person was the notable Nicholas Denys Sieur de Fronsac, who came out with Lieutenant Governor Isaac de Razilly. The date is probably 1632. Forty years afterward Denys published in Paris a book entitled, "Description Geographique et Historique des Costes de Amerique Septentrionale," in which he gives a careful account of the fisheries, together with drawings of the buildings and fortifications he had erected at St. Peters.

Denys appears first of all to have put up an establishment for the shore fishery at Port Rossignol (Liverpool) and sent his catch to Europe. This was a good business, but he was obliged to abandon it on account of dispute with the detestable Charnisay who claimed everything thereabouts. Denys then went to Chedabuctoz (Guysborough) and there began anew with great energy and intelligence. He constructed buildings and fortifications, and soon had one hundred and twenty men engaged in fishing. He did not neglect the soil, but cultivated it quite extensively, and with profit, besides. It is but a short distance from that point to St. Peters, and there he had also another station. At St. Ann's he had still another, and there he had fields and an apple orchard.

At St. Peter's he had with his usual discretion located himself on the narrow isthmus that commanded not only the fisheries, but the Indian.fur trade that came. much of it through the Bras d'Or waters. His fort stood near the old Kavanah house and its location can still be traced. Through the courtesy of Dr. Bissett of St. Peter's I have before me a plan of the fort, built in 1749. Scales on fishes, and shells on turtles and other creatures, imply enemies, and just as surely did this fort of Deny's imply them. He was not making palisades, and mounting cannon to withstand the attacks of Indians or English, but to repel the attacks of his own countrymen was the purpose of all this preparation. The next year after the completion of his fort, he was relieved by the news that Charnisay who had driven him from Port Rossignol, and had other intentions of a like nature, had been drowned in the river at Port Royal (Annapolis). There really was not much reason for relief,. when the facts became known that Charnisay had legal claims on the stations owned by Denys; and a certain creditor of his, Emmanuel Le Borgne, a merchant of Rochelle, had obtained a decree from Parliament authorizing him to take possession of Charnisay's property in Acadie, in payment of the debt. To get all this settled and in shape to enforce the claim took considerable time, a matter of three or four years, and then in 1754 Le Borgne was ready to push it in a vigorous fashion. He arrived at Canso, and despatched an officer with sixty men to seize the establishment at St. Peter's. As it happened Denys had gone to St. Ann's, and all his men were at work clearing land about the premises; they were made prisoners and he on his return was captured by a small detachment that lay in ambush for him on the way. He was at once carried to Port Royal and there shut up in a prison, with his feet in irons like the meanest criminal. The establishment was robbed and broken up at St. Peter's. Le Borgne, on maturer thought concluded that he had exceeded his proper authority, and set Denys at liberty. He made his way to France to get some measure of redress for these outrages. He did not go in vain, but returned with ample powers in the form of documents to come into the possession of his own again. He proceeded to St. Peter's, and the officer in charge for Le Borgne surrendered without opposition. That spring of 1754 Major Sedgwick acting under instructions from Cromwell laid siege to Port Royal, took it and carried Le Borgne a prisoner to Boston, just as he was planning to attack the Chedabucto station. With a fair prospect of peaceful possession Denys set to work and repaired his fort and buildings, and made his home at Chedabucto. In this expectation he was doomed to disappointment, for in less than ten years there was another claimant for his property, in the person of La Giraudiere who had a fishing establishment not fifty miles away on the river St. Mary. His fishing and fur-trading had not satisfied his greed, and he set about to secure the prosperous establishment of Deny's at Chedabucto. Being destitute of wholesome sentiments, and restraining principles he proceeded by false representations to undermine his rival, and ingratiate himself with the Company of New France until he secured a grant of the entire coast from Canso to Cape St. Louis and thereby including all of Deny's belongings. To enforce his claim he laid siege to Chedabucto, and failing in that, turned to St. Peter's and captured it. At this point they went to France with the mutual understanding that the Company should settle the dispute. The outcome was in favor of Denys, but he got no compensation for this expensive outrage. He was not able to establish himself again at Chedabucto on account of his great losses, and retired to St. Peter's where he was making a prosperous deal in furs when a fire broke out in the buildings, and completed his misfortunes by consuming everything he owned. The date of this calamity is not set down, but it was about 1765. Afterwards he went to Miramachi where his son was established, and was yet living in 1790.

From Bourinot's Cape Breton the following paragraph is extracted:.

"St. Peter's.—The French Port Toulouse is the first place of importance after leaving the Nova Scotia side of the Strait where we find ourselves on historic ground in Cape Breton. This well-known place, which still retains its importance as a geographical and commercial point, appears to have been named after the Count de Tolouse, who was an illegitimate son of Louis Quartoze and Madame Montespan, and won high distinction as a naval commander. The establishment formed at St. Peter's Bay by Denys was situated as far as can be ascertained, on a rocky neck of land in a little cove to the right of the entrance of the canal; and in this same neighborhood from the days of the French there has been always a small settlement of fishermen and traders. The new village that has grown up since the construction of the canal can be seen to the left of the canal and is a collection of white-washed wooden houses, almost bare of trees. In old times when Pinchon wrote of this locality, it was the center of communication for the whole island, and the most important post after Louisburg. In 1755 there were in this place two hundred and thirty inhabitants exclusive of officers and troops, and the people who were very industrious found constant employment in building boats and vessels, in the cutting of timber, and in the fisheries."

I am indebted to Duncan Finlayson, Esq., M. P. P., of Arichat, for the following sketch of Isle Madame and Arichat in particular, and Richmond County in general:

"Arichat, the county-seat of Richmond County, is situated on the south of Isle Madame, and at the mouth of Chedabucto Bay, at the entrance to the Strait of Canso. Isle Madame, named after one of the Queens of France, was settled probably later than Louisburg, though there is some evidence to show that Denys visited the island, and perhaps had a station there before the settlement of Louisburg. The word Arichat is of Indian origin. The first settler was Gabriel Samson, who came from Louisburg about 1712, and settled at Petit de Grat. Some of the Acadians after the expulsion made their way to the Strait of Canso, and settled at River Inhabitants, where they crossed over to Isle Madame. The first Acadian to hold lands in Richmond was Simon Foust, who received a Crown lease of what is to-day the town of Arichat.

The Jersey firm of Phillip Robui began business in Arichat in 1776, and the history of the town is closely identified with this historic house. It is said that they first started business in the island at the entrance of Arichat harbor, now known as Jerseyman's Island, and their establishment was destroyed by Paul Jones, the privateer during the American war, and they moved to the head of the harbor, where they do business to the present day. About 1812 other business concerns from Jersey and Guernsey followed, so that the majority of English speaking people on the Island Madame are of Jersey or Guernsey origins. The trade of Arichat from 1821 to 1867 was considerable, and ranked after Halifax, and Yarmouth, and Pictou. In 1863 the tonnage of the port of Arichat was 16,898 tons, 279 vessels, valued at $389,244. The trade of Arichat is insignificant to-day. The falling off was due to several causes, the chief of them being the decline of wooden shipping, as well as the opening up of the country, and the directing of trade to other centres.

VIEWS OF ARICHAT

To-day the only industry is fishing. The fresh fish industry which is now started has done much for the island, which should become one of the first fishing towns in the Province.

The population of Arichat is about 1,200, mostly of Acadian origin. Descousse and West Arichat to-day rival the Shire Town in population and importance. The other Acadian settlements in Richmond are River Bourgeois and L'Ardoise. The remaining districts of the County were settled by Highlanders who came there between the years 1821 and 1830. Grand River and Black River by Rossshire families, while Loch Lomond and Red Islands were settled by people from the Hebrides. St. Peters is rapidly growing. This is the home of The Kavanaghs, whose ancestor, Lawrence Kavanagh, was the first Catholic to take a seat in the Parliament of Nova Scotia."

GEOLOGY OF RICHMOND COUNTY.

From St. Peter's Canal westward and northward all within the county limits are carboniferous rocks, excepting an area that extends the entire length of the southerly shore of West Bay, and having a width of about four miles which is an outcrop of the vastly older Pre-Cambrian formation that does not quite reach the West Bay shore, unless it be at Big Pond, and near Pringle's Island. A narrow fringe of lower carboniferous rocks, often but a quarter of a mile in width and less, prevents the Pre-Cambrian from forming the coast line. Thus we see that the shore follows the close vicinity of the contact, as it also does in its eastern extension up the East Bay. By such occurrences as that, one may readily see how much the geological structure has determined the relative positions of land and water. On the southeastern side of this Pre-Cambrian area there is a slender border of the lower carboniferous rocks, similar to those on the shore side, and this is in contact on the southern edge with the millstone grits of the middle carboniferous series that forms a continuous area bounded by a nearly straight line drawn from Scotch Cove on the lake waters to within two miles of the Inhabitants Basin, then following the coast eastward and through the canal to the place of beginning. This millstone grit extends around the Inhabitants Basin and reaches the Strait of Canso, but nowhere makes a contact with the Pre-Cambrian.

The Isle Madame belongs to the Devonian formation, with the exception of a mile-wide strip of Lower Carboniferous on the south side of Lennox Passage that includes the small islands thereabouts.

32

On the eastern and southeastern side of the canal the Devonian and
Pre-Carboniferous occupy nearly the whole area. The exceptions are
the Lower Carboniferous, forming a narrow margin along the canal
where there are diorite intrusions here and there, including the vicinity ·
of McNab's Creek, Bar Point and Campbell's Creek and on to Irish
Cove, Loch Lomond, and eastward to the Salmon River waters and
beyond. The Pre-Carboniferous rocks are shut from the waters of
East Bay by this border of Carboniferous formation, and their width
is three and four miles. The Devonian forms the coast from St.
Peter's Bay to Lower L' Ardoise. The Cambrian, with but few
exceptions, extends to the county line in that direction.

"Coal seams of economic value are known at Coal Brook, Little
River, and Carabacou Cove. At the first named place explorations
have shown a three-foot, a four-foot, and several smaller seams cf
coal. The quality is stated to be good as far as the crop workings
were extended. At Carabacou Cove, or, as it is also called, Seal Coal
Bay, quite extensive workings were carried on about thirty years ago
in a seam of eleven feet eight inches thick, holding some layers of
shale. Reports made to the Government of Nova Scotia state that
there are in this connection at least seven other seams ranging in thickness from three feet upwards; beside a number of small ones. Owing
to the want of demand for coal, and to the heavy surface cover accompanied by the almost vertical position of the seams, little progress has
been made in tracing the seams inland towards Hawkesbury. It is
probable that they are sharply folded at no great distance from the
shore, and their nearest outcrop at Little River represents their reap-
pearance on a parallel folding. At Glendale on the upper waters cf
the River Inhabitants, there is a small well-defined coal field, a few
square miles in extent, showing from recent explorations a three-foct
and a smaller seam. It may be fairly assumed that there must undoubtedly be a large amount of coal in this field." '

This extract is from a paper entitled, "The Undeveloped Coal
Fields of Nova Scotia," by Dr. E. Gilpin, who is authority in these
matters.

CHAPTER XXXV.

Here we have a division of the Province that smacks of the Highlands of Old Scotland, and it is rather singular that it should stand alone in this respect. Both Pictou and Antigonish, in view of their Scotch settlers, might well have hit upon some name to commemorate the land of oaten cakes, fine scholars and brave soldiers, instead of adopting crude pronunciations of Indian words. In fact it is to be regretted that Sir William Alexander's choice of New Scotland failed to hold fast and was supplanted by the Latin form for the same thing, but nevertheless it does carry the charm and tang of New Scotland. From the time of Alexander till the Treaty of Utrecht (1713) this region, embracing the peninsula of Nova Scotia and New Brunswick, was generally known as New Scotland, as well as Accadie, and the name would doubtless have held fast had it not been for the boundary disputes that followed during more than forty years, and these involved a continuous reference to the Latin Treaty with its "Nova Scotia," with the result that we were cheated out of a better name than we have. Sir William Alexander, in his book entitled, "An Encouragement to Colonies" (1624), has this interesting passage that will bear introducing here, and then we will get back to Inverness County:

"Haning sundry times exactly weighed that which I haue alreadie deliured (viz., the advantage of colonization), and beeing so exceedingly enflamed to doe some good in that kinde, that I would rather betray the weaknesse of my power than to conceal the greatness of my desire, being much more encouraged hereunto by Sir Ferdinando Gorge, and some others of the undertakers for New England, I shew them that my Countrimen would neuer aduenture in such an Enterprize, vnless it were as there was a New France, a New Spain, and a New England, that they might likewise haue a New Scotland, and that for that effect they might haue bounds with a corresponrencie in proportion (as others had) with the Countrey whereof it should beare the name, which they might hold of their own Crowne, and where they might bee gouerned by their owne Lawes; they wisely considering that either Virginia or New England, hath more bounds than all his Maiesties subjects are able to plant, and that this purpose of mine

by breeding a vertuous emulation amongst us, would tend much to
the advancement of so braue a work, did yeeld to my desire, designing
the bounds for mee in that part, which had been questioned by the
French and leaning the limits thereof to bee appointed by his Mauesties
pleasure, which are expressed in the Patent granted vnto mee vnder
his gret Seale of this Kingdom of Scotland, marching vpon the West
towards Riuer of Saint Croix now Tweed (where the Frenchmen did
designe their first Habitation) with New England, and on all other
parts of it is compassed by the great Ocean, and the great Riuer of
Canada, so that though sundry other preceding Patentes are imagin-
arily limited by the degrees of Heauen. I think that mine be the first
National Patent that euer was cleerly bounded within America by
particular limits vpon the Earth."

By this quaint paragraph we may see that Sir William had set his
heart on having a worthy namesake for his country. In the division
of Cape Breton the Highlanders got the name of a large portion of
their home country tacked to a generous slice that extended the whole
length of the island from the Strait of Canso to Cape St. Lawrence,
reaching the Bras d'Or waters on the east and taking nearly half the
long northern extension that stretches to Cape North. This comprises
an area of 1,385 square miles that contains a population of 24,746.
Although this County is in the extreme north of the Province, and
appears on the map to be in the region where frost and storms hold
sway, to the exclusion of the more delightful aspects of nature, yet
the maps are misleading, since climate is the results of many factors.
While the cold season is a trifle long for those who prefer a warmer
clime, still it is a land of Spring, and Summer, and Autumn, where
each season displays its peculiar charms in forest and field, on mountains and meadows, and pastures and roadsides: a land of flowers,
and fruits, and grains, and tubers, and roots, where the farmer finds
a kindly soil, and a fostering sun to give him seed-time and harvest
from year to year. There the mountain Celts had much of the counter-
part of their own wild glens, and wind-swept heights, and soon made
themselves at home in these congenial surroundings. Had they been
the first European settlers, we may be sure that the County would
have been fairly stuccoed with the old familiar names of localities they
had left behind, but other men had preceded them, the Indians first,
· and afterwards the French and English, and they had not been at a
loss for designations that either described a locality, perpetuated an
incident, or a name, or humored a sentiment.

These Highlanders did not neglect the opportunities that remained, and named localities for themselves and their Scottish homes. Thus we have MacKenzie's River, MacIntosh's Brook, Ranald's Brook, Lake MacPherson, Campbell's Brook, MacDonald's Island, MacLean's Point, MacKay's Point, Glendale, Mull River, Glencoe, Strathlorn, Skye Glen, Claverhouse, Glenmore, and others too numerous to mention. In these localities may still be heard the old Celtic speech of Druid Priests and Highland Bards: the language that Cæsar heard from the hostile host that met him on the English shore more than two thousand years ago. It has come from far out of a source common to all the cultivated tongues of Europe, allied to Greek and Latin, Teutonic and Sanscrit and other respectable linguistic connections. In the fierce struggles of the nations, it has been hard pressed, and driven into small quarters, but like the people who used it the ground has been hotly disputed and surrendered little by little before overwhelming odds. It fits the Highlander's mouth to a nicety, it becomes him like his kilt and bonnet. It is a speech that readily sounds a note of war, and just as readily suits itself to devotional purposes; it is adapted to a fine long grace before meat or to a lusty war cry that startles the very eagles in their eyries.

The prevailing notion that all Scotchmen are the same people is a great mistake. While there is some intermingling of Lowlander and Highlander, still the division between them is clear enough as a rule. The Lowlander is simply an outlyer of the old Anglo-Saxon and Norse invaders, and the broad Scotch is but a survival of their more ancient speech. Every foot of those Lowlands was gotten by fighting the native tribes, British Celts, who were there long before the Christian era, and were also there to meet the Roman Legions and make the meetings memorable occasions. Tacitus the Roman historian of those days, tells of his father-in-law, Julius Agricola, who was first to cross the Scottish border, with warlike intentions, almost two thousand years ago. He says: "At no time had Britain been under greater combustion nor affairs there more precarious. Our veterans were slaughtered, our colonies burned down, our armies surprised and taken."

Their last refuge was the mountains. In Wales and the northern regions of Scotland they defied extermination by the hand of man. Thus we see that the Highland Gael is widely removed from the descendants of the Germanic invaders now occupying the Lowlands of Scotland. The ancestors of all Englishmen were pirates. They swarmed out of the Baltic littoral, where they farmed and fished and fought the stormy elements, and one another. In black boats, that well indicated their dark designs, they fell upon the British shores. Whatever they could get by the exercise of courage, endurance, strength, skill and intelligence they held to be theirs by the most defencible of titles. The Britains had what they wanted and would have, unless the holders, could resist their attacks, and that was beyond their ability. There was no end to their invasions; swarm after swarm was thrown off from the parent hives in the old home-land till they came to hold all England: were in fact England itself, and their kings were the rulers of the land. They were irresistible; they fought, and farmed, plowed the land. Their eyes were verily in the ends of the earth. A thousand years ago their King Alfred was sending an expedition of discovery into the White Sea, dispatching envoys to India and Jerusalem, and enriching the work of Orosius with geographical notes; and now his lineal descendant reigns over the widest and most populous empire the world has ever seen. They came into Scotland to make homes, to build towns and cultivate the soil: the fierce Highlanders fell upon them at every point of exposure. These enemies were divided into clans that were often at war with each other, but for all that they made common cause against the men who had driven them by force of superior numbers into the wild retreats that sheltered them. Their internal strifes were but schools of training to keep them well skilled in the use of arms and thoroughly seasoned for the border fray. They were fiercer than lions, unscrupulous in warfare, reckless of dangers, pushing daggers into each others ribs, and placing wedding rings on the fingers of daughters whose fathers had fallen by the hand of those who wedded them. They did not stick at trifles, nor seek for the soft side of things. Often enough the heather had been their bed, the crook of the arm a pillow, and the wide heavens their coverlet. Withal the Highlander was a poet whether he could write out verses or whether he could not. He lived near to Nature, and responded to her subtle moods and striking aspects. The lofty mountains, the lonely glens, the leaping cataracts, the secluded lakes and the savage surge of the moaning surf found responsive chords in the serious Celts, and made themselves perceptible in their characters and dispositions to a remarkable degree. There were mysterious influences in the awful solitudes of mountain heights, and the gloomy shadows of sunless glens, where the human voice seemed like an irreverent intrusion. In the midst of these surroundings the growth of superstition was favored; they saw not only the past, but "coming events cast their shadows before," leaving them not only scarred with the experiences of the past and grappling with the duties and emergencies of the present, but oppressed with the apprehensions of a future that a "second sight" had vaguely revealed. The result was a serious people, who did not take this life to be a matter for jest, and they saw but little occasion for lighter forms of mirth. They had been cradled throughout all their history amid perils of warfare, and the hard experiences of winning from a stingy soil and a stormy sea the means of subsistence. Only within a century and a half have they ceased to place themselves in battle array against the English forces on Culloden's disastrous field. They were at once thereafter stripped of their martial gear, and forbidden under heavy penalties to wear the national dress. William Pitt, the Great Commoner, with his masterful discernment, saw a better way, and opened the army lists for these Donalds, and Duncans, and Neils and Normans, and gave them a chance to exhibit their warlike prowess on bloody fields; and ever since their wild warpipes have been heard in all quarters of the world, swelling and screaming above the din of battles where the kilted clans crowded to the front, as if thus to fall was a proud distinction. Their blood has dyed the brown leaves of American forests, soaked into the field of Waterloo, stained the snows of Himalayan passes, and crimsoned the velts of the wide and wild Karoo. Their blood has done more than that, it has flowed in the veins of Shakespeare, and Milton, and Burns and Byron, and Ruskin, and Gladstone, and many another distinguished man with an English name, and adding always a dash of poetry, a touch of genius that belongs, of the same fine quality, to no other people. They are now but a small remnant of an historic host. They have outlived the rude usages of their remoter fathers, their virtues have been softened, but they have yet all the piquancy of a peculiar race whose presence in our province has been one of the greatest aids to its settlement and progress.

Perhaps we will do well to get around to Inverness County where the genuine article can still be found, and where I hope it will long remain as a useful factor in the public structure and a picturesque feature in the life of the Province.

The French had very early settled at certain points in this County as Cheticamp, Margaree, Mabou and Port Hood, but they were very much disturbed by wars and treaties that were utterly discouraging

to those who desired to make permanent homes. The demons of
misrule were ever abroad, and he who would have sowed was
restrained because there was no assurance that he, or his, would reap
in return. Something of the County and French population may be
learned from the following extract from Bourinot's Cape Breton.
"We come now to the adjacent County of Inverness, which stretches
from about the middle of Canso Strait to the heights that end with
Cape St. Lawrence, and includes the westerly section of the great
northern division of the island, so remarkable for its mountains and
rugged scenery. It is a County presenting few harbors of value compared with those in Richmond and Cape Breton.

Port Hawkesbury in the Strait of Canso has now become a more
important place than Arichat, and second only to Sydney as a port.
The County, however, has fine stretches of meadow lands, and on the
grassy slopes of its uplands and hills there are great facilities for
grazing and the rearing of fine cattle. The Mabou and Margaree
(Marguerite) in their courses run through a beautiful country, which
has not only a charm for the tourist but shows to the practical eye
of the agriculturist that energy and good farming could here reap rich
results. As I have already said, it is on the fine farming lands of the
Margaree that descendants of the French Acadians have had their
homes for a century or more.

Between Margaree and Cheticamp there is a considerable population of the same class, while in the latter district we meet with probably the best types of the Acadians, with all their simple primitive
ways, entirely free from the influences of the large Gaelic population
that elsewhere, as in Cape Breton and Victoria Counties, and even on
the Margaree, has intermingled with the Acadians and changed their
habits and methods of life in many respects. The total French
Acadian population of the County is probably between four and five
thousand souls, and the number is not likely to decrease. · Indeed, the
emigration of these people, even from the rugged hills of Cheticamp,
appears rather on the decrease with what it was thirty years ago
(1862). Since then there has been a decided improvement in the
condition of the people. While many of them cling to their primitive
habits they display much more energy and enterprise than their ancestors. As in Richmond County, the majority adhere to the French
language, especially in the Cheticamp district. though wherever they
are in the neighborhood of large English settlements they speak English with facility. Fishing and farming are the principal occupations

of the people as heretofore, but as one well-informed person writes: "While thirty years ago not a single individual among them was engaged in trade, now they take a share in all the active pursuits of life with energy, intelligence and enterprise, and are no longer apparently the subdued, timid people they were for many years after the possession of Cape Breton and Nova Scotia by the English.

Inquiring into the intellectual position of this class of people in Cape Breton, I find that they are in this respect considered somewhat inferior to other nationalities. They seem to lag behind the English-speaking members of the community from an educational point of view. English is the only recognized language of the public schools, and the Acadians are subject to a great disadvantage compared to the English children who commence their education at the same time. The character of the French spoken by the Acadians depends in a large measure upon the locality and their surroundings. They speak it ungrammatically of course, but still it is pure French, and not a mere patois, though some of the words in use amongst them are now obsolete in France as well as in the Province of Quebec."

As I have before indicated, the majority of the inhabitants of this County are of Scotch ancestry, but a generation or two removed from the old home land. I cannot pretend to tell much of the history of their various settlements. Among them is the district of Lake Ainslie, and I am indebted to Alexander Campbell, Esq., of Strathlorne, for the following sketch of the locality, that he kindly sent in response to my request, a bit of courtesy that was not extended from Margaree and elsewhere, although the parties might well have met my wishes.

"Lake Ainslie derived its name from Governor Ainslie, who administered that office when the Island of Cape Breton was a separate Province. This sheet of water is twelve miles long and six broad, and around its beautiful shores are the richest and most prosperous yeomanry in the island. It was first settled in 1820 by Scotch Highlanders. The eastern and northern sides of the Lake were from Mull, Tiree, Coll, Isle of Muck, and a few from the Isle of Skye. Campbells, MacGregors, MacMillans, MacKinnons, MacDonalds, MacKays,— genuine Celts. The settlers from the western and southern side were from South Uist, Moidart, Arisaig, and a few from Lochaber; Mac-Donalds, Walkers, MacCormics and MacLeans. These people were first attracted to this region not only for its beautiful scenery and rich soil, but for its wonderful production of fish: trout, alewives, eels, perch, etc. Trout are more abundant in this lake and rivers flowing into it than elsewhere in the island.

This beautiful fresh water Mediterranean is sure to become one of the choicest watering-places in Nova Scotia. Now that a railway has entered this region, its charms and advantages will become known to the outside world. Lake Ainslie is the source of the Margaree River, joining the northeast branch at the Forks. The east side settlements of this lake have produced more professional men, as ministers, lawyers, doctors, etc., than any other locality of its dimensions in the County, and beside has given a Governor and Senator to British Columbia.

. The first white child born at Lake Ainslie is still living, and the last of the first pioneers, John McGregor, died this winter at the age of ninety-five years."

Any good map of Cape Breton will show to interested parties the location of villages and harbors. I have therefore passed over those features in order to call attention to resources that are not so well known. In furtherance of that design I here insert an excellent letter contributed to the Halifax Herald, 1902, by J. L. McDougall, Esq.:

"Agricultural development in Inverness has hitherto been slow, but it must not be assumed thence that the place is ill-adapted to agricultural pursuits. There were many causes for the tardy progress of Inverness in that respect."

After enumerating the reasons why farming was not more extensively carried on in that County, and chief among them was the lack of proper railway facilities, he goes on to say, that: "To-day the Inverness and Richmond railway is completed and operated from the Strait of Canso to Broad Cove Mines, a distance of fifty-eight miles. This line of railroad lies exclusively in the County of Inverness, traverses ten fine farming districts, and taps in its course such valuable avenues of wealth and work as the Port Hood coal mines, the Mabou plaster quarries, the Broad Cove coal mine, the St. Rose and Chimney Corner coal mines, and several other mineral deposits which have not yet been adequately tested. This road gives us our first easy access to the world without. With these fresh railway advantages, with strikingly increased intelligence among the yeomanry, with the opening up of mines and local markets, with modern appliances and improved methods of farming, and with good ground and plenty of it, we may reasonably expect a rapid rise in the agricultural importance of this fine country. Even under the old conditions, Inverness rated high among the farming countries of Nova Scotia. I believe there is plenty of room here for four times as many farmers as we now have, and I know the place is capable of producing ten times as much as it does now. I should like to see a number of live, up-to-date farmers, with moderate means coming into the various districts of this County. What is wanted here is that our farmers should give their hearts to their calling, and do their work, and conduct their affairs on strictly business principles. I must not be understood to say that all our farmers have been thus at fault. Along the grand sweep of the River Inhabitants, down the winding courses of the rippling River Denys, in the rosy glens of Wycocomagh, through the fertile tracts of Mabou and Glencoe, among the sylvan scenes of Strathlorne, upon the hoary hills of Broad Cove, and on the majestic stretches of the Margaree you will find fine farms, as fine as can be seen anywhere, with thoroughly intelligent independent owners."

The coal mines of Broad Cove have lately come into much prominence with an excellent prospect of doing a large business that will be greatly facilitated by the entrance of the railway.

The Cheticamp district has attracted attention by its indications of valuable mineral deposits. While there are no mines in operation thereabouts, still it is almost certain that adequate prospecting will bring to light more than one valuable property. The following account was contributed to the press by a competent person not long ago, and contains interesting and valuable information about this portion of the County.

"For mining and prospecting purposes the mining district of Cheticamp may be defined as the region lying within ten miles from Eastern Harbor, and through which the Cheticamp River and other smaller streams flow. It will be convenient to describe this in three divisions: First, the northern, or Cape Rouge, which is an hour's drive from Cheticamp Harbor. The first prospect on the road is a copper deposit, abandoned many years ago in the days of high grade ores. The ore consists of copper pyrites, associated with carbonates, and is found along the walls and in wings of calc spar in a trap dyke which cuts the granite of Jerome Mountain. Some prospecting of a desultory nature has been done of late, but not enough to determine the value or extent of the deposit. About a mile further along the coast, in the slate of Puceenett's Mountain, is a promising copper deposit. Here the ore occurs in a fissure vein, and its thickness is about three feet. Half a mile to the northeast, in the slate of Presque Isle Beach, is to be seen another copper-bearing fissure vein; the ore is copper pyrites associated with Fluor spar. The prospecting has not been sufficient to determine the value of the deposit. Near this at the mouth of Corney Brook are workable deposits of barytes. About four miles in a southwesterly direction from Cheticamp Harbor is · a large area of copper-bearing, metamorphic sandstones and grits, associated with dikes of trap. Some years ago a shaft an hundred feet in depth was sunk there, but the ore seemed of too low grade, but recently a new company has covered this region where they are prospecting, not without considerable · encouragement. The most important is the L'Abime division, which is an interior locality. The ore does not occur in veins, but in masses, in lens-shaped cavities in the country rock, which consists of hydro-mica chlorite and hornblende schists. The ores mostly belong to the sulphite group, and in the order of their preponderance are mispickel, copper pyrites, galena and zinc blende, all carrying more or less gold and silver values."

Professor Woodman, an expert employed by the Provincial Government, reported in part of this region as follows:

CHETICAMP.

SITUATION. — The general situation of the ore-bearing rocks at Cheticamp is somewhat different from that at the two other places. They form a portion of a great plateau covering most of northern Cape Breton; and at their base lies, not the metamorphic portion of the lower Carboniferous, but the next succeeding group, which is unmetamorphosed. The former usually contributes both hills and valleys to the landscape; the latter only valleys, in this region. This lower portion consists at Cheticamp of a narrow strip along the coast, widening southward towards the village of Margaree Harbor; and from it the outlying spurs of the pre-Cambrian plateau rise abruptly. From the center of the upland, streams flow westward to the gulf; and the spurs are formed by branches of these streams which have cut their way downward for hundreds of feet, and separated portions of what was once a unit. In the sections exposed along these brooks, a few outcrops of galena have been found by various prospectors. The country between the waterways is rugged, with steep sides and flat tops, and either covered by dense growths of wood or abounding in preci-. pices and dangerous talus slopes. The most accessible route to the interior is Cheticamp River; and along its course prospectors have traveled to and from the east coast. Some of its branches and the small brooks of the region have been explored in part; but chiefly about two decades ago, when only slight traces of ore other than copper had been found.

ORIGIN OF THE ORES.—The distribution of the sulphides points distinctly to the conclusion that none of them were connected in their genesis with the entrance either of the bedded veins or of the gash veins. Rather it appears that the veins are in a measure accidental as far as the ores are concerned. There is little doubt that the blende and galena came from below, and probably the other sulphides as well. In general the amount of those substances increases with the metamorphism of the country rock. It is probable that not all the changes in the slates were effected by dynamic action, but that heat and soltaric action have played an important part. A study of the surrounding rocks shows the improbability of concentration by lateral secretion, and moreover, only a small percentage of the ore lies in what were clearly pre-existing fissures. The differences in the character of distribution of the various minerals does not prove a variety of sources for them, but does appear to show different periods of concentration. Thus the arsenopyrite is present elsewhere, while the galena is limited to definite bands, lenses, etc., and only now and then does the microscope or lens show particles of it at a distance in the schist. Again, in the areas now opened in mining, galena is found abundantly in a zone below the slate belt already mentioned; while blende is found in a belt several feet lower. The distribution in the margin between these two is not known. On the west side of the brook, galena occurs again in beds lower than those which contain the blende; and by means of "float" on the mountain-side to the east, and outcrops in the little canon a quarter of a mile below the mine, it is known that the ore also occurs considerably above the slate belt. It is upon this basis that the estimate of thickness given above is made.

ECONOMICS.—It is probable that here as elsewhere there is little to be gained by systematic searching for the precious metals in massive igneous rocks such as the granites. These rocks do contain gold and silver, but chiefly in irregular fissure veins whose distribution is erratic and ungoverned by any known laws. As an example of this, the cliffs immediately north of the mouth of Jerome brook show many large calcite veins which very possibly contain copper. In this case they are inaccessible, but there is no reason to suppose that this is the only portion of the granite areas which contains such veins. In general, then, it would be wise to examine carefully any such occurrences found within the granite zone. In regard to the region north of Jerome brook occupied by the schist, it is worth while to determine its extent inland and to prospect it carefully. It is highly probable that it con-

tains much more copper than has ever been found in it. Its similarity
to the schists of Faribault brook indicates also the possibility of silver-
lead ores of some importance. Those on Faribault brook remained
long unnoticed. Up Cheticamp River it appears as though little good
would be gained by extensive search. Below the first gorge outcrops
are few and unpromising. Something may be found, however, higher
up on the sides of the hills near by. Whatever may come from this
region will find easy transport to the coast, but beyond the lower end
of the gorge the valley is narrow, steep-sided, and completely filled in
times of freshets.

The schists south of Cheticamp River have been opened up sufficiently to show that they contain ores of some worth. It would be ·
profitable to extend the explorations of these, both along the strike
and also across it. In a few cases stream cuttings may serve, and in
others the outcrops on the hillside are numerous enough to be of some
aid; but artificial stripping of the surface will generally be necessary.

Owing in part, perhaps, to the later opening up of the country; in
part to the mistakes of a few investors; and in part to the fact that
there is in Cape Breton no one series of ore-bearing rocks of wide
extent, easily recognized, the island has not received in the past the
attention paid to equal areas of the mainland of Nova Scotia. In this
we must except the interest in the coal formations of the Sydney Basin
on the east. Moreover, for some reasons difficult to discover, the firm
belief appears fixed in the minds of many that nothing good of a
metallic nature can come out of the island. That this is a false impression anyone can learn by a sufficiently careful study of the rocks.
There is no doubt but that the region occupied by the older rocks is
one in which a number of districts are capable of successful development, if judiciously handled, with the proper distribution of men and
money. I am the more pleased to have arrived at this opinion because it has been reached by direct field work, influenced by no pre-
possession in favor of the region, with little hope held out except
by a few who had seen some of the territory, and with full knowledge ·
of the well-nigh universal condemnation accorded to the country in
commercial circles. I would be unjust if I were to convey the impression that I have seen anything which indicates the presence of enormous wealth in the rocks of any locality. But it is not upon such
foundations that the prosperity of a region can be based. Prosperity
if far more likely to follow the healthy development of lasting invest-
ments which yield moderate rewards; and I believe there is room for

such in the ores of Cape Breton. To make the best use of whatever may be in the rocks, however, thorough and systematic study must go hand and hand with investment. This is true both of the region as a whole and of individual prospects. The erratic and unscientific method of much of the search must be held responsible for a fair share of the failure to see any good in the country. A day does not suffice to exhaust the possibilities of a mining district, nor does the sight of two or three localities determine the worth of a prospect. Much will be gained if, instead of the common method, one be employed by the enquirer which shall include a study of the structure, the probable limits of the field in which ore is claimed to occur, and the chances that that particular method of ore formation may be duplicated in kind in the adjacent territory.

The method followed in this paper has been to describe in some detail those portions of the three selected regions which were most available, from either artificial or natural exposures; and to let these serve for some generalizations by myself, and still more by any who may find the research serviceable."

The interest in this locality has increased of late, and the "Inverness Mining Company" is displaying some energy thereabouts, and if the best hopes are to be realized, they are in the way of securing a large share of the good things.

Doubtless the railway will soon be extended from Broad Cove to Cheticamp and even beyond, and this feature will result in the development of mining and other natural resources that have long invited the coming of the iron horse.

The Cheticamp district contains about 200 inhabitants, most of whom are French Acadians. It is a fishing station of Robin & Co., an ancient and powerful commercial house on the Isle of Jersey, and was founded by them in 1784, and settled by Acadian refugees from Prince Edward Island. The harbor is suitable for small vessels and is formed by Cheticamp Island, sheltering the mouth of the Cheticamp River. There are no wagon roads much beyond this point. That still remains almost a trackless unexplored forest.

The Margaree has the reputation of being one of the best stocked salmon rivers in America.

The settled portion of this county is but a mere trifle when compared in extent with the portion that remains in a state of nature, where forests stretch unbroken a hundred miles into the far north. These are of great value, consisting of some hard woods, but for the

most part of fir, spruce and
pine, all of thrifty growth and
well adapted to be made into
lumber or pulp. Thus far this
wealth has not been drawn
upon, but the day is at hand
when the County will feel the
good results of nature's
bounty.

In this County the fish-
eries are no small item, and
with better methods and
greater enterprise, they will
figure more largely than heretofore in the industrial life of
the region. Wherever nature
has been very generous of
her store, there man has always taken the opportunity
to lay back more or less, and
do no more than would an-
swer his purpose in a small
way. Men are naturally lazy
—they are not hankering for
a heavy job. A continuous
holiday would be acceptable
to nine-tenths of the human
race. Hunger is the force that
moves the whole world of
animal life; if it were not for
that sharp reminder, most activities would speedily cease.
This domain of Inverness has
the natural resources that
many small kingdoms never
enjoyed. Gold and silver, and
iron and copper, and sulphur
and arsenic for metals; and
coal and barytes and granites
and limestone for minerals;

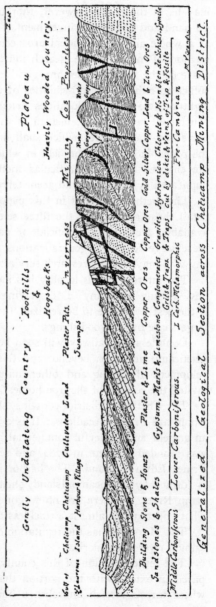

Generalized Geological Section across Cheticamp Mining District

PORT HOOD COLLIERY.

PORT HOOD COLLIERY.

FAN AT COAL MINES, PORT HOOD.

ENGINE HOUSE, PORT HOOD COLLIERY.

with soil, and forest, and sea, each and all offering large opportunities for industrial enterprises. These good things in a healthy climate, under a good form of government do not leave much to be asked for, over and above a thankful heart for such unmeasured blessings.

GEOLOGY OF INVERNESS COUNTY.

Beginning in the extreme north, from Cape St. Lawrence to the County line and thence west to the coast, the formation is lower carboniferous. From Pollet's Cove to the extreme southwestern side of Pleasant Bay the lower carboniferous forms a narrow belt from a half, to a mile and half in width and extends some four miles up the Grandanse River. From Jerome's Brook, all the way to Port Ban, some thirty miles, the carboniferous in one or another of its series forms the coast, and extends into the country about a dozen miles when abreast of Lake Ainslie, and retains that width till well up on the Margaree River, when it grows much narrower and forms a fork, one side going to the shore belt, the other extending past Sugar Loaf Mountain and ending at McInnis' Brook. In the region of Cheticamp there is a considerable area of metamorphic rocks, almost reaching the coast, and these are more or less mineralized, and present a fair field for the ever-hopeful prospector. These metamorphic rocks extend almost to the Margaree River, and thence to Lake Ainslie and across to St. Patrick's Channel. From this lake to the Strait of Canso, the County is not very unequally divided between the carboniferous, pre-Cambrian and metamorphic series. From Port Ban to within a mile of Sight Point, the pre-Cambrian forms the shore and extends backward to include an area of some twenty square miles.

CHAPTER XXXVI.

In this section there is a complete list of the birds of Nova Scotia. To those who are interested in our feathered friends, and desire to enlarge their knowledge, or even wish to make a beginning, these pages will be helpful. I have introduced the birds with some praetical directions and suggestions, because for the lack of them many persons never get at work on these lines, or they make a bad beginning and soon give up in disgust or despair.

In this section, our perching birds have received the most detailed attention because they are the most useful, the most readily observed, the most beautiful and intelligent. If it were not for the insect-eating birds the human race would starve, unless it might be that a wretched remnant could exist on fish and marine mammalia, after the manner of the Esquimaux. We will do well to keep this important fact in mind, for it is no fancied danger that menaces us. In the human race that so long was hunter and fisher, there is an almost, if not quite, an instinctive disposition to kill the wild creatures of sea and land. It has not died out with our boasted veneer of civilization. The German Emperor, out of this savage propensity, slaughters thousands of beasts and birds every year that are driven up within range of his imperial rifle, and this is called "sport." Our own King, when Prince of Wales, found it fine fun to bring down scores of pigeons in a morning. When bows and arrows were the most deadly weapons in existence, then there was not possible any great danger of killing off the birds; but now, armed with breech-loading shot-guns, the peril is serious.

It may be possible to know all the birds without the use of trap or gun, but I very much doubt if it can be accomplished without the aid of large collections of stuffed specimens, and a good library on the subject besides. There are birds enough to afford specimens to students who should, for the most part, get them by their own exertions in their native haunts. I do not mean that specimens are to be, or need be mounted on wires, but simply made into skins. 1 am thinking that a student or two in a neighborhood in the country might provide the schools with the common birds in that shape, where they can be readily examined. To make a fairly good skin is no great art;

to make them quickly will come from practice. Perhaps it may be helpful to tell how it may be done, then any person with gumption and perseverance will need no instructor beyond these directions :—

Shoot small birds with mustard seed shot. Plug up the mouth as soon as taken. Carry a little plaster of paris, or buckwheat meal, or corn meal, to absorb blood on the feathers. Roll it up in paper and place it in a basket, not in a bag, where it will be squeezed and ruined. You are in duty bound to take good care of it. That you may learn to love and appreciate birds is the only excuse for killing your specimens. Then deal tenderly with them. Place the specimen on its back, part the feathers and cut from the upper end of the breast bone nearly to the tail, have on hand some meal and throw it on the cut, and thus use it to prevent the feathers from sticking to the flesh. Now, you are not to pull the skin, but you are to push it off with the ends of your fingers, crowd it, shove it, do anything but pull it, and tear it. You may lay bare the neck and cut it away with the points of scissors, using plenty of meal. Push back the skin to the wing bones, cut them close up to the body, together with the flesh of that part, and continue backward until the legs are reached. Cut the legs off near the body; be careful of the rump, the skin is tender there and you will tear it unless much care is used. Continue till the base of the tail is reached, and cut it clear. Now, you have the skin with the body out of it, but this is only a beginning, and with practice you will be able to do that much to a jay or a robin in five minutes. Take the neck and draw it out, all the while pushing back the skin till the skull is reached. In most birds trouble will be encountered there at first. It must be a task for the thumb and finger nails. When you come to the ear-holes, they will be found to be filled with naked skin. You may pick it out with your knife and go on to the eyes. By pushing over them you will see that a thin, bluish membrane, which has a history in the animal world, is stretched over the eye; run the point of your small blade under it and cut it clear. Continue to the bill. Scoop out the eyes, cut away the base of the skull and the neck will go with it; clear out the brains, and now you have ready some arsenic, (in powder form I like best) keep it in a snug box, with a bit of a brush or rabbit's foot, and put it on the skull and eye sockets and skin of head and neck. Rub it in with the brush. Don't be afraid, but keep it out of your mouth. The use of it will prevent insects from destroying the skin. Fill up the sockets with cotton wool. Now comes a real difficulty till you have mastered it, and that is to push the skin back again without tearing it, but practice will show how to succeed.

Next comes the wings. You are to clean the meat from the upper bone, the humerus. By a close look it will be seen that on the next bone the quills are cemented by the ends to the bone; by the thumb nail they are best pushed away, and the bone, or the two bones there, skinned to the wrist joints; in small birds you need not skin further. Treat these bones and skin with arsenic as you did the head, enough will stick to the moist surface. Wind a bit, a very little cotton wool about the bones, push them into the skin again, and when both wings have been thus treated, tie them together at the elbows about the same distance apart as they were in life. A glance at the body will tell the distance.

The legs are to be cleaned of flesh, poisoned with arsenic, and then the bones wrapped in wool. With a bit of wire or smooth stick, push a small long piece of cotton wool up the neck and the end of it into the skull; if you get this too large there will be bare places on the neck. Arrange the wings closed, and their bones with the cut ends pointing to the head, and fill the skin with a piece of cotton, not full as it can hold, but full without much crowding. Sew up the skin. Put a little cotton, sprinkled with arsenic, in the mouth. Have ready a tray divided into small sections suitable to the sizes of birds, lay your specimen within on its back, with the neck straight out, but not stretched, cross the legs, tie them together and on the string fasten a label bearing the name of bird, sex, young or adult, locality and date of capture. Tuck it tenderly in with cotton and allow it to dry undisturbed. Keep them away from cats, mice and children. Keep all the skins, no matter if tattered or torn, they will prove of service and much may be learned from them. Many birds, like owls and hawks and crows, are quite readily obtained from gunners. Game birds of all kinds are to be had from sportsmen, or to be bought in markets.

A word about how to study birds in their own haunts. Interest kindled into enthusiasm will overcome all obstacles, but provided you begin without much of either, in hope of these good things following, you may succeed. Then learn their haunts, the nature of their food, their habits, their nesting and breeding, be satisfied to take them one by one. Here is a Chimney Swift, for instance, common everywhere in the Province. Notice that it never alights on the ground, or tree, or anywhere, except to cling to the side of a chimney. You will find that their food is altogether of insects taken on the wing, that their nests are made inside of chimneys and consist of small brittle twigs broken off while the birds are on the wing, and stuck together into a saucer-like scaffold by a glue secreted in their mouths. They have peculiar defective feet, their tail feathers end in bare needle-like quills, and much more I might tell of them and their close kindred. You will naturally inquire where they nested in this country before there were chimneys? In hollow trees is the answer, and other questions are also attached to that.

Learn the notes and calls of birds, till your ear will be a sure guide to their whereabouts. Become familiar with their nests, observe how they are built, and notice the species that do not build a nest at all. Don't despise a last year's nest. You may take it and be blameless. Each one has a story to tell. There is no money, no fame, in all this diligent pursuit of knowledge, but it enlarges the faculties, enriches the mind, and furnishes wholesome food for healthy thought, and these are worth more than money or fame.

If you are the possessor of an opera glass it will be found of great service in the study of birds in their native haunts. Careful observation will enable you to know many birds, their peculiar flight, also their attitude when at rest. There are real difficulties, but the charm of the work lies in that fact, for it is the overcoming that insures the triumph. Here as elsewhere, every wall will prove to have a gateway, that diligent search will reveal. The more work you have to identify a specimen, the surer you will be to remember it ever afterwards.

If you desire to mount specimens, then get a little book that will enable you to begin work. Practice and careful observation are essential to good work.

The student of birds will meet with difficulties, but the main one will be to make sure of the name of the species in hand.

The male and female, in most cases, are more or less unlike in color of plumage, and their young, even when as large as the parent birds, differ in color from them, and by reason of these unlikenesses the learner's progress is greatly arrested. When a specimen falls into your hands to be recognized, then is your opportunity for interesting work.

Begin by deciding what it is not, or in other words, use a process of elimination, by which the search becomes limited within narrow range. Corner it within a certain family at first, then make out its genus and species. If you cannot get so far at once, then label it as

far as you have gone, and find an opportunity to consult some text
book, of which there are several. Be in earnest and you will find
out all about, and enjoy the pursuit.

LIST OF BIRDS OF NOVA SCOTIA.

THRUSH FAMILY.

American Robin (Merula Migratoria).

Let us notice the thrush family, and the best known of all our
birds belongs here, viz: Our common robin. I need not describe
this bird. He is known to all because of his sociable and domestic
habits. Like all the thrushes, he is of musical turn. In the matter
of nesting, he has departed from the hard and fast rule, and builds
on fences and trees and cornices of houses, and almost anywhere a
good opportunity presents itself. This bird feeds on worms, flies,
fruit and berries—his liking for cherries and strawberries has been
fatal many a time, but it is shortsighted policy to kill a bird for eating
a pint of cherries, when he has eaten a peck of worms and insects
during the season. The robin has a special liking for angleworms,
and has consequently developed great skill in catching them.

Hermit Thrush (Turdus Analaskæ).

A common bird. The sexes alike in color. The whole upper
parts of the body an olivaceous brown, at the tail this abruptly
changes to a foxy reddish color. The under parts are white, shaded
on the sides with grayish, inside of the mouth yellow, a dull yellowish
ring around the eye, legs a pale brown, length seven inches. This bird
is the hermit of the swamps and lower woodlands, and of all the
feathered tribe in this province, he easily stands first for his musical
powers. His special time for a performance is a little before dark
and well into the gloaming. Of all the sounds of the woodlands this
is the sweetest, the most suggestive of peace and glad contentment
that greets our ears. Not to know this bird is a loss to be regretted,
and amended by making his acquaintance. The nest is generally on
the ground, mostly on a little mound, sometimes on a fallen log, more
seldom on the lowest limbs of a small spruce or fir tree. The eggs
are of a greenish blue without markings of any kind. This is a truly
common bird, often enough seen by the roadside away from the villages. In the autumn they are to be seen in the gardens after the
weather becomes somewhat cold, and food of berries and bits of fruit
are to be had near the houses. A bird of wide range over North

America, varying somewhat in different localities. In the Rocky Mountains is a variety known as Audubon's Thrush; on the Pacific coast there is another, the Western Hermit Thrush.

Olive-Backed Thrush (Turdus Ustulatus).

To all ordinary eyes this bird will not be known from the hermit thrush I have just described. His haunts are very nearly the same, rather inclined to frequent the borders of clearings than his cousin, whom he so much resembles. Once known, however, there need be no mistaking them for each other, because there is really a number of points of difference. The first is, the tail is not reddish brown, like that of the hermit thrush, the whole back, head, neck and tail, a pretty shade of olive brown, below the throat, and extending backward numerous dusky spots. A fine songster, builds in low trees, sometimes ten and fifteen feet from the ground, nest built of mosses and bark and no mud at all, the eggs have a greenish ground speckled with shades of brown.

Wilson's Thrush, Veery. Turdus fuscesens.

Cat Bird (Galeoscoptes Carolinensis).

Belonging to our family of thrushes is our Cat Bird. There is one marked structural difference that has placed him in a sub-family, by the best authority. The robins and typical thrushes have the bare portion of the leg, tarsus, as it is called, in one piece, or "booted." The Cat Bird has it scaled or scutellate in front. These are known as "mocking thrushes." Our species is of the same genus as the well known mocking bird of the cages. All the country boys know the Cat Bird, for he can mimic a cat to perfection. He is a happy, jolly fellow, loving the bushes and briers. One cannot call him black, but very dark, with a black spot on the crown, and the under tail coverts are chestnut brown. A first-class mimic is this jaunty dweller of the thicket, and he can imitate the call of a northern flycatcher, or the warbling Vireo, in a way to deceive the elect—if it were possible. He is one who does a good deal of singing in his own native fashion, mounting the tip of a bush or stake, and flirting his long tail and craning his neck before he gets fairly started, reminding one of a rural "pitcher" of tunes "in ye olden times;" but our bird can sing not only a rigmarole of his own happy vagaries, but a medley of stolen notes that moves one to laughter who knows the rightful owners.

When the hermit thrush sings, one feels that the song is his own, an expression of himself, it is sweet and sober, in keeping with the secluded haunts that he beautifies with his presence; but our cat seems to be a rollicking, merry Andrew possessed with the notion that some one is listening to his performance. The nest is concealed with a great deal of judgment in the closest thicket, and the eggs are greenish blue; if one undertakes to find it and comes close upon the secret, then the cat calls become very excited, and a fluttering protest is made to the invasion. There are other birds among us miscalled thrushes, but those I have described are the only genuine members of the family hereabouts.

SUB-FAMILY OF THRUSHES—REGULINÆ. KINGLETS.

Golden-Crested Kinglet (Regulus Satrapa).

Among the smallest of all our feathered friends are the Kinglets. The two species common among us have entirely escaped general notice, although they are as pretty and dainty as anything in our bird life. These two species are common in our woods, and,along the borders of old pastures, mostly preferring the soft-wood of firs, pines and spruces. In the winter they are almost sure to be associated with a party of chickadees. The more common of the two is the golden-crested kinglet. From tip of bill to tip of tail it is four inches; this is small measurement, for our male humming bird is three and a quarter inches long. The whole upper parts are olive green, brightest on the rump; under parts dull white, or in some cases a wash of yellowish white. Crown black; in the center of it a brilliant golden and flame color, over the eye a well defined dull white line, wings and tail dusky with yellowish borders. The tarsus or lower leg is not scaled, but booted all in one piece in front. With this description the bird will be recognized. If this bird is a songster I do not know the fact. A faint squeak is the noise I know it by. This little creature braves our rough winters, and lives wholly upon what it finds in the nests of worms and caterpillars and spiders. In pursuit of food one may see them clinging to the under sides of fir, spruce and pine branches, examining every part for some portion of meat; in this position the golden crown is conspicuous. The nest is a bulky affair for so tiny a bird, and built on evergreen trees, the eggs white, speckled with brown. It is no ordinary find to come upon the nest and eggs.

Ruby-Crowned Kinglet (Regulus Calendula).

In color this bird closely resembles the golden-crested, the most conspicuous difference is an absence of this golden crest, and the presence of a small partially concealed scarlet crown. The wings are marked by two dull white bars, and the length is about one-half inch more than the golden-crested. An interesting feature is the wonderful vocal power of this little creature. To hear him sing in June and July, one might well believe it the performance of a bird as large as a robin. I cannot describe the song in words, but I can whistle it, but not here. The nest I have never seen, the eggs were unknown till quite recently. Mr. Harry Austin, of Dartmouth, an enthusiastic collector and skillful taxidermist, has made several finds within three years. He tells me that the nest is most cunningly concealed in the thickest portion of the tops of large fir trees, and hung between the forks of a little branch. Anyone especially interested may learn particulars by communicating with Mr. Austin. This species is not so common as others, but one who knows their note in the breeding season could secure a dozen in a day.

FAMILY SITTIDÆ.

White-Bellied Nuthatch (Sitta Carolinensis).

Among our common birds of the forests is the White-bellied nut-hatch. This bird is about as large in body as our common song sparrow, but the tail is very short. Length 5½ inches. Under portion white, the whole top of the head and nape glossy black, all the rest of the upper part a bright ashy blue, wings are dark or dusky, the tail black, each feather marked with white, bill straight, strong and sharp at the end. You will not see this nimble little creature anywhere, but on the branches and trunks of trees in search of food. I read in the books that "they hop up and down the trunks of trees." My own observation is this: when they alight on a tree, they always begin and continue a downward direction, mostly in spirals around the tree or branch, all the while investigating with sharp eye and bill every possible lodgment of insects and their eggs. They are very expert, pushing their bills under bits of loose bark, and all the while uttering a sharp "quank, quank." The short tail is even with the ends of their short wings, and this is carried a little tilted up. When they reach the bottom of a tree, they at once fly to another to repeat the perform-ance. The nest is excavated from a decayed tree, the eggs are white, speckled with reddish brown. Remains here all the year round.

Red-Bellied Nuthatch (Sitta Canadensis).

One other species of Nuthatch we have in our woodlands, viz., the Red-bellied Nuthatch. This bird is not so common as the other just described. It is considerably smaller, the upper parts are like the other species, but underneath it is a rusty brown, darkest near the tail. Habits and nests and eggs very like Carolinensis. One, in fall and winter most frequently comes upon these two birds associated with chickadees, kinglets, and woodpeckers. In such a party one is almost sure to discover a quiet little bird, busy at work in quest of food on the great trunks and branches of trees. Length 4½ inches. Remains here all season◦

FAMILY PARIDÆ.

Black-Capped Chickadee (Parus Antricapillus).

This is one of the smallest of birds. The feathers cover a tiny little body, not much larger than a horse bean. It would seem impossible for this mere mite to brave the coldest weather of winter, and find food enough to sustain life in the cold bleak solitudes of the north. Surely we may say to him:

"The Providence that is most large
Takes hearts like thine in special charge."

No wonder that Emerson said of him:

"There was this atom in full breath
Hurling defiance at vast death,
This scrap of valor just for play
Fronts the north wind in waistcoat grey.",

A most sociable and fearless little creature is this dweller of the thicket, the underwood, the forest, the fence corners, and orchards. He is not a soured recluse, but a sociable companionable midget in black and grey, always, except in breeding season, in company, not only with his own kind, but entering into the friendliest relations with other species. In the winter, a chickadee party will have kinglets, and creepers, and nuthatches, and woodpeckers, all busy in their own fashion searching for food.

The chickadee is a bold frequenter of the lumber camps, investigating the barns and sheds with a saucy familiarity, diving into open pork barrels picking up scraps here and there, and living like a prince all winter long, without once having to search the frozen trees for a scanty meal. They have a very pretty note, used mostly in the breeding season, but also uttered at any time when they feel contented and at peace with themselves and the world, a very sweet note that could not come out of anything but a happy heart, and so I have ever a partial liking for it. Our chickadee breeds early. By the first of May he has pecked out a hole in a rotten stump, and by the middle of May there may be found five or six tiny, speckled eggs, resting upon a soft cushion of hairs. Length, 5¼ inches.

Hudsonian Chickadee (Parus Hudsonicus).

This bird is a rusty brown below, from the breast backward to the tail, crown is not black but dark brown, less black under the throat than the other chickadee. The call chickadee is somewhat muffled and hoarse and betrays the identity of the bird to practiced ears, even from the tree tops. These chickadees are much like miniature jays. In the far south and west there are chickadees with long crests like jays, and in this outfit they are very curious and interesting. The nest is in a hollow stub of a tree, or in the side where the decayed wood can be easily picked away. The eggs are numerous, sometimes nine and even ten in one nest. In color they are white sprinkled with brick brown. A bird of a northern range from Nova Scotia to Alaska Not common here.

FAMILY TROGLODYTIDÆ. WRENS.

Winter Wrens (Troglodytes Hiemalis).

We have at least two species of wrens, and neither of them at all common. One is the winter wren. This is a very, very small bird, a trifle larger than a hummer, and yet with a very long name, and the first part means a cave dweller, and the last part wintry. Any of my readers will be lucky to see this creature in the woods without a guide. As they dodge under old tree roots, and brush, in here and out there, they seem more like mice than birds. Wait till the breeding season comes, and you will hear this dweller of the underwood filling all the forests for a quarter of a mile around with his song. One must catch him in the very act of singing to realize the wonder of it in a creature so tiny. This is a brown bird. Tail very short and barred with light and dark brown. Carries the tail tipped upward. Long quills of the wings (primaries) barred. Nest under old roots of upturned trees, in stumps or hollow logs. Eggs white, finely dotted with brown.

House Wren (Troglodytes Domesticus).

But one individual has come under my observation here. Doubtless there are others, as it is a bird of a northern range. Brown over all the body; underneath parts rusty brown; whole plumage wavy with fine lines. Length, 5 inches. Nests in hollow trees and in old buildings. Eggs brown with fine dots. A very tame little bird, preferring the haunts of men to the forest.

FAMILY CERTHIDÆ. CREEPERS.

Brown Creeper (Certhia Familiaris).

This is a fairly common bird of the forests. He never ventures out into the borders of fields. To make his acquaintance you must pay him a visit. This description will suit him: The back is reddish brown streaked with whitish, under parts dirty white, a well-marked whitish stripe over the eye, the bill slender and curved downward, tail long and each feather stiff and sharp at the end like those of a woodpecker. This curious little bird has no note beyond a feeble chirp and squeak. It invariably, while in search for food, alights upon the base of a tree, trunk or limb, and climbs up in irregular spirals, bracing itself with the rigid tail, and peering and prying into every crevice and lodgment of insects, spiders and eggs. These birds associate in cold weather (for they winter with us as also do the nuthatches) with the chickadees and others mentioned above. The nest is oftenest found under a bit of loose fir bark clinging to a dead trunk, the eggs are numerous and speckled, and a nest is not a common find. Length 5½ inches.

FAMILY SAXICOLINÆ. BLUEBIRDS.

Eastern Bluebird (Sialia Sialis).

Unless others have been more careful in observation than myself, the eastern bluebird (sialia sialis) is a rare species in this region.

One year ago I saw a pair on the Molega Barrens. This summer I have noticed a pair nesting in the same locality, and more than these I have never seen here. This beautiful bird, so domestic in its habits, would be a welcome addition to our birds. I hope no one will be tempted by their rarity and beauty to kill a single specimen at present.

The male in full plumage is a rich azure blue on all the upper parts. The throat, breast and sides are chestnut. The under tail coverts white, extending forward a little between the legs. Somewhat larger than a sparrow, 6½ inches long. The female is duller in color, only bright blue on the rump and tail. Young ones are brown, excepting a shade of blue on wings and tails. Nests in hollow trees in stumps or posts, or even martinboxes; the eggs are light bluish, and two or three broods in one season is the usual habit. This species is the "early bluebird" of New England where it is much noticed and well known by all. They are cheerful songsters in a quiet way, and I hope to see them fairly common in our midst.

FAMILY CYPSELIDÆ.

Chimney Swallow—Chimney Swift (Chætura Pelagica).

This bird is not a swallow, as commonly supposed, and beyond a mere outward appearance at first sight they do not much resemble them and are by no means closely related to them. The toes are pecu-liar; the third and fourth have three joints like the second, and the hind toe is reversed, being turned forward. The end of each tail quill is long, bare and pointed, the leg is feathered, and the mouth is pro-vided with glands that secrete large quantities of glutinous saliva. The chimney swift never alights on the ground, or anywhere but in the chimney, where it clings to the dark sooty wall. The habit of building in chimneys is something new to them. In wild remote dis-tricts they still nest in the cliffs and in hollow trees, but for come rea-son when chimneys were built here in America these birds forsook their old haunts and selected these dark and smoky places to build and breed in, and now it is fairly an instinct with them, showing us that these little creatures do change their habits and in a measure exercise their own judgment in some things. The nest is too well known to need a detailed description. It is of entirely small dry twigs, glued together with the saliva of the birds. These twigs are plucked from the trees by the birds on the wing. I have often seen them do it, and a very nice feat it is. Their food is wholly of winged insects which they must capture in great numbers. They seem to be a jolly lot as they go chittering through the air like children just out of school with lots of noise that means nothing more than the fact that they are glad to get a chance to "holler." They are very sociable, always living in communities, and when abroad seem to have real parties, often of hundreds in a group; then watch them! see what curves and turns and dashes, what endless diversities of wing tactics, to keep out of one another's way and keep up the fun.

One member of this family, resident in the East Indies and China and Java, builds a nest in which there is more glue used than in ours. This nest is carefully prepared by the Chinese and made into soup, which is so great a delicacy that a single nest is valued at twenty-five dollars, and consequently only rich people can afford to eat them. I may say their eggs are four or five in number, of a pure white color.

Often the old birds are greatly troubled by the nest breaking away from the brick, by reason of the weight of the young birds. Then all goes to the bottom of the chimney, but there they feed them until they can crawl and shift for themselves.

FAMILY CAPRIMULGIDÆ.

Night Hawk (Chordeiles Virginianus).

We all know this fellow, with his big head, wide mouth and long wings with white bars across them. What a master of the art of flying is this dashing goat-sucker, as he is often called. Who of us has not seen him high in air, dashing down almost to the ground, and, with a quick twirl of his wings, shooting up again, making, as he turned, a singular noise like that produced by striking on a stretched wire. He scorns to pick up his bugs one by one, but away he scoots with open jaws, engulfing them as it were, in his roomy throat, dropping down upon the flocks of beetles and flies and scooping them up as if it were fun to catch them. When he comes to a standstill on a fence-rail or a dead limb, he always sits lengthwise of it. This is a protective habit. His colors agree with the object on which he rests, and his attitude is not conspicuous. On the wing he is a beauty—such quartering the air, such curves and spirals, such splendid evolutions of all kinds, that no other can distance him. He loves an eleven o'clock meal, and so comes out with his sharp squeak and slashes with his wings all the air above some grass, grain, or potato field. Then at twilight he is out again in pursuit of his food; he is a voracious eater. I shot one, from which I took over three hundred small red-and-black beetles, that he had run down in a half hour's foraging over a potato field. He does not make a nest, but scratches out a little hollow place on a bare barren or burnt land, lays two eggs of a dirty white, specked with brown of different shades. On the whole he is a stupid fellow, with fine qualities here and there. On the wing he is a beauty; in the hand he is ugly enough, with his large eyes, monstrous head, and defective feet. In his case, "distance lends enchantment to the view," and if you admire him in the air, be sure to never bring him down for a nearer look.

Whippoorwill (Antrostomus Vociferus).

This is a bird which is not often seen even where it is often heard. It is rarely abroad in the daylight, and seeks the shelter of the thick woods during that time. It very closely resembles the night hawk in general appearance, but the heavy, long bristles by the sides of its mouth are sufficient to identify it, when comparing it with the night hawk. Its peculiar cry of "whip-poor-will" has given it a name, and it has no other call except a sort of clucking sound occasionally uttered. This is a very rare bird in this portion of the Province. Only once during ten years have I met with it here. Length, 9 inches. Nest and eggs much like the night hawk.

FAMILY HIRUNDINIDÆ.

Swallows.

In all the world there are known to be about one hundred species of swallows. They are altogether insect-eating, and are therefore serviceable to man. Aside from their services, they are pretty forms of life, graceful on the wing, interesting in their nesting habits, and apparently happy in the enjoyment of existence. Being dependent upon flying insects, they come to climates like our own with the warm weather and leave on the approach of cold. They come to us from Southern climes where there is abundant food, making a journey of two or three thousand miles to build their nests and rear their young, and why they and other birds have such a habit has not yet been explained. It would seem to be an inherited habit formed when climates were different and food was differently distributed. The old spur of hunger no longer starts them, but habit keeps up the practice, and we may be glad if it does. It was an old belief in England and other countries that the swallows found a particular kind of stone on the seashore and carried it to their nests where it gave sight to their blind young. With this in view, Longfellow says in Evangeline:

" Seeking with eager eyes the wondrous stone which the swallow
  Brings from the shore of the sea to restore the sight of her fledge-
     lings."

Among old medical concoctions that were supposed to be good for "what ails you" these dainty birds were not neglected. Here are the directions:

"Take swallows and burn them, and powder them and give the drunken men thereof to drink, and he shall never be drunken hereafter." Less expensive than the present gold cure.

An old writer, more than a thousand years ago, says to anyone fearing blindness: "Look out for the first swallow, then run silently to the nearest spring, wash your eyes and pray God that you may be clear from it that year."

An old English book of knowledge has this valuable information: "Take a swallow in the month of August, look into her breast and you shall find a stone the bigness of a pease, take it and put it under your tongue and you shall have such eloquence that no man shall have power to deny thy request."

When men of learning believed all such idle stuff they were not less intelligent than we are who smile at such silly stories told in earnest. It has been the work of keen-eyed science to purify the intellectual atmosphere of such ignorance and superstition.   They are inseparable associates.   Anyone could believe in miracles in those days, and some men of learning like Sir Thomas Browne, hankered after greater than the Scriptures contained, in order that he might show his faith in them.

There is a widespread belief that some swallows do not go away to warmer regions in the autumn, but hibernate, or pass the winter like frogs under soft mire or in the mud of marshes where the water covers them in winter.   It is pretty safe to say that chimney swifts pass the winter in hollow trees where they assemble in great numbers. The foremost authority says that "I suppose the chimney swift hibernates, and could give reasons for my belief."   A great deal has been written on the subject of swallows hibernating, and Dr. Coues says of it that "The most wary or the most timid student may be assured that he will find himself in perfectly respectable company whichever side of the fence he may fall on."   I have during several years taken some interest in this matter, and if reputable persons have not lied to me then swallows do pass the winter like frogs.   Perhaps some of my readers may have experience in this direction.   I would be gratified to hear from them if they have.   Evidently there is something to be settled about the habits of these birds.   Our most common species is the

Eaves Swallow (Petrochelidon Lunifrons).

These birds are so well known to all that no extended description is called for here.   Male and female: Adults, back and top of the head and bit on the throat steel-blue, collar grey, forehead whitish, chin and sides of the head rufous or reddish.

In this species we have gregarious birds, they are a social folk, and as a rule live peacably and happily, although nest joins nest, one furnishing a wall for another.   It seems almost wonderful how each pair knows their own home although tucked away in a long row of mud tenements.   There is diversity of taste in building, some draw out the doorways into long bottle-like entrances. If this nest-building was not so common, any person would be interested in the operation where so much skill and industry are manifested by these little creatures. Oftentimes the mud is a long distance from the nest-site, and bill-full by bill-full must be carried away, and once there it must be used with some discretion or there will be no nest after all. The bulging walls must be rounded and drawn in, and a doorway provided, and to do this the two little workers must be agreed and competent for the business. Such a nest as this is the outcome of long struggles, and many makeshifts to escape enemies. Most all of our small birds have nesting habits with a careful eye to their enemies. They either hide them in trees, or on the ground, or under a bank, or beneath a cover of leaves, or deck them in lichens like the branches. Mr. Wallace tells us of a certain species of hornbill in the far East that nests in holes in trees, and when the female begins to "set" the male plasters up the door with mud, all but a small hole through which he feeds her. Doubtless a habit formed out of the struggle for existence. Even our eaves swallows, protected by the presence of man, too swift and supple for hawks to overtake, and hatching young by the nestful, with food in plenty, still do not make any noticeable gains in their numbers. The young are only enough in number to fill up the ranks made vacant by death. A swallow should naturally live at least half a dozen years. If for instance there were one hundred thousand last spring in Nova Scotia, or fifty thousand pairs, and each pair had reared two young, then in the autumn there would be two hundred thousand swallows to migrate or hibernate, and allowing that fifty thousand had perished during the winter we should have one hundred and fifty thousand arrivals the ensuing spring; but we do not. The number remains about the same, and we are thus able to see that not even one young bird out of the brood has succeeded in going to winter quarters with the parents. Making all allowances for falling nests, still the wonder is that swallows do not greatly increase in numbers. By what means so many perish we cannot very well imagine. One seldom finds an adult bird dead of disease. The most common enemies of the nests of small birds are owls, crows, blackbirds, jays, hawks, red squirrels, weasels, snakes, cats and boys. But from all of these excepting the cat the swallows have nothing to fear, and yet their numbers are kept in check by means we have largely yet to learn, as we have with other birds and animals.

Another point of great interest with this species is their change

of nesting places since man begun to build barns in America. Before
that time they had built on every "coign of vantage" that cliffs
afforded, and in localities far removed from human habitations they
still follow the old practice. I have seen on a basaltic pillar in Esgeria
Park, Col., hundreds of nests sticking fast in groups, far up the black
walls, where the rough and broken surface was best adapted to their
purpose. Such a wholesale desertion of ancient customs, wherever
buildings afford an opportunity shows us that instinct is ·not
unbending in all cases, as we have been want to believe.

Our barns are also used by another species of swallow, which
build on beams, using more or less mud in the work.   This is the   .

Inside Barn Swallow (Chelidon Erythrogastra).

The adult male is steel-blue above, the forehead and under parts
rufous. Outside pair of tail feathers long and slender. Here we
have a change of habit in this bird. Before the coming of white
men they were obliged to find natural shelters for their nests. Another common species is the

Stump Swallow, or Tree Swallow (Tachycineata Bicolor).

A beautiful bird, common wherever there are hollow stumps to
use for nests. They may be often seen about houses in search of
feathers for their nests. The adult male—all the upper parts shining
or glossy steelbluish green. Female duller, no gloss on the plumage.
Another member of this family among us is the

Bank Swallow (Clivicola Riparia).

This species is common in some localities in our Province. I
have not noticed it in my locality of North Queens. Male and female
adults—no lustrous finish to the plumage, that is a dull mouse color.
Wing and tail ashy blue, under parts white with a broad breast band.
Nests in dry sand and gravel banks.

Rough-Winged Swallow (Stelgidopteryx Serripennis).

· I have never yet found this bird, but other observers may come
across it. So here is a brief description: Very much like the bank
swallow, but lacks the band of gray across the breast and the tuft of
feather at the base of the hind toes. Nests in banks, old walls, etc.

Purple Martin (Progne Subis).

Adult male brilliant steel-blue; wings and tail a little darker.
Larger than other swallows; length 7½ inches. Nests in little boxes
and houses prepared for them by friendly hands. There are none

in my locality, but in other parts of the Province they are regular visitors. Originally nested in holes in trees and still do in some parts of the United States.

Belted Kingfisher (Ceryle Alcyon).

A common summer resident, a bird of conspicuous plumage, a harsh rattling call, and known to all in some degree. A fine crest, a long bill and short legs are noticeable at a glance. Blue grey back, and band of same color across the breast; a white collar and white beneath. Female with chestnut band and sides. This is a lone fisherman gifted with all the perseverance of the successful human angler. Perched on a branch that overhangs the river or lake's shallow margin, he keeps a keen lookout for small fry, and when the luckless victim swims into the proper place the bird dashes upon it, seizing it in his bill, and when alighted again uses his broad-soled hand-like foot to hold the slippery morsel while he enjoys the fruit of his labor.

What a cruel world is all this realm of wriggling, writhing agony of dying creatures! Nature red in tooth and claw is appalling in the magnitude and refinements of cruelty, and man exceeds all other creatures in that repulsive feature.

To get back to our kingfisher: The soles of his outer and middle toes are grown together for half their length, and other peculiarities of the feet we need not describe. When it comes to nesting, the kingfisher find a dry gravel or sand bank, and with his strong bill and handy feet makes a tunnel or burrow two or three feet long, and at the end of it lays the eggs. All things considered, a safe place. Hawks and snakes cannot get there, but weasels can enter. Length, about one foot.

FAMILY CUCULIDÆ.

Black-Billed Cuckoo (Coccyzus Erythrophthalmus).

This is one of our fairly common birds and certainly the most elegant in build, and one of the most beautiful in plumage; and yet I very much doubt if one person in fifty could name it if the creature were within reach of their hands. It is not so very small, being three inches longer than a robin, but one cannot get eyes on it. Neither is it always silent; neither does it live within deep forests far from the haunts of men. On the contrary, it loves the orchards and scrubby hardwood growths of old pastures and barrens. The fact is that this bird likes to keep under covert of friendly trees—he hides in the clump of their branches where he searches for grubs and caterpillars, not even sparing the hairy ones that other birds will not eat. If one knows readily the call of a cuckoo—ku-ku-ku (as if he had water in his throat)—if he knows the call, still he will hear a dozen birds before by chance he will see one. After hearing one it is not an easy matter to see him. He is a ventriloquist, the sound of him is where he is not. Whether he is one rod or a dozen rods away it is difficult to tell by the ear. · Wordsworth sets this all down in his well-known poem on the Cuckoo. He says:

> "O Cuckoo! Shall I call thee bird,
>   Or but a wandering voice?
>
> "Thrice welcome darling of the Spring!
>   Even yet thou art to me
> No bird, but an invisible thing,
>   A voice, a mystery.
>
> "To seek thee often did I rove
>   Through woods and on the green,
> And thou wert still a hope, a love,
>   Still longed for, never seen!"

But if you want to see him, you *can*. When you hear his call, get his direction and look *that* way. After a little he will leave his hiding place by a short flight for another. If you had him in hand this would be his appearance: One foot in length, a very long tail, a slender body, very short legs, toes parted in pairs like a parrot or common woodpecker. Upper parts bronze drabbish brown; wings marked with cinnamon; under parts white; outer tail feathers tipped with white and showing a little black. . The nest is placed on bushes or small scrub beech trees, or an apple tree sometimes. It is hardly more than a rude platform made of sticks. They evidently take no pride in it like a vireo or humming bird does, but seem to think that "any old thing will do." There is a disposition in that family to shirk the responsibility of rearing a family. The English cuckoo does not even build a nest, but drops her eggs into the nests of other birds, who must hatch and feed them. There is a scandal abroad that our cuckoo has been caught, as it were, red-handed in a trick of that kind. If there is truth in the report, then they are showing by their shabby nests the beginning of the end when they will not make any at all. It is easy to go down hill. One of the family having shown the way, all may follow in time.

Yellow-Billed Cuckoo (Coccyzus Americanus). .

A rare bird in this Province, and not readily distinguished from the preceding black-billed cuckoo, unless one have an opportunity to examine them. One mark will tell; the under portion of the bill is *yellow*. Habits, and haunts, and nesting about like the preceding . species.

FAMILY TANAGRIDÆ.

Scarlet Tanager (Piranga Erythromelas).

This is a very rare bird in Nova Scotia, but not uncommon even in sections of Eastern Maine. The male in breeding cannot be mistaken for anything else.

Somewhat smaller than a robin, a brilliant scarlet all but wings and tail, which are a dark chocolate brown or even black. The female is without any red, green above, underneath greenish yellow; wings and tail dusky. The young resemble the female. This is a family of a tropical and subtropical range, and this one species is a venturesome exception into northern regions where they remain during the summer. A bird of the woodlands and orchards, a pleasing warbler, nesting on trees. Length about seven and one-half inches.

Passenger Pigeon—Wild Pigeon (Ectopistes Migratorius).

A rare bird now, but fifty years ago it was very common. But for the greed and cruelty of men it would be still abundant. As a bird of flight it probably outdistances all others in swiftness and endurance. Forty years ago, in Michigan, Wisconsin, and other Western regions, these birds existed in numbers so great that even competent naturalists estimated that single flocks of them contained several millions. For four and five hours they would continue to cloud the sky with their numbers. Their roosting places among the trees almost destroyed the forests for miles in extent, breaking down great branches by their accumulated weight. They lived on grains, nuts and berries, and their feeding grounds extended from the shores of Hudson Bay to Mexico. Hundreds of miles were covered in a few hours. They have been killed in New York State with rice in their craws still undigested from the swamps of Georgia. Their ability to cover so large a feeding ground was the reason for their great numbers. They nested over the whole feeding range. From the great central northward flying hordes, smaller detachments visited all the Maritime Provinces of Canada in the autumn when nuts and berries were plentiful. Shotguns could never have thinned them out, but nets were spread for them in the West, and for a single netter to take twenty thousand in a year was a fair return for his pains. The young birds were also taken from their nests just before they were able to fly, as they were very fine morsels for food. The nest is placed on a branch, rather a clumsy structure. Eggs white, and but two in a nest. This indicates that the birds had exceptional advantages to reach maturity. The number of eggs bear a proportion to the chances for or against them.

The bird may be described as follows: Above greyish blue, deeper on the head and rump; back tinged with brown; large wing quills, (primaries) blackish with borders of pale blue, middle tail feathers dusky, the remainder shading through blue to white; neck with metallic reflections of golden purple and wine color. Under parts brownish red, with a purple tint shading to pink and white.

FAMILY COLUMBIDÆ.

Carolina Dove (Zenaidura Macroura).

Rather a rare summer visitor with us, but not uncommon in portions of New England. A near relative of the wild pigeon, but smaller. Length about one foot or a little less. Upper parts greyish brown; back and wings tinted with olive; crown bluish black; spot on the sides of the head; bronze and purple iridescence on the neck. Beneath dull buff, tail feathers bluish brown, outer one barred with black and tipped with white. Longest wing quills are dark. Bill black. Nest a rude affair in trees. Eggs white.

FAMILY THROCHILIDÆ.

Hummingbirds.

We are fortunate in having for a portion of the year even, one pretty representative of this elegant and beautiful family, that flourishes in the tropical world where flowers and blossoms are found in all seasons. There these feathered gems fairly revel in gorgeous hues, and marvelous diversity of feathered ornaments. The species that visit us is the

Ruby-Throated Hummingbird (Trochilus Colubris).

They come from Cuba and regions thereabouts, leaving solid banks of flowers with all their sweets, braving the dangers of sea and lands for nearly or quite 2000 miles, to visit this chilly northern country just emerging from the snow, and build their nests and rear their broods, to return again, if life is spared, with their surviving young to tropic home again. Whether one considers the accomplishments of the journey or the impulse that prompts it, he is equally at a loss for an explanation. Without chart or compass, without pilot or instructions, this little creature, not much larger than a bean, aside from feathers, makes the long journey in safety from our shores to Cuba, where they have never been before.

The nest is saddled on a branch and decked with bits of lichen to mimic the surroundings, and two eggs is the number, and pure white the color. These birds, when taken young, are easily tamed, sipping sugar and water from a quill or a cup. Their food is very largely the nectar of plants, a few insects found in the flowers do not come amiss.

In Mexico I discovered a new species of small owl, by having my attention attracted by several hummingbirds uttering an angry call and dashing past the head of the tiny owl, not much larger than a sparrow. I shot him to end the difficulty, and had a prize in my hands and relieved the hummers of an unwelcome visitor.

FAMILY LANIDÆ.   SHRIKES.

Great Northern Shrike, or Butcher Bird (Lanius Borealis).

Not a common bird. Male and female colored alike, about the size of a robin. Bill hooked and notched at the tip. Upper parts bluish gray or ash, whiter on the rump and shoulders. Under portions white, crossed with fine wavy dark lines. A black bar or stripe on the side of the head, including the eye. Bill and feet bluish black. Length 9 inches. This is a bird of savage instincts, fierce and strong and quarrelsome; although not rated among hawks, it lives largely upon birds. A most peculiar habit marks them; they kill small birds, and impale them on twigs or thorns and leave them there, and for what purpose is not known.   /

Horned Lark (Otocoris Alpestris).

A brown bird with little tufts of feathers on the head. A little larger than a sparrow.

FAMILY AMPELIDÆ.

Of this family we have but two species. It is rather a singular group of birds, in the fact that it is difficult to decide where are their nearest relatives.

Cedar Bird—Wax Wing (Ampelis Cedrorum).

Found in flocks except in nesting time. Size between a sparrow
and a robin. Length 6½ inches. General color ash. Conspicuous
marks are a long crest, a black forehead extending around the eyes, under parts whitish yellow, chin black, tail feathers tipped with yellow.
The inner wing quills are tipped with a red wax-like substance. Feeds
largely on berries. Has no song. Makes a squeaking noise during
flight. Nests on trees, frequents orchards and fields. One of our
handsomest birds, and fairly common. Eggs pale blue, marked with
dark spots. Another species, the Bohemian waxwing, may be found
as an occasional visitor, but I have not seen it nor heard of it here.
It is a larger and handsomer bird than the other.

FAMILY VIREONIDÆ.

Vireos, or Greenlets.

This is a small family of small birds. They are quite unrecognized
by people in general. In fact they are very nearly the same size and
with one exception they closely resemble each other. The male and
female and full grown young are alike in color.

Here follow certain bodily characteristics of the group: The bill
is short, flat and notched at the tip and hooked, stout bristles at base
of bill; wings have ten primary, or long quills; toes grown together to
the first joint of the middle toe; never more than seven inches long.
There are sixteen species in America, north of Mexico; of this number
we have probably six, but some of them are rare. They are all of them
included in one genus, Vireo, all of them strictly insect-eating, with a
partiality for grubs.

The Warbling Vireo, or Greenlet (Vireo Gilvus).

A very trim and elegant creature, dressed in dainty shades of
olive-green and ash and white. All the upper parts are olive-green,
except the ashy crown bordered with dark; below a pale yellowish,
whiter on the throat; no bars on the wing or tail; length from 5 to 6
inches. The nest is a hammock cradle slung in the fork of a branch.
The eggs are speckled, on a white ground.

Solitary Vireo (Vireo Solitarius).

As its specific name indicates, this is not a bird of the roadside
and lanes. One must go into the larger growths of hardwoods to
meet this species. So far as I know they are not musical, but are quick
enough to challenge an intruder with a sharp rattle as they peer from

a half hidden perch. A glance at his head with crown and sides of bluish ash and broad white line from nostrils to the eyes and around them, will be sufficient to make out his name, when taken with his dimensions of length, about 5¼ inches. Sex in color nearly alike. Under parts of body white, flanks olivaceous, under tail coverts, or crissum, pale yellow. Wing and tail-quills edged with whitish, two white bars across the wing; bill and feet dark; eye brown.

Only two birds in this region build more attractive nests than this little vireo, and they are the hummingbird and the wood pewee. The Solitary Vireo, like other members of his family, constructs a slung, or hanging, nest. Generally a limb of a small tree, often within reach of a hand, is selected, and at the forking of the twigs the work is begun with fibres of bark and strings of moss, and finished on the outside with dainty bits of paper, birch bark interwoven with the nest. These are not chosen for the purpose of hiding or disguising the nest by making it look like the birch on which it is constructed, as in the case of the hummingbird, but it must be a sense beauty that prompts to acts of pure decoration. The eggs are white, speckled with brown mostly on the larger end.

Yellow-Throated Vireo (Vireo Flavifrons).

·This is also a dweller of our deeper woods, and not very rare, so far as my experience goes. It would be called a Yellow-bird by an ordinary observer. Upper parts olive-green, rump ashy, below brighter yellow, tail coverts white, extending a little forward the same color, sides yellowish olive, yellow ring around the eye and across the forehead. Wings are dusky with white edges on the inner quills or secondaries, two white bars across the wing coverts. Tail dusky, quills edged with whitish. Length about 5 3-4 inches. Nests very like the preceding.

Red-Eyed Vireo (Vireo Olivaceous).

This is another woodland gem, musical and dainty in form and color, and the size of the last described. Above olive-green crown ash edged on the sides with blackish; a white line over the eye, a dusky stripe through the eye. Under parts white slightly shaded with yellowish. Wings and tail dusky, eyes red. Nest much like others described. About houses and shade trees.

Brotherly-Love Vireo.

This is a smaller species than the foregoing "red eye,' but general color is the same. Crown is not bordered with black, no spurious quill as in the red eye. That is a very short, useless quill, useless for flying purposes, but useful as a means of identification. I have not taken this bird here, and I am not sure that I have seen it alive in the trees, but it ranges into the far north of eastern North America, and other observers may have identified it in this Province.

FAMILY PICIDÆ.

Woodpeckers.

This is a group of birds very well represented in Nova Scotia by five genera and seven species. All of them are generally recognized as Woodpeckers, by their habit of pecking the trees in search of worms and insects. Their whole structure is admirably adapted to that purpose, and all their habits are very interesting and instructive. One soon comes to know these birds on the wing by their peculiar undulating flight, that has doubtless come about by their usual short passage from tree to tree. The bill is a perfect chisel, the tongue is a barbed spear, that divides into two branches extending over the skull, and are fastened to it a little back of the eye, in most woodpeckers. These prongs are very elastic and muscular, and by their aid the tongue can be thrust into a hole far beyond reach of the bill, and many unlucky worms are speared.

The Hairy Woodpecker (Picus Villosus).

This is the spotted black and white bird, nearly as large as a robin, that one sees so often, vainly pecking at a fence stake, or trying for rotten places in fence poles or dead trees. A pretty active noisy dweller of woods, and fields, and roadsides. Not in the least afraid, as he often holds his ground while one passes within a few feet of him, merely shifting to the other side of his tree or stake for prudence sake. This bird winters with us. The quills of the wings are spotted with white as are also the wing coverts. The male has a fine scarlet band across the back of his head. The average length hereabout is 10 inches; in still more northern regions this species is larger; in the Rocky Mountains eastern slope, the wing spots begin to disappear until in the variety known as Harris Woodpeckers, they have nearly all vanished, and this variety inhabits the regions from the Rocky Mountains to the Pacific. If one has not the whole series of specimens wherein the change of the marking takes place, he would certainly claim that the Harris Woodpecker was a good species instead of a mere variation or variety. Like all woodpeckers it nests in the trunks of trees, in holes of its own making. Eggs pure white.

The Downy Woodpecker (Dryobates Pubescens).

Another common woodpecker is the so-called "Downy Woodpecker." He is a small copy of the one I have just described, except that the tail is barred. This is also a social fearless little creature. In the winter they are oftenest seen with a company made up of Chickadees, Kinglets, Creepers and Nuthatches. They are oftener found in our orchards than the foregoing species. The range of this bird is to the Rocky Mountains, where it gradually, feather by feather, meets with such a change that it is known as Gairdner's Woodpecker, and in that form it extends to the Pacific. It is impossible to maintain the old doctrine of permanence of stability or specific form in the face of facts like these, and they abound in the whole domain of natural history.

Golden-Winged Woodpecker (Colaptes Auratus).

This bird has various common names. Here are a few of them: "yellow-hammer," "high-holer," "pigeon woodpecker," "flicker." This is one of our common and handsome birds. All the country boys know him, with wings like gold on the under side, and also the tail the same. The rump as white as snow; back of olive brown with black bars; a new-moon shaped patch of black on the breast; a scarlet band on the nape; cheek patches black in the male. Below a yellowish cream color dotted with circular spots. Length is 1 foot and the stretch of wings is eighteen inches. This species has habits not at all becoming a typical woodpecker. One often finds them in the open fields, capturing ants and other insects. In the late autumn they go southward as if conscious that when it came to making a living from worms in frozen trees, that the battle would be sorely against them.

Yellow-Bellied Woodpecker (Sphyrapicus Varius).

The next member of this family that one oftenest sees, is the yellow-bellied woodpecker. This is the genuine "sap-sucker" of the orchards. A handsome, merry bird, with a "cat-call" voice, a red back head, a red chin, a white throat, a yellow belly, and all the rest black and white. Nearly as large as the hairy woodpecker. In the winter he seeks a more genial climate. The male alone has red under the bill or on the chin. Occasionally the female shows a red feather or two in that place. This species is not a typical member of the woodpecker family. A marked difference is, that he is not wholly insect-eating, but is fond of fruits, and sweet juices, and berries, and the tender inside bark of trees. We find in his structure a corresponding difference. He cannot extend the tongue but a little way beyond the bill, because its roots do not reach the skull and over it, as in the others I have described. In the late summer and early autumn one often sees the young of this species in the orchards. A greyish, plain-looking bird, with no red markings, and but little yellow on the hinder belly.

Pileated Woodpecker (Ceophlœus Pileatus).

The largest of all our woodpeckers. Rarely to be seen outside of the old forests where it lives on the worms and insect life found in old logs and decayed trees. Our woodsmen call it the "cock of the woods." Length about 17 inches, sometimes larger. Upper parts dull black, under parts white. From the nostrils a long white stripe to the breast. Male has a long scarlet crest. This is description enough for anyone who wishes to identify this bird. A powerful bird of striking appearance, and to be sometimes found in old forests over the greater portion of North America.

Ladder-Backed, Three-Toed Woodpecker (Picoides Americanus).

This, it will be seen by the name, is of the same genus as the following arcticus, with us a rarer bird. The only difference worth noting here is that the back is barred with black and white. Length 8 inches. Range about the same as arcticus. There are other species of this genus in northern Asia and northern Europe. Sometimes the white stripe down the back is unbroken by black bars. I have a specimen of that variety taken in this vicinity, although this variety in the Rocky Mountains is the one altogether in possession, and is known as P. dorsalis, and is not supposed by the authorities to be found hereabouts. Yellow crown.

Black-Backed, Three-Toed Woodpecker (Picoides Arcticus).

This species is not one of our common birds. The entire upper parts are black, a few pairs of white spots on the wings. Underneath all white; wings barred below; flanks barred; four middle tail feathers black, others white or partly white. Male with yellow crown. Length 9 inches. The mark peculiar to this genus is the possession of only three toes. The first toe is absent, and the fourth toe is turned back. The ordinary woodpeckers have two toes forward, and two directed backward; a very curious deformity, this lack of a toe, that the habits of this bird does not now account for. Frequents the larger growths of timber, and is to be found over northern North America in favorable localities.

FAMILY SYLVICOLIDÆ.

Wood-Warblers (*Mniotllidæ*).

This group of birds is represented by about twenty species in our own Province. It is a rather loosely arranged family because its members are marked with much diversity of colors and habits. Nature knows nothing of such classification as men make of her productions. It is only a contrivance of our own to assist us in learning. With that object in view certain species are included within broad lines called a family; but often enough it is a matter of doubt where to properly place a bird that it may be classed with its nearest relatives. Our warblers differ much in habits, and somewhat in structure, but at present it is convenient to include them in one family group. These features are characteristics of them all. The wing has nine long quills, or primaries. The tail has twelve quills, or rectrices. The bare portion of the leg (tarsus) is scaled, or scutellate. They are insect-eating, small, average about five inches in length. There are about one hundred species, and in Nova Scotia about twenty species. They are generally clad in bright plumage, and some species are common, but it is a safe assertion that not one person in five hundred knows by name one of these birds. They are most useful friends of mankind, living on insects, and worms that will become insects, and devouring them by the million every summer. For the most part they ·frequent the forests, but there are notable exceptions, in the "summer yellow-bird" nesting in our gardens, in the "Maryland yellow-throat" of our lowland pastures, and the myrtle bird of our orchards in springtime. To identify one of our warblers in his forest haunt is not difficult to the advanced learner, but to a beginner it is next to impossible even with the aid of an opera glass, which is a great help. They are so nimble and restless, hiding here and there in leafy coverts, that the eye cannot well follow them. What then shall the beginner do? He may make a judicious use of a shot gun and secure a specimen of each species and take good care of them; preserve their skins and learn their characteristics of color and structure, or he (or she) may buy for a quarter of a dollar or thereabouts, of a Boston dealer, skins of all these species nicely preserved and ready for use. The word warbler may suggest considerable vocal ability but in reality the members of this family are no great singers, like the thrushes and grosbeaks, but rather indulge in quaint ditties and snatches of song, quiet repetitions of some ornamental call, apparently

for their own amusement, and in no way implying a listener. These
birds are all, only summer residents.

We must take them up one by one. Let us begin with the species
oftenest to be seen, the most domestic and therefore easiest to be
studied.

The Summer Yellow Bird (Dentroica Æstiva).

This is a common summer resident of a decidedly domestic turn.
In our rural districts he is to be found nesting in gardens among the
shrubbery, in and about old bush-grown fences and orchards. There
should be no difficulty in knowing him, because there is no other enough
like him to be mistaken for this real yellow bird. The adult male,
golden yellow, sometimes with dark streaks down the middle of the
back. Wing quills and tail dusky edged with yellow. Length about
five inches. On the first look he resembles a canary. The female is
of duller yellow than the male. Nests generally concealed in a leafy
hiding place of hedge or rose bushes. Even in towns and cities we
may hear and see these beautiful creatures. The note is a quiet bit
of contented carol, sung over and over again as they flit here and there
in search of worms and other insects. Eggs are greenish white,
dotted with rusty brown.

Black-Throated Green Warbler (Dendroica Virens).

Adult male in spring plumage is not difficult to recognize, but one
must not expect to meet him in the garden, or find him playing hide
and seek in the bushes. He is a dweller of the woods, not hardwoods,
but softwoods. He loves the tall pines, and firs, and spruces, and
keeps himself well aloft on their wide branches in search of food.
Most all the members of this family are dainty in form and beautiful
in color. They are like all other birds, in finest feather at the beginning of the breeding season. Then, the adult male we are considering
is at his best. Upper parts yellow, under parts yellowish white. Chin
and throat black extending along the sides, and that marking taken
with the size of the bird will be enough to identify him. Wings and
tail dark or dusky. In the autumn much of this courting finery has
disappeared. The black has been mostly replaced with yellowish and
the brilliancy of color has faded. Female at all times much resembles the male in fall plumage. Nests in pine trees, or some other cone-
bearing tree. Eggs creamy white with reddish brown specks and
streaks. A common bird, arriving in May from the south.

Black-Throated Blue Warbler (Dendroica Cœrulescens).

Male bird in spring, upper parts dull blue, under parts white, sides of head blue; chin, throat, sides of body black. Wing coverts blue with black edgings of quills, white spot at base of the primaries, tail with white spots on the quills. There is no good reason why the bird may not be readily known by this description. Length about five inches. Female dull green with faint bluish markings, always has the triangular white spot at the base of primaries. I do not count this as a very common bird, still I meet with them every season by merest accident in a ramble. They are birds of the riverside copse and thickets, liking the more open regions of small hardwood growths. Eggs very much like others already described in this family.

Black-Polled Warbler (Dendroica Striata).

This is one of the plainer colored warblers. Adult male has a black crown, grey and black striped and mingled, underneath white, some black streaks. Wings dusky with greenish edgings and two white bars. Tail covered like the wings. Small white spots on outer tail feathers. Female duller plumage. This is a bird of northern range even to Labrador. Prefers the softwood forests. A fairly common bird with us. Nests on trees, eggs creamy and dotted.

Yellow-Crowned Warbler (Dendroica Coronata).

So far as my own observations go this is the most common of all our warblers. In the spring and fall I see them in the orchards and by the roadsides, a pretty creature, quite tame and social, often in little groups, indulging in a ditty all their own. A yellow rump and a yellow crown are never-failing marks in both sexes and young. White line over the eye, white wing bars, white spots on tail. Female much duller in color; length about five inches. Nest built low on softwood trees generally. Eggs white with purple brownish markings.

Chestnut-Sided Warbler (Dendroica Pennsylvanica).

This is one of our smallest warblers, only about four and three-quarters inches in length. The most conspicuous mark is a yellow crown bordered with white and white with black. Sides of the head, behind the eye, neck and under portions white. A black triangular mark in front of the eye and extending backward and joining a chestnut streak that extends the length of the body along the sides. White patch on the wings, tail whitish yellow, black bluish, streaked with pale yellow. Nests low down on small bushes, eggs about like others of this genus. This is one of our common warblers, often to be met with in small growths of hardwood bushes. I do not know that it is more common than species that one seldom sees, but their haunts are not in lofty trees, or dense cone-bearing forests but more in the open and frequented localities of men.

Bay-Breasted Warbler (*Dendroica Castanea*).

Adult male, black streaked with black and grey, crown chestnut, forehead and sides of head black, chestnut on chin, throat and sides of head, belly stained rusty whitish. Female duller colors. This is a bird of northern range. They may be common, but I have not seen many of thém. Nests in cone-bearing trees. Eggs bluish green, speckled. Length about five inches.

Cape May Warbler (*Dendroica Tigrina*).

A bird of the north country as far as Hudson Bay. Rare in New England. Should be fairly common in this Province. Have not often come across them myself. They certainly breed in New Brunswick, as the nests have been found. Doubtless they breed here also. Adult male, back yellowish with dark marks; crown dark or black; rump yellow; sides of neck, sides of head, and under parts bright yellow. Patch on ear, orange-brown. Under tail coverts streaked with black, also on breast and sides. White patch on wings. Tail has white spots on the outer feather. Female duller colors; but the orange-brown ear spots is a mark that will not fail to distinguish this bird. Not an easy matter to make the acquaintance of a little creature that prefers the top-most parts of pines, spruce, fir, and hemlock trees. Length about five inches. Eggs bluish white, with brown markings.

Black and Yellow Warbler, or Magnolia Warbler (*Dendroica Maculosa*).

This is a beautiful little bird not difficult to find in his haunts, and easily identified at close range. Back black, crown ash, sides of head black with black forehead; short stripe behind the eye white; eyelids white. Entire under parts rich yellow, excepting white under the tail, and black streaks on the breast; sides heavily streaked with black. Wings yellow, tail blackish with square white spots. This is a bird of the forests, but I see them on hardwood trees as well as softwood, and sometimes low down on the branches. It is an early comer from the south. Nests in trees. Eggs much like others of this genus.

Yellow Red-Polled Warbler (Dendroica Palmarum).

Adult male, crown chestnut red; line over the eye yellow, back brownish olive streaked with dusky. Under parts yellow, sides and breast streaked with orange-brown. No white wing bars; tail spots white at the ends of the two outer quills only. This is a bird of the north country, an early comer in the spring, and late to start southward in the fall. Nest sometimes on the ground. Length 5¼ inches.

Blackburn's Warbler (Dendroica Blackburniac).

This is one of our most beautiful birds. Indeed he is a conspicuous beauty in a family where they are nearly all pretty, and none without beauty of feather or elegance of form. The name is for Mrs. Blackburn, an English lady. The adult male has all the upper parts including wings and tail black streaked with yellowish white. Now anyone can know this bird by the brilliant orange of the breast, throat, crown, and line over the eye. Sides are orange streaked with black, belly whitish yellow. In the autumn the plumage is not so brilliant. Adult female upper parts and sides of head brownish olive with black streaks. Under parts yellow where the male was orange. Wings with two white bars instead of the one white spot of the male. In spite of the fact that this is a fairly common summer bird, not one person in a thousand has ever noticed it. The reason is that the lovely creature prefers to live mostly in the forests, among the lofty branches of great hemlocks, pine, spruce, black birch, etc. I know their note and get a glimpse of them now and then. Length 5¼ inches. Nests high on softwood trees. Eggs white, speckled with reddish brown.

Pine-Creeping Warbler (Dendroica Vigorsii).

This is a large warbler, five and one-half inches in length. A plain plumaged bird. The adult male is yellowish olive above, yellowish and pale whitish or ashy below, line over the eye yellow. Wing bars white, tail blotches white on the outer quills. Female even plainer. A fairly common bird, the earliest arrived of the warblers. Appearing in April, when they may be seen in pine and other softwood forests, often creeping over the trunks of trees in search of food, like nuthatches and creepers. Eggs white, tinted pinkish, spotted rusty brown.

Oven-Bird (Seiurus Aurocapillus).

In common speech this is rather a "tame bird." One may come close upon him in his native haunts, and with us he is quite common

35

in his favorite localities.   All summer at intervals throughout the day
one may hear their note that always reminds of whetting a knife,
beginning slowly to say, "wee, chee," and rising louder and quicker
with the repetition of the same note.   In the mating season they can
do a great deal better in a musical way.   Nest on the ground concealed
and roofed with dead leaves.   The roof is an ingenious bit of work
shedding the rain and hiding the nest, but the vigilant cow-bird
will manage to drop an egg even there.   The roof is not always
added, showing that instinct does not follow such hard and fast lines
as to leave no room for taste and inclinations of individuals to operate.
The bird does not leave the nest until one has almost trodden upon it.
so secure does she feel in her little oven of leaves.   At last taking
alarm she runs away fluttering and limping, as if wanting the intruder
to follow her and leave the nest alone.

Water Thrush (*Seiurus Noveboracensis*).

This is not a thrush but a warbler.   Common names are misleading, as the scientific name shows it is of the same genus as the
last described, and a common bird of our banks and borders of rivers,
lakes, and brooks.   A plain plumage but sweet songster of swampy
thickets of alders and "hardhacks."   The sexes are quite alike in color.
Above dark olive brown, white line over the eye.   Under parts whitish
or inclined to sulphury yellow, thickly spotted with color of the back,
except the lower belly and under tail coverts.   Length five and one-
half to six inches.   This bird has a fashion of tipping and dipping as
he walks after manner of "Sand peeps."   Nests on the ground or on
old logs.   Eggs white and speckled with brown.

Maryland Yellow-Throated Warbler (*Geothlypis Trichas*).

We have here a very beautiful little bird of swamp and brake and
bushy interval, and a common resident during the breeding season.
Adult male, upper parts olive green, brighter on the rump and greyish
on the forward part.   Forehead and broad band on the sides of the
head pure black bordered above with ash.   Under parts rich yellow
fading to whitish on the belly.   Wings and tail dusky.   Female without black and ash of the head of the male; faded yellow below, obscure
ash line over the eye.   In the autumn the male has lost something of
his brilliant aspect.   Length five inches, sometimes a little less.   Nests
on the ground.   Eggs white with few spots or specks.   All summer
one may hear the notes of these birds, saying "wee cheety, wee cheety,"

faster and faster for several repetitions. They are not easily to be seen as they creep like mice, near the ground and on the ground, in and out the thickets, but once learn their note and they can be found.

Connecticut Warbler (Geothylpis Agilis).

Adult male, head, neck, and chest ashy grey. The throat and chest more or less mixed with black often forming a distinct patch; rest of lower parts yellow. Female duller in colors. This is a bird of eastern North America, not common in New England. It is a bird of our Province, but so far as my observation goes, not common. Prefers swampy grounds; nests on the ground. Length from five to five and three-fourths inches.

Nashville Warbler (Helminthophila Ruficapilla).

Here we are introduced to another genus or group of warblers. This species, the Nashville, is not a rare bird with us, but conspicuous neither in plumage nor note. Adult male, upper parts olive-green, brighter on the rump, ashy on the head with a circular crown of chestnut. Below bright yellow, paler on the belly. Pale ring about the eye. No spots on wings or tail. Length four and one-fourth to four and three-fourths inches. Nests on the ground.

Tennessee Warbler (Helminthophila Peregrina).

Adult male, upper parts yellowish olive, brighter behind, fore parts above pure ash; no crown patch; white ring about the eye. Under parts dull white, sometimes yellowish. Wings and tail dusky edged with olive like the back. Wings very long, tail very short. Length four and one-half to four and three-fourths inches. Nests in the ground. Breeds up to high latitudes. I do not find it common in my locality.

Blue Golden-Winged Warbler (Helminthophila Chrysoptera).

Adult male: above slaty blue; below white, sometimes tinged with yellowish; crown yellow; two wing bars yellow. Broad bar of black from the bill through the eye, sides of head dull white. Patch on the throat black. Length five inches. Nests on the ground. Not common with me.

Canadian Flycatching Warbler (Sylvania Canadensis).

Adult male in spring: above ashy blue with black streaks. Yellow line over the eye. Whole underparts yellow excepting the tail coverts. Black stripes along the side of the head including in it the eye.

Black streaks on the sides of the neck. No markings on wings and tail. Length five and one-fourth to five and one-half inches. Female duller. A fairly common bird of the woods and thickets. Nests on the ground.

American Redstart (*Setophaga Ruticilla*).

One of our commonest small birds and also one of the most brilliant. Adult male: above black; flanks and outer tail coverts white; sides and lining of wings rich orange sometimes extending across the black breast. Wing quills reddish orange, the outside tail feathers orange. Length 5 to 5½ inches. Female: Orange of the male replaced with yellow, and black by duller brownish. This is a bird of bush and roadside thickets as well as the deeper seclusion of the woods. In the spring they are conspicuously common in my locality. Nests on bushes and small trees.

Black and White Creeping Warbler (*Mniotilta Varia*).

Here we have a sociable warbler, common in woods, visiting orchards and roadside trees in villages, creeping over the old trunks, in search of hidden morsels. Adult male: All over streaked black and white no other colors. Crown black, white stripe through the crown and one on each side of it. Wings with two white bars. Female duller. Nests on the ground. Length, 5¼ inches.

Black-Capped Flycatching Warbler (*Sylvania Pusilla*).

Adult male: Forehead yellow; crown black; rest of upper parts, wings, and tail olive green. No wing bars, no tail patches. Under parts bright yellow; bill with bristles at the base. Female duller; no black cap as a rule. A bird of northern range, and one I occasionally meet. Not difficult to identify with his glossy black crown and yellow forehead.

SPARROW FAMILY.

Snow Sparrow (*Junco Hyemalis*).

A common sparrow and resident of our country is the locally called "blue bird," which it certainly is not. It is the "snow sparrow" of the books. On the back a dark slate color, blacker on the head, under parts white, bill pinkish white. It is a very tame domestic little bird, liking the barns and lanes, and sometimes passing all the winter with us. This bird nests under the shelter of a sod by a ditch side, or near a rock or under the side of a log, and while keeping the nest does not leave it till one has nearly trodden upon her. The eggs are reddish speckled. This bird rarely indulges in any other note but a sharp "chip, chip," but in the days of mating the male will betake himself to the tip of a fir or the top of a fence stake and do fair justice to his family connections in the way of a pleasant ditty.

Tree Sparrow (Spizella Monticola).

This bird is only a winter and early spring resident; a pretty little creature that braves the coldest seasons, and lingers all winter about stables and houses. It is as large as the song sparrow. The bill is black above and yellow below; the crown is chestnut, bordered by whitish lines; back streaked with black and reddish brown; two plain whitish bars in the wings; whitish underneath; nests on low bushes or on the ground. Breeds in the far north to the Arctic circle in mountain regions as its specific name implies. Length 6 inches. In the winter fairly common. It lives on seeds. Eggs pale green and speckled with very small dots. To find the nest in Cape Breton would be no surprise.

The Chipping Sparrow (Spizella Domesticus).

This is the next smallest of all our sparrows, and in my own locality is not common. Under parts pale ash without any markings. Back a grayish-brown streaked with darker brown; crown chestnut or almost brick-colored; over the eye a whitish line—this is always called a "supercilliary line;" a dark stripe through the eye; feet pale; forehead black. A very thin line on the extreme front is what is meant here by the forehead. Length 5 inches. Sexes appear very much alike. This little bird prefers the vicinity of houses, and always builds on the trees and shrubbery and lines the nest with hair, and for that reason it is known as the "hair bird." Eggs are greenish blue, a little speckled at the larger ends. This sparrow has a wide range and is pretty generally distributed over eastern North America.

Eastern Fox Sparrow (Passerella Iliaca).

Among our earliest arrivals from the south in the last of March or first of April is the eastern fox sparrow. The name is for his foxy color. This is the largest of our sparrows. All the upper parts are rusty red, brightest on the rump, tail and wings; the under parts are white, marked more or less with the color of the back. Breast much blotched with dark spots. Across the wings two whitish bars. Very large feet and claws. They are great scratchers, and may be seen in the spring and fall on the ground among the dead alder leaves, scratch-

ing like a flock of hens.   The nest is placed on the ground.   Eggs are
pale greenish white, speckled with reddish brown.   I presume they
breed in the extreme eastern portion of the Province, but their general
range of breeding is further north.   This is one of the most pleasing
songsters of all the sparrows.   Length 6½ to 7½ inches, that is, from
tip of bill to tip of tail.

Savanna Sparrow (*Ammodramus Sandwichensis*).

Nothing short of intimate acquaintance with our sparrows, or a
very close examination, will identify this sparrow.   In the first place
there are considerable differences in size among them, and the plumage
changes a great deal in seasons.   If one can handle a specimen, he
can soon tell what it is not among sparrows.   It may be taken for the
"yellow-winged sparrow," but close comparison will settle the matter.
Thickly streaked everywhere above with brownish grey, blackish, pale
grey, and other kindred shades.

One of the most accomplished authorities on birds remarks concerning this species: "It is not easy for an unpracticed person to dis-
criminate the small sparrows, and so variable a one as this offers special
difficulty."   Average length 5¼ inches.   Breeds from New England
to far northward.   Nests on the ground.   Eggs much clouded and
speckled with dark brown.   Frequents fields and open grounds, and
sea-shores.   Rather a feeble singer.   There are several varieties of
this species distributed over the western states and California.   Not
common in Nova Scotia.

Swamp Sparrow (*Melospiza Georgiana*).

This is one of our prettiest birds, but for all that he is not well
known, because he lives in swamps and meadows.   One can see him
from the river, on the grassy banks, or among the hardhacks and
alders that overhang the streams.   This bird is smaller than the song
sparrow, and his brick-colored crown is conspicuous; with a dark
marking on the forehead and a faint ashy stripe over the eye; a dark
stripe running around the ear feathers; back and rump brown; breast
whitish; nests and eggs like the song sparrow.   One need not look
for this bird outside of such places as I have mentioned.   He is a
pleasing and voluble songster, but all his wealth of melody is for
his chosen haunts.   An observer of birds soon learns that each species
has its own habitat or domain, and they do not wander far from its
boundaries.   They are all governed by the food supply, and each kind
has come to learn where their likings can be readiest gratified.   Our ·

sparrows are by first preference seed eaters, but they are not restricted to this diet—a worm or two does not come amiss, and some of them are quite expert flycatchers on the wing.

Song Sparrow (*Melospiza Fasciata*).

Another member of the sparrow group is the common "ground sparrow" of this locality. The "song sparrow" of students. This little bird, with its brown back, speckled breast with black in the center, with his reddish brown crown marked with dark stripes, is known to all of us if we ever cared to notice him. He comes by the last of March and no snow or rain can dampen his cheery spirits. The cold wind may turn all his feathers on end and nearly dislodge him from his airy perch, but he sings on with all his might. In the early morning he wakes with his throat full of melody, and without him our gardens, pastures and fields would seem drear indeed to the lover of these sweet phases of nature. Our little bird builds mostly upon the ground, but sometimes on a low bush of spruce or fir, and the eggs are speckled prettily with black and chocolate. Two or three broods are often reared in the season.

Yellow-Winged Sparrow (*Ammodramus Savannarum*).

The first point to distinguish this sparrow to the eye is the yellow edge of the wing; the next is a yellow line over the eye. Crown with a middle or medium stripe of brownish yellow. No streaks to be readily seen below without handling. Back and all other parts in streaks and specks of variegated brown and blackish and yellowish brown. Belly whitish. Outer tail feathers pale. Bill brown and stout. Wings short and rounded. Feet flesh-colored. Length about 4 3-4 inches, sometimes 5 inches. Lives in old fields and open places where there is grass among which it hides from the view of most people. The note is not so bird-like as one would fancy, and it is doubtless often taken for the rasping of grasshoppers. Nests on the ground. Eggs pure white speckled with brown. A rather common species over the eastern United States and Canada.

White-Throated Sparrow (*Zonotrichia Albicollis*).

Another sparrow among us escapes the eye of the general public, not because he is not a veritable gem among birds; neither is it because he is a silent dweller in our midst. I suppose it is because in the first place, he insists upon living where he can make the "waste places" glad with his charming notes and pretty cadence, as he calls out "pe pe peabody pe" from the barren lands and swamps, where old dead trees abound. This is the white-throated sparrow or "peabody bird" of New England. The adult male has a white throat and a yellow mark from the nostril to the eye, and a narrow white line runs through the crown; edge of the wing yellow; 6½ inches long; nest on the ground in a tussock of grass, cunningly hid from common eyes. If you wish to make his acquaintance you must go to his haunts, for he will never enter your garden or your dooryard; he will never salute you from the shade trees, or linger in open pasture or field, but morning and evening he mounts some outlook on a dead limb and makes his presence known in his own delightful fashion. On the barrens of the Bridgewater road, on the waste land of swampy barren of the Molega road, these are favorite places for them in the northern district of Queens.

White-Crowned Sparrow (*Zonotrichia Leucophrys*).

So far as I am aware this species does not nest in this country, but it would not be strange if on the coast they were found breeding. They make their appearance early in April in flocks, very tame, lingering around gardens and barnyards. They are then on their way to the north to Labrador, and colder localities to the northeast, where they nest, and return to us late in the fall. I have specimens taken by me in March in the lowlands of Mexico, where no snow nor frost ever comes; there they were in flocks making ready for a long northern journey to the Rocky Mountains of Colorado, or even further north. This bird one may take for a sparrow by his general appearance, size, etc., but the wide white stripe through the crown will, of itself, fix his identity; black stripes over the eyes, no yellow anywhere. With this description interested eyes will soon make him out.

Grass Finch, or Grass Sparrow, or Bay-Winged Bunting (*Pooecetes Gramineus*).

This is a bird to be found in old fields and pastures, and unfrequented roadsides. A fine tuneful fellow, making the waste places glad with his cheerful song. The first point to attract the eye about him is his streaked appearance above and below. Above brown, below whitish; a dark jaw stripe; no crown to be readily noticed. Bend of the wing bright chestnut. Outer tail feathers all or nearly all white, very readily noticed when flying and tell who he is. A widely distributed species in North America, but nests more to the northward than southward. These birds live almost wholly on the ground, subsisting, like all sparrows, largely on seeds. Nest on the ground, or in the ground, preferring a sunken place. Eggs a complete spattering of dark browns. Length of bird 6 inches, or over, sometimes. Not a common species in my locality in North Queens.

Indigo Bird (*Passerina Cyanea*).

This is a rare visitor, coming from New England. Adult male—General color plain cerulean blue, changing to bluish green in certain lights, portions of the wing coverts black, jaws black. The dimensions are those of a small sparrow., Adult female—Above plain brown, below whitish brown, dimly streaked on the breast and sides, upper mandible blackish, lower pale, some black feathers at the base of the bill, young male much like the females, but soon showing a bluish tint. A pleasing but weak songster; nests in bushes. Eggs bluish white.

Purple Finch (*Carpodacus Purpureus*).

A common summer resident. One can hardly overlook this bright-colored dweller among orchards and shady roadsides; a delightful songster, often singing as he flies, fairly bubbling over with happiness. Male—Carmine red, back streaked with dusky, underneath near the tail whitish. The female is a very plain creature, brown and streaked with dusky, below white marked with dusky, dark jaw stripes. This bird comes about our houses and builds in our orchards, and if it were not for prowling cats, these and many other species would give us much of their company. Nest on trees. Eggs dull greenish with black and lilac markings.

American Goldfinch (*Spinus Tristis*).

The male of this species is not likely to be overlooked in the early summer. It is a brilliant yellow excepting a black patch on the crown, and black wings and tail, the latter with white spots on each feather. This is the courting costume calculated to catch the eye of a little brown creature smaller than himself, without a touch of color decoration. In September, our fine fellow has lost his jaunty black cap, and the bravery of his feathered gold has faded to the obscurity of his mate. In the fall they collect in flocks and pay particular attention to the ripe thistle seeds, grappling the spiny heads just in the nick of time, before the wind lends its services to the plant that has furnished each seed with a pair of wings. A fairly common bird, with a plaintive note of "bay bee" often repeated. Nest on bushes or trees placed in a crotch. Eggs bluish white, sometimes marked.

American Crossbill (*Loxia Curvirostra*).

A fairly abundant bird in the cold season, and I have seen occasionally, a pair in the month of June in Queens County. Male—Upper parts and under parts red, wings and tail very dark. Female—Brownish, olive tinted with yellowish, below paler; bill with upper and lower mandibles crossed at the tips to facilitate the extraction of seeds from cones. Very likely they breed in our deep coniferous forests, but the nesting is so early that the nest would be taken for one of last year's, unless the birds were seen on it, or about it; perhaps they build even earlier than the Canada jay, but certainly while the winter snow remains. The nest is placed on soft-wood trees, a thick. warm structure of moss, rootlets and fine strips of bark, the eggs are pale blue, dotted with black and lilac.

White-Winged Crossbill (*Loxia Leucoptera*).

. Male—Rosy red, or sometimes crimson, obscured on the back, paler below. Wing and tail black with whitish or reddish edgings; two white cross bars on the wing. Female and young of first year duller, but all have the wing markings. Both of these species are very tame and gentle, and are found in flocks at all times but in the nesting season. A bird of more northern range than the other species. Nest and eggs very similar to the other just described.

Redpoll Linnet, or Common Linnet (*Acanthis Linaria*).

This is a common winter visitor, coming from the north in flocks. There is much variety of color among them; the adult male has a crimson crown and rose red breast, and a touch of this color on the whitish rump; below white, more or less streaked with dusky on the sides; wings and tail dusky. The female has no red unless in some instances a faint trace on the rump, breast yellowish, streaked with dusky; young much resemble the female. Breeds in the far north, nests in low trees. Eggs pale bluish. Length about 5½ inches.

Holbool's Redpoll (*Acanthis Linaria Holbællii*).

This species is colored exactly like the next preceding, but it is a decidedly larger bird; length about 6 inches. Very likely some of our students have taken this species, as it is reported in Canada and New England.

Greater Redpoll (*Acanthis Linaria Rostrata*).

Very nearly colored like the redpoll linnet but smaller, rump white and pink tinted, not streaked, or spotted. This bird should be among our Arctic visitors, and doubtless it is recorded somewhere in the Province.

Lapland Longspur (Calcarius Lapponicus).

This is another visitor from the Arctic regions, but not common in Nova Scotia. It is almost as large as the snow bunting. Male— Black crown and throat and breast the same; chestnut collar; upper parts brownish black; wings and tail dusky; the outer tail feathers with white spots. Nests on the ground.

Pine Finch, or American Siskin (Spinus Pinus).

This is a common bird of all seasons, driving hither and thither in flocks in a gusty uncertain flight, as if they were so many dry leaves. Sexes colored about alike. A very small brown bird, streaked with dull white and washed with yellowish; outer margin of tail feathers edged with yellow; bill very sharp. Nests high in coniferous trees. Eggs pale greenish, speckled with brown. Is partial to seeds of dandelions.

Snow Bunting (Plectrophenax Nivalis).

This is our common white snow bird of winter, to be seen in flocks about the roads and fields. It is an Arctic visitor, coming in the winter; a white bird with rusty brown washing; black on the back; wings and tail the same. Length 7 inches. Nests on the ground.

Pine Grosbeak (Pinicola Enucleator).

A conspicuous and common bird. They are most numerous in winter and keep in flocks. The male is nearly as large as the robin, short and plump, and bright red over mostly the whole body, underneath, towards the tail, light gray; wings and tail blackish; bill dark; length about 8½ inches. The female and young males have no red at all; head and rump clear yellow. All shades dull yellow, reddish yellow and gray may be found in a flock. These birds are conspicuous in the winter, as they feed in the roads from the grain in the offal of horses. They frequent mostly those portions of the highway that run through the deep pine and spruce woods, as they are largely dependent on the seeds of the cones for a living. I have seen them here as late as June, and am quite confident that they breed in our deep soft-wood forests. The nests are built on trees; the eggs are pale greenish, spotted with brown. This bird does well in a cage, is a fine singer, and of very tame and confiding habits. There are other American grosbeaks, and among them the blue and the evening grosbeaks; by a rare chance either or both of these species might be sometimes found here, as their migration is extensive over the north country, but I have not observed them hereabouts.

Rose-Breasted Grosbeak (*Zamelodia Ludovicianus*).

This is a fairly abundant species in the large hardwood growths. A valuable and delightful songster, and the male is the most conspicuous feathered beauty of all our woodlands. The whole breast is a brilliant rose red, the rest of the under parts white, and the upper portions black. In size somewhat smaller than a robin. Rump white, and the red of the breast extending to the shoulders, bill white and very stout; there is no other bird in the Province that comes near answering this description. The female is a very modest, demure looking creature beside this dashing mate; she is what may be called a brown bird with a whitish line through the crown, and white line over the eye, but the under parts are yellowish, and the under wing coverts are sulphur yellow; young birds of the first year resemble the females. This beautiful bird is not generally known among us, because he keeps to his haunts in the more remote woodlands, and even there prefers the tops of lofty trees where, in the breeding season, he is by no means stingy with his fine gifts of song; his notes may be heard at a greater distance than those of any other feathered creature among us. Of course I do not include the weird shouts of loons, and the muffled "too hoo" of owls. This is a common bird in my locality of North Queens. Length about 8½ inches. Nests on bushes and small trees. Eggs dull green.

Blue Grosbeak (*Guiraca Caerula*).

A very rare visitor.

FAMILY TYRANNIDÆ, OR FLYCATCHERS.

King Bird (*Tyrannus Tyrannus*).

This is a large family scattered all over the world, nearly. The best known to us is the common King Bird, not "Kingfisher." In New England he is called the "Bee Martin." Any day in the country, in summer, they may be seen and heard. They like to perch upon a stake, and dash after a fly or other winged insect, and then return to their perch again. He is not so large as the robin, dark on the back, pure white on the breast, an orange crest on the crown hidden by the dark feathers. This bird is pluck personified, for with feeble feet and thin bill he will pursue the fiercest hawks and pounce upon their defenseless heads without hesitation. Perched upon his bare lookout, with keen eyes he sights crow or hawk far away, and is off for the fray with a defiant jingling note. They are veritable tyrants, but under their vigilant. eyes many small birds enjoy a valuable protection. The nest is a loose structure of sticks placed on a limb, sometimes high and sometimes low down, but always in plain view, a sort of challenge to the boldest feathered marauders to try an encounter. The eggs are of a pale cream color. This is a bird of the open places of farms and orchards, and cleared river banks. Like all the members of this family he is no singer; indeed, they are all destitute of singing organs, but he is a regular rattler and jingler, and when he leaves his perch, he sounds the alarm, as much as to say, "I am coming." This bird lives entirely on insects and is, therefore, the farmer's friend, except when he falls in with a swarm of bees and helps himself in great style, and this indulgence has many a time secured him the contents of a shot-gun. One never meets with this bird in the forests; he prefers localities not far removed from human habitation, or in the open of shores or lakes or rivers. Length 8 inches. Distributed over the more eastern temperate North America. Sexes alike in color.

Water Pewee (Sayornis Phœbe).

Continuing the description of members of this family, we may notice the Water Pewee, or Phœbe. This bird is among the early spring arrivals, reaching here as soon as the ice clears from the rivers. A marked habit is to linger about the banks of · streams and near bridges and villages. The note is clear "phebe," uttered slowly and distinctly. It has another habit of ruffling and adjusting its feathers when alighting on a perch. In·size it is 7 inches in length, in color a dark blackish brown, darker on the head, underneath soiled white or whitish yellow in many cases, a whitish ring around the eye. The outer tail feathers edged with pale gray, bill and feet black. The nest is always near the water, under the bridge is a favorite locality, not on trees, but rocks and logs, etc., made of grass and mud and moss. Eggs white. I have omitted to mention quite a marked crest of long feathers that adds an air of consequence to our little friend, who busies himself in catching flies and moths and other winged insects. Rare.

Traill's Flycatcher (Empidonax Traillii).

Continuing the account of flycatchers, we may next notice Traill's flycatcher. This is a slender little bird, hardly 6 inches long; color olive brown, slaty brown; grayish white underneath, with a touch of sulphur; yellow below, and near the tail felt black; a difficult bird for a beginner to identify by his general appearance, but he is a dweller of the bushy thicket, liking the alders in damp localities; not often seen, his note is "phe-be," uttered with a hoarse, frog-in-the-throat manner that settles his name to practiced ears. The nest is in the crotch of a bush, a very well-made affair; eggs creamy white and spotted. This is not a rare bird. I could get three or four in a day if it seemed desirable, but this must be done by locating them first by the ear.

Wood Pewee Flycatcher (*Contopus Virens*).

These flycatchers in many cases are so nearly alike that one would think they would get mixed among themselves and scarcely know who was who. Here we have the wood pewee flycatcher, merely a reduced copy of the water pewee, I first described in this article. The difference in size, an inch shorter, will be noticeable. Of course, with the two birds in your hands, there will be some small difference. The habits are very different. This bird likes the deep woods, where, at intervals through the day, he utters the cry "pee-wee" in a most lonely and dismal fashion. They are rather shy and obscure in appearance. To see one, he must be marked down by ear and then still-hunted. They are not very common, but I come upon a half dozen in a day, by looking in their proper haunts. They seem to eat no other food but what they can take on the wing. The nest is a fine affair, the prettiest of all in our woods; it is saddled on a limb and stuck all over with lichens to make it look like the limb or a knot, which, at first sight it resembles. The eggs are creamy white, marked with reddish brown.

Least Flycatcher (*Empidonax Minimus*).

We come next to another member of this genus, almost in detail the color of the one just described; it is a trifle shorter, not quite so slender and is the least flycatcher. This little, obscure bird is much more common than the other; he lives in the large, open woods, liking the lower limbs of old pines, where he perches all day long, uttering a harsh snapping "che-pec," with the accent strong on the last syllable. He seems out of humor, leaving his perch to snap at every passing insect. He will come out to the skirts of pastures or nest in the trees near barns, if the trees are large enough to suit him. The nest in the crotch of a tree or limb, very neat and deep. Eggs white, no marking as a rule, sometimes lightly speckled. The gray ring about the eye is very distinct, and will help to make him out.

Yellow-Bellied Flycatcher (Empidonax Flaviventris).

A much rarer bird is the yellow-bellied flycatcher. This is a rare bird with us; about the size of Traill's flycatcher; all the upper part olive green, underneath yellow, ring about the eye yellow, under mandible of bill yellow, feet black. Nests in swamps in a stump or on a log or tree roots; a bulky nest. Eggs spotted. The note of this bird is a slowly uttered "pe-a."

Olive-Sided Flycatcher (Contopus Borealis).

The next member of this family I shall notice is the olive-sided flycatcher, a rarer bird than the phœbe and noticeably larger; dusky brown on the back; head little darker; under parts sulphury yellow. This is an exceedingly shy bird, difficult to find, and it is still more difficult to get within shooting range of him. His favorite haunts are burnt woods and borders of new clearings, where he always mounts the topmost twig of the highest dead tree, and calls out from minute to minute "uck-phebe"—a dreary, monotonous sound, in full keeping with his desolate surroundings. By dint of creeping and hiding one gets under him and sees his crest erected, and turning his head first one way and then the other in the most nervous, uneasy manner, till an insect is sighted and away he goes, fluttering and darting and cracking his bill till his prey is secured, and then he comes back to his perch to pounce upon the next unfortunate fly or beetle. A most unsocial, crabbed fellow, with nothing admirable about him; no song to make the waste places glad, but with a doleful, unmeaning cry that deepens the solitude. He seems like some banished creature, a Pariah among birds, doomed to forsake the leafy coverts and abide among the lonely nooks and corners of the world. His cousin, the king bird, is sociable, noisy and plucky; his other cousin, the phœbe, is retired, to be sure, but is not averse to company; but this old *contopus borealis* seems either to be afraid of everybody or feels himself too good for other folks; or, what seems more likely, he is a waspish, unsocial, glum fellow, who wants to be let alone. They are not common anywhere. They will fight with each other in the most ferocious manner, and if they don't pursue other birds it probably arises from their aversion to the whole of them. Their nests are much like those of the king bird. Eggs cream colored. Sometimes a pair will sneak into an orchard and select the scraggiest half dead tree in the lot and build in it.

FAMILY CORVIDÆ.

The Raven (Corvus Corax).

Of this family we will give precedence to the largest and most noted member, and so call up the raven. Distributed over almost the whole earth, he has been woven into the earliest legends, and associated with the grossest superstitions. Somewhat rare. Length 2 feet. Eggs greenish, blotched and dotted.

Common American Crow (Corvus Frugivorous).

Of this bird we have but one species and that is enough. In the Rocky Mountain region they have Clarke's Crow and the blue pine crow not larger than jays.

Our own bird is known to all. He is a conspicuous feature in our landscapes. Intelligent as a monkey, destructive and noisy to a provoking degree. He can do many things well,—he is a fair flyer, he can run well, walk well and jump well; he can live on frozen apples in midwinter, or revel in young robins, strawberries and eggs in summer. He knows a gun from a stick, can count three, and pull up corn, and rob nests, and do many other objectionable things. He can eat worms and grasshoppers, but he very seldom puts in an honest day's work in that fashion.

There are rogues and rascals in the world of birds. As a group of creatures they are at their best when engaged in some way that is not destructive to other birds. The crow is a bad fellow from our standpoint. He will pounce on a nest of young birds or eggs, and, despite all remonstrance, proceed to make a meal of the contents. Among small birds, the nest of the little king bird escapes, because he knows that when they would be done with him, he would have no eyes. The crow is very destructive to our small birds.

Blue Jay (Cyanocitta Cristata).

A large group of birds comprising many species, is the sub-family of jays. They are by habit and structure closely allied to the crow family. About a dozen species are found in North America. We have but two. One of them is known to everybody—the Blue Jay (Cyanocitta cristata), which only signifies the crested blue jay, after all the hard words. This bird is a character; he is individual and striking both in appearance and manners. Dressed in his bright jacket of blue, and black, and white, his shiny crest and black collar, he seems the dandy of the thickets and woodlands. He is a fearless marauder, driving robins and other small birds from their nests by sheer fright, and seizing upon eggs or young birds with equal appetite. All summer long they are scouring the woods for nests, and helping themselves to insects and berries when other rations are short. In the autumn they feed upon beech nuts and oak nuts. The beech nut they free from its hull, and the acorn is seized in the claws with the soft end upward, from which they have taken the cap or "saucer," and drive the bill into it, and then send it home by pounding it upon a limb till the acorn splits open. In this they show great intelligence and have a comical appearance as they make a mallet of their bills and pound away like little carpenters. I would regret the absence of these flashy gay colors in our woods and fields, but I have been so much annoyed by their destructive cruelty that I have sometimes felt like encouraging a shot-gun war upon the whole of them. They are intelligent and watchful and manage to keep out of the way of their worst enemies. These birds remain with us all the year. In the winter they are often reduced to the scantiest fare, and then come about the houses for any scrap of meat or bread that may chance in their way. I feed some of these noisy fellows every winter, nail up a box, and put in it a meat bone, and they will be sure to find it out and become very tame, and they are always pretty and interesting. The nest is a clumsy affair on a tree or brush, eggs a dull bluish with brown spots.

Rusty Blackbird (*Scoleocophagus Carolinus*).

This species is generally distributed over the Province. One of the first arrivals in the spring, when they announce their coming by a cheerful whistle. They frequent rivers and lakes where insect food is then most readily found. One may see them examining the margins of waters and piles of driftwood and overhanging branches in search of insects. Later on they are guilty of robbing the nests of other birds and helping themselves to eggs or young. Their own nests are placed low on bushes or old stumps, a clumsy structure of sticks and mud. Eggs greenish blue mottled with brown. Male black, with some glossiness of plumage. Female faded black. Length about nine and a half inches; eyes. or iris, light brassy yellow.

Bronzed Grackle Crow-Blackbird (*Quiscalus Quiscula*).

Male black, iridescent purple and bronze. Female smaller, and duller; bill and feet black; length about one foot. Not a common

36

bird 'throughout the Province.   Have never seen it on the Atlantic slope.   An elegant noisy species frequenting streams and meadows, and intervales and fields.

Red-Winged Blackbird (*Aegelaius Phœnicus*).

Male black, with a scarlet patch on the bend of the wing bordered with buff.   Female brownish black; under parts ashy streaked with darker, all but the throat.   Length about nine and one-half inches. Nests on bushes; eggs greenish blue, marked with brown.   Not common.

American Titlark—Pipit (*Anthus Pennsilvanicus*).

A brown bird about the size of hermit thrush.   A migrant from the north in the fall.   Not common.

FAMILY ICTERIDÆ.   STARLINGS.

Meadow Starling (*Sturnella Magna*).

This is often known as the "meadow lark," a conspicuously colored bird, ten inches in length.   Brown, yellow and black are the colors.   Back brown, chin yellow; black streaks on the crown; a dark line behind the eye; black bars on wing and tail.   Feet large, wings short; tail very short.   Sexes colored alike.   Lives on the ground, never on trees.   Not common in Nova Scotia.

Bobolink (*Dolichonyx Oryzivorus*).

In a sub family of American starlings is the bobolink or rice bird of the Southern States, which means long clawed rice-eater.   It is not easy to describe for untrained eyes this happy dweller of the fields and meadows.   To begin with, the male is black, white and buff in breeding season, and he sings while on the wing, a delirious medley of whims and fancies; at such times his wings are wide outspread and quivering, as he slants away into the deep grass where a little brown mate has been admiring his amorous performance.   The bobolink is not so large as the robin.   Length from end of bill to end of tail, seven inches.   At first jet black is the most conspicuous color, the back of the neck, cervix, as that part is called, is buff; over the shoulder blades, or scapulars, rump and upper tail coverts white; between the shoulder blades, or inter-scapulars, streaked with black and yellowish brown.   This plumage is for the courting season.   In the late summer and fall all this conspicuous dress is changed for another color of. yellowish brown like the females always wear.   In the winter this bird is the victim of sportsmen who slaughter them for fine eating they afford and call them "rice birds." Savage pastime at best!

The nest is placed on the ground among tall grass and hidden with great care. The eggs are grayish and mottled with brown. Not common in the Atlantic counties.

Canada Jay (Perisoreus Canadensis).

This is the common "meat bird" of Nova Scotia, the "moosebird" of Maine, and "camp robber" of Colorado. "Canada jay" is the proper name for every day use. I have heard this bird called the "dumb jay," which he certainly is not when he chooses to break the silence. In the country he is always around in butchering time, his ability to scent afar a bit of fresh meat can hardly be excelled. Let one make up a fire in the woods and begin to prepare a meal and he will soon have the company of these birds although he may have never seen one in a day's tramp. They are very inquisitive and tame at such times, picking up the crumbs near at hand. Their flight is slow and noiseless like an owl's. In the winter they are sore pressed for food, living almost entirely upon the pickings from caterpillars' nests. They are first to nest, in March and first of April. Build in trees, pines, hemlocks, firs and spruce. Eggs greenish white speckled fine with brown.

Cow-Pen Bird (Molothrus Ater).

I come to notice now a bird that is an object of peculiar interest to a naturalist. It belongs as nearly to the jay and blackbird family as anywhere; and on many accounts it might be rated with the sparrows. It is the cow-bird or cow-pen bird. It is from seven to seven and one-half inches long. The male is almost black with a shining plumage, a little faded to chocolate brown about the head. The female is of a light uniform slate color. In the far west they are seen in great numbers around the herds of cattle, feeding on the offal and waste, and picking the parasites from the brutes. This habit alone renders them of more than usual interest. But the most peculiar point is to come. They neither build a nest nor rear their young. They are parasites of the first water. They lay their eggs in the nest of other birds and leave them to their luck. This is the only American bird with such a habit. Our cuckoo builds and breeds; the European cuckoo is a parasite like the cow-bird. Eggs greenish white. Rare in Nova Scotia.

FAMILY STRIGIDÆ.   OWLS.

This group of birds is very well represented in Nova Scotia. With the exception of one species they are all night birds of prey. When almost all nature is off guard and asleep, these creatures seize the opportunity to find their food. Their peculiar soft plumage renders noiseless their flight, and their large cat-like eyes are adapted to darkness, that is never complete. These advantages, coupled with sharp, strong claws and acute senses, make them formidable enemies to rabbits and mice and sleeping birds. ·

Great Horned Owl (Bubo Virginianus).

Perhaps one of the most common of our species is the great horned owl. This is the "hoot owl," or "cat-owl," of our rural districts. A large bird, two feet in length, with long ear tufts. Large yellow eyes, white throat, and whole body tawny yellowish mottled and mixed with black and white. Claws long and sharp, legs and feet thickly feathered to the claws. That is description enough to identify him at some distance. One often sees these birds in the day time and hears them, too, if he is much about the larger forest growths. Nests in trees, hollow stubs and cliffs. Eggs white. ·

Great Grey Owl (Strix Cinerea).

As far as I can learn, about the rarest of our owls is another very large bird, the great grey owl. This species is of Arctic distribution, and not a regular resident of the southwestern portion of this Province, but may be of Cape Breton in the higher altitudes. Length sometimes over two feet; extent of wings about three feet; color greyish white much marbled and barred. Bill and eyes yellow; no ear tufts; feathered to the claws. The facial disc, or eye patches, in· concentric rings of light and dark.

Barred Owl (Syrnium Nebulosum).

One of our common owls belongs to the same genus. It is the barred owl. It is easily known from the great gray owl, firstly by its size, length 18 inches; then the eyes are black, not yellow; general plumage grey, barred on the breast; striped on the belly. Nests in hollow trees.

Snowy Owl (Nyctea Nyctea).

Conspicuous among our largest owls is the snowy owl. This is a bird of Arctic regions, and in the winter ranging southward, mostly along the coasts, even to the Southern States. As large as the great horned owl, two feet in length. Color white spotted and barred with black. Bill and claws black, iris or eye yellow; no plumicorns or ear tufts. I do not know that they breed in this Province. Nests on the ground.

Little Horned Owl, Screech Owl, or Red Owl (Megascops Asio).

Not at all common is the "little horned owl," "screech owl," or "red owl." It is a small copy of the great horned owl. Length about ten inches. Eye yellow. Bill slate colored. Claws dark.

American Long-Eared Owl (Asio Wilsonianus).

Length about fourteen inches. Upper parts blackish mottled with whitish. Under portions blackish brown with grey. Long ear tufts, eyes yellow. This is one of the rarest owls of our Province, as far as my observations go.

Short-Eared Owl (Asio Acciptrinus).

This species seems more abundant than the long-eared. One finds them in the twilight by the borders of unfrequented streams. It is a trifle longer than the other just described. Ear tufts much smaller. Color in general much like the long-eared. If there is doubt about determining it from the other, then examine the wing, the long quills of which are called primaries. In the long-eared owl the first primary is emarginate, that is, the feather portion or web is abruptly narrowed on the inner edge nearest the point. In the short-eared the first and second primaries are emarginate.

American Hawk, or Day Owl (Surnia Ulula).

While the snowy owl can and does pick up a dinner by daylight, it prefers the night for hunting, but the American hawk-owl makes a regular practice of securing his prey in daylight. I have shot them in Northern Maine, but only a single species has come under my notice here in ten years. In spite of his daylight propensities, he is in structure an owl but with hawk-like aspect that is unmistakable. The facial disc is not well developed; the tail is very long; eyes are more on the sides of the head than in typical owls. Length fifteen inches. Bill and legs yellow; claws blackish; head grey and thickly spotted with white. A bird of wide northern distribution. Nests in trees.

Acadian Owl, or Saw-Whet Owl (Nyctale Acadica).

We complete our list by noticing two species of very small owls. The first is the Acadian owl, or saw-whet owl. This is fairly common for a bird of prey. A very interesting little creature, only seven and one-half inches in length, but thoroughly owl-like in appearance and habits. In our rural districts cold weather and hard times drive them into barns in search of mice. Color grey; under parts almost white, streaked and otherwise marked with darker shades; feet feathered and whitish; eye yellow. There is no danger of taking this bird for any other but the next to be described. In the spring one may hear the breeding call, and it is very like the filing of a saw at a distance. Nests in hollow trees.

Arctic American Saw-Whet, or Richardson's Owl (Nyctala Richardsoni).

Another owl of this genus is the Arctic American saw-whet, or Richardson's owl. It is larger than the Acadian owl. Length about eleven inches, and this difference in size is enough to determine its name. I have not yet seen this species in Nova Scotia, but in the northern part of the State of Maine, more than once they have fallen into my hands, and as they have a wide northern range, I do not doubt their existence in this Province. Altogether the owls make up a very interesting group of birds, and the species that fall to our·share are well worth a great deal of study. To make a collection of them would be a fine bit of work for some of our younger students: Bringing together a pair of each kind in adult stage, and as many pairs as possible in immature stages, together with eggs of each species, and nests, when at all convenient to obtain them.

FAMILY FALCONIDÆ. HAWKS, BUZZARDS, EAGLES.

These are all birds of prey. They are fully fitted out with claws and beaks and strong wings to enable them to capture their victims. If we seriously study the forms of animal life we readily see that a great proportion of species can only live by eating some other creatures. Nearly all fishes live in this way. Inanimate forms of microscopic life in the water are also found swallowing each other. On the land all the great cat-like lions, tigers, leopards, etc., are purely flesh-eating, and the number of animals destroyed by them is something startling to contemplate. Then all the minks and otters, and sables, and weasels are entirely dependent upon other animals for food. Whales and seals and alligators, and all lizards and serpents are flesh eating. For the most part birds are predatory. They kill in order to live. Our dainty warblers and thrushes and woodpeckers and swifts and swallows and fly-catchers are so many hunters of weaker forms of life. They mercilessly kill all the day long. To escape them insects have taken many shapes, resorted to many devices: to catch them, birds have also become equipped with special features of color and bill and wings and feet all varying as their prey and · hunting grounds were.

The woodpecker's chisel bill, the woodcock's long probing bill, the nighthawk's wide mouth, are all special equipments for capturing prey. Hawks and owls are calculated for larger game, and the smaller and weaker birds are generally their victims. As a rule the small birds are of great service to mankind as destroyers of insect pests, and if it were not for the hawk and owls the numbers of small birds would be greatly increased. An incredible number of small birds are devoured in one year by one pair of hawks. In some counties there is a bounty offered for the heads of hawks on the ground that they kill hens and chickens; but the fact is that the damage done by them to our wild bird friends is by far the best reason for putting a price on their scalps. In this Province we may find fourteen or fifteen species; not all to be found in one locality, but doubtless they could all be collected in Nova Scotia.

Here follows a brief but sufficient description of each species. Within one order of raptores all birds of prey are included; and that would take in the owls. Within the order is the family falconidæ, embracing hawks, buzzards, eagles, vultures. We begin with the

Sharp-Shinned Hawk (Accipiter Velox).

Plumage of male and female about the same. Upper parts dark slate, a little darker on the wings and tail. Tail crossed by four dark bars; in some cases five bands, the first somewhat hidden by the upper tail coverts. Primary quills marked by dark bands. Under parts of body white barred with reddish and rusty brown. Under tail coverts white, lining of wings white with dark spots. Young of the first year brown above with reddish brown edgings of the feathers. White spots on the scapulars or shoulder blade feathers; in the adults these spots are concealed. Under parts white tinged with rusty yellowish striped lengthwise with brown. Among hawks the female is generally larger than the male. Length of male eleven inches or a little less; female thirteen to fourteen inches. Nests on trees. Eggs white splashed thickly with shades of brown. This is one of our small hawks, sometimes called chicken hawk. Generally they prey on mice, squirrels and small birds, but chickens will suffer from their attacks when an opportunity offers. It may be added that the eye or iris is yellow.

Cooper's Hawk (Accipiter Cooperii).

This, as the name indicates, is a close relative of the sharp-shinned above described. Colored very nearly the same, the crown a little darker than the back in the adults; the tail more definitely white at the tip. A distinctly larger bird than sharp-shinned. Males about fourteen inches in length; female sixteen inches. Iris yellow. Nests on trees. Eggs not distinctly marked with brown. This bird is not so common with us as the sharp-shinned hawk, but occasionally one comes my way near enough to call him by name.

American Goshawk (Astur Atricapillus).

If courage, audacity, strength, fine plumage, and elegance of form are admirable in birds, then this hawk is fairly to be admired. The year through the goshawk remains with us, but is not the most common of his tribe. Rather shy and reserved unless hunger drives him to some desperate raid on domestic fowls, he is more a dweller of deep woods than otherwise. Partridges, rabbits, and squirrels are his principal victims for food. His light colored plumage enables him to secure his prey in the snow-clad forests with greater certainty. In the summer the food supply is more plentiful. Young birds by the nestful are to be had then without great effort. In the winter this hawk is wilder, and he holds to the remoter haunts. I have seen him emerge from a fierce squall of snow and wind with a defiant whistle as if he were tempest-born and loved the wild uproar. The north is his home. Once a man brought me a trapped specimen in a large box, where he had been confined for several days. He would not eat, but defiantly threw himself backward into an attitude of defence with wide open talons and upraised wings and gleaming eyes. I opened the box after a few hours and allowed him to escape. Half-starved and with battered pinions and tail, yet he showed no signs of damaged condition; but laid his course for the mile away forest with an energy and rapidity truly surprising. I do not know his opinion of the fellow who reduced him to captivity, but for myself there was a chance for him to think well of me to the last. Now we will try to describe him, or them, as the sexes are colored alike. Adults, upper parts dark slaty blue, darker on the head; white line over the eye; under parts closely barred in wavy lines of white and dark; feathers with black shafts; tail colored like the back, and banded with four or five dark bars; bill dark bluish; feet yellow; claws black. Length about two feet for the female. The male about twenty-two inches. Young of the first year dark brown above, streaked with yellowish brown on the head. Below yellowish or tawny white with club-shaped brown markings.

Marsh Hawk (*Circus Hudsonius*).

This is a fairly common hawk during the summer. Generally to be seen flying low over bogs and meadows in search of frogs and snakes. Not the largest of hawks; but with a wide extent of wings on a slender body. Adult male bluish ash above; upper tail coverts white; five outer primaries, mostly blackish, all of them and the secondaries with white at the base on the inner webs of the quills. Tail banded with five or six dusky bars. Lining of wings white, under parts principally white with rufous or reddish spots. One oftener sees the young and females than the older males of this hawk. They are much alike in color, thus: Above dark brown, varied with reddish brown; upper tail coverts white; under parts brownish yellow, streaked with another shade of brown; tail barred; iris yellow; bill dark; claws black. Length of adults seventeen inches; extent of stretched wings, forty inches. Nests on ground. Eggs dull white with a bluish shade, sometimes blotched with brownish. This hawk has an owl-like face with ruffs, and large ear openings.

American Continental Gyrfalcon (*Falco Sacer*).

One of the largest hawks, more likely to be found in the more northern portions of our Province. Adults, male and female: Upper parts barred with dark brown and pale ash; tail closely barred with light and dark brown. Lower parts white spotted and streaked with dusky, all but the throat. Length twenty-four inches. Tarsus or "shank" feathered half way down in front. Nests in trees or cliffs and preys on hares and partridges and ptarmigans, principally. I do not know that it has been observed in Nova Scotia.

Duck Hawk, or Great-Footed Hawk (*Falco Peregrinus*).

One of the rare hawks. Length about eighteen inches. Above blackish ash with pale edgings of feathers. Forehead white or whitish; under parts white with yellowish tinge and dark bars or spots; black cheek patches extending a little down the neck; toes very long; tarsus feathered a little way down in front, and barred with dusky; throat white between the cheek patches. Nests on cliffs.

Pigeon Hawk (Falco Columbarius).

This is one of our small hawks and fairly common. Adult male: Above ashy blue, varying from dark to light with individuals. Under parts rusty yellowish; on the throat white or whitish; sides and breast marked with dark spots, dark shaft lines to feathers; inner webs of primaries with seven or eight white spots; tail tipped with white and barred with dark; cere, or waxy, covering of base of the bill greenish yellow; feet yellow. Female: Back ash brown; no blue like the male; whitish bands on the tail. Iris brown in both sexes. Length about thirteen inches. A bird of northerly range.

White Gyrfalcon (Falco Islandus).

Rare visitor.

Sparrow Hawk—Rusty-Crowned Falcon (Falco Sparverius).

This is the smallest of our hawks and also one of the most common. Adult male: Back reddish cinnamon; wing coverts ashy blue; tail bright chestnut with white tips and black bars; under parts white tinged with tawny; cere and feet yellow; length male, ten inches; female, eleven inches. . Female: Back with black bars; wing coverts reddish barred with black. The small dimensions of this hawk is sufficient to identify it. Nests in hollow trees, old woodpeckers' holes, etc. Eggs yellowish brown blotched with dark brown.

Red-Tailed Buzzard—Hen-Hawk (Buteo Borealis).

This is our commonest hen-hawk, inland in Queens County. Male and female colored nearly alike. Adults dark brown above; upper tail coverts whitish; below white or reddish-white; upper sides tail bright chestnut red with a black bar at the end; under side of tail grey; wings covert dark. Young birds of the first and second years, no red on the tail. Length twenty-three inches. One of the largest of hawks, a terror of the domestic fowls. I have known one to attack a full-grown gander—a better exhibition of pluck than judgment. Hens instinctively know these hawk enemies. The dread and fear of them is born with them. The murderous attacks have been made for so many ages that the sight of the old enemy, or any other large bird. awakens the sleeping transmitted fears of their ancestors. Even the shadow of a hawk will scatter a flock of hens to cover in the wildest alarm.

Red-Shouldered Buzzard (Buteo Lineatus).

This is one of our hen-hawks to be seen in nearly all seasons. Adults, male and female: General plumage brownish yellow; above reddish brown; wing coverts chestnut; bend of wing chestnut; feet light yellow. Length of female, twenty-two inches; male, nineteen inches. The size and chestnut on the wings will be sufficient to identify this species.

Rough-Legged Buzzard (Archibuteo Lagopus Sancti-Johannis).

A very large hawk, two feet in length. Tarsus, or "shank," or "shin," feathered to the toes; general color, dark brown to blackish; tail barred. A bird of northern range. Prefers the seaboard; frequents marshes and bogs for frogs and reptiles. Not common. Sometimes black, a rather frequent occurrence in this species. The feathered tarsus and great dimensions are enough for identification. A rare bird.

Broad-Winged Buzzard (Buteo Latissimus).

Male and female alike. Upper parts umber brown; feathers with ashy edgings; tail with three or four dark bars alternating with white; under parts white to tawny, streaked, and spotted or barred with rusty; lining of wings mostly white; feet yellow; claws black. Length of male, fourteen inches; female, seventeen to eighteen inches. Extent of outstretched wings from tip to tip, thirty-three inches. A fairly common hawk. Nests on trees.

FAMILY PANDIONIDÆ.

Fish Hawk—Osprey (Pandion Haliætus).

This species is known to all who care to observe birds. If one had never seen such a performance as the fish hawk exhibits it would seem impossible of accomplishment. There he is one or two hundred feet above the water, hovering in search of a fish. His eyes are adapted to the purpose, and that is a most admirable adjustment. In order to gain the velocity and momentum needed to swiftly enter the water, a great height must be reached from which the plunge must be made. Meantime the eye becomes adjusted to a long range, becomes in fact a telescope. One would think that the bird would be almost killed by the headlong fall, that often buries it entirely under water; but it is not even dazed or confused, for in the fierce scuffle beneath the waves the swift and slippery victim is seized in the grip of those terrible feet and claws and dragged from his native element in triumph. One cannot imagine how this is performed. Fish are so ready to be alarmed that it would seem incredible that they do not escape when the hawk strikes the water directly over him, or even at sight of the bird in the air. Certain it is that the hawk cannot see in the splash and uproar of water, and how he manages to fasten on his prey in a blind encounter is a matter for curious speculation. Very true it is that there are many failures, but success comes often enough to feed them and give a large share to eagles besides.

Male and female adults dark brown above; head, neck and under parts white; iris yellow; claws black; sole of feet with sharp horny points, to better fix and hold the fish. Nests on trees. Length, two feet.

Bald Eagle (*Haliætus Leucocephalus*).

This is the American eagle of our national neighbors. "The bird of freedom," that spreads his wings on coins and banners and all manner of patriotic devices where the "lion and unicorn" answers a similar purpose among Britons. Benjamin Franklin strongly urged upon the founders of the great Republic the turkey instead of the eagle. It is distinctly an American bird, handsome, useful, domestic, quiet, and unique as a national emblem. He was over-ruled, and the fierce, piratical, parasitical, carrion-eating tyrant of the sky was given the place of honor. This was following the fashion of old monarchies where savage beasts and birds once expressed the ferocity of bloody chiefs and despot kings; but the new world and the new republic might well have left all that barbaric finery behind forever.

There are two species of eagles in North America—the bald or white-headed eagle, and the golden eagle. The latter belongs to the western portion of the continent; the former is generally distributed over eastern North America, principally along the sea coasts and shores of great lakes where fish can be found. It also seizes rabbits and partridges, etc. When a fish-hawk has secured a fish it is common enough that an eagle runs him down in mid-air until he drops his prey for the benefit of his assailant.

Length three feet. Body dark brown; head white; tail white; eyes and feet yellow; young all brown. Nests on trees and cliffs.

Golden Eagle (*Aquila Chrysætos*).

About the dimensions of the bald eagle. No marking; feathers reaching the toes. A rare visitor.

FAMILY TETRAONIDÆ.

The Canada Grouse, or Spruce Partridge (*Canace Canadensis*).

This is a rare species and withal an object of much interest, if one cares to do more than name and label the birds. It is not so large as the ruffed grouse, and the male in good plumage is a handsome bird; almost black, with red eyelids; a slight crest; tail tipped with rich brown. The female distinctly smaller, decidedly reddish brown and barred with blackish shades. These birds are said to be very tame; the fact is they are very stupid. One can capture them alive by placing a snare on the end of a trout pole and slipping it over their necks while they sit on a limb, and apparently wonder what you are about. At first sight one would think this species should be very plentiful, instead of very scarce, for they almost entirely, and so far as I can tell, entirely subsist on spruce needles. The supply of food is thus never failing and abundant. A flock of them will remain all winter in a small clump of spruce. It was an unlucky departure from family habits when a branch of the family by necessity fell upon the spruce leaves for a living. That way lay the doom of extinction. When food could be obtained without effort or the use of more intelligence than was required to pluck it, then intelligence declined, brain structure dwindled, faculties not used became unusable, vigilance slumbered and slept. Without the prick of hunger they went on no foraging expeditions to meet new dangers and keep alive all their instincts and faculties, and now the owls pluck them from their roosts, the wildcats seize them, the hawks pounce on them in broad daylight, and the boys pelt them to death with rocks, if they happen to find them, and already they are far on the road to extinction. Our ruffed grouse is alert, cautious, vigilant, quick to run to cover, or fly away to some retreat. A few weeks ago I opened the "crop" of this bird and found the following: A few thorn berries, two cranberries, some bits of mushroom, a little wild celery, a beetle, and a nibble of grass. To secure such a variety called into action all his intelligence; and so the great law holds everywhere in the domain of life; use your faculties, your organs, your gifts, and something shall be added; cease to use them and the outcome is degeneration and death. There are not only "sermons in stones and books in brooks,' but Nature thunders the gospel of responsibility in our dull ears from unlikely and unlooked for quarters, and "let him who has ears to hear, hear."

Ruffed Grouse, or Birch Partridge (*Bonasa Umbellus*).

This common bird needs no description; but it needs strict protection from shotguns and snares.

FAMILY ARDEIDÆ. HERONS.

The Great Blue Heron (*Ardea Herodias*).

This bird is commonly known as a crane, which it is not. All the upper parts slaty blue; eyes yellow; under parts lighter. Length about four feet. Nests on high trees in colonies. This species is distributed along the lakes and rivers of our Province. They live on frogs and snakes and small fish.

Night Heron (Ardea Virescens).

So far as my information goes this is rather a rare bird in Nova Scotia. In New England fairly common. Length, twenty-three inches. Adults: Upper parts, crown and forehead dark green; other portions of the back bluish grey; under parts whitish; eyes red; bill black; legs yellow. Nests on trees.

American Bittern—Stake-Driver (Botaurus Lentiginosus).

This member of the heron family is a common resident of our meadows and marshes. Upper parts brown or yellowish brown; head slaty, under parts lighter; sides of neck with a black streak; bill yellowish; eyes yellow; legs greenish yellow. Length about twenty-eight inches. A stupid bird, and easily approached. When one comes suddenly upon him he takes to his wings in a clumsy fashion, uttering a squawk as he rises. Nests on the ground. Eggs brown. Feeds on snakes, toads, frogs, fish, salamanders, and aquatic insects.

Green Heron (Ardea Virescens).

A rare bird in Nova Scotia, a fairly common summer resident of New England. Upper parts green, dull blue and whitish; crown and markings about the head greenish black; other parts of head chestnut; under parts greyish; throat lighter; bill black above, yellow below; feet and legs yellow. Length seventeen inches—most all of that is in legs and neck. Habits very much like other herons.

Little Blue Heron, *Ardea Cocruela.* Very rare.

American Egret, *Ardea egretta.* Casual.

Snowy Heron, *Ardea candidissima.* Very rare.

Virginia Rail, *Rallus virgianus.* Rare.

Carolina Rail, *Porzana caroline.* Rare.

Yellow Rail, *Porzana novaboracensis.* Rare.

The following shore birds are representatives of three families, viz.: Phalaropes, Snipes and Plovers. For the most part they are migrants. In fact, these groups of birds are noted for their wonderful migrating journeys. The little Golden Plover, directly to be mentioned on this list, breeds in Arctic America and winters in Patagonia, thus taking a flight of eight thousand miles. A Tattler, Heteractitis incanus, and a sanderling Calidris arenaria, breed on islands in the Bering Sea and winter in the Sandwich Islands, more than two thousand miles distant, with no intervening land, and as these birds are not swimmers they are obliged to fly all the way without resting or eating.

Upland Plover, *Bartramia longicauda.*
Golden Plover, *Charadirus dominicus.* Rare.
Wilsons Plover, *Aegiolites wilsonia.*
Kildeer Plover, *Acgialitcs vocifera.* Very rare.
Semipalmated Plover, *Aegialites semipalmata.*
Piping Plover, *Aegalites mcloda.* Common.
Black-bellied Plover, *Charadius squaterola.*
Turnstone, *Arenaria interpres.* Quite rare.
American Avocet, *Recurvirostra americana.* Very rare.
Northern Phalarope, *Phalaropus lobatus.* Occasional.
Red Phalarope, *Crymophilus fulicarus.* Rare.
American Woodcock, *Philohela minor.* Common.
English Snipe, *Gallinago delicata.* Common.
Red-breasted Snipe, *Tringa canutus.*
Purple Sandpiper, *Tringa maritima.* Not common.
Curlew Sandpiper, *Tringa ferruginea.* Very rare.
Jack Snipe, *Tringa Maculata.* Common.
Least Sandpiper, *Tringa minutella.* Common.
White-rumped Sandpiper, *Tringa fusciollis.* Common.
Red-backed Sandpiper, *Dunlin tringa alpina.*
Sanderling, *Colidas arenaria.* Common.
Semipalmated Sandpiper, *Exoeunetes pusillus.* Rare.
Spotted Sandpiper, *Actis macularia.* Very common.
Solitary Sandpiper, *Totanus solitarius.* Common.
Greater Yellow-legs, *Totanus melanoleucus.*
Yellow-legs, *Totanus flavipcs.*
Hudsonian Godwit, *Limosa haemastica.* Common.
Willet, *Symphemia semipalmata.* Common.
Buff-breasted Sandpiper, *Trygnites subruficollis.* Rare.
Hudsonian Curlew, *Numcnius hudsonicus.* Common.
Esquimaux Curlew, *Numenius borealis.* Common.

Ducks and Geese.

Shoveller Duck, *Spatula clypcata.* Rare; migrant.
Ring-necked Duck, *Aythya collaris.* Rare.
Canvas-back Duck, *Aythya vallisncria.* Rare.
Greater Black-head Duck, *Aythya marilla.* Rare; migrant.
American Scaup Duck, *Aythya marilla.* Near Arctica.

Little Black-head Duck, *Aythya affinis.* Rare; migrant.

Red-head Duck, *Aythya, americana.*

Velvet Scotor Duck, *Oidemia deglandi.* Rare.

Surf Duck, Surf scotor, *Oidemia perspicillata.* Common; migrant.

Black Scotor Duck, *Oidemia americana.* Very common; migrant.

Eider Duck, *Somateria dresseri.*

King Eider, *Somateria spectabilis.* Rare.

Gadwall, Gray Duck, *Anas strepera.*

Baldpate, Widgeon, Duck, *Anas americana.* Rare.

Summer Duck, *Aix sponsa.* .Fairly common.

Barrows Golden-eye Duck, *Glaucionette islandica.* Rare.

American Golden-eye, Whistler Duck, *Glaucionette clangula.*
Common.

Buffle-head, Dipper Duck, *Charitonetta albeola.* Common.

Harlequin Duck, *Histrionicus histrionicus.* Rather common.

Old Squaw Duck, *Clangula hyemalis.* Very common.

Ruddy Duck, *Erismatura rubida.* Common.

Shelldrake, *Merganser americanus.* Common.

Red-breasted Merganser, *Merganser serrator.* Common.

Hooded Merganser, *Lophdytes cucullatus.* Not common.

Mallard Duck, *Anas boschas.* Rare.

Green-winged Teal, *Anas carolinensis.* Abundant.

Blue-winged Teal, *Anas discors.* Rare.

Black duck, *Anas obscura.* Very common.

Canada Goose, *Branta canadensis.* Common.

Snow Goose, *Chen hyperborea.* Rare.

Brant, *Branta bernicla.* Not common.

Whistling Swan, *Olor columbianus.* Very rare.

Loons.

Loon, *Urinator imber.* Common.

Red-throated Loon, *Urinator lumme.* Not common.

Grebes.

Red-necked Grebe, *Colymbus hoeleellii.* Rare migrant.

Pied-bill Grebe, *Podilymbus podicepts.* Occasional.

Horned Grebe, *Colybus auritus.*

Purple Gallinule, *Inornis Martinica.* Rare. A fine specimen was taken alive at Liverpool, Nova Scotia, after a great southerly gale. The writer presented it a few weeks afterwards, in May,. 1902, to Miss Marshall Saunders, of Halifax, the well-known authoress, who has it in good health, now two months later.

Several families are represented by the following species, but I have not attempted to separate them, and only set them down as sea birds. In many instances the common name will indicate the family relation, as, for instance, Gulls, Petrels, Auks, Grebes, Loons, etc.

Brunnichs Murre, *Uria lomvia.*

Sea-dove, *Dovekie, Alle alle.* Rare.

Gannet, Solan Goose, *Sula passana.* Common.

Cormorant, Shag, *Phalacrocorax carb.* Not common.

Man-of-War Bird, *Fregata aquila.* Very rare.

Double-crested Cormorant, *Phalacrocorax dilophus.* Rare.

Gannet, *Sula bassana.*

Leaches Petrel, *Oceanodroma leucorhoa.*

Wilsons Petrel, *Oceanites oceanicus.*

Lesser Fulmar Petrel, *Fulmari glacialis.*

Greater Shearwater, *Puffinus major.*

Sooty Shearwater, *Puffinus stricklandi.*

Buffons Skua, *Stercorarius parasiticus.*

Pomarine Jaeger, *Stercorarius pomarinus.*

Parasitic Gull, Sea Falcon, *Megalestris skua.*

Razor-billed Auk, *Alca torda.*

Puffin, Sea Parrot, *Fratercula arctica.*

Black Guillemot, *Ceppha grylle.* Very common.

Foolish Guillemot, *Uria troile.*

Common Guillemot, *Uria lomvia.*

Ivory Gull, *Gavia alba.*

White-winged Gull, *Larus leucopterus.*

Glacuous Gull, *Larus glaucus.*

Great Black-backed Gull, *Larus marinus.*

Sabines Gull, *Xema sabinii.*

Herring Gull, *Larus argentatus.*

Ring-billed Gull, *Larus delewarensis.*

Laughing Gull, *Larus atricilla.*

Bonaparte's Gull, *Larus philadelphia.*

Kittiwake Gull, *Rissa tridactyla.*

Wilson's Tern, *Sterna hirundo.*

Arctic Tern, *Sterna paradisea.*

Black Tern, *Hydrochelidon nigra surinamensis.*

Least Tern, *Sterna antillarum.*

Roseate Tern, *Sterna dougalli.*

Caspian Tern, *Sterna tschegrava.*

This list might be lengthened by adding here and there an alien bird, like the Lapwing and Least Bittern, but the addition would not add to the value of what has been given.

37

CHAPTER XXXVII.

GAME LAW FOR NOVA SCOTIA.

MOOSE AND CARIBOU.

Close season from January 1st to September 15th. No person shall kill more than two moose and two caribou. Meat must be taken from the woods within ten days from time of killing. Penalty for breach of foregoing provisions, $50 to $200.

No person shall have in possession any green hide or fresh meat from January 5th to September 15th. Penalty, $25 to $50.

No person shall set a snare or trap for moose or caribou. Penalty, $50 to $100.

No person shall hunt or kill moose or caribou with dogs. Penalty, $50 to $100

All dogs hunting moose may be destroyed by any person.

Close season for American elk or red deer till October 1, 1904. Penalty, $50 to $100. Provision protecting cow moose repealed.

BIRDS.

Partridge.—Till October 1, 1901, no person shall hunt, kill, buy, sell or have in possession any partridge, whether killed in this Province or elsewhere. Penalty, $5 to $10 for each offence.

No person shall kill woodcock between sunset and sunrise.

No snare, trap or net shall be used for partridge or any other game bird, at any time. Penalty for breach of provisions as to birds, $5 to $10 for each bird.

PHEASANTS.

It is unlawful to hunt, kill, have in possession any pheasant, blackcock, capercailzie, spruce partridge, or sharp-tailed grouse. Penalty, $5 for each spruce partridge, $25 for each of the other birds. Unlawful to have in possession, buy or sell eggs, or injure or destroy the nests of any native birds. Penalty, $5 to $10.

RABBITS, HARES.

Close season from February 1st to October 1st. No person shall have them in possession from February 5th to October 1st.

No snares shall be set for rabbits or hares in close season. All

578

snares shall be of "rabbit wire," not slighter than number 21. Clear space of 100 feet must be left between each hedge and the nearest hedge. All snares or hedges unlawfully set may be destroyed. No hedge shall exceed 50 feet in length. Penalty for each offense, $5.

BEAVER.

No person shall hunt or kill any beaver until after the first day of November, 1900. Penalty for each offense, $100.

MINK.

Close season from March 1st to November 1st.

OTHER FUR-BEARING ANIMALS.

Close season for all other fur-bearing animals, except bear, wolf, loupcervier, wild cat, skunk, mush quash, raccoon, fox, woodchuck, otter and weasel, from April 1st to November 1st. Penalty, $5. Unlawful to hunt any of the foregoing animals with dogs between the 1st of February and 1st of October. Penalty, $30 to $80.

LICENSES.

No person not domiciled in Nova Scotia shall hunt without a license.

License fee for birds, hares, rabbits, $10; for all other game, $30. Licenses may be had at Provincial Secretary's Office, Halifax, from all clerks of counties, and from all the agents of the game society in various parts of the Province. Penalty for hunting without license, $50 to $100, in addition to license fee. The hunter, guide or companion of any such person hunting without a license, is liable to the same fine as himself.

Whenever a fine is imposed by the game laws, the person fined is liable to imprisonment if the fine is not paid; judgment may be recovered in the county courts for amount of fine and costs, and may be recorded so as to bind the lands of the defendant. When he is imprisoned he shall remain in jail one day for each dollar of the fine.

SALMON.

Close season from August 15th to March 1st, except that salmon may be fished with fly from February 1st to August 15th.

TROUT.

Unlawful to fish for or have in possession any speckled trout, lake trout, or land-locked salmon between October 1st and April 1st.

Unlawful to fish for trout by any other means than angling with hook and line. Penalty, $20. The use of explosives to kill any kind of fish is prohibited under a penalty of $20.

FOREIGNERS.

No person, not a British subject, shall fish in Canadian waters for bass, pike, perch, or trout, without an angler's permit. Penalty, $20. Permit, $5 for three months, $10 for six months. Permits not transferable.

No person holding a permit shall kill in one day more than —— pike, perch, or 20 trout.

No person holding a permit shall export or sell any fish caught with hook and line. Foreigners temporarily domiciled in Canada, and employing Canadian boats and boatmen, not required to take permit.

BASS.

Close season from 1st March to 1st of October, except by angling with hook and line.

SHAD AND GASPERFAUX.

Close season from sunset Friday evening to sunrise Monday morning in each week. Penalty, $20.

CHAPTER XXVIII.

INSTITUTIONS FOR THE BLIND AND THE DEAF AND DUMB.

By Superintendent Fraser.

Previous to the year 1871, the boys and girls of Nova Scotia who were deprived of sight were without educational facilities. Forty years earlier, schools for the blind were established in Boston, New York, and Philadelphia, but their growth was slow and the results of the training given were far from satisfactory.

In the year 1867, Mr. Wm. Murdock, a retired merchant and banker of Halifax, died in London, and by will bequeathed the sum of 5,000 pounds Nova Scotia currency ($19,466.67) toward the endowment of a school for the blind in Halifax, upon condition that a building should be erected at a cost of not less than 3,000 pounds.

Steps were immediately taken by the Hon. M. B. Almon and other prominent gentlemen of Halifax to procure an act of incorporation, and a strong committee was selected to canvass the city for subscriptions.

The Act of Incorporation of the Halifax School for the Blind was passed on May 7, 1867, and the requisite sum for the erection of the building having been subscribed, his Excellency, J. H. Francklyn, C. B., Administrator of the Government of Nova Scotia, on April 11, 1868, issued a proclamation declaring the act to be in operation, and the corporation was thereby authorized to meet on April 27, 1868, as a body corporate, and elect a Board of Managers and other officers.

By the Act of Incorporation the school was placed under the control of a Board of Managers, consisting of twelve members, who were elected annually by the members of the corporation. The offices of the Board of Managers and the officials of the school were appointed by the Board. Some modifications of the constitution have taken place which will be referred to later on; but in the main the government of the institution remains as it was originally constituted, and it may be said that it has been found to work satisfactorily to all concerned, and in our judgment in the best interests of the education of the blind

The school was opened with four pupils on the first of August, 1871, since which time the number has slowly but steadily increased.

In 1874 applications were received and accepted for the admission of pupils from the Provinces of New Brunswick and Prince Edward Island and the Board of Managers of that year applied to the Government of these Provinces to join with Nova Scotia in helping to maintain the institution by annual appropriations towards its support. The Legislatures of the two Provinces named responded liberally to the request for assistance, and thus the school became Maritime Provincial in the extent of its usefulness.

In 1877 the growth of the school demanded an increase of accommodation, and through the liberality of the public a commodious building was erected. This building contained a fine gymnasium and workshop, both of which have been in constant use for the past twenty-five years.

In the year 1882 the "Act in relation to the education of the Blind" was adopted by the Provincial Legislature, by which this institution was recognized as a special academy for those deprived of sight, and the Provincial Secretary, as representative of the Government, became, ex officio, member of the Board of Managers.

In 1887 two pupils were received from the Province of Newfoundland, and in that year for the first time pupils from all the four Provinces, namely, Nova Scotia, New Brunswick, Prince Edward Island, and Newfoundland were in attendance at the school. In 1891 the increased number of applications for the admission of pupils caused the Board of Managers to make a strong effort to secure additional accommodations, which resulted in the erection of a fine new wing to the main building at a cost of $15,954. The Provincial Legislature of Nova Scotia liberally appropriated $4,000 toward paying for the building, and this sum being supplemented by the bequests of the late J. P. Mott, Esq., and the late S. A. White, Esq., and being further augmented by the handsome subscriptions of the many friends of the blind throughout the Maritime Provinces, the Board of Managers was gratified to find that but a small balance of debt had to be incurred, which has since been wiped out.

In 1892 the Provincial Legislature of New Brunswick enacted a law providing for the free education of the blind youth of that Province in this school. The increase in the number of pupils in the early nineties was phenomenal and necessitated the erection of the west wing of the building, which was completed and occupied in February, 1897.

During the thirty-one years since the inception of the school its standard of education has been high and its training effective.

In most respects the course of instruction is similar to that followed in the more advanced institutions for the blind in Great Britain and the United States. It is based upon the idea that our pupils, notwithstanding their lack of sight, are to be educated with a view of becoming self-supporting men and women. Were it possible for blind persons to perform ordinary labor or to market hand-made articles in competition with the output of mills and factories equipped with steam and machinery, we might be justified in limiting their education to the rudimentary branches of learning and be satisfied with the result. We have, however, to face the fact that the blind cannot perform ordinary labor to advantage and cannot hope to become so skilled in manual work as to be able to undersell machine-made products. It is therefore a fundamental principle with the best educators of the blind that every effort should be made to train and develop the mental faculties of their pupils, so as to prepare them for such professions and occupations to call for intellectual acumen.

To the educated blind person the loss of sight is a handicap but not a barrier to success. His trained sense of touch and hearing and even of smell make up to him in a great measure for his loss of sight, while his intellectual powers are none the less strong, keen and effective, because he is deprived of vision. Bearing the foregoing facts in mind, our course of study has been carefully arranged so as to place within reach of our pupils a broad and liberal education which is in all respects equal to that imparted in the best public schools in Canada. This education is supplemented by a careful training in music, piano-forte tuning, and such other branches as the pupils can turn to practical account when they graduate from the school.

Aim of the School.—It is the aim of the school to give each pupil such an education and training as will enable him to become self-supporting. The teaching staff keeps this aim well in mind, and while all of the graduates of the school may not be able to maintain themselves, the great majority of them do so successfully, and the lives of all of them are the happier and better for the instruction which they have received.

Graduates.—The following table shows the occupations now followed by those who have been under instruction in this school, with the percentage of the graduates in each calling:

Teaching music (piano-forte, organ or voice)..........39 per cent
Piano-forte tuning ....11 per cent
Manufacturing (willow baskets, brushes and chair seating...................... ....15 per cent
Engaged as shopkeepers, traders, agents, lecturers, teachers, caterers and manufacturers...'...............15 per cent
At home (partially self-supporting)..................:...20 per cent

Generous Benefactors.—Since the inception of the school many persons have evinced their deep interest in the welfare of the blind by freely giving of their time or means to further the objects for which it was established. In addition to the large sums of money which have been contributed towards our buildings, library equipment and other special objects; the institution has received seventy-two bequests amounting in all to $72,149.66. These legacies have been invested by the Board of Managers in securities of undoubted value, and the dividends and other receipts therefrom have been used to meet the current expenses of the school.

Increased Accommodations.—In the report of the Board of Managers of the school recently published, the following reference is made to the present overcrowded state of the building, and to the need for additional accommodation:

"The buildings, although extensive and well adapted for their purpose, are nevertheless too small to meet the present needs of the school. It must be remembered that our household, including officers, members of the teaching staff, the domestics and pupils, numbers 144 persons, and that to provide dormitories, school rooms, music rooms, sitting rooms, dining rooms and other requisite accommodations, is under present circumstances no easy matter. We have utilized every available space, have used our music rooms at night for bed-rooms, have turned our hallways and reading rooms into practice rooms and our sitting rooms into class rooms. In fact we have done everything that can be done to keep the doors of the school wide open to those for whom it was intended. We fully realize that in the very near future an effort must be made to provide increased accommodation, and we believe that when the friends of the school appreciate the fact that increased accommodation is absolutely essential, they will, as hitherto, gladly aid us with their subscriptions, and will do all in their power to help us in extending the grand educational work which is being carried on."

Proposed Extension.—After mature consideration it has been decided to erect a new school building, so that the present building will be connected with it by a covered way or corridor. In the new school building will be concentrated all the regular work of the school. The building will contain in addition to school rooms, music rooms and an assembly hall, a printing office, manual training department, gymnasium for boys, gymnasium for girls, lavatories, etc. In the southern portion there are to be dormitories and other accommodation for pupils in the kindergarten and primary divisions. The present buildings will be utilized for residence purposes, and will enable the Board of Managers to provide library, reading room and sitting room accommodation which is at present urgently required.

The school for the blind has proved a blessing to scores of boys and girls without sight. It has given to them a broad and liberal education and a thorough practical training so that at least 80 per cent of its graduates are able to support themselves in comfort. The school has been kept well abreast of similar institutions in other countries and is recognized as a progressive and practical part of the educational system of the Maritime Provinces.

The religious training of the pupils is considered of vital importance and each church or denomination provides for the instruction of its adherents or members.

Among the members of its Board of Managers are to be found some of the most prominent business men in the City of Halifax and the corporation includes among its members and life members a large number of gentlemen and ladies resident in different parts of the Maritime Provinces.

The several departments of the school are admirably equipped and officered with talented and energetic teachers. It is the aim of the Board of Managers and Superintendent to broaden the scope of the training given at the school so that the graduates may be fitted to follow other occupations and may find profitable employment in the work-a-day world side by side with their fellow citizens blessed with sight.

CHAPTER XXXIX.

MANUFACTURING CONCERNS.

When the plan of this book was arranged, it was determined best not to insert business advertisements, because in the nature of things many of them would seem be out of date and misleading. Furthermore, if the door was once opened to that kind of material there would soon be no room for the main matter of the work. However it is not desirable to altogether pass over the fact that there are in the Province · many manufacturing interests, and some of them on a considerable scale. There has been no systematic effort to secure a complete list of them, but Mr. Brown during his canvass for the sale of stock throughout the Province incidentally gained some information of the various concerns, and I have made such additions as occurred to me.

Amherst comes alphabetically first, and its manufacturing interests are of enough importance to lead the list.

Very likely that the Rhodes, Curry & Co., Ltd., is the largest concern in that town. Their premises cover ten acres, and eight of them are occupied by the car-building plant. They also operate a foundry and planing and lumber mills and extensive blacksmith's shops, and have branches of the business in Halifax and Truro, and ·Little Forks. On the pay roll there are 425 at Amherst, 35 at Little Forks, 40 at Halifax, and 200 at Sydney and Glace Bay, about 100 at various points engaged on building contracts.

One of the most enterprising concerns in Canada is the Robb Engineering Co., Ltd., well known as manufacturers of· high grade engines. The most important product of the company is the Robb-Armstrong engine, designed with especial reference to driving electric generators. This is constructed after the design of Mr. E. J. Armstrong, an American engineer whose services were secured for that purpose. This concern does a large export business, sending their goods to Europe and South America, besides a thriving home trade.

The firm of Christie Bro. & Co., manufacturers of coffins, dealers in undertakers supplies of all kinds, and manufacturers of trunks, travelling bags and valises, now employs about fifty hands and carries on· a good business with Maritime Provinces, Newfoundland and the West Indies.

The Amherst Boot and Shoe Manufacturing Company was incorporated in 1867, it has a capital of $50,000 and employs 200 hands and carries on a prosperous business.

At Oxford, Cumberland County, is the Oxford Manufacturing Company, devoted to the making of woolen goods. It has been in operation about thirty-five years and established an excellent reputation for superior products that are wholly fashioned from wool raised in the Maritime Provinces, and no shoddy has ever been used there. About sixty-five hands are employed the year through, and about one-quarter of a million pounds of wool consumed annually.

At Oxford there are also a furniture factory and a foundry and machine shop, of which I have no further knowledge than is here set down.

New Glasgow is one of the towns that has rapidly come to the front in the manufacturing line, and very likely the firm of J. Matheson & Co., Limited, is among the foremost concerns. They are makers of engines and boilers, gold mining machinery of all kinds, marine and stationary engines and boilers. This company has secured an excellent trade on an extensive scale.

The Munroe Wire Works are also in New Glasgow, where they make woven wire fencing in many varieties, and other kinds of wire goods.

The Trenton Iron Works are located in New Glasgow.

In the town of Truro is the well-known concern of the Truro Foundry and Machine Company. They are manufacturers of mining machinery of all kinds, makers of boilers and engines, etc., producing about 700 tons of castings annually. The number of employees is about fifty, and sometimes the number is considerably increased.

The Truro Condensed Milk and Canning Co., Ltd., is a concern that was established in 1883, and in spite of a disastrous fire four years ago, the business is in a prosperous condition, handling several tons of milk daily.

The Truro Knitting Mills Co. was established in the year 1882. About 1,200 pounds of wool are handled daily. That amount is spun into thread about four millions of miles in length, and then taken to the knitting rooms, where it produces some 2,500 yards of underwear. There are over 100 employees constantly at work, and 300,000 pounds of Nova Scotian wool is consumed annually in the establishment.

In the Town of Pictou there are a tannery and a biscuit factory in operation.

In Windsor there are a cotton factory, a furniture factory, and foundry and machine shops. No further knowledge of them is at hand.

In the City of Halifax and the Town of Dartmouth there are a large number of manufacturing concerns, of which I cannot give a complete list, but here is very likely a close approximation:

 Acadia Powder Company.

 Acadia Sugar Refining Company.

 Dominion Electrical Works.

 Nova Scotia Fertilizing Company.

 Dartmouth Rolling Mills, Ltd.

 Nova Scotia Furnishing Company.

 Hillis & Son Foundry.

 The Starr Manufacturing Company, skates.

In Yarmouth there are several manufactories known as the

 New Burrell and Johnson Foundry and Machine Shops.

 Crosby's Shoe Factory (Hebron).

 Kinney and Haley's Sash and Door Factory.

 Patterson's Shoe Factory.

 Redding's Shoe Factory.

 Allan's Barrel and Box Factory.

 Yarmouth Duck & Yarn Co., Ltd., manufacturers of cotton sail, duck, wide duck sail.

In Kentville the Nova Scotia Carriage Company has established a flourishing business, where they turn out fine carriages and sleighs.

The Lloyd Manufacturing Company, of Kentville, saw-mill outfits of all kinds.

At Milton, Queens County, there are in operation two pulp mills owned by the Acadia Pulp and Paper Mills Company, Ltd., where a fine water power is turned to account.

Several saw mills are operated in Milton and various kinds of lumber are turned out in considerable quantities. The principal operator is Mr. John Millard, who is also largely engaged in ship building in Liverpool.

The Thomson Bros. are the proprietors of a superior machine shop in Liverpool, where engine, mill and mining machinery are made and repaired.

The Liverpool Foundry, operated by Thomas Quinn, manufactures ship, mill, and general castings.

The Eureka Mills, of Liverpool, are owned and operated by Elisha More. Cornmeal is ground and kept on sale, and oats, buckwheat and barley are ground for customers for feed purposes.

J. H. Fraser, of Liverpool, manufactures carriages and sleighs.

Edward A. Cowie represents the tannery business established by his grandfather in 1821, in Liverpool.

The Barrington Woolen Mills, of Shelburne County, are reputably known as manufacturers of tweeds, homespuns, dress goods, blankets, yarns.

At Bridgewater the Davisons have long carried on a very extensive manufacture of lumber—the largest concern of the kind in the Province.

There is in Bridgewater a small foundry operated by Mr. Rieves.

R. C. Durland, of Bridgewater, carries on a carriage manufactory business there.

The Lunenburg Foundry Company, Ltd., is operated in that town.

In Antigonish is the Canada Milk Condensing Company.

The large steel and iron concerns of Cape Breton have been noticed elsewhere in this volume, when treating of iron ores.

At Weymouth there is a pulp mill in operation.

At New Germany, Lunenburg County, is a pulp mill owned by the Acadia Pulp and Paper Mills Company, Ltd.

CHAPTER XL.

HOW NOVA SCOTIA IS GOVERNED.

BY THE HON. J. W. LONGLEY, ATTORNEY GENERAL OF NOVA SCOTIA, CONTRIBUTED TO MARKLAND.

Since July 1st, 1867, Nova Scotia has been a part of the Dominion of Canada and subject to the provisions of the British North America act. That act is the constitution of Canada and all parts are subject to the provisions of this constitution. It is essentially a Federal system, the central authority being the government and parliament of Canada, with headquarters at Ottawa and having exclusive control of certain subjects which are regarded of a larger and more national character. To each of the provinces is assigned another class of subjects, supposed to be more local in character, and, as will invariably occur under a Federal system, the line of demarkation is very frequently doubtful and leads to a conflict of authority in many cases.

Although, under the constitution of Canada, the evident design was to strengthen and make permanent the power of federal authority, and to this end a provision was made that all matters not classified, that is, all residuary power, should be vested in the Dominion authorities, and not in the provincial, yet experience has shown that the subjects allotted to the provincial authorities are of the gravest possible importance, and that the provincial interests are thoroughly safeguarded under the constitution. The power to amend the provincial constitution is vested absolutely in the provincial governments and legislatures, but no such power is invested in the Federal. The allotment of all property and civil rights to the provincial legislature and not the Dominion, also confers upon the former tremendous powers, so far reaching in their character as to make the provincial arena one of great importance in the development of national life.

The class of subjects assigned to the Dominion are: Military affairs, shipping and commerce, tariffs, fisheries, banking and currency, etc., etc., the provincial authorities are assigned property and civil rights, constitution and procedure of courts, education, mines, local and police requirements, the power to issue licenses for the purposes of revenue and the administration of local public works.

Nova Scotia is, therefore, governed partially from Ottawa and partially from Halifax. The Ottawa authority is vested in the Governor General and Senate and House of Commons. The Senate is composed of eighty members, holding office for life; the House of Commons, consisting of two hundred and fifteen members, distributed according to population. The full term of the House of Commons is five years, subject, however, to dissolution by the Governor General at an earlier period. The Governor General's functions are exercised in reality by the Cabinet, composed of the Prime Minister and twelve Associate Cabinet Ministers. The Departments are: President of the Council, Minister of Justice, Minister of Finance, Minister of Public Works, Minister of Railways and Canals, Minister of Commerce, Minister of Inland Revenue, Minister of Customs, Postmaster General, Minister of Marine and Fisheries, Minister of the Interior, Secretary of State and Minister of Militia.

The provincial affairs are administered through the Lieutenant Governor, appointed by the Governor General on the advice of his Ministers, who holds office for five years; a Legislative Council, composed of twenty-one members, who hold office for life; and a House of Assembly, composed of thirty-eighty members, the term of which, under the law, is five years. The functions of the Lieutenant Governor are exercised through and by the advice of an Executive Council, composed of three Departmental Ministers and six members without office.

In addition to the Dominion and provincial governments, there is also a system of municipal government throughout Nova Scotia. Each municipality has a system of municipal government by a municipal council, chosen every three years by the people. Twenty-five towns have also become incorporated as towns, with Mayor and Council to transact the municipal business of the towns. But though these municipal bodies exercise important functions and transact a great deal of business pertaining to the well-being of the people, it would be scarcely correct to say that they constitute a distinct system of government. The municipal council is not recognized or provided for by the B. N. A., as a part of the constitution. Under that act the provincial governments and legislatures have power to create municipal institutions and these municipal institutions so referred to are the creatures of the provincial legislature; it is merely a delegation of certain powers by the provincial legislature to municipal bodies. It is an enlargement of the principal and policy of self-government carried to the utmost limit.

The revenues of the Dominion authorities are derived chiefly from customs and excise supplemented by the receipts of the post-office department, the revenues from railways and other public works. The revenues of the provincial government of Nova Scotia are derived:—

First. A subvention from the Federal government amounting to $480,000 a year.

Second. Royalty from mines, amounting at present to about $500,000.

Third. Sales of Crown lands, amounting, last year, to $90,000.

Fourth. Succession duties, averaging $40,000.

Fifth. Fees from incorporated companies, "Royal Gazette," etc., etc.

In the province of Nova Scotia there is no provincial taxation, whatever.

Justice is administered by a Supreme Court, composed of Chief Justice, and six Puisne Judges, who have jurisdiction from $20.00 upwards in all civil suits, appellate jurisdiction from all inferior courts and from trials at Nisi Prins, and it is also a court of review in criminal cases.

County courts, of which there are seven judges in Nova Scotia, divided into seven judicial districts. The County court has jurisdiction in civil matters from $20.00 up to $40.00, and the right to try criminals for all, except capital offenses, upon consent of the accused.

County court judges have also appellate jurisdiction from the decisions of Justices of the Peace.

Probate courts, of which there is one in every county, to provide for the execution of wills and the administration of intestate estates.

Magistrates and Justices of the Peace, who have jurisdiction in civil matters up to $80.00, and also in petty offenses, and for preliminary enquiry into criminal offenses.

Nova Scotia has a Court of Divorce, with full jurisdiction to annul the marriage tie. The Judge in Equity is the Judge in Ordinary to this Court.

Nova Scotia has also an Admiralty Court, over which the Chief Justice presides and disposes of all questions naturally pertaining to the Admiralty Court.

CHAPTER XLI.

THE COMMON SCHOOL SYSTEM OF NOVA SCOTIA.

BY A. H. MACKAY, LL. D., SUPERINTENDENT OF EDUCATION.

Written Especially for "Markland."

Provision is made for the free instruction of all children from five years of age upwards. Courses of study are prescribed covering a period of twelve years. The first eight years or grades are known as the common school grades, the remaining four years or grades as the high school grades. In the high school grades there is a wide range of choice between linguistic, literary, mathematical and scientific subjects allowed to students.

Free education is also provided for the deaf and dumb of the Province in the modern and well-appointed "Halifax Institution for the Deaf and Dumb;" and for all the blind in the progressive and splendidly equipped "Halifax School for the Blind."

Liberal provision is made by the Provincial authorities for the support of manual training schools of two varieties at every centre of population such as a large village, town or city, namely: Mechanic Science (woodwork mainly), and Domestic Science (cooking, etc.). And in the smaller and rural schools teachers are being prepared to give object lessons on nature and science and when possible manual training exercises of greater or lesser extent, with the object of developing the industrial sentiment in the schools and awakening the industrial genius in the pupils.

Provision is made for the free instruction of the teachers of the public schools in the Provincial Normal School at Truro, with which are affiliated the Provincial School of Agriculture, the Macdonald Mechanic Science School and the Truro Domestic Science School.

Provision is also made for free technical instruction in agriculture, horticulture and allied subjects at the Provincial School of Agriculture and Experimental Farm at Truro; in horticulture at the School of Horticulture, Wolfville, and in mining at the local mining schools near each mining centre.

The Council of Public Instruction, which is the supreme authority under the Legislature, consists of the members of the Executive

Council with the Superintendent of Education as their secretary. It has extensive powers under the statutes to frame regulations for the general educational administration.   /

The Superintendent of Education is the executive officer of the Council, and is charged with the general supervision and direction of the educational system.

The Territorial Divisions of the Province recognized in the educational system are as follows, proceeding from the greater to the less.   Ten *inspectorial divisions,* each under the special charge of an inspector, through whom the teachers and school boards receive their public moneys as well as by whom their work is inspected and reported upon.

Eighteen *counties,* each of which can have one of its high schools, if properly equipped and open free to all qualified students in the county, ranked as a County Academy and therefore in receipt of a special grant.

Thirty-four *districts,* each under a board of commissioners whose main duty is now the delimitation of the boundaries of the ultimate subdivisions of the Province—the school section.

Nearly 1,900 *school sections* which are self-governing corporations, normally including a territory swept by a two-mile radius around the school house as a centre, each (except in incorporated towns) presided over by an elective school board of three trustees.

The size, location and relation of these subdivisions to each other are shown at one view in the table following:

Commissioners' Districts.	Counties.	Divisions.	Sections.	Schools (1901).	Pupils (1901).	Inspector.
1 Halifax, West. 2 Halifax, East. 3 Halifax, Rural 4 Halifax City*	Halifax.......	No. 1	133	305	15,117	C. Creighton, Halifax.
5 Lunenburg .... 6 Chester........ 7 South Queens. 8 North Queens.	Lunenburg... Queens.	No. 2	192	242	9,550	H. H. MacIntosh, Lunenburg.
9 Shelburne..... 10 Barrington .... 11 Yarmouth ..... 12 Argyle	Shelburne.... Yarmouth.	No. 3	138	206	8,503	J. H. Munro, Yarmouth.
13 Digby .... 14 Clare........... 15 Annapolis, W. 16 Annapolis, E. .	Digby......... Annapolis.	No. 4	168	229	9,259	L. S. Morse, Digby.

*Halifax City, which is one school section with 147 schools, in 1901, has the District and School Board powers virtually combined in their Board of School Commissioners, consisting of six members of the City Council and six members appointed by the Governor-in-Council, each member serving three years.

Commissioners' Districts.	Counties.	Divisions.	Sections.	Schools (1901).	Pupils (1901).	Inspector.
17 Kings .... 18 Hants, West.. 19 Hants, East...	Kings .... Hants.	No. 5	201	255	9,685	C. W. Roscoe, Wolfville.
20 Antigonish .... 21 Guysboro....... 22 St. Mary's	Antigonish ... Guysboro.	No. 6	161	181	6,778	A. G. Macdonald, Antigonish.
23 Cape Breton .... 24 Richmond.......	Cape Breton. Richmond.	No. 7	203	237	11,229	M. J.T. Macneil, Riv. Bourgeois
25 Inverness, S... 26 Inverness, N... 27 Victoria	Inverness .... Victoria.	No. 8	222	191	6,844	J. McKinnon, Whycocomah.
28 Pictou, South.. 29 Pictou, North.. 30 Colchester, S. :.	Pictou........ Colchester.	No. 9	193	260	10,093	E. L. Armstrong, Pictou.
31 Colchester, W. 32 Stirling .... 33 Cumberland .. 34 Parrsboro	Colchester ... Cumberland .	No. 10	217	281	11,300	I. C. Craig, Amherst.
Totals (1901).....			1,848	2,387	98,410	

The Boards of District School Commissioners consist of at least seven persons appointed by the Council of Public Instruction, three of whom form a quorum, in each of the thirty-three districts specified in the foregoing table. Originally these boards had supreme authority in educational matters within each district, subject to the Provincial Legislature. Now their chief functions are the determining or changing of the boundaries of the school sections, the condemning of defective school houses, and the creation or consolidation of school sections, subject to the ratification of the Council. The secretary of each board is *ex officio*.

The Inspector of Schools, who is appointed by the Council on the recommendation of the superintendent. His duties include the regular inspection of and report upon all schools and educational institutions receiving public money within his jurisdiction, the reception and approval of the returns from each school, the payment of the public funds to teachers and school boards according to the instructions of the Superintendent of Education, the summation of the statistics of the schools under his charge, and the general oversight and direction of educational matters under the superintendent within his inspectorate.

The School Boards are the local authorities in charge of the administration of the law in the school sections. Except in incorporated towns they consist of three trustees elected at the annual (or when necessary at a special) meeting of the school section. The

term of service is three years, one trustee retiring at each annual
meeting. In towns the school board is formed of three commissioners elected from its members by the town council in like manner,
together with two persons appointed by the Governor-in-Council
for two years, one retiring each year. The most important officer
of the school board is the secretary, who may or may not be also a
member of the board.

: *The Annual Meeting* is the parliament and election day of each
school section, which is in nearly all respects a free and independent
corporation with respect to local taxation for school purposes, the
selection and appointment of licensed teachers, etc., subject to the
Provincial statutes and the regulations of the Council of Public Instructions. The date of the annual meeting is fixed generally on
the last Monday of June. In certain regions where the ratepayers
leave early in the spring to engage in deep sea fishing, the Council
has fixed the last Monday of March for the annual meeting.

The Financial Support of the Schools is derived from three
sources, the Provincial Aid, the Municipal Fund and Section Assessment.

The Provincial Aid is a provincial grant of $190,000 to be di-
vided among licensed teachers according to their class of license and
time taught. The object of this provision is to encourage the employment of teachers of higher scholarship while aiding to some extent
those of elementary qualifications. The distribution is made propor-
tional to the following scale: Class D, $60 per annum; Class C, $90;
Class B, $120; Class A (in a superior school), $150; Class A in high
school grades $180, and principals of high schools $210. The actual
grants for each class was during the year ended July, 1901, about
five per cent less than the scale figures; $10,000 additional are dis-
tributed among the county academies which are the high schools
open free of charge to all qualified students in each county.

The Municipal School Fund is raised by assessment on each
municipality of an amount equal to thirty cents on each inhabitant
according to the last census. For the last ten school years the sum
total of these funds for the Province was nearly $120,000. The scale
of distribution is $25 to each school board for each licensed teacher
employed, $75 for each pupil from the municipality attending the
School for the Blind or the Institution for the Deaf and Dumb, *payable to these institutions,* the balance to be distributed to the school
boards in proportion to the attendance of pupils. The actual dis-

tribution for 1901 was as follows: On account of teachers, $53,974; on account of attendance, $55,739; on account of Blind, $4,237; on account of Deaf and Dumb, $5,925.

Sectional Assessment.—The sum of the amounts voted by the ratepayers of the school sections at their annual meetings, to be levied on the income and on the real and personal property of the residents of the sections, together with the poll tax of one dollar on each male resident between the ages of twenty and sixty, amounted during the school year of 1901 to $470,108, of which $86,532 were for building and repairs, and $370,934 to supplement to Provincial Aid and the Municipal Fund for the teachers' salaries.

Courses of Study are outlined for fully graded schools as well as the several classes of "miscellaneous" or rural schools. For purposes of statistics all pupils are classified into grades, each of which represents the average work of one year. Of these the first eight are known as *common* school, and the last four as *high* school grades. The distribution of pupils in these was, for the school year of 1901, as follows: I, 19,185; II, 13,089; III, 11,975; IV, 12,655; V, 10,590; VI, 8,700; VII, 8,292; VIII, 6,628; IX, 4,461; X, 1,850; XI, 878; XII, 107. Total, 98,410.

Provincial Certificates of Scholarship are awarded to those who choose to take and who pass the annual Provincial High School examination on each of the four high school grades. For 1901 the awards were as follows: IX, 947; X, 659; XI, 394; XII, 38. Total candidates, 3,470.

Manual Training schools are aided by a Provincial grant which may be $600 to a school section which can qualify for the maximum. It is provided that pupils can be withdrawn from the ordinary school for half a day per week, and each pupil who attends regularly once a week enables the section to draw about $6 per annum. One hundred pupils in regular attendance can thus qualify, so far as attendance is required, for the maximum grant. The equipment must be up to the standard also. The Manual Training schools are divided into two classes, namely *Mechanic Science* schools, devoted mainly to woodwork at present, and *Domestic Science* schools devoted mainly to cookery and other domestic arts. They are now being established in nearly all of the large and progressive towns of the Province. For such schools specially trained teachers are required.

Teachers are of two classes so far as their general preparation for the profession is concerned. In 1901 there were 1,545 employed who merely passed the 'high school scholarship examinations and the minimum professional qualification examination; and only 945 who passed the scholarship examinations and the Provincial Normal School course. Five hundred and forty were male and 1,952 female teachers. Of the total 2,492 teachers, there were 1,063 of Class D, 903 of Class C, 422 of Class B, and 104 of Class A.

The Provincial Normal School, which was established at Truro in 1855 for the training of teachers, was merely a high school with special emphasis laid upon the theory and practice of teaching. In 1893 it became a professional training school for teachers who were required to pass the prescribed high school examinations before admission. Scholarship qualifications with the subsequent training course of the Normal School admits a teacher to a standing one class higher than the scholarship qualifications without Normal School training.

It is affiliated with the public schools of Truro for the purpose of teaching practice in regular public schools, with the Truro School of Domestic Science with the Macdonald School of Mechanic Science for Manual Training, and with the Provincial School of Agriculture and Experimental Farm for Nature-Study and the elements of Agriculture and Horticulture.

The number of students in attendance during the school year 1901 was 240, of which seven received diplomas of Academic rank, ninety of First rank, eighty of Second rank, and fifty-five of Third rank.

FACULTY.

David B. Soloan, B. A., Principal,

Principles of Pedagogy, Language, History, German.

John B. Calkin, A. M.,

Emeritus Professor of Psychology and Pedagogy.

James B. Hall, Ph. D.,

Psychology, History of Education and Method in Geography.

Hermon W. Smith, B. Sc. (Principal, School of Agriculture),

Botany, Biology and Agriculture.

Ottie A. Smith,

Drawing and Calisthenics.

L. C. Harlow, B. S., B. S. A.,

Chemistry, Mineralogy and Geology

J. Alphonse Benoit, B. A.,

Method in Mathematics and Physics, French.

Edward W. Connolly, B. A.,
  Hygiene, Physiology, Math. Drawing, Commercial Branches.
Mina A. Reade,
  Elocution and Music.

AFFILIATED SCHOOLS.

T. B. Kinder, F. B. I. C., &c., Director of Macdonald Manual
  Training Fund for Nova Scotia.
F. G. Matthews, Macdonald Manual Training School.
Bertha Grace Turner, Truro School of Domestic Science.
Winnifred Maud McKeand, Truro School of Domestic Science.
Mrs. S. B. Patterson, Truro Kindergarten.
Directors of Teaching-practice in the Public Schools:—W. R.
  Campbell, M. A., and James Little, County Academy, Truro.

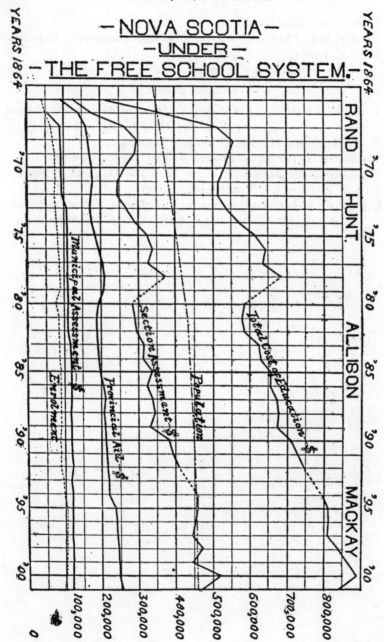

— NOVA SCOTIA —
— UNDER —
— THE FREE SCHOOL SYSTEM. —

APPENDIX.

NOVA SCOTIA.

BY MOSES H. NICKERSON, CLARKE'S HARBOUR, N. S.

O land of the mayflower and birch
Where my sires paid their homage to God,
What time neither schoolhouse nor church
Bestudded the wilderness broad.

With Britain supreme in their thoughts,
They heeded no danger nor toil;
And the tenderest affections they brought
Took root in thy stoniest soil.

How simple, how few, the delights
They found in this tenantless coast;
Yet the land of Arabian Nights
Not deeper contentment could boast.

They faced with a Puritan psalm
The roughest encounters of life,
And bore in their bosoms a calm
Through the winds and the waters at strife.

Though Winter may scowl on thee rude
And Summer be fickle at times,
Thy children with vigor endued,
Never envy the sun-gilded climes.

And wherever distinction is sought,
Though boldly and widely they roam,
Their sweetest and holiest thought
Is when they are dreaming of home.

I behold thee when fairest thou art
With a lover's devotion to pride,
And the climate ne'er changes the heart
Ever warm with a patriot's pride.

601

E'en the deep, unmelodious tunes,
　　When the crags with the storm-echoes rang,
Always had the brave dash of the runes
　　That Thorfinn, saluting thee, sang.

Neither title nor lordly domain
　　With vassalage cumbers thy soil,
But the forest, the mine and the plain
　　Present thee with the tribute of toil.

And here where the storm-braving Cape*
　　Reaches out its white arms to the sea,
Old Proteus puts on the shape
　　Of a ministering angel to thee.

Dear land, may the years as they roll
　　Still view thy just fortunes increase,
Placed under no harsher control
　　Than that which gives Freedom and Peace.

THE MAYFLOWER, OR TRAILING ARBUTUS.

BY THE LATE JOHN M'PHERSON, OF QUEENS COUNTY.†

Sweet child of many an April shower,
First gift of Spring to Flora's bower,
Acadia's own peculiar flower,
　　I hail thee here;
Thou com'st like Hope in sorrow's hour,
　　To whisper cheer.

I love to stray with careless feet,
Thy balm on morning breeze to meet—
Thy earliest opening bloom to greet—
　　To take thy stem
And bear thee to my lady sweet,
　　Thou lovely gem.

---

*Cape Sable Island, home of the poet.
†He was author of a volume of poems published and praised by Joseph Howe.
He died in 1848. His wife yet survives.

What though green mosses o'er thee steal,
And half thy lovely form conceal—
Though but thy fragrant breath reveal
  Thy place of birth—
Gladly we own thy mute appeal,
  Of modest worth.

Thy charms so pure a spell impart,
Thy softening smiles so touch my heart,
That silent tears of rapture start,
  Sweet flower of May.
E'en while I sing devoid of art
  This simple lay.

SABLE ISLAND, THE GRAVEYARD OF THE ATLANTIC.

BY CROFTON UNIACKE M'LEOD, BROOKFIELD, N. S.

A lonely isle in a hapless sea
  Where the nipping north winds blow:
A sodless isle in a southern sea
  Of current and undertow.

A treacherous isle in a frost-swept sea
  Where a chill mist blears the eyes:
A barren isle in a merciless sea,
  Where deadly danger lies.

Beware, beware, of its shifting sands,
For many a good ship strikes and strands:
  And hearts grow cold forever;
Where billows beat the live-long while
Upon the bars of Sable Isle
  With demon-like endeavor.

Among the products of Nova Scotia are these bits of verse with a local coloring. They are not here because the best lines of the several writers, but the topics they touch decided their selection.

THE END.